Japanese/Korean Linguistics
Volume 19

Japanese/Korean Linguistics

Volume 19

edited by

Ho-Min Sohn

Haruko Minegishi Cook

William O'Grady

Leon A. Serafim

Sang Yee Cheon

*Published for the
Stanford Linguistics
Association by*

CSLI
PUBLICATIONS
Center for the Study of
Language and Information
Stanford, California

Library of Congress Cataloging-in-Publication Data

Conference on Japanese/Korean Linguistics (1st : 1989 :
University of Southern California)
  Japanese/Korean Linguistics / edited by Hajime Hoji.

  Volume 19 / edited by Ho-min Sohn, Haruko Cook,
  William OGrady, Leon Serafim, and Sang Yee Cheon

    p.   cm.

  Includes bibliographical references and index.
  ISBN-13: 978-1-57586-619-2
  ISBN-13: 978-1-57586-618-5 (pbk.)

  1. Japanese language—Congresses. 2. Korean
language—Congresses. 3. Japanese language—Grammar,
Comparative—Korean—Congresses. 4. Korean language—Grammar,
Comparative—Japanese—Congresses. 5. Linguistics—Congresses.
I. Hoji, Hajime. II. Stanford Linguistics Association. III. Center for
the Study of Language and Information (U.S.) IV. Title.
PL503.C6 1989
495.6–dc20   90-2550
                                                                   CIP

For a list of volumes in this series, along with a cumulative table of
contents, please visit

http://cslipublications.stanford.edu/site/JAKO.shtml

CSLI was founded in 1983 by researchers from Stanford University, SRI
International, and Xerox PARC to further the research and development of
integrated theories of language, information, and computation. CSLI headquarters
and CSLI Publications are located on the campus of Stanford University.

CSLI Publications reports new developments in the study of language,
information, and computation. Please visit our web site at
http://cslipublications.stanford.edu/
for comments on this and other titles, as well as for changes
and corrections by the author and publisher.

Contents

Part I
Phonetics and Phonology

Part II
Syntax

v

Part III
Semantics

Part IV
Pragmatics, Discourse and Sociolinguistics

Part V
Historical Linguistics and Grammaticalization

Part VI
Psycholinguistics and L1/L2 Acquisition

Acknowledgment

The 19th Japanese/Korean Linguistics Conference was held in Honolulu at the Center for Korean Studies of the University of Hawaii at Manoa on November 12-14, 2009. There were 53 presentations during the three days in session, including four by invited speakers, eight by scholars on a panel on old writing systems organized specifically for that purpose by Alexander Vovin and Ross King, and four by scholars on a panel on Okazaki Survey on Honorifics III. Invited speakers were Chung-Hye Han (Simon Fraser University), Sun-Ah Jun (UCLA), Yoshihisa Kitagawa (Indiana University), and Shigeko Okamoto (UC Santa Cruz). The remaining 37 presentations were chosen by blind review from the 154 abstracts submitted. A total of 35 papers (including 33 peer-reviewed and 2 invited papers) appear in this volume. Our thanks go to all of the presenters and session chairs at the meeting.

As in all previous J/K conferences, J/K 19 owed greatly to the scholars who generously agreed to referee the abstracts. We are grateful to 57 referees whose perceptive evaluations of the abstracts led to the successful organization of the J/K 19 program. We also send our appreciation to the Standing Organizing Committee, especially to Pat Clancy, Hajime Hoji, Shoichi Iwasaki, and Sung-Ock Sohn, for their valuable advice and encouragement.

J/K 19 was supported by funds from the Center for Korean Studies, Japanese Studies Endowment (Center for Japanese Studies), and National Resource Center-East Asia of the University of Hawaii at Manoa and the Academy of Korean Studies in Korea. We take this opportunity to extend our appreciation to these organizations for the generous support.

Preparation of conference materials, conference logistics, registration, and on-site support were provided by some two dozen capable volunteers from the Center for Korean Studies, Department of East Asian Languages and Literatures, Department of Linguistics, Department of Second Language Studies, and the Korean Language Flagship Center. We wholeheartedly thank them for their willingness to help.

Finally, we are also grateful to Dikran Karagueuzian and Emma Pease at CSLI for helping us get the manuscript into publishing shape.

Ho-min Sohn, Haruko Cook, William O'Grady, Leon Serafim,
and Sang Yee Cheon
University of Hawaii at Manoa

Part I

Phonetics and Phonology

Integrated Accounts on Consonant Cluster Simplification

MIYEON AHN
University of Michigan

1. Introduction

Speakers frequently drop one consonant of a cluster (e.g. $/C_1C_2/ \rightarrow [C_1]$ or $[C_2]$) and they do so mostly for the goal of 'simplification'.[1] Much of previous research has been concentrated on describing which consonant is deleted (e.g. /stb/ $\rightarrow$ [sb] in *must be*), on analyzing why a consonant is deleted (e.g. *COMPLEXCODA in Optimality Theory), or on explaining a general pattern of deletion (e.g. voiceless plosives are deleted more often than voiced), Cho (1999), Steriade (1999a, 1999b), McCarthy (to appear), amongst others.

This research examines the conditions under which consonant deletes and provides integrated accounts on consonant cluster resolution based on

---

[1] Browman and Goldstein (1991) suggest that speakers actually produce every segment in a consonant cluster. Instead of dropping a specific segment, speakers resolve the cluster in a way of overlapping gestures. The segment is, therefore, 'hidden' rather than 'deleted' due to gestural overlap with the flanking consonants. I acknowledge this issue and by 'simplification', I mean the segment may be articulartorily still present but acoustically absent (because it is masked by neighboring segments).

Japanese/Korean Linguistics 19.
Edited by Ho-min Sohn, Haruko Cook, William O'Grady, Leon A. Serafim, & Sang Yee Cheon.

data analysis in Ahn (to appear). Referring to the study, I will review one thread of previous research regarding consonantal phonotactics (perceptually grounded phonology) and discuss its implications for Korean consonant cluster resolution. I further explore how Korean speakers resolve consonant clusters for the purpose of simplification in their native language.

1.1 Consonant Clusters in Korean

Korean does not allow tautosyllabic consonant clusters. When a consonant-initial suffix is attached, the suffixation yields a triconsonantal cluster wherein the three consonants in a row generate a /VC$_1$C$_2$-C$_3$V/ sequence. In such sequences, Korean speakers simplify the consonant cluster by deleting either C$_1$ or C$_2$ such that the pronunciation is either [V(C$_1$)C$_2$-C$_3$V] or [VC$_1$(C$_2$)-C$_3$V].

(1)   /palk-/   'bright'
     /-ta/ suffixation   /palk-ta/ → [pak-ta ~ pal-ta]   'to be bright'
     /-ki/ suffixation   /palk-ki/ → [pal-ki ~ pak-ki]   'brightness'

The discussion in this study is focused on /lk-t/ or /lk-k/ clusters in Korean. As shown above, when /-ta/ is suffixed to a /lk-/ cluster, it is C$_1$ /l/ that is preferentially deleted, whereas when /-ki/ is suffixed, it is C$_2$ /k/.

The above consonant cluster simplification is of interest because it shows that there is more than one simplification pattern, even for the same cluster in the same stem. Both of the simplified representations are well-formed, which indicates that consonant cluster simplification in Korean is a phonologically variable phenomenon.[2] Although phonologically variable, one representation – for instance, to delete [k] and preserve [t] – is preferred to the other – to delete [t] and preserve [k] – depending on the conditions. What are the conditions to have influence on phonological variation?

2. Previous Studies

2.1 Perceptual Accounts

There is a large body of recent research that relies on perceptual considerations in order to explain a variety of phonological phenomena. These argue that 'knowledge of differential perceptibility enters the grammar' (Steriade 1999a: 17). These accounts have been used to explain

---

[2] It has been described in the Korean literature that there are three variants in consonant clusters; [VC$_1$-C$_3$V], [VC$_2$-C$_3$V], and [VC$_1$C$_2$-C$_3$V] (Cho,Y.-M. 1990, Jun 1995, Cho 1999). If this is true, it would mean that Korean speakers pronounce both of the tautosyllabic consonants, which are not usually allowed in the phonetic level. It might be that the speakers are influenced by the Korean orthography. However, since this study is focused on consonant cluster simplification, I do not take this [VC$_1$C$_2$-C$_3$V] variant into consideration and leave this issue for future study.

phonological alternations that involve consonantal phonotactics, including loanword adaptation (Kang 2003, Shinohara 2006), assimilation (Jun 1995, Steriade 2001), and neutralization (Steriade 1999c, Wilson 2001), as well as consonant cluster reductions (Cho 1999, Côté 2000). The shared assumptions and arguments among these studies are that (i) perceptibility depends on auditory cues, (ii) cue salience depends on segmental context (relative perceptibility), and (iii) segments with weak perceptual cues are targets of phonological alternation, (subject to neutralization in assimilation and a deletion in cluster reduction, for instance).

Consider an intervocalic biconsonantal sequence $/VC_1C_2V/$. Ideally, the best corresponding output is $[VC_1C_2V]$ because it is fully faithful to its input and it carries maximum cues. However, if deviation from input is required, (i.e. if one of the two consonants must be deleted due to phonotactic constraints) the output will be either $[VC_1V]$ or $[VC_2V]$. Neither of these two outputs preserves all the perceptual cues from the fully faithful input $[VC_1C_2V]$. Some loss of perceptual information necessary to recovering the input cannot be avoided due to the consonant deletion.

Perceptual accounts claim that when the fully faithful output is not considered to be well-formed, the relative perceptual similarity between the faithful output and the less faithful ones plays a role in determining the speaker's choice. Perceptual similarity is based on perceptual cues, which include various phonetic properties such as release burst, silence, voicing, C-to-V or V-to-C formant transitions, and other acoustic cues (Steriade 1999a, Cho 1999). It is assumed in perceptual accounts that the perceptual similarity is hierarchical in terms of these acoustic cues (Shinohara 2006). Between the two outputs $[VC_1V]$ and $[VC_2V]$, the one that preserves more salient acoustic cues from the faithful output $[VC_1C_2V]$, is considered to be perceptually more similar to the input. Consider (4).

(2)   Cue preservation in $[VC_1C_2V]$, $[VC_1V]$ and $[VC_2V]$

		$[VC_1C_2V]$	$[VC_1V]$	$[VC_2V]$
↑	A	✓	✓	
cue salience	B	✓	✓	✓
↓	C	✓		✓

Let us assume that the faithful output $[VC_1C_2V]$ carries three kinds of cues A, B and C in which cue A is more salient than cue B and C, and cue B is more salient than cue C. Compared to $[VC_1C_2V]$, the one less faithful output $[VC_2V]$ does not carry cue A, the most perceptually salient cue, and the other less faithful output $[VC_1V]$ misses cue C, the least salient one. Because A is more salient cue than C, the cue loss in $[VC_1V]$ and $[VC_2V]$ is not equivalent, regardless of losing the same number of cues. [VC$_2$V] shows more perceptual cue loss than [VC$_1$V]; accordingly, the one with less perceptual cue loss [VC$_1$V] is perceptually 'more similar' to the fully faithful output [VC$_1$C$_2$V] than [VC$_1$V] is.

This assumption regarding the hierarchy of perceptual similarity is formally expressed in a 'perceptibility scale'. This perceptual similarity scale has been incorporated into grammars so that perceptual effects can directly influence phonological alternations. The perceptual difference can be formalized as follows:

(3) Δ (VC$_1$C$_2$V ~ VC$_1$V)   < Δ (VC$_1$C$_2$V ~ VC$_2$V)

The above formula indicates that the perceptual difference of [VC$_1$C$_2$V] ~ [VC$_1$V] is smaller than [VC$_1$C$_2$V] ~ [VC$_2$V] (i.e. [VC$_1$C$_2$V] and [VC$_1$V] are perceptually more similar than [VC$_1$C$_2$V] and [VC$_2$V]). This implies that [VC$_2$V] has greater cue loss from [VC$_1$C$_2$V] than [VC$_1$V]. It also implies that [VC$_2$V] carries fewer and weaker perceptual cues than [VC$_1$V] does. Perceptual accounts claim that language users' repair preference is for the relation that perceptually costs less; therefore, [VC$_1$V] has more robust perceptual correlates to the faithful output than [VC$_2$V] does and [VC$_1$V] is a perceptually preferred output.

2.2 Perceptual Accounts in Korean Cluster Simplification

What are the implications of these accounts for Korean consonant cluster simplification? The clusters that we are interested in are intervocalic triconsonantal clusters as in /VC$_1$C$_2$-C$_3$V/, wherein C$_1$C$_2$ is /lk/ and C$_3$ is either /-t/ or /-k/. The cluster, then, is /Vlk-tV/ or /Vlk-kV/ and the same principle applies to both.

Let us consider /Vlk-tV/ first. The faithful output of this input is [Vlk-tV] but since the faithful output [Vlk-tV] is phonotactically illegal, the other two less faithful but legal ones are [Vl-tV] (i.e. with preserving C$_1$ /l/ and deleting C$_2$ /k/) and [Vk-tV] (i.e. with preserving C$_2$ /k/ and deleting C$_1$ /l/). There are several perceptual cues that the faithful output [Vlk-tV] carries.

(4)   Cue preservation in [Vlk-tV], [Vl-tV] and [Vk-tV]

		[Vlk-tV]	[Vl-tV]	[Vk-tV]
more salient	V-to-[l]	✓	✓	
	[l]-to-[k]	✓		
	[t]-to-V	✓	✓	✓
	[t] burst	✓	✓	✓
less salient	[k]-to-[t]	✓		✓

The most obvious ones are V-to-[l], [l]-to-[k], [k]-to-[t] and [t]-to-V transitions, closure, release burst, and other acoustic cues. Some of them are given in (4).

The acoustic cues that the faithful output [Vlk-tV] carries are incompletely preserved in both [Vl-tV] and [Vk-tV], which means both [Vl-tV] and [Vk-tV] lack some perceptual correlates to the faithful output. However, the perceptual similarities of the two outputs to the faithful output are not identical. Specifically, [Vk-tV] lacks more salient perceptual correlates to [Vlk-tV] than [Vl-tV] does. The above table illustrates cue preservation in the three outputs. Among several cues, V-to-[l], [l]-to-[k], [t]-to-V and [t] release burst are most salient cues in [Vlk-tV]. The transitional cues from the preceding vowel to C_1 /l/ are preserved in [Vl-tV] but not in [Vk-tV], which means [Vk-tV] loses one perceptual cue while [Vl-tV] does not. The transition from [l]-to-[k] is missing in both [Vl-tV] and [Vk-tV]. In terms of these cue losses, [Vk-tV] is the subset of [Vl-tV], which means that [Vk-tV] loses more perceptual correlates to [Vlk-tV] than [Vl-tV] does.

On the other hand, there is a cue that is absent in [Vl-tV] but present in [Vk-tV], which is [k]-to-[t] transition. The transition from one stop to another is not as salient as the previous four salient cues. Also, the gestural overlap for release burst of [k] to the following [t] increases the non-salience of this transitional cue. Thus, even though this cue is missing in [Vl-tV], this loss does not make a big difference.

Therefore, arguably, the [Vlk-tV] is perceptually more similar to [Vl-tV] than it is to [Vk-tV], and [Vl-tV] is considered to be a better repair. The perceptual similarities between the input and the two output variants are formulated below:

(5) Δ (Vlk-tV ~ Vl-tV)   < Δ (Vlk-tV ~ Vk-tV)

The formula captures the claim that the strategy to preserve C_1 /l/ and to delete C_2 /k/ costs less perceptually.

In terms of the /Vlk-kV/ input, a similar account applies. The most important perceptual cues that this input carries include V-to-[l], [l]-to-[k], and [k]-to-V transitions, closure, and release.

(6)   Cue preservation in [Vlk-kV], [Vl-kV] and [Vk-kV]

		[Vlk-kV]	[Vl-kV]	[Vk-kV]
more salient	V-to-[l]	✓	✓	
	[l]-to-[k]	✓	✓	
	[k]-to-V	✓	✓	✓
	[k] burst	✓	✓	✓
less salient	[k]-to-[k]	✓		✓

The faithful but phonotactically ill-formed output [Vlk-kV] is excluded so that the two possible outputs are [Vl-kV] and [Vk-kV]. Compared to [Vl-kV], [Vk-kV] carries fewer and weaker acoustic cues of the faithful output [Vlk-kV], because the spectral (non-temporal) cues of [Vl-kV] are virtually identical to those corresponding to the faithful output, whereas the spectral cues in [Vk-kV] are very different from those expected from the faithful output. For instance, [Vl-kV] preserves almost all the acoustic cues of the input but many of the acoustic cues are absent in [Vk-kV]. One acoustic cue that is absent in [Vl-kV] but present in [Vk-kV] is the temporal cue differentiating C_2 [k] and C_2C_3 [kk], which is not as salient as V-to-[l] and [l]-to-[k], I suspect.[3] In the long run, [Vk-kV] carries less perceptual correlates to the faithful output [Vlk-kV] than [Vl-kV] does; thus, this output is perceptually fewer and less similar than [Vl-kV] is to the input. The reasoning yields the following perceptual scale:

(7) Δ (Vlk-kV ~ Vl-kV)   < Δ (Vlk-kV ~ Vk-kV)

In summary, according to perceptual accounts represented here, Korean should have a tendency to resolve /Vlk-tV/ and /Vlk-kV/ clusters in the same way: namely, as [Vl-tV] and [Vl-kV]: both of them should preserve C_1 /l/ and delete C_2 /k/.

---

[3] I am grateful to Patrice S. Beddor for raising the point that this assumption is not uncontroversially true. I acknowledge that spectral and temporal properties are inherently different perceptual cues so that it is hard to compare the perceptual saliency between these two kinds of cues. Also, I admit that cues cannot be simply counted and compared without perceptual data. The next step of research, therefore, should be to run the perceptual experiment and investigate what the actual cues are that language users adopt.

2.2 Experimental Accounts on Korean Consonant Cluster Simplification

In fact, many /lk/ cluster-embedded words appear to support perceptual accounts. Ahn (to appear) showed an experimental study on consonant cluster simplification in Korean. The results of the study suggest that consonant cluster resolution in Korean generally conforms to perceptibility accounts and that simplification pattern is influenced by several non-grammatical factors such as word frequency, OCP and dialectal differences.

The general tendency regarding word frequency is that /l/ is deleted more often in low-frequency morphemes than in high-frequency morphemes. This tendency is shown both by Seoul Korean (SK) and Pusan Korean (PK) speakers. However, for both frequencies, speakers preserve more /l/ than /k/: /l/-deletion does not exceed 50% for either low-frequency or high-frequency morphemes and in either SK or PK, which shows that to delete /k/ is less preferred, in general. PK in particular showed much less /k/ retention compared to SK in both the low- and the high-frequency morphemes. Across dialects, the low-frequency morphemes deleted more /l/ than the high-frequency morphemes. The /l/-deletion in the high-frequency morphemes was higher in SK than PK and /l/-deletion in the low-frequency morphemes was also higher in SK than PK. The fact that /l/-deletion in PK low-frequency morphemes was lower than SK high-frequency morphemes means that /l/-deletion is much more preferred in SK than PK.

The OCP effect was found to be a significant factor in consonant cluster simplification. When a cluster was placed in the OCP environment, i.e. a /lk-/ cluster followed by a /k/, SK speakers deleted /k/ much more frequently than they did in the Non-OCP environment, i.e. a /lk-/ cluster followed by /t/. PK speakers showed a similar tendency.

Different dialects of Korean also seem to have different simplification patterns. SK and PK speakers showed an overall difference in cluster simplification. Both SK and PK speakers preferred to preserve /l/ and delete /k/. However, as illustrated in Figure 2, SK speakers were overall more likely to preserve /k/ than were PK speakers.

In Ahn (to appear), it was suggested that consonant cluster simplification cannot be explained by one single factor. Instead, the simplification is a complex phonological process influenced by several factors. The factors that we found to be relevant, as non-grammatical factors, are frequency, OCP effects and the speaker's dialect. This outcome suggests that language users incorporate knowledge from these factors in resolving phonotactically impossible clusters. It also suggests that consonant cluster resolution is not a random phenomenon and that language users do rely on knowledge about these factors when deciding which strategy to employ in cluster simplification.

3. Integrated Accounts

Perceptual accounts predict that Korean speakers would resolve clusters by preserving /l/ and explain the general pattern. However, it is not necessarily the case that perceptual accounts alone can explain the whole phenomenon. It seems that some speakers often deleted /l/, whereas others often deleted /k/ for the same /lk/ cluster resolution (i.e. inter-speaker variation was found). In addition, it seemed that even one speaker often deleted /l/ in one case but /k/ in another (i.e. intra-speaker variation was found), although the general pattern of consonant cluster simplification in Korean is consistent with perceptual accounts, that is, /l/-preservation should be preferred across the board.

The idea that perceptual similarity is incorporated into grammar seems well-motivated, and furthermore, the general tendency found in various phonological phenomena supports the effect of perception on human language use. Therefore, research incorporating perceptual effects into grammar has been extensively discussed in the literature on phonological variation. Perceptual accounts claim that perceptual similarity between input and output plays a role in phonological variation.

The findings of Ahn (to appear), however, suggest that Korean speakers' consonant cluster resolution is sensitive to several factors in addition to perceptibility. The results indicate that phonological variation, particularly consonant cluster resolution, may not be linked exclusively with perceptibility but with the interaction between perceptibility and other non-grammatical factors. That is, consonant cluster resolution in Korean is a linguistic phenomenon in which several both grammatical and non-grammatical factors are integrated.

This suggests that a kind of upgraded model to explain consonant cluster simplification in Korean. Coetzee (2009) has suggested an integrated grammatical/non-grammatical model to explain phonological variation. Concerning that consonant cluster simplification in Korean is a phonologically variant phenomenon, the model can incorporate the cluster resolution.

Coetzee (2009) argued that both grammatical and non-grammatical influences on variation should be explained and suggested a noisy Harmonic Grammar model of variation in which the influences of non-grammatical factors are explained by *scaling factors*.[4]

---

[4] See Coetzee (2009) for the calculation of scaling factors.

One of the factors that we found to be significant in Korean consonant cluster resolution was OCP violation. It might be the case that OCP is a kind of perceptual property rather than an independent factor that influences linguistic variation. This OCP effect can be explained as a grammatical influence in the suggested model. The other two factors – frequency and dialects – can be explained as non-grammatical influences.

Language usage reflects the interaction of many rules, the lexicon, and other linguistic knowledge. I have shown that there can be other factors that are involved other than perceptibility. The fact that frequency is important in cluster resolution means language users are influenced by linguistic experience. Also, that OCP violation and perceptual similarity are involved in cluster resolution may reflect the influence of a universal preference for preserving robust cues. Language users employ all these aspects of grammatical knowledge for cluster resolution. Additionally, the fact that cluster resolution differs according to dialectal regions suggests that social information, which is a language-external factor, is also involved in the same phenomenon. As a result, I argue that both grammatical and non-grammatical factors should be accounted for in a theory of phonological variation and that the model suggested in Coetzee (2009) can be one of the kind.

4. Concluding Discussion

Phonological variation is the result of a cognitive process in which language users employ both grammatical and non-grammatical knowledge. This argument was supported with acoustic data analysis from carefully designed production experiments. In future research, perception experiments on consonant cluster resolution should follow. Assuming that language users employ the same grammar for production and perception (Smolensky 1996), similar cluster resolution is expected in the perception of consonant clusters.

The motive for Korean speakers to resolve consonant clusters lies on representational mismapping between the morphophonemic and the phonetic levels wherein phonotactic knowledge is involved, saying /VCCCV/ is not an allowable structure on the surface level. As described in the introduction, consonant deletion is not the only strategy for simplification. Korean speakers could have employed another strategy, vowel insertion, for instance. In fact, some English loanwords that contain /-lk/ or /-lp/ such as *bulk* and *pulp* are borrowed as [pəlki][5] and [pʰəlpi], respectively. It will be interesting to see whether language users apply different grammar for native cluster resolution (i.e. cluster resolution only)

---

[5] A word-initial voiced stop becomes a voiceless in Korean.

and for borrowed cluster resolution (i.e. cluster resolution plus nativization), even though the overall goal in both cases is 'simplification'.

References

Ahn, M. to appear. *Experimental Investigation of Consonant Cluster Simplification, Harvard Studies in Korean Linguistics* 13.

Browman, P. and Goldstein, L. 1991. Tiers in Articulatory Phonology, with Some Implications for Casual Speech. In J. Kingston and M. E. Beckman (eds), *Papers in Laboratory Phonology I: Between the Grammar and the Physics of Speech.* Cambridge, U. K.: Cambridge University Press.

Cho, T. 1999. Intra-dialectal Variation in Korean Consonant Cluster Simplification: A Stochastic Approach. In Mattew K. Gorden. ed., *UCLA Working Papers in Linguistics*, vol. 1. *Papers in Phonology* 2.

Cho, Y.-M. 1990. *Parameters of Consonantal Assimilation.* Doctoral dissertation, Stanford University.

Coetzee, A. W. 2009. An Integrated Grammatical/non-grammatical Model of Phonological Variation., eds. *Current Issues in Linguistic Interfaces.* Y.-S. Kang, J.-Y. Yoon, H. Yoo, S.-W. Tang, Y.-S. Kang, Y. Jang, C. Kim, K.-A. Kim, & H.-K. Kang, 267-294. Seoul: Hankookmunhwasa.

Côté, M.-H. 2000. Consonant Cluster Phonotactics: A Perceptual Approach, Ph. D. dissertation, Massachusetts Institute of Technology, Cambridge, MA.

Jun, J. 1995. Perceptual and Articulatory Factors in Place Assimilation: An Optimality Theoretic Approach. Doctoral dissertation, University of California, Los Angeles.

Kang, Y. 2003. Perceptual Similarity in Loanword Adaptation. *Phonology* 20: 219-273.

McCarthy, J. 2008. The Gradual Path to Cluster Simplification. *Phonology* 25: 271-319.

Shinohara, S. 2006. Perceptual Effects in Final Cluster Reduction Patterns. *Lingua* 116: 1046–1078.

Smolensky, P. 1996. On the Comprehension/production Dilemma in Child Language. *Linguistic Inquiry* 27: 720-731.

Steriade, D. 1999a. Alternative to Syllable-based Accounts of Consonantal Phonotactics. In Osamu Fujimura, Brian D. Joseph & Bohumil Palek (eds.) *Proceedings of LP '98: Item order in language and speech,* Prague: Charles University in Prague – The Karolinum Press, vol. 1: 205-245.

Steriade, D. 1999b. Grammar of Perceptibility Effects: Direction in Assimilation and Cluster Simplification. Paper delivered at the Phonology 2000 Symposium, Massachusetts Institute of Technology / Harvard University, Cambridge, MA.

Steriade, D. 1999c. Phonetics in Phonology: The Case of Laryngeal Neutralization. *UCLA Working Papers Linguist 2*; Papers Phonology 3: 25-246.

Steriade, D. 2001. Paradigm Uniformity and the Phonetics-Phonology Boundary. In Michael B. Vroe and Janet B. Pierrehumbert (eds.) *Papers in Laboratory Phonology V: Acquisition and the Lexicon* (313-334). Cambridge: Cambridge University Press.

Wilson, C. 2001. Consonant Cluster Neutralization and Targeted Constraints. *Phonology* 18(1): 147-197.

A Statistical Model of Korean Loanword Phonology

HAHN KOO
San José State University

The paper presents a statistical model of Korean loanword phonology which predicts the adapted form in Korean for a given word in English. In essence, the model is a first-order hidden Markov model, where the states represent Korean phoneme strings of variable length and emit English phonemes as observation. The parameters of the model are trained on pairs of English word and the corresponding form in Korean according to maximum likelihood estimate. The most likely sequence of Korean phonemes given an English phoneme string is found by applying the Viterbi algorithm. Performance of the model is evaluated on a subset of Korean loanword database compiled by the National Institute of the Korean Language. As the model incorporates virtually no linguistic knowledge, the evaluation results can be used as baseline performance for future research in developing linguistically sophisticated models.

1. Introduction

Recent studies in loanword phonology have addressed specific issues for which there is no simple phonological explanation such as whether the neutral vowel /i/ is inserted word-finally when an English word that ends with a

Japanese/Korean Linguistics 19.
Edited by Ho-min Sohn, Haruko Cook, William O'Grady, Leon A. Serafim, & Sang Yee Cheon.
Copyright © 2011, CSLI Publications

stop is adopted in Korean (Kang 2003). Needless to say, such studies are crucial in developing a theory. However, another type of effort one should make in developing a theory is to assess its overall quality by implementing a model and testing it against reasonably large data. For example, if one were to develop a generative model of Korean loanword phonology in terms of rewrite rules of the form X -> Y / W_ Z, one should not only identify the phonological context in which /i/ is inserted word-finally, but also assess how accurately the entire set of such rewrite rules explain a large collection of Korean loanwords.

To evaluate the overall quality of a model, one needs data and performance of other models to compare with. In response, the current study presents a simple statistical model whose performance on a database of Korean loanwords can be compared with those of more linguistically sophisticated models in the future. In brief, the model is a first-order hidden Markov model that predicts the most likely sequence of Korean phonemes given an English phoneme string. As we shall see, the model incorporates virtually no linguistic knowledge, so the performance level reported in this study can be used as baseline performance for comparison.

The paper is organized as follows. In Section 2, I present a statistical interpretation of the adaptation process in loanword phonology. In Section 3, I introduce a few simplifying assumptions I made to build a working model of the adaptation process. I describe how the idea is implemented as a first-order hidden Markov model in Section 4. The implemented model is evaluated on a Korean loanword dataset in Section 5. I conclude the paper in Section 6.

2. A Statistical Interpretation of the Adaptation Process

In this paper, I assume that predicting how the form of a word in the source language is adapted in the recipient language is equivalent to identifying the most likely adapted form in the recipient language given the source form. That is, predicting how a source form s is adapted in the recipient language where potential candidates are enumerated in a set R is equivalent to solving the equation in (1) and identifying what $\hat{r}$ is.

$$\hat{r} = \arg\max_{r \in R} P(r \mid s) \tag{1}$$

By Bayes' rule, solving (1) is equivalent to solving (2).

$$\hat{r} = \arg\max_{r \in R} P(s \mid r) \cdot P(r) \tag{2}$$

The two conditional probabilities $P(s|r)$ and $P(r)$ are often called the likelihood and the prior, respectively, in the computational linguistics literature. In this context, the likelihood $P(s|r)$ is the probability that the source form of a given candidate r is s, as opposed to some other source forms. The prior $P(r)$ is the probability of observing r as an adapted form that corresponds to some source form, whatever the source form may be.

For example, assuming that the source language is English and the recipient language Korean, the likelihood $P(/\text{bɹɑɪəɹ}/ \mid /\text{pɨɾɑiʌ}/)$ is the probability that /pɨɾɑiʌ/ is how the English word /bɹɑɪəɹ/ ('briar') is adopted in Korean rather than some other English word. The prior $P(/\text{pɨɾɑiʌ}/)$ is the probability of observing /pɨɾɑiʌ/ in a list of Korean loanwords. To predict how 'large' is adopted in Korean, one would calculate $P(/\text{bɹɑɪəɹ}/ \mid r) \cdot P(r)$ for every candidate form r and choose the one that maximizes the product of the two probabilities.

By making several assumptions including the independence assumption and the bigram assumption, I solve the equation in (2) with a first-order hidden Markov model whose states represent component units of the recipient language and generate component units of the source language as their observation. The most likely candidate form can be identified by running the Viterbi algorithm on the given source form. Details of the assumptions and the hidden Markov model implementation are described in the next two Sections.

3. Assumptions

One major issue with the statistical approach in Section 2 is how to estimate the likelihood and the prior specified in (2). A straightforward approach would be to get their maximum likelihood estimates from pairs of source form and the corresponding adapted form in the recipient language. That is, the likelihood and the prior can be estimated according to (3) and (4) as follows, where $C(s,r)$ denotes the number of times s is paired with r, $C(r)$ denotes the number of times r appears as an adapted form, and N denotes the total number of adapted forms.

$$P(s \mid r) = \frac{C(s,r)}{C(r)} \tag{3}$$

$$P(r) = \frac{C(r)}{N} \tag{4}$$

For example, suppose we had a database of Korean loanwords, like the one in Section 5, consisting of English words paired with their adapted form in Korean. The likelihood $P(/\text{bɹaɪəɹ}/ \mid /\text{pɨɾɑiʌ}/)$ can be estimated by dividing how often /bɹaɪəɹ/ is paired with /pɨɾɑiʌ/ by how often /pɨɾɑiʌ/ appears in the database as the adapted form. The prior $P(/\text{pɨɾɑiʌ}/)$ can be estimated by dividing how often /pɨɾɑiʌ/ appears in the database as the adapted form by the total number of adapted forms in the database.

However, the problem with (3) and (4) is that the frequencies $C(s,r)$ and $C(r)$ will be very small. It would be realistic to assume that each adapted form in the database appears at most once and is paired with just one word in the source language. That is, it is highly likely for most r that $C(r)=1$, and $C(s,r)=1$ or even $C(s,r)=0$ for many pairs. As a result, using the maximum likelihood estimates of the probabilities as in (3) and (4) for prediction would be meaningless.

In response, for a given pair of s and r, I rewrite each of the forms as a string of smaller component units and make the independence assumption and the bigram assumption to estimate the likelihood and the prior. Assuming that s and r are respectively rewritten as strings of n component units $s_1 s_2 ... s_n$ and $r_1 r_2 ... r_n$, the likelihood and the prior can be approximated as in (5) and (6). Note that in approximating the prior, we first pad the adapted form with the word boundary symbols <s> and </s> at the beginning and the end, respectively. That is, $r_0 = <s>$ and $r_{n+1} = </s>$ in (6).

$$P(s \mid r) \approx \prod_{i=1}^{n} P(s_i \mid r_i) = \prod_{i=1}^{n} \frac{C(s_i, r_i)}{C(r_i)} \qquad (5)$$

$$P(r) \approx \prod_{i=0}^{n} P(r_{i+1} \mid r_i) = \prod_{i=0}^{n} \frac{C(r_i, r_{i+1})}{C(r_i)} \qquad (6)$$

As long as the pair of component units (s_i, r_i) and the bigram of component units of an adapted form (r_i, r_{i+1}) are frequently found in the given database, the approximated likelihood and the prior will be robust.

Thus, the final issue to be resolved is how to define and identify the component units of the source form and the adapted form. In this paper, I assume that the component units of the source form are its component phonemes and that the component units of the adapted form are the sequences of zero or more of its phonemes that correspond to the component phonemes of the source form.

Note that the assumption I made for defining the component units of the adapted form requires alignment between the source form and the adapted form. Given that both the source form and the adapted form are initially written as strings of phonemes, the forms can be aligned using dynamic programming after defining the costs of following three edit-operations: substituting a phoneme in the source language with a phoneme in the recipient language, inserting a phoneme in the recipient language after a phoneme in the source form, deleting a phoneme in the source form.

In the current study, the substitution cost is assumed to be inversely proportional to the phonological similarity between the two phonemes; the more similar the two phonemes are, the more expensive substituting one phoneme for the other is. To calculate the phonological similarity, every phoneme in both languages is specified in terms of features listed in Table 1 and the similarity between every phoneme pair is calculated according to Frisch et al. (1997) using the script by Albright (2003).

Table 1. List of phonological features in terms of which all phonemes in both the source language and the recipient language are specified.

Phonological features
consonantal, sonorant, continuant, strident, lateral, labial, coronal, dorsal, round, anterior, distributed, front, central, back, high, mid, low, diphthong, nasal, advanced-tongue-root, spread glottis, constricted glottis, voiced

The resulting similarity score lies between zero and one. The substitution cost is defined as one minus the similarity score. Insertion and deletion are assumed to be as bad as substitution that involves two phonemes with zero similarity. As a result, the insertion cost and the deletion cost are assumed to be one in this paper. Table 2 illustrates how /bɹɑɪəɹ/ in English and its adapted form /piɾaiʌ/ in Korean are aligned using dynamic programming with the cost parameters thus defined.

Table 2. Illustration of how the phonemic transcription of the English word 'briar' is aligned with that of its adapted form in Korean.

Language	Phonemic transcription						
English	b		ɹ	ɑ	ɪ	ə	ɹ
Korean	p	i	ɾ	ɑ	i	ʌ	

The alignment example in Table 2 entails that the component units of the source form are its constituent phonemes /b/, /ɹ/, /ɑ/, /ɪ/, /ə/, and /ɹ/, while the component units of the adapted form are /pi/, /ɾ/, /ɑ/, /i/, /ʌ/, and *NULL*. Note that the unit /pi/ consists of two phonemes and that *NULL* stands for a unit of zero length. In turn, the likelihood $P(/bɹɑɪəɹ/ \mid /piɾaiʌ/)$ is estimated by multiplying the following component likelihoods: $P(/b//pɨ/)$, $P(/ɹ//ɾ/)$, $P(/ɑ//ɑ/)$, $P(/ɪ//i/)$, $P(/ə//ʌ/)$, and $P(/ɹ//NULL/)$. The prior $P(/pɨɾɑiʌ/)$ is the product over the following bigram probabilities: $P(/pɨ//<s>)$, $P(/ɾ//pɨ/)$, $P(/ɑ//ɾ/)$, $P(/i//ɑ/)$, $P(/ʌ//i/)$, $P(NULL//ʌ/)$, and $P(</s>/NULL)$. The maximum likelihood estimates of the component likelihoods and the bigram probabilities can be derived after all the pairs of source form and adapted form in the database are aligned.

4. Implementation as a First-order Hidden Markov Model

Once we have the likelihood and the prior, we need to identify the candidate form that maximizes the product of the two probabilities. One efficient way is to use a first-order hidden Markov model and the Viterbi algorithm.

The states of the model in the current study represent the set of constituent units in the recipient language, including the word-boundary symbols $<s>$ and $</s>$ described in Section 3. It should be clear that the set of constituent units can be identified by aligning all the pairs of source form and adapted form in a database of loanwords.

The model is in the initial state representing $<s>$ at the beginning. It probabilistically changes its state, possibly to the same state, one at a time. In the current study, the transition from a state to another state is bound by the bigram probabilities described in Section 3. For example, the probability of transition from the state representing $<s>$ to the state representing /pɨ/ is equal to $P(/pɨ//<s>)$.

The model probabilistically generates a phoneme in the source language while it is in a particular state as observation. In the current study, the emission of an observation is bound by the component likelihood in Section 3. For example, the probability of emitting /b/ as observation while in the state representing /pɨ/ is equal to $P(/b//pɨ/)$.

The probability of a particular state sequence generating a given observation sequence is calculated by multiplying all the transition probabilities and emission probabilities along the way. As the transition probabilities are equivalent to the component bigram probabilities and the emission probabilities are equivalent to the component likelihood, this is in fact equivalent to multiplying the likelihood and the prior approximated in (5) and (6).

Transition along a number of different state sequences can generate the same observation sequence, but with different probabilities. By running the Viterbi algorithm on the observation sequence, one can identify the state sequence that can generate the given observation sequence with the highest probability (Rabiner 1989: 263-4). In other words, running the Viterbi algorithm will essentially solve the equation in (2).

In this context, the given observation sequence would be the phoneme sequence of the source form. Our goal is to find the most likely sequence of states from the initial state representing <s> to the final state representing </s> that can generate the source form. Concatenating the component units in the recipient language that the states in the identified sequence represent will yield the most likely adapted form predicted by the model.

4.1. Monophones vs. Triphones

The hidden Markov model described above emits a single phoneme, or a monophone as observation while in each state. One can certainly enrich the content of the observation in various ways by representing it as a vector of multiple feature values instead of a single discrete value; the feature vector would consist of a monophone plus values of other features related to the monophone.

The feature I consider in this paper is the identity of phones immediately adjacent to a given monophone. The idea is that this will capture the effect of coarticulation on how listeners in the recipient language perceive the individual phones in the source form. The resulting model generates triphones as observation instead of monophones.

The difference between the monophone model and the triphone model is best illustrated by comparing how they calculate the likelihood. The monophone model calculates the likelihood as formulated in (5), which is repeated in (7) below for ease of comparison.

$$P(s \mid r) \approx \prod_{i=1}^{n} P(s_i \mid r_i) = \prod_{i=1}^{n} \frac{C(s_i, r_i)}{C(r_i)} \qquad (7)$$

In (7), the component likelihood $P(s_i|r_i)$ is the emission probability of the monophone model, where s_i is the ith phoneme in the source form and r_i the corresponding component unit in the adapted form. The triphone model, on the other hand, computes the likelihood according to (8).

$$P(s \mid r) \approx \prod_{i=1}^{n} P(s_{i-1}s_i s_{i+1} \mid r_i) = \prod_{i=1}^{n} \frac{C(s_{i-1}s_i s_{i+1}, r_i)}{C(r_i)} \qquad (8)$$

In (8), the component likelihood $P(s_{i-1}s_i s_{i+1}|r_i)$ is the emission probability of the triphone model, where $s_{i-1}s_i s_{i+1}$ is a triphone consisting of the ith phoneme in the source form and its neighboring phonemes. The 'phonemes' at the edge, s_0 and s_{n+1} are word boundary symbols <s> and </s>.

While a richer representation of observation can in principle lead to a more accurate model, it faces the risk of data sparseness. For example, the number of triphone types would be the number of monophone types cubed, in theory. It is possible that some triphones have no token in a given database. In such cases, their emission probability would be zero for every state in the model.

Zero emission probability is problematic because when the model computes the probability of a given observation sequence being generated by a particular state sequence, it multiplies the emission probabilities as well as bigram probabilities. If the emission probability of a triphone were zero for every state in the model, the probability of any state sequence generating the observation sequence including that triphone would be zero. As a result, it would be impossible to identify the most likely state sequence that generated the given observation sequence.

There are several ways to deal with this problem (Jurafsky and Martin 2008: 97-107). For the triphone model in this paper, I use a back-off method such that if every state in the model has zero emission probability for a given triphone, the model backs-off and uses the monophone emission probability as formulated in (9) below. For example, if every state in the triphone model has zero emission probability for the triphone /pzt/, the model uses the emission probability for the monophone /z/ instead.

$$P(s_{i-1}s_i s_{i+1} \mid r_i) = \begin{cases} P(s_i \mid r_i) & \forall r_k : P(s_{i-1}s_i s_{i+1} \mid r_k) = 0 \\ P(s_{i-1}s_i s_{i+1} \mid r_i) & Otherwise \end{cases} \qquad (9)$$

5. Evaluations

Both monophone and triphone models were evaluated in terms of how accurately they predicted the adapted form in Korean for a given English word after being trained on a subset of a Korean loanword database.

5.1. Data

The data used to train and evaluate the model is a subset of the database of Korean loanwords compiled by the National Institute of the Korean Language (NIKL 2008). The original database is a list of 24865 foreign words adopted as Korean loanwords along with information such as the adapted form spelled in Hangul, the domain in which the word is used, the source language, etc. Example entries look like the following:

#1chase#2 체이스#3 #4 편수일반, 용일
#1chashao[叉燒]#2 차사오#3 중국어#4 표준
#1chassis#2 새시#3 #4 편수일반, 용일, 표준
#1chateaubriand#2 샤토브리앙#3 프랑스어#4 표준

A total of 5812 entries that do not violate the following exclusion criteria were selected from the database:

- The source language is not English.
- The source word is an abbreviation.
- The source pronunciation is not available in a pronunciation dictionary for look-up.
- The adapted form reflects pragmatic knowledge of the word usage (e.g. Adapting 'Auckland' as '오클랜드국제공항' meaning 'Auckland international airport').
- The adapted form is the result of loanword shortening process (e.g. Adapting 'accelerator' as '악셀' which is the result of shortening the source word to 'accel.').

Each of the selected entries was rewritten as a pair of phonemic transcriptions, one for the original word in English and the other for the Korean loanword. The original source pronunciations were transcribed by looking up the CMU Pronouncing Dictionary, while the adapted forms were phonemically transcribed by applying letter-to-sound rules to their Hangul representation specified in the database. Ultimately, the data consisted of 5812 English-Korean pronunciation pairs.

5.2. Methods

Both the monophone and triphone models were evaluated in terms of prediction accuracy using five-fold cross validation. The dataset of 5812 pronunciation pairs described above was randomly shuffled and split into five sets of similar size. Two of these five sets had 1163 pairs each and the remaining three sets had 1162 pairs each. Each model was evaluated on one of the five sets after its emission probabilities and bigram probabilities were estimated from pairs in the remaining four sets. As there were five sets, this procedure was repeated five times, once for each set.

Prediction accuracy was measured in terms of word accuracy. For a given phonemic transcription of an English word, each model identifies the most likely underlying state sequence by running the Viterbi algorithm. Each state represents a substring of zero or more Korean phonemes. Concatenating the substrings results in a string of Korean phonemes, which was interpreted as the model's prediction of how the English form will be adapted in Korean. The model's prediction was deemed correct only if it is exactly identical to the Korean phonemic transcription in the dataset.

5.3. Results

The results are summarized in Table 3. Roughly speaking, the monophone model predicted a little less than half of the test items correctly, while the triphone model predicted a little more than half correctly. Paired t-test showed that the triphone model performed significantly better than the monophone model ($t(4)=18.198$, $p<0.0001$).

Table 3. Prediction accuracy of the monophone and the triphone models measured in terms of word accuracy using five-fold cross validation.

	Mean word accuracy	Standard Deviation
Monophone	48.07%	1.673
Triphone	52.65%	1.668

5.4. *N*-best predictions

While the mean word accuracy of the model is more or less than fifty percent, a closer look at the prediction errors reveals that some of them might be alternative answers although they are different from the ones suggested in the original database. For example, consider how some model predictions compare with the "correct" adapted forms in Table 4. There are predictions which might correspond to how some Korean speakers might use the word such as predictions of the triphone model /kʰaɾiko/ for 'cargo' or /ʌptʰeik/ for 'uptake'.

Table 4. Example prediction errors compared with the correct adapted forms suggested by NIKL (2008).

Source form		Correct	Prediction	
Spelling	Pronunciation		Monophone	Triphone
cargo	kaɹgo	kʰako	kʰoɾiko	kʰaɾiko
novelty	navəlti	nopeltʰi	nopʌltʰi	nopiltʰi
pixel	pɪksəl	pʰiksel	pʰiksil	pʰiksail
uptake	ʌpteɪk	ʌptʰeikʰi	ʌpʰitʰeikʰi	ʌptʰeik

In other words, there may be alternative forms in which a source form is adapted, but the given database suggests only one of them. As a result, model's performance may have been underestimated in the results in Section 5.3. One way to deal with this issue is to recruit native speakers of Korean to evaluate the model's prediction. However, this would be too costly. Another way is to let the model suggest multiple hypotheses and see if the form suggested in the database is one of them.

The Viterbi algorithm can be modified to return the *N*-best list, or a list of *N* most likely underlying state sequences, rather than the single most likely state sequence (Jelinek 1999: 86-89). So a second experiment was conducted with the same data and methods except for the following. The model was modified to return ten best hypotheses instead of the single best hypothesis. The model's prediction was deemed correct if the "correct" form was included in the ten best hypotheses.

The results are summarized in Table 5. On average, the ten best hypotheses from the model included the correct answer a little less than seventy percent of the time for the triphone model and a little more than sixty five percent of the time for the monophone model. Paired *t*-test showed that the triphone model performed significantly better than the monophone model ($t(4)=6.120, p=0.0018$).

Table 5. Prediction accuracy of the models measured in terms of the percentage of times the correct answer was one of the ten-best hypotheses from each model.

	Mean word accuracy	Standard deviation
Monophone	65.78%	1.355
Triphone	69.32%	0.880

6. Conclusion

In sum, I presented a statistical interpretation of the loanword adaptation process which was implemented as a first-order hidden Markov model. As its prediction, the model identifies the most likely sequence of phonemes in the recipient language given the phoneme string representing the source form. The prediction is based on the maximum likelihood estimates of the likelihood of the source form given the adapted form and the prior of the adapted form, where the estimates are derived from a list of pairs of source form and adapted form. Performance of the model was evaluated in terms of how accurately it predicts how English words are adapted in Korean after observing English-Korean pronunciation pairs.

The proposed model is meaningful in two ways. First, the reported performance of the statistical model provides a baseline performance level with which performance of other models can be compared. The proposed model is only one of many potential models of loanword phonology. Furthermore, it is a simple model in that incorporates virtually no linguistic knowledge. Second, it provides the means to evaluate various hypotheses on how the source form is perceived by the listeners of the recipient language. One can represent the source form in different ways and compare how different representation schemes affect the performance of the model. The current study compared the monophone representation scheme with the triphone representation scheme, but more phonologically interesting representation schemes can be evaluated and compared in the future.

One aspect of the model that is not desirable is that it is supervised. To determine the structure of the hidden Markov model and its parameters, one needs a set of examples of how source forms are adapted in the recipient language. The model must first learn from the examples before it generalizes what it learned to new source forms. This is problematic for two reasons. First, such example data may not be available for some language pairs. In addition, the probabilistic parameters of the model will be more robustly estimated if there are more examples. Even if some example data were available for a given language pair, it may not be large enough. Second, upon hearing a foreign word for the first time, human listeners can come up with some version of the adapted form without recourse to how other foreign words are adopted. An ideal model must mimic the behaviors of the listeners in this regard. Future research should be directed towards making the current model less supervised.

References

Albright, A. 2003. Similarity Calculator.pl. *Segmental Similarity Calculator, using the "shared natural classes" method of Frisch, Broe, and Pierrehumbert* (1997).

Frisch, S. A., Brow, M. B., and Pierrehumbert, J. B. 1997. Similarity and phonotactics in Arabic. *Rutgers Optimality Archive [Online]*. ROA-223-1097.

Jelinek, F. 1999. *Statistical Methods for Speech Recognition*. Cambridge: The MIT Press.

Jurafsky, D., and Martin, J. H. 2008. *Speech and Language Processing*. 2nd ed. Prentice-Hall.

Kang, Y. 2003. Perceptual Similarity in Loanword Adaptation: Adaptation of English Post-vocalic Word-final Stops in Korean. *Phonology* 20: 219-273.

NIKL. 2008. *Survey of the Loanword Usage*. The National Institute of the Korean Language.

Rabiner, L. R. 1989. A Tutorial on Hidden markov Models and Selected Applications in Speech Recognition. *Proceedings of the IEEE* 77: 257-286.

Variation and Noun-verb Asymmetry in Consonant Cluster Simplification in Seoul Korean

KYUWON MOON
Stanford University

1. Introduction

Korean consonant cluster simplification (henceforth CCS) is a phenomenon in which a consonant undergoes deletion when two consonants occur before a consonant or word boundary. This follows from a phonotactic condition on Korean syllable structure that does not allow more than one consonant to be in coda position.

When consonant clusters are followed by vowel-initial suffixes, resyllabification occurs, and the second consonant in the coda becomes the onset of the following syllable, as illustrated in (1b) and (2b). When clusters are followed by a pause or a consonant initial suffix, however, one of the consonants needs to be deleted to preserve the syllable condition (V, CV, VC, CVC), as shown in (1a) and (2a).

(1) C1C2 > C1
    a. /kaps/ → [kap]   'price'
    b. /kaps + -i/ → [kap.si]   'price' 'subject marker'

Japanese/Korean Linguistics 19.
Edited by Ho-min Sohn, Haruko Cook, William O'Grady, Leon A. Serafim, and Sang Yee Cheon.
Copyright © 2011, CSLI Publications

(2) C1C2 > C2

    a. /salm- + -ta/ → [sam.t'a]   'boil' 'declarative ending'

    b. /salm- + -a/ → [sal.ma]   'boil' 'connective ending'

The main characteristics of CCS in Korean are fourfold: First, the deletion process is completely obligatory. Unlike CCS in English, which is optional and is more frequent in casual speech than in formal speech, Korean CCS is required as part of the phonotactic constraints on syllable structure. Because Korean does allow consonant clusters across syllables but not within the syllables, and also because the onset of the following syllable (C3 in C1C2C3) is never affected by the deletion processes, Korean CCS is traditionally viewed as a syllable condition requirement, not as a phenomenon caused by consonant contact.

Second, when CCS occurs, the selection of which consonant is deleted varies according to the type of cluster. Below is the complete list of consonant clusters in Korean, divided by noun and verb, with the consonant that undergoes deletion in parentheses:

(3) Consonant Clusters in Korean (shaded where variation is observed)

	ks	ps	lk	lm	lp[1]
Noun	k(s)	p(s)	(l)k	(l)m	l(p)
	/saks/ [sak]	/kaps/ [kap]	/talk/ [tak]	/salm/ [sam]	/yedelp/ [yedel]
Verb		p(s)	(l)k~l(k)	(l)m	l(p)~(l)p
		/ops-/ [op-]	/ilk-/ [il-~ik-]	/kulm-/[kum-]	/yelp-/ [yel~yep]

	ls	lt^h	lh	nc	nh
Noun	l(s)				
	/tols/ [tol]				
Verb		l(t^h)	l(h)	n(c)	n(h)
		/halt^h-/ [hal-]	/alh-/[al-]	/anc-/ [an-]	/manh-/ [man-]

Third, as shown in (3), some consonant clusters show variation where the others do not. In /lk/ and /lp/ clusters, the surface representations of the verbs /ilk-/ and /yelp-/ vary in terms of realization as either the liquid or the stop. Fourth, the variation is only found in verbs, not in nouns, causing noun-verb asymmetry. These two characteristics, variation and noun-verb asymmetry, have been puzzling problems for Korean phonology.

The goal of this paper is to provide phonological explanation to these issues. For the solution, it is shown that in CCS the phonological conditioning plays a dominant role, but morphological conditioning is also

---

[1] In this paper I will not distinguish /p/ and /pʰ/, which are two different phonemes in Korean, because due to coda neutralization the two phonemes are identical in coda position, and because there is only one stem that contains /pʰ/ in consonant cluster: /ilpʰ-/.

important when phonology fails to determine the output (Anttila 2002). Based on this insight I argue that a morphologically driven OT approach is suitable for explaining variation and noun-verb asymmetry in CCS. Rather than addressing each issue individually and seeking a separate solution to the each problem, I suggest that a unified approach driven by both phonology and morphology sheds light on many controversial puzzles in Korean phonology.

Rejecting the dominant view that different outputs can be explained by reordering the constraints in an ad-hoc manner, I argue that variation caused by the competition of two phonological constraints is enough to explain the seemingly complicated phenomenon. Moreover, I show that the different phonological processes that apply to verbs and nouns, also known as noun-verb asymmetry, is in fact caused by morphological inflection; and therefore should be treated in morphologically-driven OT.

2. CCS Data: Production Experiment

There are as many different analyses of CCS as there are different descriptions of CCS data of Seoul Korean. The abundance of analyses and the often conflicting assumptions about the basic data make it difficult to use extant data to suggest new generalizations about the phenomenon.

The variation pattern in Korean that was discussed in the previous section has often been dealt with as a dialectal variation showing consistent patterns within the same dialect, but varies across different dialects (Iverson and Lee 1994, S. Cho 2000, Oh 1994). This observation mainly comes from the prescriptive grammar (NIKL 1988) or the generalization of the past dialectology studies, thus failing to capture the intra-regional variation patterns. In the studies where natural speech data are collected and intra-regional variation patterns are recognized, however, the data are only limited to the recordings of words in isolation (Hong 1991), or sentence completion task (T. Cho 1999). Therefore, the primary goal of the current production experiment is to demonstrate that Korean speakers show variation in pronouncing /lk/ and /lp/ consonant clusters, and to show that these patterns of variation are in fact systematic.[2]

For the experiment, 17 Seoul Korean speakers, aged between 22 and 32, were asked to read aloud the given texts with two distinct styles: i) prose

---

[2] Conducting an experiment is necessary with this phonological phenomenon because the existing corpus data are only written, and the deletion process is not shown orthographically. Furthermore, because the number of words that contain the two consonant clusters in question – /lk/ and /lp/ – is very small (about 15 stems in total, of which I chose 9 target stems for recordings), and because I am only looking at cases where a consonant follows the coda consonant clusters, it was impossible to find any existing and reliable data that have large amount of consonant cluster data.

reading style (PRS); ii) word-list reading style (WRS).[3] There were seven females and ten males. Because all of them are the interviewer's friends or relatives who are in the same age group as the interviewer, and because all the interviews were either conducted in their own house or their friends' house, it was easy to get less formal interview data.

Twenty-three or twenty-seven words[4] with stems of /lk/ and /lp/ clusters were embedded in the passage-reading style (PRS) sheet, and the same words were reproduced in the word-list reading style (WRS) sheet. Word lists contained fillers as well as stimuli, and the fillers were placed between the stimuli to avoid a possible familiarity effect. The number of fillers was twice as large as the number of stimuli, and the fillers also have the same inflectional paradigms as the stimuli. Nine stems, five with /lk/ clusters and four with /lp/ clusters, were provided with three inflectional morphemes, each starting with /-ta/, /-ko/, and /-ci/.[5] (See Appendix A for the complete list of stems and inflectional suffixes)

Below are the results of the production experiment. The overall patterns are shown in Fig.1, and Fig.2 and Fig. 3 show the patterns by phonological environments – following onsets – and styles. (See Appendix B for the full figures)

In the data collected, the variation patterns are found from both clusters: [l]~[k], [l]~[p]. Also, it is confirmed that young speakers of Seoul Korean have more tendency to preserve [l] than [k] or [p] variants in both /lk/ and /lp/ clusters. The stylistic patterns are also observed. In both /lk/ and /lp/ clusters speakers tend to preserve [l] more in the less formal style ($p < .01$, Pearson's chi square). For the following phonological environments effect, there is no effect of phonological environments except for _/k/ environment (cf. Jun 1995, T. Cho 1999).

This result strongly suggests not only the existence of variation in contemporary Seoul Korean speakers' speech, but also the systemic nature of it.

---

[3] All of the speakers are highly educated, having graduated from four-year universities. Most of them are M.A or Ph.D. students in Stanford University.

[4] Four more sentences with four more words were added for later interviews in order to reflect the whole inflection paradigm.

[5] The morphemes used in reading passage style are not necessarily the same ones as ones in word-lists; for /-ta/, /-tago/ and /-taga/, two different morphemes are used. It was inevitable to use the different morphemes in order to obtain natural speech that closely resembles informal speech. Since I am only looking at the effect of the following consonant, and the vowels following the consonants are identical among them (-ta-), it will not make any difference to the results.

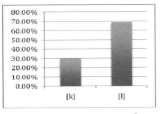

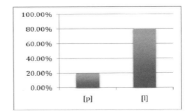

Figure 1. Overall patterns [6]

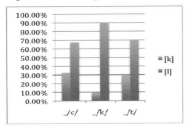

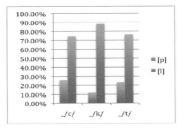

Figure 2. Phonological Environments

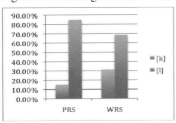

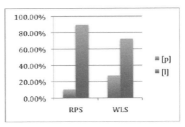

Figure 3. Style pattern

From Fig.1-2, it is shown that /lk/ and /lp/ clusters share the same pattern, contrast to the descriptions of many other studies (Iverson and Lee 1994, S. Cho 2000, Oh 1994, among others) where /lk/ and /lp/ patterns are treated separately, following the description of the prescriptive grammar.[7] Also, the /lp/ pattern in Fig.3 shows that code-switching from the less to more formal style does not result in more normative speech, which suggests that style

---

[6] [lk] and [lp] variants, that were argued to exist in some studies (Jun 1995, T. Cho 1999, among others) are ignored in this study because i) there was no evidence of [lk] and [lp] in spectrogram, and ii) non-Korean speakers cannot hear any [k] or [p] even in the most exaggerated speech, which suggests native speakers' bias might play a role.

[7] According to Korean Pronunciation Rule, published by National Institute of Korean Language, the proper pronunciation for /lk/ is /[k] while it is [l] for /lp/ (with the exception of /palp-/ → [pap-]).

differences in Fig.3 have an independent phonological motivation that is common to /lk/ and /lp/.

In general, it is apparent from the data that /lk/ and /lp/ show a similar pattern across the board. The motivation for the variation in /lk/ and /lp/ clusters, along with the explanations of the acquired patterns, will be discussed in the next section.

3. Phonological Conditioning: Emergence of Variation

In this section the phonological conditions for CCS are discussed. I argue that the emergence of variation in CCS is brought about by the different ranking of two phonological constraints, PERIPHERALITY and CODA SONORITY, as proposed in Iverson and Lee (1994) in the discussion of dialectal patterns in Korean. With the support of my data, however, it is shown that the variation is observed not only between different dialects but also in the same dialect. I show this to be the case in Seoul Korean. Thus, I argue that variation should be explained as a totally natural phenomenon that is caused by the competition of these two constraints, not by the ad-hoc application of different constraint rankings according to different environments.

In explaining the mechanism of CCS, Iverson and Lee (1994) introduced two relevant constraints – PERIPHERALITY and CODA SONORITY:

(4)   Constraints proposed (Iverson and Lee 1994)
        PERIPHERALITY: Parse Peripheral specifications (Or Parse marked specifications).
        CODA SONORITY: In syllable codas, parse segments with high sonority.

The motivation of PERIPHERALITY can be supported by the status of peripheral ([-coronal]) consonants in Korean, which can be seen in other phonological processes in Korean as well. For instance, in place assimilation, coronals assimilate to non-coronals, but not vice versa. The data also show that labials assimilate to velars, but not vice versa.

(5)   a. /sinpal/ → [simbal]   'shoe' (p→b:inter-sonorant voicing)
        b. /pat- + -ko/ → [pak.k'o] 'receive' 'conjuctive ending' (k→k':
                                      post-obstruent tensification)
        c. /nop- + -ta/ → *[not.t'a] 'high' 'declarative ending'

In fact, Korean assimilation is not an eccentric one considering assimilation patterns found in English, German, and Catalan (hot cake vs. cup cake), which gives the case cross-linguistic generalization (Kiparsky 1994). Unmarked segments, coronals in this case, assimilate to marked segments, which are non-coronals. In deletion, unmarked segments are deleted while marked segments are retained. This pattern also can be found in many other phenomena in various languages including English t/d deletion. The PERIPHERALITY constraint, therefore, reflects a natural phonological process in language and is not a language-specific constraint.

The perceptual salience ranking suggested by Jun (1995), which is grounded in phonetic data, also provides support for the PERIPHERALITY constraint in Korean. In analyzing the gradient pattern of CCS, he proposes the perceptual salience ranking as in (11):

(6)   Perceptual salience hierarchy in coda:
        dorsal > labial > coronal

It is argued in Jun (1995) that coronals are the least salient group among stops, and it is supported by the CCS data. This proposal is also supported by the more detailed perceptual analysis by Hume et al. (1999). Thus, the PERIPHERALITY constraint in Korean has significant independent motivation, grounded in both cross-linguistic generalizations and perceptual salience.

For the CODA SONORITY constraint, it has also been reported that many languages prefer segments of higher sonority in syllable codas (Vennemann 1988, Goldsmith 1990). According to these analyses, it is natural to delete non-sonorant (or less sonorant) segments in the coda, because the end of a syllable has to be higher in sonority than the beginning of the following onset. This generalization has been supported by many experiments that show higher probability for sonorants than obstruents as codas (Blevins 1995, Content et al. 1990), and cross-linguistic evidence of a preference for sonorants in the coda.

In Iverson and Lee (1994) and in the following OT-driven analyses (Cho 2000, Oh 1994, among others), however, the ranking between PERIPHERALITY and CODA SONORITY is applied for in ad-hoc manner, to account for the inter-regional variation of Korean CCS. In Seoul dialect, according to Iverson and Lee (1994), PERIPHERALITY dominates CODA SONORITY because [k]-variant is a winning output of /lk/ cluster. This analysis, however, not only fails to capture the [l]-variant pattern of Seoul Korean as shown in the earlier section, but also fails to provide the general insight to the problem – that variation emerges where phonology is at its weakest (Anttila 2002).

Let us reconsider the whole consonant clusters in Korean. PERIPHERALITY and CODA SONORITY constraints, when working together, can account for all the categorical deletions of CCS. Tableau (1) is repeated below as (7), omitting the clusters that show variation – /lk/ and /lp/.

(7)   Categorical conditioning (no variation)

	ks	ps	lm	ls	lt^h	lh	nc	nh
Noun	k(s)	p(s)	(l)m	l(s)				
	/saks/ [sak]	/kaps/ [kap]	/salm/ [sam]	/tols/ [tol]				
Verb		p(s)	(l)m		l(t^h)	l(h)	n(c)	n(h)
		/ops-/ [op-]	/kulm-/ [kum-]		/halt^h-/ [hal-]	/alh-/ [al-]	/anc-/ [an-]	/manh-/ [man-]

The CODA SONORITY constraint explains ([+sonorant], [+coronal]) and ([-sonorant], [+coronal]) clusters: ls (→l), lt (→l), lh (→l), nc (→n), nh (→n). The PERIPHERALITY constraint accounts for ([-sonorant], [-coronal]) and ([-sonorant], [+coronal]) clusters, along with ([+sonorant], [-coronal]) and ([+sonorant], [+coronal]): ks (→k), ps (→p), lm (→m). The OT analysis with each of these examples is shown in (8).

(8)   A. manh-   'much'
       B. salm   'life'

A. /manh-/	*COMPLEX	PARSE	PERIPHERALITY	CODA SONORITY
a. manh-	*!			
b. mah-		*	*	*!
c. ☞ man-		*	*	
B. /salm/	*COMPLEX	PARSE	PERIPHERALITY	CODA SONORITY
a. salm	*!			
b. sal		*	*!	
c. ☞ sam		*		

In (8A), c. [man-] can be a winner because b. [mah-] violates the CODA SONORITY constraint while [man-] do not. In (8B), c. [sam] can be a winner because b. [sal] does not satisfy the PERIPHERALITY constraint. Therefore, all the clusters in (7) can be explained with these two constraints.

However, the problem arises when these two constraints compete with each other: ([+sonorant], [-coronal]) and ([-sonorant], [+coronal]). /lk/ and /lp/ clusters fall into these cases, and not surprisingly, these two clusters are the ones that show variation in Seoul Korean. The variation is a totally expected and natural phenomenon, because there are two competing constraints in the same class of words (in the CCS system), and they ensure that different member of the clusters will be preserved. The competition between PERIPHERALITY and CODA SONORITY leads to variation.

(9)   Ranking for the variation account
        /lk/: il.t'a ~ ik.t'a
        /lp/: nel.t'a ~ nep.t'a
        → CODA SONORITY ~ PERIPHERALITY

By (9), it becomes clear that variation is in fact the most optimal choice, involving not only the designated cluster but also the whole consonant cluster system. Among all the clusters, /lk/ and /lp/ are the only clusters in which PERIPHERALITY and CODA SONORITY compete with each other. This competition, therefore, is resolved by freely ranked constraints, which lead to surface variation. There is no need to posit different rankings for the two clusters, for the variation occurs as a result of un-ordering of the two constraints. Thus, the variation arises when two cross-linguistic markedness constraints are at work together in shaping a phonological process. Although Korean CCS seems like the exception to the axiom that language changes to reduce variation, it is in fact an example of optimization of the broader phonological system.

4. Morphological Effects

So far we have seen that the choice between [k]/[p] and [l] is primarily conditioned by phonology – competition between two markedness constraints. The phenomenon, however, is more complicated, because nouns do not seem to act like verbs; the variation that was illustrated in the earlier sections is only found in verbs, not nouns. This asymmetrical pattern that is found in Seoul Korean is summarized below:

(10) Noun and verb pattern for /lk/ and /lp/ in Seoul dialect

	lk	lp
Noun	k	l
	/talk/ [tak] 'chicken'	/yedelp/ [yedel] 'eight'
Verb, Adjective	l~k	l~p
	/ilk-/ [il-]~[ik-] 'read'	/nelp-/ [nel-]~[nep-] 'wide'

This noun-verb asymmetry in (10) suggests that phonology alone cannot provide a solution. With respect to this issue, I argue that the asymmetry occurs not because of the genuine difference in noun and verb phonology in Korean, but because they go through the CCS process in different stages in derivation. Phonological variation, therefore, is motivated and constrained by morphological processes, which is a central assumption of Stratal OT (Kiparsky 2000, 2001).

4.1 Nominal and Verbal Inflection

The noun-verb asymmetry has been one of the primary issues in Korean phonology (Kang 2006, Ko 2006, Yun 2008, among many others). The asymmetry has been treated as a non-trivial issue in studies in which a unified analysis for nouns and verbs is presented. This asymmetry is observed in various phonological processes, including CCS.

(11) CCS

    a. Verbs: /ilk- + -ta/ → [ik.t'a]~[il.t'a]   'read' 'declarative ending'
    b. Nouns: /talk + -to/ → [tak.t'o]~*[tal.t'o]   'chicken' 'additive ending'

(12) Glide Formation

    a. Verbs: /s'o- + -a/ → [s'oa] ~ [s'wa]   'shoot' 'declarative ending'
    b. Nouns: /so + -e/ → [soe] ~ *[swe]   'cow' 'locative ending'

(13) i-deletion

    a. Verbs: /kʰi- + -ə/ → [kʰə], *[kʰiə]   'big' 'declarative ending'
    b. Nouns: /ki + -ege/ → [kiege], *[kege]   'he' 'directive ending'

As shown in (11)-(13), nouns and verbs seem to show different behaviors in some phonological processes. It should be noted that all the noun and verb asymmetry cases are found in derived environments, and never in non-derived environments. The fact that there is no noun-verb asymmetry inside of a single morpheme gives us positive evidence that the asymmetry is not caused by the inherent dissimilarity between nouns and verbs, but is motivated by morphological derivation.

Then how should this asymmetry be treated in a phonological theory that seeks for a unified account? (12) and (13) are the cases that are described as "underapplication" in some studies (Kang 2006, Ko 2006, Yun 2008) because nouns do not go through the same phonological processes – glide formation and i-deletion – as verbs. The underlying assumption of calling it "underapplication" is that nouns show "special" or "eccentric" behavior, so some processes that are supposed to take effect do not have an effect on nouns. However, this view gives us crucial insight into the noun-verb asymmetry issue. This "underapplication" process suggests that some phonological processes seem to be "blocked" in nominal inflection, and as a result, the processes cannot operate in the domain of nominal inflection. This observation is a key to the solution because it explains why there are only examples of "underapplication of nominal inflection," and no examples of "overapplication of nominal inflection."[8]

---

[8] There are, in fact, processes that are called "overapplication" in the literature (Kang 2006, Ko 2006, Yun 2008):

The motivation of analysis can be found from the generalization that nouns seem to be "blind" to some phonological processes. Thus, the solution to this issue is related to the properties of verbal and nominal inflection in Korean, namely that verbal inflection takes place at an earlier stage than nominal inflection. First, I will illustrate how verbs and nouns show different behavior in inflection due to their different status in morphology:

(16) Inflectional pattern of verbs and nouns (adopted from Yun 2008)
      a. Verbal Inflection: [Vstem]$_{Stem}$ending]$_{Stem}$]$_{Word}$
      b. Nominal Inflection: [Nstem] $_{Stem}$] $_{Word}$]particle] $_{Word}$

According to (16), the difference between verbs and nouns is that verbs can never be independent words without the help of endings (inflectional suffixes), while nouns can be independent words without the help of inflectional particles. This insight has led many scholars to consider invoking "Base" as a solution to the noun-verb asymmetry. The argument is that nouns and verbs behave differently because only nouns are Base (Kenstowicz 1997, Ko 2006), or because nouns and verbs have different kinds of Bases (Kang 2006, Albright and Kang in press). However, what is crucial in this inflectional pattern is that the inflected verb forms can be embedded in the nominal inflection. In other words, inflected verb stems, which can then function as an independent word, can be combined with a nominal particle and construct a word. The reverse, however, is not possible. This is shown with examples in (17):

(17)   Verbal and nominal inflection:
        [Vstem]$_{Stem}$ending]$_{Word}$]particle]$_{Word}$
        e.g. [ilk- + -ə] + -neun]   'read' 'conjunctive ending' 'topic

Thus, it can be concluded that verbs and nouns do not just show different behavior in inflection, but that they undergo different stages of inflection. This generalization is supported by the morphological fact that

---

(14) CCS
  a. Nouns: /kaps + -i/ → [kap.si] ~ [ka.bi](p→b: inter-sonorant voicing) 'price' 'subj.maker'
  b. verbs: /əps- + -ə/ → [əp.sə] ~ *[ə.bə] (inter-sonorant voicing) 'absent' 'declarative ending'

(15) Laryngeal neutralization
  a. nouns: /ip^h + -i/ → [i.p^{h}i] ~ [i.bi] (inter-sonorant voicing)   'leaf' 'subj.marker'
  b. verbs: /kip^h- + -ə/ → [ki.p^{h}ə] ~ *[ki.bə] (inter-sonorant voicing) 'deep' 'declarative ending'

In (14) and (15), it may seem like CCS and laryngeal neutralization are "over-applied" only to nouns. However, these cannot be examples of noun-verb asymmetry and are not analogous to (12) and (13), because the "over-applied" outputs, namely [ka.bi] and [i.bi] in (14a) and (15a), are the results of restructuring of verb stems (stems: /kap-/ and /ip-/). Therefore, they should be dealt with as a diachronic restructuring process, not as a synchronic derivation process.

nominal particles can be attached to inflected verbs, and the inflected verbs occupy the same status as bare nouns, in terms of their stage of inflection.

4.2 A Stratal OT Approach

Given the morphological characteristics that have been discussed in 4.1, I propose a Stratal OT approach (Kiparsky 2000, 2001), assuming that the phonological differences of nouns and verbs are affected by their morphological differences. Stratal OT, an OT version of Lexical Phonology and Morphology, assumes three levels of representations that are called "strata." The three levels consist of stem, word, and phrase levels, and they provide different constraint rankings for each stratum. The output of each ranking is linked to the next stratum, functioning as the input to the next stratum.

The principle of parallelism in classical OT is maintained in each stratum of the Stratal OT model. What it does for our analysis of noun-verb asymmetry is to explain why nouns are blind to some phonological processes that take effect on verbs. I assume that verbal inflection takes place at the Stem Level while nominal inflection takes place at the Word Level. Because nominal particles are only attached at the Word Level, the nouns are blind to the processes that verbs go through at the Stem Level.

In another Stratal OT approach to CCS, Yun (2008) assumes that the CCS process takes place at the same level (Word Level) for both nouns and verbs. This analysis can deal with the opacity problem that is caused by the interaction with tensification, but not the asymmetry between nouns and verbs.

(18) Proposed rankings in Yun 2008:

Verb: /ilk-/	'read'	Noun: /talk/ 'chicken'
	ilk- + -ta	talk
Stem Level	*OO [9] >> MAX-IO-C >> IDENT-IO(tense),* COMPLEX, VOICING	
	ilk.t'a	talk + -to
Word Level	*COMPLEX, *OO, VOICING >> MAX-IO-C >> IDENT-IO (tense)	
	il.t'a ~ ik.t'a	tal.do ~ tak.t'o

Because the rankings in (18) do not have any constraints that specify which segment survives in coda position, it cannot block outputs like *tal.do, so the ranking yields a wrong output. Although we can try to modify the analysis by incorporating PERIPHERALITY and CODA SONORITY constraints in the model, we cannot get the correct outputs because there is no way in

---

[9] *OO: no lax obstruent sequences

this analysis to get different outputs for nouns and verbs in terms of selection of consonants in the coda.[10]

The analysis proposed here, however, can successfully deal with variation and noun-verb asymmetry because it assumes that CCS occurs at different levels for nouns and verbs.

(19)   Proposed Ranking

        Verb: /ilk-/ 'read'   Noun: /talk/ 'chicken'

                ilk + ta   talk

        Stem Level   *COMPLEX >> MAX-IO-C >> *POBS-ONSE[11] >> VOICING,

                            CODA SONORITY ~ PERIPHERALITY

                            il.t'a ~ ik.t'a   talk + -to

        Word Level   *COMPLEX >> MAX-IO-C >> PERIPHERALITY >> CODA

                            SONORITY, *POBS-ONSET, VOICING

                            il.t'a ~ ik.t'a   tak.t'o

(20) OT Analysis: Stem Level

/ilk- + -ta/	*COM PLEX	MAX-IO-C	*POBS-ONSET	VOICING	CODA SONORITY	PERIPHE RALITY
a. ilk.ta	*!		*			
b. ilk.t'a	*!					
c. il.ta		*	*!	*		*
d. ☞ il.t'a		*				*
e. il.da		*	*!			*
f. ☞ ik.t'a		*			*	

In (20), because CODA SONORITY and PERIPHERALITY are unordered at the Stem Level, the input /ilk- + -ta/ yields two outputs: il.t'a and ik.t'a. They then go into the Word Level and yield the same output as the Stem Level because they are the most faithful candidates.

---

[10] Yun (2008) adopts a Stratal OT approach for a very different motivation from this paper. It is proposed to solve an opacity puzzle of CCS, regarding noun-verb asymmetry, namely that the obstruent in the onset ([t] in [ta]) is tensed after a lateral [l], which is not an expected phonological process. It is pointed out that this opacity is only shown in verbs (so /ilk- + -ta/ → il.t'a) but not in nouns (/yedelp + -to/ → yedel.do). Although this analysis seems to work well with the opacity problem in verbs, it has not solved the noun-verb asymmetry puzzle for two reasons. First, the word *yedeldo*, which is an example of non-opacity in nouns, is the only noun that has a /lp/ cluster. Therefore, it is questionable to call it a systematic noun-verb asymmetry, for it might only be a lexical exception. Second, /yedelp + -to/ can actually be pronounced with a tensified onset, as 6 people out of 17 in my data did in my data ([yedel.t'o]).

[11] *Pobs-onset: No plain obstruent in onset.

(21) OT Analysis: Word Level

1) /il.t'a/	*COM PLEX	MAX- IO-C	PERIPHE RALITY	*POBS- ONSET	VOICING	CODA SONORITY
a. ☞ il.t'a			*			
b. ilk.t'a	*		*			
2) /ik.t'a/	*COM PLEX	MAX- IO-C	PERIPHE RALITY	*POBS- ONSET	VOICING	CODA SONORITY
a. ☞ ik.t'a						*
b. ilk.t'a	*			*		*
/talk + -to/	*COM PLEX	MAX- IO-C	PERIPHE RALITY	*POBS- ONSET	VOICING	CODA SONORITY
a. talk.to	*!			*		
b. talk.t'o	*!					
c. tal.to		*	*!	*	*	
d. tal.t'o		*	*!			
e. tal.do		*	*!	*		
f. tak.to		*		*!		*
g. ☞ tak.t'o		*				*

For nouns, it is shown in (21) that a nominal particle -to is attached at the Word Level and undergoes a simplification process. Because PERIPHERALITY dominates CODA SONORITY at the Word Level, the ranking yields the correct output, tak.t'o.

It should be noted that the constraints that are involved in noun-verb asymmetry –CODA SONORITY and PERIPHERALITY – are the very constraints that shape the phonological conditioning of CCS, as discussed in section 3. Thus, it seems to echo the generalization of Finnish variation data that Anttila (2002) discusses. In Anttila (2002), it is shown that morphological effects emerge where phonology cannot decide which variant should surface. In CCS in Korean, noun-verb asymmetry occurs because different constraint rankings seem to be responsible for nouns and verbs; CODA SONORITY and PERIPHERALITY constraints are competing with each other in verbal inflection, but PERIPHERALITY wins out over CODA SONORITY in nominal inflection. In other words, CODA SONORITY and PERIPHERALITY, the two constraints proposed for CCS, are unordered at the Stem Level, thus yielding two outputs for verbs. At the Word Level, however, the PERIPHERALITY constraint dominates the CODA SONORITY constraint, thus yielding only one output for nouns.[12]

---

[12] The analysis proposed in this paper is by no means a complete solution to Korean CCS, because it does not deal with opacity problem caused by an interaction with tensification (Tak

5. Conclusion

In this paper, I have shown a case in which variation emerges where phonology is weak in its predictive power, with Consonant Cluster Simplification data in Korean. It is argued that the intra-regional variation shown in /lk/ and /lp/ clusters in Seoul Korean is caused by the competition between two cross-linguistically motivated constraints, and so the variation is a result of un-ordering of the two constraints.

The locus of variation is where morphological effects apply. The variation is only observed with verb stems, but not in nouns. This seemingly complex puzzle of noun-verb asymmetry is explained by a morphologically driven OT analysis. The advantage of a Stratal OT analysis is that morphological processes strictly motivate the phonological processes, so there is no need to posit anything else other than different strata.

This paper has shown how variation is conditioned by both phonology and morphology. I argue that proposing different rankings without an adequate motivation should be avoided in analyzing variation, for variation is part of strictly regulated linguistic system, not a random and unexpected process. More studies on various kinds of phonological processes in Korean will be needed to confirm the wider applicability of my analysis.

References

Albright, A. and Kang, Y. in press. Predicting Innovative Alternations in Korean Verb Paradigms. *Proceedings of CIL18: The 18th International Congress of Linguists.* John Benjamins.

Anttila, A. 2002. Morphologically Conditioned Phonological Alternations. *Natural Language and Linguistic Theory* 20: 1-42.

Cho, S. 2000. Choycekseng ironey uyhan caumgwun tansunhwa hyensanguy pangen chai pwunsek (An analysis on dialectal differences of Korean consonant cluster simplification by the optimality theory). *Sahoy enehak* 8 (1): 497-523.

Cho, T. 1999. Intra-dialectal Variation in Korean Consonant Cluster Simplification: A Stochastic Approach. *Chicago Linguistic Society* 35: 43-57.

Goldsmith, J. 1990. *Autosegmental and Metrical Phonology.* Oxford: Basil Blackwell.

Hong, Y. 1991. *A Sociolinguistic Study of Seoul Korean.* Seoul: Research Center for Peace and Unification of Korea.

2001, Sohn 1999, Yun 2008). In my analysis tensification was handled with the *Pobs-onset constraint that forces a tensified consonant to appear in the onset. This treatment, however, is only an intermediate step toward an analysis that can incorporate the opacity issue with the current analysis. Tensification itself is a notoriously complicated process in Korean, and only by looking at this issue from a broader perspective that incorporates tensification can we arrive at a comprehensive analysis of CCS.

Hume, E., Johnson, K., Seo, M., Tserdanelis, G., and Winters, S. 1999. A Cross-linguistic Study of Stop Place Perception. *Proceedings of the XIVth International Congress of Phonetic Sciences*: 2069-2072.

Iverson, G. K. and Lee, S. 1994. Variation as Optimality in Korean Cluster Reduction. *Proceedings of ESCOL 94*.

Jun, J. 1995. Perceptual and Articulatory Factors in Place Assimilation: an Optimality Theoretic Approach. PhD dissertation, UCLA.

Jun, J. 1998. Restrictions on Consonant Clusters. *Enehak* 23: 189-204.

Kang, Y. 2006. Neutralizations and Variations in Korean Verbal Paradigms. *Harvard Studies in Korean Linguistics XI*, ed. S. Kuno et al., 183-96. Seoul: Hanshin Publishing.

Kenstowicz, M. 1997. Base Identity and Uniform Exponence: *Alternatives to Cyclicity. Current Trends in Phonology: Models and Methods*, ed. J. Durand and B. Laks. 363-394. Salford: University of Salford.

Kiparsky, P. 1994. Remarks on Markedness. Handout from TREND 2.

Kiparsky, P. 2000. Opacity and Cyclicity. *The Linguistic Review* 17: 351-367.

Kiparsky, P. 2001. Stratal OT vs. Sympathy. Ms., Stanford University.

Ko, H. 2006. Base-Output Correspondence in Korean Nominal Inflection. *Journal of East Asian Linguistics* 15 (3): 195-243.

Oh, M. 1994. A Reanalysis of Consonant Cluster Simplification and S-neutralization. *Theoretical Issues in Korean Linguistics,* ed. Y. Kim-Renaud. 157-174. Stanford: CSLI.

Sohn, H. 1999. *The Korean Language*. Cambridge: Cambridge University Press.

The National Institute of the Korean Language (NIKL). 1988. *Phyocwun palumpep* (Standard pronunciation). The National Institute of the Korean Language.

Tak, J. 2001. Opacity in Korean: A Sympathy Approach. *Korean Journal of Linguistics* 26: 587-602.

Yun, J. 2008. A Stratal OT Approach to a Noun-Verb Asymmetry with respect to Opacity in Korean. paper presented at the 32nd Penn Linguistics Colloquium, University of Pennsylvania.

Vennemann, T. 1988. *Preference Laws for Syllable Structure and the Explanation of Sound Change*. Berlin: Mouton de Gruyter.

Japanese Velar Allophones Revisited: A Quantitative Analysis Based on Speech Production Experiments*

SHIN-ICHIRO SANO
Dokkyo University

1. Introduction

This research reexamines the voiced velar allophones of /g/ in Japanese through a quantitative analysis based on speech production experiments, taking phonological factors governing the distribution of these allophones into account.[1] It has been traditionally assumed that velars in Japanese realize as either plosives [g] or nasals [ŋ] (Kindaichi 1942, Otsu 1980, Kato 1983, Shibatani 1990, Hibiya 1995, 1999, Inoue 1998, Okada 1999, Kindaichi and Akinaga 2001, Inoue and Yarimizu 2002, Vance 1987, 2008, among others). The distribution of velar allophones has been assumed to be

* I would like to thank Ross Krekoski, Ichiro Yuhara, Timothy Vance, Natsuko Tsujimura, the audience at the 19th conference, and reviewers for their valuable comments. Special thanks also go to the members of Sophia Phonetics Lab and Frank Scott Howell for their help and support on this and an earlier version of this paper. Any remaining faults are, of course, mine.

[1] In the following, I refer to voiced velars (allophones) as simply velars (allophones).

Japanese/Korean Linguistics 19.
Edited by Ho-min Sohn, Haruko Cook, William O'Grady, Leon A. Serafim, & Sang Yee Cheon.

governed by contextual factors. The fundamental restriction is concerned with position within a word: velars realize as plosives in word-initial positions as in *gakuhi* 'tuition' (Figure 1); on the other hand, in word-internal positions as in *dokuga* 'venom fang,' velars realize as nasals (Figure 2).[2]

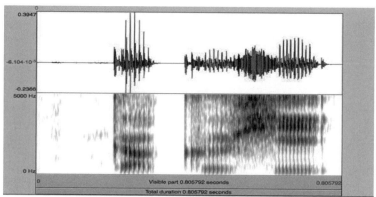

Figure 1. Waveform and spectrogram of [g] in *gakuhi* (speaker #03)

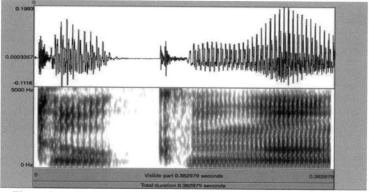

Figure 2. Waveform and spectrogram of [ŋ] in *dokuga* (speaker #01)

The positional restriction interacts with some other factors such as lexical strata (e.g. Sino-Japanese, Yamato Japanese, or loanwords), and word-internal structure in compounds (Kindaichi 1942, Vance 1987, among others).[3] The intricate interactions of contextual factors define the variable dis-

---

[2] For the details of the recording and the phonetic analysis, see Section 2.

[3] At this point, I consider the reason for the idiosyncratic distribution of velar allophones in onomatopoeic words. Japanese onomatopoeic words involve reduplication as in *garagara*, *mogumogu*. The allophonic realization of velars in these words obeys distinct rules: 1) in ini-

tribution of velar allophones. However, a few works point out that velars can realize as fricatives [ɣ] as in Figure 3 (spirantization, Kintaichi 1942, Kamei 1956, Hattori 1957).

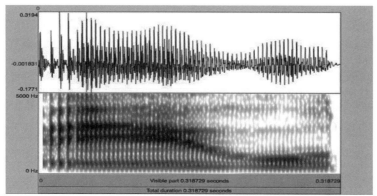

Figure 3. Waveform and spectrogram of [ɣ] in *eigo* 'English'(speaker #02)

Furthermore, the distribution of velar allophones shows some variation and change. In terms of dialectal difference, in Tohoku dialect nasals are remarkable; on the other hand, in Kansai dialect, velars categorically realize as plosives, and in Kanto dialect the situation is intermediary (Vance 1987, among others). Thus, the dialectal difference of velar allophones is characterized as Tohoku dialect > Kanto dialect > Kansai dialect, with respect to nasals. As for a change, a decline of velarnasalization has been reported, namely, cases have been increasing where velars in word-internal positions realize as plosives instead of supposed nasals, in violation of the aforementioned restrictions (Kindaichi 1942, Hibiya 1995). Specifically, Kindaichi (1942) claims that the rate of velar nasals has been declining starting with

---

tial positions of each constituent (a base and a reduplicant), velars categorically realize as plosives as in ([garaɡara]), even though the initial position of the second constituent is a word-internal one; 2) velars categorically realize as nasals, only if the velars appear in final positions of each constituent as in [moŋumoŋu] (Vance 2008). Based on the assumption that the Japanese reduplication involves the process where the first constituent functions as the base and the second one functions as the reduplicant obtained by copying the base, I argue that in the former case the reduplicant is obtained by copying a base that includes velars in word-initial positions ([gara]); it follows that the reduplicant also includes word-initial velars and all velars realize as plosives, even though the velars in the reduplicant themselves position word-internally; on the other hand, in the latter case the reduplicant is obtained by copying a base that includes velars in word-internal positions ([moŋu]); it follows that the reduplicant also includes word-internal velars and all velars realize as nasals. Thus, the difference between the former case and the latter one can be attributed to whether the process involves the copying of word-initial velars or of word-internal velars.

speakers born in the 1910s;[4] Hibiya (1995) claims that 48% of all the velars in word-internal positions realized as nasals in the data collected in 1986.

However, as we saw above, in-depth analysis of the data has been insufficient, phonetic/phonological aspects of the distribution of velar allophones have been underresearched, and crucially velar fricatives have been overlooked, as previous studies had mainly been based on the "word" as their units of analysis. The goals of the present research, therefore, include: 1) to challenge the claims of previous studies such as the traditional plosive/nasal dichotomy and the decline of velarnasalization; 2) to examine the effects of factors, that govern the distribution of velar allophones. Specifically, the analysis focuses on the following points: distributions 1) in word-initial position, 2) in post-nasal position, 3) in sequential contexts; 4) the effects of following vowels; 5) dialectal difference. Throughout the analysis, I assume a trichotomy among plosives, nasals and fricatives following the claim of spirantization.[5]

This paper is organized as follows: Section 2 introduces the details of the experiments; in Section 3, I summarize the results; in Section 4, I present the analysis and discussion; Section 5 concludes the discussion.

2. Method

2.1 Target Words

In the speech production experiments, I selected target words exclusively from Sino-Japanese words with three mora length for the purpose of eliminating the effects of word length and of lexical strata. In addition, in Sino-Japanese words the distribution of velars is relatively free, allowing us to set up various contexts. Specifically, I arranged target words focusing on the following factors: phonological contexts such as word-initial velars, post-nasal velars, and sequential velars; and the types of following vowels. The target words include the following six phonological contexts:

(1) [$_U$ g (no carrier sentence)   e.g. *gakuhi*   'tuition'
(2) [$_ω$ g   e.g. *gimmi*   'review'
(3) Vg   e.g. *dokuga*   'venom fang'
(4) Ng   e.g. *ginga*   'galaxy'
(5) VgVg   e.g. *eigo-ga*   'English-case particle'
(6) NgVg   e.g. *rongo-ga* 'Analects-case particle'

---

[4] Kindaichi (1942) did not record audio data.

[5] In the present data, some velar allophones, characteristics similar to voiced velar approximants were observed. I include these allophones showing among the fricatives, instead of establishing an extra independent category.

Velars, in themselves, appear in word-initial positions both in (1) and (2). In (1), however, target words are not embedded in carrier sentences (*kare-wa* '......' *to itta* "He said ' ...... '"), yielding velars in utterance-initial positions; on the other hand, in (2) target words are embedded in carrier sentences, yielding velars in word (prosodic word, accentual phrase) -initial positions. Every target word is presented as embedded in carrier sentences except for (1). In (3) velars appear in post-vocalic positions. In (4) velars appear in post-nasal positions. (5) and (6) include the sequential contexts where syllables involving velars are adjacent. (5) involves two post-vocalic velars; on the other hand, (6) involves post-nasal velars followed by post-vocalic velars. Every sequential context includes the case-particle *ga*.

For each context listed above, I arranged five extra contexts with respect to the types of following vowels (/gi/, /ge/, /ga/, /go/, /guɯ/).

2.2 Participants

I randomly sampled three participants according to the following criteria:[6] 1) age: under 25; 2) gender: male/female; 3) hometown: Tohoku/Kanto/Kansai areas; 4) experience abroad: less than one month. Specifically, in order to examine the progress of loss of velarnasalization, I focused on younger speakers; for the examination of dialectal differences, I sampled one speaker from each of these areas; and to eliminate the influence of foreign languages, I limited experience abroad to a short time-period. In the prior questionnaire, no participants reported auditory impairments.

2.3 Recording

The recording were conducted in a soundproofed room at the Sophia University phonetics lab, for each participant individually. The recording conditions are as follows: recorder: SONY linear PCM recorder; Microphone: SONY ECM-959DT (directionality: 90°); Sampling frequency: 48 kHz; Quantization: 16bit; monaural digitization. In the recordings, I randomly presented target words and distracters embedded in carrier sentences one by one; participants read the whole sentence according to the presented script. I recorded at least five tokens for each target word/distracter.[7]

2.4 Segmentation

The recorded audio data were in turn analyzed by Praat (version. 4.5.08, Boersma and Weenink 2006). Spectrogram settings were as follows: View range: 0~5000Hz; Window length: 0.005s; Dynamic range: 50dB. I extract-

---

[6] The attributes of participants are shown in the Appendix. In the pilot study, I conducted the recording as well as the analysis of audio data of one extra participant gender.

[7] Although in some cases I recorded more than six tokens for a certain word, only five out of six tokens were subjected to analysis.

ed the parts corresponding to velar allophones from the audio data and classified these into plosives, fricatives, and nasals. The criterion for the classification of velar allophones is schematized below.

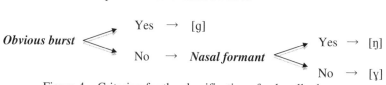

Figure 4. Criterion for the classification of velar allophones

Firstly, if an obvious burst (closure and release) was observed with respect to the waveform (e.g., Figure 1), the velar allophone was categorized as a plosive; if no obvious burst was observed, then I checked for a nasal formant; if a nasal formant was observed (e.g., Figure 2), the velar allophone was categorized as a nasal; if no nasal formant was observed (e.g., Figure 3), then the velar was categorized as a fricative.[8]

3. Results

As mentioned above, I arranged six phonological contexts and five contexts for the types of following vowels. In addition, each target word in sequential contexts included two velars. Thus, the total tokens I focused on amount to 600 (6 phonological contexts × 5 vowels × 5 tokens × 3 speakers + 2 phonological contexts × 5 vowels × 5 tokens × 3 speakers). The overall distribution of velar allophones is summarized in Table 1.

Table 1. Distribution of velar allophones

	frequency	%
	277	46.17
	269	44.83
	54	9
Total	600	100

As Table 1 shows, the frequency (269) as well as the probability (44.83%) of fricatives are almost the same as those of plosives (frequency: 277; probability: 46.17%); on the other hand, the frequency (54) and the probability (9%) of nasals are extremely low. The result shows that velar fricatives, which have been overlooked in previous works, are frequently observed in actual utterance and that the decline of velarnasalization has been accelerated, considering the younger age of participants.

---

[8] The discrimination between velar nasals and velar fricatives in post-nasal positions (Ng) involved some difficulties.

Next, I show the distribution of velar allophones by six phonological contexts arranged in the target words.

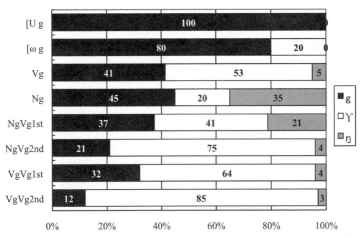

Figure 5. Distribution of velar allophones by phonological contexts[9]

In Figure 5, "NgVg$_{1st}$" and "VgVg$_{1st}$" represent the preceding velars in sequential contexts (e.g. *rongo-ga*, *eigo-ga*), and "NgVg$_{2nd}$" and "VgVg$_{2nd}$" represents the following velars (e.g. *rongo-ga*, *eigo-ga*).

As Figure 5 shows, the probability of plosives is 100% in utterance-initial position and 80% in word-initial position. In word-initial position, plosives are shown to be predominant; on the contrary, no nasals are observed. In postnasal position nasals show a relatively higher probability (Ng: 35%; NgVg$_{1st}$: 21%) compared with other positions. In sequential contexts, we can observe the higher probability for fricatives (NgVg$_{2nd}$: 75%; VgVg$_{1st}$: 64%; VgVg$_{2nd}$: 85%).

Based on the results, I make a rough generalization for the distribution of velar allophones with respect to phonological context: 1) word-initial positions – [g]; 2) post-nasal positions – [ŋ]; 3) sequential contexts – [ɣ].

4. Analysis

In this section, I will conduct detailed analyses as well as discussions for each context.

---

[9] Every distribution in the following figures was shown to be statistically significant, although I omit the details due to space limitations.

4.1 Word-initial Position

Firstly, I examine the effect of word-initial position. Although previous studies claim that velars realize as plosives in word-initial position, it is unlikely that words are uttered separately in spontaneous speech; instead, words are usually surrounded by preceding and following constituents in a continuous stream of utterances. Given that Japanese basically takes the CV syllable structure, it follows that velars are surrounded by preceding and following vowels (CV**g**V) even in word-initial position, and velars can realize as fricatives according to the aforementioned spirantization. To verify this hypothesis, I examine the distribution of velar allophones by word-initial and other positions. The result is shown below.

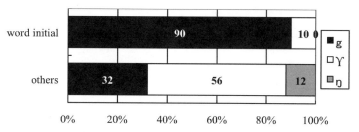

Figure 6. Distribution of velar allophones by word-initial/others

As shown in Figure 6, in word-initial position the probabilities of plosives and of fricatives are 90% and 10%, respectively, and no nasals are observed, demonstrating that plosives are predominant in word-initial position. In other positions, on the other hand, the probability of plosives is 32%, that of fricatives is 56%, and that of nasals is 12%, showing that fricatives are more frequent and plosives are less frequent than in word-initial position. Thus, word-initial position was shown to have a strong impact on the distribution of velar allophones; however, the claim of spirantization was also verified in actual utterances, considering the fact that velar fricatives, albeit only slightly, were attested.

Next, I examine the distribution within word-initial positions. Specifically, I examine the difference between utterance-initial positions ([$_U$ g) and word-initial positions ([$_\omega$ g) with respect to their effects on the distribution of velar allophones. I illustrate the distribution of velar allophones by utterance-initial and word-initial positions in Figure 7.

As Figure 7 shows, every velar categorically realizes as plosive in utterance-initial position; on the other hand, in remaining word-initial position the probability of plosives is 80% and that of fricatives is 20%, and no nasals are observed. The result slightly differs from the claims of previous studies: although plosives are predominant, not a few fricatives are observed in word-initial position.

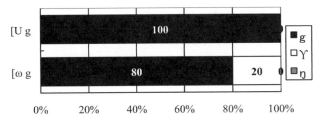

Figure 7. Distribution of velar allophones in word-initial position

Thus, we can argue that the difference in utterance-initial and other word-initial positions affects the distribution of velar allophones, and that velars can realize as other allophones than plosives due to some phonological factors even if they are in the same position within a "word." The result further shows that in word-initial position velar allophones are not categorically restricted to plosives; rather, the distribution should be characterized in a gradient manner; for example, plosives are more frequent than fricatives in word-initial positions.

At this point, I consider the reason for the different distributions in utterance-initial and after word-initial positions in terms of the difference in levels of strengthening in prosodic structure: initial segments of each prosodic category undergo strengthening; the degree of strengthening depends on the level of the category in prosodic structure: the higher the level, the stronger the strengthening (e.g. utterance > intermediate phrase > accentual phrase > prosodic word) (Keating 2006, among others). In the present case, the utterance-initial positions are higher, while word-initial positions, which are categorized as accentual phrases or prosodic words, are lower with respect to the levels in prosodic structure. This gives more chance for word-initial positions to be spirantized, where weaker strengthening is expected.

4.2 Post-nasal Position

I turn now to the examination of the distributions in post-nasal positions, where it can be predicted that velars are likely to realize as nasals, being affected by the preceding nasals. To verify this hypothesis, I examine the distribution of velar allophones by post-nasal and other positions. The result is shown in Figure 8.

Focusing on the distribution of nasals, we can recognize that nasals show a higher probability in post-nasal positions (28%) than in other positions (3%). In post-nasal positions, velars preferentially realize as nasals compared with other positions, in support of the hypothesis.

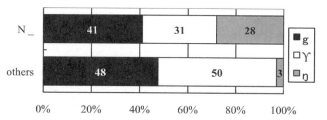

Figure 8. Distribution of velar allophones by post-nasal position/other

This process can be thought of as a kind of progressive assimilation. All in all, however, the probability of nasals is lowest in either context compared with that of plosives and of fricatives, showing that the higher likelihood of nasalization in post-nasal positions is suppressed by the effect of the decline of velarnasalization. The interaction among factors is demonstrated to play a crucial role in defining the distribution.

4.3 Sequential Context

In this part, I examine the distribution in sequential contexts. In sequential contexts, it can be hypothesized that time for tongue movement is insufficient, resulting in halfway closure, and more fricatives are observed. To verify this hypothesis, I examine the distribution of velar allophones by sequential and single contexts. The result is shown below.

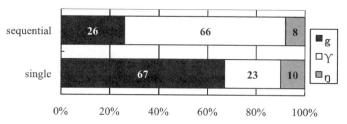

Figure 9. Distribution of velar allophones by sequential/single contexts

As shown in Figure 9, in single contexts the probability of fricatives is 23% and plosives show the highest probability (67%); on the other hand, in sequential contexts fricatives show the highest probability (66%). The result shows that in sequential contexts velars are more likely to realize as fricatives, as hypothesized.

Next, I analyze the distribution within sequential contexts. Firstly, which one is more likely to realize as fricatives, preceding velars or following velars? Preceding velars cannot be affected by other preceding velars as there are no other preceding velars; on the other hand, following velars may well be affected by preceding velars, yielding more fricatives. I illustrate the distribution of velar allophones by preceding/following distinction.

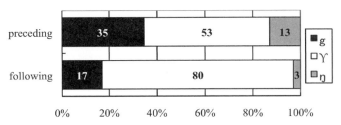

Figure 10. Distribution of velar allophones by preceding/following

As Figure 10 shows, the probability of fricatives is extremely high in following velars (80%), as predicted; however, the high probability of fricatives is also observed in preceding velars (53%). The result shows that in sequential contexts following velars are more likely to realize as fricatives, and that preceding and the following velars are interacting with each other. Note that in the present analysis the following velars are all included in case particles, and most of the following velars realize as fricatives, contrary to the claims of previous studies that velars in case particles categorically realize as nasals (Kindaichi and Akinaga 2001, and others). The result suggests the importance of phonological factors rather than grammatical factors.

Secondly, I take a closer look at the relationship between preceding and following velars. Specifically, I examine whether preceding and following velars in a single token match or mismatch with respect to the allophonic realization. Given the result that the distributions of preceding velars and of following ones are different, I hypothesize that preceding and following velars mismatch. I verify the hypothesis by cross-tabulation.

Table 2. Cross-tabulation of the distributions of preceding and of following

following \ preceding			
	15 (60%)	6 (24%)	4 (16%)
	37 (31%)	73 (61%)	10 (8%)
	0 (0%)	0 (0%)	5 (100%)
Total	52	79	19

$\chi^2 = 47.03$, $d.f. = 4$, $p = 1.504e-09$, fisher's exact test: $p = 6.664e-07$

In Table 2, cases where preceding and following velars match show a higher probability (shaded cells). Furthermore, putting all tokens together, the probability of "match" constitutes 62% of all cases ("mismatch": 38%), showing that preceding and following velars in sequential contexts are more likely to match, contrary to the hypothesis. Note that in sequential contexts velars are not adjacent as there is an intervening vowel as in *eigoga*. Therefore, I argue that the matching in the present case is an instance of assimilations in nonlocal contexts, in support of the Long Distance Consonant Agreement (LDCA: Rose and Walker 2004), which assumes the agreement of consonantal features in nonlocal contexts.

4.4 Effects of Following Vowels

A number of phonetic/phonological researches to date point out that consonants undergo some changes with respect to their features, because they are affected by following vowels (Keating et al. 1994, Ladefoged 2006, among others). If this is on the right track, the distribution of velar allophones should vary according to the types of following vowels. I examine the distribution of velar allophones for the five Japanese vowels.

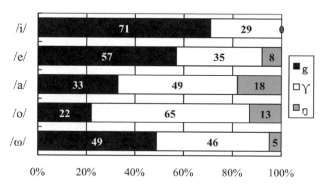

Figure 11. Distribution of velar allophones by types of following vowels

As shown in Figure 11, the probability of plosives is higher before /i/ and /e/; on the other hand, the probabilities of fricatives and nasals are higher before /a/ and /o/. The result shows that the distribution of velar allophones is affected by types of following vowels as expected: specifically, plosives are more compatible with high and front vowels, while fricatives and nasals are more compatible with low and back vowels. This can be attributed to articulatory reasons: to articulate velars followed by low and back vowels, a relatively larger tongue movement is required, compared with high and front counterparts, resulting in halfway-closure, and velars are likely to realize as fricatives or nasals, rather than plosives.

4.5 Dialectal Difference

Finally, I examine the distribution in terms of dialectal difference. As mentioned above, the dialectal difference of velar allophones is characterized as Tohoku dialect > Kanto dialect > Kansai dialect, with respect to nasals. Even with the decline of velarnasalization, is the characterization of dialectal difference still valid? If so, we would obtain a distribution similar to the above even in the present analysis, which focuses on utterances of younger speakers. For the examination, I classified velar allophones according to the region of origin of speakers. The result is shown below.

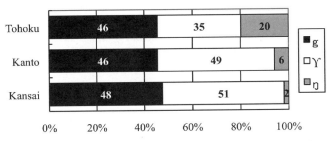

Figure 12. Distribution of velar allophones by speakers/origin

As Figure 12 shows, with respect to nasals Tohoku shows remarkably higher probability (20%), and nasals are frequent in the following order: Tohoku > Kanto > Kansai, showing that the characterization of dialectal difference remains valid. Although no significant difference is observed with respect to plosives, the following tendency is observed concerning fricatives: fricatives are most frequent in Kansai, least in Tohoku, and Kanto is in between. This order is the exact opposite of the one in nasals.

5. Conclusion

In this paper, I presented an analysis of Japanese velar allophones. Specifically, I challenged their traditional categorization, and I examined their distribution taking phonetic/phonological factors into account. The examinations brought forth the following findings: 1) the decline of velarnasalization has been accelerated; 2) word-initial velars can realize as fricatives, although plosives are predominant (contra Kindaichi 1942; the distribution is governed by the prosodic structure (cf. Keating 2006)); 3) post-nasal velars preferentially realize as nasals; 4) velars in sequential contexts preferentially realize as fricatives; 5) progressive assimilation is observed in post-nasal positions and sequential contexts (LDCA, Rose and Walker 2004); 6) velars preceding front and high vowels preferentially realize as plosives, while those preceding low and back vowels are more likely to realize as fricatives or nasals; and 7) the characterization of dialectal difference is still valid (nasals: Tohoku dialect > Tokyo dialect > Kansai dialect). Incidentally, the distribution of velar allophones in Japanese shows some similarity with those in Spanish with the plosive/fricative dichotomy, except for nasals (Japanese: utterance-initial positions: plosives, post-nasal positions: nasals, other contexts: fricatives; Spanish: utterance-initial/post-nasal positions: plosives, other contexts: fricatives) (cf. Hualde 2005).

I propose that the traditional plosive/nasal dichotomy is insufficient to account for the nature of the velar allophones in Japanese; instead, the velar allophones need to be discussed in terms of the trichotomy with fricatives; the distribution of velar allophones is defined by the interaction between language changes and phonological factors. Furthermore, it can even be predicted that nasal will disappear; the velar allophones will be comprised only of plosives and fricatives.

Appendix: attributes of participants

Speaker #	age	gender	hometown
01	19	male	Iwate
02	25	female	Kanagawa
03	22	male	Nara

References

Boersma, P. and Weenink, D. 2006. *Praat: Doing Phonetics by Computer* (Version 4.5.08) [Computer program]. Retrieved December 20, 2006, from http://www.praat.org.

Hattori, S. 1957. Nihongo no Boin. *Kobayashi Rigaku Kenkyûjo Hôkoku* 7. (Reprinted in T. Shibata et al. eds. 1980. *Nihongo no Gengogaku, Dainikan: On'in*, 68-99. Tokyo: Taisyûkan syoten.)

Hibiya, J. 1995. The Velar Nasal in Tokyo Japanese: A Case of Diffusion from Above. *Language Variation and Change* 7(2): 139-152.

Hibiya, J. 1999. Variationist Sociolinguistics. *Handbook of Japanese Linguistics*, ed. N. Tsujimura, 101-120. Oxford: Blackwell.

Hirayama, T. 1960. *Zenkoku Akusento Jiten*. Tokyo: Tôkyôdô syuppan.

Hualde, J. I. 2005. *The Sounds of Spanish*. Cambridge: Cambridge University Press.

Inoue, F. 1998. *Nihongo Watching*. Tokyo: Iwanami syoten.

Inoue, F. and Yarimizu, K. 2002. *Jiten <Atarasii Nihongo>*. Tokyo: Tôyô syorin.

Kamei, T. 1956. Ga-gyô no Kana. *Kokugo to Kokubungaku* 39(9): 1-14.

Kato, M. 1983. Tokyo niokeru Nenreibetsu Onsei Tyôsa. *'Sinhôgen' to 'Kotoba no Midare' nikansuru Shakaigengogaku-teki Kenkyû*, ed. F. Inoue, Kakenhi hôkokusyo.

Kawakami, S. 1977. *Nihongo Onsei Gaisetsu*. Tokyo: Ohû.

Keating, P. 2006. Phonetic Encoding of Prosodic Structure. *Macquarie Monographs in Cognitive Science, Speech Production: Models, Phonetic Processes, and Techniques*, eds. J. Harrington and M. Tabain, 167-186. New York and Hove: Psychology Press.

Keating, P., Byrd, D., Flemming, E., and Todaka, Y. 1994. Phonetic Analyses of Word and Segment Variation Using the TIMIT Corpus of American English. *Speech Communication* 14: 131-142.

Kent, R. D. and Read, C. 1992. *The Acoustic Analysis of Speech*. San Diego: Singular.

Kindaichi, H. 1942. Ga-gyô Bionron. *On'in no Kenkyû*. (Reprinted in Kindaichi 1967)

Kindaichi, H. 1967. *Nihongo On'in no Kenkyû*. Tokyo: Tôkyôdô.

Kindaichi, H. and Akinaga, K., eds. 2001. *Sinmeikai Nihongo Akusento Ziten*. Tokyo: Sanseidô.

Ladefoged, P. 2006. *A Course in Phonetics*, 5th ed. Boston: Thomson Wadsworth.

Leben, W. 1973. *Suprasegmental Phonology*. Ph.D. dissertation, MIT.

Martin, S. 1952. *Morphophonemics of Standard Colloquial Japanese*. Language Dissertation 47. Linguistic Society of America.

McCawley, J. 1968. *The Phonological Component of a Grammar of Japanese*. The Hague: Mouton.

NHK Hôsôbunka Kenkyûzyo ed. 1966. *Nihongo Akusento Ziten*. Tokyo: Nihon Hôsô Syuppan Kyôkai.

Okada, H. 1999. Japanese. *Handbook of the International Phonetic Association*, ed. International Phonetic Association, 117-119. Cambridge: Cambridge University Press.

Otsu, Y. 1980. Some Aspects of Rendaku in Japanese and Related Problems. *MIT Working Papers in Linguistics* 2: *Theoretical Issues in Japanese Linguistics*, eds. Y. Otsu and A. Farmer, 207–227.

Rose, S. and Walker, R. 2004. A Typology of Consonant Agreement as Correspondence. *Language* 80: 475-531.

Selkirk, E. 1984. *Phonology and Syntax: The Relation between Sound and Structure*. Cambridge, MA: MIT Press.

Shibatani, M. 1990. *The Languages of Japan*. Cambridge: Cambridge University Press.

Stevens, K. 1998. *Acoustic Phonetics*. Cambridge, MA: MIT Press.

Vance, T. 1987. *An Introduction to Japanese Phonology*. Albany: State University of New York Press.

Vance, T. 2008. *The Sounds of Japanese*. Cambridge: Cambridge University Press.

Part II

Syntax

Decomposing Overt Syntax*

YOSHIHISA KITAGAWA
Indiana University

1. Introduction and Background

The goals of this work are: (i) to direct our attention to the existence of prosody-information synchronization in linguistic expressions, and propose an approach to capture it in the grammar, and (ii) to explore the implications of the proposed approach for the reorganization of grammar, redefining the notion 'overt syntax'. In particular, it will be pointed out that overt syntax, including overt movement, should be regarded as nothing but the two related but independent computational processes that induce the synchronized effects at PF and LF.

* I am grateful to the organizing committee of JK 19 for providing me with this wonderful opportunity to present my research. I would also like to thank Phil LeSourd, Miguel Rodríguez-Mondoñedo and Satoshi Tomioka for helpful comments, and Sang Yee Cheon for her patience and cooperation while I prepared this article. The usual disclaimer applies. This material is based upon work supported by the National Science Foundation (NSF) under Grant No. 0650415.

Japanese/Korean Linguistics 19.
Edited by Ho-min Sohn, Haruko Cook, William O'Grady, Leon A. Serafim, & Sang Yee Cheon.

2. Prosody-Information Synchronization

2.1 Wh-focus

In semantico-pragmatic terms, wh-interrogatives and their answers have long been analyzed as foci (Hamblin 1973). Independently, it has also been pointed out that wh-interrogatives are often accompanied by a distinct focus prosodic pattern, for instance as in Tokyo Japanese illustrated in (1) (Kori 1989, Maekawa 1991).

(1) Kanozyo-wa ano-ban $\boxed{\text{DA}}$re-to   atteita-*no*?
    she-TOP   that-night who-with seeing-COMP$_{\text{Wh}}$

    'Who$_1$ was she seeing t_1 that night?'

'Focus Prosody' (henceforth **FPD**) involved here can be characterized by 'Wh-focus prominence' (indicated by a boxed portion of a wh-word) followed by 'post-focal reduction', which significantly compresses the pitch range of all subsequent items in the FPD domain (indicated by an underline). All matrix questions also involve the utterance-final 'Interrogative Rise' (indicated by a question mark).[1]

More recently, Deguchi and Kitagawa (2002) and Ishihara (2003) pointed out that the grammar of Japanese induces even finer correspondence between the prosody and the interpretation of Wh-focus —the domain of FPD coincides with the scope domain of Wh-focus in such a way that the final word of FPD (i.e. COMP) corresponds to the syntactic head of the Wh-scope domain (CP). Thus, a wh-interrogative sentence that is potentially ambiguous in its scope can be disambiguated by two distinct patterns of FPD as illustrated below. First, if the FPD terminates at the subordinate COMP as in (2), the wh-phrase in the subordinate CP takes subordinate scope.

(2) [$_{\text{CP}}$ Keesatu-wa [$_{\text{CP}}$ kanozyo-ga ano-ban $\boxed{\text{DA}}$re-to   atteita-*ka*]
     police-TOP   she-NOM   that-night   who-with   seeing-COMP$_{\text{Wh}}$
     kaKUNIN-SIYOoto-siteiru-*no*]?
     confirm-try.to-doing-COMP$_{\text{Y/N}}$
     'Are the police trying to confirm [*who*$_1$ she was seeing t_1 that night]?'

In (2), the post-focal reduction and hence FPD terminates at the subordinate COMP (henceforth **Local FPD**), and the entire utterance is interpreted as a yes-no question. The end of the post-focal reduction in Local FPD is signaled by the Initial Rise applying in the first post-COMP element in the

---

[1] FPDs of distinct kinds have been also reported on other dialects of Japanese. See Kubo (2001), Smith (2005) and Igarashi (To appear) among others. In this work, I concentrate on Tokyo Japanese, which I simply refer to as "Japanese" throughout. I also examine only the examples including lexically accented Wh-phrases and post-COMP items for clarity.

matrix clause (e.g. *kaKUNIN-SIYO'oto* 'confirm-try.to' in (2)). If, on the other hand, FPD is extended in the same sentence up to the matrix COMP as in (3) below (henceforth **Global FPD**), the Wh-focus takes the matrix scope. The entire utterance therefore is interpreted as a wh-interrogative (with the subordinate COMP *-ka* interpreted as 'whether'.)

(3) [$_{CP}$ Keesatu-wa [$_{CP}$ kanozyo-ga ano-ban DAre-to atteita-*ka*] kakunin-
    who-with -COMP$_{Wthr}$ confirm-

siyooto-siteiru-***no***]?
trying.to-COMP$_{Wh}$

'**Who$_1$** is such that the police are trying to confirm [*whether* she was seeing **him$_1$** that night]?'

One crucial property of Global FPD worth paying attention to is that its domain does not necessarily correspond to any syntactic constituent, as can be seen in (3), while it is prosodically indicating that the matrix CP is the Wh-scope domain. Such a twisted correlation between the two domains indicates that the sound-meaning synchronization in question cannot be captured solely in terms of hierarchical syntactic analyses. The pitch-track diagrams in Figure 1 and Figure 2 below (reproduced from Ishihara (2003: 61) with permission) illustrate the tonal properties of Local and Global FPD, respectively. (The Wh-focus prominence is indicated by an upward arrow, the post-focal reduction by an oval, and the pos-COMP rise by a box.)

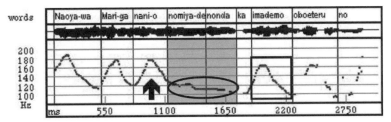

'Does Naoya still remember [**what$_1$** Mari drank *t$_1$* at the bar]?'
Figure 1: Pitch-track diagram of *Local* FPD for *Subordinate* Wh-scope

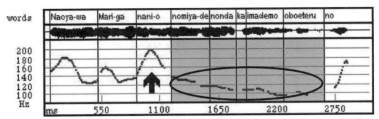

'**What$_1$** is such that Naoya still remembers [whether or not Mari drank **it$_1$** at the bar]?'
Figure 2: Pitch-track diagram of *Global* FPD for *Matrix* Wh-scope

In short, the grammar of Japanese permits the interpretive scope of information packaging involving a Wh-focus in Tokyo Japanese to be synchronized with the focus prosody domain starting from a wh-phrase and ending with COMP.

The successful synchronization of matrix wh-scope and Global FPD as in (3) (as well as in the sentence in Figure 2) has very important implications for the syntax of Japanese. Since a wh-phrase located in a wh-island can provide an acceptable matrix scope interpretation, we should *not* consider that Subjacency as a grammatical constraint is at work in Japanese, contra Nishigauchi (1990) and Watanabe (1992). It has also been pointed out, on the other hand, that the matrix wh-scope interpretation in a potentially ambiguous sentence like (3) is heavily handicapped because of multiple extra-grammatical biases toward the subordinate wh-scope interpretation as summarized in (4).

(4) a. The matrix scope interpretation for the wh-in-situ located within a wh-island is pragmatically uncommon, and it generally needs to satisfy a more elaborated presupposition than the subordinate scope interpretation.

    b. Global FPD to accompany the matrix wh-scope is prosodically more marked than Local FPD. As a result, Local FPD as a default prosodic pattern is generally assigned in production as well as in perception through silent reading (in accordance with the Implicit Prosody Hypothesis argued for by Fodor (1998), Bader (1998), and Fodor (2002), among others.

    c. For the matrix wh-scope interpretation, the wh-item in the subordinate clause would have to be associated with the non-local COMP in defiance of the locality requirement imposed by the on-line processing strategy (Miyamoto and Takahashi 2002).

    d. The critical prosodic cue *listeners* need in the on-line processing of the matrix wh-scope interpretation often fails to be encoded by *speakers*.

Such multiple extra-grammatical biases against the matrix wh-scope interpretation in a potential ambiguous sentence often induces awkwardness when the sentences is presented for judgment, typically in a null discourse context without appropriate prosody assigned. The awkwardness induced this way has been repeatedly misinterpreted as ungrammaticality and misattributed to Subjacency in the literature. For relevant discussion, see Kitagawa and Fodor (2003), Kitagawa (2005), and Kitagawa and Fodor (2006) for (4a-c) and Hirose and Kitagawa (2008) for (4d).

2.2 The Syntax of Prosody-Scope Synchronization

How can we capture these (and possibly other) cases of prosody-information (i.e. sound-meaning) synchronization? Since the model of generative grammar has been designed to let syntax mediate sounds and meanings, the most obvious answer is that such synchronization is established in syntax, that is, in the course of computation in I-languages. Some core working hypotheses of the minimalist program prescribe that computation in I-languages have the following properties. First, computational operations are characterized as nothing but an algorithm to simply *map lexical information onto PF and LF*, which is not allowed to append any other information (='Inclusiveness Requirement'). Second, computation must *completely split* lexical information into PF and LF representations (='Legibility Requirement'). Third, computational operations are induced *only to achieve legitimacy at the interface* (= 'Least Effort Requirement').

Adopting this view, I would like to hypothesize that whatever information which ensures sound-meaning synchronization is encoded in lexical items and comes to be split into part of PF and LF in the course of syntactic derivation. In particular, I postulate what I call 'Physical/Logical Feature Complex (henceforth **PL-Complex**), which takes the form [f_P, f_L]. A PL-Complex consists of two parts — a feature legitimate for sounds [f_P] and one legitimate for meanings [f_L]. I tentatively assume that a PL-Complex is an interpretable feature complex motivated by information packaging, and that it is assigned to lexical items when Numeration (or Lexical Array) is formed, just as formal features are assigned there. A PL-Complex then comes to be split into [f_P] and [f_L] in the course of computation, and [f_P] at PF provides some instruction to the performance system for sounds and [f_L] at LF provides some instruction to the performance system for meanings. In this way, the sound-meaning synchronization can be established in the grammar effectively and naturally.

In order to achieve the prosody-scope synchronization involved in wh-interrogatives, I propose the following analyses. First, the grammatical concept of 'Wh-focalization' is introduced into Numeration as what I call the 'WC-pair', consisting of a wh item and a COMP, each of which is specified with a PL-Complex as indicated in (5).[2]

(5) a. *dare* 'who':   [$\mathbf{W_P}$, $\mathbf{W_L}$]
    b. *-ka* 'COMP$_{Wh}$': [$\mathbf{C_P}$, $\mathbf{C_L}$]

---

[2] To be precise, the PF-Complexes for the WC-pair should probably be analyzed as consisting of the Wh-question feature inherent to a Wh-word and what should be called 'Focus' PL-Complexes. For simplicity, however, I treat them as if they were inseparable, which is probably true only in the unmarked case.

Introduction of a grammatical unit/concept into syntax in the form of a pair of lexical items is nothing unusual. The aspectuals and passive in English, for instance, require the appropriate pairing of an auxiliary verb and a participle (e.g. perfect expressed with *have* and *-EN*).

The synchronization of Global FPD and matrix wh-scope we observed in (3) above, for example, will be represented as in (3') below with these PL-Complexes.

(3) **PF**: [$_{CP}$ Keesatu-wa [$_{CP}$ kanozyo-ga ano-ban $\boxed{DA}$ re$_{WP}$-to   atteita-ka]

  kakunin-siyooto-siteiru-*no*$_{CP}$]?   **Beginning of FPD**

  End of FPD

LF: [$_{CPL}$ Keesatu-wa [$_{CP}$ kanozyo-ga ano-ban $\boxed{DA}$ re$_{WL}$-to atteita-ka]

Scope domain   **Wh as focus**

  kakunin-siyooto-siteiru-*no*$_{CL}$]?

  Head of scope domain

'**Who**$_1$ is such that the police are trying to confirm [*whether* she was seeing **him**$_1$ that night]?'

At PF, the domain of FPD is defined *linearly*, W$_P$ indicating the initial point of FPD and C$_P$ its terminal point. As pointed out earlier, this prosodic domain does not have to correspond to any syntactic constituent. At LF, W$_L$ indicates the focused wh-item and C$_L$ indicates the head of the scope domain of this focus. Grammar then must fulfill a rather difficult task of synchronizing the domain of FPD (linear information) with the Wh-scope domain (hierarchical information). The introduction of PL-Complexes, however, can fulfill this task properly and achieves the prosody-information synchronization.

3. Implications for the Model of Grammar

The proposed approach to prosody-information synchronization has great potential for the improvement of the minimalist program, permitting us to eliminate some undesirable theoretical constructs from the grammar.

3.1 Current Deviation from the Minimalist Standards

While the notion 'movement', especially 'overt movement', perhaps had long been the strongest drive for the advancement of generative syntax, its justification became rather difficult — at least unofficially so — when the framework made the 'minimalist' turn. In the minimalist program, overt syntax has been characterized as the computation that takes place *before Spell-Out*, and thereby affects both PF and LF rather than LF alone. First, in order to justify its inclusion into the grammar, the EPP-feature was postulated (Chomsky 2000, 2001), which bluntly requires various functional heads to attract some item to their Spec positions. This theoretical device, however, simply is a restatement of the problem rather than its solution. Furthermore, in order to justify why movement occurs overtly, i.e. why it applies before Spell-Out, it had to be assumed that the EPP property is a 'virus,' which needs to be eliminated before any larger constituent is created by Merge. Movement is made overt, in other words, at the expense of the postulation of an imperfect entity that needs to be eliminated even before it reaches the interface, disregarding the major tenet of the framework, i.e. the legibility requirement imposed only on the interface. Note also that movement was made to induce displacement effects at both PF and LF *accidentally* because of this tailor-made imperfection to be eliminated before Spell-Out. It does not seem to be overly brash, therefore, to state that the EPP approach to overt movement was a rather desperate attempt, with the absence of any other good alternative, to achieve the displacement effects anticipated at PF as well as LF.

Miyagawa (2010) attempted to substantiate this approach by identifying EPP as agreement features on the target heads. He claimed that EPP triggers overt movement because it needs to agree and this agreement must take place locally with its Spec.[3] Chomsky (2001: 5) assumes that 'Agree' must apply before Spell-Out since valued agreement features on the target heads may provide phonetic effects at PF while they cannot play any role at LF. The combination of these assumptions would in effect provide some substance to both EPP and virus. Note, however, that overt movement applies in this approach basically for providing phonetic effects at PF, and if it induces any effect on LF, it takes place only *incidentally* or merely as a *by-product*.

Bošković (2007) also pointed out that EPP characterized as 'I need a Spec' would inevitably induce a "look-ahead" problem in Chomsky's phase approach when movement applies in a successively cyclic fashion. In (6) below, for instance, the Phrase Impenetrability Condition would require *what* to have moved to the intermediate Spec-CP for further movement to the matrix Spec-CP.

(6) [$_{CP}$ **What**$_1$ do-**C** you think [$_{CP}$ **t**$_1$ that$_C$ Mary bought **t**$_1$]?
　　　　　　　EPP　　　　　　　　　　EPP

This also means that EPP must have been introduced under the subordinate C in (6). There are cases such as (7) below, on the other hand, in which wh-movement cannot take place within the subordinate CP.

---

[3] See Borer (1986), Kitagawa (1986: 236), and Kuroda (1988) for the earlier proposals that EPP is reducible to obligatory agreement.

(7) *[$_{CP}$ **Who$_2$ C** t_2 thinks [$_{CP}$ **what$_1$** that$_C$ Mary bought **t$_1$**]?
     EPP   ~~**EPP**~~

The introduction of EPP under the subordinate C in (7) therefore would incorrectly permit this sentence. Since EPP for the subordinate C is introduced only when the item in its Spec must move further to the matrix Spec-CP, a decision with 'look-ahead' would inevitably be needed.

To avoid this problem, Bošković proposed an alternative approach, in which he argues that the EPP property should be regarded as the 'I need to be a Spec (of the target head)' property of the *moving* element rather than the 'I need to have a Spec' property of the target head. In particular, it was argued that an uninterpretable feature assigned to the moving element as a checkee is required to move to the Spec-position of the target head as a checker so that it can c-command and induce a proper feature checking relation. Bošković further claims that the uninterpretable feature of the moving item in question is a Case feature on NP ([uK]) in NP-movement, and identifies the checking relation imposed on it as (a reincarnated version of) the Case Filter. It is also claimed that overt wh-movement is induced by another type of uninterpretable feature [F] ([uF]) on the wh-item, which must be checked by [uF] of COMP at its Spec position as in (8a).

(8) a.   I wonder [$_{CP}$ **who$_1$** COMP [$_{IP}$ **t$_1$** bought **what**]]
                         ~~**[uF]**~~   ~~**[uF]**~~   **[iF]**
     b. *I wonder [$_{CP}$ COMP [$_{IP}$ John bought **what**]]
                              [uF]   **[iF]**

A sentence like (8b) is ruled out in English since the interrogative COMP is assumed to have [uF] universally, and it would remain unchecked with the absence of the movement of a wh-phrase with [uF]. Bošković argues that this analysis eliminates the 'lookahead' problem of successively cyclic movement. A wh-phrase with [uF] has its own motivation to start and keep moving until it becomes the Spec of an appropriate head. This means that movement can launch and continue without having to anticipate the introduction of any target head into the syntactic object.

Note that in order for the proposed 'I need to be a Spec' features to induce movement in overt syntax, they must have some relevance to both PF and LF. It is difficult to see, however, what roles the proposed uninterpretable features play at LF. For instance, the idenitity of [F] assigned to wh-phrases is left unspecified except that it is assumed to be "related to focus" (p. 631). While moved wh-phrases have been assigned [uF], the 'in-situ' wh-phrases have been assigned [iF], as in (8a) above. If the uninterpretable [F]s ([uF]s) undergo deletion after they induce wh-movement and checking in overt syntax, they would not remain on either of the moved wh-phrase and the target COMP at LF. The same feature [F], on the other hand, would be interpreted at LF on the in-situ wh-phrases. It then would have to be the case that the wh-phrases as foci are interpreted in distinct ways between what seem to be synonymous wh-questions in (9a-b).

(9) a. **What**₁ did-COMP John eat **t**₁?
   [uF]   [uF]

 b. John-wa **nani**-o   tabeta-no?
    John-TOP what-ACC ate-COMP_Wh
       [**iF**]

The role of [F] at LF, in other words, is unclear and appears inconsistent.[4] Case ([K]) for A-movement, especially structural Case, hardly seems to play any role in semantic interpretation, either. The true motivation for the proposed features therefore seems to reside in the displacement effects they induce at PF. Other than that, it is not very clear if these features have any consistent role to play at PF.[5] The sole contents of [F] and [K], in other words, seem to be the property 'I need to be located at the Spec-position of the target head at PF (i.e. must be pronounced there),' and overt movement is assumed to apply before Spell-Out solely to achieve this anticipated displacement effects at PF.[6] Once again, if any simultaneous LF effects arise, they are incidental. In short, none of the EPP approaches examined above seem to be capable of providing satisfactory answers to the fundamental questions involved in the postulation of overt movement in the minimalist program 'Why overtly move?' (i.e. 'Why move before Spell-Out?') without failing to attain the minimalist standards.

The only consistent picture that emerges when we examine the analyses of overt movement offered in the literature seems to be that the true motivation for such movement lies in the effects it causes at PF and whatever simultaneous LF-effects that may arise are all by-products. An approach that is consistent with this generalization has been proposed by Richards (2010), who attempted to advocate the view that some syntactic operations are motivated (or licensed) by phonology. For instance, overt wh-movement applies to satisfy the universal condition on wh-prosody, which requires that "the wh-phrase and the corresponding complementizer are separated by as few prosodic boundaries as possible" (p. 145). This approach distinguishes itself from the previous ones, identifying direct interface (PF) incentives for overt movement. As Richards himself is aware, however, his approach would inevitably induce a 'look-ahead' problem in

---

[4] If [F] is identified as some question/Wh property relevant only to LF, on the other hand, why Wh-movement must apply overtly cannot be accounted for.
[5] The only exception that comes to mind is the sporadically observed phonetic effects of Case on the target heads in languages like Latin and Turkish (Blake 2001).
[6] Cyclicity of overt displacement is forced in Bošković's approach with an appeal to the prohibition against the linear order contradicting among distinct Spell-Out domains (Fox and Pesetsky 2005), which also is a PF constraint.

the minimalist model of grammar, this time not only in regards to successively cyclic movement but also to the reference to phonology by overt wh-movement, which he regards as a syntactic rather than PF operation. Richards implies the need to modify the model of grammar to let syntactic operations directly refer to phonology (p. 205, p. 215 (footnote 1)) but virtually no concrete proposals have been made to materialize that idea.[7] Richards, in other words, still seems to have to maintain the position that wh-movement itself is directly triggered syntactically, perhaps by postulating EPP, even if the true incentive behind this operation is prosodic in nature. His approach therefore is also subject to the same problems/restrictions pointed out above with respect to the different versions of the EPP approach.

3.2 Proposals

3.2.1 Overt Syntax Redefined

I consider that the problem we have observed in the approaches appealing to EPP or phonology-induced syntax resides in the design of the grammatical model itself, in which simultaneous effects at both interface levels can be achieved only when computation takes place before Spell-Out even when there is no genuine motivation behind it. With the postulation of PL-Complexes, however, we can synchronize the PF- and LF-effects by inducing a PF-derivation and LF-derivation separately and independently, each of which is enacted strictly by its own motivation. Pursuing this new perspective, I would like to propose the reanalysis of overt syntax as follows. First, the 'overt' syntactic effects of wh-interrogatives (and possibly other constructions) are to be analyzed as the synchronized PF- and LF-effects induced by PL-Complexes. Second, as a specific case of overt syntax, overt movement is also analyzed as involving a type of sound-meaning synchronization achieved by PL-Complexes. That is, the PF-effect of displacing the phonetic contents of some linguistic expression is synchronized with some semantic interpretive effects at LF. Third, the model of grammar is revised in such a way that syntax inducing PF-effects and syntax inducing LF-effects do not overlap. They are completely separate and operate in this order, reflecting one of the core minimalist theses, i.e. computational operations are induced solely to achieve legitimacy at the interface.

---

[7] He briefly mentioned the possibility that multiple Spell-Out might be capable of offering a solution if it can permit phonology to return to the syntax an object annotated for prosodic structure at each phase edge (pp. 201-2, 206), but this idea was not developed in any substantial way, either.

3.2.2 Remodeling with P-Syntax and L-Syntax

I propose the model of grammar and derivation as illustrated in Figure 3.

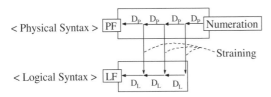

Figure 3: Proposed Model of Grammar

The reorganized model of grammar consists of two subcomponents of syntax, Physical-syntax (henceforth **P-syntax**) and Logical-syntax (henceforth **L-syntax**), each operating independently and fulfilling distinct tasks. The goal of P-syntax is to derive a well-formed PF, which starts with the generation of linguistic expressions by merging and projecting features encoded in the lexical items and their derivatives. At any stage of its derivation, a computational operation may be triggered by those features relevant to PF ('**P-features**'), which include [f_P] of a PL-Complex, and affect the syntactic projection containing it. While the operations in P-syntax may eventually induce the effects at LF, they apply strictly in the course of derivation of PF, solely motivated and triggered by P-features.[8] In a nutshell, P-syntax determines the physical properties of syntactic expressions relevant to PF. It determines, for example, the domain of prosodic activities. (e.g. FPD domain) and also the linear relation of syntactic elements (e.g. displacement).

At any derivational stage of P-syntax, any portion of logical and semantico-pragmatic properties of lexical items ('**L-features**') may be extracted away from P-features and fed into L-syntax 'as needed' for interpretation. I will refer to this mapping process as '**Straining**'. L-syntax then derives well-formed LF, operating on L-features, which include [f_L] of a PL-Complex. The derivation in L-syntax determines, for example, the hierarchical relations and dependency among syntactic constituents (e.g. predicate-argument relation, operator-variable relation and scope). In each of P- and L-syntax, legitimacy of a linguistic element is achieved 'opportunistically' as needed at any stage of derivation, and in the end, the most economically derived well-formed representation is selected. The information on each and every lexical item must also be completely split into those relevant to PF and those relevant to LF so that the legibility condition comes to be satisfied at each interface level.

While the proposed reorganization of grammar may appear to be drastic at first sight, the revisions in fact are relatively on a small scale. First, it

---

[8] Phonology is regarded in this model as a component totally independent of P-syntax.

simply decomposed overt syntax by untangling and separating its PF-effects and LF-effects, while permitting them to be synchronized with an appeal to PL-Complexes. Second, 'Straining' applies merely in the opposite way to Spell-Out, stripping away L-features rather than P-features from the feature complexes of lexical items. In the proposed approach, P-syntax is induced strictly for the PF-effects and L-syntax solely for LF-effects. It thus meets the minimalist standards that were not appropriately attained in the EPP approaches discussed above.[9]

3.2.3 PL-syntax for Wh-interrogatives

I will label the synchronization of P-syntax and L-syntax achieved by PL-Complex as **PL-syntax**, and sketch out the way PL-syntax applies in a wh-interrogative construction in Japanese and other languages. First, I hypothesize that the PL-Complexes for the WC-pair in (5) (repeated below as (10)) become legitimate objects at PF and LF, respectively, only when each of its features is 'signified' in the way relevant to the respective interface.

(10) a. *dare* 'who': $[W_P, W_L]$
     b. *-ka* 'COMP$_{Wh}$': $[C_P, C_L]$

I also assume that the way the signification of P-features (henceforth P-signification) is carried out is subject to certain variations cross-linguistically, which possibly is parametric in nature. The P-signification in the grammar of Japanese, for example, is stated as in (11).

(11) The P-signification of the WC-Pair (Japanese):

   At PF, the WC-Pair is P-signified when it is *identified as the domain of FPD.*

Whenever both lexical items making up the WC-pair are introduced into a sentence in Japanese, the P-syntax operation in (12) may apply.

(12) The FPD Identification:

   In the linear string of words, identify W_P as the initiator of FPD and C_P as its terminator.

This operation will properly identity the domain of FPD starting with W_P and ending with C_P, for instance in (13) below, while failing to establish such a domain when W_P and C_P are introduced in the opposite linear order.

---

[9] In the earlier stage of this work, I assumed that syntax involving 'merger and projection' constitutes a separate subcomponent of syntax. I have incorporated it into P-syntax, following the suggestion made by Miguel Rodríguez-Mondoñedo (p.c.), to whom I am grateful. I would also like to make clear here that what is illustrated in Figure 3 is *not* an acquisition model.

(13) [$_{CP}$ Kanozyo-wa ano-ban   **dare$_{WP}$-to**   atteita-**no**$_{CP}$]?
     she-TOP   that-night   who-with   seeing-COMP$_{Wh}$

'Who was she seeing that night?'

In the PF of (13), the WC-pair is properly P-signified in accordance with (11), and the phonetic rules apply to the specified domain of FPD in this PF, phonetically realizing it as focus prominence followed by post-focal reduction.

The P-signification in English, on the contrary, is carried out as in (14).

(14) P-signification of the WC-pair (English):

At PF, the WC-pair is P-signified when it *initiates CP*.

When both lexical items making up the WC-pair are introduced into a sentence in English, for example as in (15) below, the WC-pair is yet to be P-signified.

(15) [$_{CP}$ C$_P$ [$_{IP}$ she was seeing **who**$_P$ that night]?

I claim that it is this potential PF-problem which induces wh-displacement in P-syntax of English as in (16).

(16) [$_{CP}$ **who**$_P$ C$_P$ [$_{IP}$ she was seeing _____ that night]?
        ↑_____|

In (16), the WC-pair comes to initiate CP and is properly P-signified in accordance with (14). Note also that this approach permits us to avoid the 'look-ahead' problem of successively cyclic movement since (14) requires W$_P$ to start and keep moving in P-syntax until it comes to initiate CP together with C$_P$. We have no need to appeal to any version of EPP, either. We have identified the triggering property of phonetically visible displacement which has a genuine PF motivation and induces computation strictly in the course of the syntactic derivation of PF.

In short, with the availability of a prosodic means, the grammar of Japanese establishes the 'physical marking' of the domain of a wh-focus interpretation non-locally between W$_P$ and C$_P$. In the grammar of English, on the other hand, an appeal must be made to wh-displacement in order to let W$_P$ and C$_P$ unite and establish such physical marking in a local fashion. [10] In both cases, what grammar attempts to do is to provide visible clues for language users which, for instance, they can appeal to when they process and interpret sentences. The proposed approach also allows us to unify the analyses of overt wh-movement and the prosody-information

---

[10] See Sections 4 below for a brief discussion on wh-in-situ in English and the mixture of wh-displacement and wh-in-situ in some languages.

synchronization observed in a wh-in-situ construction under the single concept of P-signification.

The L-feature of the PL-Complex for the WC-pair must also be signified at LF, this time in accordance with (17) below, which possibly is universal in nature.

(17) The L-signification of the Wh-C Pair:

> At LF, the WC-pair is L-signified when it is identified as "Focus and Domain."

Whenever the L-features of both lexical items making up the WC-pair have been 'strained', the L-syntax operation in (18) may apply.

(18) The "Focus and Domain" Identification:

> When W_L is dominated by the *label* of C_L (= CP), identify the former as a focus and the latter as its scope domain.

This operation will properly identity W_L as the focused item and the CP, the label of C_L, as its scope domain, for instance both in (19) and (20).

(19) $[_{CP}$ Kanozyo-wa ano-ban **dare$_{WL}$**-to a'tteita-*no*$_{CL}$]?
       she-TOP   that-night who-with seeing-COMP$_{Wh}$

'Who was she seeing that night?'

(20) $[_{CP}$ **who$_L$** C_L $[_{IP}$ she was seeing ____ that night]?
     ↑_____|

In the LF of (19) and (20), the WC-pair is properly L-signified in accordance with (17), and the identified "Focus and Domain" in this LF comes to be semantico-pragmatically interpreted.

In short, the required P-signification of the WC-pair guarantees that the domain of 'wh-focalization' is visually identified while the required L-signification of the WC-pair ensures that this domain be submitted to the C-I system for proper interpretation. Such successful pairing of sounds and meanings is established thanks to the twin properties of a PL-Complex, a physical and semantico-pragmatic feature complex motivated by information packaging.

Various interactive effects of the P- and L-signification of the WC-pair can be illustrated with the examples below. The Japanese sentence in (21) cannot be interpreted as a subordinate wh-question since the WC-pair does not involve the appropriate dominance relation and fails to be L-signified.

(21) $[_{CPM}$ **DA** re-ga $[_{CPS}$ Bill-ga siken-ni ukatta-**ka**] taZUneta(-no?)]
      who-NOM   Bill-NOM test-DAT passed-**COMP$_{Wh}$** asked(-COMP$_{Y/N}$)

    *Subordinate wh-question: P-signified but *not* L-signified

(21) contrasts with (22), in which the WC-pair is properly L-signified.

(22) [$_{CPM}$ DA re-ga [$_{CPS}$ Bill-ga   siken-ni ukatta-ka]   tazuneta-no]?
       who-NOM   Bill-NOM test-DAT passed-COMP$_{Wthr}$ asked-COMP$_{Wh}$

'Who asked whether Bill passed the test?'

okMatrix wh-question: P-signified *and* L-signified

The WC-pair in sentence (23) below, on the contrary, cannot yield a matrix wh-question since it does not involve the appropriate linear relation and fails to be P-signified even if it may be L-signified.

(23) [$_{CPM}$ John-ga t$_1$ tazuneta-no, [$_{CPS1}$ dare-ga   siken-ni   ukatta-ka]]?
       John-NOM asked-COMP$_{Wh}$ who-NOM test-DAT   passed-COMP$_{Wthr}$

    *Matrix wh-question: L-signified but *not* P-signified

(23) contrasts with (24), in which the WC-pair is properly P-signified.

(24) [$_{CPM}$ John-wa [$_{CPS1}$ DA re-ga siken-ni ukatta-ka]   tazuneta-no]?
       John-TOP   who-NOM test-DAT passed-COMP$_{Wthr}$ asked-COMP$_{Wh}$

'Who$_1$ was such that John asked whether s/he$_1$ passed the test?'

okMatrix wh-question: L-signified *and* P-signified

The English sentence in (25) below is ungrammatical since the WC-pair fails to be signified simultaneously at PF and LF whether the pair involves the COMP in the matrix clause or that in the subordinate clause — no CP-initiation is involved anywhere (and no appropriate dominance relation, either, in the subordinate CP).

(25) *[$_{CPM}$ C$_M$ [John asked whom [$_{CPS}$ C$_S$ [Bill passed the test]]]]

    *Matrix/subordinate wh-question: *Not* P-signified
                                        (also *not* L-signified in CP$_S$)

Finally, the sentence in (26) below can be interpreted as a subordinate but not matrix wh-question.

(26) [$_{CPM}$ C$_M$ [John asked [$_{CPS}$ what$_1$ C$_S$ [Bill had bought t$_1$]]]]

    okSubordinate wh-question: P-signified *and* L-signified
    *Matrix wh-question: L-signified but *not* P-signified

Crucially, the WC-pair initiates CP only in the subordinate clause here, even though it can be L-signified in both CPs.

4. Variations in the P-Syntax of Wh-Interrogatives

P-signification of the WC-pair in English as in (14) would not necessarily be satisfied in multiple wh-interrogatives like (27):

(27) [$_{CP}$ Who$_1$ do-COMP [$_{IP}$ you think t$_1$ bought **what**]]?

Here, while the fronted wh-phrase satisfies (14), the in-situ wh-phrase does not. The condition for P-signification in (14), therefore, must be revised to accommodate this fact. One possible revision suggests itself when we recall that multiple wh-questions and their answers are required to make up a pair (or set). The question in (27), for instance, can be answered with A$_1$ but not with A$_2$ or A$_3$ in (28).

(28) A$_1$: (I think) **John** bought **wine**, **Bill** bought **flowers**, and ...
     A$_2$: (I think) **John** did.
     A$_3$: **Flowers**(, I think).

This suggests that the question involved in a multiple wh-construction can be completed only when all of the fronted and in-situ wh-phrases are interpreted as the segments making up a single semantic unit. Reflecting this property of multiple wh-questions, (14) can be revised as in (29).

(29) At PF, the WC-pair is P-signified when the sequence of *at least one segment of W$_P$* and C$_P$ initiates CP.

Further specifications will be necessary, however, to capture the distinction between single wh-fronting languages like English and multiple wh-fronting languages like Bulgarian. The example in (30) is from Rudin (1988: 449).

(30) [$_{CP}$ **Koj kogo** COMP viz#da]?
     who whom   sees

    'Who sees **whom**?'

This can be achieved, for instance, by further specifying (29) into (31) for the former and (32) for the latter.

(31) English:

    At PF, the WC-pair is P-signified when the sequence of *exactly one segment of W$_P$* and C$_P$ initiates CP.

(32) Bulgarian:

    At PF, the WC-pair is P-signified when the sequence of *all segments of W$_P$* and C$_P$ initiates CP.

At this point, it may be a little impetuous to discuss the universality of the proposed approach, especially that of P-signification. Nonetheless, the general picture emerging from the comparison of Japanese and English in regard to the P-signification of the WC-pair seems promising. The 'physical marking' of the domain of a wh-focus interpretation can be fulfilled non-locally by W_P and C_P when some prosodic means for such marking is available. When no such prosodic means is available, on the other hand, it must be established locally by the sequence of W_P and C_P with an appeal to wh-displacement. There seems to exist the general division of labor, in other words, between prosody and displacement in achieving the P-signification of the WC-pair, though the split is not always complete and the two may occasionally be mixed in intricate ways. This general picture is supported by the well-known observation that displaced wh-items themselves generally do not carry focus prominence in wh-movement languages (Ladd 1996: 170-172).[11]

Richards (2010:189) offers typology of wh-interrogative constructions, cross-classifying languages in terms of the linear directions of prosodic boundaries and those of COMPs as in (33).

(33)	C to right of TP	C to left of TP
Prosodic boundaries on right of XPs	Basque	Chichew\$a
Prosodic boundaries on left of XPs	Japanese	Tagalog

We may reinterpret (33) as the typology of P-signification of the WC-pair, appealing to the two options of physical marking in P-syntax (prosody and displacement) and the directions of COMP (left and right), as in (34).

(34) a. Japanese: $[_{CP} \ldots \boxed{\text{Wh} \ldots \text{C}}]$ (prosody, right)

    b. English: $[_{CP} \text{C} \ldots \text{Wh} \ldots]$ (displacement, left)

(35) a. $[_{CP} \ldots \text{Wh} \ldots \text{C}]$ (displacement, right)

    b. $[_{CP} \boxed{\text{C} \ldots \text{Wh}} \ldots]$ (prosody, left)

We obviously must also permit both of the two options of physical marking to be available in some languages (e.g. French and Brazilian Portuguese).

---

[11] Though sporadically, it has been observed in the literature (e.g. Pesetsky 1987) that the in-situ wh-phrases in multiple wh-questions may receive noticeable focus prominence as in (ib) below in contradistinction to the general absence of focus prominence in the displaced wh-word as in (ia).

(i) a. *What$_1$* did you buy t$_1$?
    b. *Who$_1$* t$_1$ gave **WHAT** to **WHOM**?

While this observation is still compatible with (31), it may suggest that the P-signification of the WC-pair with the application of wh-displacement may have to be supplemented by a secondary means appealing to prosody for those segments of W_P that remain in-situ just as in wh-in-situ languages like Japanese.

There clearly are many questions that remain unanswered in this approach. I must, however, leave further pursuit of this topic to the future research. See Richards(2010) for highly relevant observations and discussion.

5. Summary and Conclusions

In this work, I first examined the prosody-information synchronization phenomenon involving wh-interrogatives in Japanese, and proposed that it can be properly and straightforwardly captured when 'PL-Complex', a physical and semantico-pragmatic feature complex motivated by information packaging, is postulated. I then pointed out that PL-Complexes would also permit us to redefine overt syntax, including overt movement, as two related but independent computational processes that induce the synchronized effects at PF and LF. This approach led us to reorganize grammar in such a way that overt syntax is decomposed into P-syntax and L-syntax, which would permit us to eliminate the EPP property from the grammar.

The proposed approach can also be extended to the overt syntax of Spec-TP when we postulate a PL-Complex for what we may call the Top(ic)-T(ense) pair. It would then allow us to explore the possibility that at least all instances of phrasal overt movement (and possibly all overt syntactic operations) are induced by PL-Complexes motivated by information packaging. The pursuit of this topic must also be left for the future research.

References

Bader, M. 1998. Prosodic Influences on Reading Syntactically Ambiguous Sentences. In *Reanalysis in Sentence Processing (Studies in Theoretical Psycholinguistics, Vol. 21)*, ed. Fodor and Ferreira, Dordrecht: Kluwer Academic Publishers.

Blake, B. J. 2001. *Case (Second Edition)*. Cambridge: Cambridge University Press.

Borer, H. 1986. I-subjects. *Linguistic Inquiry* 17: 375-416.

Bošković, Ž. 2007. On the Locality and Motivation of Move and Agree: An Even More Minimal Theory. *Linguistic Inquiry* 38(4): 589–644.

Chomsky, N. 2000. Minimalist Inquiries: the Framework. In *Step by Step: Essays on Minimalist Syntax in Honor of Howard Lasnik*, ed. Martin, 89-155. Cambridge, Massachusetts: The MIT Press.

Chomsky, N. 2001. Derivation by Phase. In *Ken Hale: A Life in Language*, ed. Kenstowicz, 1-52. Cambridge, MA: MIT Press.

Deguchi, M. and Kitagawa, Y. 2002. Prosody and Wh-questions. In *Proceedings of the Thirty-second Annual Meeting of the North-Eastern Linguistic Society*, 73-92. GLSA, University of Massachusetts at Amherst.

Fodor, J. D. 1998. Learning to Parse? *Journal of Psycholinguistic Research* 7: 285-318.

Fodor, J. D. 2002. Prosodic Disambiguation in Silent Reading. In *Proceedings of the Thirty-second Annual Meeting of the North-Eastern Linguistic Society*, 113-137. GLSA, University of Massachusetts at Amherst.

Fox, D. and Pesetsky, D. 2005. Cyclic Linearization of Syntactic Structure. *Theoretical Linguistics — Special Issue on Object Shift in Scandinavian, ed. by É. Kiss, Katalin* 31: 1-45.

Hamblin, C. L. 1973. Questions in Montague English. *Foundations of Language* 10: 41-53.

Hirose, Y. and Kitagawa, Y. 2008 of Conference. Asymmetry between Encoding and Decoding of Wh-scope in Japanese. In Proceedings of the 27th Westcoast Conference on Formal Linguistics, ed. by Ryan, Kevin, UCLA Working Papers in Linguistics Poster Session, http://www.linguistics.ucla.edu/faciliti/wpl/, Los Angeles.

Igarashi, Y. To appear. Typology of Intonational Phrasing in Japanese Dialects. In *Prosodic Typology II: The Phonology of Intonation and Phrasing*, ed. Jun, Pp. 45. New York: Oxford University Press.

Ishihara, S. 2003. *Intonation and Interface Conditions*. Doctoral dissertation, Massachusetts Institute of Technology.

Kitagawa, Y. 1986. *Subjects in Japanese and English*. Doctoral dissertation, University of Massachusetts at Amherst (available as Kitagawa (1994) with annotations).

Kitagawa, Y. 2005. Prosody, Syntax and Pragmatics of Wh-questions in Japanese. *English Linguistics* 22: 302-346.

Kitagawa, Y. and Fodor, J. D. 2003. Default Prosody Explains Neglected Syntactic Analyses of Japanese. In *Japanese/Korean Linguistics* 12: 267-279. CSLI Publication.

Kitagawa, Y. and Fodor, J. D. 2006. Prosodic Influences on Syntactic Judgments. In *Gradience in Grammar: Generative Perspectives*, ed. Fanselow, et al., 336-358. Oxford, UK: Oxford University Press.

Kori, S. 1989. Kyocho-to Intoneshon (Emphasis and Intonation). In *Koza Nihongo-to Nihongo-kyoiku 2: Nihongo-no Onsei · On'in Vol. 1*, ed. Sugito, 316-342. Tokyo: Meiji-Shoin.

Kubo, T. 2001. Syntax-Phonology Interface in the Fukuoka Dialect. *Journal of the Phonetic Society of Japan* 5: 27-32.

Kuroda, S.-Y. 1988. Whether We Agree or Not: A Comparative Syntax of English and Japanese. *Linguisticae Investigationes* 12: 1-47.

Ladd, R. 1996. *Intonational Phonology*. New York: Cambridge University Press.

Maekawa, K. 1991. Perception of intonation characteristics of WH and non-WH questions in Tokyo Japanese. In *Proceedings of the XXIInd International Congress of Phonetic Science* 4: 202-205. Ain-en-Provence, France: Universite de Provence.

Miyagawa, S. 2010. *Why Agree? Why Move?—Unifying Agreement-Based and Discourse-Configurational Languages*. Cambridge, MA: The MIT Press.

Miyamoto, E. T. and Takahashi, S. 2002. The Processing of Wh-phrases and Interrogative Complementizers in Japanese. In *Akatsuka, Noriko M. and Susan Strauss (eds.) Japanese/Korean Linguistics* 10: 62-75. CSLI Publications.

Nishigauchi, T. 1990. *Quantification in the Theory of Grammar*. Dordrecht: Kluwer Academic Publishers.

Pesetsky, D. 1987. Wh-in-Situ: Movement and Unselective Binding. In *The Representation of (In)definiteness*, ed. Reuland and Meulen, 98-129. Cambridge: The MIT Press.

Richards, N. 2010. *Uttering Tress*. Cambridge, MA: MIT Press.

Rudin, C. 1988. On Multiple Questions and Multiple WH Fronting. *Natural Language and Linguistic Theory* 6: 445-501.

Smith, J. L. 2005. On the WH-Question Intonational Domain in Fukuoka Japanese: Some Implications for the Syntax-Prosody Interface. In *Papers on Prosody, UMOP*, ed. Kawahara, 219-237. Amherst, MA: GLSA.

Watanabe, A. 1992. Subjacency and S-structure Movement of WH-in-situ. *Journal of East Asian Linguistics* 1: 255-291.

An Experimental Study of the Grammatical Status of *caki* in Korean

CHUNG-HYE HAN
Simon Fraser University

DENNIS RYAN STOROSHENKO
Simon Fraser University

R. CALEN WALSHE
Simon Fraser University

1. Introduction

In the existing literature, the Korean long-distance anaphor *caki* is often described as subject-oriented, meaning that its antecedent is always a clausal subject (Yang 1985, Cole and Sung 1994). But the potential for non-subject antecedents has also been noted elsewhere (Kim 2000, Madigan and Yamada 2006). In (1), any of the c-commanding DPs in the sentence can serve as an antecedent for *caki*, including the non-subject *Mary*.

(1) *John$_i$-i   Mary$_j$-eykey [Tom$_k$-i   caki$_{i,j,k}$-lul cohaha-n-tako]*
    John-NOM Mary-DAT Tom-NOM self-ACC like-PRES-COMP
    malha-yess-ta.
    say-PAST-DECL
    'John told Mary that Tom likes self.' (Sohng 2003, ex 11a)

In light of this fact, the question arises as to how the antecedent for *caki* is determined when more than one potential antecedent is available in the

Japanese/Korean Linguistics 19.
Edited by Ho-min Sohn, Haruko Cook, William O'Grady, Leon A. Serafim, & Sang Yee Cheon.
Copyright © 2011, CSLI Publications.

same sentence. In this paper, we present our experimental study that tests the hypothesis that the DP referring to the most salient entity in the discourse is chosen as the antecedent, in the same manner as the antecedent for a pronoun is chosen. The data from our experiment show that while discourse context has an effect on the reference resolution of pronouns, it has little effect on the choice of antecedent for *caki*.

This paper is organized as follows. In section 2, we present data that illustrate pronoun-like qualities of *caki*, motivating our experimental hypothesis and research questions. Section 3 presents behavioral and eye-tracking data obtained from the experiment comparing the behaviour of *caki* with the third person pronouns *ku* ('he') and *kunye* ('she'). We conclude in section 4 with a discussion on the implications of our findings.

2. Framing the Issue: Pronouns and *Caki*

Condition B of the binding theory states that pronouns must be free within their binding domain (Chomsky 1981). So, pronouns can be coreferential with other entities in the sentence, whether they are c-commanded by the antecedent or not, as long they are free within their binding domain. They can also refer to entities established in discourse, from previous sentences. With these potentials for ambiguity, it is generally assumed that discourse context plays a role in ultimately resolving the reference of a pronoun.

Though typically treated as a long-distance anaphor, *caki* has pronoun-like qualities (Cho 1996). First of all, it can have a non-c-commanding antecedent within the same sentence. In (2), although *caki* is not c-commanded by genitive *Suni* embedded in a DP *Suni-uy sinpal-un* ('Suni-GEN shoes-TOP'), it is read as being coreferential with that genitive.

(2) $Suni_i$-uy   sinpal-un $caki_i$-uy   pal-pota   hwelssin   khu-ta.
     Suni-GEN   shoes-TOP   self-GEN   foot-than   a lot   big-DECL
     'Suni's shoes are a lot bigger than self's feet.' (Kim 2000, ex 2a)

Secondly, *caki* seems to demonstrate split antecedence (Huang 2000). For example, in (3), *caki-tul* ('self-PL') finds its reference from a composite of matrix subject and the dative argument. This type of split antecedence is generally considered to be a diagnostic for a pronominal-like element.

(3) $John_i$-un $Mary_j$-eykey   [$caki$-tul_{i+j}-i   iki-lke-lako]
     John-TOP   Mary-DAT   self-PL-NOM   win-FUT-COMP
     malha-yess-ta.
     say-PAST-DECL
     'John told Mary that selves would win.' (Huang 2000, ex 2.179).

Thirdly, *caki* doesn't even require an antecedent within the same sentence. In (4), *caki* is co-referential with *Suni* from the previous sentence.

(4) *Na-nun Suni$_i$-eykey chayk-ul   pillye cwu-ess-ta.   Kulentey*
    I-TOP   Suni-DAT   book-ACC lend   give-PAST-DECL and yet

    sasil   ku   chayk-un   caki$_i$ oppa-ka   ceney   nay-key
    in fact that book-TOP self   elder brother-NOM before me-DAT

    pillye cwun kes   i-ta.
    lend   give thing be-DECL

    'I lent a book to Suni. But the fact is that self's brother had lent it to me before.' (Kim 2000, ex 2b)

Given the apparent similarities between pronouns and *caki*, we might expect the discourse context to have an effect on determining the antecedent of *caki* in a similar way that it influences reference resolution on pronouns. We thus designed an experiment to address the following two questions:

1. Can we manipulate context to influence reference resolution on pronouns?
2. Given the noted similarities, will *caki* show the same pattern as pronouns?

3. The Experiment

To test these questions, we designed an experiment which combined an online processing measure, in the form of visual world eye-tracking, with a delayed behavioural measure in the form of a forced-choice questioning task. By making use of this dual approach, we were able to observe participants' reactions to stimuli as they were presented, as well as their considered judgements of those same stimuli. Because the data reported in the previous literature are all the result of considered grammaticality judgements, we were interested in seeing whether speakers presented with a pronoun or *caki* with multiple possible antecedents would consider more options for reference resolution than simply the one which they would report in our forced-choice task. Our reasoning that eye-tracking would be useful in addressing this issue is based on the demonstration by existing research that eye movements to objects that are potential referents of a referring expression are closely time-locked to the linguistic input (Cooper 1974, Tanenhaus et al. 1995).

3.1. Material

The stimuli used in this experiment combined audio and visual presentation. The visual portion consisted of a series of 18 still images (2 for training and 16 for experimental trials), a sample of which is given in Figure 1. Each image contained two characters, standing on either side of the scene. Between the characters is a scene-anchoring item, a blackboard in Figure 1. Others were items such as a gas range to suggest a kitchen, a tree to suggest a park, or a treadmill to suggest a gymnasium. In all cases, the setting is further reinforced

FIGURE 1 Sample Visual Stimulus (Classroom Scene)

by the clothing of the characters. For all the images, one character was male and the other female, and their positions (left or right) in the image were evenly counterbalanced across the whole set of images used.

The audio portion of the stimuli consisted of a five-sentence recorded narration, spoken by a native speaker of Korean. The first two sentences provided background information, naming the characters and establishing the setting. The background information for the scene in Figure 1 is given in (5).

(5) *Jongwu-wa   Yuli-ka   kyosil-ey   iss-ta.   Jongwu-wa*
     Jongwu-and Yuli-NOM classroom-DAT be-DECL Jonguw-and
     Yuli-nun   pangkum sihem-ul chi-less-ta.
     Yuli-TOP   just   test-ACC take-PAST-DECL

     'Jongwu and Yuli are in their classroom. Jongwu and Yuli just took a test.'

The following two sentences gave further information about either one of the characters, or about the item in the centre of the image. For the scene in Figure 1, further information about Jongwu (6a), Yuli (6b), or the blackboard (6c) is given.

(6)   a. *Jongwu-nun mayil pam   yele   sikan tongan*
       Jongwu-TOP every night several hour   while
       kongpwuha-yess-ta. Kuliko Jongwu-nun cinan sihem-eyse
       study-PAST-DECL   And   Jongwu-TOP last   test-at

iltung-ul   ha-yess-ta.
first-ACC   do-PAST-DECL

'Jongwu studied for many hours every night. And Jongwu was the top student on the last test.'

b. *Yuli-nun   wutungsayng-i-ta.   Yuli-nun   sihem-eyse*
Yuli-TOP   honour student-COP-DECL   Yuli-TOP   test-at
90cem   iha   mat-un   cek-i
90 point   below   score-ADNOM   experience-NOM
eps-ta.
non exist-DECL

'Yuli is an honour student. Yuli has never scored below 90 on a test.'

c. *Kyosil-ey   chilphan-i   iss-ta.   Chilphan-ey-nun*
classroom-at   blackboard-NOM   be-DECL   blackboard-at-TOP
amwukesto   ssuyye   iss-ci   anh-ta.
anything   written   be-CONNECT   not-DECL

'There is a blackboard in the classroom. The blackboard doesn't have anything written on it.'

The final sentence of the narration was our target sentence. Again, there were three different possible versions of this sentence, depending upon the anaphor type used as the subject of the embedded clause, as in (7).

(7)   *Jongwu-ka   Yuli-eykey   chilphan   yeph-eyse*
Jongwu-NOM   Yuli-DAT   blackboard   beside-at
caki/ku/kunye-*ka   sihem-ul   cal   chi-less-tako*
self/he/she-NOM   test-ACC   well   take-PAST-COMP
malha-n-ta.
tell-PRES-DECL

'Jongwu tells Yuli beside the blackboard that self/he/she did well on the test.'

Crucial here is that there are two potential antecedents for the embedded clause subject; either Jongwu or Yuli could serve as the antecedent for *caki*. For *ku* and *kunye*, there is less room for ambiguity, as the sentence contains one male and one female referent. Target sentences were constructed to be counterbalanced by gender, with half male and half female matrix subjects, equally distributed across the images where the positions of the male and female characters were also counterbalanced.

Once the audio presentation was completed, the image disappeared from the screen, replaced by a black screen presenting a comprehension question written in Korean, as in (8).

(8) *Jongwu-nun   nwu-ka   sihem-ul   cal   chi-less-tako*
Jongwu-TOP   who-NOM   test-ACC   well   take-PAST-COMP
malha-yess-supnikka?
tell-PAST-INT
'Who did Jongwu say did well on the test?'

Beneath this sentence were two clickable boxes, labelled for the names of the two characters in the given scene. Through the answers to this comprehension question, we were able to determine the participants' considered judgements as to the antecedent of the potentially ambiguous embedded clause subject.

As soon as an answer was entered, a cross would appear in the centre of the screen, which the participants would have to click before the image for the next item would appear, and the audio playback for that item would begin. This fixation cross was used to control the gaze of the participant at each trial.

For each of the 16 images used in the experimental trials, 3 scripts were prepared foregrounding the female character, male character or the scene-anchoring item in the middle, corresponding to (6). Each of the 3 scripts were presented with a target sentence containing *caki*, and a target sentence containing either *ku* or *kunye*, corresponding to (7). This produced 96 experimental trials in total.

3.2. Design

Our study consisted of two independent variables, each with three levels. The first of these variables was Contextual Bias. In examining the target sentence (7), Jongwu is the matrix subject, Yuli is the matrix indirect object, and the blackboard is mentioned as a locative adjunct. Contextual Bias was manipulated in the choice of which sentence pair from (6) was presented in a given trial. For the classroom scenario, (6a) placed additional emphasis on the target sentence subject, (6b) on the target sentence object, and (6c) on the locative adjunct. This manipulation was designed to make one or the other character more salient in the discourse. The emphasis on the locative adjunct was included as a control, to observe what happens where there has been no additional emphasis placed on either character. These three conditions were coded as the Subject, Object, and Neutral Biases, respectively.

The second independent variable, Anaphor Type, was represented in the form of the target sentence itself. As shown in (7), there were three possibilities for the embedded clause subject: *caki*, *ku*, or *kunye*. Taking the two independent variables in combination, the result is a 3 X 3 within-subjects design with 9 conditions, shown in Table 1.

Our experiment also had two dependent variables. The first of these was the on-line measurement of participants' gaze during the audio presentation of the target sentence. Specifically, we measured the proportion of fixations

TABLE 1 Experiment Design - Independent Variables

	caki	*ku*	*kunye*
Subject Bias	Condition 1	Condition 4	Condition 7
Object Bias	Condition 2	Condition 5	Condition 8
Neutral Bias	Condition 3	Condition 6	Condition 9

on either of the two characters, as well as fixations on the adjunct item in the centre of the image. We were interested in the gaze of participants at two key timepoints. The first of these was after the utterance of a proper name in the target sentence; this was an important control, as it would allow us to establish whether or not participants' gaze was indeed responding to the audio stimulus. The second timepoint of interest was the interval after the utterance of the embedded clause subject in the target sentence. This was the most important measure, as it would show where a participant's gaze shifts upon hearing *caki* or a pronoun. Following similar research on English (Runner et al. 2003; 2006), we focused our analysis of the eye-tracking results on the time interval 300ms to 1000ms after the onset of the proper name or embedded clause subject. This interval was selected to allow for enough time for the execution of the saccadic eye movement, while remaining restricted to a period close to the utterance of the word in question.

The second dependent variable in our experiment was the behavioural measure. For this, responses were coded according to whether the participants selected the target sentence subject or indirect object as the antecedent for the embedded clause subject. Selections of the subject were scored as 1, and selections of the indirect object were scored as zero.

3.3. Participants and procedure

For this experiment, we recruited 27 native speakers of Korean, none of whom had any education outside of Korea after age 12. All were university-age residents of Vancouver, and all were paid $10 for their participation.

Eye-tracking measures were taken using tabletop Tobii X100 eyetrackers, sampling at 60Hz. Experiments were conducted using three different eye-trackers, all operating with the same specifications and settings. Upon arriving at the lab, participants were briefed on the nature of their task, and first introduced to the eye-tracking equipment by way of a calibration routine. After calibration, participants were instructed to remain as still as possible throughout the experiment.

Participants then saw two practice trials using images and narrations which were not repeated during the experiment. These trials were designed to familiarise participants with the audio-visual combination, and to get them accustomed to the self-pacing of the experiment by way of their responses to the comprehension questions and the fixation crosses. Each participant saw 96 experiment items in total, presented in two randomly ordered blocks of 48. Periodically during the experiment, a screen would appear between trials displaying the eyetracker's image of the participants' eyes, as a reminder to return to the position of the original calibration.

Though participants were aware of the operation of the eyetracker, tracking was only done for the duration of the target sentence. The target sentences were specifically constructed to keep the eye-tracking as unobtrusive as possible. Rather than interrupt the flow of the narrative by re-introducing the fixation cross at the beginning of the target sentence, or during the target sentence, the mention of the locative adjunct was intended to serve as a cue to draw the participants' gaze back to the centre of the screen. Furthermore, without this locative adjunct, there would be no time delay between the target sentence indirect object and the embedded clause subject, which could have influenced the gaze results at the onset of the embedded clause subject.

Once the entire experiment was completed, participants were given an optional written debriefing form, as well as an informal verbal debriefing with the experimenter.

3.4. Results

Eye-tracking results are reported for only 14 of the 27 total participants. For 13 participants, more than 25% of the total eye-tracking data was lost due to calibration or equipment errors, and those participants' entire eye-tracking data sets were discarded. However, full behavioural data was collected for all 27 participants. We first examine the eye-tracking results, then turn to the behavioural data.

Our first concern with the eye-tracking results was to check our control test: the proper names. Figure 2 shows the proportions of fixations after the utterance of a proper name, aggregating across all proper names in all target sentences. The duration of the proper names is indicated by the arrows; at the onset, participants show roughly equal proportions of fixations to either character, and a higher proportion of looks to the adjunct item in the centre of the image. As shown in the graph, looks to the correct character spike upward approximately 300ms after the onset of the name, and looks to the other character and the adjunct item show a corresponding decline. We take this as evidence that the eye-tracking methodology is sound, and participants' gaze does indeed respond to the audio stimulus.

From this, we proceeded to examine the proportions of fixation after the

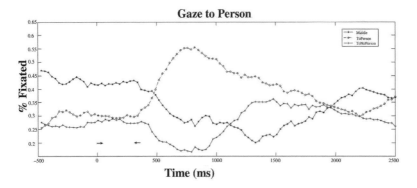

FIGURE 2 Proportions of Fixations in Image after Proper Names

utterance of *caki* in the target sentence. Eye-tracking results for *caki* in all three Contextual Bias conditions are shown in Figure 3. Again, the duration of *caki* is indicated by the arrows, though the graph lines now correspond to looks to the target sentence subject, object, and the adjunct (middle) item. What we observe is that in all three bias conditions, there was a greater proportion of looks to the subject than the object or the adjunct after the utterance of *caki*. Similar results were obtained for *ku* and *kunye*. Figure 4 combines the proportions of fixations for all nine conditions, averaging over the 300ms to 1000ms time duration. While there are some small variations in the numbers the general trend is clear: regardless of Anaphor Type of the embedded clause subject or Contextual Bias, participants tend to look at the image of the subject upon hearing the embedded clause subject, even when either character is a potential antecedent.

To confirm this observation, we conducted a three-way ANOVA, comparing the variables of Contextual Bias, Anaphor Type, and Target of Fixation. The ANOVA revealed a main effect of Target of Fixation ($F(1,13) = 27.610$, $p = .000$) indicating that participants looked significantly more often at the image corresponding to the subject than anything else, regardless of Anaphor Type and Contextual Bias. There was no main effect of Anaphor Type or Contextual Bias. The ANOVA also revealed significant interactions between Anaphor Type and Target of Fixation ($F(2,26) = 4.179$, $p = .027$), and between Contextual Bias and Target of Fixation ($F(2,26) = 4.317$, $p = .024$). The first interaction is due to the slight increase in looks to the subject in the *caki* conditions than in the pronoun conditions. It may be that this is a

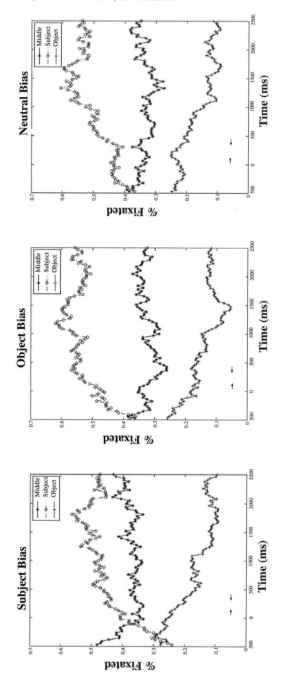

FIGURE 3 Proportions of Fixations in Image after *caki* for each Bias

reflection of the fact that while *caki* is gender-neutral, *ku* and *kunye* are not, although we'll see later that this gender effect on pronouns can be overridden by context. The second interaction is due to the increase in the looks to the subject in the Object Bias conditions with all anaphor types. We have no explanation for this other than the speculation that the increase in looks to the subject here is spurious.

We then turned to the analysis of the behavioural results. For this, the mean score on each of the nine conditions was calculated for each participant. Recalling our scoring scheme, a mean closer to 1 would translate to more frequent selection of subjects as antecedents for the embedded subject, and a mean closer to 0 would translate to more frequent selection of objects. Because the target sentences were counterbalanced with respect to the gender of the subjects, *ku* and *kunye* selections based purely upon gender agreement would be reflected by a mean of 0.5. The mean scores in each condition, averaged over all participants is reported in Figure 5.

Regardless of the Contextual Bias, subjects were selected as the antecedent for *caki* 99% of the time. For *ku*, there was an effect of the contextual manipulation, as objects were selected more often in the Object Bias condition. There was a similar effect for *kunye*, though it was much less pronounced. A 2-way ANOVA was conducted on the means for each participant comparing the factors of Anaphor and Contextual Bias. A main effect of Anaphor Type was observed ($F(2,52) = 305.180$, $p = .000$), with all three levels significantly different on pairwise comparisons. Similarly, there was a main effect of Contextual Bias ($F(2,52) = 7.788$, $p = .001$), though on pairwise comparisons, it was only the case that the Object Bias was significantly different from the other two. There was no significant difference between the Subject and Neu-

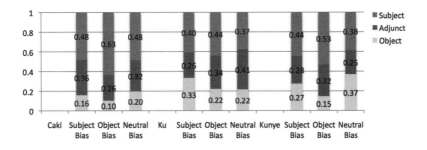

FIGURE 4 Proportions of Fixations in all Conditions

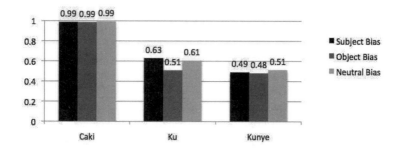

FIGURE 5 Average Means for each Anahpor/Bias Combination

tral Bias conditions. Finally, a significant interaction between Anaphor Type and Contextual Bias was found ($F(4,104) = 5.809$, $p = .000$), with *ku* showing the greatest sensitivity to Contextual Bias, less so for *kunye*, and virtually none at all for *caki*.

4. Discussion and Conclusion

Returning to our first research question in section 2, our experiment showed that it is possible to manipulate context and affect the choice of antecedent for an ambiguous pronoun. From the eye-tracking results, we conclude that there is a default setting to consider sentential subjects upon first hearing a pronoun or *caki*, reflected in the observation that there was a greater proportion of fixations on the images of subjects than objects (or adjuncts) regardless of Anaphor Type and Contextual Bias. However, the results for the behavioural test clearly showed an effect of context for pronouns. Though the average means for *ku* and *kunye* hovered around 50% due to the gender agreement effect, we observed subjects being chosen most often in the Subject and Neutral Bias conditions. For *ku*, this effect was so strong that it overrode gender considerations, and there were selections of a female antecedent. The same overriding of gender was present for *kunye*, though to a lesser extent. In debriefing, participants were very conscious of this gender effect, reporting that it was possible for both *ku* and *kunye* to have gender-mismatched antecedents, and even speculated that this had been the underlying research question of the experiment. So, the eye-tracking and the behavioural results taken together show that for pronouns, in the early stage of processing, the sentential subject is considered as a default antecedent, but this default selection can be overriden in the later stage of processing by contextual effects despite strong gender agreement effects.

Adding strength to our conclusion that subjects are a default antecedent was the finding that there was no significant difference between the Subject and Neutral Bias conditions in the behavioural data. If subjects are default antecedents, then adding emphasis to the subject should have no effect on the final decision of which antecedent to choose. Placing additional emphasis on the locative adjunct, adding no more input about either potential antecedent, yielded results that were the same as in the Subject Bias condition, revealing the effect of the default interpretation. Where neither potential antecedent was emphasised, the result was the same as though the default has been emphasised.

Turning to our second research question, we clearly see that it is not the case that *caki* is subject to the same effect of context. Devoid of any confounds of gender, the default subject antecedent is in full force with *caki*, resulting in 99% selections of subject antecedents across the board in the behavioral data. This finding corresponds with the general tendency in the literature to consider *caki* a subject-oriented anaphor.

This however does not mean that the subject is the only grammatically possible antecedent for *caki*. It merely means that the subject was the preferred choice by our participants in the given forced-choice task. In fact, there was still not 100% acceptance of subjects as antecedents for *caki*. In all three Contextual Bias conditions, there were selections of the indirect object as the antecedent for *caki*. While the effect was so small in our experiment that it could be dismissed as extraneous noise in the data, such readings are repeatedly reported in existing literature, and our experiment attests to the possibility of such readings. What is clear though is that antecedent resolution of *caki* is not subject to those factors which can influence pronouns, speaking to the larger question of whether or not *caki* should be considered a pronoun or a bound anaphor. Our conclusion is that the results of this experiment can be added to the case for claiming that *caki* should not be grouped together with referential pronouns, despite the putative evidence for making this claim outlined in Section 2. Having established that *caki* is not subject to the same contextual influences as pronouns, future research will focus on determining what are the factors which will induce a non-subject reading for *caki*.

Acknowledgments

We thank the audience at the 19th Japanese/Korean Linguistics Conference for their helpful questions and comments. We are also grateful to Yue Wang for her helpful comments on the design of the experiment in the initial stage of the project. This research was partially funded by SSHRC Standard Research Grant #410-2007-2169 to Han.

References

Cho, D. 1996. Anaphor or Pronominal. *Language Research* 32:621–636.

Chomsky, N. 1981. *Lectures on Government and Binding.* Dordrecht: Foris.

Cole, P., and L. Sung. 1994. Head Movement and Long-distance Reflexives. *Linguistic Inquiry* 25:355–406.

Cooper, R. 1974. The Control of Eye Fixation by the Meaning of Spoken Language: A New Methodology for the Real-time Investigation of Speech Perception, Memory and Language Processing. *Cognitive Psychology* 6:84–107.

Huang, Y. 2000. *Anaphora.* Oxford University Press.

Kim, S. 2000. Acceptability and Preference in the Interpretation of Anaphors. *Linguistics* 38:315–353.

Madigan, S., and M. Yamada. 2006. Asymmetry in Anaphoric Dependencies: A Cross-linguistic Study of Inclusive Reference. In *University of Pennsylvania Working Papers in Linguistics 13-1: Proceedings of Penn Linguistics Colloquium 30,* 183–196.

Runner, J., R. Sussman, and M. Tanenhaus. 2003. Assignment of Reference to Reflexives and Pronouns in Picture Noun Phrases: Evidence from Eye Movements. *Cognition* B1–B13.

Runner, J., R. Sussman, and M. Tanenhaus. 2006. Processing Reflexives and Pronouns in Picture Noun Phrases. *Cognitive Science* 30:193–241.

Sohng, H. 2003. Topics in the Syntax of East Asian Languages: Long-distance Anaphora and Adverbial Case. Doctoral Dissertation, University of Washington.

Tanenhaus, M., M. Spivey-Knowlton, K. Eberhard, and J. Sedivy. 1995. Integration of Visual and Linguistic Information in Spoken Language Comprehension. *Science* 268:1632–1634.

Yang, D. 1985. On the Integrity of Control Theory. In *Papers in Korean Linguistics: Commemorating the Eightieth Birthday of Prof. Hyonggi Kim.* Research Society of Omun. Taejon, Korea.

"AMOUNT" Relativization in Japanese*

SHUN'ICHIRO INADA
University of Tokyo / JSPS Research Fellow

1. Introduction

This paper considers the properties of subordinate CPs in Japanese as exemplified in (1).

(1)　a.　John-wa [DP[CP Bob-ga　　yatin-ni　tukau]　*hanbun*]-o
　　　　　John-TOP　　　　Bob-NOM　rent-for　uses　　half-ACC
　　　　　gyanburu-ni　tukau.
　　　　　gambling-for　uses
　　　　　'John uses for gambling half as much money as Bob uses for the rent.'
　　　b.　Mary-wa [DP[CP teisyu-ga　　　hitotuki-ni　　kasegu] *bai*]-o
　　　　　Mary-TOP　　　husband-NOM　one.month-in　earns　　double-ACC
　　　　　hantuki-de　　kasegu.
　　　　　half.month-in　earns

* I am grateful to Noriko Imanishi and Akira Watanabe for invaluable comments on earlier versions of this paper. My thanks also go to Toshiaki Inada, Sakumi Inokuma, and Chuu Yong Teo for their helpful comments. This research is supported by JSPS Research Fellowships for Young Scientists. Needless to say, all remaining inadequacies are mine.

Japanese/Korean Linguistics 19.
Edited by Ho-min Sohn, Haruko Cook, William O'Grady, Leon A. Serafim, & Sang Yee Cheon.
Copyright © 2011, CSLI Publications

'In half a month Mary earns twice as much as her husband earns in one month.'   (Ishii (1991: 222))

In Ishii (1991), these examples are called *Half* Relatives. The name comes from the amount/degree expressions of these sentences, such as *hanbun* 'half' or *bai* 'double.' These amount/degree expressions are nominal in Japanese. Thus, CPs "modifying" them have been treated as an instance of the relative clause, although the interpretation assigned to them is similar to that of the comparative clauses, as is shown in the English translations.

The comparative-like interpretation of the *Half* relatives calls to mind so-called Amount Relatives (ARs) in English. The relative clause in (2) is potentially ambiguous between a restrictive relative (RR) reading and an amount relative (AR) reading, as illustrated in (2).

(2)   It would take days to drink [$_{DP}$ the champagne they spilled that evening].
        AR reading: the same (amount) as much amount of champagne they spilled that evening
        RR reading: the very champagne that was spilled that evening
                                                                        (Heim 1987: 38)

In the RR reading, the argument DP of the matrix clause denotes the same entity as the relativized DP which would have been base-generated within the relative clause. On the other hand, in the AR reading, DP is interpreted as denoting amounts or degrees, but not individual entities. Thus, in (2) the champagne that they spilled and the champagne that somebody would drink can be different in the an AR reading, or they can be the same champagne in the RR reading.

(3)   John-wa [$_{DP}$ Bob-ga yatin-ni tukau hanbun]-o gyanburu-ni tukau.
        AR reading: half as much money as Bob pays for the rent
        RR reading: the half of Bob's money that will be used to pay for
        the rent   (Inada 2009: 85)

Half Relatives are ambiguous in the same manner. In (3) the bills that John uses can be different from Bob's, or they can be the same.

One can argue that ARs and *Half* Relatives have the same structure that induces AR reading. However, although ARs involve the nominal Head, *Half* Relatives do not seem to involve the Head, otherwise the nominal amount/degree expressions such as *hanbun* 'half' are the Head (Okutsu

1974, Inoue 1976, Ishii 1991, Kuroda 1999, Hasegawa 2002).* This paper claims that the Head of the *Half* Relatives is not the visible amount/degree expression such as *hanbun* 'half,' but a covert nominal expression such as AMOUNT. The covert noun AMOUNT is an unpronounced, covert lexical item, lacking phonetic content. These Heads are often small nouns, which are considered to be semilexical items with functional meaning. They can be covert in various languages (Corver and Riemsdijk 2001, Kayne 2005).†

The article is organized as follows. In Section 2 I will consider some other properties of the *Half* Relatives and argue that *Half* Relatives are a subtype of the clausal modifiers which modify *Sootai Meishi* 'Relational Nouns' in Japanese (Okutsu 1974). In Section 3 I will examine the internal structure of the temporal/locative PPs (Geis 1970, Haegeman 2009, Larson 1990, Nomura 2008, and Watanabe 1993, 2009) and show that we cannot assign an appropriate interpretation to the *Half* Relatives without postulating a covert Head. In Section 4 I will present the Headed-relative analysis and discuss the derivation and the structure of the *Half* Relatives. Section 5 concludes the paper.

2. Some Properties of *Half* Relatives

2.1 Sortal on the Degree/Amount

Let us first look at the so-called identity requirement on the Head of the relative clause. The fact that ARs obey the requirement on the identity of sortal is shown by the infelicity of (4b) (Grosu and Landman 1998, McNally 2008).

---

* Ishii (1991) points out that Japanese quantifiers, such as *hanbun* 'half,' are Q-quantifiers, which do not contain a head noun and express only the quantity, whereas English quantifiers do not express just the quantity, but rather the whole DP including the head noun. He argues that this difference explains why English does not have relative constructions that correspond to (1).

Kuroda (1999) and Hasegawa (2002) point out that Ishii's (1991) *Half* Relatives are head-internal relatives. Hasegawa proposes that the internal head is licensed via AGREE with the CP-external probe D⁰, such as *hanbun* 'half.' The internal Head is given a theta-feature by its lexical governor of the matrix. However, Hasegawa's analysis cannot account for the fact that *Half* Relatives can involve the overtly pronounced semilexical Head in the left-periphery, as will be discussed in this paper. Moreover, the analysis presented in this paper can account for why *Half* relatives have comparative-like interpretation, as observed above. Notice that Kuroda observes the important distinction between *Hanbun* 'half' relatives and *Hanbun-no* 'half-GEN' relatives. See Kuroda (1999) for detailed discussion.

† Semilexical nouns cannot appear alone, e.g. *Taro-wa gaku-o kaseida*, (Lit.) 'Taro earned *gaku*.' or *Haha-wa toki-ni shinda*'(Lit.) 'My mother died *toki-ni*.'

(4) a. It will take us the rest of our lives to drink [the *champagne* that they spilled that evening].

    b.# It will take us the rest of our lives to drink [the *champagne* that they spilled *beer* that evening].

What the English ARs denote is not just the property of amounts or degrees. The Head noun *champagne* must be interpreted internally and provides a sortal on the degree.‡ The identity-of-sort requirement is, however, not imposed on the *Half* Relatives as shown in (5) and (6).

(5)   Taro-wa [[Jiro-ga   biiru-o   nonda] *hanbun*] sake-o
            Taro-TOP Jiro-NOM beer-ACC drank   half   sake-ACC
            nonda.   (Inada 2009a: 100)
            drank
            'Taro drank half as much sake as Jiro drank beer.'

(6)   John-wa [[Mary-ga *mado-o*   aketa] bai] *doa*-o
            John-TOP Mary-NOM window-ACC opened double door-ACC
            aketa.   (Ishii 1991: 236))
            opened
            'John opened twice as many doors as Mary opened windows.'

For instance, the example in (5) involves the nominal *biiru* 'beer' inside the relative clause, which is different from *sake*.

2.2 Relational Nouns in Japanese

The amount/degree expressions such as *hanbun* and *bai* have been considered to be one type of *Sootai Meishi* 'Relational Nouns (RNs).' The RNs are the class of the nouns in Japanese which denote a relative amount or degree. Look at the examples in (7). *Mae* 'front' in (7b) and (7c) is also considered an RN (Okutsu 1974).

(7) a. John-wa [DP[CP Bob-ga yatin-ni tukau] *hanbun*]-o gyanburu-ni tukau.

    'John uses for gambling half the amount Bob uses for the rent.'

---

‡ Grosu and Landman (1998) and McNally (2008) point out that the relativization out of existentials (which are also considered to be ARs) requires not only the identity-of-quantity but also the identity-of-individuals, as in RRs.

(i)   I read all the books there were on the table.
       #'When there were five books on the table and I read five books, but not those that were on the table.'

If so, the identity requirement cannot distinguish ARs from RRs. This leads us to conclude they are the same construction, i.e. ARs in English are derived by restrictive relativization.

b. [[_CP_ sensou-ga owaru] 3kka *mae*]-ni haha-wa sinda.
   war-NOM ended 3.days front-at mother-TOP died
  'My mother had died 3 days before the war ended.'

c. [[_CP_ roujin-ga suwatteiru] *mae*]-de hato-ga
   old.man-NOM is.sitting front-at pigeons-NOM
  mame-o tabeteiru.
  beans-ACC are.eating
  'Pigeons are eating beans in front of the place where the old man is sitting.'

Suppose the RNs function as an apparent Head of the relative clause. Then, the *Half* Relatives can be analyzed as one type of relative clause modifying the RN. Henceforth, I refer to the structure involving the subordinate CP modifying the RN, an RNRC. I will show in Section 3 that the modifying subordinate CP will be reanalyzed as a relative clause involving the (covert) Head distinct from the RN.

The question arises here whether the RNRC as a whole can really be treated as a kind of relative clause. We would expect that (7a) and (7b)/(7c) are derivationally related to the "reconstructed" sentences (8) and (9).

(8) Bob-ga hanbun yatin-ni tukau.
    Bob-NOM half rent-for uses
    'Bob uses the half (amount of the money) for the rent.'

(9) Sensou-ga 3kka mae-ni owatta.
    war-NOM 3.days front-at ended
    'The war ended 3 days ago.'

If the RNs are the Head, we expect that they would be interpreted in the base position within the relative clause, but they are not. For example, (7b) does not mean "the war ended three days ago." What (7b) really means is 'three days before the war ended.' But if this is the case, what does the "relative clause" modify? Where is its Head?

3. Relativization of Covert Nouns

3.1 Relativization of Semilexical Noun

The RNRCs sometimes involve overt semilexical nouns such as *gaku* 'amount (of price)' or *toki* 'time/instance,' as shown in (10) and (11).

(10) [_DP_ [[Taro-ga kasegu] *gaku*]-no hanbun-o _DP_]
    Taro-NOM earns AMOUNT-GEN half-ACC
   'half as much money as Taro earns'

(11)   [PP [[kyuuryou-o uketoru] *toki*]-no   mae-ni PP]
        salary-ACC   receives TIME-GEN   front-at
        'before one receives his salary'

My claim is that the modifying CPs in (7) are indeed relative clauses, though the RNs modified by these CPs are not the Head. The Head is a semilexical noun which can be seen in (10) and (11). The schema is illustrated in (12).

(12)   [DP2/PP [DP1 [TP ...t_{HEAD}...] [HEAD] D1^0] RN D2^0/P^0]

There is a covert Head of the relative clause which raises for relativization from within the TP. Then, DP1, which involves the covert Head, becomes the internal argument of the RN, being interpreted as its covert reference point. What is reconstructed into the relative clause is not the Relational Noun, but the covert reference point.[§]

3.2 The Covert Temporal Operator in English Temporal PPs

The analysis of the RNRCs as Headed relatives finds crosslinguistic support. Geis (1970) and Larson (1990) propose that temporal adverbial clauses are derived by the movement of the operator to the left-periphery. Look at the examples below.

(13)   I saw Mary in New York [PP before [CP1 she claimed [CP2 that she would arrive]]].

The temporal PPs containing CPs are ambiguous. For example, (13) may mean that I saw Mary in NY before she made the claim, or prior to "some time t that she alleged would be the time of her arrival" (Larson 1990: 170). Larson claims that the ambiguity in (13) patterns with that of the adverbial clause involving *when*, as illustrated in (14).

(14) a. [CP1 when [TP she claimed [CP2 she would arrive] *t*]]
     b. [CP1 when [TP she claimed [CP2 she would arrived *t*]]]

[§] Section 4 will discuss the derivation and structure of the RNRC in detail. The precise position of the promoted Head NP is, however, under discussion: [Spec, DP] in Kayne (1994), but [Spec, TopP] of the relative clause in Bianchi (1999), and Aoun and Li (2003). In any case, the movement of the Head from within the raised DP may not be counter-cyclic, otherwise it should be motivated theoretically and empirically. In this paper, I leave this issue open.

(i)   [DP2 the [CP[DP1[NP book] which t_{NP}] C^0 [IP I read [DP1 which [NP book]] yesterday]]]

The ambiguity comes from the structural difference concerning the position of the variable in (14a) and (14b). Larson takes (15) to be the LF of (13), where the moved element is the empty operator of category NP generated in adjunct position occupied by the bare-NP adverb.[**]

(15)   [$_{PP}$ before [$_{CP1}$ Op$_i$ she claimed [$_{CP2}$ t_i' that she would arrive t_i]]].

The observed ambiguity does not depend on whether the relevant PP is a temporal PP or not. The temporal PP headed by *while* does not show the ambiguity.

(16)   I didn't see Mary in New York [$_{PP}$ while [$_{CP1}$ she said [$_{CP2}$ she was there]]].   (Larson 1990: 174)

It is worth noticing that Larson's (1990) analysis is based on a fact about the Case-assigning property of P. Larson claims that the null operator Op of the temporal adjunct clause must be Case-marked, assuming that the specifier position of the complement clause is the selection domain of P. The analysis is based on the selectional property of P.

(17) a. {before, after, since, until}   { John arrived
                                               that day
     b. while   { John slept
                                               *that day

The contrast in (17) indicates that the lower reading is available when the temporal P can select DP.

The Case condition Larson assumes is analogous to the one that holds in adverbial relatives as shown in (18). The clausal complement of *before* is then reanalyzed as a DP that involves the relative clause, as shown in (19a). The complement of *while*, on the other hand, cannot be a DP because *while* does not select DP, and thus PP does not involve A'-movement of the temporal operator, as shown in (19b).[††]

[**] Geis (1970) notes that the lower reading is not available when the extraction of the null operator from the lower position violates the island condition, as in (i).

(i)   *I saw Mary in New York [$_{PP}$ before [$_{CP1}$ Op she made the claim [$_{CP2}$ that she had arrived t]]].

[††] Haegeman (2009) also argues, following Demirdache and Uribe-Exebarria (2004), that (ia) has the same underlying structure as (ib).

(i) a. [$_{PP}$ Ø [$_{ZeitP}$ Ø [$_{CP}$ when Zooey arrived]]]
    b. [$_{PP}$ at [$_{ZeitP}$ the time [$_{CP}$ when Zooey arrived]]]   (Haegeman 2009: 391)

In her analysis, the landing site of *when* is that of the relative pronouns.

(18)   [$_{DP}$ the day   [$_{RC}$ Op [I left t]]].
(19) a. [$_{PP}$ before [$_{DP}$ Ø$_{the day}$ [$_{RC}$ Op [I left t]]]]
     b.* [$_{PP}$ while [$_{DP}$ Ø$_{the day}$ [$_{RC}$ Op [I left t]]]]

There is also crosslinguistic support (Demirdache and Uribe-Exebarria 2004, Haegeman 2009). In Dutch, *toen* 'then' originates within TP and moves to the left-periphery, as shown in (20).

(20) a. Hij woonde toen in Londen.
        he   lived   then in London
        'At the time he lived in London.'
     b. Toen hij in Londen woonde, ...
        then he in London lived
        'When he lived in London ...'   (Haegeman 2009: 387)

In Hungarian, temporal adjunct clauses contain relative *wh*-phrases, as illustrated bellow.

(21) a. (A)mikor   Peter nincs otthon
        REL-what-at Peter is.not home
        'When Peter is not at home'
     b. A   nap [amikor   Anna megjött]
        The day REL-what-at Anna arrived
        'The day when Anna arrived'   (Lipták 2005: 142)

3.3 The Fine Structure of Temporal/Locative PPs

Watanabe (2009) and Nomura (2008) investigate the structure of the temporal/locative PP and consider the semantic roles which functional categories of PP bear, within the cartographic approach. Based on the vector-space semantics for the interpretation of the temporal/locative PPs (Zwarts 1997), Watanabe claims that each of the atomic information (semantic roles) of the vector-space semantics corresponds to the function of the functional heads of the temporal/locative PP, as illustrated in (22).

(22)   [$_{PP}$ [$_{#P}$ [$_{MP}$ ...] [$_{PnP}$ [$_{RP}$ R^0] Pn^0] #^{0}] P^0]

The topmost PP layer is the locus of the position of the vector. #P represents the length of the vector. PnP represents the direction of the vector. RP represents the reference object of the vector. The Measure Phrase (MP) may further specify the degree of Pn^0 numerically. The MP is located in [Spec,#P].

Let us look at some examples. Watanabe decomposes the morphologically complex postposition such as *no-mae-ni* 'in-front-of' into two parts, Pn^0 and P^0. A Relational Noun such as *mae* 'front' is the head of PnP, which determines the type of the dimension/direction of PP. Then, #P, which is the functional projection above PnP, specifies the degree of Pn^0.

(23) a.   b.

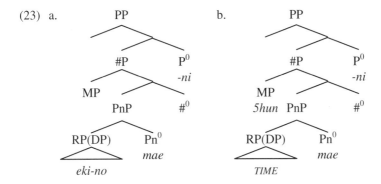

What is important here is that the reference point of the RN is signified by the complement of PnP: It is R(eference)P, which immediately dominates DP. It functions as the source of the temporal/locative vector. Even if RP is phonetically missing, the complement position must be occupied by a covert noun such as PLACE or TIME, as illustrated in (23b), for the appropriate temporal/locative interpretation.[‡‡]

Given the fine structure of PP in (22), the temporal/locative RNRCs in Japanese and the English temporal PPs can be analyzed in the same way. With the clausal complement, both of them involve the relative clause and the Head is the (covert) reference point.

4. Headed-relative Analysis of the RNRCs

4.1 The Derivation and the Structure of the RNRCs

In order to express the reference point, we must have DP in the most embedded complement position of PP. This DP is the Head of the relative clause. In the temporal/locative RNRCs, this Head DP signifies the reference point of PP. The covert Head is also motivated by the scope construal of the temporal P in English. Based on the analysis of the temporal/locative RNRCs, we can say that there is also a covert Head in the amount RNRCs.

[‡‡] Furthermore, Watanabe (2009) and Nomura (2008) assume DimP, whose head assigns the information of dimension, representing, for example, whether PP is temporal or locative.

(24) a. $[_{CP} \text{[HEAD]} \; [_{TP} \ldots t_{\text{HEAD}} \ldots] \; C^0]$

b. $[_{DP1}[_{TP} \ldots t_{\text{HEAD}} \ldots] \; [_{CP} \text{[HEAD]} \; t_{TP} \; C^0] \; D1^0]$

c. $[_{PP}[_{PnP} \; [_{DP1}[_{TP} \ldots t_{\text{HEAD}} \ldots] \; [_{CP} \text{[HEAD]} \; t_{TP} \; C^0] \; D1^0] RN(Pn^0) \;]P^0]$

d. $[_{DP2} \; [_{DP1}[_{TP} \ldots t_{\text{HEAD}} \ldots] \; [_{CP} \text{[HEAD]} \; t_{TP} \; C^0] \; D1^0] \; RN \quad D2^0]$

Under the promotion analysis of relative clauses, the Head raises to the [Spec,CP] of the relative clause (Kayne 1994). TP also raises to [Spec,DP] in languages like Japanese with the relative clause-Head order. Then $D1^0$ merges with CP, projecting DP1. The RNs are external to DP1.[§§],[***]

Let us consider the following examples. The subordinate CP, e.g. *sensou-ga owaru*, involves the covert semilexical noun *TIME*, as in (25a) below. With this covert noun, the subordinate CP is analyzed as being a relative clause. The subordinate CP in (25b) also involves the relativization of the covert semilexical noun *AMOUNT*.

(25) a. $[_{PP}[_{PnP}[_{DP1}[_{TP} \text{sensou-ga} \; t_i \; \text{owaru}] \; [_{CP} \; \text{TIME}_i \; t_{TP} \; C^0] \; D1^0]$

mae]-ni]

b. $[_{DP2} \; [_{DP1}[_{TP} \text{Bob-ga} \; t_i \quad \text{tukau}] \quad [_{CP} \text{AMOUNT}_i \; t_{TP} \; C^0] \; D1^0]$

hanbun-o]

The most embedded CP of the amount RNRC must move to [Spec,CaseP] for oblique Case-checking within DP1, as shown in (26) (cf., Watanabe 2008b). The DP1 is then assigned genitive Case in the temporal/locative RNRC via phrasal movement within PP, as shown in (27).

(26) $[_{DP1}[_{TP} \text{Hanako-ga} \; t_i \; \text{kaseida}] \; [_{CaseP} \; [_{CP} \text{AMOUNT}_i \; t_{TP} \; C^0]$

$[_{\#P} \; t_{CP} \;] \; \text{Case}^0] \; D^0]$

'(Lit.) the amount (of money) that Hanako earned'

(27) $[_{PP} \; [_{DP1} \text{sensou-ga} \; t_i \text{owaru TIME}_i \;]$

$[_{\#P} \; [_{MP} \text{3kka}] \; [_{PnP} \; t_{DP1} \quad \text{mae}] \; \#^0] \; \text{-ni}]$

'three days before the war ended'

[§§] There is a question as to whether the raised Head is a fully projected DP or some smaller projection. Inada (2008) argues that, based on the reconstruction effects concerning the scope of the universal quantifier of the Head, the raised Head is considered #P, which at least involves numerals, but not universals.

[***] As a consequence, this derivation of the Head-final relative clause partially accounts for the TP properties of the relative clause in Japanese. See Murasugi (1990) for the detail.

The most embedded RP(DP1) of the temporal/locative RNRC must move to the position higher than #P, that is, [Spec,PP], as in (27).[†††] Through these movements for Case checking, the well-formed order is obtained.

4.2 On the Distribution of Overt Heads

Measure phrases can replace semilexical Heads as shown in (28), or occur internally within the relative clause as shown in (29).

(28)   [$_{DP}$[[Taro-ga t_i kaseida]   100man yen$_i$]-no   hanbun $_{DP}$]
        Taro-NOM   earned   a.million yen-GEN   half

(29) a.   [$_{DP}$[Taro-ga   100man yen   kaseida](*-no)   hanbun $_{DP}$]

   b.   [$_{DP}$[Taro-ga   100man yen   kaseida]   gaku-no   hanbun $_{DP}$]
        Taro-NOM   a.million yen   earned   GAKU   half
        (Lit.) 'half of a million yen that Taro earned (a million yen)'

The measure phrases in (29) are, however, not the internal Head of the relative clause. Look at the examples in (30).

(30) a.   syakkin-ga   (sono)   (gaku)   100man   yen-ni   tassita.
        debt-NOM   that   amount   a.million yen-to   reached
        'The debt has amounted to a million yen.'

   b.   [$_{DP}$ [gaku/AMOUNT] 100man yen]

The example shows that the semilexical noun *gaku* and numerical expression *100man yen* constitute one DP, as illustrated in (30b). Given this analysis, the measure phrases in-situ in (29) are considered to be the remnant of A'-movement of the semilexical Head, as shown in (31).

(31) a.   [$_{DP}$[$_{TP}$ [$_{DP}$ g̶a̶k̶u̶]$_i$ 100man yen-o] kaseida] [$_{CP}$ [gaku]$_i$ t_{TP}]]

   b.   [$_{DP}$[$_{TP}$ [$_{DP}$A̶M̶O̶U̶N̶T̶]$_i$ 100man yen-o] kaseida] [$_{CP}$[AMOUNT]$_i$ t_{TP}]]

The RNRC with the measure phrase Head in (28) is derived via the relativization of the whole DP in (30b), as illustrated in (32).[‡‡‡]

(32)   [$_{DP}$[$_{TP}$ [$_{DP}$A̶M̶O̶U̶N̶T̶/̶g̶a̶k̶u̶]̶ 1̶0̶0̶m̶a̶n̶ ̶y̶e̶n̶]̶$_i$ kaseida]
                [$_{CP}$ [$_{DP}$[AMOUNT/gaku]100 man yen]$_i$ t_{TP}]]

[†††] The Case can also be checked via PnP movement. See Nomura (2008) for details.

[‡‡‡] In this respect, the fact that relative clauses such as *amount that they drank champagne* is ruled out in English is due to the violation of the Left Branch Condition, which is operative in Japanese in this case.

4.3 On the Identity Requirement on the Head

The Headed-relative analysis of RNRCs sheds light on the fact that the amount RNRCs show the "nonidentity" effect that we have discussed in Section 2. Remember that in ARs the Head is imposed on the so-called Identity Requirement.

(33)   # It will take us the rest of our lives to drink [the *champagne* that they spilled *beer* that evening].   (Grosu and Landman 1998)

Grosu and Landman (1998) observe that the Head *champagne* must be interpreted internally in some sense and that it provides a sortal on the degree. This is shown by the infelicity of (33). However, the requirement is not observed in the case of the amount RNRCs, as repeated below.§§§

(34) a.   Taro-wa[[Jiro-ga *biiru*-o nonda] hanbun] *sake*-o nonda.
         'Taro drank sake half as much as Jiro drank beer.'
    b.   John-wa [[Mary-ga *mado*-o aketa]bai] *doa*-o aketa.
         'John opened twice as many doors as Mary opened windows.'

The present analysis accounts for the presence of the sortal that is different from the Head. The RNRCs in (34) have a covert Head, as illustrated in (35).

(35) a.   [$_{DP}$ [$_{DP}$Jiro-ga   [(AMOUNT) *biiru*-o] nonda] (AMOUNT)]]   hanbun]
    b.   [$_{DP}$ [$_{DP}$Mary-ga [(NUMBER) *mado*-o] aketa] (NUMBER)]]   bai]

Now we can see why a problem does not arise concerning the lack of an identity requirement in the RNRCs. The sortal is not a part of the Head. Instead, the Head only comprises the semilexical covert noun, which denotes the amount/degree.****

---

§§§ This identity-of-sort requirement is also not imposed on the sub-comparatives.
(i)   It will take us the rest of our lives to drink as much *champagne* as they spilled (*beer*)
       that evening.   (Grosu and Landman 1998)
**** When the degree word AMOUNT with the sortal on it as a whole is relativized (as in English ARs), the identity requirement (re)emerges as is shown in (i), where the Head including the sortal is overtly relativized as shown in (i).
(i)   *[$_{DP}$ [$_{DP}$[$_{CP}$ Taro-ga *t* nonda] [(AMOUNT/ryou-no) sake]]-no biiru-o nonda.
       '(Lit.) (Someone) drank beer that Taro drank (the amount of) sake.'

4.4 The Partitive Structure of the Amount RNRC

We have seen that the relative clause involved in the amount RNRC (*Half Relatives*) is derived via the relativization of the covert noun *AMOUNT* as shown in (36a). The amount RNRC as a whole then has a partitive structure, "half of the AMOUNT," as shown in (36b).

(36) a. $[_{DP1}[_{TP}...t_i...] [_{CP}$ AMOUNT$_i$ t_{TP} $C^0]_{DP1}]$

     b. $[_{DP2} [_{DP1}[_{TP}...t_i...] [_{CP}$ AMOUNT$_i$ t_{TP} $C^0]_{DP1}]$(-no)hanbun $_{DP2}]$

In the partitive structure, the covert nominal Head cannot be replaced with a proper name. This prediction is borne out as shown in the difference between the amount RNRCs with common nouns in (37) and those with proper names in (38).

(37) a.   Jiro-wa [[[Taro-ga   kyousitu-de   atta] gakusei]-no   hanbun](-ni)
            Jiro-TOP Taro-NOM   classroom-at saw student-GEN   half-DAT
            koutei-de   atta.
            playground-at saw

    b.? Jiro-wa [[[Taro-ga gakusei-ni   kyousitu-de atta]] hanbun](-ni)
            Jiro-TOP Taro-NOM student-DAT   classroom-at saw   half-DAT
            koutei-de   atta.
            playground-at saw
            'Jiro saw at the playground half the number of the students that
            Taro saw in the classroom.'

(38) a.# Jiro-wa [[[Taro-ga   kyousitu-de   atta] Hanako]-no   hanbun](-ni)
            koutei-de   atta.

    b.# Jiro-wa [[[Taro-ga Hanako-ni kyousitu-de atta]] hanbun](-ni)
            koutei-de   atta.
            '(Lit.) Jiro saw at the playground half of Hanako that Taro saw in
            the classroom.'

The examples in (38) are infelicitous because we cannot "meet" some proper part of *Hanako* in the actual world. Compare (38) with the following. The relativization of the proper name itself is possible.

(39)   Jiro-wa [[Taro-ga   kyousitu-de   sakki   atta] Hanako]-ni
            Jiro-TOP Taro-NOM   classroom-at   a.little.ago saw   Hanako-DAT
            ima   koutei-de   atta.
            now   playground-at   saw
            'Jiro saw Hanako at the playground just now, who Taro saw at the
            classroom a little while ago.'

5. Concluding Remarks

Given the Headed-relative analysis of the RNRCs presented in this paper, the comparative-like interpretation of them is accounted for. According to Carlson (1977), an AR reading of the relative clause CP in (40a) is obtained not by restrictive relativization as shown in (40b), but by relativization of the degree operator as in (40c). The comparative clause CP also involves A'-movement of the degree operator, as shown in (41b).

(40) a. It would take days to drink the champagne [$_{CP}$ that they spilled ...].
  b. they spilled THAT champagne ...
  c. they spilled THAT MUCH (*d-many*) champagne ...
(41) a. There are more women in high school [$_{CP}$ than there are in college].
  b. there are THAT MANY (*d-many*) women in college.

It is clear that the relative clause with an AR reading is derived in the same way as the comparative construction.

This observation demonstrates that the amount RNRC, which is derived via the relativization of AMOUNT, serves as the clausal modifier of nominal element, like a relative clause, and at the same time as the clausal modifier of the amount/degree, like a comparative clause.

(42) a. [$_{CP}$ [AMOUNT]   [$_{TP}$ ...[DP-no <AMOUNT>]...] Ø$_C$]
  b. [$_{CP}$ [*d*-many N] *that*$_C$ [$_{TP}$ ...<*d*-many N>...   ]]
  c. [$_{CP}$ *d*-Op   *than*$_C$ [$_{TP}$ ...[<*d*-many-x> Adj.]...   ]]

The relativization of the (covert) semilexical noun AMOUNT in (42a) is considered an example of the ARs because, as in (42b), what undergoes A'-movement denotes 'nominal.' (42a) is also considered an example of the comparative clauses because, as in (42c), what undergoes A'-movement only denotes 'amount/degree.' In Japanese, the covert semilexical degree word AMOUNT is nominal. Thus, the clausal modifier that involves A'-movement of AMOUNT results in the structure of the relative clause, and has the AR reading, that is, the comparative-like interpretation.

References

Carlson, G. 1977. Amount Relatives. *Language* 53: 520-542.
Corver, N. and van Riemsdijk, H. 2001. Semi-lexical Categories. *Semi-Lexical Categories: The Function of Content Words and the Content of Function Words*, eds. N. Corver and H. van Riemsdijk. 1-20. Berlin: Mouton de Gruyter.
Demirdache, H. and Uribe-Etxebarria, M. 2004. The Syntax of Time Adverbs. *The Syntax of Time*, eds. J. Guéron and J. Lecarme 143-80. Cambridge, MA: MIT Press.

Geis, M. 1970. Adverbial Subordinate Clauses in English. Doctoral dissertation, MIT.

Grosu, A. and Landman, F. 1998. Strange Relatives of the Third Kind. *Natural Language Semantics* 6: 125-170.

Haegeman, L. 2009. The Movement Analysis of Temporal Adverbial Clauses. *English Language and Linguistics* 13: 385-480.

Hasegawa, N. 2002. Syuyoobu Naizaigata Kankeisetsu: DP Bunseki (Head-internal Relative Clauses: DP Analysis). *Scientific Approaches to Language* 1: 1-33. Kanda University of International Studies.

Heim, I. 1987. Where does the Definiteness Restriction Apply? Evidence from the Definiteness of Variables. *The Representation of (In)definiteness*, eds. E. Reuland and A. Meulen. 21-42. Cambridge, MA: MIT Press.

Inada. S. 2008. Unexpected Narrow Scope and Reconstruction into Relative Clause. *Linguistic Research* 24: 1-11. University of Tokyo.

Inada, S. 2009a. On the 'AMOUNT' Relativization and Its Relatives. *Linguistic Research* 25: 85-102. The University of Tokyo.

Inada, S. 2009b. Relativization of Covert Nouns and Their Structural Position in Japanese. Paper read at 139th Conference of Linguistic Society of Japan, Kobe University.

Inoue, K. 1976. *Henkeibunpoo to Nihongo Joo: Toogo Koozou o Tyuusin ni (Transformational Grammar and Japanese: focusing on the Syntactic Structure)*. Tokyo: Taishukan.

Ishii, Y. 1991. Operators and Empty Categories in Japanese. Doctoral dissertation, University of Connecticut.

Kayne, R. 1994 *The Antisymmetry of Syntax*. Cambridge, MA: MIT Press.

Kayne, R. 2005. *Movement and Silence*. Oxford: Oxford University Press.

Liptak, A. 2005. Relativization Strategies in Temporal Adjunct Clauses. *LIVY Yearbook* 5: 133-185. Amsterdam: John Benjamins.

Kuroda, S.-Y. 1999. Syubu Naizai Kankeisetu (Head-internal Relative Clauses. in S.-Y. Kuroda and M. Nakamura. eds). *Kotoba no Kaku to Syuhen (Core and Periphery in Language)*, 27-103. Tokyo: Kurosio.

Larson, R. 1990. Extraction and Multiple Selection in PP. *The Linguistic Review* 7: 169-182.

McNally, L. 2008. DP-Internal *Only*, Amount Relatives, and Relatives out of Existentials. *Linguistic Inquiry* 39: 129-161.

Murasugi, K. 1990 Noun Phrases in Japanese and English: A Study in Syntax, Learnability, and Acquisition. Doctoral dissertation, University of Connecticut.

Nomura, J. 2008. Locative Arguments with Measure Phrases in Japanese. MA Thesis. University of Tokyo.

Okutsu, K. 1974. *Seisei Nihon Bunpooron, (Generative Japanese Grammar)*, Tokyo: Taishukan.

Watanabe, A. 2009. Measure Phrases in PP. *The Proceedings of the Tenth Tokyo Conference on Psycholinguistics*. 1-25. Tokyo: Hituzi Syoboo.

Zwarts, J. 1997. Vectors as Relative Positions: A Compositional Semantics of Modified PPs. *Journal of Semantics* 14: 57-86.

Is Genitive Subject Possible in Modern Korean?*

YIN-JI JIN
Gifu University

1. Introduction

It has been assumed that genitive subjects were possible in Middle Korean around the 15 century (Suh 1977, 1981 and Jang 1995, among others), but it is impossible in Modern Korean (Korean, hereafter). However, there are a few researchers who claim that the genitive subject is possible in Korean as well. They include Huang et al. (1988) and Kim (2006), among others. In this paper, I first review two of the previous studies by Sohn (1997) and Maki et al. (2006), both of whom claim that a genitive subject is not allowed in Korean, and then present the relevant data with a genitive subject from Kim (2006) and Huang et al. (1988), who claim that a genitive subject is allowed in Korean. Then, I put the data in a certain structure in order to guarantee that the genitive subject is within the relative clause, and point out

---

* An earlier version of this paper was presented at the 19th Japanese/Korean Linguistics Conference held at the University of Hawai'i at Mānoa on November 12, 2009. I would like to thank the audience at the conference, Jessica Dunton, Heejeong Ko, and Hideki Maki for their valuable comments. All errors are my own.

Japanese/Korean Linguistics 19.
Edited by Ho-min Sohn, Haruko Cook, William O'Grady, Leon A. Serafim, & Sang Yee Cheon.

that all the data that were claimed to allow genitive subjects are ungrammatical in that structure.

I then turn to the data in Middle Korean, and point out that those examples with a genitive subject do not have a structure which guarantees that the genitive subject is within the relative clause. Based on these findings, I claim that even Middle Korean did not allow genitive subjects. Finally, I consider these findings from the viewpoint of a comparative Altaic study, taking into account genitive subjects in Old and Modern Japanese.

The organization of this paper is as follows. Section 2 reviews two previous studies, and shows that genitive subjects are impossible in Korean. Section 3 first reviews two relatively recent studies that show that genitive subjects are possible in Korean, and then examines whether they really represent genuine genitive subjects. After showing that they are not genuine genitive subjects, genitives subjects in Middle Korean are examined in Section 4, and shown that they are actually not genitive subjects. Section 5 considers, following Maki, Uchibori, and Jin (in progress), the origin of the difference between Korean and Japanese, in which genitives subjects are considered to be allowed. Finally, Section 6 concludes this paper.

2. Previous Studies by Sohn (1997) and Maki et al. (2006)

Sohn (1997) argues that there is no nominative/genitive alternation in Korean, on the basis of the examples with an adverb placed in front of the genitive subject, as shown in (2). (1b) is far worse than (1a).

(1) a.   ecey   John-i   san   chayk
               yesterday   -NOM bought book
               'the book John bought yesterday'

     b.   ?*   ecey   John-uy   san   chayk
               yesterday   -GEN bought book
               'the book John bought yesterday'

Sohn (1997) concludes that the construction with a genitive subject is not legitimate, and is just "felt" to be grammatical due to its resemblance to normal NPs/DPs.

Maki et al. (2006) conducted a statistics-based investigation, and examined whether the case marker alternation might take place in the structures shown in (2)-(5) in Korean.

(2) a.   [NP-NOM V] N
     b.   [NP-GEN V] N

(3) a. [ADVP NP-NOM V] N
    b. [ADVP NP-GEN V] N

(4) a. [NP-NOM ADVP V] N
    b. [NP-GEN ADVP V] N

(5) a. [ADVP NP-NOM ADVP V] N
    b. [ADVP NP-GEN ADVP V] N

They used intransitive verbs only, as transitive verbs may cause Transitivity Restriction effects (Watanabe 1996). They collected data from Korean college students by asking them to complete the questionnaire designed for this study, and then analyzed the data by Analysis of Variance (ANOVA). A series of ANOVAs was conducted on ratings (1 to 5) (1= totally ungrammatical and 5 = perfectly grammatical) for two Case marker (Nominative/Genitive) types. The results showed a significant effect on Case marker: in each pair in (2)-(5), the rating was far higher for Nominative Case sentences than for Genitive Case sentences. The results of the analyses are shown in Table 1.

Table 1 Results of ANOVAs for Two Case Marker (NOM/GEN)Types

	Structure	Average Rating	F	P
(2a)	[NP-NOM V] N	3.73	1088.87	.000
(2b)	[NP-GEN V] N	1.90		
(3a)	[ADVP NP-NOM V] N	3.79	1245.54	.000
(3b)	[ADVP NP-GEN V] N	1.92		
(4a)	[NP-NOM ADVP V] N	3.46	1217.33	.000
(4b)	[NP-GEN ADVP V] N	1.80		
(5a)	[ADVP NP-NOM ADVP V] N	3.62	1394.31	.000
(5b)	[ADVP NP-GEN ADVP V] N	1.85		

The results suggest that it is highly plausible to conclude that there is no nominative/genitive alternation in Korean, in favor of Sohn's (1997) claim, and that apparent "genitive subjects" in Korean are not actually subjects of the sentences modifying the head nouns, but ought to have other grammatical functions within the given contexts.

However, there have been some studies in Korean linguistics that show the availability of genitive subjects since Sohn's (1997) work. In the next section, I extract the relevant data from Huang et al. (1998) and Kim (2006), among others, and carefully examine the structures of the examples.

3. Korean Data from Huang et al. (1998) and Kim (2006)

The original data from the studies by Huang et al. (1998) and Kim (2006) are shown in (6)-(12). They all have genitive subjects in the prenominal sentential modifiers to nouns. The examples from (6) to (9) involve relativization of the argument NPs in the clauses, and the examples from (10) to (12) involve relativization of non-argument phrases in the clauses.

Argument Relativization

(6) [Na-uy salanghanun] anay-eykey y   kul-ul   ssessta.
     I-GEN love   wife-to   this sentence-ACC writing
     'I am writing these sentences to my wife who I love.'
     (Huang et al. 1988)

(7) [Na-uy salanghanun] mikuk-uy   tongphoeyyo.
     I-GEN love   America-GEN friend
     'The American friends who I love.' (Kim 2006)

(8) [Sensayngnim-uy hasin] malssum-un cengmallo coun kyohwun-i
     teacher-GEN   told   story-TOP   really   good lesson-to
     toy-essta.
     become
     'The story which the teacher told me became a really good lesson.'
     (Kim 2006)

(9) [Sekubon-uy ssun] kulssi-nun   myengphil-lo yumyenghata.
     Sekubon-GEN wrote character-TOP masterpiece-as famous
     'The characters which Sekubon wrote are famous as a masterpiece.'
     (Kim 2006)

Non-Argument Relativization

(10) [Bocho-ui gyodeahar] sigan-i   doe-otta.
     guard-GEN change   time-NOM came
     'The time when the guards change came.' (Huang et al. 1988)

(11) [Na-uy salten] kohyang-un   kkochphi-nun sankol.
     I-GEN lived   hometown-TOP blooming mountain
     'The hometown where I lived is in the blooming mountain.' (Kim 2006)

(12) [Aitul-uy   nonun] mosup-i   yeypputa.
     children-GEN play   appearance-NOM cute.
     'Children look cute when they play.' (Kim 2006)

All of these examples have genitive subjects, and given their frequent occurrence, we may be convinced that genitive subjects should be possible in Korean. Interestingly enough, however, no genitive subject in (6) to (12) is preceded by any other element. Maki and Uchibori (2008), among many others, point out, following the essential claim by Sohn (1997), that it may be possible to assume that genitive subjects in such examples would be placed in DP SPEC, and there may be *pro*'s corresponding to them in the relative clauses, as schematically represented in (13).

(13) [$_{DP}$ DP$_i$-GEN [$_{NP}$ [$_{IP/TP}$ pro$_i$ Predicate] N] D]

They claim that in order to ensure that the genitive subject is within the relative clause, elements such as adverbs need to be placed in front of it, as in (14).

(14) [$_{DP}$ [$_{NP}$ [$_{IP/TP}$ Adverb DP-GEN Predicate] N] D]

Following this insight, I embedded the relative clauses in (6) to (12) in the structure in (14) in order to guarantee that the genitive subjects are within the relative clauses. I then examined their grammaticality by comparing them with the nominative subject counterparts. The result was that the examples with a genitive subject were all ungrammatical, as shown below.

Argument Relativization

(15) [cinsimulo ne-ka/*na-uy salanghanun] anay-eykey i   kul-ul
     heart from I-NOM/I-GEN love   wife-to   this sentence-ACC
     ssunta.
     writing
     'I am writing these sentences to my wife who I love from the bottom of my heart.'

(16) [kiphi   ne-ga/*na-uy saranghanun] mikuk-uy   tongphoeyyo.
     deeply I-NOM/I-GEN love   America-GEN friend
     'The American friends who I love very much.'

(17) [Kyosil-eyse sensayngnim-i/*-uy hasin] malssum-un cengmallo coun
     class-in   teacher-GEN   told   story-TOP really   good
     kyohwun-i toy-essta.
     lesson-to become
     'The story which the teacher told me in class became a really good lesson.'

(18) [Sumusalcek-ey Sekubon-i/*-uy ssun] kulssi-nun   myengphil-lo
     20 years old-at Sekubon-GEN   wrote character-TOP masterpiece-as
     yumyenghata.
     famous
     'The characters which Sekubon wrote when he was 20 years old are
     famous as a masterpiece.'

Non-Argument Relativization

(19) [kwungcen-aph-eyse pocho-ka/*-uy kyotayhal] sikan-i   toy-essta.
     palace front-at   guard-GEN   change   time-NOM came
     'The time when the guards change in front of the palace came.'

(20) [e-lilcek-ey ne-ka/*na-uy salten] kohyang-un   kkophi-nun
     childhood-at I-NOM/I-GEN lived   hometown-TOP blooming
     sankol.
     mountain
     'The hometown where I lived in my childhood is in the blooming
     mountain.'

(21) [kongwen-eyse aitul-i/*-uy   nonun] mosup-i   yeypputa.
     park-at   children-NOM/-GEN play   appearance-NOM cute.
     'Children look cute when they play at the park.'

    In the examples from (15) to (21), the subjects in the relative clauses are
all preceded by an adverb phrase, and the examples with a nominative subject are all perfectly grammatical, while those with a genitive subject are all
ungrammatical, which indicates that there is a clear contrast in grammaticality between the two types of sentences. Therefore, I conclude that genitive subjects, which appear to be possible, are actually not allowed in Korean. This again supports Sohn's (1997) and Maki et al.'s (2006) claims, that
genitive subjects are not possible in Korean.
    With this conclusion, let us examine Middle Korean data in the next sec-
tion.

4. Middle Korean Data from Suh (1977, 1981)

Suh (1977, 1981) examined the 15th century Korean, which I call Middle
Korean in this paper, and provided data with a genitive subject. Consider the
examples in (22)-(26). (22)-(24) involve relativization of argument NPs, and
(25)-(26) involve nominalized clauses followed by the accusative case
marker.

Argument Relativization

(22) [Asasewang-uy seywun] thap-ey   sali-lul ta…
     Asase King-GEN built tower-in sari-ACC all
     '…all of sari to the tower which King Asase built' (Suh 1977)

(23) I   Dongsan-un [Sekutal-uy   san]   kes-io.
     this Dongsan-TOP Sekutal-GEN bought Nominalizer-be
     'This Dongsan is what Sekutal bought.' (Suh 1977)

(24) a.   [ceypul-i   ta melisye chanthanha-si-nun mal]-ila
          Buddhists-NOM all from far praise-Hon-RC   words-is
          '(the above) is the words that all the Buddhists praise.'
          [welinsekpo 18, 57b] (Suh 1981)
     b.   [ceypul-s   ta melisye chanthanha-si-nun mal]-ila[1]
          Buddhists-GEN all from far praise-Hon-RC   words-is
          '(the above) is the words that all the Buddhists praise.'
          [pephwakyung 6, 179a] (Suh 1981)

Nominalized Clauses

(25) a.   [taman ttong-i   talmye ssum]-ul maspolkesila
          only   excrements-NOM sweet   sour-ACC tastes-DC
          '(he) tastes whether the excrements are sweet or sour'
          [sohakenhay 6, 28a-b] (Suh 1981)
     b.   [taman ttong-uy   talmyessum]-ul maspoa
          only   excrements-GEN sweet sour-ACC tastes
          '(he) tastes whether the excrements are sweet or sour'
          [tongsinsok, hyo 4, 62b] (Suh 1981)

(26) nwuy   [tanglang-uy nunghi swulwuy kesul-um]-ul   polio
     who-NOM tanglang-GEN easily cart-(Acc) push-NML-ACC see
     'Who can see Tanglang's easily pushing the cart?'
     [nammyung 2, 73b] (Suh 1981)

There were just a few examples with a genitive subject in Middle Korean. However, just like the Korean data examined in Section 3, no Middle Korean example with a genitive subject is preceded by an adverb. Regarding this matter, Jang (1995: 228) states the following: "My investigations (of

---

[1] According to Jang (1995), -s is an honorific form of the genitive case marker -uy in Middle Korean.

Suh 1981) have revealed no cases in which a sentential adverb precedes the genitive subject in Middle Korean."

The same comment applies to Suh (1979), where I found no genitive subject preceded by an adverb. Therefore, it is highly plausible to assume that the genitive subjects in (22)-(26) are placed in DP SPEC, and there are *pro*'s corresponding to them in the relevant clauses, as schematically represented in (13), reproduced as (27).

(27) [$_{DP}$ DP$_i$-GEN [$_{NP}$ [$_{IP/TP}$ pro$_i$ Predicate] N] D] (= (13))

Therefore, the examples in (22)-(26) do not constitute genuine evidence for the claim that genitive subjects were possible in Middle Korean, and I tentatively conclude, based on the data in Sections 3 and 4, that no genitive subject has ever been possible in the history of Korean since the 15th century.

If it is correct, this conclusion poses an interesting question as to what the difference is between Korean and Japanese, which has been claimed to allow genitive subjects. In the next section, following Maki, Uchibori, and Jin's (in progress) hypothesis, I will discuss the origin of this difference between Korean and Japanese by considering data from Old Japanese as well as Modern Japanese (Japanese, hereafter).

5. Origin of the Difference Between Korean and Japanese

Harada (1971) and Miyagawa (1993), among many others, show that genitives subjects are allowed in Japanese. In the following, I will show genitives subjects in Old Japanese and Japanese first. Then, I will show an important historical change in the transition from Old Japanese to Japanese. Finally, based on this change that happened in Japanese, but not in Korean, I will provide a hypothesis about the origin of the visible difference between Korean and Japanese in terms of the case marker alternation.

First of all, Old Japanese and Japanese have genuine genitive subjects, as shown below.

Old Japanese

(28) kono ahida-ni,   aru hito-no   kakite   idaseru uta,
     this period-during some person-GEN write(CONT) turn in poem
     'the poem which some person has written and turned in during this period,' (Tosa Nikki 018-06)[2]

---

[2] The Old Japanese data in the text are cited from the data base Koten Soogoo Kenkyuujo (2009). The name in the parentheses indicates the name of the book, and the numbers indicate

(29) imijiku   hito-no   shiritaru gen nare domo
    very well person-GEN know   word be   but
    'although (it is) the word which people know very well'
    (Makura no Sooshi 328-11 Joo)

Japanese

(30) [Sukkari   kizu-ga/-no   naotta neko]-wa kono neko desu.
    completely injury-NOM/-GEN cured cat-TOP   this   cat   be
    'The cat which was completely cured of the injury is this cat.'
    (Maki et al. 2009)

(31) [Totemo raamen-ga/-no   oishikatta mise]-wa   kono mise
    very   noodle-NOM/-GEN delicious restaurant-TOP this   restaurant
    desu.
    be
    'The restaurant where noodles were very delicious was this restaurant.'
    (Maki et al. 2009)

Example (28) is from *Tosa Nikki* written by Kino Tsurayuki around the middle 10th century, and example (29) is from *Makura no Sooshi* written by Seishoo Nagon during the late 10th to the early 11th century. Examples (30) and (31) are cited from Maki et al. (2009). All these examples have a genitive subject which is followed by an adverb within the relative clauses. Therefore, it is plausible to assume that a genitive subject has been possible in the history of the Japanese language at least since the middle 10th century.

Interestingly enough, Old Japanese has another genitive case marker: *ga*. In Japanese, *ga* is a nominative case marker, but in Old Japanese, it was a genitive case marker only for the 1st and 2nd person pronouns. Maki, Uchibori, and Jin (in progress) present the following data with a 1st person singular pronoun.

(32) tada wa-ga tatetaru   koto
    just I-GEN paid due respect fact
    'the fact that I paid due respect (to him)'
    (Genji Monogatari (277-13(4)))

---

the page number, the line number, and the volume number (or volume name), if any, in this order.

(33) tsurezureto   wa-ga naki   kurasu natsu-no   hi-o
without doing anything I-GEN cry(CONT) live   summer-GEN day-ACC
'the summer day when I live crying without doing anything'
(Genji Monogatari (542-14(4)))

In each of (32) and (33), the genitive case marker *ga* is preceded by an adverb, and appears within a sentential modifier to a noun. However, the nominative case marker for the 1st person singular pronoun was not *ga*, but -∅ (zero), as shown below.

(34) Mazu,   ware   sarubeki tokoro-e iku
first of all I-NOM the   place-to go
'First of all, I will go to the place'
(Makura no Sooshi (035-09/-010 Ge))

(35) Kimi-no on-kami-wa   ware soga-mu
you-GEN Hon-hair-TOP I-NOM cut-will
'I will give you a haircut'(Genji Monogatari (027-15(2)))

Note that the nominative case marker for nominals was also -∅ (zero), as shown below.

(36) ...Taketori-no-okina to   iu   mono-∅   ari-keri.
Taketori-no-okina that say man-NOM be-Past
'There was a man called Taketori-no-okina...'
(Taketori Monogatari (017-04))

Therefore, in Old Japanese, subjects were not morphologically marked in root structures, but they were marked with the genitive case marker *ga* or *no* in prenominal sentential modifiers, depending on the person feature of the subject.

Let us now consider what happened in the history of the Japanese language. In Old Japanese, predicates that are not in prenominal sentential modifiers take a conclusive form, and predicates in prenominal sentential modifiers take an attributive form. This is shown by the contrast between the predicate form in (36) and that in (37).

(37) ari-keru mewarawa-namu, kono uta-o   yomeru.
be-Past girl-FOCUS   this poem-ACC read
'the girl who was there read this poem'(Tosa Nikki (028-01/02))

(36) contains *ari-keri* 'be-Past' in the root clause, which is of the conclusive form, while (37) contains *ari-keru* 'be-Past' in the prenominal sentential modifier, which is of the attributive form.

According to Ikawa (1998), among others, around the 16th century, there was an influential language change in Japanese, where the distinction between the two predicate forms gradually became lost. Ikawa (1998) proposes that in Old Japanese, subjects in root structures have an abstract nominative Case, which is checked against INFL, as in English. This indicates that there was an agreement relation between the subject and the predicate (or INFL). However, the distinction between the two predicate forms gradually became lost, probably as a consequence of the loss in the agreement relation between the subject and the predicate. Furthermore, the loss in the agreement relation between the subject and the predicate is plausibly linked to the loss in the agreement relation between the person feature and the type of genitive case marker. If this is true, the subject in a prenominal sentential modifier must have become able to be either *ga* or *no*, irrespective of the type of person feature of the subject. This historical change seems to be the origin of the nominative/genitive alternation in post-Old Japanese.

Note further that during this historical language change, the two predicate forms converged to the attributive form, instead of the conclusive form. Therefore, the subject in root clauses could not stay bare, as it became unable to be licensed by INFL, and it came to be licensed by one of the case markers, that is, *ga*. It is still unclear why *ga* was chosen over *no* for the subject in root clauses, but our speculation is as follows.

Both *ga* and *no* became able to freely appear in prenominal sentential modifiers. Therefore, there seemed to be a close relation between *ga* and *no* on the one hand, and the outer noun to which the sentential modifier is attached. However, while *no* can freely appear in the possessor position of an NP/DP, as in (38), the appearance of *ga* in such a context is strictly restricted, as shown in (39).

(38) a.   neko-no shippo
        cat-GEN tail   'cat's tail'

     b.   te-no   nagasa
        arm-GEN length   'the length of the arm'

(39)a.   wa-ga ya
        I-NOM home   'my home'

     b.   wa-ga ko
        I-NOM child   'my child'

In (38), the possessor position can host virtually any type of NP/DP. However, in (39), what can be in the possessor position can be the first person pronominal element, and the phrases in (39) sound like idiomatic expressions, a sort of residue from Old Japanese. Thus, the number of phrases such as (39a, b) is extremely limited, so that the relation between *no* rather than *ga* and a nominal element had been established. Consequently, in root structures, which are not projections of nominals, *ga* was chosen over *no* for subjects, out of the two possible options.

Let us now turn to Korean with the above mentioned claims. In the history of Korean, there were not two genitive subjects that correspond to *ga* and *no* in Old Japanese, and there was no strong piece of evidence that suggests a comparable historical language change, such as the one that took place in the history of Japanese. If this is correct, and if it is this kind of language change that constitutes the origin of the nominative/genitive alternation, it suggests that no genitive subject has been ever possible in the history of Korean. Therefore, I conclude that genitive subject is impossible in Korean, and it was impossible in Middle Korean as well. This is the origin of the visible difference between Korean and Japanese in terms of the case marker alternation.

6. Conclusion

In this paper, I argued that there has been no genuine genitive subject in the history of Korean. On the other hand, Japanese had two types of genitive subject markers, *ga* and *no*, which appeared depending on the person feature of the subject, and around the 16th century, there was an influential language change in Japanese, which caused the situation where *ga* and *no* could freely alternate within prenominal sentential modifiers, no matter what person feature the subject had. I claimed, following Maki, Uchibori, and Jin (in progress), that this historical change, which took place in Japanese, but not in Korean, is the origin of the visible difference between Korean and Japanese in terms of the case marker alternation.

References

Harada, S.-I. 1971. Ga-No Conversion and Ideolectal Variations in Japanese. *Gengo Kenkyu* 60: 25–38.

Huang, C.-H., Lee, K.-S., Chang, S.-J., and Lee, G.-R. 1988. *Han Iro Dejo Bunsuk (Contrastive Analysis of Korean and Japanese)*, Eohak-Yeonguso (Language Research Office), Seoul National University.

Ikawa, H. 1998. On Kakarimusubi in Old Japanese: A Possibility under a Perspective of Generative Grammar. *Journal of Japanese Linguistics* 16: 1–38.

Jang, Y.-J. 1995. Genitive Subjects in Middle Korean. *Harvard Studies in Korean Linguistics* VI: 223–234.

Kim, S.-G. 2006. *Gwan-hyung-gyeok-josa 'Ui'-ui Tong-o-jeok Umi Bunsuk (A Syntactic Analysis of the Meaning of the Genitive Case 'Uy')*. Kyungjin Munhwa.

Koten Soogoo Kenkyuujo. 2009. http://genji.co.jp/

Maki, H., Jin, Y.-J., Yokoyama, S., Hamasaki, M., and Ueda, Y. 2009. The Nominative/Genitive Alternation in Modern Japanese: A Visual Analogue Scale (VAS) Evaluation Method-Based Analysis. Paper read at *the 19th Japanese/Korean Linguistics*. University of Hawai'i at Mānoa.

Maki, H., Shin, K.-S., and Tsubouchi, K. 2006. A Statistical Analysis of the Nominative/Genitive Alternation in Modern Korean: A Preliminary Study. *Proceedings of the 133rd Meeting of the Linguistic Society of Japan*, 71–76.

Maki, H. and Uchibori, A. 2008. *Ga/No* Conversion. *Handbook of Japanese Linguistics*, ed. S. Miyagawa and M. Saito, 192–216, Oxford: Oxford University Press.

Maki, H., Uchibori, A., and Jin, Y.-J. To appear. The Origin of the *Ga/No* Conversion in the History of the Japanese Language. Ms., Gifu University and Nihon University.

Miyagawa, S. 1993. Case-Checking and Minimal Link Condition. *MIT Working Paper in Linguistics 19: Papers on Case and Agreement II*, ed. C. Phillips, 213–254, Cambridge, MA.: MIT Working Papers in Linguistics.

Sohn, K.-W. 1997. Some Notes on the So Called Nominative-Genitive Conversion. *Proceedings of the Fourth Seoul International Conference on Linguistics*, 533–541, Seoul: The Linguistic Society of Korea.

Suh, J.-M. 1977. Sibosegi guk-o Sok-gyeok Yeongu (A Study of Genitive Case in the 15th Century Korean). *Guk-ea Yeongu (The Korean Language Research)* 36: 65–81.

Suh, J.- M. 1981. 15 Seyki Kwuke Tongmyngsa Nayphomwunuy Cwueuy Kyekey Tayhaye (On the Case of the Embedded Clause in the 15th Century Korean). *Cintanhakpo* 53.54: 171–192.

Watanabe, A. 1996. Nominative-Genitive Conversion and Agreement in Japanese: A Cross-Linguistic Perspective. *Journal of East Asian Linguistics* 5: 373–410.

Texts

Genji Monogatari: written by Murasaki Shikibu around the early 11th century. A. Abe, K. Akiyama, G. Imai, and H. Suzuki. 1994. *Shinpen Nihon Koten Bungaku Zenshuu (21) Genji Monogatari (2)*, Tokyo: Shogakukan.

Genji Monogatari: written by Murasaki Shikibu around the early 11th century. A. Abe, K. Akiyama, G. Imai, and H. Suzuki. 1996. *Shinpen Nihon Koten Bungaku Zenshuu (23) Genji Monogatari (4)*, Tokyo: Shogakukan.

Makura no Sooshi: written by Seisho Nagon during the late 10th to the early 11th century. B. Hagitani. 1977a. *Makura no Sooshi Joo: Shinchoo Nihon Koten Shuusee*, Tokyo: Shinshosha.

Makura no Sooshi: written by Seisho Nagon during the late 10th to the early 11th century. B. Hagitani. 1977b. *Makura no Sooshi Ge: Shinchoo Nihon Koten Shuusee*, Tokyo: Shinchosha.

Taketori Monogatari: written during the late 9th to the early 10th century. Y. Katagiri, S. Takahashi, S. Fukui, and Y. Shimizu. 1994. *Shinpen Nihon Koten Bungaku Zenshuu (12) Taketori Monogatari, Ise Monogatari, Yamato Monogatari, Heichuu Monogatari*, Tokyo: Shogakukan.

Tosa Nikki: written by Kino Tsurayuki around the middle 10th century. Y. Kikuchi, T. Imuta, and M. Kimura. 1995. *Shinpen Nihon Koten Bungaku Zenshuu (13) Tosa Nikki, Kageroo Nikki*, Tokyo: Shogakukan.

Selective Reproduction in NP-Ellipsis*

OCK-HWAN KIM
Indiana University

YOSHIHISA KITAGAWA
Indiana University

1. Introduction

In this paper, we are concerned with the interpretation of NP-Ellipsis (henceforth **NPE**) in Korean (and Japanese). Taking various observations made by S. Kim (1999) as our starting point, we first examine some unexpected interpretive and grammatical properties that NPE exhibits when it replaces the reflexive pro-form *caki* 'self' or a name. We then briefly review some of the major approaches to NPE proposed in the literature and point out their problems. As an alternative approach, we propose and argue for a novel analysis. We argue in particular that NPE involves reproduction at LF in which referential features of an antecedent nominal expression are 'selectively copied' onto the ellipsis site.

---

* An earlier version of this paper was presented at the 19th Japanese/Korean Linguistics Conference held at the University of Hawai'i at Mānoa on November 12, 2009. I would like to thank the audience at the conference, Jessica Dunton, Heejeong Ko, and Hideki Maki for their valuable comments. All errors are my own.

Japanese/Korean Linguistics 19.
Edited by Ho-min Sohn, Haruko Cook, William O'Grady, Leon A. Serafim, & Sang Yee Cheon.

2. Puzzles: Interpretive and Grammatical Contrasts

When the first utterance in a discourse involves *caki* 'self' in its object position as in (1A) below, a puzzling interpretive contrast arises between the two alternative second utterances, (1B) and (1B').

(1) A: John-un   caki-lul   chaykmanghaysse
      John-TOP self-ACC   blamed
      'John blamed himself.'

   B: Bill-to   **caki**-lul   chaykmanghaysse
     Bill-also self-ACC   blamed
     = Bill blamed **Bill**, too
     ≠ Bill blamed **John**, too   (Strict identity **unavailable**)

   B': Bill-to   **[E]**   chaykmanghaysse
     Bill-also   blamed
     = Bill blamed **Bill**, too
     = Bill blamed **John**, too   (Strict identity **available**)

Before addressing the contrast here, let us reconfirm three well-known properties of *caki*, which we will pay close attention to throughout this work. First, as a 'dependent' reflexive pro-form, *caki* must be syntactically bound within an utterance (the 'obligatory binding condition'). Second, unlike reflexive anaphors like *himself/herself* in English, *caki* need not observe Binding Condition A insofar as it is bound (even by a non-local antecedent). Third, unlike *zibun* 'self' in Japanese, *caki* has an antecedent restriction which requires its antecedent to be a third-person nominal expression. That is, *caki* cannot take as its antecedent a first- or second-person nominal expression ('the antecedent condition'). With these properties of *caki* clarified, we now are ready to return to the paradigm in (1) above. When the overt *caki* is repeated as in (1B), it cannot be interpreted with strict identity (i.e. referring to *John*). When *caki* in the object position is elided as in (1B'), on the other hand, this ellipsis site (indicated by [E]) can be interpreted with strict identity. The 'obligatory binding condition' imposed on *caki*, in other words, apparently need not be satisfied in this NPE construction. If we simply take [E] in (1B') to be interpreted on a par with its antecedent *caki*, we would be misled to the incorrect prediction that [E] would permit only a sloppy identity interpretation (i.e. as *Bill*). Let us call this mysterious interpretive contrast between *caki* and its elided counterpart the 'strict *caki* puzzle'.

Another interpretive puzzle, which was first pointed out by S. Kim (1999: 272), concerns the interpretive restrictions imposed on *caki* in the second utterance of a discourse as in (2).

(2) A: John-un   caki-lul   chaykmanghaysse
      John-TOP   self-ACC   blamed
      'John blamed himself.'

    B: *Na-to   **caki**-lul   chaykmanghaysse
      I-also   self-ACC   blamed
      ≠ I blamed **myself**, too   (Sloppy identity **unavailable**)
      ≠ I blamed **John**, too   (Strict identity **unavailable**)

    B': Na-to   **[E]**   chaykmanghaysse
      I-also   blamed
      = I blamed **myself**, too   (Sloppy identity **available**)
      = I blamed **John**, too   (Strict identity **available**)

When *caki* is overt in the second utterance as in (2B), the sentence is not even grammatical. The subject *Na* 'I' in (2B) is not third-person, and hence cannot serve as the binder of *caki* due to its 'antecedent condition'. The subject *John* in (2A) cannot serve as the binder of *caki* in (2B) either because of the 'obligatory binding condition' on *caki*. *Caki* in (2B) therefore remains to be unbound and hence is not interpretable. Quite surprisingly, however, in the NPE construction in (2B'), the 'elided' counterpart of *caki* ([E]) can be bound by the first person *Na* and yield a sloppy identity interpretation in addition to a strict identity interpretation. We refer to this interpretive contrast as the 'sloppy *caki* puzzle'.

Still another puzzle involving NPE was observed in a discourse as in (3) below, again by S. Kim (1999: 268).

(3) A: Na-nun   [John$_J$-uy   imo]-lul   cohaha-nuntey,
      I-TOP   John-GEN   aunt-ACC   like-but

    B: **ku**$_{*J}$-nun [**John**$_J$-uy   imo]-lul   cham   silhehanta
      he-TOP   John-GEN   aunt-ACC   much   hates
      ≠ 'I like John's aunt, but he (= John) hates John's aunt very much.'

    B': **ku**$_J$-nun   **[E]**   cham   silhehanta
      he-TOP   much   hates
      = 'I like John's aunt, but he (= John) hates John's aunt very much.'

When the name *John* is bound by a pro-form *ku* as in the second conjunct (3B), the sentence is ruled out by the Binding Condition C (Condition D, to be precise). Interestingly, however, in a similar sentence but with its object noun phrase elided as in (3B'), such binding seems to be permitted and the sentence becomes grammatical. Let us call this grammatical contrast the 'Condition C puzzle.'

The interpretive/grammatical contrasts between NPE and their overt counterparts observed so far lead us to offer some novel generalization on NPE: (i) Elided nominals are often not subject to some conditions imposed on their overt counterparts — e.g. the 'obligatory binding condition' or the 'antecedent condition' on *caki* and the Binding Condition C on names. (ii) As a result, NPE tends to exhibit more freedom in its interpretations. This generalization suggests that the ellipsis site in NPE ([E]) need not necessarily be interpreted 'entirely on a par' with its antecedent while the way its lexical contents are retrieved suggests that it must still be interpreted 'more or less on a par' with its antecedent. In what follows, we first point out that none of the approaches previously offered in the literature seem to be capable of capturing this generalization. We then attempt to demonstrate that the interpretive flexibility observed on NPE can be attributed to the interactions between the feature system of nominal expressions and the syntactic processes involved in the proper derivation of the LF for NPE.

3. Previous Analyses of NPE and Their Problems

3.1 A PF Deletion Approach

Perhaps the most popular approach to the ellipsis constructions in general is a PF-deletion approach, in which the ellipsis site is argued to be base-generated with a full-fledged internal structure and lexical contents that are identical to those of its antecedent. The surface effect is then achieved by the full deletion (or non-pronunciation) of these materials at PF. The PF-deletion analysis can handle properly the VP-ellipsis construction (henceforth, VPE) in English that involves a pronoun as in (4).

(4) John will [$_{VP}$ wash his car], and Bill will [$_{VP}$ e], too

The elided VP in (4) is argued to have an identical representation as its antecedent VP in every stage of derivation in narrow syntax and then ends up being deleted at PF as in (5).

(5) a. **LF**: John$_J$ will [$_{VP}$ wash his$_J$ car] & Bill$_B$ will [$_{VP}$ wash his$_{J/B}$ car], too

    b. **PF**: John$_J$ will [$_{VP}$ wash his car] & Bill$_B$ will [$_{VP}$ ~~wash his car~~], too

When *his* in the first conjunct refers to *John*, *his* in the second conjunct can be interpreted with either sloppy identity (i.e. *Bill*) or strict identity (i.e. *John*). The pronoun *his* in the second conjunct, in other words, is interpreted in the same way whether it is pronounced or not pronounced, sharing the same LF representation as in (5a). When the elided pro-form and its overt counterpart give rise to an identical range of interpretations as in this case, the PF-deletion approach does not encounter any problem.

Crucially, however, the PF-deletion approach cannot be directly extended to the analysis of the NPE in Korean (and Japanese), as has already been pointed out by S. Kim (1999: 273). A problem arises when the overt and elided pro-forms are not interpreted in an identical way, for instance, as in the case of the 'strict *caki* puzzle' discussed in (1) above. In the PF-deletion approach, the ellipsis site at LF has the full-fledged contents and internal structure identical to those of its antecedent NP, while this NP is deleted at PF under some type of identity condition. The LF and PF representations of (1B') then would look like (6a) and (6b), respectively.

(6) a. **LF**: Bill-to [$_{NP}$ **caki**-lul] chaykmanghaysse   ⇒   **Interpreted**
   b. PF: Bill-to [$_{NP}$ ~~caki-lul~~] chaykmanghaysse   ⇒   Pronounced

The prediction under this approach thus is that the overt *caki* and its elided counterpart ([E]) in (1) would yield the same range of interpretations based upon the identical LF representation (6a). As observed earlier, however, the overt *caki* in (1B) prohibits a strict identity reading while NPE in (1B') permits it. This contrast suggests that the LF representation of the NPE should not be identical to that of the overt *caki* contrary to what is expected in the PF-deletion analysis. The same problem is encountered when we apply the PF-deletion analysis to the paradigms that induced the 'sloppy *caki* puzzle' as in (2) and the 'Condition C puzzle' as in (3) above. We are, therefore, led to the conclusion that [E] in NPE is not a mere gap created at PF by a phonetic deletion operation.

3.2 An Empty Pronominal Approach

One may try to solve the 'strict *caki* puzzle' hypothesizing that NPE involves a base-generated null pronominal argument which simply corefers with the antecedent in the previous utterance, as in (7B).

(7) A: **John$_J$**-un   caki-lul   chaykmanghaysse
     John-TOP   self-ACC   blamed
     'John blamed himself.'
  B: Bill-to   **pro$_J$**   chaykmanghaysse
     Bill-also   blamed

This approach, however, would fail to account for the strict identity interpretation available in (8B).

(8) A: [John-kwa Bill]$_X$-un   [*caki*$_X$-uy komwun]$_Y$-ul conkyenghay
     John-and Bill-TOP   self-GEN advisor-ACC   respect
     'John respects **John's** advisor and **Bill** respects **Bill's** advisor.'

  B: [talun   haksayng-tul]-to   **[E]$_Y$**   conkyenghay
     other   student-PL-also   respect

   =   Each of other students also respects **his or her own advisor**
   = Other students also respect **them** (= **John's advisor & Bill's advisor**)

Here, $[E]_Y$ can be interpreted as collectively referring to a plural entity 'John's advisor and Bill's advisor' (with strict identity). This interpretation, however, would have to be established by associating $[E]_Y$ with the NP_Y *caki-uy komwun* 'self's advisor', which is singular because *caki* interpreted as a variable bound by a plural antecedent as in (8A) is singular-denoting. $[E]_Y$ analyzed as *pro*, in other words, would have to denote a plural entity by coreferring with a singular entity NP_Y.[1] This clearly is an impossible task to be fulfilled, and the strict identity reading in (8B) would be incorrectly prohibited.[2]

3.3 A Dependency Theory Approach

Fiengo and May (1994) propose a Dependency Theory approach to handle mostly the interpretation of VPE in English. In their approach, an index of a nominal expression is a complex object consisting of an indexical 'type' as well as an indexical 'value'. An index may also have multiple 'occurrences' in a syntactic structure, and each such occurrence may be either dependent on another occurrence or independent of other occurrences. The occurrence bearing a **dependent** indexical type is called a **β-occurrence**, and that bearing an **independent** one an **α-occurrence** (indicated by a superscripted α or β as in (9A) below). The indexical 'value' of a β-occurrence is determined based upon the indexical value of its antecedent (e.g. his^{β}_1 in (9A-i)); and that of an α-occurrence is determined inherently and independently of other occurrences (e.g. his^{α}_1 in (9A-ii)).

(9) A: (i) $Mike^{\alpha}_1$ $[_{VP}$ loves his^{β}_1 $wife^{\alpha}_2$].
        (ii) $Mike^{\alpha}_1$ $[_{VP}$ loves his^{α}_1 $wife^{\alpha}_2$].

   B: $John_2$ does $[_{VP}$ **e**], too.

      (i) $John_2$ does $[_{VP}$ love his^{β}_2 $wife^{\alpha}_2$] $\Rightarrow$ Sloppy identity
      (ii) $John_2$ does $[_{VP}$ love his^{α}_1 $wife^{\alpha}_2$] $\Rightarrow$ Strict identity

---

[1] A coreferential construal of *caki* with a plural (referential) subject can only be made possible by attaching the plural marker *–tul* '-PL' to the end of *caki* (i.e. *caki-tul* 'self-PL').

[2] It is not the case, however, that we deny the existence of a phonetically empty pronominal category. In fact, we postulate it at least in a sentence like (i) (and its equivalent in Korean).

(i)   sonna tokoro-de **pro** nani-o   sagasiteru-no?
       such place-at   what-ACC searching-Q
       'What are **you** looking for in a place like that?'

With these assumptions, it is claimed that, if the reconstructed contents of the elided VP involve a nominal that bears a β-occurrence, sloppy identity arises (e.g. (9B-i) while a nominal that bears an α-occurrence is involved, strict identity arises (e.g. (9B-ii).

This approach was directly extended to the interpretation of NPE in Korean by S. Kim (1999). He argues that NPE involves a genuine empty phrase-marker which is base-generated without any internal contents and, hence, must undergo reconstruction of the indexical structure of the antecedent nominal expression. In particular, it is claimed: (i) that *caki* can bear either a β-occurrence or an α-occurrence, and (ii) that the sloppy-strict ambiguity of *caki* in (10) is ascribed to the possibility that the indexical structure of *caki* in the antecedent clause (10a) can have either of the two distinct LF representations as in (11) below.

(10) a. Mike-ka　[**caki**-uy　ai]-lul　　　ttayly-ca
　　　　 Mike-NOM　self-GEN　child-ACC　　hit-when
　　　　 'When Mike hit his own child,'

　　 b. Jeanne-to　　　[$_{NP}$ **E**]　　　　ttaylyessta
　　　　 Jeanne-also　　　　　　　　　 hit
　　　　 = Jeanne hit **Jeanne's** child, too　(Sloppy identity)
　　　　 = Jeanne hit **Mike's** child, too　　(Strict identity)

(11) a. Mike$^{\alpha}_{1}$-ka [$_{NP}$ **caki**$^{\beta}_{1}$-uy　ai]-lul　ttayly-ca　$\Rightarrow$　Sloppy identity
　　 b. Mike$^{\alpha}_{1}$-ka [$_{NP}$ **caki**$^{\alpha}_{1}$-uy　ai]-lul　ttayly-ca　$\Rightarrow$　Strict identity

The object NP in LF representation (11a) involves *caki* with a β-occurrence. When this NP is reproduced into [E] (with a new indexical value '2' established in the course of reconstruction) in (10b), a sloppy interpretation arises. When the object NP in (11b) is reproduced into (10b), on the other hand, a strict identity interpretation arises because this NP involves *caki* with an α-occurrence with the indexical value '1'.

We would like to point out, however, that this approach encounters a system-internal problem when it is confronted with a discourse like (12).

(12) A: [John-kwa Bill]-un　　[**caki**-uy ai]-lul　　chingchanhaysse
　　　　 John-and Bill-TOP　　　self-GEN child-ACC　praised
　　　　 'John praised John's child, and Bill praised Bill's child.'

　　 B: Harry-to　　　　　　　　　[E]　　　chingchanhaysse
　　　　 Harry-also　　　　　　　　　　　　 praised
　　　　 = Harry praised **Harry's** child, too
　　　　 = Harry praised **those** children (= John's child and Bill's child), too

In (12B), a strict identity reading of the reconstructed *caki* ('Harry praised **John's** child and **Bill's** child.') is clearly available. In the antecedent clause (12A), however, the singular-denoting *caki* is interpreted as a variable bound by a plural antecedent (just as in (8) above). It follows then that *caki* in (12A) cannot bear an α-occurrence, and the only indexical type available to *caki* is a β-occurrence. The legitimate LF representation of (12A) therefore must be (13A) below, and the LF representation for the strict identity in (12B) would have to be (13B), in which the reproduced interpretive contents of [E] involve *caki*$^{\beta}_1$.

(13) A: [John-kwa Bill]$_1$-un [**caki**$^{\beta}_1$-uy ai]-lul   chingchanhaysse
                         self-GEN   child-ACC

     B: Harry$_2$-to   [**caki**$^{\beta}_1$-uy   ai-lul]   chingchanhaysse

In (13B), *caki* bears a β-occurrence and hence must be dependent on the subject *Harry$_2$-to* 'Harry also' within its sentence. The indexical value '1', which it must inherit from (13A) for strict identity, however, inevitably causes a conflict with the indexical value '2' on its antecedent. This approach therefore makes an incorrect prediction that the strict identity reading is not possible, contrary to the fact observed in (12) above.[3]

     S. Kim (1999: 274) attempts to justify the postulation of an α-occurrence of *caki* by presenting a proverb-like sentence in (14).

(14) **caki**-ka   caki-uy   il-ul   an   tolpo-myen,
      self-NOM   self-GEN   work-ACC   not   take.care.of-if

      nwu-ka   tolpokeyss-nunka
      who-NOM   take.care.of-Q
      'If one does not take care of one's own business, who would?'

Directing his attention to the *caki* in boldface in (14), he argues that this *caki* can stand alone without any antecedent that binds it and hence must be analyzed as an α-occurrence. What is regarded as an 'unbound' *caki* as in (14), however, is quite limited in use. As S. Kim himself is aware, it must be interpreted as arbitrary or generic people. The bold face *caki* in (14), for instance, can be quite naturally paraphrased as *salam-tul* 'person-PL'. If this seemingly unbound *caki* must always be associated with such particular

---

[3] Fiengo and May (1994: 167-9) do assume that strict identity can be derived when a β-occurrence is reconstructed without its indexical value altered from the antecedent clause. This option, however, is claimed to be available only when the antecedent clause and the ellipsis clause happen to share an identical antecedent of the reproduced β-occurrence as well as a parallel syntactic structure. In the case of (13B), for example, its subject would have to be 'John and Bill' rather than 'Harry' for strict identity to arise with a β-occurrence.

interpretations, it clearly deviates from the general use of *caki* and is hardly analyzable as a reflexive anaphoric item. Such arbitrary/generic interpretations never seem to be required for the $caki^\alpha$ that is postulated to capture the strict identity of [E] in (10b)/(12B), either.

Instead of postulating $caki^\alpha$, whose property is quite elusive, we would rather appeal to what seems to be a more viable alternative analysis as in (15) below, in which a more familiar entity **PRO$_{arb}$** is postulated.

(15) **PRO$_{arb}$**   [**caki**-ka   caki-uy il-ul an tolpo-myen], ...
    |___Bind___|
   'Speaking of people, if each of them does not take care of his or her own business, ...'

Alternatively, we could also adopt the analysis in (16), in which a generic operator (**OP$_{gen}$**) is postulated.

(16) **OP$_{gen}$**   [**caki**-ka   caki-uy il-ul an tolpo-myen], ... [4]
    |___Bind___|
   'Generally, if one does not take care of one's own business, ...'

In either of these analyses, *caki* is bound by the item to which we can comfortably ascribe the arbitrary/generic readings *caki* comes to acquire. We thus conclude that the validity of the α-occurrence of *caki* is highly questionable. To sum up, the Dependency Theory approach encounters a problem when it attempts to capture strict identity interpretations in the NPE in Korean (and Japanese), whether it postulates $caki^\beta$ or $caki^\alpha$.

4. Proposals

We have seen so far the inadequacy and/or the insufficiency of the three popular analyses of NPE proposed in the literature. In this section, we propose and argue for an alternative analysis resorting to what we call 'selective feature copy' at LF. To be more specific, we argue that covert computation for NPE involves the reproduction of **minimally** necessary features rather than **total** lexical contents of the antecedent NP. We first propose to postulate a new feature system for nominal expressions and then describe the way selective feature copy applies.

4.1 A Referential Feature [REF]

In order to be semantically interpreted, NPs generally must either 'refer' by itself or be 'dependent' on some other NP. We propose to capture this

---

[4] See Han (2009: See this volume) and Han and Storoshenko (2009) for a bound variable analysis of *caki* by the generic operator.

property of NPs by postulating two subtypes of a semantic feature [REF]. In particular, we hypothesize that a name always bears [REF] with its 'referential value' inherently specified (indicated as, e.g. [REF$_J$] for *John*) while an anaphoric item like *caki* is introduced into syntax with [REF] with its referential value unspecified (indicated as [REF$_{< >}$]). [5] The referential value of [REF$_{< >}$] on anaphoric items comes to be specified when it is syntactically dependent on its antecedent, with the application of a computational process that we call '(Referential) Valuation', as illustrated in (17 i-ii). [6]

(17) (i) John ... caki ...   (ii) John ... caki ...

     REF$_J$ **REF$_{< >}$** == Valuation $\Rightarrow$ REF$_J$ **REF$_{<J>}$**

     |............|

After Valuation takes place, a referentially 'valued' [REF] (indicated as [REF$_{<J>}$]) comes to be derived, as shown in (17ii). We may consider that the referentially underspecified nature of [REF$_{< >}$] is the source of the referential dependency of anaphors, and that its valuation is mandatory to satisfy the Principle of Full Interpretation at the LF-interface. We may consider, in other words, that [REF$_{< >}$] in *caki* enacts its 'obligatory binding condition'.

In addition to this [REF] feature, we also postulate the feature [PR], whose presence distinguishes 'pro-form' NPs from lexical NPs. We can now characterize various types of NPs with these features as in (18), where only those features relevant to our analyses are indicated.

(18) a. *John*:   [REF$_J$, ...]
     b. *caki* 'self':   [PR, REF$_{< >}$, +3P, ...]
     c. *ku* '3.S.M':   [PR, REF$_V$, ...]   (V = referential value)
     d. [E]:   [PR]

Note in particular the following. First the 'antecedent condition' on *caki* discussed in Section 2 is represented as its inherent feature [+3P] in (18b). Second, *ku*, which is often translated into *he* in English, is specified with the inherently valuated [REF$_V$] in (18c). While we cannot provide the full justification for this analysis in this work, the contrast between *caki* and *ku*

---

[5] We are leaving 'operator' NPs out of consideration here.

[6] This referential valuation should be distinguished from the "valuation" of uninterpretable formal features in Chomsky (2001).

in (19) below provides the initial motivation — *ku*, unlike *caki*, here cannot be interpreted as a variable bound by a quantified antecedent. [7]

(19) taypwupwun-uy salam-tul-i { **caki-/ku-**}uyhim-ul   kwasinhanta
     most-GEN   people-NOM self-/3.S.M-GEN ability-ACC overrate

> With *caki*:   Each of most people overrates his own ability.
> With *ku*:   Most people₁ overrate his₂ ability.

With *ku*:   Most people$_1$ overrate his$_2$ ability.

Finally, the elided object ([E]) in NPE is specified as [PR], i.e. a pro-form, with no [REF] feature involved ((18d)). [8] We will argue below that [PR] of [E] plays a key role in permitting one type of interpretive flexibility of NPE ('Condition C Puzzle').

4.2 Selective Feature Copy at LF

Our approach to NPE incorporates this feature system into what we call the 'selective feature copy' analysis, in which the interpretive contents of a base-generated [E] are covertly copied from its antecedent NP in the form of a feature bundle. [9] We crucially assume that (i) covert copy for NPE does not necessarily have to reproduce the entire contents of the antecedent NP at the ellipsis site [E], (ii) the [REF] feature can be copied separately from other features of an NP, (iii) such selective feature copy does not take place arbitrarily but is regulated by a type of economy constraint, and (iv) the covert feature copy may freely mingle with other computational processes, in particular with Valuation of [REF] (see Kitagawa (1991) for VPE and Kitagawa (1999a) for NPE). The economy constraint mentioned in (iii) can be stated as in (20) below, which probably is a corollary of a more fundamental economy constraint imposed on lexical information in general (Kitagawa (1999b)).

(20) Economy on feature reproduction:
     Reproduction of features is **minimized** (up to full interpretation).

In the remainder of this paper, we will attempt to demonstrate that this 'selective feature copy' approach correctly solves the three puzzles on NPE introduced in Section 2.

---

[7] *Ku* in Korean seems to be closer to the demonstrative *that* rather than to the pronoun *he* in English, just as *kare* in Japanese is (Hoji 1991).

[8] The assumption that [E] is specified with the PR feature distinguishes our approach from S. Kim's (1999), in which [E] is analyzed as a genuine empty phrase-marker base-generated without any internal contents (see subsection 3.3 above).

[9] See Kitagawa (1991) and Oku (1998) for an approach incorporating the partial/selective copy of formal features such as Φ-features in dealing with the VPE in English.

First, the strict identity interpretation in (1) (repeated below as (21)) is made possible when Copy applies **after** Valuation applies. That is, it arises when the [REF$_{<J>}$] of *caki* as in (17 ii) is selectively copied onto [E]. This derivation is illustrated by the 'oval and arrow' on the right end in (21).

(21) A: John-un**caki**-lul   chaykmanghaysse *John ... caki*

      John-TOP self-ACC blamed

      'John blamed himself.'

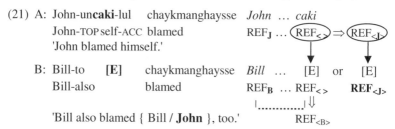

  B: Bill-to   **[E]**   chaykmanghaysse *Bill ...*   [E]   or   [E]

      Bill-also   blamed

      'Bill also blamed { Bill / **John** }, too.'

A sloppy identity interpretation ([E] = REF$_{<B>}$), on the other hand, arises when Copy applies **before** Valuation does — that is, when [REF$_{<>}$] in (17 i) is copied onto [E] and then undergoes Valuation. This derivation is illustrated by the other 'oval and arrow' in (21). On the contrary, when the **overt** *caki* appears instead of [E] in the second utterance (21B), it must be bound by *Bill* due to the 'obligatory binding condition', and there is no room for strict identity to arise. This is how we can solve the 'strict *caki* puzzle'.

The surprising sloppy identity observed in (2) (repeated below as (22)) also follows from the 'selective feature copy'.

(22) A: John-un   **caki**-lul chaykmanghaysse *John ... caki*

      John-TOP self-ACC blamed

      'John blamed himself.'

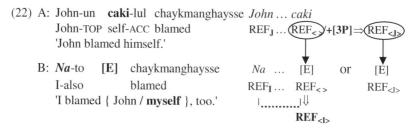

  B: *Na*-to   **[E]**   chaykmanghaysse   *Na ...*   [E]   or   [E]

      I-also   blamed

      'I blamed { John / **myself** }, too.'

Again, sloppy identity becomes possible when Copy applies **before** Valuation does. Crucially, [REF$_{<>}$] on the antecedent *caki* in (22A) can be selectively copied onto [E], leaving behind the [+3P] feature. The referential value of the copied [REF$_{<>}$] thus can be provided by the first-person subject *Na* in (22B) without disturbing the 'third-person antecedent condition'. This derivation is illustrated by the left-hand side 'oval and arrow' in (22). On the contrary, when the **overt** *caki* appears in place of [E] in the second utterance (22B), the lexical requirement [+3P] imposed on *caki* would prohibit its [REF$_{<>}$] from undergoing Valuation with the first-person antecedent *Na*. This is how we can solve the 'sloppy *caki* puzzle'.

Finally, the unexpected amelioration of the Condition C violation in (3) (repeated below as (23)) also follows from the covert feature copy incorporating the proposed referential feature specification of NPs.

(23) Na-nun [**John**$_J$-uy imo]-lul cohaha-nuntey,   ... [***John's aunt***]
    I-TOP   John-GEN aunt-ACC like-but   (REF$_J$)

    ku$_J$-nun   **[E]**   cham silhehanta   *ku* ...   [E]
    3.S.M-TOP   much hates   PR   **PR**
                                                 REF$_J$ **REF$_J$**
    'I like John's aunt, but he (= John) hates his own aunt very much.'

We argued briefly in Section 4.1 that *ku* in Korean, unlike *he* in English, has its referential feature inherently valued just as names do. *Ku* referring to *John*, for instance, is inherently specified with [REF$_J$]. The name *John* and *ku* are crucially distinct, however, in that only *ku* (but not *John*) has the [PR] feature, being a pro-form (see (18a/c)). Exploiting the similarity as well as the asymmetry between these two items, we argue that when the 'pro-form' feature [PR] is added to [REF$_J$] of *John*, this name comes to function on a par with *ku* specified with [REF$_J$]. Recall also that we have characterized the null object [E] as a 'skeletal pro-form', which is specified only with [PR] (see (18d)). When [REF$_J$] of *John* as the antecedent is copied onto [E] in (23), therefore, it comes to be combined with the inherent [PR] feature of [E], deriving an LF that is 'referentially' equivalent to that containing *ku*$_J$ in the object NP, as in (24). [10]

(24) **ku**$_J$-nun   [**ku**$_J$-uy   imo]-lul   cham silhehanta
    3.S.M-TOP   3.S.M-GEN   aunt-ACC   much hates
    'He$_J$ hates his$_J$ aunt very much.'

In this way, [E] in (23) evades the Condition C violation even if it is interpreted on a par with 'John's aunt'. This is how we solve the 'Condition C puzzle'.

We can provide independent support for the claim that [E] in (23) indeed comes to be interpreted as referentially equivalent to *ku*. Compare (23) with (25).

---

[10] We assume here that [PR] of [E] spreads to both of the possessor NP and the head N.

(25) Na-nun **John$_J$**-ul cohaha-nuntey,   ... *John*
    I-TOP   John-ACC like-but

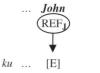

    'I like John, but ...'

    ***ku$_J$**-nun   **[E]**   cham silhehanta   *ku* ...   [E]
    3.S.M-TOP   much hates   PR   **PR**
    'John hates John very much.'   REF$_J$ **REF$_J$** $\Rightarrow$ ***BT(B)**

In (25), [REF$_J$] of the antecedent *John* is copied, and [E] comes to be represented as [PR, REF$_J$]. This derivation gives rise to an LF representation which is 'referentially' equivalent to the LF for (26).

(26) ***ku$_J$**-nun   **ku$_J$**-lul   cham silhehanta   *ku* ...   *ku*
    3.S.M-TOP 3.S.M-ACC much hates   PR   **PR**
    'He$_J$ hates him$_J$ very much.'   REF$_J$ **REF$_J$** $\Rightarrow$ ***BT(B)**

Clearly, (26) induces the violation of Condition B while (24) does not. The contrast between (23) and (25) therefore suggests that the [REF$_J$] copied onto [E] and amalgamated with [PR] indeed becomes referentially equivalent to *ku$_J$*.

    One may consider that the Condition C violation can be avoided in (23) if we postulate a base-generated empty pronominal instead of [E], and let it corefer with its antecedent NP in the previous sentence (i.e. *John's aunt*). This approach, however, is insufficient since the amelioration of the Condition C violation as observed in (23) takes place even in (27).

(27) [John-kwa Bill]$_X$-un [$_{NP}$ *caki$_X$*-ka **Mary$_1$**-eykey sensahan panci]$_Y$-lul
    John-and Bill-TOP   self-NOM Mary-DAT   gave   ring-ACC

    ceykakki usitayess-ciman, **kunye$_1$**-nun **[E]**$_Y$ kkiko siphci anhassta
    each   boasted-but   she-TOP   wear   want   not.DECL

    'Each of John and Bill boasted of the ring **he** gave to Mary as a gift, but she did not want to wear **them** (= the ring John gave and the ring Bill gave).'

Here, [E]$_Y$ can be interpreted as collectively referring to the plural entity 'the ring John gave to Mary and the ring Bill gave to Mary', but this interpretation would have to be established by associating [E]$_Y$ with the singular NP *caki$_X$-ka Mary$_1$-eykey sensahan panci* 'the ring self gave to Mary'. [E]$_Y$ analyzed as *pro* therefore would be required to fulfill the impossible task of denoting a plural entity by coreferring with a singular entity NP$_Y$ (just as in (8) above). We cannot consider, in other words, that [E] in (27) merely corefers with its antecedent. This in turn suggests that the interpretive contents of the antecedent NP must somehow be reconstructed at the ellipsis site in this case as well. The empty pronominal analysis of [E] therefore would send us back to the 'Condition C puzzle'. In our approach, on the other hand, we can capture the Condition C amelioration in (27) in the same way as in (23). [11]

Since we capture the contrast between (23) and (25) by turning, in effect, a name into a pronoun, one may also consider that an appeal to 'vehicle change' is appropriate. Vehicle change was originally devised by Fiengo and May (1994) as a general label of mysteriously permitted cases of PF-deletion under 'loosened identity conditions' in ellipsis constructions. S. Kim (1999: 272) reinterpreted it as an LF operation that allows the syntactic form of the antecedent NP to be altered freely (as long as its indexical type and value are not altered) when its contents are covertly reconstructed onto an ellipsis site. The vehicle change approach, however, proves to be overly permissive. Since there is no reason why it cannot permit a name to be altered into (or identified with) *caki* in the process of the LF reconstruction of [E] (or PF-derivation of [E]), it should be capable of turning the name *John* into *caki* even in the ellipsis site of (25). The Condition B violation therefore should be evaded in (25), which is contrary to the fact. This indicates that an appeal to (whichever version of) vehicle change in this problem is inadequate. Our approach appealing to the [PR] feature of [E], on the contrary, allows us to derive the 'vehicle change **effects'**, and crucially only those effects that are permitted, without actually adopting the 'vehicle change **operation/permission'**, a quite enigmatic and highly powerful device, to say the least.

5. Summary

We have proposed a novel analysis of the NP-Ellipsis in Korean (and Japanese) in which a computational process of feature copy selectively reconstructs some features of the antecedent NP onto a base-generated skeletal pro-form [E]. We have argued: (i) that this analysis can provide natural solutions to various puzzles involving NPE when we let it interact with the 'referential' feature system of NPs we postulated, and (ii) that it overcomes the obstacles some other alternative approaches encounter.

---

[11] The 'covert feature copy' applies in (27) after *caki* undergoes variable binding and the valued

feature [REF$_{<X>}$] is derived. See Kitagawa (2003) for the motivation to copy 'bound and licensed variables' at LF, which are claimed to induce 'strict variables' to be interpreted on a par with demonstratives in various constructions.

References

Chomsky, N. 2001. Derivation by Phase, in Kenstowicz, M. ed., *Ken Hale: A Life in Language*, 1-52. Cambridge, Mass: MIT Press.

Fiengo, R. and May, R. 1994. *Indices and Identity*. Cambridge, Mass: MIT Press.

Han, C.-H. 2009. Semantics of a Korean long-distance anaphor, Paper presented at *The 19th Japanese/Korean Linguistics Conference*. University of Hawaii at Mānoa.

Han, C.-H. and Storoshenko, D. R. 2009. A bound-variable analysis of the Korean anaphor *caki*: evidence from corpus. In *Current Issues in Unity and Diversity of Languages: Collection of the Papers Selected from the 18th International Congress of Linguistics*, The Linguistic Society of Korea, Seoul.

Hoji, H. 1991. *Kare* in Georgopolous, C. and R. Ishihara eds., *Interdisciplinary Approaches to Language: in Honor of Prof. S.-Y. Kuroda*, 287-304. Dordrecht: Reidel.

Kim, S.-W. 1999. Sloppy/strict identity, empty objects, and an ellipsis. *Journal of East Asian Linguistics* 8: 255-284.

Kitagawa, Y. 1991. Copying identity. *Natural Language and Linguistic Theory* 9: 497-536.

Kitagawa, Y. 1999a. VP-ellipsis and NP-ellipsis. In *Linguistics in Search of Human Mind —A Festschrift for Kazuko Inoue*, ed. Muraki, M. and E. Iwamoto, 347-372. Tokyo: Kaitakusha.

Kitagawa, Y. 1999b. Economy of lexical information. Paper presented at *LICSSOL 1—Economy in Language Design, Computation and Use*, The Lyon Institute of Cognitive Science.

Kitagawa, Y. 2003. "Copying Variables," in Li, A. and A. Simpson eds., *Functional Structure(s), Form and Interpretation — Perspectives from East Asian Languages*, 28-64. London: Routledge Curzon.

Oku, S. 1998. *A Theory of Selection and Reconstruction in the Minimalist Perspective*. Doctoral dissertation, University of Connecticut.

NPI and Predicative Remnants in Japanese Sluicing

Hiroko Kimura
Tohoku University

Daiko Takahashi
Tohoku University

The phenomenon called sluicing has received much attention in the field of generative syntax in recent years. We can observe a construction in Japanese that appears to involve what is similar to sluicing (see Inoue 1976 and Takahashi 1994). Though the standard analysis of sluicing assumes that it involves deletion of TP subsequent to *wh*-movement (Ross 1969 and Merchant 2001), it has been controversial how the Japanese counterpart is treated: While Takahashi (1994) proposes to assimilate it to the standard analysis of sluicing, researchers like Kuwabara (1996), Nishiyama, Whitman, and Yi (1996), Saito (2004), and so on argue that it should be analyzed as deriving from the cleft construction (henceforth, the cleft analysis). The purpose of this article is to provide novel data pertaining to Japanese sluicing that are difficult to accommodate under the cleft analysis and to suggest an alternative analysis of the phenomenon in question in terms of nonconstituent deletion (van Craenenbroeck and den Dikken 2006).

Japanese/Korean Linguistics 19.
Edited by Ho-min Sohn, Haruko Cook, William O'Grady, Leon A. Serafim, & Sang Yee Cheon.
Copyright © 2011, CSLI Publications

This article is organized as follows: In Section 1, we will briefly review the cleft analysis of Japanese sluicing in order to set on the stage for the discussion thereafter. In Section 2, we will provide data where negative polarity items (henceforth, NPIs) occur as remnants of Japanese sluicing, pointing out that they cannot be accounted for by the cleft analysis. In Section 3, we will propose an alterative way to handle the phenomenon in question, which crucially assumes nonconstituent deletion, and present an additional supportive argument for our analysis. In Section 4, we will strengthen our hypothesis further by considering data where small clause predicates appear as remnants. In the final section, we will summarize our discussion, concluding the present work.

1. Japanese Sluicing and the Cleft Analysis

Inoue (1976) and Takahashi (1994) observe that a phenomenon similar to sluicing exists in Japanese. They provide cases like the following:

(1)   a.   Ken-ga   dareka-ni   atta   sooda.
          Ken -NOM   someone-DAT   met   I-heard
          'I heard Ken met someone.'
      b.   Boku-wa   [dare-ni   ka]   soozoodekinai.
          I-TOP   who-DAT   Q   imagine.cannot
          'I cannot imagine who.'
      c.   Boku-wa   [Ken -ga   dare-ni   atta   ka]
          I-TOP   Ken -NOM   who-DAT   met   Q
          soozoodekinai.
          imagine.cannot
          'I cannot imagine who Ken met.'

In the context where (1a) precedes (1b), the embedded clause in (1b) is a reduced indirect question, which consists only of the *wh*-phrase and the question marker (henceforth, Q-marker). Though truncated, it has the same interpretation as the full-fledged form in (1c). This superficially resembles what is called sluicing in English, exemplified below:

(2)   a.   John dated someone.
      b.   I cannot imagine who.
      c.   I cannot imagine who John dated.

Anteceded by (2a), (2b) has a reduced indirect question composed just of the *wh*-phrase, which is understood in the same way as the full-fledged form in (2c). Ross (1969) proposes an analysis of sluicing in English, according to which sluiced clauses are derived from their complete forms by deletion of TP. This idea has recently been reinforced by Merchant (2001), and has become the standard analysis.

As for Japanese sluicing, the predominant view at present is that it arises from the cleft construction, which is illustrated below:

(3) a. Ken-ga   Hana-ni   atta.
       Ken-NOM Hana-DAT met   'Ken met Hana.'

    b. [CP Ken-ga   e   atta no]-wa   Hana-ni   da.
          Ken-NOM   met that-TOP Hana-DAT be
       'It was Hana that Ken met.'

    c. [CP Ken-ga   e   atta no]-wa   dare-ni   desu ka?
          Ken-NOM   met that-TOP who-DAT   be   Q
       'Who was it that Ken met?'

The example in (3a) is a normal sentence conforming to the basic word order in Japanese (SOV). Its cleft counterpart is given in (3b), where the object is focused and dislocated from the clause it belongs to. The cleft construction typically consists of a clausal subject headed by the complementizer *no*, followed by the topic marker, a focused element, and the copula, as shown in (3b). The clausal subject serves as the presupposition and contains a gap inside (indicated as *e* above), which is associated with the focus. We note that *wh*-phrases also can appear as foci in cleft sentences, as exemplified in (3c).

Saito (2004) argues that sluiced sentences in Japanese are derived from corresponding cleft constructions (we consider Saito's (2004) analysis as representative of the cleft analysis). This is illustrated in (4), which shows the analysis of (1b):

(4) Boku-wa [CP [CP ~~Ken-ga~~   *e* ~~atta no]~~-ga   dare-ni
    I-TOP   Ken-NOM   met that-NOM who-DAT
    (da) ka] soozoodekinai.
    be   Q   imagine.cannot
    'lit. I cannot imagine *Q* it was who ~~that Ken met~~.'

The embedded clause in (4) is a cleft construction. The presuppositional clausal subject may be elided because Japanese generally allows ellipsis of arguments. Further, the copula may be omitted optionally in embedded contexts, as independently indicated below:

(5) Boku-wa [CP Ken-ga   gakusei (da/dearu) ka] kiita.
    I-TOP   Ken-NOM student be   Q   asked
    'I asked whether Ken was a student.'

These yield the form in (1b).

That cleft structures underlie Japanese sluicing is supported by the fact that the copula can optionally appear in sluiced clauses (Takahashi 1994, Saito 2004). Thus, (1b) has the following alternative form:

(6)   Boku-wa [dare-ni   da/dearu ka] soozoodekinai.
        I-TOP   who-DAT   be   Q   imagine.cannot
        'I cannot imagine who.'

The copula appears between the *wh*-phrase and the Q-marker, and this is exactly what the cleft analysis expects.

2. Negative Polarity Items as Remnants

The cleft analysis should predict that only those expressions that can be foci in cleft constructions should be able to be remnants in Japanese sluicing. In this regard, we consider data involving the NPI *sika* 'anything/anyone but', which is illustrated below (just for convenience, we gloss it as *SIKA*):

(7)   a.   Ken-wa   Hana-ni-sika   awanakatta.
           Ken-TOP   Hana-DAT-SIKA   met.not
           'Ken did not meet anyone but Hana. / Ken met only Hana.'
      b.   *Ken-wa   Hana-ni-sika   atta.
           Ken-TOP   Hana-DAT-SIKA   met
           *' Ken met anyone but Hana.'

Here the NPI is attached to the object. While it is allowed in the negative sentence in (7a), it results in ungrammaticality without negation as in (7b).

Kizu (2005) observes that NPIs generally fail to occur in focus positions in cleft constructions. Thus, the following examples are degraded:

(8)   a.   *[Ken-ga *e* awanakatta no]-wa   Hana-ni-sika   da.
           Ken-NOM   met.not   that-TOP Hana-DAT-SIKA   be
           lit. 'It was anyone but Hana that Ken did not meet.'
      b.   *[Ken-ga *e* awanakatta no]-wa   dare-ni-sika   desu
           Ken-NOM   met.not   that-TOP who-DAT-SIKA   be
           ka?
           Q
           lit. 'Anyone but who was it that Ken did not meet?'

The sentence in (8a) is obtained if the object in (7a) is put in the focus position in the cleft construction. It is unacceptable. The status does not change if the object is switched to a *wh*-phrase as in (8b). NPIs in Japanese are subject to the requirement that they be clausemates with the negation marker (Muraki 1978). In (8), the NPI is dislocated out of the presuppostional clauses, violating the condition.

Let us now construct an example of Japanese sluicing where an expression accompanied by the NPI appears as the remnant, to see whether the prediction made by the cleft analysis is borne out. The following is a relevant case:[1]

(9)   a.   Ken-wa   hitori-no   onnanoko-ni-sika   awanakatta sooda.
                  Ken-TOP   one-GEN   girl-DAT-SIKA   met.not   I-heard
                  'I heard Ken did not meet anyone but one girl.'

        b.   Dare-ni-sika   ka osiete-kudasai.
                  who-DAT-SIKA   Q tell-please
                  'lit. Please tell me anyone but who.'

Anteceded by (9a), (9b) has a reduced indirect question. Although the NPI occurs with the remnant *wh*-phrase, the sentence sounds fairly acceptable, in sharp contrast with (8a-b). This is confirmed by the following data:

(10)   a.   Ken-wa   hitori-no   onnanoko-kara-sika   tyoko-o
                  Ken-TOP   one-GEN   girl-from-SIKA   chocolate-ACC
                  morawanakatta   sooda.
                  received.not   I-heard
                  'I heard Ken did not receive chocolate from anyone but one girl.'

---

[1] Nishigauchi and Fujii (2006) observe that the NPI cannot occur in remnants in fragment answers, on the basis of the following data:

(i)   a.   Kono neko-wa   nani-sika   tabenai no?
                this   cat-TOP   what-SIKA   eat.not Q   'Only what does this cat eat?'
        b. *   Maguro-sika   desu.
                tuna-SIKA   be   'Only tuna.'

The sluicing counterpart sounds fairly acceptable to us, however:
(ii)   a.   Kono neko-wa aru   syu-no   sakana-sika tabenai   sooda.
                this   cat-TOP a.certain kind-GEN   fish-SIKA   eat.not   I-heard
                'I heard this cat does not eat anything but a certain kind of fish.'
        b.   Donna sakana-sika   ka osiete-kudasai.
                what   fish-SIKA   Q   tell-please   'lit. Please tell me anything but what fish.'

We have no explanation of this discrepancy between fragment answers and sluicing at the moment.

    b.   Boku-wa dare-kara-sika   ka   soozoodekinai.
           I-TOP   who-from-SIKA Q   imagine.cannot
           'lit. I cannot imagine anyone but who.'

The truncated embedded clause in (10b) contains a *wh*-phrase remnant accompanied by the NPI: Nonetheless, the sentence is acceptable.

    The observation that (9b) and (10b) are possible would not be explained by the cleft analysis, which would predict them to be degraded just like those cases where the NPI accompanies the foci in the cleft constructions in (8a-b).

    Before leaving this section, we should mention the fact that the copula may still appear in (9b) and (10b) though they are unlikely to involve cleft structures. Thus, (9b) and (10b) may be expressed alternatively as in (11a-b), respectively.

(11)   a.   Dare-ni-sika   **da** ka osiete-kudasai.
             who-DAT-SIKA be Q   tell-please
        b.   Boku-wa dare-kara-sika   **da** ka soozoodekinai.
             I-TOP   who-from-SIKA be Q imagine.cannot

The source of these sluiced clauses, whatever it may be, must be a construction that can optionally contains the copula and allows the NPI to accompany *wh*-phrases.

3. Proposal

Basically following Hiraiwa and Ishihara (2002), we propose that the cases of Japanese sluicing above be derived from the so-called *no da* 'that be' construction (Kuno 1973), which is illustrated below:[2]

(12)   a.   Ken-ga   Hana-ni   atta.
             Ken-NOM Hana-DAT met
             'Ken met Hana.'
        b.   Ken-ga   Hana-ni   atta no   da.
             Ken-NOM Hana-DAT met that be
             'It was that Ken met Hana.'

---

[2] Hiraiwa and Ishihara (2002) assume that the sluicing construction is derived from the *no da* construction via cleft formation, and hence their analysis is another instance of the cleft analysis of Japanese sluicing. We depart from them in not assuming the involvement of cleft formation in the derivation of Japanese sluicing (see below).

The example in (12a) is a normal transitive sentence. Its *no da* counterpart is given in (12b). While the cleft construction must dislocate foci in the designated focus position, the *no da* construction allows focused elements to remain *in situ*: Thus, the subject *Ken* or the object *Hana* can be focused in (12b) without causing a word order shift (for details about this construction, see the references above). We just assume that the *no da* construction has the following configuration (see Hiraiwa and Ishihara 2002 for a more elaborate structure):

(13) $[_{TP}$ *(pro)* $[_{T'}$ $[_{VP}$ $[_{CP}$ $[_{TP}$ Ken-ga Hana-ni atta] no$_C$] da$_V$] T]]

Here the TP in (12a) is selected by the complementizer *no*, and the resulting CP is the complement of the copula verb *da*. The matrix TP may or may not contain a null expletive subject: If it does, the whole structure directly corresponds to the English construction given as the translation in (12b).

Let us note that the *no da* construction can be embedded, as below:

(14)   Boku-wa [Ken-ga   Hana-ni   atta no   (da) ka] kiita.
         I-TOP   Ken-NOM Hana-DAT met that be   Q   asked
         'I asked whether it was that Ken met Hana.'

In (14), the construction in question is embedded in the indirect question. What is noteworthy is the fact that the copula is optional in this environment too. Further, phrases accompanied by the NPI *sika* can appear in the *no da* construction.

(15)   Ken-ga   dare-ni-sika   awanakatta no   (da) ka
         Ken-NOM who-DAT-SIKA met.not   that be   Q
         osiete-kudasai.
         tell-please
         lit. 'Please tell me *Q* it was that Ken did not meet anyone but who.'

In (15), the *wh*-phrase is attached to by the NPI, and the entire sentence is acceptable, which is natural because the NPI is in the same clause as the negation marker. As seen in (14), the copula is optional here too.

Capitalizing on those properties of the *no da* construction, we assume that it underlies the cases of Japanese sluicing considered in the previous section. Our analysis of (9b) and (11a) is shown below:

(16) $[_{CP}$ $[_{TP}$ $[_{CP}$ ~~Ken-ga~~   dare-ni-sika   ~~awanakatta no~~]
                Ken-NOM who-DAT-SIKA met.not   that

(da) ka] osiete-kudasai
be   Q   tell-please
lit. 'please tell me *Q* it was ~~that Ken did not meet~~ anyone but who'

We have a *no da* construction inside the embedded question in (16). The CP headed by the complementizer *no* is affected by nonconstituent deletion so that the part excluding the *wh*-phrase plus the NPI is elided. The result yields (9b) or (11a) depending on whether the copula is omitted or not.

Nonconstituent deletion is independently motivated by van Craenenbroeck and den Dikken (2006) in their analysis of fragmentary answers such as the following:[3]

(17) a.   What didn't work?
      b.   Any of the printing equipment.

The fragment in (17b) is intended as an answer to the question in (17a). It might be thought that (17b) stems from the nonelliptic form in (18).

(18) *Any of the printing equipment didn't work.

As indicated, however, this cannot be the source of (17b). It is ungrammatical because the NPI *any* is not c-commanded by the negation marker. The authors mentioned above propose that (17b) be derived rather from the structure below by nonconstituent deletion:

(19)   [TP ~~T not~~ [VP any of the printing equipment ~~work~~]]

Here the subject remains in VP without moving to the specifier position of TP, and deletion applies to TP so that the elements except the subject are elided. This analysis can account for the grammaticality of (17b) since it posits that the subject stays in VP so as to be c-commanded by the negation marker. According to van Craenenbroeck and den Dikken (2006), the subject can remain in situ in (19) because T is deleted and consequently the EPP requirement, which is arguably associated with T, becomes void.

We now adduce an argument for our analysis of Japanese sluicing depicted in (16). It is based on the observation made by Hasegawa (1994) with regard to cases like the following:

---

[3] In fact, Ross' (1969) formulation of sluicing assumes nonconstituent deletion.

(20) a.   Ken-wa   Hana-ni   manga-sika   yomanai
             Ken-TOP   Hana-DAT comic.book-SIKA read.not
             yooni   iwanakatta.
             to   told.not
             'Ken did not tell Hana not to read anything but comic books.'

      b.   Manga-sika   Ken-wa   Hana-ni   yomanai
             comic.book-SIKA Ken-TOP   Hana-DAT read.not
             yooni   iwanakatta.
             to   told.not
             lit. 'Anything but comic books, Ken did not tell Hana not to read.'

In (20a), the embedded object is accompanied by the NPI *sika* and the matrix clause and the embedded clause are negated. The sentence is ambiguous between the two readings in (21) depending on which negation the NPI is associated with.

(21) a.   It was only comic books that Ken told Hana not to read.

      b.   Ken did not tell Hana that she should read only comic books.

In (20b), the embedded object is preposed into the matrix clause by scrambling. Hasegawa (1994) observes that the sentence loses ambiguity and is confined to the interpretation in (21a).

    Bearing this in mind, let us consider the following data:

(22) a.   Ken-wa   Hana-ni   aru   syu-no   hon-sika
             Ken-TOP   Hana-DAT a.certain kind-GEN   book-SIKA
             yomanai yooni iwanakatta.
             read.not to   told.not
             'Ken did not tell Hana not to read anything but a certain kind of book.'

      b.   Donna   hon-sika   (da) ka osiete-kudasai.
             what.kind book-SIKA be   Q   tell-please
             lit. 'Please tell me anything but what kind of book.'

The sentence in (22a) is like (20a) in that the embedded object is modified by *sika* and may be associated with either negation. (22a) antecedes (22b), where the embedded clause is sluiced and the *wh*-phrase remnant is accompanied by the NPI. We find (22b) to be ambiguous with regard to the association of the NPI with negation in parallel with (22a): It has either of the two readings in (23).

(23) a.   Please tell me only what kind of book Ken told Hana not to
           read.
      b.   Please tell me only what kind of book Ken did not tell Hana to
           read.

The ambiguity of (22b) is expected by our remnant-in-situ analysis of Japanese sluicing, according to which it is analyzed as follows:

(24)   [[~~Ken-ga   Hana-ni~~   donna   hon-sika   ~~yomanai~~
          Ken-NOM   Hana-DAT   what.kind book-SIKA   read.not
          ~~yooni iwanakatta no~~]   (da) ka]   osiete-kudasai
          to   told.not   that be   Q   tell-please
          lit. 'please tell me [Q (it) was [~~that Ken did not tell Hana not~~
          ~~to read~~ anything but what kind of book]]'

Here again, to account for the fact that the copula may optionally appear in
(22b), we assume that the *no da* construction underlies the sluiced embedded clause. Nonconstituent deletion applies to the CP headed by *no*, eliding everything in the clause except the *wh*-phrase. Note that the NPI accompanying the *wh*-phrase is in situ, so that it is expected to be able to be associated with either negation just as in (20a).

On the other hand, if one were to derive (22b) by constituent deletion,
he/she would have to treat it in the following way:

(25)   [donna   hon-sika   [~~Ken-ga   Hana-ni   yomanai~~
          what.kind book-SIKA Ken-NOM   Hana-DAT   read.not
          ~~yooni iwanakatta no~~]   (da) ka]   osiete-kudasai
          to   told.not   that be   Q   tell-please
          'lit. please tell me [Q anything but what kind of book (it) was
          [~~that Ken did not tell Hana not to read~~]]'

In (25), the remnant *wh*-phrase is dislocated out of the *no* clause (it is immaterial exactly where it is located), and deletion applies to the whole clause to elide everything contained there. Notice that this analysis would predict that (22b) should not be ambiguous because the NPI is dislocated out of the clause it originally belongs to just as in (20b). Thus, the analysis assuming constituent deletion could not accommodate the ambiguity of (22b), whereas our analysis in terms of nonconstituent deletion makes the right prediction for the example.

4. Small Clause Predicates as Remnants

In this section we provide a further supportive argument for our analysis of Japanese sluicing. It has to do with cases where predicates of small clauses occur as remnants. As a preliminary, let us review some basic properties of small clauses in Japanese. They typically appear as complements of such verbs as *omow* 'think,' *kanzi* 'feel,' and *su* 'make' (see Kikuchi and Takahashi 1991). Below are representative cases:

(26) a.   Ken-wa   [Hana-o   kawaiku] omotta.
            Ken-TOP Hana-ACC pretty   thought
            'Ken considered Hana pretty.'

      b.   Ken-wa   [Hana-no   te-o   atuku]   kanzita.
            Ken-TOP Hana-GEN hand-ACC hot   felt
            'Ken felt Hana's hand hot.'

      c.   Ken-wa   [gakusei-o   sake-ni   totemo tuyoku] sita.
            Ken-TOP student-ACC liquor-DAT very   strong   made
            'lit. Ken made his students very strong in liquor.'
            'Ken made his students able to hold their liquor.'

The parts surrounded by brackets in (26a–c) are small clauses, where the subjects are marked accusative and the predicates are adjectives without a tense marker. Kikuchi and Takahashi (1991) observe that predicates of small clauses resist movement. Let us try dislocating the predicate in (26c) in the following way:

(27) a.   *Totemo tuyoku Ken-wa   gakusei-o   sake-ni   sita.
            very   strong Ken-TOP student-ACC liquor-DAT made
            'lit. Very strong, Ken made his students in liquor.'

      b.   *Ken-ga   gakusei-o   sake-ni   sita   no-wa
            Ken-NOM student-ACC liquor-DAT made that-TOP
            totemo tuyoku da.
            very   strong be
            lit. 'It was very strong that Ken made his students in liquor.'

The predicate is preposed by scrambling in (27a), while it is dislocated by cleft formation in (27b). Both examples are quite degraded.[4] With this in mind, let us consider the following case of Japanese sluicing:

---

[4] We are not concerned about the reason for the observed failure. See Kikuchi and Takahashi 1991 for this matter. It suffices for our purpose that predicates in question are immobile.

(28) a. Ken-wa gakusei-o sake-ni tuyoku si-tai
          Ken-TOP student-ACC liquor-DAT strong make-want
          sooda.
          I-heard
          'lit. I heard Ken wanted to make his students strong in liquor.'
      b. Kimi-wa [dorekurai tuyoku (da) ka] soozoodekimasu ka?
          you-TOP how   strong be Q imagine.can   Q
          'Can you imagine how strong?'

Preceded by (28a), (28b) contains a sluiced embedded clause, where the small clause predicate occurs as a remnant. The cleft analysis would predict that (28b) should be impossible just like (27b), but the fact is that it is perfectly acceptable. Also, if one were to try to derive (28b) by constituent deletion, he/she would analyze it as follows:

(29)   *kimi-wa [dorekurai tuyoku [Ken ga   gakusei o
         you-TOP how   strong Ken-NOM   student-ACC
         sake-ni   si-tai   no] (da) ka] soozoodekimasu ka
         liquor-DAT make-want that   be Q   imagine-can   Q
         'lit. can you imagine Q (it) was [how strong [that Ken wanted
         to make his students in liquor]]'

In (29), the remnant *wh*-phrase is assumed to be moved out of the CP headed by *no* (we do not have to be concerned about the precise location of the *wh*-phrase), and then deletion elides the whole CP as a unit. Although this analysis could adhere to constituent deletion, it would not be able to rule in the sentence because we know from (27a) that the predicate cannot be moved in the way depicted in (29).

On the other hand, our analysis can handle the example easily. We analyze it as follows:

(30)   kimi-wa [Ken ga   gakusei o   sake ni   dorekurai
         you-TOP Ken-NOM student-ACC liquor-DAT how
         tuyoku si-tai   no] (da) ka] soozoodekimasu ka
         strong make-want that   be Q   imagine-can   Q
         lit. 'can you imagine Q (it) was [that Ken wanted to make his
         students how strong in liquor]]'

Here the small clause predicate remains in situ. Nonconstituent deletion applies to the *no* clause, eliding everything except the *wh*-phrase. Since the predicate is not moved, the structure should be deemed to be wellformed, as is desired.

5. Conclusion

To summarize, we have considered those cases of Japanese sluicing that have phrases accompanied by the NPI *sika* or small clause predicates as remnants, arguing that they cannot be accounted for by the cleft analysis. We have proposed an alternative analysis of Japanese sluicing, according to which the relevant cases are derived from *no da* constructions by nonconstituent deletion. To the extent that our analysis is successful in handling the data the previous analyses have difficulty accommodating, it provides support for the existence of deletion that affects nonconstituents. There are languages like Japanese that have *wh*-phrases in situ in *wh*-questions and nonetheless exhibit sluicing. Previous approaches have postulated *wh*-movement or some other operations that dislocate *wh*-phrases, such as cleft formation, to explain the phenomenon in question. The idea offered in this article, on the other hand, does not take recourse to such movement operations, shedding new light on the issue.

Acknowledgments

The material reported in this article was presented in one form or another at the 2nd International Workshop on Chains in Minimalism held at Yokohama National University in August, 2009, at the 5th Workshop on the International Research Project on Comparative Syntax and Language Acquisition held at Nanzan University in September, 2009, and at the 19th Japanese/Korean Linguistics Conference held at University of Hawai'i at Mānoa in November, 2009. For their valuable comments and/or questions, we are grateful to the audiences at those meetings, especially to Jun Abe, Tomohiro Fujii, Roger Martin, Keiko Murasugi, Mamoru Saito, and Hideaki Yamashita. All the remaining errors are ours, needless to say.

References

Craenenbroeck, J. van, and den Dikken, M. 2006. Ellipsis and EPP Repair. *Linguistic Inquiry* 37: 653-664.

Hasegawa, N. 1994. Economy of Derivation and A'-movement in Japanese. *Current Topics in English and Japanese*, ed. M. Nakamura, 1-25, Tokyo: Hituzi Syoboo.

Hiraiwa, K. and Ishihara, S. 2002. Missing Links: Cleft, Sluicing and '*No Da*' Construction in Japanese. *MIT Working Papers in Linguistics* 43: 35-54.

Inoue, K. 1976. *Henkei Bunpoo to Nihongo* (Transformational Grammar and Japanese). Tokyo: Taisyukan.

Kikuchi, A. and Takahashi, D. 1991. Agreement and Small Clauses. *Topics in Small Clauses*, ed. H. Nakajima and S. Tonoike, 75-105., Tokyo: Kurosio Publishers.

Kizu, M. 2005. *Cleft Constructions in Japanese Syntax*. New York: Palgrave Macmillan.

Kuno, S. 1973. *The Structure of the Japanese Language*. Cambridge, Mass.: MIT Press.

Kuwabara, K. 1996. Multiple *Wh*-Phrases in Elliptical Clauses and Some Aspects of Clefts with Multiple Foci. *Formal Approaches to Japanese Linguistics 2: MIT Working Papers in Linguistics* 29: 97-116.

Merchant, J. 2001. *The Syntax of Silence: Sluicing, Islands, and the Theory of Ellipsis*. Oxford: Oxford University Press.

Muraki, M. 1978. The *Sika Nai* Construction and Predicate Restructuring. *Problems in Japanese Syntax and Semantics*, ed. J. Hinds and I. Howard, 155-177. Tokyo: Kaitakusha.

Nishigauchi, T. and Fujii, T. 2006. Short Answers: Ellipsis, Connectivity, and Island Repair. Ms. Kobe Shoin Graduate School and University of Maryland.

Nishiyama, K., Whitman, J., and Yi, E. 1996. Syntactic Movement of Overt *Wh*-phrases in Japanese and Korean. *Japanese/Korean Linguistics* 5: 337-351.

Ross, J. R. 1969. Guess Who? *Papers from the 5th Regional Meeting of the Chicago Linguistic Society*, ed. R. Binnick, A. Davison, G. Green, and J. Morgan, 252-286, Chicago: Chicago Linguistic Society.

Saito, M. 2004. Ellipsis and Pronominal References in Japanese Clefts. *Nanzan Linguistics* 1: 21-50.

Takahashi, D. 1994. Sluicing in Japanese. *Journal of East Asian Linguistics* 3: 241-265.

Parametric Variation in Classification of Reflexives

MAKI KISHIDA

University of Maryland, College Park

1. Introduction

Several languages have more than one type of reflexive anaphors and those reflexives induce different kinds of reflexivity when locally bound: Lidz (2001a,b) distinguishes 'Pure reflexivity' and 'Near reflexivity.' Liu (2003) shows that there is another type of reflexivity: 'Pure identity.' We assume that there are only two types of anaphor: 'Pure reflexive anaphors' and 'Near reflexive anaphors,' and what looks like the third type of anaphor is a subcase of Near reflexive anaphor. We further propose that how anaphors are classified into the two types is parametric among languages and that this variation depends on how reflexivity marking occurs.

2. Lidz (1996, 2001a,b)

2.1 Two Types of Reflexivity

Lidz (1996, 2001a,b) demonstrates that, when they are locally bound, refexives in a language can induce different reflexivity using two diagnostics: (i) availability of statue readings in the Madame Tussaud context (Jackendoff, 1992) and (ii) availability of non-sloppy identity readings in

Japanese/Korean Linguistics 19.
Edited by Ho-min Sohn, Haruko Cook, William O'Grady, Leon A. Serafim, & Sang Yee Cheon.

comparative deletion constructions. First, let us see the Madame Tussaud context diagnostic, comparing the two expressions in Dutch. Imagine a situation in which Ringo Starr goes into a wax museum. He is standing in front of a statue that depicts him. The statue has a beard and he does not like that. If Ringo shaves the statue, in Dutch, it is felicitous to say (1b) in which the anaphor *zichzelf* 'selfself' is used, but not (1a) with *zich* 'self.' On the other hand, if he shaves his face, it is fine to say either (1a) or (1b). Reinhart and Reuland (1993) claim that the predicate *scheert* 'shaves' in (1) is doubly specified in the lexicon: the predicate in (1a) is specified as reflexive and the predicate in (1b) is as nonreflexive. A reflexive interpretation is available in (1b), though the predicate is not lexically reflexive. Reinhart and Reuland account for this by assuming that the predicate itself lacks reflexivity but that it gets reflexivity by taking a *reflexivizer anaphor* in their term, namely *zichzelf*, in syntax. Predicates that are specified as reflexive in the lexicon are called 'lexically reflexive predicates,' and predicates that get reflexivity in syntax are called 'syntactically reflexive predicates.' If we follow Reinhart and Reuland's (1993) analysis, we can say that the syntactically reflexive predicate in (1b) induces an additional 'statue' reading, compared to the lexically reflexive predicate in (1a).[1]

(1) a.   Ringo   scheert   zich (*zich* = Ringo,*statue)   [Dutch]
       Ringo   shaves   self
       'Ringo shaves himself.'

    b.   Ringo   scheert zichzelf (*zichzelf* = Ringo, statue)
       Ringo   shaves selfself
       'Ringo shaves himself.'   (Lidz, 2001a, (29))

    The other diagnostic is availability of non-sloppy identity interpretations in comparative deletion constructions. Compare the two expressions in (2). The sloppy identity reading (the deleted structure contains a local reflexive reading) is allowed in both cases, while the non-sloppy identity reading (the object of the deleted structure is the same as the one in the matrix clause) is available only in (2b). Here again, the syntactically reflexive predicate in (2b) has an additional reading.

(2) a.   Zij   verdedigde zich beter dan Peter
       She defended   self better than Peter
       'She defended herself better than Peter defended himself' (sloppy)
       *'She defended herself better than Peter defended her' (non-sloppy)

---

[1] Jackendoff (1992, p.16), who first discusses 'statue' readings in the Madame Tussaud context restricts what an anaphor can refer to 'physical representations' such as pictures, statues recordings and portraying actors, and excludes tales or legends (they are not physical) or cars (that are not representational).

b.   Zij   verdedigde zichzelf beter dan Peter
     She defended   selfself better than Peter
     'She defended herself better than Peter defended himself'
     'She defended herself better than Peter defended her'

(Lidz, 2001a, (30))

Based on the results of these diagnostics, Lidz claims that lexically re-flexive predicates and syntactically reflexive predicates have different se-mantics. He proposes that lexically reflexive predicates are 'Pure reflexive predicates' that have the semantics schematized in (3a). He calls what a Pure reflexive predicate induces 'Pure reflexivity.' On the other hand, syntactical-ly reflexive predicates are 'Near reflexive predicates' that have the seman-tics in (3b). Near reflexive predicates induce 'Near reflexivity.'

(3) a. $\lambda x [P (x,x)]$ (semantic / pure reflexive)
    b. $\lambda x [P (x,f(x))]$ (near reflexive)   (Lidz, 2001a, (15))

Further, Lidz categorizes anaphors into types. Anaphors that occur with lexically reflexive predicates, such as *zich* 'self' in (1a), are 'Pure reflexive anaphors' that require complete identity with their antecedents. This type of anaphor functions as a variable (the second argument of the formula x in (3a)). By contrast, anaphors that occur with syntactically reflexive predi-cates, such as *zichzelf* 'selfself' in (1b), are 'Near reflexive anaphors' that are referentially dependent on their antecedents but are not necessarily iden-tical with them. This type of anaphor introduces the 'Near reflexive func-tion' (the second argument $f(x)$ in (3b)) that takes the antecedent (the first argument x) as input and returns an entity that is representationally related to that argument, such as 'a statue of Ringo' in (1b). When the Near reflexive function returns the input itself, namely, the antecedent itself, a Pure reflex-ive reading is induced. That is, Pure reflexivity is a subcase of Near reflex-ivity. Lidz (2001a,b) claims that an individual anaphor is lexically specified as introducing the Near reflexive function or not. If an anaphor is specified as introducing the function, it can refer to an extension of the antecedent and Near reflexivity is induced. To regulate Pure reflexivity, he proposes 'Con-dition R' given n (4).

(4)   Condition R:
      $\lambda x [P(x,x)]$ $\leftrightarrow$ $(\theta 1 = \theta 2)$
      semantics   theta-grid   (Lidz, 2001a, (17))

The left side of the condition shows the semantics of reflexivity, and the right side indicates the theta-grid of a lexically reflexive predicate. The two thematic roles of a lexically reflexive predicate must be coindexed. Condi-tion R says that if a predicate is semantically reflexive, it must be lexically reflexive. Also, if a predicate is lexically reflexive, it must be semantically reflexive.[2]

2.2 Reflexivity Marking

In this subsection, we see how lexical and semantic reflexivity is marked on verbs. In Lidz's (2001a,b) discussion, there is only one way to mark semantic reflexivity among languages: a verb is semantically reflexive when it takes a Pure reflexive anaphor. By contrast, there seem to be three ways that lexical reflexivity is marked on verbs. A first way of lexical reflexivity marking is that verbs are inherently specified as reflexive in the lexicon. This way is observed in Dutch. Recall (1). The predicate *scheert* 'shaves' in (1a) is specified as reflexive in the lexicon, and lexical reflexivity is marked. The verb occurs with the Pure reflexive anaphor *zich*, so semantic reflexivity is also marked. In (1a), Condition R is satisfied and only a Pure reflexive reading is induced. By contrast, the predicate in (1b) is specified as non-reflexive. Lexical reflexivity is not marked. Semantic reflexivity is not marked either, as the verb occurs with a Near reflexive anaphor *zichzelf*. Condition R does not operate, so a Near reflexive interpretation is allowed.

A second way is to attach a verbal reflexive marker on verbs (see Lidz, 1995). Kannada takes this way: as in (5b), the verbal reflexive marker -*koND* is attached to the verb to mark lexical reflexivity. The predicate in (5a) is semantically reflexive since it takes a Pure reflexive anaphor *tann*, but it lacks lexical reflexivity on the verb. The sentence is excluded due to the violation of Condition R. By contrast, the condition is satisfied in (5b) since the predicate is now marked for lexical reflexivity by -*koND*. In (5c), the condition vacuously applies: the predicate is neither semantically nor lexically reflexive marked.

(5)a. *Hari tann-annu hoDe-d-a   [Kannada]
        Hari self-Acc   hit-Past-3sm 'Hari$_i$ hit himself$_i$.' (*tann* = Hari)
    b.   Hari tann-annu hoDe-du-koND-a
         Hari self-Acc   hit-PR-Refl.Past-3sm
         'Hari$_i$ hit himself$_i$.' (*tann* = Hari,*statue)

---

[2] Burzio (1994) also notices that different types of anaphor induce different reflexivity. Under his analysis, morphologically complex anaphors are called as 'strong anaphors' and simplex anaphors are called as 'weak anaphors.' He proposes the 'Weak Anaphor Principle' given in (i). This principle says that inherent coreference (similar notion to Lidz's 'Pure reflexivity') requires weak(er) anaphors, and weak anaphors induce inherent coreference. He proposes that morphologically simpler anaphors such as Italian reflexive clitic *si* 'self' or morphologically simplex anaphor *sé* are 'weaker' than the morphologically complex anaphor *se stesso* 'self-same.'

    (i) Weak Anaphor Principle
        Inherent coreference ↔ weak anaphora
        (semantics)   (morphology)   (Burzio, 1994, (3))

   c.   Hari tann-annu-taane hoDe-d-a
       Hari self-Acc-self   hit-Past-3sm
       'Harii hit himselfi.' (*tannu-tanne* = Hari, statue) (Lidz, 2001a, (12))

A third way is observed in Russian: a Pure reflexive anaphor marks lexical reflexivity as well as semantic reflexivity. In (6a), only a Pure reflexive reading is induced. Condition R is operative. Even though the same verb is used, the additional statue reading is available in (6b). So, we reason that the verb in (6) lacks any reflexivity and that the anaphor -*sja* in (6a) is Pure reflexive and it marks both semantic and lexical reflexivity. We regard *sebja* in (6b) as a Near reflexive anaphor.

(6) a.   Yeltsin zastrelil-sja.   [Russian]
        Yeltsin shot-self
        'Yeltsini shot himselfi.' (-*sja* = Yeltsin,*statue)
    b.   Yeltsin zastrelil   sebja.
        Yeltsin shot   self
        'Yeltsini shot himselfi.' (*sebja* = Y, statue)   (Lidz, 2001a, (26))

3. Liu (2003)

Arguing against the two-type distinction of anaphor proposed in Lidz (2001a,b), Liu (2003) claims that Pure reflexivity and Near reflexivity are not the only options that are induced in the Madame Tussaud context. (7) illustrates that two types of anaphors in Chinese: *ziji* 'self' and *ta-ziji* 'himself,' can refer to statues, but another type *ziji-benshen* 'self-self' cannot.

(7) a.   Jiang Jie-Shi henhen-de   da-le   ziji   yi-xia.
        Jiang Jie-Shi furiously   hit-Asp self   one-Cl
        'Jiang Jie-Shii hit himselfi furiously.' (*ziji* = JJS, statue)
    b.   Jiang Jie-Shi henhen-de   da-le   ta-ziji   yi-xia.
        Jiang Jie-Shi furiously   hit-Asp him-self one-Cl
        'Jiang Jie-Shii hit himselfi furiously.' (*ta-ziji* = JJS, statue)
    c.   Jiang Jie-Shi henhen-de   da-le   ziji-benshen yi-xia.
        Jiang Jie-Shi furiously   hit-Asp self-self   one-Cl
        'Jiang Jie-Shii hit himselfi furiously.' (*ziji-benshen* = JJS, *statue)
                                                   (Liu, 2003, (11))

Liu claims that what looks like Pure reflexivity in (7c) is 'Pure identity' between the anaphor and its antecedent. His claim is that this anaphor is not a Pure reflexive anaphor but a 'focus operator anaphor.' While Pure reflexivity in Lidz's (2001a,b) sense is as a consequence of Condition R, Pure identity arises as a consequence of the semantic composition of the anaphor *zijibenshen*: (a) the Near reflexive function of *ziji* 'self,' (b) a focus function of -*benshen* '-self,' and (c) the operator status of the anaphor *ziji-benshen*.

(8) shows that the suffix *-benshen* functions as a focus marker that involves a notion of scalarity with respect to the expectations of the speaker (see Rooryck and Vanden Wyngaerd 1998). The speaker of the sentence has not expected that the subject NP (*zongtong* 'president') did the action, but he/she actually did. What was done was beyond the speaker's expectation. Thus, the focus marker is attached to the subject NP. Without the focus marker, the sentence sounds pragmatically odd.

(8) Wei-le jiaqiang liang-guo jian de bangyi, zongtong benshen
  For-Asp reinforce two-state between DE friendship president self
  yao dao jichang lai yingjie meiguo guowuqing.
  want arrive airport come welcome United States Secretary of State
  'In order to reinforce the diplomatic relationship between the Unit
  ed States and us, the president *himself* will come to the airport to
  welcome the U.S. Secretary of State.' (Liu, 2003, (27))

Liu explains how the Pure identity reading is induced in the Madame Tussaud context, such as (7), as follows. There is a set of what the Near reflexive function of *ziji* denotes (referential extensions of the antecedent or the elements that could be construed as the antecedent) and the focus marker *-benshen* picks out an element that is highest on the scale among the set. As a consequence, the antecedent itself is selected as the reference of the anaphor. Pure identity does not necessarily imply Pure reflexivity but not vice versa. So, Pure reflexivity is a subcase of Pure identity.

Liu notes that *ziji-benshen* shows a different behavior compared with the other anaphors in a comparative deletion construction as well. While *ziji* in (9a) allows both sloppy and non-sloppy identity readings, *zijibenshen* in (9b) allows only a sloppy identity reading. Liu accounts for this by claiming that *ziji-benshen* functions as an operator because this anaphor has a 'semantic range,' namely the range of the Near reflexive function of *ziji* (cf. Katada, 1991). The possession of semantic range is a property shared by other operators such as quantifiers, wh-words, and null operators.

(9)a. Zhangsan xianzai bi Lisi guoqu geng quanxin ziji-de liyi
   Z   now compare L past more care-about self-DE benefit
   'Z_i cares about his_i benefit more than L_j cared about his_j benefit.'
   'Z_i cares about his_i benefit more than L_j cared about his_i benefit.'
 b. Z xianzai bi L guoqu geng quanxin ziji-benshen-de liyi
   Z now compare L past more care-about self-self-DE benefit
   'Z_i cares about his_i benefit more than L_j cared about his_j benefit.'
   *'Z_i cares about his_i benefit more than L_j cared about his_i benefit.'
               (Liu, 2003, (32))

He assumes that the operator *ziji-benshen* undergoes LF movement, namely, adjunction to VP (cf. Huang and Tang, 1991). Under his analysis, the deleted structure of (9b) has an LF representation like (10). The anaphor constitutes an Operator-variable relation with its trace (cf. Heim and Kratzer, 1998): *Ziji-benshen* adjoins to VP, and its trace can be bound only by the local subject *Lisi* because the anaphor is subject to predication or strong binding by an appropriate local subject (cf. Chomsky, 1986).

(10)   [[Lisi$_i$] [$_{VP}$ *ziji-benshen*$_i$ [$_{VP}$ t_i]]]   (Liu, 2003, Footnote 26)

Further, he claims that *ziji-benshen* is not a Pure reflexive anaphor from the viewpoint of the semantic contents of anaphor. Pure reflexive anaphors (e.g. *zich* 'self' in Dutch) are variables without any content, while the focus operator anaphor has a richer semantic/pragmatic content as a focus marker.

It seems that there are three types of anaphor in languages: Pure reflexive anaphors, Near reflexive ones and ones with a special function. Liu (2003)'s claim is that there are two ways to induce Pure identity reading in languages: Pure reflexivity as a consequence of Condition R and Pure identity as a consequence of the properties of anaphor. He proposes that a language disjunctively selects one of the two ways. For instance, Dutch selects the first way: it has the Pure reflexive anaphor *zich* as well as the Near reflexive anaphor *zichzelf*. On the other hand, Chinese selects the second way: it has the focus operator anaphor *ziji-benshen* as well as Near reflexive anaphors *ziji* and *ta-ziji*. Then, we wonder what decides whether a language select the first or second way as a way to induce Pure identity reading. At the same time, we have another question: do the two ways need to be disjunctive?

4. Proposal

We claim that a language can have both of the two ways to induce Pure identity reading: Pure reflexivity and Pure identity, contrary to Liu's (2003) claim. Further, we propose that there are only two types of anaphor: Pure reflexives and Near reflexives, and that what looks like a third type; e.g. an anaphor with a focus function, is a subcase of Near reflexive anaphor. Our assumption is that when a Near reflexive anaphor has a special function, its Near reflexive anaphor status is counteracted by the special function and Near reflexive readings are not induced. These claims are based on the observations in Japanese in Section 4.1. Further, we propose that there is parametric variation among languages in the two-type classification of anaphor as in (11).

(11) a.   morphologically simplex anaphor = Pure reflexive anaphor
          morphologically complex anaphor = Near reflexive anaphor

    b. bound-morpheme anaphor = Pure reflexive anaphor
        free-morpheme anaphor = Near reflexive anaphor

In languages like Dutch, Kannada and Malayalam, the morphological composition of an anaphor distinguishes Pure and Near reflexive anaphors: morphologically simplex anaphors are Pure reflexive anaphors (e.g. *zich* 'self' in Dutch), while complex ones are Near reflexives (*zichzelf* 'self-self').[3] On the other hand, in languages like Russian and Japanese, a bound-morpheme anaphor is a Pure reflexive anaphor and a free-morpheme anaphor is a Near reflexive anaphor. We attribute this proposal to a predication made in Lidz's Condition R analysis given in (12).

(12)   If an anaphor can be bound by a coargument (in the absence of lexical reflexivity), then that anaphor is a Near-reflexive.

                                                  (Lidz, 2001a, 237)

Although Lidz refers to only Near reflexive anaphors, we can paraphrase this as 'an anaphor is bound by a coargument in the presence of lexical reflexivity, then that anaphor is Pure-reflexive.' As we have reviewed above, there are several ways to mark lexical reflexivity: a verb is marked as reflexive in the lexicon (e.g. Dutch), a verb takes a verbal reflexive marker (Kannada) and a verb takes a Pure reflexive anaphor (Russian). Semantic reflexivity is, on the other hand, marked on verbs by a Pure reflexive anaphor in all languages. We assume that if lexical reflexivity marking occurs independently from semantic reflexivity marking as in Dutch and Kannada, a Pure reflexive anaphor is a free-morpheme. By contrast, if lexical reflexivity marking occurs simultaneously with semantic reflexivity marking as in Russian, a Pure reflexive anaphor is a bound-morpheme that has to be morphologically incorporated into verbs. Our proposal is that how anaphors are classified into types in a language depends on how reflexivity marking occurs. In section 4.2, we see that our proposal is compatible with the date from several languages.

---

[3] We regard Malayalam as the language in which the morphological composition of anaphor distinguishes types of anaphor. However, the language does not mark lexical reflexivity on verbs and coargument binding of the anaphor *tan* 'self' is always excluded by Condition R as in (i). We would not regard this anaphor as a Pure reflexive. On the other hand, another anaphor *tan-tanne* 'self-self' in (ii) can be bound by its coargument and induce a statue interpretation. This anaphor is a Near reflexive anaphor.

    (i)*Raaman tan-ne   kshauram ceytu   [Malayaram]
         Raaman self-Acc shaving   did
         'Raaman shaved.'
    (ii) Raaman tan-ne-tanne kshauram ceytu
         Raaman self-Acc-self   shaving   did
         'Raaman shaved himself.' (*tan-tanne* = Raaman, statue)   (Lidz, 2001a, (32))

4.1 Japanese

In this subsection, we discuss why we claim that there are only Near reflexives and Pure reflexives and that what looks like the third type of reflexivity is a subcase of Near reflexive. We examine three types of anaphor in Japanese that lack phi-feature specification: *zibun* 'self,' *zibun-zisin* 'self-self' and bound morphemes *zi-/ziko-* used in Sino-Japanese complex verbs.[45]

Recall the prediction made by Condition R in (12). The verb *hihan-suru* 'criticize' in (13) lacks an overt object argument, and the sentence induces a transitive reading but not a reflexive reading. In (14), the same verb overtly takes an object *Mary*, and the sentence is perfect. Based on (13) and (14), we reason that this verb lacks lexical reflexivity and it is transitive in nature. Now, in (15), *zibun* and *zibun-zisin* can each be bound by its coargument *John* though the verb lacks lexical reflexivity. So, following the prediction in (12), we regard *zibun* and *zibun-zisin* as Near reflexive anaphors in Japanese.

(13) John-ga   hihan-si-ta.
      John-Nom   criticism-do-Past
      'John criticized {someone / something / *himself }.'
(14) John-ga   Mary-o   hihan-si-ta.
      John-Nom Mary-Acc   criticism-do-Past
      'John criticized Mary.'
(15) John-ga   {zibun / zibun-zisin}-o   hihan-si-ta.
      John-Nom {self-Acc / self-self}-Acc   criticism-do-Past
      'John criticized {self / self-self}.'

---

[4] Verbs that incorporate the bound-morphemes *zi-/ziko-* are called *zi*-verbs /*ziko*-verbs. Following Kishida and Sato (2009), we assume that these morphemes are incorporated into verbal nouns (VNs) such as *satu* 'killing' in (i) and *hihan* 'criticism' in (16) in syntax and that these complexes are supported by the light verb *suru* 'do' as *zi-satu-suru* 'do self-killing, kill oneself' and *zikohihan-suru* 'do self-criticism, criticize oneself.' Our assumption is that *zi-* and *ziko-* are object arguments of the complex predicate (*satu-suru* 'do killing' and *hihan-suru* 'do criticism') because, as in (ii), the *zi*-verb cannot take an object argument.
      (i) John-ga   zi-satu-si-ta.
      John-Nom self-killing-do-Past
      John$_i$ killed himself$_i$'
      (ii)*John-ga   zibun-o   zi-satu-si-ta.
      John-Nom self-Acc   self-killing-do-Past
      'John$_i$ killed himself$_i$.'

[5] Japanese has one more type of anaphor that is phi-feature specified and composed of a pronoun and the *-zisin* '-self' suffix such as *kare-zisin* 'him-self' and *kanojo-zisin* 'her-self.' This type of anaphor is, however, rarely used, so we exclude this type from our examination.
      (i) John-ga   kare-zisin-o   hihan-si-ta.
      John-Nom him-self-Acc   criticism-do-Past
      'John$_i$ criticized himself$_i$.'

In (16), the same verb occurs with the bound-morpheme anaphor *ziko-*. This anaphor is bound by its coargument *John*, and a reflexive interpretation is exclusively induced. We assume that if an anaphor marks lexical reflexivity by incorporating to a verb root, the verb root gains semantic reflexivity too. So, we regard this anaphor as a Pure reflexive anaphor.

(16) John-ga   ziko-hihan-si-ta.
     John-Nom   self-criticism-do-Past
     'John criticized {self / *someone / *something}.'

Our prediction based on the observations above is that Japanese anaphors are classified as listed in (17).

(17) a. *zibun* 'self' = Near reflexive anaphor
     b. *zibun-zisin* 'self-self' = Near reflexive anaphor
     c. bound-morpheme *zi-/ziko-* 'self-' = Pure reflexive anaphor

Now, to see if the classification in (17) is correct, we apply the two diagnostics that distinguish Near and Pure reflexives proposed in Lidz (2001a,b): availability of statue readings in the Madame Tussaud context in (18) and availability of non-sloppy identity readings in comparative deletion constructions in (19) (Cf. Shimada (2006), Miura (2008)).

(18) a. John-wa   zibun-o   hihan-si-ta.
         John-Top self-Acc   criticism-do-Past
         'John criticized self.' (*zibun* = John, statue)
     b. John-wa   zibun-zisin-o   hihan-si-ta.
         John-Top self-self-Acc   criticism-do-Past
         'John criticized self-self.' (*zibun-zisin* = John, *statue)
     c. John-wa   ziko-hihan-si-ta.
         John-Top   self-criticism-do-Past
         'John criticized self.' (*ziko-* = John, *statue)

(19) a. Mary-wa   John yorimo hagesiku zibun-o hihan-si-ta.
         Mary-Top John than   severely self-Acc criticism-do-Past
         'M criticized herself more severely than J criticized himself.'
         'M criticized herself more severely than J criticized her.'
     b. Mary-wa   John yorimo hagesiku zibun-zisin-o hihan-si-ta.
         Mary-Top John than   severely self-self-Acc criticism-do-Past
         'M criticized herself more severely than J criticized himself.'
         *'M criticized herself more severely than J criticized her.'
     c. Mary-wa   John yorimo hagesiku ziko-hihan-si-ta.
         Mary-Top John than   severely self-criticism-do-Past
         'M criticized herself more severely than J criticized himself.'
         *'M criticized herself more severely than J criticized her.'

In (18), *zibun* can refer to a statue of the antecedent, but each *zibun-zisin* and *ziko-* refers to only its antecedent. If *zibun* is a Near reflexive anaphor and *ziko-*is a Pure reflexive anaphor as in the proposed classification in (17), the (un)availability of statue reading in (18a) and (18c) can be straightforwardly accounted for. The Near reflexive anaphor *zibun* introduces the Near reflexive function and it takes the antecedent *John* as its input and returns 'statue of John,' and the Pure reflexive anaphor *ziko-* excludes the statue reading and only the reading in which it refers to its antecedent is allowed. However, there seems to be a contradiction in (18b). *Zibun-zisin* is categorized as Near reflexive in (17b), but it does not induce a statue reading in (18b). In (19), only *zibun* induces a non-sloppy identity reading as well as a sloppy identity reading. *Zibun-zisin* and *ziko-* induce only sloppy identity readings. The explanation for (19a) and (19c) is straightforward. While *ziko-* is a variable so it can bound only by the local subject *John*, *zibun* not being a variable can have its own index and it can induce a non-sloppy identity reading. Here again, we notice the same contradiction: why doesn't the Near reflexive anaphor *zibun-zisin* behave like a Near reflexive in (19b)?

To dispense with this contradiction, we claim that *zibun-zisin* functions as a focus operator anaphor, following Liu's (2003) analysis of *ziji-benshen* 'self-self' reviewed in Section 3. *Zibun-zisin* also consists of two parts: the Near reflexive anaphor *zibun* 'self' and the suffix *-zisin* 'self.' The suffix-*zisin* functions as a focus marker that involves a notion of scalarity with respect to the expectations of the speaker, as (20) illustrates.

(20)   Amerika to   wagakuni-no   gaikoo kankei-o   kyooka-suru tame
        America and our country-Gen diplomatic relation-Acc reinforce to
        syusyoo-**zisin**-ga Amerika-no kokumutyookan-o kuukoo-e
        president-self-Nom America-Gen secretary of state-Acc airport-to
        mukaeni it-tta.
        welcome go-Past
        'In order to reinforce the diplomatic relationship between the
        United States and us, the president *himself* will come to the airport
        to welcome the U.S. Secretary of State.'

What is induced in (18b) is Pure identity as a consequence of the semantic composition of *zibun-zisin*: the focus function of *-zisin* selects one element that is highest on the scale of these elements that could be construed as the antecedent from the set of what the Near reflexive function of *zibun* denotes. As a consequence, the antecedent itself is selected. From the viewpoint of semantics/pragmatics as well, what is induced by *zibun-zisin* in (18b) and what is induced by *ziko-* in (18c) differ. *Zibun-zisin* functions as a focus marker and has richer a semantic/pragmatic content, and the sentence means 'John criticized HIMSELF, not anyone else.' By contrast, *ziko-* is just a variable without any content. (18c) does not mean the same as (18b).

We account for the unavailability of non-sloppy identity reading in (19b) by saying that *zibun-zisin* is an operator anaphor since it has the semantic range, namely the range of the Near reflexive function of *zibun*. Following Liu (2003), we assume that *zibun-zisin* undergoes an operator movement at LF as in (21) and it is subject to strong binding so only the local subject *John* can be the reference of *zibun-zisin*.

(21)   [[John] [$_{VP}$ *zibun-zisin*$_i$ [$_{VP}$ t_i]]]   (the elided part of (19b))

The observations above show that Japanese has both Pure reflexivity induced by *ziko-* and Pure identity induced by *zibun-zisin*. Therefore, we claim that the two ways to induce Pure identity readings are not disjunctive in a language. Though *zibun-zisin* is a Near reflexive anaphor being a free-morpheme, its Near reflexive anaphor status is counteracted by its special function as a focus. So, *zibun-zisin* does not behave similarly with *zibun*.[6]

The classification of Japanese anaphors under our proposal is as follows: *Zibun* 'self' and *zibun-zisin* 'self-self' are Near reflexive anaphors as they are free-morphemes, but the latter one has a special function as a focus so its Near reflexive anaphor status is counteracted by the function. The bound-morpheme anaphors *zi-* and *ziko-* are Pure reflexive anaphors.

4.2 Chinese

Liu (2003) discusses that Chinese is a language that uses a focus operator anaphor to get a Pure identity reading. However, this language also has a Pure reflexive anaphor *zi-* 'self' that functions as a variable as in (22). This anaphor is regarded as a Pure reflexive because, unlike *ziji-benshen*, it has no semantic/pragmatic content.

(22)   Xiang-Yu zuihou zi-jin-le.
         Xiang-Yu finally   self-killing-Asp
         'Xiang finally killed himself' (*zi-* = X, *statue)

                                               (Liu, 2003, Footnote 30 (ii))

---

[6] It is not always that *zibun-zisin* semantically functions as a focus as in (i). In that case, *zibun-zisin* can be used interchangeably with *zibun* that lacks the *-zisin* part as in (ii). I would have to say that there are two types of *zibun-zisin*: one with a focus meaning and the other without it. I leave this for future research. Thanks to Yoshihisa Kitagawa for pointing out this.
     (i) Dare-ga   zibun-zisin-o hihan-si-ta no.
         who-Nom self-self-Acc   criticism-do-Past Q
         'Who criticized himself?'
    (ii) Dare-ga   zibun-o   hihan-si-ta no.
         who-Nom self-Acc   criticism-do-Past Q
         'Who criticized himself?'

Then, the classification under our proposal holds true in this language. As we have seen in (7), free-morpheme anaphors *ziji* 'self' and *ta-ziji* 'him-self' are Near reflexives that can refer to statues. *Ziji-benshen* 'self-self' is also Near reflexive being a free-morpheme, but it refers only to the antecedent as a consequence of the semantic composition of the anaphor.

4.3 Other Languages

Our proposal that in some languages, bound-morpheme reflexives are Pure reflexive anaphors and free-morpheme ones are Near reflexive, and a Near reflexive anaphor with a special function does not behave like a Near reflexive anaphor, is compatible with the data below from other languages.

In Russian, as seen in (6), the bound-morpheme anaphor *-sja* '-self' behaves like a Pure reflexive anaphor, while the free-morpheme anaphor *sebja* 'self' behaves as a Near reflexive. In Korean, as in (23), the bound-morpheme *caki-* 'self' is Pure reflexive that excludes a Near reflexive interpretation, while the free-morpheme *caki* 'self' is Near reflexive and can induce a statue reading. In Spanish, the bound-morpheme anaphor *se-* 'self' cannot be used to induce Near reflexive reading as in (24). English has just the free-morpheme type anaphor such as *himself* and *herself*. *Himself* can refer to a statue as in (25).

(23) Chelswu-ka {caki-piphan-ha-yss-ta / caki-lul piphan-ha-yss-ta}.
      C-Nom   {self-criticism-do-Past-Dec / caki-lul piphan-ha-yss-ta.}
      'Chelswu criticized himself.' (*caki-* = C,*statue) (*caki* = C, statue)
                                                      (Kang 2001:18)

(24) El zorro   se- lavó.
      The zorro   self washed
      'Zorro washed himself.' (*se-* = Zorro,*statue) (Shimada, 2006, 60)

(25) Reagan dressed himself in the museum. (*himself* = Reagan, statue)
                                                      (Lidz, 2001a, (22b))

We believe that the data here shows the validity of our proposal.[7]

---

[7] That the bound-/free-morpheme distinction corresponds to the Pure-/Near-reflexive distinction seems to be true with reciprocal pronouns in Japanese. The free-morpheme reciprocal pronoun *otagai* 'each other' allows a Near reflexive interpretation as in (i), while the bound-morpheme *sougo-* 'each other' does not as in (ii).

      (i) Ringo to John -wa   otagai-o   hihan-si-ta.
          Ringo and John -Top each other-Acc   criticism-do-Past
          'Ringo criticized John and John criticized Ringo.'
          'Ringo criticized the statue of John and John criticized the statue of Ringo.'
      (ii) Ringo to John -wa   sougo-hihan-si-ta.
          Ringo and John -Top each.other-criticism-do-Past
          'Ringo criticized John and John criticized Ringo.'
          *'Ringo criticized the statue of John and John criticized the statue of Ringo.'

5. Conclusion

We have observed that several languages have more than one form of reflexive anaphor and that they are classified based on their semantics into 'Pure reflexive anaphors' that require complete identity with their antecedents and 'Near reflexive anaphors' that are referentially relevant to their antecedents but not necessarily identical with them, in Lidz (2001a, b)'s sense. There is a third type of reflexivity: Pure identity, as shown in Liu (2003). We claim that what looks like the third type of anaphor is a subcase of Near reflexivity. The Near reflexive anaphor status of a free-morpheme anaphor is counteracted if the anaphor has a special function, such as focus as Chinese *zijibenshen* and Japanese *zibun-zisin* do. We have also proposed that the Pure / Near reflexive anaphor classification is parametric among languages: in some languages (e.g. Japanese, Russian, Chinese etc.), bound-morpheme reflexives are Pure reflexives and free-morpheme ones are Near reflexives, while in others (Dutch, Kannada etc.), morphologically simplex anaphors among free morpheme reflexives are Pure reflexive and complex ones are Near reflexive. We assume that the parametric variation depends on how reflexivity marking occurs in the language. Our proposal sheds new light on typological research into reflexivity and coreference in generative grammar.

Acknowledgments

This paper is a revised version of a section in Kishida (2009). I would like to express my gratitude to Jun Abe, Tonia Bleam, Norbert Hornstein, Howard Lasnik, Jeff Lidz, Chizuru Nakao, Akira Omaki, Kamil Ud Deen, Juan Uriagereka and Masaya Yoshida and the audience at the 11th SICOGG and the 19th JK Conference for their valuable comments and suggestions.

References

Burzio, L. 1994. Weak Anaphora. In *Paths toward Universal Grammar: Studies in honor of Richard Kayne*, 59–84. Georgetown University Press.

Chomsky, N. 1986. *Knowledge of Language: Its Nature, Origin and Use*. Praeger.

Heim, I. and Kratzer, A. 1998. *Semantics in Generative Grammar*. Blackwell.

Huang, C.-T. James and Jane Tang, C.-C. 1989. The Local Nature of the Long-Distance Reflexive in Chinese. *Proceedings of NELS* 19:191–206.

Jackendoff, R. 1992. Mme Tussaud Meets the Binding Theory. *Natural Language and Linguistic Theory* 10:1–31.

It is important to see if the proposed classification of reflexive anaphors holds with reciprocal anaphors, and more generally, with pronouns. These, however, would go beyond the issue in this paper so I leave them for future research. I appreciate Keiko Murasugi and John Whitman for pointing these out.

Kang, B. 2001. The Grammar and Use of Korean Reflexives. *Informational Journal of Corpus Linguistics* 6(1):134–150.

Katada, F. 1991. The LF Representation of Anaphors. *Linguistic Inquiry* 22: 287–314.

Kishida, M. 2009. Anti-Reflexivity in Japanese. Generals paper, University of Maryland, College Park.

Kishida, M, and Sato, Y. 2009. Zi-verbs in Japanese: Description and explanation. Ms. University of Maryland, College Park and National University of Singapore.

Lidz, J. 1995. Morphological Reflexive Marking: Evidence from Kannada. *Linguistic Inquiry* 26:705–710.

Lidz, J. 1996. Dimensions of Reflexivity. Ph.D. dissertation, University of Delaware.

Lidz, J. 2001a. Anti-Antilocality. In *Long Distance Reflexives*, ed. G. Hermon P. Cole and J. C.-T. Huang, 227–254. Academic Press.

Lidz, J. 2001b. Condition R. *Linguistic Inquiry* 32:123–140.

Liu, C. L. 2003. Pure Reflexivity, Pure Identity, Focus and Chinese *Ziji-Benshen*. *Journal of East Asian Linguistics* 12:19–58.

Miura, H. 2008. Grammatical Relations, Reflexives and Pseudo-Raising in Japanese. Ph.D. dissertation, State University of New York at Buffalo.

Reinhart, T. and Reuland, E. 1993. Reflexivity. *Linguistic Inquiry* 24:657–720.

Rooryck, J. and VandenWyngaerd, G. 1998. The Self as Other: A Minimalist Approach to Zich and Zich-zelf in Dutch. *Proceedings of NELS 28* 359–373.

Shimada, M. 2006. Reflexives in Competition. M.A. thesis, University of Calgary

A Hybrid Approach to Floating Quantifiers: Experimental Evidence

HEEJEONG KO
Seoul National University

EUNJEONG OH
Sangmyung University

The non-local dependency between a noun and its associate quantifier has been widely discussed. The details may differ, but the formal analyses of floating quantifiers can be divided into three schools of research. One is an adnominal approach, which argues that the noun and the quantifier are externally-merged together (at some point of the derivation), and that the noun has undergone leftward movement in a later derivation (e.g. Kuroda 1983, Sportiche 1988, Ueda 1990, Bošković 2004). Another is an adverbial approach, which claims that the quantifier modifies the event structure of the verb phrase, and that the noun and the quantifier are not related to each other by movement (e.g. Kayne 1975, Fukushima 1991, Bobaljik 1995, 2003, Brisson 1998, Nakanish 2003, Kim and Yang 2006). The other is a hybrid approach (e.g. Ishii 1998, Kang 2002, Ko 2005, 2007, Fitzpatrick 2006) which argues that some floating quantifiers are adnominals while some are adverbials. This paper evaluates the predictions and validity of the three

Japanese/Korean Linguistics 19.
Edited by Ho-min Sohn, Haruko Cook, William O'Grady, Leon A. Serafim, & Sang Yee Cheon.
Copyright © 2011, CSLI Publications

approaches with new experimental data, and provides evidence for the hybrid approach from on-line processing and off-line judgment data.

1. The Issues

The three major approaches to capture the non-local dependency between a noun and its associate quantifier have different predictions and implications.

On the adnominal approach, floating Q(uantifier) constructions are transformationally related to a corresponding non-floating Q construction. For instance, *the students* in (1a) is externally-merged with *all* in base position, and has undergone leftward movement, as in (1b).[1]

(1) a. [$_{TP}$ ___ [$_T'$ have [$_{VP}$ [$_{DP}$ all [$_{DP}$ the students]] had lunch]]]

  b. [$_{TP}$ [$_{DP}$ the students] $_1$ [$_T'$ have [$_{VP}$ [$_{DP}$ all t$_1$] had lunch]]]

This approach has some advantages in explaining the close relationship between floating and non-floating Q constructions. The semantic similarities between (1a) and (1b) straightforwardly follow from the claim that they share the base structure. The fact that the floating Q shows the same agreement pattern with its host noun as the non-floating Q is also naturally explained by the adnominal approach (e.g. Shlonsky 1991, Merchant 1996). It also explains the fact that floating Qs appear in the original or intermediate positions of its host noun (e.g. Bošković 2004). Floating Qs were also taken as evidence for the predicate-internal subject hypothesis (e.g. Sportiche 1988; see Fitzpatrick 2006 for a summary).

Under the adverbial approach, on the other hand, the quantifier modifies the event structure of the verb phrase, and crucially, the noun and its associate Q are not directly related to each other by syntactic movement. For instance, (1a) and (1b) are not related to each other by syntax. Instead, the "apparent" ability of the adjunct Q to modify the noun is derived *indirectly* by the semantics. Due to its lexical meaning, *all* "maximizes" the external argument of the verbal phrase, as stated in (2) (Dowty and Brody 1984, adopted by Bobaljik 1995).

(2) [[all]] = λ P<e,t>. λ x P(max(x))

The adverbial approach has some advantages, too. When a floating Q appears in non-argument position, the adverbial approach claims to best explain the distribution of the floating Q. Some semantic differences between

---

[1] In the strict sense, *all* is "stranded" in its base position rather than "floated" in an arbitrary place. For the sake of simplicity, however, we use the term *floating* theory-neutrally to denote a non-local dependency between a noun and its associate Q.

floating and non-floating Q constructions are also naturally explicable by the adverbial approach (see a detailed discussion by Bobaljik 1995, 2003).

Lastly, the hybrid approach argues that both adnominal and adverbial approaches are basically on the right track. It argues that in languages, some floating Qs are adnominal while some are adverbial, and that the two types of floating Qs show different semantic and syntactic properties. For instance, Ishii (1988) argues that floating Qs are ambiguous between a stranded Q and adverbial Q, and that systematic counterexamples to the adnominal Q approaches are limited to the cases where the floating Qs bear a distributive reading, which should be analyzed as an adverbial Q. Fitzpatrick (2006) argues that the split between the two types of floating Qs exists not only between languages (e.g. Japanese vs. English), but also within a single language (e.g. Korean, West-Ulster English). Fitzpatrick (2006) further shows that adverbial floating Qs are characterized by the A-movement-like properties of the host noun, whereas adnominal floating Qs are diagnosed by A'-movement-like properties of the host noun. Fitzpatrick (2006) also shows that exhaustivity is systematically related with the Q types. Ko (2005, 2007) focuses more on syntactic properties of floating Qs, and argues that while the distribution of adnominal Qs is affected by various syntactic factors (e.g. grammatical function of the host noun, argument structure of the verb, and position of the intervening element), the distribution of adverbial Qs is not restricted by those syntactic factors.

The predictions of the three approaches to floating Qs are divergent. Under the adnominal approach, we predict that the distribution of floating Qs will be restricted by the locality conditions on NP-movement. Under the hybrid approach, on the other hand, only a subset of floating Qs would show such locality effects. On the adverbial approach, floating Qs may appear rather freely as long as event quantification is possible.

Though the predictions can be clearly stated, there has been lack of consensus on which prediction is supported by quantifiable empirical data. Each approach often discusses different sets of data in different languages, and researchers occasionally report different judgments on the same data set, too (e.g. Hoji and Ishii 2005, Miyagawa and Arikawa 2007 for debates on Japanese floating Q data). Moreover, it has been unclear what we mean by "unacceptability". It remains unclear whether "unacceptability" of floating Q constructions comes from mere processing difficulty or quintessential ungrammaticality (cf. Miyagawa and Arikawa 2007 for a suggestion that prosody plays a crucial role in processing floating Q constructions). If the former is correct, we expect that the unacceptability can be overcome in off-line judgment tasks. If the latter is correct, however, we predict that the unacceptability will be maintained both in on-line and off-line tests.

To tackle the issue of judgment variations more properly, we need a controlled experiment on floating Q constructions so that we may apply a statistical analysis on the data. Furthermore, to test whether unacceptability originates from processing difficulty or ungrammaticality, we need both real time and off-line data. It may be worth noting, however, that linguistically-informed processing studies on floating Qs are in fact quite rare. Miyagawa and Arikawa (2007) properly addressed the issue of prosody in processing floating Qs but conducted a pilot study only. Kang (2002) pointed out the effects of discourse focus, but experimental evidence is yet to be given (see also Kim and Yang 2006 for discussion).

The goal of our study is to evaluate the predictions and validity of the three approaches to floating Q constructions with new experimental data from Korean. Korean is a language that is claimed to have both adnominal and adverbial Qs (see Kang 2002, Ko 2005, 2007, Fitzpatrick 2006). Thus, some systematic correlations between various syntactic factors and Q-types are expected. Furthermore, the two types of floating Qs are claimed to be only minimally different from each other in morphology: the adnominal Qs are Caseless and the adverbial Qs are Case-marked. Otherwise, they look the same. Thus, Korean floating Qs may provide an ideal background to test the hypotheses concerning the syntactic differences associated with Q-types.

2. Experimental Design

2.1 Theoretical Background

Ko (2005, 2007) argues that (at least) three factors in (3) are involved in licensing floating adnominal Qs, and claims that the distribution of floating adnominal Qs conforms to the *Edge Generalization*, stated in (4).

(3) a. Grammatical function of the host noun (e.g. subject vs. object)
   b. Type of the quantifier (e.g. adverbial vs. adnominal Q)
   c. Argument structure (e.g. unergative vs. unaccusative verb)

(4) *Edge Generalization*
   Elements that are externally merged as a constituent in syntactic edges cannot be separated by their domain-mates.

Ko (2005) argues that the Edge Generalization is a consequence of *Cyclic Linearization* (Fox and Pesetsky 2005) and a *probe-goal Search* (Chomsky 2001). As described in (5), when the two elements A and B are base-generated as a constituent at the syntactic edge of αP, their domain-mate C may precede or follow them. Crucially, however, A or B would not be able to move over C within αP since they are not in the search domain (i.e. c-command domain) of the head α (Chomsky 2001). Consequently, A and B are not separable by C within αP. If αP is a Spell-out domain, the linear orderings in αP must be preserved in the higher domains, due to Cyclic Linearization (Fox and Pesetsky 2005). Hence, A and B are not separable by their domain-mate C in the higher domains, either. As in Ko (2005), we call this ordering restriction the *Edge Effect*.

(5) *[A ... C ... B]: *Edge Effect*

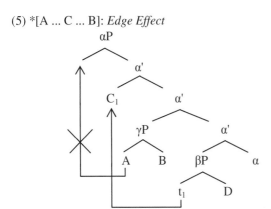

If (4) is correct, we make a particular prediction about the distribution of floating Qs. If the floating Q is adnominal (e.g. B in (5)), we predict that the floating Q will show Edge Effects. More specifically, if *v*P is a Spell-out domain (Chomsky 2001), we predict that the external argument (e.g. transitive subject, unergative subject) cannot be separated from its associate Q by their domain-mate (e.g. object). We also predict that the internal argument (e.g. unaccusative subject, transitive object) can be separated by *v*P-internal elements from its associate Q since it may undergo *v*P-internal movement (just like C in (5)). Ko shows that Caseless N(umeral) Qs in Korean show the Edge Effects, as expected for adnominal Qs. Some examples are given in (6).

(6) a. *__Haksayngtul-i__ maykcwu-lul __sey-myeng__ masiessta
   Students-NOM beer-ACC   3-CL$_{person}$ dränk
   'Three students drank beer.' [see B in (5)]
 b. __Maykcwu-lul__ John-i __sey-pyeng__ masiessta
   Beer-ACC J-NOM   3-CL$_{bottle}$ drank
   'John drank three bottles of beer' [see D in (5)]

Ko (2005) further argues that when two elements are merged at the edge as non-constituents, they are separable by their domain-mate, in contrast to

(5). This is illustrated in (7). As shown in (7), the domain-mate C may be merged above B before A is merged (or tuck-in between A and B) within αP. Hence, A<C<B ordering is possible in split edges. As named in Ko (2005), we call this the *Split Edge Effect*.

(7) √[A ... C ... B]: *Split Edge Effect*

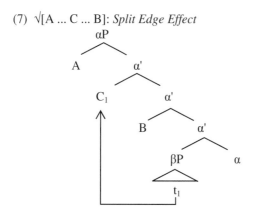

Ko (2005) argues that Case-marked Qs show Split Edge Effects described in (7) (inspired by the proposals of O'Grady 1991 and Kang 2002). Unlike Caseless NQs, the subject-oriented Case-marked Qs may be separated by *v*P-internal elements (e.g. object) from its host noun, as illustrated in (8).[2]

(8) **Haksayngtul-i**   maykcwu-lul   **sey-myeng-i**   masiessta
    Students-NOM   beer-ACC   3-CL$_{person}$-NOM drank
    'Three students drank beer.' (cf. Caseless NQ in (6a))

    Though Ko provides evidence that the predictions depicted in (5) and (7) are borne out, large-scale experimentation has not been conducted before. Furthermore, on-line processing data have not been provided in the previous studies, either. In this paper, we evaluate Ko's proposal with experimental data more thoroughly, and tie the experimental results with the general discussion of floating Qs presented in Section 1.

---

[2] In this paper, we categorize the Case-marked Q into an adverbial-type. To be precise, however, the Case-marked Qs may be a different type from adverbial Qs. As long as it is merged as a non-constituent from it host noun (e.g. secondary predicate; Miyagawa 1989), it would show the *Split Edge Effect* (7). Ko (2005) has also argued that focus-marked Qs, universal Qs, and noun-associated NPIs also show the same distribution as Case-marked Qs. For the sake of space, we limit our discussion to Case-marked Qs here. See Ko and Oh (in prep.) for further discussion.

2.2 Stimuli and Predictions

In the experiment, we examined how the three factors in (3) affect on-line and off-line judgments of floating Q constructions. The stimuli consist of 16 types of floating Qs, with 4 tokens each (64 main items). There were 16 fillers. The items were matched in word length. In this paper, we report the results, focusing on the contrast between Caseless NQs and Case-marked NQs.[3] The schema of the main item is given in (9). As depicted in (9), we tested the effects of verb types (argument structure), Q-types, and the grammatical function of the host noun in processing and judging floating Q constructions. (In (9e-h), vP-internal adverbs were used to test the ordering in intransitive verb constructions. See also Ko (2005, 2007) for the behavior of vP-external adverbs. See (10) for representative examples for each item.

(9) Stimuli Items

V ＼ Q	Transitive Verb		Intransitive Verb	
	Subject-oriented NQ	Object-oriented NQ	Unergative subject-NQ	Unaccusative subject-NQ
Caseless NQ	a. $S\text{-}O\text{-}NQ_{subj}$	c. $O\text{-}S\text{-}NQ_{obj}$	e. $S\text{-}adv\text{-}NQ_{subj}$	g. $S\text{-}adv\text{-}NQ_{subj}$
Case-marked NQ	b. $S\text{-}O\text{-}NQ_{subj}$	d. $O\text{-}S\text{-}NQ_{obj}$	f. $S\text{-}adv\text{-}NQ_{subj}$	h. $S\text{-}adv\text{-}NQ_{subj}$

(10) Sample Stimuli Items

a. $S<O<NQ_{subj}$ [transitive subject-oriented Caseless NQ] (cf. (9a))

Haksayngtul-i	kongchayk-ul	**ney-myeng**	sassta
Students-Nom	notebook-Acc	4-Cl	bought

'Four students bought a notebook'

b. $S<O<NQ_{subj}$ [transitive subject-oriented Case-marked NQ] (cf. (9b))

Haksayngtul-i	kongchayk-ul	**ney-myeng-i**	sassta
Students-Nom	notebook-Acc	4-Cl-Nom	bought

'Four students bought a notebook'

c. $O<S<NQ_{obj}$ [transitive object-oriented Caseless NQ] (cf. (9c))

Kongchayk-ul	haysayngtul-i	**han-kwen**	sassta
Notebook-Acc	students-Nom	1-Cl	bought

'Students bought one notebook'

---

[3] In the experiment, we also examined the distribution of universal Qs (e.g. *motwu* 'all') and focus-marked NQs (e.g. *two-myeng-man* 'two-Cl-only'), which are claimed to show *Split Edge Effects* by Ko (2005). The results from these items are as expected by Ko (2005) (but with some complications for universal Qs). For the sake of space, we omit the discussions on these items. See Ko and Oh (in prep.) for detailed discussion.

   d. O<S<NQ_{obj} [transitive object-oriented Case-marked NQ] (cf. (9d))

Kongchayk-ul	haysayngtul-i	**han-kwen-ul**	sassta
Notebook-Acc	students-Nom	1-Cl-Acc	bought

   'Students bought one notebook'

   e. S<Adv<NQ_{subj}[unergative subject-oriented Caseless NQ] (cf. (9e))

Haksayngtul-i	culkepkey	**ney-myeng**	wusessta
Students-Nom	happily	4-Cl	laughed

   'Four students laughed happily'

   f. S<Adv<NQ_{subj}[unergative subject-oriented Case-marked NQ] (cf. (9f))

Haksayngtul-i	culkepkey	**ney-myeng-i**	wusessta
Students-Nom	happily	4-Cl-Nom	laughed

   'Four students laughed happily'

   g. S<Adv<NQ_{subj}[unaccusative subject-oriented Caseless NQ] (cf. (9g))

Haksayngtul-i	coyonghi	**ney-myeng**	tulewassta
Students-Nom	quietly	4-Cl	came

   'Four students came in quietly'

   h. S<Adv<NQ_{subj}[unaccusative subject-oriented Case-marked NQ](cf. (9h))

Haksayngtul-i	coyonghi	**ney-myeng-i**	tulewassta
Students-Nom	quietly	4-Cl-Nom	came

   'Four students came in quietly'

Under the hybrid approach proposed by Ko (2005), we predict that only the shaded cells in (9) (*i.e.* items (9a) and (9e)) would show Edge Effects. Under the adnominal approach, differences related to argument structure and the host noun may be relevant. However, no differences between the Q-types are expected. Hence, we expect that (9a), (9b), (9e), and (9f) would show the same Edge Effect. Under the adverbial approach, we expect that the floating Q constructions listed in (9) would behave in the same way (as long as their event structure is not different from each other). The predictions of each approach are summarized in (11).

(11) *Predictions*

A. Hybrid Approach: Stimuli (9a) and (9e) will show Edge Effects. Hence, a processing delay and/or ungrammaticality is expected only for these items.

B. Adnominal Approach: Stimuli (9a), (9b), (9e), and (9f) [namely, all the transitive/unergative subject-related NQs] will show Edge Effects. Hence, processing delay and/or ungrammaticality is expected only for these items.

C. Adverbial Approach: No differences among the stimuli types in (9) are expected (unless a theory of event structure leads us to the contrary).

To test the predictions in (11), we conducted on-line processing (self-paced reading task) and off-line judgment tests (scaled judgment task) with native speakers of Korean. In section 3, we report the results.

3. Experiment

3.1 On-line Study

A time course study was conducted with 74 native speakers of Korean (male 37; female 37) to test when and where, if at all, anomaly occurs with floating Q constructions. On-line test stimuli were randomized and presented by the DMDX program (a Windows display program with millisecond accuracy: Foster and Foster 2003). After reading a stimulus, subjects were asked to answer a follow-up question about the stimulus. In our data analysis, we filtered out trials with wrong answers to check-up questions and responses that took more than 2500ms as errors. Consequently, results from 70 subjects were analyzed after filtering. We found statistically significant processing effects in verb position, but not in quantifier position. The mean Response Time (RT) on the verb position is summarized in (12). For statistical analysis, a paired-sample t-test was conducted.

(12)   Results: Processing data

	Transitive Verb		Intransitive Verb	
	Subject- NQ	Object-NQ	Unergative	Unaccusative
Caseless NQ	a. **556.17ms** S-O-NQ$_{subj}$	c. 413.97ms O-S-NQ$_{obj}$	e. **501.30 ms** S-adv-NQ	g. 461.30ms S-adv-NQ
Case-marked NQ	b. 444.54ms S-O-NQ$_{subj}$	d. 481.15ms O-S-NQ$_{obj}$	f. 437.72 ms S-adv-NQ	h. 550.79ms S-adv-NQ

Consider first the mean RT for the subject-oriented NQs in (12a) and (12b). As shown above, the mean RT for Caseless NQ constructions (12a) was much slower than the corresponding Case-marked NQs (12b). The contrast between (12a) and (12b) is significant ($p<.0001$). Consider also the contrast between the unergative NQs in (12e) and (12f). Similar to the transitive subject patterns, the mean RT for Caseless NQ constructions (12e) was much slower than the corresponding Case-marked NQs (12f) ($p=.003$). We also found a contrast due to the host noun. As shown in the contrast between (12a) and (12c), the subject-oriented NQs slowed down the processing, in comparison to the object-oriented NQs ($p<.0001$). The same type of pattern was also observed in (12e) and (12g). The unergative subject-oriented NQ slowed down the processing, in comparison to the unaccusative subject-oriented NQ ($p=.083$, approaching significance).

Turning to the object-oriented NQs in (12c) and (12d), we found a very interesting inhibition effect due to Case-marking. As demonstrated in (12c) and (12d), Caseless NQs triggered faster RTs than Case-marked NQs (p=.003). This is surprising given the exactly opposite effects of Case for the subject-oriented NQs in (12a) and (12b). The same type of inhibition effects was also observed with unaccusative subject-oriented NQs in (12g) and (12h). Caseless NQs triggered faster RTs than Case-marked NQs when the NQ is associated with the unaccusative subject (p=.002) (cf. the contrast between (12e) and (12f) with the unergative subject-oriented NQ).

Overall, the experimental results support the hypotheses of the hybrid approach (3-4). First, the experiment shows that the type of host noun matters in processing floating adnominal Qs. The transitive subject-oriented NQ triggered slower RTs than the object-oriented NQ. Second, the result also confirms the prediction that Caseless subject-oriented NQs (adnominal Qs) showed slower RTs than Case-marked Qs (adverbial Qs). Third, the result also shows that the type of argument structure matters. The unergative subject-oriented NQ triggered slower RTs than the unaccusative subject-oriented NQ. All of these effects were predicted by the hybrid approach proposed by Ko (2005, 2007). Note that the results reported here are not expected either by the adnominal approach or adverbial approach. On the adnominal approach, we would not expect differences due to Q-types, contrary to facts. On the adverbial approach, we have no principled reasons to expect differences reported here.

Very interestingly, we also found inhibition effects due to Case-marking, which has not been observed in any of the previous studies (to the best of our knowledge). When an NQ is associated with a (deep) object, the Caseless NQ is processed faster than the Case-marked NQ. Note, crucially, that in exactly those environments, we expect that there will be no Edge Effects with Caseless NQs (see (5) and (6b)) and that the sentences will be grammatical. Put differently, the result shows that when both adnominal (Caseless) Qs and adverbial (Case-marked) Qs are grammatical, adnominal Qs are processed faster than adverbial Qs. We speculate that this is due to the additional information conveyed by the Case-marker on the NQ. If Case marking carries the semantics of focus and exhaustivity, it is expected that Case-marked NQs will be processed slower than Caseless NQs (when both structures are grammatical).[4]

---

[4] As William O'Grady (p.c.) pointed it out, it would be interesting to test whether Case-marking in general (without an NQ) would trigger the same processing delay. Since Korean allows Case drop, it would be interesting to test whether Case-dropped sentences are processed faster than Case-marked ones. For clarification, when an NQ is associated with a transitive subject, Edge Effects are obtained (e.g. (12a), (12e)). The NQ is simply ungrammatical when

3.2 Off-line Study

To test how the grammaticality judgment holds at the off-line level, we also tested 64 native speakers of Korean (35 males; 29 females) with the same types of stimuli as the on-line study. The participants were asked to judge a sentence with a floating Q with respect to 3 other types of floating Q constructions (scale of 1-4). There were 24 quadruple set of sentences, and the test order was randomized. The off-line test results are summarized in (13).

(13) Results: Judgment data ["4" means absolutely grammatical]

	Transitive Verb		Intransitive Verb	
	Subject-NQ	Object-NQ	Unergative	Unaccusative
Caseless NQ	a. **1.78** S-O-NQ$_{subj}$	c. 2.91 O-S-NQ$_{obj}$	e. **2.14** S-adv-NQ	g. 2.65 S-adv-NQ
Case-marked NQ	b. 1.96 S-O-NQ$_{subj}$	d. 2.75 O-S-NQ$_{obj}$	f. 2.37 S-adv-NQ	h. 2.55 S-adv-NQ

Consider first the contrast between the subject-oriented NQs in (13a) and object-oriented NQs in (13c). The subject-oriented NQs were much less acceptable than the object-oriented NQs (p<.0001). Note also that the subject-oriented Caseless NQs in (13a) were also less acceptable than the subject-oriented Case-marked NQs in (13b) (p=.028). The same types of patterns were obtained with intransitive verbs. Unergative Caseless NQs in (13e) were significantly less acceptable than unaccusative Caseless NQs in (13g) (p<.0001), or unergative Case-marked NQs in (13f) (p<.0001).

Note also that the processing delay due to Q-types associated with object-oriented NQs disappeared in off-line judgment tests. As shown in (13c) and (13d), object-oriented Caseless and Case-marked NQs were both judged grammatical, and the difference between the two was not statistically significant (p=.269). The same results were obtained with unaccusative NQ pairs in (13g) and (13h). Unlike the on-line test, Caseless (13g) and Case-marked NQs (13h) were judged grammatical, and the difference between the two was not statistically significant (p=.146).

The results support for the hybrid approach from quantifiable off-line data. First, we obtained a significant effect of the host noun. The subject-oriented NQs were significantly less acceptable than the object-oriented NQs when separated from its host noun by a vP-domain-mate. Second, a significant effect of Q-types was also obtained. Caseless subject-oriented floating NQs (adnominal Qs) were judged significantly less acceptable than adverbial Qs (Case-marked Qs). Third, the predictions on verb types were

---

separated from its host subject by a vP-domain-mate. Hence, the processing delay due to Case-marking cannot be observed with the transitive/unergative subject-oriented NQs.

also borne out. The unergative NQs showed Edge Effects and were judged significantly less acceptable than unaccusative NQs when separated from its host by a *v*P-domain-mate. The off-line data confirm all the predictions of the hybrid approach adopted in Ko (2005, 2007). Under the hybrid approach, it is also expected that there will be no difference between adnominal and adverbial Qs when they are associated with the object. Since they are not merged on the edge of a Spell-out domain, we expect that both types of floating Q constructions would be grammatical. This is in fact what we have observed in the off-line test.

4. Conclusion

In this paper, we evaluated three major approaches to floating quantifiers, with special attention to Korean numeral quantifier constructions. We have seen significant effects of grammatical function, argument structure and Q-types in processing and judging floating quantifiers, exactly in the direction expected by the hybrid approach. We also found a previously unnoticed fact that when a sentence is grammatical, adnominal floating Qs trigger faster RTs than adverbial floating Qs in processing. The overall results provide empirical support for the *Edge Generalization* advanced in Ko (2005).

We also found an interesting asymmetry between processing and judgment data due to the host noun. The processing delay obtained with transitive/unergative subject-oriented Qs was also observed with off-line data (ungrammatical sentences with *Edge Effects*). In contrast, the inhibition effects with object-oriented Case-marked NQs in processing disappeared in the off-line test (grammatical sentences with temporary processing delay). Hence, the current results provide some challenges to the claim that the Edge Effects obtained with the subject-oriented NQs reflect processing difficulty, but not grammaticality (cf. Miyagawa and Arikawa 2007).

At the same time, the results reported in this paper challenge the "across-the-board" adnominal or adverbial approaches, which do not predict such intricate interactions among syntactic factors in processing and judging floating Q constructions. Korean speakers find both processing difficulty and ungrammaticality where we expect Edge Effects under the hybrid approach. Under the adnominal approach, we expect that there would be no differences associated with Q-types. Hence, the differences attributed to Q-types cannot be explained. This result also poses serious challenges to the adverbial approach since there is no obvious reason why the NQ_{subj} and unergative NQ_{subj} are not qualified as an event modifier.

Turning to a more general issue, our study supports the claim that experimental syntax not only provides a large-scale empirical data but also provide a useful probe into theoretical concern. A controlled experiment helps us to sort out various factors that underlie one phenomenon. Statistical analysis helps us to investigate subtle distinctions. In our case, by conducting a structured experimentation, we were able to evaluate various predictions by competing theories on floating Q constructions. Through experimentation, we may also uncover new patterns which lead to new theoretical questions. Our results suggest that the role of particles attached to a numeral quantifier is a new area of research in processing. In the offline-tests, more studies are needed on discourse effects such as distributivity and exhaustivity in licensing floating Qs. We hope that the current study provides a useful background to deepen our understanding of the processing and grammar of floating quantifier constructions.

Acknowledgement

We thank the participants of our experiments (138 undergraduate and graduate students at Korea University). Thanks also to Mun Hyong Kim, Sunju Kim, and Daeyoung Sohn for their help with data collection and analysis. We are also grateful to the audiences of SICOGG-10 and JK 19, especially Kamil Ud Deen, Marcel den Dikken, and William O'Grady for their helpful questions and comments. All errors are of our own, of course.

References

Bobaljik, J. D. 1995. Morphosyntax: The Syntax of Verbal Inflection. Doctoral dissertation, MIT, Cambridge, Mass.

Bobaljik, J. D. 2003. Floating Quantifiers: Handle with Care, in *The Second GLOT International State-of-the-Article Book: The Latest in Linguistics*, eds. by Lisa Cheng and Rint Sybesma, 107-148. Berlin: Mouton de Gruyter.

Bošković, Ž. 2004. Be Careful Where You Float Your Quantifiers. *Natural Language and Linguistic Theory* 22(4): 681-742.

Brisson, C. 1998. Distributivity, Maximality, and Floating Quantifiers. Doctoral dissertation, Rutgers University, New Brunswick, N.J.

Chomsky, N. 2001. Derivation by Phase. In *Ken Hale: A Life in Language*, ed. by Michael Kenstowicz, 1-52. Cambridge, Mass.: MIT Press.

Dowty, D. and Brody, B. 1984. A Semantic Analysis of "Floated" Quantifiers in a Transformationless Grammar'. In *Proceedings of WCCFL 3*, 75-90. Stanford University, Stanford, Calif.

Fitzpatrick, J. 2006. The Syntactic and Semantic Roots of Floating Quantification. Doctoral dissertation, MIT, Cambridge, Mass.

Foster, K. I. and Foster, J. C. 2003. DMDX: A Window Display Program with Millisecond Accuracy. *Behavior Research Methods, Instruments and Computers* 35: 116-124

Fox, D. and Pesetsky, D. 2005. Cyclic Linearization of Syntactic Structure. In Object shift, ed. Katalin É. Kiss, special issue, *Theoretical Linguistics*, 31(1-2): 1-46.

Fukushima, K. 1991. Phrase Structure Grammar, Montague Semantics and Floating Quantifiers in Japanese. *Linguistics and Philosophy* 14: 581-628.

Hoji, H. and Ishii, Y. 2005. What Gets Mapped to the Tripartite Structure of Quantification in Japanese. In *Proceedings of WCCFL 23*, 346-359. Somerville, Mass.: Cascadilla Press.

Ishii, Y. 1998. Floating Quantifiers in Japanese: NP Quantifiers, VP Quantifiers, or Both?. Researching and Verifying on Advanced Theory of Human Language, Grant-in-Aid for COE Research Report 2 (No. 08CE1001): 149-171. Kand, Japan: Graduate School of Language Sciences Kanda University of International Studies.

Kang, B.-M. 2002. Categories and Meanings of Korean Floating Quantifiers – with some References to Japanese. *Journal of East Asian Linguistics* 11: 375-398.

Kayne, R. 1975. *French Syntax: The Transformational Cycle*. Cambridge, Mass.: MIT Press.

Kim, J.-b. and Yang, J. 2006. Processing Korean Numeral Classifier Constructions in a Typed Feature Structure Grammar. Ms. Kyung Hee University, Kangnam University, Korea.

Ko, H. 2005. Syntactic Edges and Linearization. Doctoral dissertation, MIT, Cambridge, Mass.

Ko, H. 2007. Asymmetries in Scrambling and Cyclic Linearization. *Linguistic Inquiry* 38: 29-83.

Kuroda, S.-Y. 1983. What can Japanese Say about Government and Binding?. In *Proceedings of WCCFL 2*, ed. Michael Barlow, Daniel P. Flickinger, and Michael T. Westcoat, 153-164. Stanford Linguistics Association, Stanford University, Stanford, Calif.

Merchant, J. 1996. Scrambling and Quantifier Float in German. In *Proceedings of NELS 26*, ed. by Kiyomi Kusumoto, 179-193. Amherst: University of Massachusetts, GLSA.

Miyagawa, S. 1989. *Structure and Case Marking in Japanese: Syntax and Semantics 22*. San Diego, Calif.: Academic Press.

Miyagawa, S. and Arikawa, K. 2007. Locality in Syntax and Floating Numeral Quantifiers. *Linguistic Inquiry* 38:645-670.

Nakanishi, K. 2003. The Semantics of Measure Phrases. In *Proceedings of NELS 33*, ed. by Makoto Kadowaki and Shigeto Kawahara, 225-244, Amherst: University of Massachusetts, GLSA.

O'Grady, W. 1991. *Categories and Case: The Sentence Structure of Korean.* Amsterdam/Philadelphia: John Benjamins Publishing Company.

Shlonsky, U. 1991. Quantifiers as Functional Heads: A Study of Quantifier Float in Hebrew. *Lingua* 84: 159-180.

Sportiche, D. 1988. A Theory of Floating Quantifiers and its Corollaries for Constituent Structure. *Linguistic Inquiry* 19: 425-449.

Ueda, M. 1990. Japanese phrase structure and parameter setting. Doctoral dissertation, University of Massachusetts, Amherst.

The Nominative/Genitive Alternation in Modern Japanese: A Visual Analogue Scale (VAS) Evaluation Method-Based Analysis*

HIDEKI MAKI
Gifu University

YIN-JI JIN
Gifu University

SATORU YOKOYAMA
Tohoku University

MICHIYO HAMASAKI
Aichi University of Education

YUKIKO UEDA
Akita University

1. Introduction

The objective of the present study is to examine whether the hypothesis proposed by Miyagawa (to appear) will be correct in terms of the nominative/genitive alternation in modern Japanese (Japanese, hereafter) by using a Visual Analogue Scale (VAS) evaluation method.

Miyagawa (1993) proposed a hypothesis of genitive case licensing in Japanese on the basis of earlier works by Harada (1971) and Nakai (1980), among others. His main claim was that genitive subject was licensed by D/N. At that time, Miyagawa did not take into consideration the nature of the predicates that co-occur with a genitive subject. Therefore, genitive subject may appear with any type of predicate in the relative clause, and within the relative clause, it may freely alternate with nominative subject. Miyagawa

* An earlier version of this paper was presented at the 19th Japanese/Korean Linguistics Conference held at the University of Hawai'i at Mānoa on November 12, 2009. We would like to thank the audience at the conference and Jessica Dunton for their valuable comments. All errors are our own.

Japanese/Korean Linguistics 19.
Edited by Ho-min Sohn, Haruko Cook, William O'Grady, Leon A. Serafim, & Sang Yee Cheon.
Copyright © 2011, CSLI Publications

(to appear) refines his 1993 hypothesis, and claims that genitive subject licensing is affected by the nature of the predicates that co-occur with a genitive subject. His main claim is that genitive subject may co-occur with stative predicates, but may not co-occur with eventive predicates.

However, since the data used in Miyagawa (to appear) was collected by intuitive judgments from a small number of informants including the author, it will be desirable if it is confirmed that these data are generally acceptable to other Japanese native speakers as well. Therefore, in order to examine whether his hypothesis will be correct or not, in this study, we collected a large number of data from Japanese native speakers, and analyzed it by using the Visual Analogue Scaling (VAS) evaluation method.

The organization of this paper is as follows. Section 2 reviews Miyagawa (1993) and Miyagawa (to appear) as the background to the subsequent sections. Section 3 presents the methodology of this study, and Section 4 analyzes the data. Section 5 discusses what the results of the analysis suggest and point out remaining issues. Finally, Section 6 concludes this paper.

2. Background: Miyagawa (1993) and Miyagawa (to appear)

2.1 Miyagawa (1993)

Maki and Uchibori (2008) provide a concise summary of Miyagawa (1993), which is given below. Miyagawa (1993) proposes the two hypotheses in (1).

(1) a. The genitive subject in a prenominal gapless clause raises into Spec,DP.
  b. This movement takes place in LF.

The first hypothesis (1a) is motivated by scope interactions between the nominative/genitive subject and the head noun. The example in (2a), which has a nominative subject, only has the reading in which the head noun *kanoosee* 'probability' takes scope over the nominative subject *rubii-ka sinzyu* 'ruby or pearl.' Maki and Uchibori (2008) call this reading the "in-situ" reading. The example in (1b), which has a genitive subject, allows an additional reading in which the subject takes scope over the head noun *kanoosee* 'probability.' They call this reading the "raising" reading.

(2) a. [[[Rubii-ka sinzyu]-ga yasuku-naru] kanoosee]-ga   50% izyoo
    ruby-or pearl-NOM cheap-become probability-NOM 50% over da.
    i. 'The probability that rubies or pearls become cheap is over 50%.'
    ii. *'The probability that rubies become cheap or the probability that pearls become cheap is over 50%.'
      probability>[ruby or pearl]; *[ruby or pearl]>probability

b. [[[Rubii-ka sinzyu]-no yasuku-naru] kanoosee]-ga 50% izyoo
ruby-or pearl-GEN cheap-become probability-NOM 50% over da.

    i.   'The probability that rubies or pearls become cheap is over 50%.'
    ii. 'The probability that rubies become cheap or the probability that pearls become cheap is over 50%.'
    probability>[ruby or pearl]; [ruby or pearl]>probability

Miyagawa (1993) points out that (2a) is unambiguous because the nominative subject does not raise out of the prenominal sentential modifier and is c-commanded by the head noun, as schematically shown in (3).

(3) [$_{DP}$ [$_{NP}$ [$_{IP}$ [ruby or pearl]-NOM predicate] N] D]

However, (2b) allows scope ambiguity because the genitive subject raises into Spec,DP at some point in the derivation and c-commands the head noun, as schematically shown in (4).

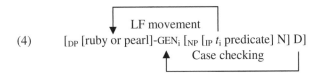

(4)   [$_{DP}$ [ruby or pearl]-GEN$_i$ [$_{NP}$ [$_{IP}$ t_i predicate] N] D]

The second hypothesis is motivated by Nakai's (1980) observation that the genitive subject may be preceded by other elements in the prenominal sentential modifier, as shown in (5).

(5) [kotosi sinzyu-no yasuku-naru] kanoosee
    this year pearl-GEN cheap-become probability
    'the probability that pearls become cheap this year'

In (5), the adverb *kotosi* 'this year' is at the left edge of the sentential modifier, preceding the genitive subject *sinzyu* 'pearl.' Therefore, the genitive subject cannot be in Spec,DP in overt syntax. This led Miyagawa to conclude that the genitive subject raises out of the sentential gapless clause into Spec, DP at LF.

Thus, Miyagawa (1993) proposed a D-licensing analysis of a genitive subject in Japanese. The claim that D licenses a genitive subject applies to a genitive subject in a relative clause as well as to a prenominal gapless clause.

2.2 Miyagawa (to appear)

In the mechanisms proposed in Miyagawa (1993), a genitive subject may appear in a relative clause, irrespective of what type of predicate the clause with the genitive subject may contain. However, Miyagawa (to appear) refines his 1993 hypothesis, based on the observation that predicates such as *tuita* 'attached/had' have two readings, that is, eventive and stative, but the stative reading disappears with a genitive subject, when the relative clause contains an adverb that emphasizes the event, as shown in (6).

(6) [Totsuzen shimi-ga/*-no tsuita   shatsu]-o misete kudasai.
     suddenly stain-NOM/-GEN attached/had shirt-Acc show please
     'Please show me the shirt that was suddenly stained.'

Based on this, Miyagawa (to appear) claims that genitive subject licensing is affected by the nature of the predicates that co-occur with a genitive subject. His main claim is that a genitive subject is licensed by D, as in Miyagawa (1993), and it may co-occur with stative predicates, but may not co-occur with eventive predicates. Pushing this claim further, Miyagawa (to appear) argues that the size of the clause where a genitive subject may appear is "smaller" than that of the clause where a nominative subject may appear. To be precise, he argues that the clause with a genitive subject is a TP with a defective T, which does not assign nominative Case, and the clause with a nominative subject is a CP, where T assigns nominative Case.

3. Methodology

In order to test Miyagawa's (to appear) hypothesis precisely, the present study used the Visual Analogue Scale (VAS) Evaluation Method. According to Gould et al (2001), VAS is defined as in (7).

(7) *Visual Analogue Scale* (VAS) (Gould et al. 2001: 706, slightly edited)
     A VAS is a measurement instrument that tries to measure a characteristic or attitude that is believed to range across a continuum of values and cannot be directly measured. Operationally, a VAS is usually a horizontal line, 100 mm in length, anchored by word descriptions at each end, as illustrated in Fig 1. When responding to a VAS item, respondents specify their level of agreement to a statement by indicating a position along a continuous line between the two end-points. The VAS score is determined by measuring in millimeters from the left hand end of the line to the point that the respondent marks.

How severe is your pain today? Place a vertical mark [\]on the line below to indicate how bad you feel your pain is today.

No pain |_____| Very severe pain

Figure 1: Effects of the interpersonal, technical and communication skills of the nurse on the effectiveness of treatment

> "From the patient's perspective, this spectrum appears continuous - their pain does not take discrete jumps, as a characterization of none, mild, moderate and severe would suggest." (Gould et al (2001: 706))

We used the VAS because the subjects taking part in this survey would have the same perspective as the above mentioned patient in the sense that their grammaticality judgment does not take discrete jumps, as a characterization of the 5-point scale such as (8) would suggest.

(8)   Totally ungrammatical (1) < ... (2) < ... (3) < ... (4) < ... Completely grammatical (5)

Actually, it is hard to choose labels for (2), (3), and (4). In order to avoid this problem, we used the VAS method, and used the scale in Fig. 2. after showing one example of a totally unnatural sentence and another example of a completely natural sentence.

How would you judge the naturalness of the sentence as Japanese? Place a vertical mark [\] on the line below to indicate how natural you feel the sentence is.

Totally unnatural |_____| Completely natural
as Japanese   as Japanese

Figure 2: The scale used in this study

As for the materials, the data set consisted of the three types of predicates in (9).

(9)   a.   Type 1:   verbs with a stative reading
       b.   Type 2:   adjectives with a stative reading
       c.   Type 3:   verbs with an eventive reading

(9b) was included in the questionnaire, because adjectives are stative in nature, so that it would be guaranteed that the verbs with a stative reading in (1) are really stative in nature by a comparison between the two types of predicates. Also, the predicates are consistently in the past tense in order to control any effect caused by a difference in tense.

Furthermore, in order ensure that the subject is really within the relative clause, we used the structure in (10) for all the target sentences, where the subject is preceded by an adverb.

(10) [Adverb Subject-NOM/-GEN Predicate(Past)] N-TOP *this* N be.

The typical example with structure (10) is something like (11) in English.

(11) The book [that John read yesterday] is this book.

Also, in (10), the head noun preceded by the materials in the parentheses is followed by the topic marker, which excludes the possibility of allowing the subject within the parentheses to be marked with another topic marker, and also ensures that the most natural case marker to be assigned to the subject in the parentheses is either nominative (with the meaning of neutral description in the sense of Kuno 1973) or genitive.

We used 60 target sentences in total, and 10 predicates were used for each of Types 1, 2, and 3, with two types of case markers in (9). We also included 15 benchmark sentences, all of which had been judged as totally unnatural as Japanese with the VAS method by 6 native speakers of Japanese in advance. Three examples of the target sentences are illustrated in (12a-c), where the predicate types are (9a), (9b), and (9c), respectively.[1]

(12) a. [Sukkari   kizu-ga/-no   naotta neko]-wa kono neko desu.
         completely injury-NOM/-GEN cured cat-TOP this cat   be
         'The cat that was completely cured of the injury is this cat.'

     b. [Totemo raamen-ga/-no   oishikatta mise]-wa   kono
         very   noodle-NOM/-GEN delicious restaurant-TOP this
         mise   desu.
         restaurant be
         'The restaurant where noodles were very delicious was this restaurant.'

     c. [Yonaka-ni Yuuta-ga/-no   sakenda riyuu]-wa kono riyuu
         midnight-at Yuuta-NOM/-GEN screamed reason-TOP this   reason
         desu.
         be
         'The reason why Yuta screamed at midnight was this reason.'

---

[1] The actual test sentences and benchmark sentences do not contain parentheses.

Also, three examples of the benchmark sentences are illustrated in (13).

(13) a.   [Sukoshimo fuku-ga   yabureta ningyoo]-wa kono ningyoo desu.
        little   cloth-NOM torn   doll-TOP   this doll   be
        'The doll whose cloth is torn at all is this doll.'

    b.   [Saraishuu   hige-ga   mijika-katta neko]-wa kono
        two weeks from now whisker-NOM short-PAST cat-TOP   this
        neko desu.
        cat   be
        'The cat whose whisker was short two weeks from now is this cat.'

    c.   [Shiasatte   Natsuko-ga   katta   terebi]-wa kono
        the day after tomorrow   -NOM bought TV-TOP   this
        terebi desu.
        TV   be
        'The TV which Natsuko bought the day after tomorrow is this TV.'

A counterbalanced design was used in order to prevent the problem of the participants' repeatedly encountering the stimuli with the same patterns. For this purpose, we made 8 different questionnaires, each of which contained 30 target sentences and 15 benchmark sentences.

We administered the survey from April to June of 2009. We provided the questionnaires to 264 native speakers of Japanese (97 males and 167 females with the age range from 18 to 29), who were undergraduate students studying at Japanese universities. Out of the 264 subjects, we abstracted 100 subjects (37 males and 63 females with the age range from 18 to 21), all of whom marked a vertical line on the 0 cm point of the scale on each of the 15 benchmark sentences, which indicates that these 100 subjects did not randomly put vertical lines on the scales for the sentences, and they were completely consistent in terms of their judgments of the naturalness of the given sentences.

We then conducted a 3x2 ANOVA (Predicate Type x Case Type) on the scores measured by the VAS. To summarize, the methodology used in this study is as follows.

(14) a.   A total of 100 university undergraduate students participated in this study.

    b.   The structure in (10) was used for all the target sentences (60 in total) in the questionnaires.

    c.   A counterbalanced design was used.

    d.   The VAS evaluation method was used.

    e.   An ANOVA was conducted on the scores measured by the VAS.

Before going to the analysis of the data, we would like to mention one important thing about dealing with data. It has been a common practice in generative grammar to judge the grammaticality of the given sentence based on the contrast in grammaticality with the minimal pair counterpart. For instance, we cannot simply judge the grammaticality of examples such as (15).

(15) She came.

Apparently, (15) is a perfect English sentence. However, this does not mean anything in terms of theory construction in generative grammar. The status of (15) is determined by a comparison with a minimal pair counterpart such as (16).

(16) Her came.

One finds a clear contrast in grammaticality between (15) and (16), and we say that there is a contrast between (15) and (16), which clearly suggests that there is no absolute grammaticality for a given sentence. The grammaticality status of the sentences is only determined by a comparison with its minimal pair counterpart.

However, a questionnaire-based study such as the present one forces the subject to determine the absolute value or absolute naturalness of the given sentence in terms of the length of the scale, and in this sense, this is not consistent with the common practice of generative grammar.

Nonetheless, there is a point which generative grammarians, including ourselves, should keep in mind and carefully deal with. There are some minimal pairs which are difficult to judge. The extent to which some would say that there is a contrast in the pair may vary, and some may even feel there is not a contrast at all. One individual could claim that there is a contrast in the given minimal pair for her/him, and based on this, she/he could posit a hypothesis or even construct a theory, while other people say something else based on a different grammaticality judgment of the same minimal pair. In such a case, a questionnaire-based study should come into play, as this will be the last resort to determine whether there is a contrast in the pair. Of course, as stated above, this method forces the subject to determine the absolute value of the given sentence. However, it can collect a large number of data from the target population, and it is possible to show a rough tendency concerning the naturalness of the given sentence.

We regard Japanese nominative/genitive subject examples as those which fall under the category mentioned above, and we assume that it will be necessary to make a generalization based on this method for this phenomenon to make a crucial contribution to theory construction in generative grammar. It will also be desirable if the result obtained from a questionnaire-based study matched the one obtained from the study based on the common practice of generative grammar, because this would make the generalization solid.

Finally, we used data only from participants who signed the consent form for this study, and agreed to our intention regarding this project. With this much in mind, let us analyze the data in the next section.

4. Analysis

As stated in Section 1, Miyagawa (to appear) claims that genitive subject may co-occur with stative predicates, but may not co-occur with eventive predicates. Therefore, our predictions are summarized in (17).

(17) Predictions

a.   There will be no statistically significant difference in naturalness between sentences with the nominative case marker and sentences with the genitive case marker with Type 1 predicates, that is, verbs with a stative reading.

b.   There will be no statistically significant difference in naturalness between sentences with the nominative case marker and sentences with the genitive case marker with Type 2 predicates, that is, adjectives with a stative reading.

c.   There will be a statistically significant difference in naturalness between sentences with the nominative case marker and sentences with the genitive case marker with Type 3 predicates, that is, verbs with an eventive reading.

The basic statistics for the data obtained are shown in Table 1.

Table 1.The basic statistics for the data

Predicate Type	Case Type	Count	Average in millimeters (STD)
1. Stative Verb	Nom	100	83.88 (22.81)
	Gen	100	84.68 (21.79)
2. Adjective	Nom	100	80.11 (22.50)
	Gen	100	79.73 (22.90)
3. Eventive Verb	Nom	100	94.91 (23.95)
	Gen	100	82.79 (21.93)

The results of the analyses are as follows. First, we conducted a two-factor ANOVA (3x2), and found a statistically significant main effect for each of the two factors, Predicate Type (Types 1, 2, and 3 (Stative Verb, Adjective, and Eventive Verb)) and Case Type (Types 1 and 2 (Nom and Gen)), that is, a statistically significant difference among the three levels within factor Predicate Type ($F(2,99)=7.76$, p=0.00) and between the two levels within factor Case Type ($F(1,99)=4.43$, p=0.04), and we also found a statistically significant interaction between the two factors ($F(2,99)=4.97$, p<0.01). We then conducted multiple comparisons (Bonferroni), and found statistically significant differences in the pairs shown in (18).

(18) a.   at the level of **eventive verb**:
        the pair between the cluster of **nominative case** and the cluster of **genitive case**
    b.   at the level of **nominative case**:
        i.   the pair between the cluster of **eventive verb** and the cluster of **stative verb**, and
        ii.   the pair between the cluster of **eventive verb** and the cluster of **adjective**

The results of the analyses are shown in Tables 2 and 3.

Table 2. The differences in case types at the level of predicate types

Predicate Type	Case Type 1	Case Type 2	Difference
	Type 1 (Nom)	Type 2 (Gen)	
Type 1 (S.V.)	Type 1 (Nom)	Type 2 (Gen)	-.80
Type 2 (A.)	Type 1 (Nom)	Type 2 (Gen)	.38
Type 3 (E.V.)	Type 1 (Nom)	Type 2 (Gen)	12.12*

(*statistical significance threshold, $p < .05$, by Bonferroni correction)

Table 3. The differences in predicate types at the level of case types

Case Type	Predicate Type 1	Predicate Type 2	Difference
Type 1 (Nom)	Type 1 (S.V.)	Type 2 (A.)	3.77
		Type 3 (E.V.)	-11.03*
	Type 2 (A.)	Type 3 (E.V.)	-14.80*
Type 2 (Gen)	Type 1 (S.V.)	Type 2 (A.)	4.95
		Type 3 (E.V.)	1.89
	Type 2 (A.)	Type 3 (E.V.)	-3.06

(*statistical significance threshold, $p < .05$, by Bonferroni correction)

In the next section, we will discuss what these results suggest.

5. Discussion

Let us start with the finding in (18a) and the related findings in terms of the predictions in (17). The findings are shown in (19).

(19) Findings
    a.   There was no statistically significant difference in naturalness between the sentences with the nominative case marker and the

sentences with the genitive case marker with Type 1 predicates, that is, verbs with a stative reading, as PREDICTED.

b. There was no statistically significant difference in naturalness between the sentences with the nominative case marker and the sentences with the genitive case marker with Type 2 predicates, that is, adjectives with a stative reading, as PREDICTED.

c. There **WAS** a statistically significant difference in naturalness between the sentences with the nominative case marker and the sentences with the genitive case marker with Type 3 predicates, that is, verbs with an eventive reading, as PREDICTED.

These results strongly suggest that Miyagawa's (to appear) hypothesis was correct, and genitive subjects are allowed with stative predicates, whether they are verbs or adjectives.

Let us then turn to the finding in (18b) and the related findings summarized in (20).

(20) Findings

a. At the level of **nominative case**:

    i. there **WAS** a statistically significant difference in naturalness between sentences with **eventive verbs** and sentence with **stative verbs**.

    ii. there **WAS** a statistically significant difference in naturalness between sentences with **eventive verbs** and sentences with **adjectives**.

    iii. there was no statistically significant difference in naturalness between sentences with **stative verbs** and sentences with **adjectives**.

b. At the level of **genitive case**:

there was no statistically significant difference in naturalness among the sentences with **eventive verbs**, those with **stative verbs**, and those with **adjectives**.

Let us now consider what (20a) may suggest. We started this survey with an emphasis on the occurrence of genitive case rather than the occurrence of nominative case, and assumed that nominative case would be consistently rated more or less the same among the structures with the three predicate types. However, contrary to our expectation, (20a) shows that there is a clear distinction in judgments between the nominative case of eventive verbs and that of stative predicates (verbs and adjectives). This distinction seems to suggest that there should be two types of **nominative case**, one which goes with eventive predicates, and another with stative predicates, in Japanese. This finding is important, since it raises an interesting question as to where the two subject positions are placed in the clausal structure of Japanese under the Internal Subject Hypothesis (ISH) advocated by Fukui (1986), Kitagawa (1986), Kuroda (1988), and Diesing (1992), among others, under the traditional version of which Japanese subjects are VP/*v*P internal (probably throughout the derivation).

Of course, there remains a mystery as to the difference in naturalness between the eventive sentences with the nominative case marker and the stative sentences with the nominative case marker, because if there were really two types of nominative case as linguistic entities, one may expect that the naturalness of these two could be identical. At the present stage of our understanding, we cannot provide any adequate explanation for this issue, but we suggest one possible way to deal with it.

All of the examples used in this study have an adverb in sentence-initial position. In order to make the test sentences with the nominative case marker perfectly natural as Japanese, we put a time adverbial in the sentences with an eventive predicate, and a degree adverbial in the sentences with a stative predicate. Consider the examples in (12) again, reproduced as (21).

(21) a.   [Sukkari   kizu-ga/-no   naotta neko]-wa kono neko desu.
          completely injury-NOM/-GEN cured cat-TOP   this   cat   be
          'The cat that was completely cured of the injury is this cat.'

    b.   [Totemo raamen-ga/-no   oishikatta mise]-wa   kono
          very   noodle-NOM/-GEN delicious restaurant-TOP this
          mise   desu.
          restaurant be
          'The restaurant where noodles were very delicious was this restaurant.'

    c.   [Yonaka-ni Yuuta-ga/-no   sakenda riyuu]-wa   kono riyuu
          midnight-at Yuuta-NOM/-GEN screamed reason-TOP this   reason
          desu.
          be
          'The reason why Yuta screamed at midnight was this reason.'

Note here that in the most strict sense of the term "minimal pair," (21a, b) and (21c) do not genuinely constitute a minimal pair, because the type of adverbs used in the sentences was different. It may be the case that the position of the degree adverbials in (21a, b) affected the naturalness of the sentences, probably because they may have a specific position in the clause. Further research is required in order to see if such an adverb position effect does exist in sentences with stative predicates.

The finding in (20b), reproduced as (22), also poses an interesting issue for the naturalness of genitive case.

(22) At the level of **genitive case**:
there was **NO** statistically significant difference in naturalness among the sentences with **eventive verbs**, those with **stative verbs**, and those with **adjectives**.

Miyagawa's (to appear) main claim was that a genitive subject may co-occur with stative predicates, but may not co-occur with eventive predicates. Therefore, along with the predictions in (17), which were all shown to be correct, one could have had another prediction in (23).

(23) Another Prediction:
There will be a statistically significant difference in naturalness between genitive subject sentences with stative predicates (Type 1 and 2 predicates) and genitive subject sentences with eventive predicates (Type 3 predicates).

The result of the analysis was (22), and thus the prediction in (23) apparently turned out to be incorrect.

However, again, in the most strict sense of the term "minimal pair," (21a, b) and (21c) do not genuinely constitute a minimal pair, because the type of adverbs used in sentences was different, and the adverb position effect suggested above may be at work in (22). At the case type level, no matter which type of predicate is used, the subject, whether it is nominative or genitive, is preceded by an adverb, so that adverb position effect is not expected. On the other hand, at the predicate type level, the adverb position effect observed with the stative predicates (stative verbs and adjectives) with the nominative case marker, might arise for the sentences with stative predicates with genitive case marker as well, so that the scores on these sentences might have been restrained and lowered, no matter which case marker the subject had. Without the adverb position effect, we might have had the hypothetical basic statistics represented in Table 4, where the scores on the predicate types 1 and 2 are shifted higher.

Table 4. The hypothetical basic statistics for the data

Predicate Type	Case Type	Average in millimeters
1. Stative Verb	Nom	90.00
	Gen	90.00
2. Adjective	Nom	90.00
	Gen	90.00
3. Eventive Verb	Nom	90.00
	Gen	80.00

Note, however, that it will be extremely difficult to control for an adverb position effect for sentences with stative predicates (stative verbs and adjectives), because in order to ensure that the subject is within the relative clause, some other element, such as an adverb, must be placed in the sentence initial position, which will not be likely to be the canonical position of the element. We will therefore leave this important issue for future research.

6. Conclusion

In this paper, we examined Miyagawa's (to appear) hypothesis by using the VAS evaluation method, and confirmed that it was essentially correct. We also found that there seemed to be two types of nominative case in Japanese. The latter finding needs further confirmation by further investigation controlling for the adverb position effect for in sentences with stative predicates.

References

Diesing, M. 1992. *Indefinites*. Cambridge, MA.: MIT Press.

Fukui, N. 1986. A Theory Category Projection and Its Application. Doctoral dissertation, MIT.

Gould, D., Kelly, D., Goldstone, L., and Gammon, J. 2001. Examining the Validity of Pressure Ulcer Risk Assessment Scales: Developing and Using Illustrated Patient Simulations to Collect the Data. *Journal of Clinical Nursing* 10: 697–706.

Harada, S.-I. 1971. Ga-No Conversion and Idiolectal Variations in Japanese. *Gengo Kenkyu* 60: 25–38.

Kitagawa, Y. 1986. *Subjects in Japanese and English*. Doctoral dissertation, University of Massachusetts, Amherst.

Kuno, S. 1973. *The Structure of the Japanese Language*. Cambridge, MA.: MIT Press.

Kuroda, S.-Y. 1988. Whether We Agree or Not: A Comparative Syntax of English and Japanese. *Linguisticae Investigationes* 12: 1–47.

Maki, H. and Uchibori, A. 2008. *Ga/No* Conversion. *Handbook of Japanese Linguistics*, ed. S. Miyagawa and M. Saito, 192–216, Oxford: Oxford University Press.

Miyagawa, S. 1993. Case-Checking and Minimal Link Condition. *MIT Working Paper in Linguistics 19: Papers on Case and Agreement II*, ed. C. Phillips, 213–254, Cambridge, MA.: MIT Working Papers in Linguistics.

Miyagawa, S. To appear. Genitive Subjects in Altaic and Specification of Phase. *A Special Lingua Volume* ed. J. Kornfilt and J. Whitman.

Nakai, S. 1980. A Reconsideration of *Ga-No* Conversion in Japanese. *Papers in Linguistics* 13: 279–320.

On the Morphosyntactic Transparency of *(S)ase* and GETP*

TAKASHI NAKAJIMA
Toyama Prefectural University

This paper proposes a novel approach that uniformly accounts for the in-choative–causative alternations and causative formation in Japanese. The crucial idea lies in the realization that /a/, /s/ and /e/ that compose so-called causative morpheme *(s)ase* are not members of the same morpheme: i.e. they are heads with their own morphosyntactic and semantic import. I will show that /a/ is basically the equivalent of the verb *be* and is the morphological realization of 'little' v (Marantz 1997) that determines the grammatical category of roots (√ROOT) as V. /s/ is the causativizing morpheme that appears as the head of *v*. Its main function is to provide a spec position to a head that lacks it. /e/ is equivalent to the grammaticalized verb *e-ru* 'get' and optionally projects GETP on top of *v*P. By so doing, it plays two important functions: first, it licenses a beneficiary subject in its spec position that establishes various relations with the event embodied in the lower *v*P,

---

* I am deeply indebted to the comments and suggestions I received from the following people: Chung-hye Han, Yoshiharu Kitagawa, J. Marshall Unger, Alexander Vovin, Ichiro Yuhara, John Whitman and the audience of the 19th JK Linguistics Conference. Remaining errors and short-comings belong to me.

Japanese/Korean Linguistics 19.
Edited by Ho-min Sohn, Haruko Cook, William O'Grady, Leon A. Serafim, & Sang Yee Cheon.
Copyright © 2011, CSLI Publications

and second, it may alter the properties of *v*P. This approach for the first time uniformly relates the intuitively clear relationships between morphological inchoative–causative alternations and the causative construction.

1. Problems with Past Analyses

It has been assumed that the inchoative–causative alternations (ICA) in Japanese verbal morphology are related to the formation of the causative construction (CC). These two phenomena have been investigated extensively in separation or in conjunction with various theoretical perspectives.[1]

Despite the effort, however, the nature of ICA and the relationships it has with CC have remained for the most part unclear. One of the main reasons for this, as Teramura (1982: 306) put it, is that the isolated morphophonemes of ICA and CC inevitably resemble one another no matter whose analysis one takes, since linguists rely on the same surface verbal morphology. As a consequence, the main focus has been on how to implement such morphemes under a particular theoretical framework they happened to employ. The burden of proof was shifted elsewhere from lexical semantics to mapping rules between LCS and syntax and to syntactic apparatus. Thus, there are just as many explanations as the number of theories that are currently available, and it is difficult to give fair evaluations as to which one reveals the true nature of ICA and CC.[2]

Another problem is that the relations between so-called causative morpheme *(s)ase* and the ICA morphemes have not been investigated in detail in spite of the fact that *(s)ase* contains *as* and *e*, which play crucial roles in ICA (Jacobsen 1992). This is so because since Kuroda's (1965) seminal work, the causative morpheme has been thought to be *(s)ase,* monomorphemic and opaque to further decomposition. However, the fact that *(s)ase* shares *as* and *e* with ICA is highly suggestive: it may be that as long as we take *(s)ase* as a single causative morpheme, the morphosyntactic relevance between ICA and CC may never be captured. I argue here that this is exactly what went wrong with the past analyses.

In this work, I argue that *(s)ase* is not morphologically opaque but is composed of three parts, /a/, /s/ and /e/. Each one of them is a head and predicate of its own subject in the spec position. The relations of these sub-

---

[1] The number of works on this issue is too large to cover comprehensively. See, for example, Motoori Haruniwa (1806), Okutsu (1995), Teramura (1982), Jacobsen (1992), Kageyama (1993, 2000) and many others on approaches from morphology. For the Generative approaches, see Kuroda (1965, 1993, 2002), Shibatani (1976), Kuno (1973), Inoue (1976), Miyagawa (1989), Saito and Hoshi (2000), Pylkkänen (2008) to name just a few. As for non-Generative perspectives, see, for example, Matsumoto (1996) for LFG, Manning, Sag and Iida (1999) for GPSG and Yuhara (this volume) for Autolexical Syntax.
[2] See Kuroda (2002: 472) for a similar view.

jects and the properties of roots compositionally derive the complex syntax and semantics of ICA and CC in a systematic fashion.

2. Three Steps to Sort Things Out

To pursue a decompositional account of morphosyntax on ICA and CC, I follow the general architecture of the Minimalist Program (Chomsky 1995, 2007). In particular, two theories are crucial; one is Distributed Morphology developed by Marantz (1984, 1997) and Marantz and Noyer (2008), and the other is the Root Hypothesis (Pesetsky 1997, Ramchand 2003). In addition, I assume that the following syntactic template compositionally embodies events.

(1)

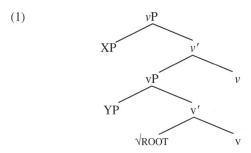

v is the 'little' v that determines the category of the root as V (Marantz 1997). The subjects of unaccusative and the objects of transitive roots are predicated in this position. v is equivalent to Voice (Kratzer 1996) or Initiation (Init.) (Ramchand 2008). The subjects of unergative and external arguments of transitive roots are predicated in this position. This v head could be defective in the cases of unaccusative verbs. In the next three subsections, I will show how /a/, /s/ and /e/ fit into the template.

2.1 /a/ as the Morphological Instantiation of the 'Little' v

Let us begin with /a/. This vowel has been considered to be a theme vowel that is inserted to break CC hiatus that is caused by roots that end in consonants and consonantal suffixes that follow them (e.g. /gs/: √kog –> √kog-*a*-s u 'burn, tr.', /ks/: √kak –> √kak-*a*-se ru 'make write'). There are, however, other vowels that appear in the same position, namely, /i/ and /o/. For example, the root √ot 'fall' below takes /i/ and /o/ as theme vowels.

(2)		√	?	?	T	
	a.	ot	ø	ø	u	'fall, intr. (archaic)'
	b.	ot	**o**	s	u	'fall, tr.'
	c.	ot	**i**		ru	'fall, intr.'
	d.	ot	**o**	r	u	'be inferior to'

The most natural interpretation of this situation is that there is a position right after the root in which the vowels appear, and the morphological environment determines its phonetic content. Incidentally, this position overlaps with the position in which the 'little' heads n, v, and a to appear under Distributed Morphology. I claim that the vowels (including the zero form) are the phonetic representation of the 'little' v that determines the category of roots as V. If this view is on the right track, it predicts that these vowels have to have [+V] feature. This is, in fact, correct; they constitute variants of the verb *be* with some designating features in Japanese.[3]

(3)   a.   a-ru   'be, [-animate]'
        b.   i-ru   'be, [+animate]'
        c.   o-ru   'be, [+animate], [-honorific]'

This shows that Japanese verbs all have the following internal structure.

(4) $[[\sqrt{\text{ROOT}}]\,be]_V$

A piece of syntactic evidence for the root analysis in (4) comes from adverbial modification. In Japanese, as in French, VP adverbs may intervene between a verb and its direct object.

(5)   a.   Je mange$_i$ souvent t$_i$ des   pommes.
               I   eat   often   of-the apples.
               (I often eat apples.)
        b.   Taro ga ringo o yoku tabe ru.
               NOM apples ACC often eat PRES
               (Taro often eats apples.)

It is widely assumed that in French, the verb *mange* 'eat' moves up to T, passing the adverb *souvent* 'often'. That is, the verb *mange* and the DP *des pommes* are sisters before the movement, and the adverb appears in a V' adjunct position above them. Japanese allow why, then, does the adverbial intervention? This is a natural consequence according to the current analysis. In (4) the verbal root √*tabe* 'eat' and v are sisters, and assuming binary branching, the direct object is licensed in the spec of vP. The word order in (5b) is derived directly because the adverb *yoku* 'often' appears between the predicate $[\sqrt{tabe}\text{-}ø^V]$ and its direct object *ringo* 'apples' in its specifier position. See (6). Here, v is null (ø) since the root ends in a vowel.

(6) $[_{vP}$ ringo o $[_{v'}$ yoku $[_{v'} \sqrt{tabe}\text{-}ø^V]]]$ ru

---

[3] One may argue that the allomorphs for the verb *be* are derived secondarily due to phonological conditions like the ones in (6). The current approach differs from Embick (ms. Dec. 2008), where he argues that theme vowels have no syntactic or semantic import.

Adverbs cannot appear to the right of the [√ROOT–v] constituent because doing so would prevent other functional suffixes such as tense to form a predicate.[4]

Another piece of supporting evidence for (4) comes from semantics. Under this analysis, it is predicted that words in a paradigm gain idiomatic interpretations, since only root derivations show such alternation (Marantz 1997, Ramchand 2003). This prediction is borne out.

(7)   a.   kata   o   ot-o-s   u
                 shoulder ACC drop-v-*v* PRES
                 ((One is) deeply disappointed.)

       b.   hu   ni   ot-i ru
                 intestines DAT fall PRES
                 (That makes sense.)

These data strongly supports the root analysis. Let us turn to /s/ next.

2.2 /s/ as *v*

Among the traditional Japanese grammarians, /s/ has been recognized as a morpheme that licenses an agentive argument (Sakakura 1985, Ohno et al. 1974, and many others). Thus, I consider /s/ as the equivalent of *v*. The full paradigm is shown in (8).

(8)

	√	v	*v*	T	
a.	ot	ø		u	'fall, intr. (archaic)'
b.	ot	o	s	u	'drop, tr.'
c.	ot	i		ru	'fall, drop, intr.'
d.	ot	o	**r**	u	'be inferior to'

The paradigm (8) contains all the possible ICA patterns with the root √ot. In (8d), the passive morpheme /r/ is shown in the *v* position for an expository purpose.[5] Sentences with this root and their analyses are shown in (9)–(10). The root is unaccusative in (9a), and (9b) shows its transitivization.

(9)   a.   Isi   ga   ot-i ru.
                 stone NOM fall PRES
                 (Stones fall.)

       b.   Taro ga   isi   o   ot-o-s u.
                  NOM stone ACC drop PRES
                 (Taro drops stones.)

---

[4] The proposed analysis directly accounts for the OV order as well. v and T are suffixes, and as a result, spec must appear on the left of the root for the reason discussed in the text. See Mirror Theory (Brody 1995, 2000) for a similar view.

[5] /s/ and /r/ compete for the same position. The localization of /s/ and /r/ supports the view that *v* comes with a variety of features (Kallulli 2007).

(10)

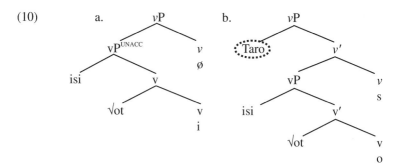

In (10a), the unaccusative predicate [√ot-i]_vP predicates of the subject *isi* 'stone' in its spec position. Due to the unaccusative nature of the root, *v*P is inactive and does not license an external argument. This is the default derivation for the root. In (10b), *v*P is activated by the overt insertion of /s/ in *v*. It makes the specifier position in *v*P available in which the agentive subject *Taro* is predicated of. It also affects the v head and alters its properties so that ACC case becomes available. As a result, *isi* 'stone' gains two characteristics; it is the subject of the unaccusative root, but is also the object of the composite transitive structure. The root √ot retains its unaccusative nature even under the transitivization. Semantically, (10b) means *Taro* causes (or triggers) the stones to fall (√ot-o-s, fall-cause, i.e. 'drop, tr.').

2.3 Unergative Roots and the Nature of Transitivization

Basically the same mechanism works for unergative roots as well. Take, for example, the root √*narab* 'line up' below.

(11)   a.   Taro ga narab-ø-ø   u (koto)
                    NOM line up-v-*v* PRES fact
                    ((the fact that) Taro lines up.)

        b.   Hanako ga Taro o narab-a-s   u (koto)
                    NOM   ACC line up-v-*v* PRES fact
                    ((the fact that) Hanako makes Taro line up.)

(12)   a.

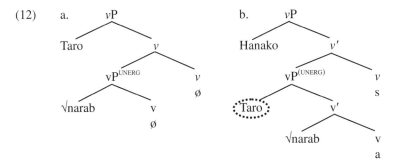

b.

The default case is shown in (12a) in which *v*P lacks its specifier position due to the unergative nature of the root, and the only argument is that of the subject in spec *v*P. When /*s*/ surfaces in (12b), it affects the v head below it and creates a specifier position, and as a result, the *v*P predicates its own subject, *Taro*, in the specifier position. This argument, again, has two crucial semantic properties: on the one hand, it is the object of the newly created transitive predicate, but on the other hand, it retains the important properties of an unergative subject, i.e. it is [+animate]. The animacy requirement can be verified by substituting *Taro* with an inanimate object *isi* 'stone'. The result is completely ungrammatical.

(13)   *Hanako ga   isi   o   narab-a-s   u   (koto)
         MOM stone ACC line up-v-*v* PRES (fact)
         ((the fact that) *Hanako makes stones line up.

The observations above show that /*s*/ affects v, the head that is immediately below it, and alters its properties to suit the transitivization requirements. It makes a new specifier position available in the projection of a head that lacks it. New external and internal arguments are predicated in spec of *v*P and vP for unaccusative and unergative roots, respectively. The roots are, however, unaffected. This gives the arguments in spec vP dual syntactic and semantic identities. So, for example, *isi* 'stone' in (10b) is the unaccusative subject as well as the object of Taro's action, and this is exactly what it means in the sentence. This supports the view that causativization is basically monotone increasing (Koontz-Garboden 2009). Another important point is that creating multiple specifiers in a projection is prohibited in ICA. This is so because there are very tight syntactic and semantic relations between a head and its subject in the spec position. Licensing multiple subjects with the same properties would only be ungrammatical. I argue that this *is* ICA.

2.4 /e/, the GETP

Finally, let us turn to the identity of /e/. /e/ has been used as a main verb *e-ru* 'get' throughout the history of Japanese. It has also been the affix of potential as in √*kak-e ru* 'write-can: X can write' in modern Japanese.

It is a well-known fact that the verb *get* becomes grammaticalized in languages (Heine and Kuteva 2002), and when it happens it gains various meanings such as ability, change-of-state, obligation, passive, permissive, possibility and others. English sentences such as *I have got to go* (obligation), *It gets softer over time* (change-of-state), *I get to choose what I want* (permission), *John got busted* (passive) etc. show the point.

In ICA, however, /e/ has been problematic, for it shows some contradictory properties. For instance, the transitive *hag-u* (√*hag*) in (14b) becomes intransitive *hage-ru* (√*hag-e*) in (14a) by the attachment of /e/.

(14) a. Posutaa ga hage-ru.
          poster NOM peel-PRES
          (The poster peels off.)
      b. Taro ga posutaa o   hag-u.
          Taro NOM poster ACC peels off-PRES
          (Taro peels off the poster.)

In other words, it shows anticausativization effect. However, /e/ seems to causativize the root √*narab* 'line up' in (15b).

(15) a. Taro ga narab-ta.
          Taro NOM line up-PST
          (Taro lined up.)
      b. Taro ga ishi o narab-e-ta.
          Taro NOM stones ACC line up-*e*-PST
          (Taro lined up some stones.)

Thus, we are confronted with contradictory pieces of evidence on the function of /e/. Okutsu (1995: 70) notes, rightly so, that we cannot assign these contradictory properties to the same morpheme /e/. He therefore concludes that /e/ is not directly relevant to ICA processes. In this paper, I differ from Okutsu and show that /e/ projects GETP and plays a vital role in ICA.

2.4.1 GETP and Unaccusative Roots

Let us return to the unaccusative root √*ot* 'drop, intr.' in (8). With this root, we could have √*ot-o-s-e ru* 'being able to drop, tr.' in the paradigm. This makes the sentence *Taro ga isi o ot-o-s-e ru* 'Taro can drop the stone'. See (16) on the next page in which /e/ projects GETP.

I assume that GETP represents Outer Event, and that the *v*P Inner Event for causation is a composite event of a causing event and a resulting event/state. /e/ predicates of a subject *Taro* in its spec GETP position and complements the *v*P.[6] The two instances of the subject *Taro* are identified as the same individual, i.e. the causative is reflexive (Chierchia 2004, Koontz-Garboden 2009).[7] Let us call this GET–Reflexive (GET[R]) Causative. The same *v*P calculi of the unaccusative root apply to the Inner Event.

(16)

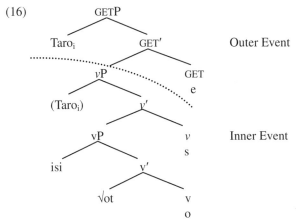

Here is the summary of the paradigm with the root √*ot*. Since specs and heads line up on the opposite sides of a root, I put the root in the middle, arguments in specs on the left, and the heads on the right. If arguments are indexed, the ones that are not in parentheses are pronounced (17c, d). If an argument does not have any index but is in parentheses, it is oblique (17d).

(17)

	Arguments in Spec		√ROOT	Heads				
	GETP	*v*P	vP		v	*v*	GET	T
a.			isi ga	ot	i	∅		ru (drop, intr.)
b.		Taro ga	isi o	ot	o	s		u (drop, tr.)
c.	Taro$_i$ ga	(Taro$_i$)	isi o	ot	o	s	e	ru (drop, tr.)
d.	Isi$_i$ ga	(Taro ni)	(isi$_i$)	ot	o	s	e	ru (GET–Pass.)

---

[6] Pylkkänen (2008: 84) argues that in Japanese the Voice and CAUS heads appear separately. Under the proposed analysis in the text, /s/ is the Voice (*v*) *and* the causative heads, contrary to her claim. If this view is correct, Japanese causative is always "verb-selecting", one of the three varieties of causative structures in her analysis (ibid: 105).

[7] The appearance of /e/ creates what are called in the literature the 'short' and the 'long' causatives *sas* and *sase*, respectively. The former is said to have more direct sense of causation. This and other differences are presumably related to the absence of /e/ in the short form. I do not go into analyzing the differences in this paper for the sake of space reason. See Kuroda (1993) for details.

The versatility of /e/ 'get' is observed in Japanese, as well. For example, it is known to create what is called GET–Passive. See (18 (=17d)).

(18)   Kono isi   ga (Taro ni (yotte)) ot-o-s-e   ru (koto).
        this stone NOM   DAT by   drop-v-v-GET PRES fact
        ((the fact that) this stone is drop-able (by Taro))

In (18), the object *isi* 'stone' is promoted to the subject position, and the agentive subject becomes oblique just like the passive. I take this process to be a result of interactions between the composite *v*P event and /e/. Recall the monotonicity condition. The argument in spec vP *isi* 'stone' is both the subject of the unaccusative root and the object of the derived transitive predictae. When /e/ projects, it may affect the *v* head and intervene in the transitive forming function of /s/. This has two consequences; first the *v* subject *Taro* becomes oblique, and second *isi* 'stone' in spec vP loses its case. /e/ predicates a beneficiary subject *isi* 'stone' in the spec GETP, and it is coindexed with the subject in spec vP. It is *isi* 'stone' in the spec GETP that is pronounced since the lack of case prevents *isi* 'stone' in the spec vP from surfacing.

2.4.2 GETP and Unergative Roots

Let us turn next to the unergative root √*narab* 'line up'. When /e/ appears, it derives the following sentences.

(19)   a.   Taro ga narab-ø-ø-e   ru
                   NOM line up-v-v-GET PRES
              (Taro can line up.)

        b.   Taro ga Hanako o narab-a-s-e   ta.
                   NOM   ACC line up-v-v-GET PST
              (Taro made Hanako line up.)

In both (19a) and (19b), /e/ predicates the beneficiary argument in much the same way that it does in (16). In the former the absence of v and *v* heads results in the potential interpretation while in the latter the surface appearance of the heads adds the causer interpretation to the subject, *Taro*.

There are, however, complications. The verbal form √*narab-e ru* in (19a) is actually ambiguous between intransitive and transitive uses. This occurs because of the surface phonological requirement of the language. The root ends in the consonant /b/, and since /e/ is a vowel, the root and /e/ could line up next to each other. Thus, v and *v* heads may optionally be null. Also, the direct object may be dropped due to the extremely common null argument phenomenon. When /s/ appears, it disambiguates the transitivity, and the theme vowel /a/ must also appear to break the CC hiatus /bs/.

This optional phonological absence of /s/, however, has unexpected effects. When /s/ is null, two things happen: the *v*P subject must also be null

(20a), and the vP subject has to be [–animate] (20b). The semantics of (20b) suggests that this is GET^R–Causative in which *Taro* in spec GETP and that of spec vP are the same. When /s/ is overt, the vP subject can be overt, and the vP subject has to be [+animate] (20c).

(20) a.   Taro ga (*Hanako ni) isi   o   narab-ø-ø-e   ru
          NOM   DAT   stone ACC line up-v-v-GET PRES
          (Taro lines up stones.)

     b.   Taro$_i$ ga   (Taro$_i$) isi/*?gakusee o   narab-ø-ø-e   ru
          NOM   stone/students ACC line up-v-v-GET PRES

     c.   Taro ga Hanako ni *isi/gakusee   o   narab-a-s-e   ta.
          NOM   DAT stone/students ACC line up-v-v-GET PST
          (Taro made Hanako line up stones/students.)

(20a, b) are problematic because the root √*narab* is unergative and predicates of [+animate] subjects in spec vP and vP as in (12b). I argue that this happens because the absence of *v* and v heads allows /e/ to penetrate deeper into the inner event all the way down to the root. It determines the semantics of the root to 'arrange' rather than unergative 'line up'. In other words, with the presence of a [–animate] object, /e/ makes the root pure transitive.

(21)

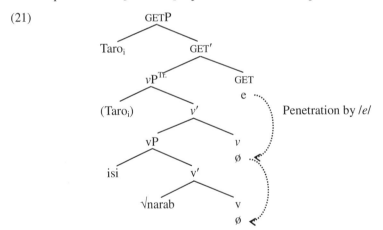

When /s/ as well as /a/ are overt, this penetration is blocked, and the unergative nature of the root prevails as in (20c). This analysis gives a very natural account for seemingly complex grammatical phenomena.

2.5 Lexical Causative and Productive Causative

There is one sentence type that we have not touched upon yet. See below.

(22)   Taro ga Hanako ni   isi   o   narab-ø-ø-e   sase ta.
        NOM   DAT stone ACC line up-v-*v*-GET *sase* PST.
        (Taro made Hanako line up some stones.)

In (22), the morpheme *sase* appears in full outside of the verbal complex. This is a typical example of the so-called "productive" or "syntactic" causative in the literature. Substituting the complex predicate with the simper "lexical" causative √*narab-a-s-e ru* would result in ungrammaticality.

(23)   *Taro ga Hanako ni   isi   o   narab-a-s-e   ru.
        NOM   DAT stone ACC line up-v-*v*-GET PRST.
        (Taro makes Hanako line up some stones.)

This ungrammaticality stems from the causativization processes of the unergative root. We have seen that in order for unergative roots to predicate of an inanimate subject such as *isi* 'rock' in spec vP, the *v* head must be null. If so, however, the only causative it can produce is GET^R–Causative as shown in (21). This means that interpretation as a coercive causative by a third person is impossible within the same GETP. To solve this problem, the grammar makes use of the causative predicate *sase* to predicate of a coercive causer.[8] (24) below is the analysis for (22).

(24)

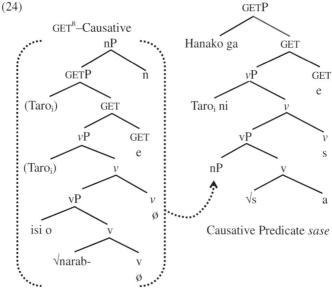

---

[8] This does not happen with unergative roots such as √*odor-u* 'dance', √*nak-u* 'cry' and √*oyog-u* 'swim' because these roots never predicate of inanimate vP subjects in ICA. The semantic ambiguity of the root √*narab* makes this construction necessary.

In Nakajima (to appear) it is argued that /s/ alone can be a root for the verb *suru* 'do' in relation to the Light Verb Construction. (See also Miyagawa 1989.) If this is correct, /s/ should be able to go under causativization √*s-a-s-e* just like any verbal root. I argue that this is indeed the case. Thus, (25) is derived by taking the GET^R–Causative event in spec *v*P of *sase*. This can be verified by the fact that the topic marker *wa* and some particles like *sae* 'even' and *mo* 'also' that attach only to nouns may intervene between the two.

(25)   Taro ga Hanako ni isi o   narab-ø-ø-e   wa/sae/mo s-a-s-e ta.
            NOM   DAT stone ACC line up-v-*v*-GET TOP/even/also CAUS PST.
            (Taro even/also made Hanako line up some stones.)

2.6 *Ni*–Causative and *O*–Causative

It is well known that there are two types of causative construction, *ni*–causative and *o*–causative, depending upon which case particle a causee takes. This alternation is possible only with unergative verbs.

(26)   a.   Taro ga Hanako ni/o   narab-a-s-e ru (koto)
                        NOM   DAT/ACC line up-v-*v*-GET PRES
                    ((the fact that) Taro makes Hanako line up.)
        b.   Taro ga isi   *ni/o   ot-o-s-e   u (koto)
                      NOM stone DAT/ACC fall-v-*v*-GET PRES
                    ((the fact that) Taro drops the stone.)

In (26a), in which the root is unergative, the causee *Hanako* may be marked either by *ni* or *o*, but this is not possible in (26b) in which the root is unaccusative. It is further said that when the causee is marked with *ni*, the sentence has the 'let' interpretation while when it is marked with *o*, the sentence only has simple coercive causative interpretation. The current analysis gives a well-disciplined derivational account for this phenomenon.

Recall that unergative roots initially lack spec *v*P, but that the position is secondarily derived by the transitivization by /s/. See (27).

Let us assume that *Taro* is the beneficiary and appears in spec GETP. There are different possibilities as to what arguments appear in the spec of *v*P and *v*P positions in (27b). In one case, *Hanako* appears in both. When this happens, the causative relation is again reflexive, and *Hanako* brings herself to line up. Let us call this *v*–Reflexive (v^R) Causative. The argument *Hanako* that appears in spec *v*P is marked with *ni*, and the one in spec *v*P with *o*. One or the other is pronounced. The semantic differences between the two follow automatically. *Ni*-causative has the 'let' interpretation because *Hanako* in spec *v*P is a volitional agent while *o* causative has the 'coercive' reading because *Hanako* in spec *v*P is deeply embedded in the event that is controlled by the beneficiary argument *Taro*. A third person, say, *Ziro* can be predicated of in spec *v*P. In this case, the sentence would mean *Taro* made *Hanako* line up *Jiro* as expected.

(27) a.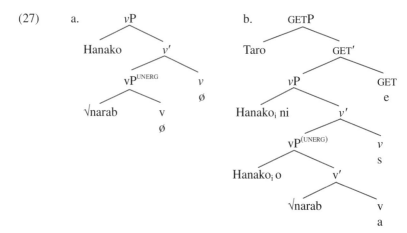

2.7 /S/ Spreading: Nishiyama (1998)

Finally, I would like to discuss one more peculiarity concerning causative predicates in Japanese with respect to /s/. The causative morpheme has been thought to have the form *(s)ase* in which the first instance of /s/ disappears with consonant ending verbal roots. Under the current approach in which /a/, /s/ and /e/ are all heads, this is problematic because it is not clear what status this initial /s/ has.

Fortunately, Nishiyama (1998) shows that this /s/ is a result of phonological spreading of /s/ to break VV hiatus when vowel ending roots meet with the v head. See one example of such roots √*tabe* 'eat' in (28) below. I assume that the order of the phonemes /a/ and /s/ is determined at the interface.

(28)

A piece of supporting evidence for this analysis comes from the cauative–passive morpheme *sare* 'made to do X'. Here is the analysis of *sare*.

(29) Taro ga Hanako ni tegami o kak-a-s-a-r-e   ta.
      MOM   by letter ACC write-v-*v*^CAUS-v-*v*^PASS-GET PST
      (Taro was made to write a letter by Hanako.)

Here, /r/ projects on top of v^{CAUS} and marks it as a passive predicate. Surprisingly, this *sare* cannot appear with vowel ending roots.

(30) *Taro ga Hanako ni yasai o tabe-s-a-r-e ta.
  MOM by vegetables ACC write-v^{CAUS}-v-v^{PASS}-GET PST
  (Taro was made to eat vegetables by Hanako.)

The reason for this ungrammaticality, I argue, is because /s/ in (30) is interpreted as the phonologically duplicated causative /s/ just like the one in (28). Therefore, there should be another /s/ in the *v* position. This is, however, not the case.

(31) √ROOT v v^{PASS} GET T
  V CV C V
  tabe- s a r e ru

If this mismatch is dissolved as in *tabe-sase-ru* 'make X eat' or *tabe-rare-ru* 'is eaten', (31) becomes acceptable as expected. The full-fledged causative–passive form is √*tabe-sase-rare*.

3. Conclusion

In this study, I argued that the causative morpheme *sase* is not monomorphemic but is the combination of functional heads v, *v* and GET. What ICA and CC reveal is how extremely compositional predicate formation processes are: each head forms a micro predicate and predicates of its subject in the spec position. These heads and roots interact in the tightly configured event structure. The proposed analysis, if correct, uncovers an elegant design of grammar. I believe that the simplicity, the depth and the empirical coverage of the analysis give it advantage and desired level adequacy over other accounts that have been proposed in the literature.

References

Arad, M. 2003. Locality Constraints on the Interpretation of Roots: The Case of Hebrew Denominal Verbs, *NLLT*, Vol.21, Num.4, Springer, Dordrecht, The Netherlands: 737–778.

Chierchia, G. 2004. A Semantics for Unaccusatives and its Syntactic Consequences. Alexiadou, Artemis, Elena Anagnostopoulou & Martin Everart (eds.), *The Unaccusative Puzzle*. Oxford: Oxford University Press. 22–59.

Chomsky, N. 2001. Derivation by Phase. M. Kenstowicz. (ed.), *Ken Hale: A Life in Language*. 1–52. Cambridge MA: MIT Press.

Embick, D. Dec. 2008. Localism and Globalism in Morphology and Phonology. University of Pennsylvania. (ms.)

Kallulli, D. 2007. Rethinking the Passive/Anticausative Distinction, *Linguistic Inquiry* 38: 4, Cambridge, MA: MIT Press: 770–780.

Koontz-Garboden, A. 2009. Anticausativization. *Natural Language and Linguistic Theory 27*: 77–138. Springer.

Kratzer, A. 1996. Serving the External Argument from its Verb. J. Rooryck. & L. Zaring (eds.), *Phrase Structure and the Lexicon*: 375–414. Dordrecht: Kluwer

Kuroda, S.-Y. 2003. Complex Predicates and Predicate Raising, *Lingua* 113: 447–480. Elsevier

Miyagawa, S. 1989. *Structure and Case Marking in Japanese*. New York: Academic Press.

Nakajima, T. To appear. Loan Words Get-by with a Little Help from *Do*, Proceedings of *30. Jahrestagung der Deutschen Gesellschaft für Sprachwissenschaft*. Universität Bamberg, Bamberg, Germany.

Nishiyama, K. 1998. The Morphosyntax and Morphophonology of Japanese *Predicates*. Doctoral dissertation. Cornell University.

Okutsu, K. 1995. Zidoka, Tadoka Oyobi Ryokyokukatenkei. K. Suga & H. Emiko (eds.) *Doshi no Zita*. Tokyo, Hitsuji Shyobo. 57–81.

Pylkkänen, L. 2008. *Introducing Arguments*. Cambridge: MIT Press.

Teramura, H. 1982. *Nihongo no Sintakusu to Imi I*. Tokyo. Kuroshio.

On Null Subjects in Embedded Jussive Clauses in Korean*

JONG UN PARK
Georgetown University

1. Introduction

Some recent studies on control have observed that when three types of clauses such as imperatives, promissives and exhortatives (labeled 'jussive clauses' by Pak 2006) are embedded in Korean, an obligatory control (OC) dependency between (one of the) matrix argument(s) and null subjects can be obtained (Choe 2006, Gamerschlag 2007, Madigan 2008a,b, Park 2009b). For example, the embedded imperative triggers object control, as in (1), the embedded promissive subject control, as in (2), and the embedded exhortative split control, as in (3).

* I wish to thank the audience at JK 19 for their useful comments: in particular, Chung-hye Han, Sean Madigan, William O'Grady and Jaehee Bak. I am also grateful to Raffaella Zanutti-ni, Miok Pak, Paul Portner, Michael Diercks, Sun Hee Hwang and Myung-Kwan Park for their feedback and/or judgments. Of course, any remaining errors are mine.

Japanese/Korean Linguistics 19.
Edited by Ho-min Sohn, Haruko Cook, William O'Grady, Leon A. Serafim, & Sang Yee Cheon.

(1)   John₁-un   Mary₂-eykey   [e₂ ttena-**la**-ko]   seltukhay-ss-ta.
        John-TOP   Mary-DAT   leave-IMP-C   persuade-PST-DEC
        'John persuaded Mary to leave.'

(2)   John₁-un   Mary₂-eykey   [e₁ ttena-**ma**-ko]   yaksokhay-ss-ta.
        John-TOP   Mary-DAT   leave-PRM-C   promise-PST-DEC
        'John promised Mary to leave.'

(3)   John₁-un   Mary₂-eykey   [e₁₊₂ hamkkey   ttena-**ca**-ko]
        John-TOP   Mary-DAT   together   leave-EXH-C
        ceyanhay-ss-ta.
        propose-PST-DEC
        'John proposed to Mary to leave together.'

Given that overt pronouns can be substituted for the controlled null subjects in (1)-(3), a natural question that would arise is whether null subjects in jussive control complements can be **PRO**, which is assumed not to alternate with the overt elements (Williams 1980, Hornstein 2001). Against this backdrop, this paper aims to address two questions: (i) what is the categorical status of null subjects in Korean jussive control complements?; and (ii) why can overt subjects appear in place of controlled null subjects in jussive control? As for (i), this paper claims that the controlled subjects in (1) through (3) are **pro**, which departs from the previous analyses (Madigan 2008a,b). In answering (ii), I suggest that jussive clauses subordinated by directive verbs, verbs of commitment and utterance verbs are 'subjunctive-like' clauses, which normally allow overt subjects across languages (cf., Uchibori 2000 for Japanese).

2. Embedded Jussives Are OC Complements

Among five relatively uncontroversial clause types in Korean, imperatives, promissives and exhortatives share several morphosyntactic and semantic properties (Pak 2006, Pak et al. 2008a,b). Let me rehearse some of their arguments here. First, in contrast to their declarative and interrogative counterparts, tense markers cannot be attached to the imperative, promissive and exhortative particles, as in (4).

(4)   a. *Hakkyo-ey   ka-ess-**la**/ka-ul-**la**/ka-nun-**la**.   (Imperative)
            school-LOC   go-PST-IMP/go-FUT-IMP/go-PRS-IMP
        b. *Hakkyo-ey   ka-ess-**ma**/ka-ul-**ma**/ka-nun-**ma**.   (Promissive)
            school-LOC   go-PST-PRM/go-FUT-PRM/go-PRS-PRM
        c. *Hakkyo-ey   ka-ess-**ca**/ka-ul-**ca**/ka-nun-**ca**.   (Exhortative)
            school-LOC   go-PST-EXH/go-FUT-EXH/go-PRS-EXH

Second, the copular-like predicate *–iss* 'be/exist' in Korean expresses not only location but also possession (Park 2009a and references therein). While this predicate can be licensed in declaratives and interrogatives, it cannot be in imperatives, promissives and exhortatives, as in (5).

(5)   a. *You-eykey   ttal-i   iss(e)-**la.**   (Imperative)
             You-DAT   daughter-NOM   exist-IMP
             Intended: 'You have a daughter!'
      b. *Na-eykey   ttal-i   iss(u)-**ma.**   (Promissive)
             I-DAT   daughter-NOM   exist-PRM
             Intended: 'I promise to have a daughter.'
      c. *Ne-wa   nay-ka ttal-i   iss-**ca.**   (Exhortative)
             you-and   I-NOM   daughter-NOM   exist-EXH
             Intended: 'Let you and I have a daughter.'

Finally, the three clause types under discussion are minimally different in that the person value of the (null) subject is encoded by the clause-typing particle, as in (6a-c), which does not necessarily hold for declaratives and interrogatives, as in (6d-e).

(6)   a. [e]   cemsim   mek(e)-**la.**   (SUBJ = 2nd)
                 lunch   eat-IMP
         '(You) have lunch!'
      b. [e]   cemsim   mek(e)-**ma.**   (SUBJ = 1st)
                 lunch   eat-PRM
        'I promise to have lunch.'
      c. [e]   cemsim   mek-**ca.**   (SUBJ = 1st inclusive)
                 lunch   eat-EXH
        'Let us have lunch'
      d. [e]   cemsim   mek-ess-**ta.**   (SUBJ = not fixed)
                 lunch   eat-PST-DEC
        'I/we/he/she/they had lunch.'
      e. [e]   cemsim   mek-ess-**ni?**   (SUBJ = not fixed)
                 lunch   eat-PST-INT
        'Did you/he/she/they have lunch?'

To summarize, the data in (4) through (6) demonstrate that the three clause types have some grammatical properties in common, which distinguish them from the other two major clause types, declaratives and interrogatives. Based on these properties, Pak (2006) and Pak et al. (2008a,b) propose to group them 'jussive clauses,' which is adopted by the current paper for the complement clauses in (1)-(3).

A few researchers have claimed that Korean (and Japanese) employs a unique option of subordinating jussive clauses to establish OC dependency, which is rare in many other languages (Gamerschlag 2007, Madigan 2008a,b, Park 2009b; cf., Uchibori 2000). In support of their claim, they have shown that the sentences in question pass the standard diagnostics for OC that are listed in (7) (from Williams 1980, Hornstein 2001).

(7)　　Diagnostics distinguishing OC from NOC　　**OC**　**NOC**
　　　　a. allows arbitrary reading.　　　　　　　　　×　　✓
　　　　b. allows a non-local controller.　　　　　　　×　　✓
　　　　c. allows a non-commanding controller.　　　×　　✓
　　　　d. allows strict identity under VP ellipsis.　×　　✓
　　　　e. requires a covariant reading with　　✓　　×
　　　　　only-NP as its controller.
　　　　f. requires a *de se* reading.　　　　　　　✓　　×

Due to space reasons, I will not repeat the actual data showing that the control sentences with the jussive complements can pass the diagnostics above. Notice, though, that the previous studies hold different views on the categorial status of null subjects in jussive complements, and this issue will be taken up in Section 3.1.

3. Controlled Subjects in Jussive Control

3.1 Previous Analyses

As for the categorial status of controlled subjects, many studies under the Principles and Parameters framework have maintained Chomsky's (1981) view that controlled null subjects are neither **A-traces** nor **pro** but **PRO** (i.e. pronominal anaphors), as their distribution is restricted to the subject position of infinitives, namely, the ungoverned position, and they cannot alternate with overt elements in English (Manzini 1983, Chomsky and Lasnik 1993, Martin 1996; cf., Landau 1999). So they assume the following two conditions on the distribution of PRO: (i) controlled subjects cannot be assigned structural Case; and (ii) they cannot be overtly realized.

However, these two distributional conditions underlying the PRO-based approaches have been challenged by crosslinguistic data. For example, Icelandic allows controlled subjects to be assigned structural Case (Sigurðsson 1991), and overt controllees are attested in Modern Greek where control complements are subjunctives (Spyropoulos and Philippaki-Warburton 2001, Landau 2006). Korean appears to provide the most extreme cases, as overt controllees are not only permitted but also marked with nominative Case

(Yang 1984, 1985, Borer 1989, Kim 1994, Choe 2006, Gamerschalg 2007, Madigan 2008b).[1]

Although the aforementioned works acknowledge that the PRO-based approaches assuming the two distributional conditions may not be empirically correct, their conclusions about how controlled subjects can be analyzed do not converge. Roughly speaking, some of them nevertheless take the controlled subjects to be **PRO**, while others reanalyze them as **pro**. Due to space limitations, our focus will be placed on those that directly deal with the Korean data, particularly, jussive control data, and their shortcomings will be briefly pointed out in order to show why the controlled subjects in jussive control are better analyzed as **pro** than **PRO** or **A-traces**.

First, based on the observations by Lee (1973), Yang (1984, 1985) and Borer (1989), Kim (1994) claims that controlled subjects in Korean are **pro**, as overt controllees are available, and that their interpretation is determined by linguistically or pragmatically. In particular, if there is a mood marker in the embedded clause, the referent of the null or overt controllee is determined by the type of the mood marker: subject control with –*keyss* or –*lye* 'will', as in (8), and object control with the imperative –*la* (e.g. (1)).

(8) a. John$_i$-i   [{pro/caki-ka}$_i$ cikcep   Mary-lul

   John-NOM   self-NOM   in.person   Mary-ACC

   manna-**lye**-ko]   hay-ss-ta.   (Subject Control)

   meet-will-C   do-PST-DEC

   'John (himself) tried to meet Mary in person.'

  b. John$_i$-i   Bill$_j$-eykey   [{pro/ku-ka/caki-ka}$_{i/*j}$

   John-NOM   Bill-DAT   he-NOM/self-NOM

   ttena-**keyss**-ta-ko]   malhay-ss-ta.   (Subject Control)

   leave-will-DEC-C   say-PST-DEC

   'John$_i$ told Bill$_j$ that (he$_{i/*j}$/caki$_{i/*j}$) would go.'

                 Kim (1994: 83, 93)

Kim's (1994) claim that the controlled subjects are **pro** and that some mood markers (other than –*ma* and –*ca*) play a crucial role in determining the controller seems to be on the right track. But without developing a full-fledged system, she simply argues that both –*lye* and –*keyss* induce subject control since they convey the speaker's volition. Given that the mood markers in (8) express the volition of the speakers of the 'reported' speech, something elaboration is required in order for her idea to work.

---

[1] Citing Yang's (1984) and Borer's (1989) observation on Korean, Landau (1999: Ch 2) makes an interesting point that, unlike the traditional view (Williams 1980), it might not be true that an infinitival subject cannot be **PRO** iff an overt element can be substituted for it.

Secondly, Choe (2006) argues against Monahan's (2003) analysis of Korean *tolok*-control sentences, which suggests under Hornstein's (1999, 2001) Movement Theory of Control that forward or backward control can be achieved depending on which copy of the moved controller is deleted. She particularly claims that what looks like control dependency in Korean is an instance of syntactic or pragmatic binding, and that controlled subjects in the language are actually **pro** with which overt nominals alternate. To support her claim that Korean does not involve obligatory control, she brings up the data similar to those under discussion, where *–la* induces object control, *-ca* split antecedent control, and *–n-ta* and *–kela* subject control. However, her analysis runs into some problems. According to Choe, if **pro** is not c-commanded by a DP, not only pragmatic coreference but also a deictic interpretation should be available when the DP is referential, while a bound variable interpretation is not available when the DP is not referential. But it is unclear how her system captures the availability of the bound variable reading in (9), not to mention the lack of the deictic reading in (10).

(9) John-un   [pro$_i$ ttena-tolok]$_k$ nwukwu$_i$-lul t_k
    John-TOP   leave-COMP   someone-ACC
    seltukhay-ss-ni?
    persuade-PST-Q
    'For which x, x is a person such that John persuaded x that x
    would leave?'   cf. Choe (2007: (36a))

(10) John-un   [pro$_{*i/j/*k}$ ttena-**la**-ko]$_m$ Bill$_j$-eykey t_m
     John-TOP   leave-IMP-C   Bill-DAT
     malhay-ss-ta.
     say-PST-DEC
     'John told Bill that he (Bill/*John/*someone else) would leave.'

Third, in his survey paper on Korean control, Gamerschlag (2007) discusses various instances where overt controllees are available, some of which particularly undermine the Movement Theory of Control-based analysis. His idea is that the semantic meanings of control predicates or the type of mood particles are important factors for determining the controllers in Korean. Although his observations seem quite correct, some clarifications are required: first, it is not made clear what the categorial status of controlled subjects is; second, just as in Kim (1994), he defines *–keyss*, rather than *–ma*, as the modal marker triggering subject control, but the former sometimes denotes possibility, not the speaker's volition, which makes it less natural to group *–keyss* together with *–la*, *-ca*, and *–ma*.

Finally, Madigan (2008b) provides the most comprehensive discussion on the availability and possible range of overt controllees in Korean jussive control contexts. Based on Pak's (2006) and Pak et al.'s (2008b) analysis, Madigan argues that the interpretation patterns in (1)-(3) can be derived through the pragmatic functions of the embedded clauses as well as the semantic meanings of the matrix clauses. He treats controlled subjects as **PRO**, but he acknowledges the problem with the standard PRO accounts where the availability of overt elements is not naturally predicted, without additional stipulations. So he proposes to tie the availability of the overt controllees to focus effects.[2] Though his finding reflects native speakers' intuition quite well, his analysis runs into the same problem as Gamerschlag (2007). For example, he groups not only *–la, -ca* and *–ma* but also *–keyss* and *–lye* as a class of Control Creating Markers dominated by the same head, Speaker/Addressee[0], but the latter two do not have the same properties as the former three, in that they do not convey any sentential force (Seo (1996)); they can co-occur with the other clause-typing particles such as the declarative or interrogative one; and *–lye* cannot appear in the root context.

In summary, the discussions so far suggest that other things being equal, any analysis taking controlled subjects in jussive complements in (1)-(3) to be **pro** can make better predictions for the data with overt controllees than other approaches treating them as **PRO** or **A-traces**.

3.2 Types of Overt Controllees in Jussive Control

We have just seen that null subjects in jussive control complements in Korean can alternate with overt counterparts, which would not be easily explained if the controlled subjects were treated as **PRO** or **A-traces**. In this subsection I will introduce some more data with overt controllees, not all of which have been discussed in previous works, so that we can draw generalizations about what kinds of overt elements are allowed and when they can be licensed.

To begin with, the long-distance (LD) anaphor *caki* can be substituted for a controlled null subject in cases of subject and object jussive control, as in (11a,b), and its plural counterpart *caki-tul* can occur in the case of split antecedent control, as in (11c).

(11)   a. John$_1$-un   Mary$_2$-eykey   [caki$_2$-ka honca nonmwun-ul
          John-TOP   Mary-DAT   self-NOM alone   paper-ACC
          ssu-**la**-ko]   malhay-ss-ta.
          write-IMP-C say-PST-DEC
          'John told Mary that self (Mary) would write a paper alone.'

---

[2] Although he notes that many languages may allow overt controllees, Landau (2006) views the controlled subjects as PRO, proposing the calculus system for control interpretation. As Madigan (2008b: Ch 5) points out, however, Landau's system fails to explain some Korean control data with personal pronouns or complex reflexives (e.g. *ku-casin* 'he-self').

b. John$_1$-un   Mary$_2$-eykey   [caki$_1$-ka   tangcang

    John-TOP   Mary-DAT   self-NOM   immediately

    nonmwun-ul   ssu-**ma**-ko]   malhay-ss-ta

    paper-ACC   write-PRM-C   say-PST-DEC

    'John told Mary that self (John) would write a paper immediately.'

c. John$_1$-un   Mary$_2$-eykey   [caki-tul$_{1+2}$-i   hamkkey

    John-TOP   Mary-DAT   self-PL-NOM   together

    nonmwun-ul   ssu-**ca**-ko]   malhay-ss-ta.

    paper-ACC   write-EXH-C   say-PST-DEC

    'John told Mary that selves (John and Mary) would write a paper together.'

However, there seem to be some restrictions that regulate the occurrence of *caki* in jussive complements. *caki* can appear in place of a controlled null subject as long as its controller is not 1st person, which is in accordance with the long-standing observation about the use of the LD anaphor *caki* (Hong (1991)). Second, the occurrence of *caki* in place of controlled null subjects is judged more natural if it is heavily stressed or is given contrastive focus (Madigan (2008b), Pak et al. (2008a,b)). For example, the sentences in (11a,b) above may sound unnatural if uttered out of blue, but most speakers tend to judge the same sentences more natural if specific contexts are provided, as in (12a) and (12b) for (11a) and (11b), respectively ((12a) adapted from Madigan (2008b: pp 205-1)).

(12)   a. **Scenario A**: John is an advisor of Mary and Bill. Mary wanted to collaborate with Bill, but John didn't want her to do so. So John told Mary to write a paper alone.

       b. **Scenario B**: Mary is the editor of a handbook of comparative syntax. In search of writers of chapters, she solicited a paper from John, her former professor. Since it is a good chance to publish his recent work, John promised to do it right away.

Secondly, first and second person singular pronouns can appear in place of controlled subjects in jussive complements, as in (13a,b), and the first person plural is also available, as in (13c).

(13)   a. John$_i$-un   ne$_j$-eykey $^?$(ecey)   [ney$_{*i/j}$-ka   nonmwun-ul

       John-TOP   you-DAT   yesterday   you-NOM   paper-ACC

       ssu-**la**-ko]   sultukhayssta

       write-IMP-C   persuaded

       'John persuaded you (yesterday) that you would write a paper.'

b. Na$_i$-nun   Mary$_j$-eykey   [nay$_{i/*j}$-ka   nonmwun-ul
  I-TOP   Mary-DAT   I-NOM   paper-ACC
  ssu-**ma**-ko]   yaksokhayssta.
  write-PRM-C   promised
  Lit. 'I promised Mary that I would write a paper.'

c. Na$_i$-nun   ne$_j$-eykey   [wuli$_{i+j}$-ka   hamkkey   nonmwun-ul
  I-TOP   you-DAT   we-NOM   together   paper-ACC
  ssu-**ca**-ko]   ceyanhayssta.
  write-EXH-C   proposed
  Lit. 'I proposed to you that we would write a paper together.'

Notice also that the occurrence of first or second person pronouns is not entirely free, and the following two restrictions seem to work. First, in order for the first or second person pronouns to be substituted for null subjects, the controllers must be the same kinds of pronouns. Second, just like the LD anaphor *caki*, the occurrence of these two pronouns is judged more natural if they are to be given stress or focus (particular scenarios not provided due to the lack of space).

Finally, although it is controversial, third person pronouns, singular or plural, can also be substituted for null subjects in jussive control complements, as illustrated in (14).

(14)   a. John$_i$-un   Mary$_j$-eykey [kunye$_{*i/j}$-ka   swukcey-lul
        John-TOP   Mary-DAT   she-NOM   homework-ACC
        ha-**la**-ko]   sultukhayssta
        do-IMP-C   persuaded
        Lit. 'John persuaded Mary that she (Mary) would do home work.'

     b. John$_i$-un   Mary$_j$-eykey   [ku$_{i/*j}$-ka   swukcey-lul
        John-TOP   Mary-DAT   he-NOM   homework-ACC
        ha-**ma**-ko]   yaksokhayssta.
        do-IMP-C   promised
        Lit. 'John promised Mary that he (John) would do homework.'

     c. John$_i$-un   Mary$_j$-eykey   [kutul$_{i+j}$-i   hamkkey
        John-TOP   Mary-DAT   they-NOM   together
        swukcey-lul   ha-**ca**-ko]   ceyanhayssta.
        homework-ACC   do-EXH-C   proposed
        Lit. 'John proposed to Mary that they (John and Mary) would do homework together.'

Just like the LD anaphor *caki* and first and second person pronouns, the third person pronouns are also subject to a couple of constraints. First, the controllers cannot be first or second person pronouns. Second, the occurrence of the third person pronouns is also affected by the interpretive restriction that can be characterized as contrastive focus.

It has been shown in Section 3.2 that controlled null subjects in jussive control complements can be replaced with various pronominal elements while some restrictions str imposed depending on their type. But, once again, the previous approaches reviewed in Section 3.1 do not seem to be able to accommodate the jussive control data with overt controllees. For this reason, I claim that controlled subjects in jussive complements in Korean are **pro**, an answer to the first question brought up in the introduction.

4. Analysis of Issues regarding Overt Controllees

4.1 Determining the Referents of pro in Jussive Complements

Recently, Pak et al. (2008b,c) provide an intuitive analysis of three subtypes of Korean jussive clauses in root contexts, and their core idea can be summarized by the following three claims. First, there is a functional category called 'Jussive Phrase' in the three clause types at issue, which encodes the person features of null subjects. Second, the null subjects of the three jussive clauses are **pro**, and their person feature values are determined by a syntactic Agree relation with the Jussive head. Third, rejecting Chomsky's (2001) Valuation/Interpretable Biconditional (i.e. "A feature F is uninterpretable iff F is unvalued"), they take Pesetsky and Torrego's (2007) view, arguing that either uninterpretable but valued, or interpretable but unvalued, features are also available (see Pak et al. (2008c) for a detailed discussion).

These claims can be illustrated by the abstract structure in (15), where x can be first, second, or first person inclusive according to whether the clause is a promissive, imperative or exhortative.

(15)   a. Before Agree   b. After Agree

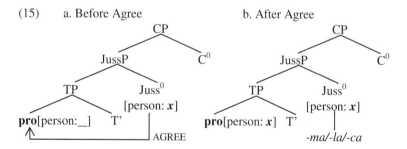

In addition to Pak et al.'s (2008b,c) claims above, this paper makes a couple of more assumptions. First, the pragmatic function of promissives, imperatives and exhortatives is to update the To-do List of the speaker, the addressee or both, and second, this function imposes syntactic restrictions on the person feature of the null subject of each clause type, as evidenced by the binding facts in (16).

(16) a. Emma$_i$-ka   nay$_i$/*kunye$_i$-uy   chinkwu-lu
       Mommy-NOM my/her   friend-ACC
       teyliko.o-**ma**.
       bring.come-PRM
       'Mommy will bring her friend' (Mommy = speaker)
     b. Inho$_i$-ka   ney$_i$/*ku-uy$_i$ chinkwu-lul
        Inho-NOM   your/his   friend-ACC
        teyliko.o-**ala**.
        bring.come-IMP
        'Inho bring your friend!'
     c. [Emma-wa   Inho]$_i$-ka   wuli$_i$/*ku$_i$-uy   chinkwu-lul
        Mommy-and   Inho-NOM   our/his   friend-ACC
        teyliko.o-**ca**.
        bring.come-EXH
        'Mommy and Inho will bring our friend' (Mommy = speaker)
                                          Pak et al. (2008b: 16)

While the analysis sketched above is aimed at the jussive clauses in root contexts, what we are concerned with in this paper are jussive clauses that are embedded under utterance verbs, directive/manipulative verbs or verbs of commitment. In extending the aforementioned analysis to embedded jussive clauses, this paper adopts Pak et al.'s (2008a: Sec 4) additional hypotheses: first, the jussive head and null pronouns have shiftable person features; second, overt pronouns have unshiftable person features; and finally, a verb like 'say' in Korean is a context-shifter. These hypotheses are rooted in previous works (e.g. Baker (2008) and references therein), which claim that while person features in a root context refer to the speakers or addressees of the actual discourse, those in an embedded context can refer to the speakers or addressees of the reported speech, as shown in the famous data in (17).

(17) ǰon   [jəgna   nə-ññ]   yɨl-all   (Amharic)
      John hero   be.PF-1sO   3M.say-AUX.3M
      'John says that he is a hero.' (Lit. 'John says that I be a hero.')
                                          Baker (2008: 125)

With these assumptions we are now in a position to analyze some of the data discussed in the previous sections. Let us begin with the subject control case in (2) where the controlled subject is null. **pro** is assumed to have the [shiftable] feature but is unvalued in person before Agree applies (i.e., [shiftable:_]), as in (18a).

(18)   a. Before Agree

$[_{CP} [_{JussP} Juss^0{}_{[shiftable: 1]} [_{TP} pro_{[shiftable:\_]} \cdots$

   b. After Agree

$[_{CP} [_{JussP} Juss^0{}_{[shiftable: 1]} [_{TP} pro_{[shiftable: 1]} \cdots$

The acceptability of (2) naturally follows from the proposed system since the features of the null subject become identical with those of the $Juss^0$ after Agree takes place, as in (18b) where [shiftable: 1] in both the head and **pro** refers to the matrix subject.

Second, consider the object control sentence in (11a) where the controlled subject is *caki,* which has the [unshiftable] feature but needs to be non-first person (i.e. [unshiftable: -1]) before Agree takes place, as in (19a).

(19)   a. Before Agree

$[_{CP} [_{JussP} Juss^0{}_{[shiftable: 2]} [_{TP} caki_{[unshiftable: -1]} \ T^0 \cdots$

   b. After Agree

$[_{CP} [_{JussP} Juss^0{}_{[shiftable: 2][unshiftable: -1]} [_{TP} caki_{[unshiftable: -1][shiftable: 2]} \ T^0 \cdots$

On the current analysis, (11a) is predicted to be OK since the combination of features [shiftable: 2] and [unshiftable: -1], which is made possible through Agree, as in (19b), does not yield any conflict, as the [shiftable: 2] refers to the matrix object and the [unshiftable: -1] requires any person other than first person. Due to space limitations, how the current analysis works for the other data introduced in Section 3.2 will not be discussed.

4.2 Why Are Jussive Complements Special?

The typical properties of OC subjects (e.g. requirements of local and c-commanding antecedents, sloppy identity for resolution of VP anaphora, and *de se* interpretation, etc.) are mostly limited to the subjects of infinitival clauses with an unrealized tense (Martin 1996, Landau 1999, Hornstein 1999, 2001). Therefore, from a theoretical perspective, the occurrence of overt controllees in control complements is puzzling, which forces us to seek a reasonable answer to the second question raised in the introduction: What makes overt subjects appear in place of controlled null subjects in jussive control? I tentatively propose that the three jussive control complements under discussion are not like control infinitives in English but analogous to subjunctive clauses found in Indo-European languages, in that they do not allow for overt tense markers (cf., (4)) but a weak form of agreement takes place in between the subjects and the Jussive head (cf. Uchibori 2000 for Japanese).

Notice that promissive, imperative and exhortative clauses in Korean can be formed with more diverse sentence-final forms than what has been discussed as core data in this paper: that is, each clause type employs at least six different kinds of speech styles. Some characteristic properties of the plain speech style particle deserve to be mentioned. First, only the jussive clauses marked by the plain speech styles can be embedded under utterance verbs or typical control-creating predicates (cf., (1)-(3)). Secondly, a closer look at the meaning of the plain jussive clauses in root contexts leads us to conclude that the use of this type of imperatives conveys a different meaning than that of other types: (i) the plain imperative or exhortative sentences are often used as slogans or mottos, as in (20) ((a) from Pak et al. 2008b: 32), and (ii) they can also function as optatives, as in (21).

(20)   a. Cengcikha-la!   b. Iki-ca!
            Be.honest-IMP   win-EXH
            'Be honest!'   'Let's win (the game)!'

(21)   a. Yengsayngha-la!   b. Yengwenha-la!
            Live.long-IMP   Be.eternal-IMP
            'May you live long!'   'May it be eternal!'

There are some independent crosslingusitic studies that seem to support the current analysis. First, given that imperatives in English are divided into two according to whether overt subjects are allowed, Han (2000: Ch 4, Sec 4.4) suggests that the imperatives with the overt subject can be analyzed as (mandative) subjunctives, while those without are normal (control) infinitives with an unrealized tense—i.e., an [irrealis] feature in her terminology.

Second, a similar idea can be found in Uchibori (2000), according to whom the two instances of control in (22) can be analyzed as embedding subjunctives. Uchibori (2000: Ch 2) discusses the following data where complement clauses are used as weak imperatives or optatives.

(22)   a. John-ga   Mary$_i$-ni   [$_{XP}$ e$_i$ Bill-o
            John-NOM   Mary-DAT   Bill-ACC
            susensu-ru-**yoo(-ni(-to))**)   tanon-da.
            recommend-NONPST   ask-PST
            'John asked Mary to recommend Bill.'   Uchibori (2000: 13)
        b. koochoo-ga   sense$_i$-ni   [e$_i$ Mary-o
            principal-NOM   teacher-DAT   Mary-ACC
            suisensu-ru   koto]-o motome-ta.
            recommend-NONPST   fact-ACC request-PST
            'The principal requested the teacher to recommend Mary.'

5. Conclusion

By examining a wide range of data where overt controllees are available in jussive complements, as well as restrictions imposed on each type of overt elements, this paper has claimed that controlled subjects in Korean jussive control are **pro**. I have tentatively suggested that the reason overt controllees are allowed in Korean jussive complements may be that the three plain-style jussive clauses exhibit properties that are closer to subjunctives than infinitives.

Notice, though, that there are some issues left open for future research: first, how OC properties can be maintained in Korean jussive control sentences with overt controllees still awaits an answer (cf. Madigan 2008b); second, what the exact nature of focus or contrastiveness licensing overt controllees is has been left unanswered.

References

Baker, M. 2008. *The Syntax of Agreement and Concord.* Cambridge: Cambridge University Press.

Borer, H. 1989. Anaphoric AGR. *The Null Subject Parameter,* eds. O. Jaeggli and K. J. Safir, 69-109. Dordrecht: Kluwer.

Choe, H.-S. 2006. On (Backward) Object Control in Korean. *Harvard Studies in Korean Linguistics XI,* eds. S. Kuno et al., 373-86.

Chomsky, N. 1981. *Lectures on Government and Binding.* Dordrecht: Foris.

Chomsky, N. 2001. Derivation by Phase. *Ken Hale: A Life in Language,* ed. M. Kenstowicz. Cambridge, MA: MIT Press.

Chomsky, N. and Lasnik, H. 1993. The Theory of Principles and Parameters. *Syntax: An International Handbook of Contemporary Research,* eds. J. Jacobs et al., 506-569. Berlin: Mouton de Gruyter.

Gamerschlag, T. 2007. Semantic and Structural Aspects of Complement Control in Korean. *ZAS Papers in Linguistics* 47, ed. B. Stiebels, 61-123.

Han, C.-H. 2000. *The Structure and Interpretation of Imperatives: Mood and Force in Universal Grammar.* New York: Garland.

Hong, K.-S. 1991. Argument Selection and Case Marking in Korean. Doctoral Dissertation, Stanford University.

Landau, I. 1999. Elements of Control. Doctoral Dissertation, MIT.

Landau, I. 2006. Severing the Distribution of PRO from Case. *Syntax* 9/2: 153-170.

Madigan, S. 2008a. Obligatory Split Control into Exhortative Complements. *Linguistic Inquiry* 39.3: 493-502.

Madigan, S. 2008b. Control Constructions in Korean. Doctoral Dissertation, University of Delaware.

Manzini, R. 1983. On Control and Control Theory. *Linguistic Inquiry* 14: 421-446.

Martin, R. 1996. A Minimalist Theory of Control. Doctoral Dissertation, University of Connecticut, Storrs.

Monahan, P. 2003. Backward Object Control in Korean. *WCCFL 22 Proceedings, eds.* G. Garding and M. Tsujimura, 356-369. Somerville, MA: Cascadilla Press.

Pak, M. 2006. Jussive Clauses and Agreement of Sentence Final Particles in Korean. *Japanese/Korean Linguistics* 14, eds. T. Vance and K. Jones, 295-306. Stanford, CA: CSLI Publications.

Pak, M., Portner, P., and Zanuttini R. 2008a. Agreement and the Subjects of Jussive Clauses in Korean. *Proceedings of NELS 37, eds.* E. Elfner and M. Walkow. Amherst, MA: GLSA.

Pak, M., Portner, P., and Zanuttini, R. 2008b. A Syntactic Analysis of Interpretive Restrictions on Imperative, Promissive, and Exhortative Subjects. Ms., Georgetown University.

Pak, M., Portner, P., and Zanuttini, R. 2008c. The Interpretation and Licensing of Null Imperative Subjects in Korean. Paper presented at the 16th International Conference on Korean Linguistics.

Park, J. U. 2009a. Decomposition of *–iss* in the DAT-NOM Construction in Korean. *Proceedings of the 2nd International Conference on East Asian Linguistics.*

Park, J. U. 2009b. Obligatory Control by Jussive Particles in Korean. *Proceedings of the 9th Seoul International Conference on Generative Grammar,* ed. S-W Kim. Seoul: Hanshin Publishing Co.

Pesetsky, D. and Torrego, E. 2007. The Syntax of Valuation and the Interpretability of Features. *Phrasal and Clausal Architecture: Syntactic Derivation and Interpretation*, eds. S. Karimi, V. Samiian and W. Wilkins. Amsterdam: Benjamins.

Hornstein, N. 1999. Movement and Control. *Linguistic Inquiry* 30: 69-96.

Hornstein, N. 2001. *Move! A Minimalist Theory of Construal.* Malden: Blackwell.

Kim, S.-H. 1993. Division of Labor between Grammar and Pragmatics: The Distribution and Interpretation of Anaphora. Doctoral Dissertation Yale University.

Sigurðsson, H. 1991. Icelandic Case-Marked PRO and the Licensing of Lexical Arguments. *Natural Language and Linguistic Theory* 9: 327-363.

Spyropoulos, V. and Philippaki-Warburton, I. 2001. Subjunctive, Coreference, and the Module of Control in Greek. Paper Presented at the 5th International Conference on Greek Linguistics, Paris, 13–15 September 2001.

Uchibori, A. 2000. The Syntax of Subjunctive Complements: Evidence from Japanese. Doctoral Dissertation, University of Connecticut, Storrs.

Yang, D.-W. 1984. The Extended Control Theory. *Language Research* 20.1, 19-30.

Yang, D.-W. 1985. On the Integrity of Control Theory. *In Proceedings of NELS* 15, 389-408.

Williams, E. 1980. Predication. *Linguistic Inquiry* 11: 203-238.

The Role of Merger and Typology of *v* Heads in Serialization

DAEYOUNG SOHN
Massachusetts Institute of Technology

HEEJEONG KO
Seoul National University

This paper investigates the role of merger and typology of *v* in serialization with special attention to Serial Verb Constructions (SVCs) in Korean. Some SVCs with a derivational suffix (e.g. causative and passive *v*) in Korean display behavior distinct from simple SVCs. We argue that this is due to different merger sites of the derivational *v* head in SVCs. A H(igh)-SVC results when a causative or passive *v* head is merged to a verbal stem before it is serialized with another verb; a L(ow)-SVC results when the verbal serialization occurs prior to the merger of the *v* head. We extend our discussion to a condition on verbal serialization, and propose that verbs can be serialized only when their *v* heads bear an identical property in introducing an external argument. We show that our matching condition coupled with the proposed dichotomy of SVCs has broader empirical coverage than previous analyses. Theoretically, our study supports the line of approaches arguing that the morphology and the syntax are intertwined so that the attach-

Japanese/Korean Linguistics 19.
Edited by Ho-min Sohn, Haruko Cook, William O'Grady, Leon A. Serafim, & Sang Yee Cheon.

ment site of derivational suffixes can vary in syntax. Our argument also provides support for the finer-grained classification of v heads (e.g. Folli and
Harley 2005, Harley 2006, Son 2006).

1. Different Merger Sites of v Heads in Serialization

1.1 Two Types of Serial Verb Constructions in Korean

By Serial Verb Construction (SVC), we refer to a construction where two or
more lexical verbs appear in a clause without an overt marker of coordination or subordination in-between. Also, one or more arguments are shared
by the verbs and only one tense marker appears in the serialized verbal
complex. Representative examples of Korean SVCs are given in (1). For
convenience, we call the first verb in an SVC V_1, and the second verb V_2.
For instance, in (1a), *palp-a* 'to trample' is referred to as V_1 and *cwuk-i* 'to
kill' as V_2.

(1) a. *John-i   kaymi-lul palp-a   cwuk-i-ess-ta.*
        John-NOM ant-ACC   trample-LK die-CAUS-PAST-DECL
        'John trampled an ant to death.'
     b. *John-i   Mary-lul   kkwulh-e anc-hi-ess-ta.*
        John-NOM Mary-ACC kneel-LK   sit-CAUS-PAST-DECL
        'John made Mary kneel down.'

Note that the V_2 *cwuk-i* 'to kill' in (1a) and *anc-hi* 'to seat' in (1b) are morphologically complex verbs, where a causativizer marker (*i* or *hi*) is suffixed
to an intransitive verbal stem *cwuk* 'to die' in (1a) and *anc* 'to sit' in (1b).
The major concern of the paper lies on the role of the derivational suffixes
in the formation of SVCs.

On the surface, SVCs in (1a) and (1b) do not seem to contrast with each
other, but in fact they show a different syntactic distribution with respect to
a variety of separability tests. It is well-known that simple SVCs may be
separated by a connective *se*, roughly meaning 'and then' (Choi H. 1929,
Sohn 1976, Lee S. 1992, Choi 2003, Lee Y. 2003, Borer 2004, and many
others). This is shown in (2):

(2) *John-i   kom-ul   cap-a-(se)   mek-ess-ta.*
       John-NOM bear-ACC catch-LK-(SE) eat-PAST-DECL
       'John caught and ate a bear.'

Interestingly, however, the complex SVCs in (1) show a different behavior with respect to *se*-insertion. The morpheme *se* may separate V_1 and V_2
in (1a), but not in (1b). The contrast is shown in (3).

(3)   a. *John-i   kaymi-lul   palp-a-se   cwuk-i-ess-ta.*
        John-NOM   ant-ACC   trample-LK-SE   die-CAUS-PAST-DECL
        'John trampled an ant to death.'
        b. **John-i   Mary-lul   kkwulh-e-se   anc-hi-ess-ta.*
        John-NOM   Mary-ACC   kneel-LK-SE   sit-CAUS-PAST-DECL
        'John made Mary kneel down.' (intended)

The same type of asymmetry is observed with an adverb test. As shown in (4), (1a) allows an adverb *kuphi* 'quickly' to intervene between V_1 and V_2, whereas (1b) does not.

(4)   a. *John-i   kaymi-lul   palp-a   kuphi   cwuk-i-ess-ta.*
        John-NOM   ant-ACC   trample-LK   quickly die-CAUS-PAST-DECL
        'John trampled an ant to death quickly.'
        b. **John-i   Mary-lul   kkwulh-e   kuphi   anc-hi-ess-ta.*
        John-NOM   Mary-ACC   kneel-LK   quickly sit-CAUS-PAST-DECL
        'John made Mary to kneel down quickly.' (intended)

The contrast shown in (5) further suggests the possibility that (1a) and (1b) are distinct from each other. In (5a), the object and the preceding verb V_1 can be scrambled together to the left of the subject, whereas in (5b), they cannot.

(5)   a. *kaymi-lul   palp-a   John-i   cwuk-i-ess-ta.* [cf. (1a)]
        ant-ACC   trample-LK   John-NOM   die-CAUS-PAST-DECL
        'John trampled an ant to death.'
        b. **Mary-lul   kkwulh-e   John-i   anc-hi-ess-ta.* [cf. (1b)]
        Mary-ACC   kneel-LK   John-NOM   sit-CAUS-PAST-DECL
        'John made Mary kneel down.' (intended)

We propose that the observed contrast between (1a) and (1b) is not accidental, and the two examples represent two different types of SVCs in Korean. We, in particular, capitalize on the fact that the scope of the causative markers in (1a) and (1b) is distinct in each case. In (1a), the causative marker *i* scopes over V_2 'to die', but not over V_1: (1a) means that 'John trampled an ant, and (he) caused the ant to die'. The agent of the preceding verb *palp* 'to trample' is John who is also the causer of an ant's dying event. In contrast, in (1b), the causative marker *hi* scopes over both V_1 *kkwulh* 'to kneel' and V_2 *anc* 'to sit': (1b) means that 'John caused Mary to kneel and sit'. We argue that the semantic differences in (1a) and (1b) are rooted in the underlying syntactic structures. In (1a) type sentences, the causative marker is directly attached to the V_2, whereas in (1b) type sentences, the causative marker is attached to the serialized verbal complex (V_1 and V_2).

More generally, we propose that SVCs in Korean can be divided into two types: H(igh)-SVC and L(ow)-SVC. The two types differ from each other depending on the merger site of the derivational suffix in relation to the serialization site of verbs. In H-SVCs, merger of the derivational morpheme occurs prior to verbal serialization, as depicted in (6). In L-SVCs, in contrast, the derivational morpheme is merged after the completion of serialization, as schematized in (7) (we will slightly revise the structure in (6) and (7) in Section 1.2, in accordance with Baker and Stewart 2002)

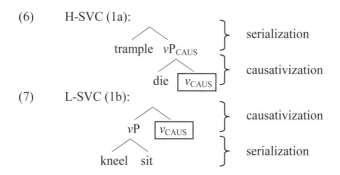

(6)   H-SVC (1a):

(7)   L-SVC (1b):

The structural difference between the sentences in (1a) and (1b) is represented using brackets in (8).

(8)   a. *John-i   kaymi-lul [palp-a]   [cwuk-i]-ess-ta.*
            John-NOM ant-ACC [trample-LK] [die-CAUS]-PAST-DECL
            'John trampled an ant to death.'
        b. *John-i   Mary-lul   [kkwulh-e   anc]-hi-ess-ta.*
            John-NOM Mary-ACC [kneel-LK   sit]-CAUS-PAST-DECL
            'John made Mary to kneel down.'

In (8a), the V_2 *cwuk* 'to die' is merged with the causative morpheme *i* first and then serialized with the V_1 *palp* 'to trample.' In (8b), in contrast, the V_2 *anc* 'to sit' is serialized with the V_1 *kkwulh* 'to kneel' first and then the serialized verbal complex is merged with the causative morpheme *hi*.

The proposed analysis is in good concert with the different interpretation of the causative morpheme in (8a) and (8b). By definition, a causative construction consists of two sub-events: a causing and a caused one. If contained in the c-command domain of the causative head, a constituent constitutes the caused sub-event; if outside the c-command domain, it constitutes the causing sub-event. Then it follows that in H-SVCs such as (8a), where the causative morpheme is merged directly with V_2, V_1 constitutes the causing sub-event; in L-SVCs such as (8b), in contrast, the causative morpheme is merged with a serialized verbal complex, and consequently both V_1 and V_2 constitute the caused sub-events.

The same distinction between H- and L-SVC with a morphological causative verb extends to morphological passive SVCs as well. Examples of H- and L-SVC with a morphological passive verb are given in (9).

(9) a. *kkoch –i*   [*situl-e*]   [*ppop-hi*]-*ess-ta*.
     flolwer-NOM [wither-LK] [break-PASS]-PAST-DECL
     'A flower withered and was pulled up.'
   b. *John-i*   (*kom-eykey*)   [*cap-a   mek*]-*hi-ess-ta*.
     John-NOM (bear-BY)   [catch-LK eat]-PASS-PAST-DECL
     'John was caught and eaten (by a bear).'

(9a) is an example of a passive H-SVC, where the passive morpheme *hi* scopes over V_2 only. The morpheme cannot scope over V_1 as it is an unaccusative verb which cannot be passivized. (9b) is an example of a passive L-SVC, where the passive morpheme *hi* scopes over both V_1 and V_2. In (9b), V_1 *cap* 'to catch' behaves as if it carries an invisible passive morpheme within it in that the nominative subject *John* is interpreted as the Theme of both catching and eating events. This can be straightforwardly explained by assuming that (9b) belongs to an L-SVC, where serialization occurs between *cap* 'to catch' and *mek* 'to eat' and then the passive morpheme *hi* is merged with the resultant serialized verbal complex.

As shown in (10), the passive H-SVC in (9a) patterns with the causative H-SVC in (1a) and pass the separability tests such as *se*-insertion, intervening adverbial, and νP scrambling. The passive L-SVC in (9b), on the other hand, patterns with the causative L-SVC counterpart in (1b) in that it fails to pass these tests. This is shown in (11).

(10) Passive H-SVC:
   a. *kkoch –i   situl-e-se   ppop-hi-ess-ta*.
     flower-NOM wither-LK-SE pull.up-PASS-PAST-DECL
     'A flower withered and then was pulled up.'
   b. *kkoch –i   situl-e   kuphi   ppop-hi-ess-ta*.
     flower-NOM wither-LK quickly pull.up-PASS-PAST-DECL
     'A flower withered and was pulled up quickly.'

   c. ?*situl-e   kkoch –i   ppop-hi-ess-ta*.
     wither-LK flolwer-NOM pull.up-PASS-PAST-DECL
     'Withered, a flower was pulled up.'

(11)   Passive L-SVC:
   a. *John-i   (kom-eykey)   cap-a-se   mek-hi-ess-ta.
      John-NOM   (bear-BY)   catch-LK-SE eat-PASS-PAST-DECL
      'John was caught and then eaten (by a bear).' (intended)
   b. *John-i   (kom-eykey) cap-a   kuphi   mek-hi-ess-ta.
      John-NOM   (bear-BY)   catch-LK quickly eat-PASS-PAST-DECL
      'John was caught and eaten quickly (by a bear).'
   c. * (kom-eykey)   cap-a   John-i   mek-hi-ess-ta.
      (bear-BY)   catch-LK   John-NOM   eat-PASS-PAST-DECL
      'Caught by a bear, John was eaten.' (intended)

Though it may not be a logical necessity, the correlation between the distinct scope of the derivational suffix and separability tests is now rather straightforwardly expected with one premise: derivational v heads cannot tolerate a syntactic modifier such as *se* connective or event adverbs. In an H-SVC type (6), V_1 and V_2 form independent domains from each other and it is natural to expect that they can be separated from each other (unless other syntactic factors block it). For instance, in (1a), v_{CAUS} is merged with 'to die' directly, and V_2 'die-CAUS' forms an independent verbal domain from V_1 'to trample'. Hence, other elements such as the *se* connective and an adverb may intervene between the two, as in (3a) and (4a). Also, the projection of V_2 may undergo movement to the left of the V_1 without a problem, as in (5a). Note, crucially, that when interveners such as the *se* connective and an adverb are placed between the two verbs, it is always outside the derivational v head.

In an L-SVC type, in contrast, V_1 and V_2 are merged together within the SVC below the derivational v head. For instance, in (1b), the argument structure is not complete yet for either 'to starve' or 'to die' before v_{CAUS} is merged. We assume that in such cases, V_1 and V_2 cannot be separated from each other by a modifier. In other words, the causative head v_{CAUS} cannot tolerate the *se* connective or an event modifier such as 'quickly' within its complement domain, as in (3b) and (4b). In the same vein, V_1 and V_2 cannot escape the complement domain of v_{CAUS} via movement, separated from its selector v head, as in (5b).

It requires further research why v heads cannot tolerate the *se* connective or an event modifier in its complement position. At this moment, we leave it as a premise. Given that, however, the point we would like to highlight here is quite clear. The connection between two verbal projections in L-SVCs is much tighter than the one in H-SVCs due to the attachment site of the derivational morpheme, and thus separation is harder for L-SVCs than for H-SVCs.

Given our discussion of morphological complex SVCs, let us turn to a consequence of our proposal for simplex SVCs in Korean. A representative example is given in (12).

(12)   *John-i   yene-lul   cap-a   mek-ess-ta.*
        John-NOM salmon-ACC catch-LK eat-PAST-DECL
        'John caught and ate a salmon.'

In (12), two verbs are serialized and there is no causative or passive morpheme to scope over them. Since there is no derivational v head higher than the serialization site, we argue that all the simple SVCs belong to the H-SVC type – it is impossible to form an L-SVC in the absence of a derivational v head in the first place. We then predict that all simple SVCs must pass the separability tests, just like the morphologically complex H-SVCs (e.g. (1a), (9a)). Indeed, they pass the separability tests involving *se*-insertion, intervening adverbial, and vP scrambling. This is shown in (13).

(13)   a. *John-i   yene-lul   cap-a-se   mek-ess-ta.*
           John-NOM salmon-ACC catch-LK-SE eat-PAST-DECL
           'John caught a salmon and then ate the salmon.'
    b. *John-i   yene-lul   cap-a   kuphi mek-ess-ta.*
           John-NOM salmon-ACC catch-LK quickly eat-PAST-DECL
           'John caught and ate a salmon quickly.'
    c. *yene-lul   cap-a   John-i   mek-ess-ta.*
           salmon-ACC catch-LK John-NOM eat-PAST-DECL
           'John caught and ate a salmon.'

1.2 Internal Structure of Serialized Verbal Complex

Before moving on to the next section, we further elaborate on our dichotomy with reference to the theory of serialization couched in Baker and Stewart (2002). Our proposals on the internal structure of serialized verbal complex are built on two crucial assumptions.

First, we assume that SVCs in Korean involve a vP-vP adjunction structure, adopting Baker and Stewart's (2002) proposal. Baker and Stewart argue that there are three types of SVCs in Edo, Nupe and Yoruba, Niger-Congo languages of West Africa: consequential, purposive and resultative SVCs. They argue that the consequential SVC is formed by adjoining a vP to another vP. Since the SVCs we deal with in this paper belong to this type of SVC in terms of their interpretation, we adopt the vP-vP adjunction structure: the preceding vP$_1$ adjoins to the following vP$_2$.

Second, we follow a decompositional approach to morphologically derived verbs. The causative and the passive morphemes are phonetic realizations of syntactic heads. Specifically, we assume that they are realizations of v_{CAUS} and v_{PASS} heads, each of which takes another vP as its complement. On this view, morphologically derived verbs involve two layers of vPs while non-derived ones involve only one vP which takes a VP as its complement.

Given the two assumptions addressed above, it follows that causative or passive SVCs in principle contain two sites available for verbal serialization - the lower level of vP and the higher one. If we couple our proposal on the dichotomy of SVCs above with the vP adjunction structures, we obtain a more elaborate picture of two types of SVCs in (14) and (15). If the serialization occurs at the lower vP level and the $v_{CAUS/PASS}$ is merged subsequently, we obtain an L-SVC, as in (14). If the serialization targets the higher vP, an H-SVC results, as in (15a). If there is no causative or passive v to be introduced in the first place, it belongs to an H-SVC type, where the serialization targets the highest (and the only) light verbal projection, as in (15b).

(14)   L-SVC: vP$_{CAUS/PASS}$

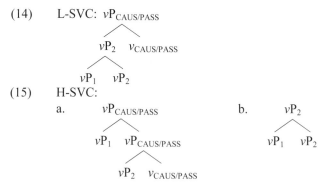

(15)   H-SVC:

Under the proposals in (14) and (15), the examples discussed in the previous section can be analyzed as in (16) and

(17), with labels specified. The tree structures in (16) represent the H-SVCs in (1a) and (12), and those in

(17) represent the L-SVCs in (1b) and (9b).

(16)   H-SVC

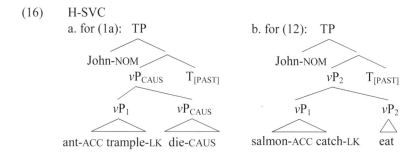

(17) L-SVC

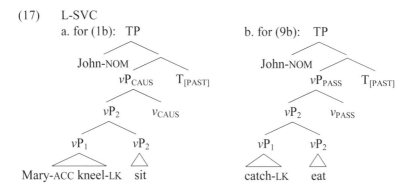

2. Different Types of *v* Heads in Serialization

In this section, we discuss a condition on verbal serialization. We argue that the condition on verbal serialization must be understood with reference to the merger site of *v*, as proposed in (14)-(15), as well as the typology of *v*. We also show that the proposed condition has broader empirical coverage than the ones proposed in previous studies.

2.1 Condition on Serialization

The contrast in (18) suggests that not any random combination of verbs can form a legitimate SVC, but there must be a condition to license verbal serialization. (18a) shows that *palp* 'to trample' and *cwuk* 'to die' cannot be serialized, and (18b) shows that *palp* 'to trample' can be serialized with *cwuk-i* 'to die-CAUS'.

(18) a. **John-i   kaymi-lul palp-a   cwuk-ess-ta.*
           John-NOM ant-ACC   trample-LK die-PAST-DECL
           'John trampled an ant and the ant died.' (intended)
      b. *John-i   kaymi-lul palp-a   cwuk-i-ess-ta.*
           John-NOM ant-ACC   trample-LK die-CAUS-PAST-DECL
           'John trampled an ant to death.'

In fact, which combination of verbs can be serialized together has been a recurrent issue in Korean syntax (e.g. Chung 1993, Kang 1997, Lee 2003, Lee 2006, Zubizarreta and Oh 2007). A number of previous studies tried to seek a better generalization to capture the condition on serialization. The previous studies state the condition in different terms. One influential approach, represented by Chung (1993), argues that the condition in SVCs must be stated in terms of θ-roles. Another approach by Kang (1997) argues that the condition hinges on the syntactic type of the verbs. The other approach by Lee (2003) argues that the semantic type of the verbs plays a role in serialization.

All of the three previous studies refer to the argument structure of the verb in order to explain a condition for SVCs in Korean. We believe that this idea is basically on the right track. However, we argue that the key to understanding the condition on SVCs lies in the typology of the v head, rather than in the θ-roles, the syntactic or semantics type of verbs.

Specifically, we propose a Matching Condition on verbal serialization as in (19):

(19)   *Matching Condition on Verbal Serialization*
        Verbs can be serialized with each other only when their v heads have the same property in introducing an external argument.

We posit different types of v heads, adapting Harley's (2006) classification of v. In the preceding section, we used v_{CAUS} and v_{PASS} responsible for forming a morphological causative and passive verb respectively. Here, we add two more types into the inventory: v_{DO} and v_{INCH}. The list of v heads we employ is illustrated in (20).

(20)   a. v_{DO}: introduces an external argument carrying an Agent θ-role.
        b: v_{INCH}: carries an inchoative meaning and does not introduce an external argument.
        c. v_{CAUS}: carries a causative meaning and gives its external argument a Causer θ-role.   (cf. Harley 2006: 16)
        d. v_{PASS}: does not introduce an external argument and demotes one introduced by the head of its complement, vP_{DO}.

Among the four types in (20), v_{DO} and v_{CAUS} introduce an external argument, and v_{INCH} and v_{PASS} do not. For convenience, we call the verbal heads that introduce an external argument [+EA class], and those which do not [-EA class]. That is, v_{DO} and v_{CAUS} belong to the [+EA class] and v_{INCH} and v_{PASS} the [-EA class]. If (19) is correct, we expect that vP_{DO} can be serialized with another [+EA class], vP_{DO} or a vP_{CAUS}, but not with vP_{INCH} or vP_{PASS}. Similarly, vP_{INCH} can be serialized with another [+EA class] vP_{INCH} or vP_{PASS}, but not with [-EA class] verbs.

Possible and impossible combinations of vPs are summarized in (21) for H-SVCs.

(21)   Prediction for H-SVC:

$V_1 \diagdown V_2$	$v\text{P}_{DO}$	$v\text{P}_{INCH}$	$v\text{P}_{CAUS}$	$v\text{P}_{PASS}$
$v\text{P}_{DO}$	✓	*	✓	*
$v\text{P}_{INCH}$	*	✓	*	✓
$v\text{P}_{CAUS}$	✓	*	✓	*
$v\text{P}_{PASS}$	*	✓	*	✓

According to the table in (21), the contrast in grammaticality in (18) can be successfully explained. In (18a), the preceding verb, *palp* 'to trample' is $v\text{P}_{DO}$ and the following one, *cwuk* 'to die' is $v\text{P}_{INCH}$ - hence, [EA] mismatch. In (18b), on the other hand, the preceding verb, *palp* 'to trample' is $v\text{P}_{DO}$ and the following one, *cwuk-i* 'to kill' is of $v\text{P}_{CAUS}$ - conforming to (19). (See Sohn and Ko 2009 for a comprehensive list of examples which show that the predictions in (21) are borne out.)

Turning to L-SVCs where the causative/passive v takes the serialized verbal complex as its complement, possible and impossible combinations of vPs in L-SVCs are listed in table (22).[1] The prediction is largely borne out, as described in (23). (There are three cases where our prediction seems to fail, which are marked as unexpectedly bad. See Section 2.3.).

(22)   Prediction for L-SVC:

higher v V_1+V_2	v_{CAUS}	v_{PASS}
$v\text{P}_{DO}$-$v\text{P}_{DO}$	✓	✓
$v\text{P}_{CAUS}$-$v\text{P}_{DO}$	✓ -unexpectedly bad	✓ -unexpectedly bad
$v\text{P}_{INCH}$-$v\text{P}_{INCH}$	✓	* (v_{PASS} does not select $v\text{P}_{INCH}$)
$v\text{P}_{PASS}$-$v\text{P}_{INCH}$	✓ -unexpectedly bad	* (v_{PASS} does not select $v\text{P}_{INCH}$)
$v\text{P}_{DO}$-$v\text{P}_{INCH}$	*	* (v_{PASS} does not select $v\text{P}_{INCH}$)
$v\text{P}_{INCH}$-$v\text{P}_{DO}$	*	*
$v\text{P}_{PASS}$-$v\text{P}_{DO}$	*	*
$v\text{P}_{CAUS}$-$v\text{P}_{INCH}$	*	* (v_{PASS} does not select $v\text{P}_{INCH}$)

(23)   Grammatical L-SVC

    a. [$v\text{P}_{DO}$–$v\text{P}_{DO}$]-v_{CAUS}:

       John-i   Mary-lul [kkwul-e anc]-hi-ess-ta

       John-NOM Mary-ACC [kneel-LK   sit]-CAUS-PAST-DECL

       'John made Mary kneel down.'

---

[1] Throughout the paper, we assume that in L-SVCs, the second vP is subcategorized for by the higher v_{CAUS} or v_{PASS}, and that $v_{CAUS/PASS}$ cannot select another $v\text{P}_{CAUS}$.

b. $[vP_{INCH}-vP_{INCH}]-v_{CAUS}$:

John-i   *kaymi-lul* [*kwulm-e*   *cwuk*]-*i-ess-ta.*

John-NOM ant-ACC   [starve(intr.)-LK die]-CAUS-PAST-DECL

'John starved an ant to death.'

(24)   Ungrammatical L-SVCs (Sohn and Ko 2009 for more examples)

    a. $[v_{DO}-v_{INCH}]-v_{CAUS}$:

        **John-i*   *Bill-ul*   *ciloy-lul*

        John-NOM Bill-ACC landmine-ACC

        [*palp-a*   *cwuk*]-*i-ess-ta.*

        [trample-LK die]-CAUS-PAST-DECL

        'John made Bill step on a landmine and die.' (intended)

    b. $[v_{INCH}-v_{DO}]-v_{CAUS}$:

        **John-i*   *Mary-lul*   *laymen-ul*

        John-NOM Mary-ACC noodle-ACC

        [*kkulh-e*   *mek*]-*i-ess-ta.*

        [boil(intr.)-LK eat]-CAUS-PAST-DECL

        'John boiled noodle and feed it to Mary.' (intended)

2.2 Comparison

The merit of our approach can be clearly seen when the same sequence of verbal heads are serialized in different ways. Suppose that three v heads, v_1, v_2, v_{CAUS}, are combined together to form a complex SVC. If vP_1 and vP_2 are projected and combined together before the causativization (L-SVC), we expect that [EA class] matching must occur between vP_1 and vP_2. In contrast, if v_{CAUS} is merged to vP_2 first and then serialization happens later (H-SVC), we predict that [EA class] matching must occur between vP_1 and vP_{CAUS}. That is, even though we have the same linear sequence of v_1, v_2, v_{CAUS}, we predict different matching effects, depending on the merger site of the derivational head. This prediction is borne out, as shown by (25).

The sequence $v_{DO}-v_{INCH}-v_{CAUS}$ ('trample-die-CAUS') in (1a), repeated in (25a), forms a legitimate SVC, while the exactly same sequence does not form a grammatical SVC in (25b).

(25)   a. *John-i*   *kaymi-lul* [*palp-a*]   [*cwuk-i*]-*ess-ta.*

        John-NOM ant-ACC [trample-LK] [die-CAUS]-PAST-DECL

        'John trampled an ant to death.'

    b. **John-i*   *Bill-ul*   *ciloy-lul*

        John-NOM Bill-ACC landmine-ACC

        [*palp-a*   *cwuk*]-*i-ess-ta.*

        [trample-LK die]-CAUS-PAST-DECL

        'John made Bill$_i$ trample a landmine to death.' (intended)

On our view, the contrast in (25) can be explained by different structures. (25a) represents an H-SVC, where the causative morpheme scopes over *cwuk* 'to die', not over *palp* 'to trample'. Thus, we are led to assume that serialization occurs between vP_{DO} 'to trample' and vP_{CAUS} containing vP_{INCH} 'to die-CAUS'. Since both vP_{DO} and vP_{CAUS} belong to the [+EA class], we predict that (25a) would be grammatical.

By contrast, (25b) is intended to represent an L-SVC, where the causative morpheme scopes over both *palp* 'to trample' and *cwuk* 'to die'. Since serialization occurs between vP_{DO} 'to trample' and vP_{INCH} 'to die' prior to the merger of v_{CAUS}, we predict that (25b) is ruled out by our matching condition (19): the heads of the two vPs do not match in class (i.e. v_{DO} belongs to the [+EA class] and v_{INCH} belongs to the [-EA class]). The contrast between (25a) and (25b) cannot be explained without positing the two different types of SVCs that we propose.

Our matching condition coupled with the dichotomy of complex SVCs also has broader empirical coverage than the previous analyses (e.g. Chung 1993, Kang 1997, and Lee 2003). First, it is not clear how the previous analyses would explain the grammaticality of L-SVCs in (23)-(24). The previous analyses implicitly or explicitly assume that the internal structure of morphologically derived verbs is opaque in syntax. If the morphological causative and passive verbs are not different from lexical verbs in syntax, however, there is no way for the serialization to precede the merger of the causative or passive morpheme. Hence, the contrast between the two types of SVCs cannot be properly explained. Second, a contrast such as (25) is not expected unless previous studies incorporate our proposal for the two types of SVCs. Lastly, even if one rejects our L-SVC analysis and accommodates the L-SVC data with other mechanisms, it would remain a mystery why scopal differences between H-SVCs and L-SVCs correlate with their different syntactic behavior.

We have seen that all the asymmetries and symmetries observed here can be naturally explained by our Matching Condition on serialization.

2.3 Unexpected Gaps

Finally, let us turn to the three unexpectedly bad patterns in L-SVCs. These are L-SVCs made up of two vPs from the same [EA class], but are judged ungrammatical. The problematic examples are given in (26).

(26)   a. $[vP_{CAUS}\text{-}vP_{DO}]\text{-}v_{CAUS}$:
          *yene-ka   [kkulh-i-e   mek]-hi-ess-ta.
          salmon-NOM   [boil-CAUS-LK eat]-PASS-PAST-DECL
          'A salmon was boiled and eaten.' (intended)

b. [v_{PASS}-v_{INCH}]-v_{CAUS}:

   *John-i   kaymi-lul   [palp-hi-e   cwuk]-i-ess-ta.
   John-NOM ant-ACC   [trample-PASS-LK die]-CAUS-PAST-DECL
   'John made an ant trampled and die.' (intended)

c. [v_{PCAUS}-v_{PDO}]-v_{PASS}:

   *lamyen-i   [kkulh-i-e   mek]-hi-ess-ta.
   noodle-NOM [boil-CAUS-LK eat]-PASS-PAST-DECL
   'Noodle was boiled and eaten.' (intended)

We do not have a fully developed answer for these exceptions, but the type of v seems to matter in capturing the generalization. In (26), the vPs contain a derivational head v (e.g., v_{CAUS} or v_{PASS}) embedded under another derivational v, unlike (23). For some reason, it seems that a derivational v head cannot be embedded under another derivational v head: in other words, causatization of causativized/passivized verbal complex and passivization of causativized/passivized verbal complex seem to be banned for independent reasons. There may be many ways of deriving this generalization from other consideration. At this moment, we simply stipulate that the derivational causative/passive v head does not select another derivational v in its domain.

3. Concluding Remarks

In this paper, we have argued that Korean SVCs must be divided into two types, depending on whether a causative or passive morpheme is merged before or after verbal serialization. We also argued that the condition on verbal serialization must be understood with reference to the type of v, and showed that when coupled with the dichotomy of SVCs, it can successfully account for the grammaticality of SVCs in Korean.

Theoretically, our study supports the line of approaches which maintain that the morphology and the syntax are intertwined (e.g. a model represented by Distributed Morphology). That the merger of the derivational suffixes (e.g. causative and passive suffixes) can follow the verbal serialization strongly suggests that the former can occur in the syntax if the latter is a syntactic operation. Our arguments also provide support for the finer-grained classification of v (e.g. Harley 2006). In addition to the v_{CAUS} and v_{PASS}, we assumed two more varieties of v, v_{DO} and v_{INCH}, borrowing from Harley (2006). We believe the classification of v gets strong support from its usefulness in stating the matching condition on verbal serialization as well as in the dichotomy of SVC.

There are other remaining issues that have not been dealt with here. We have not discussed how the shared argument reading obtains in SVC. For example, if SVCs indeed involve a vP-vP adjunction structure, one of the vPs should contain empty categories, but we remained inconclusive about their position and identity. We also kept silent about how Case-checking or assignment occurs in SVCs. Also left undiscovered is the issue of what other types of SVC there could be in Korean besides the consequential type. We hope that more complete answer will be given to these questions in future studies.

References

Baker, M. and O. T. Stewart. 2002. A Serial Verb Construction Without Constructions. Ms., Rutgers University.

Borer, H. 2004. *Structuring Sense*. Oxford: Oxford University Press.

Choi, H.-B. 1929/1989. *Wuli Malpon* (Our Grammar). Seoul: Cheungumsa.

Choi, S. 2003. Serial Verbs and the Empty Category. *Proceedings of the Workshop on Multi-Verb Constructions*. Trondheim Summer School 2003.

Chung, T. 1993. Argument Structure and Serial Verbs in Korean. Doctoral dissertation, University of Texas, Austin.

Folli, R. and H. Harley. 2005. Consuming Results in Italian and English: Flavors of v. *Aspectual Inquiries*, eds. P. Kempchinsky and S. Slabakova. Dordrecht: Springer.

Harley, H. 2006. The Morphology of Nominalization and the Syntax of vP. To appear in *Quantification, Definiteness, and Nominalization*, eds. A. Giannakidou, and M. Rathert. Oxford: Oxford University Press.

Kang, S.-M. 1997. A Comparative Analysis of SVCs and Korean V-V Compounds. Ms., University of Florida.

Lee, S.-H. 1992. The Syntax and Semantics of Serial Verb Constructions. Doctoral dissertation, University of Washington, Seattle.

Lee, Y. 2003. Two Kinds of Structural Relationships in SVCs. *Proceedings of ICKL 13*.

Lee, C.-H. 2006. Word Formation Rule and Category Conversion. *Journal of Korean Linguistics* 91: 129-161.

Sohn, H.-M. 1976. Semantics of Compound Verbs in Korean [in Korean]. *Linguistic Journal of Korea* 1(1): 142-150.

Sohn, D. and H. Ko. 2009. Condition on Verbal Serialization: The Role of Merger and Typology of *v* Categories, Ms. MIT& SNU.

Son, M. 2006. Causation, and Syntactic Decomposition of Events. Doctoral dissertation, University of Delaware, Delaware.

Zubizarreta, M. L. and E. Oh. 2007. *On the Syntactic Composition of Manner and Motion*. Cambridge, MA: MIT Press

Kuroda's (1978) Linear Case Marking Hypothesis Revisited

ICHIRO YUHARA
Keio University

1. Introduction

Haj Ross once told me that he had learned two *kooan* (Zen parables) from Shige-Yuki Kuroda in their MIT days. Which one they were is irrelevant to the following discussion, but this anecdote is suggestive to me in that Kuroda's work always reminds me of another conundrum for Zen meditation: What is new is actually old.

In this paper, I would like to reconstruct Kuroda's Linear Case Marking hypothesis [henceforth LCM] from the perspective of Autolexical Syntax [ALS] (Sadock 1991).[1] In my view, Kuroda (1978) *Case marking, canonical sentence patterns and counter equi in Japanese* is replete with important observations and original proposals concerning the realization of morphological case accompanied by complex predicate formations. Nevertheless, many important insights of that paper have been neglected over 30 years presumably because his syntactic theorizing was out of step with the

---

[1] Although the term "Linear Case Marking" first appeared in Kuroda (1986), Kuroda has since used the name (abbreviated LCM) in reference to his earlier work in Kuroda (1978). In this paper, I follow the latter convention.

Japanese/Korean Linguistics 19.
Edited by Ho-min Sohn, Haruko Cook, William O'Grady, Leon A. Serafim, & Sang Yee Cheon.
Copyright © 2011, CSLI Publications

then-latest conception of transformational generative grammar. I consequently suspect that our understandings of the Japanese language might have considerably been delayed compared to those of other languages.

For example, Kuroda (1978) was one of the earliest published articles on Japanese syntax that correctly identified the Double-*o* Constraint, be it syntactic or phonological, as insufficient (or even irrelevant to some speakers) for eliminating two accusative nominals at surface structure when it is discussed with the productive causative construction.[2] Moreover, Kuroda (1978) is also one of the few works that successfully formalizes a way of treating a variety of case frames produced by the interaction of *o*-causatives and *ni*-causatives without losing the insight of classical transformational grammar that information is fed to interpretation both from a bipropositional semantic structure (later known as "Logical Form") and a monoclausal syntactic structure. Furthermore, by arguing for separation of morphological case particles from certain syntactic configurations, or "Government" (the crux of the LCM hypothesis), the article anticipates the Case-in-Tier hypothesis (Yip, Maling, and Jackendoff 1987) and Backward Control (Polinsky and Potsdam 2002).

The purpose of the present paper is to defend Kuroda's LCM rule as applied to the productive causative construction alone. I do not attempt to extend it to complex potential predicates, to which his case marking rule applies best (in my view) together with the Counter Equi NP Deletion rule. I defend this position using ALS, which argues for the constraints in grammar that work by comparing multiple, parallel grammatical representations, rather than transformationally deriving one level of analysis from another (e.g. constraints on movement). The following discussion is thus limited in scope, and my proposed analysis is technically very different from his original proposal (e.g. no deletion rules, no subject -*ni* Raising, etc). Despite such apparent differences, however, I find that there are a great many of conceptual affinities between the architecture of ALS and remarks that Kuroda had addressed as to what universal grammar would look like were it based more properly on the structure of the Japanese language.[3] I would hence like to propose incorporating the LCM rule into ALS since it natural-

---

[2] Kuroda's own proposal to avoid double-*o* is to cyclically throw out the embedded accusative nominal through recourse to the Canonical Sentence Pattern filter (Kuroda 1978:35). The possibility of surfacing double-*o* in questions is thus eliminated in the course of derivation in Kuroda's framework.

[3] In fact, Kuroda favorably mentions some ideas behind ALS. See Kuroda (1981:103) and Kuroda (2003: 461) for example. What strikes me as conceptually similar in the context of the present paper is (i) that one mode of signaling grammatical relations is morphological case particles (Kuroda 1992: 7-8) and (ii) that (so-called) syntactic principles and wordhood are two logically independent issues (Kuroda 2003: 452-458).

ly and effectively works with multi-modular grammar in reference to productive causative sentence.[4]

To anticipate, I will propose that the distribution of morphological case particles is a function of corresponding rules, which linearly relate over nominal expressions to arguments and participant roles across distinct grammatical modules. I also contend that in order to account for the much-discussed case alternations with the causative construction (e.g. on causee nominal), we are required to elevate a hitherto relegated conceptual-semantic level of representation to a fundamental linguistic construct and to allow denotational aspects of meaning to play a formal role in grammar (cf. Dowty 1991). Crucially, I will formalize the conditions under which such a cognitive level of analysis is invoked as justification for the grammatical architecture of ALS.

The organization of this paper is as follows. Section 2 describes the basic facts of the productive causative construction accumulated over the past few decades. Section 3 provides a very brief overview its analytic history in mainstream generative grammar and points out the limit of such approaches in critically reviewing Miyagawa's (1999) LF A-Movement analysis. Section 4 offers an Autolexical proposal for the causative construction and similar phenomena and Section 5 summarizes the present work.

2. Two Major Issues in the Japanese Productive Causative

Since the 1960s, much work on the Japanese causative sentence has mainly centered on two issues. The first is concerned about the defining characteristic of complex predicates, a way to simultaneously capture monoclausal and biclausal properties in syntactic derivation. The derived causative verb is a morpho-phonologically integrated word, and as such, it undoubtedly projects a simplex sentence. There are at least five pieces of evidence that argue for monoclausality in syntax.

(1) Monoclausal Properties
    a. case array for simplex sentences
    b. scrambling
    c. the double-*o* constraint (cf., Shibatani 1973; Harada 1973)
    d. licensing of NPI *sika* ('only') (cf., Muraki 1978; Kitagawa 1986)
    e. licensing of subject honorification (cf. Shibatani 1977)

---

[4] This is a legitimate application. As mentioned in Kuroda (1992:5), the LCM hypothesis resembles the Case-in-Tier hypothesis (Yip, Maling, and Jackendoff 1987). The latter adopts the basic idea from Autosegmental Phonology (Goldsmith 1976), which in turn shares its guiding philosophy with ALS.

On the other hand, the complex causative verb also presents compelling evidence of projecting biclausal structure, which is often interpreted as incongruous with the monoclausal properties listed above.

(2) Biclausal Properties
  a. ambiguous interpretation of the subject-controlled *zibun* reflexive (cf., Kuroda 1965; Kuno 1973).
  b. scope differences of manner adverbials (cf., Shibatani 1976)
  c. ambiguity of *soo suru* ('do so') replacement (cf., Shibatani 1976)
  d. scope differences that *-sase* takes externally or internally to the base verb (cf., Kitagawa 1986)
  e. coordination between a simplex verb and a derived verb where the former is under the scope of causation (cf., Kuroda 2003).

These facts have been extensively discussed in the development of generative grammar in Japanese, and thus, it is beyond the scope of the present paper to provide a review of each of these phenomena. In both the classical Transformational Generative Grammar [TGG] and (early) Principles and Parameters [P&P] theories, a biclausal structure is assumed at the level of Deep Structure [DS]. They are then reduced into a monoclausal structure at Surface Structure [SS] by means of a Transformation rule such as Predicate Raising and Verb Raising. Although theories diverge as to when, how and what type of underlying structure undergoes a restructuring, the transformational approach is schematically represented roughly as Figure 1 below.

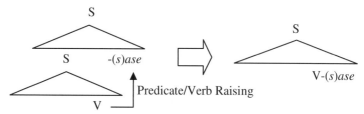

Figure 1. Transformational Approach (1960s - mid 1980s)

The second issue concerning the *V-sase* causative construction is how to account for subtle differences in meaning associated with the *ni*-causee nominal and the *o*-causee nominal in derivation, which are most visible with intransitive stems. Note that the use of *let* (for *ni*-causatives) and *make* (for *o*-causaives) in glossing of the present article (following Kuno 1973) does not describe a difference in Japanese that corresponds exactly to English.

(3)　　Taroo-ga　　　　Hanako-ni/o　　　　hatarak-ase-ta.
　　　　Taro-NOM　　　　Hanako-DAT/ACC　work-CAUSE-PAST
　　　　Taro let/made Hanako work.

The semantic boundary between *ni*-causatives and *o*-causatives depends ultimately on the way the speaker construes the causative event in question but there is a certain tendency for *ni*-marked causees to have a more volitional or self-controllable interpretation compared to *o*-marked causees, which entail a more coercive or uncontrollable reading (cf. Shibatani 1973, 1976). Therefore, if unaccusative verbs such as *kizetusuru* ('faint') and *kusaru* ('rot') enter into the *V-sase* construction, the causee will be likely to receive -*o*, inasmuch as the participant thematic role of the base verb is patientive and it is pragmatically at odds with the volitional reading that the *ni*-marked causee provides by default. On the other hand, when a transitive stem makes its way into the causative construction, the opposition between *ni*-causee and *o*-causee becomes formally neutralized due to the existence of the (so-called) Double-*o* Constraint in Japanese, which restricts two internal arguments from figuring in a simplex sentence with the accusative case -*o* (cf. Shibatani 1973, Harada 1973).

(4)　　Taro-ga　Hanako-ni　tegami-o　kak-ase-ta
　　　　Taro-NOM Hanako-DAT　letter-ACC　write-CAUSE-PAST
　　　　Taro let/made Hanako write a letter.
(5)　　*Taro-ga　　　　Hanako-o　　tegami-o　kak-ase-ta.

Thus, even though Japanese may not allow the causee nominal to receive -*o* with a transitive stem as in (5), it is plausible to think that there is a semantic counterpart of the *o*-causee at some level of analysis of (4). In other words, the sentence can arguably be conceived of as ambiguous between *o*-causative and *ni*-causative interpretations (cf. Kuroda 1965). The fact that *ni*-marked causees with transitive underlying verbs are modified by adverbials such as *muriyari* ('coercively') and *iyaiya* ('reluctantly') may confirm this conjecture that they do have an *o*-causative, or coercive, interpretation.

(6)　　Taro-ga　Hanako-ni　*muriyari*　tegami-o　kak-ase-ta
　　　　Taro-NOM Hanako-DAT coercively　letter-ACC　write-CAUSE-PAST
　　　　Taro coercively made Hanako write a letter.

3. A Brief Analytic History of the Japanese Causative in Transformational Generative Grammar

Based on the assumption in TGG and P&P that DS is the input level that determines predicative relations for the subsequent syntactic derivation, the semantic difference between coerced and volitional causees must be accounted for at DS. Hence, generative analyses of the Japanese causative construction argue vehemently which causative is best represented in what type of DS. Two proposed underlying structures are diagrammed below with simple classical notations for expository purposes.

(7) Two Types of Deep Structure
    a. Control (or Equi) type
          $[_S$ NP $[_{VP}$ NP$_i$ $[_S$ NP$_i$ VP] -sase-]]
    b. ECM (or Raising) type
          $[_S$ NP $[_S$ NP VP] -sase-]

Few generative grammarians have questioned positing two DS representations like (7a) and (7b). Some have argued that the coerced causee (or *o*-causative) derives from a Control type (the matrix VP complement headed by -*sase* in (7a)), and the volitional causee (or *ni*-causative) from an ECM type of syntactic configuration (the embedded subject position in (7b)). And others have argued the reverse. Tonoike (1978) dubs the former "the *o* extra-NP analysis" and the latter "the *ni* extra-NP analysis." These two camps are summarized in the table below.

Table 1. Two Opposing Views on Deep Structure

	Control type VP complement	ECM type embedded subject
the *o* extra-NP analysis	the *o*-causative (=coercive causee)	the *ni*-causative
the *ni* extra-NP analysis	the *ni*-causative	the *o*-causative (=coercive causee)

Researchers in both camps have taken great pains to adduce syntactic reasons in support of their analyses. Each interpretation may have offered certain advantages over the other but it is probably safe to say that neither perspective has arrived at a decisive conclusion despite forty odd years of detailed research.

The reason for this unsatisfactory situation seems to arise from a very simple assumption underlying these approaches. To put it somewhat boldly, the difficulty is intrinsic to the grammatical architecture in mainstream generative grammar. Recall that complex predicates represented by the *V-sase* causative bear simultaneously monoclausal and biclausal properties in the mainstream generative analytic tradition. Given that, to the extent that one discusses the dual, incongruous properties in terms of translating one representational level into another in a step-by-step fashion, the result is more or less the same. That is to say, such a grammar is logically unable to provide simultaneously available levels of representation, so that it demands a terminal representation (or "Spell-Out" in current terminology) to be necessarily categorical in character.[5] In other words, solutions to the case assignment problems cannot simply be localized in either an *o*-extra NP analysis or a *ni*-extra NP analysis, but rather must be sought in the manner in which one asks whether the grammatical architecture s/he espouses is optimal in dealing with the two apparently incompatible properties that simultaneously exist in the grammar of the Japanese language.

With this in mind, let us briefly review a recent proposal in the TGG and P&P tradition, Miyagawa's (1999) LF A-Movement analysis. There are four major proposals in the LF-A Movement analysis, which are listed below.

(8) The LF A-Movement Analysis (Miyagawa 1999)
    a. supports the *ni* extra-NP analysis for the Japanese productive causative: The volitional (his "let") causee derives from the matrix VP complement position headed by *-sase* (=7a) and the coerced (his "make") causee the subject of the embedded clause (=7b).
    b. The matrix and embedded clauses never undergo restructuring, so biclausal structure remains intact throughout the derivation.
    c. The coerced causee nominal checks off its Object Case at LF by raising to the specifier position of AGRoP in the manner of an ECM construction (= LF A-Movement).
    d. The Double-*o* Constraint is a constraint on PF, but not on syntax.

Miyagawa claims on the basis of Binding effects that the matrix and embedded clauses never undergo restructuring so that biclausal structure remains intact throughout the derivation (=8b). In order to explain the Double-*o* Constraint on monoclausal syntax, he assumes that the *o*-marked causee nominal is generated at the embedded subject position. After Spell-Out, or at LF, it is covertly raised to the matrix object position so as to check off its accusative case feature (or the like in support of the grammatical architecture of the Minimalist Program (=8c). As a corollary, when the base verb

---

[5] In my view, Kitagawa (1986) is the sole work in derivational grammar that ingeniously avoids this problem by introducing "Affix-Raising" to LF.

is transitive, both the *o*-marked causee nominal and the embedded object nominal legitimately figure in the same embedded clause at surface. Under this view, the Double-*o* Constraint is not a syntactic but a PF constraint, which removes the double-*o* sequence immediately after it is Spelled-Out, or at the PF component (=8d).

Plausible as this proposal may sound, several empirical facts contradict this analysis. First, the *V-sase* complex does project a monoclausal syntax. As is well known, the negative polarity item *-sika* (*...nai*) is licensed only within a simplex sentence. The LF A-Movement analysis incorrectly predicts that whereas *o*-marked causee nominals and *-sika* are permitted by *V-sase-nai* within the embedded clause, *ni*-marked causee nominals and *-sika* are not, because NP-*ni-sika* and *V-sase-nai* are supposed to figure in two separate clauses in isolation throughout the derivation. In fact, both kinds of causee nominals do allow *-sika* to be licensed by *V-sase-nai* as in the following pair of examples.

(9)   Taro-ga   Hanako-sika musume-to   aw-ase-nak-atta.
         Taro-NOM Hanako-SIKA daughter-with meet-CAUSE-NEG-PAST
         Taro made only Hanako meet with his daughter.

(10)   Taro-ga   Hanako-ni-sika   musume-to   aw-ase-nak-atta.
         Taro-NOM Hanako-NI-SIKA   daughter-with meet-CAUSE-NEG-PAST
         Tao let only Hanako meet with his daughter.

The way *-sika* concatenates to the preceding formative is somewhat different between the two sentences, but of importance here is that (10) is a perfectly acceptable sentence.

Another presumably more serious problem for this analysis is that if two *o*-marked nominals are handled as violating the PF Double-*o* Constraint, the *o*-marked nominal in the elided sentence must be sanctioned and interpreted as ambiguous between causee and patient.

(11)   Taro-ga   Hanako-o   [e]   koros-ase-ta
         Taro-NOM   Hanako-ACC   kill-CAUSE-PAST
    a.   *Taro made Hanako kill [someone].
    b.   Taro made [someone] kill Hanako.

However, this ambiguous interpretation is unavailable. The *o*-marked nominal (*Hanako*) must be understood as the victim of a murder case (=11b). Crucially, there is no interpretation available that *Hanako* is the killer

(=11a).[6] Likewise, if one of two *o*-marked nominals is supplanted by the topic marker *-wa*, the resulting sentence should be judged as grammatical in Miyagawa's treatment, which is again contrary to the intuitions of most speakers.[7]

(12)   *biiru-wa   Taro-ga   Hanako-o   nom-ase-ta.
        beer-TOP   Taro-NOM   Hanako-ACC   drink-CAUSE-PAST
        As for beer, Taro made Hanako drink [it].

What matters here is not merely connecting the accusative case *-o* with a relatively more proto-patient like argument. Such a linking must also be flexible enough to concede functional demands for the language that eschew two identical formatives. This is particularly important to the causative in question because the causee nominal may receive *-o* for *ni*-causatives (*contra* (6)) when the base is a transitive verb that is subcategorized for *ni* marked object as in *soodansuru* ('consult') and *au* ('meet').

(13)   Taro-ga   Hanako-o   bengosi-ni   soodans-ase-ta.
        Taro-NOM   Hanako-ACC   lawyer-DAT   consult-CAUSE-PAST
        Taro let/made Hanako consult a lawyer.

Taken together, these examples clearly show, contrary to much work represented in Miyagawa (1999), that (i) the derived causative sentence cannot possibly be biclausal, (ii) the Double-*o* Constraint is a necessary but not sufficient condition for avoiding double-*o* in the causative, and (iii) morphological case particles cannot always be identified with certain syntactic configurations (or abstract Case positions), all of which are properly recognized in Kuroda's work presented at Hawaii in the summer of 1977.

4. An Autolexical Treatment of the Japanese Productive Causative

Although Kuroda's LCM hypothesis was largely overlooked, I suggest that it can easily be incorporated into the grammatical architecture of ALS. First, given many incompatible or contradictory properties within syntax, we may seriously want to reconsider the organization in derivational grammar that Jackendoff (2002) describes as "Syntactocentric." ALS proposes multiple, highly autonomous generative components, or modules, in grammar. The idea behind this multimodular view is that by reducing apparently complex grammatical behavior to the interaction of an individually simple, compet-

---

[6] To my knowledge, this fact is pointed out first in Ueno (1994) as a potential problem for his LFG analysis. I present data and arguments in support of what is essentially the conclusion drawn by Ueno.

[7] Miyagawa (1999) does recognize this observation as originally due to William Poser.

ing structure of informationally distinct kinds (such as syntax, semantics, morphology, and phonology), it should be possible to provide a conceptually very simple account of some otherwise quite difficult phenomena. For example, the biclausal properties of the *V-sase* causative introduced early in this paper (=2) are arguably all related to combinatorial semantic phenomena that researchers like James D. McCawley argued for the existence of natural language semantics. Therefore, if we regard what are assumed, for biclausal properties as bipropositional, and further recognize that such a combinatorial semantic level, function-argument structure [F/A], exists in parallel with syntactic structure, it becomes possible to simultaneously represent the bipropositional and monoclausal properties of the *V-sase* causative with two distinct grammatical components in the following Figure 2 (next page). Because ALS regards morphology as a separate module, the morphological case particles *-ga, -o,* and *-ni* are irrelevant for these two dimensions.[8]

What is significant in Figure 2 is the lack of isomorphism between two levels of representations presumed in ALS (*contra* the Projection Principle in P&P). The *V-sase* complex in question is bipropositional in F/A and monoclausal in Syntax concurrently. Furthermore, the following categorial correspondence conditions between the two levels are assumed in ALS grammar.

Table 2. Categorial Correspondence Condition (preliminary)

F/A structure	Syntax
Proposition	S
Argument	NP

From Figure 2 and Table 2, it follows that *V-sase* (or actually any complex predicate) can be defined as a categorial mismatch in terms of the lower proposition. That is to say, in Figure 2, whereas the higher proposition (the top node) in the F/A structure is represented as an S (the top node) in Syntax, the lower proposition has no corresponding (embedded) S. In such a situation, the grammar of natural language seems to calculate the value of the arguments (*Hanako* and *letter*) and assign accusative case (or postverbal position) to the more patientive argument cross-linguistically (*letter* here), as Dowty (1991) proposes for the argument-selection principle on the basis of his proto-role analysis (cf., Ackerman and Moore 1999). I call role struc-

---

[8] I assume *-sase-* to be a transitive operator (i.e. $<t, <e, t>>$), for there is little evidence to support another type of F/A structure (e.g. $<t, <e, et>>$). The presence of a VP node is a moot point. I assume a flat structure below.

ture [RS] a level where cognitive-semantic roles play a role, and expand Table 2 to Table 3.

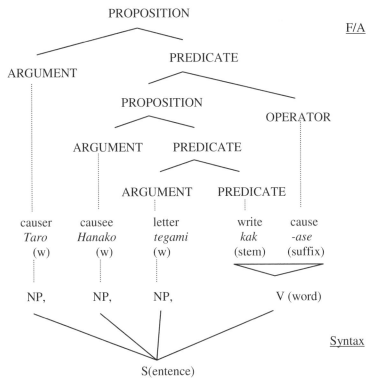

Figure 2. The Japanese Causative Representation in ALS

Table 3. Categorial Correspondence Condition (default condition)

F/A	Syntax	RS
Proposition	S	Event
Argument	NP	Participant Role

Furthermore, notice that there are hierarchical correspondences in Figure 2. The (subject) nominal *Taro* is an external argument in F/A and a proto-agent in RS. Likewise, the (object) nominal *tegami* ('letter') is an internal argument and a proto-patient. Thus, in addition to the Categorial Correspondence Condition, we also have the following Linear Correspondence Condition.

Table 4. Linear Correspondence Condition (default condition)

F/A	Syntax	RS
external Arg.	subject NP	Proto-Agent
internal Arg.	object NP	Proto-Patient

Languages differ as to how to represent "subject NP" and "object NP." Japanese as well as Korean employ morphological case particles, which are also linearly organized in the morphological module.

Table 5. Linear Organization in Morphology (accusative language)[9]

Morphology
nominative case
accusative case

Under this conception, the distribution of morphological case, which Kuroda (1978) attempts to explain without recourse to syntax, is re-characterized as the function of correspondence rules which linearly (or hierarchically) relate overt nominal expressions (in Syntax) to arguments (in F/A) and participant thematic roles (in RS). Autolexically speaking, (so-called) biclausal and monoclausal properties are respectively attributed to F/A and Syntactic structural phenomena, and the nuance in meaning accompanied by -o and -ni alternations on the causee nominal is thus characterized in RS independently of F/A and Syntax. This automodular view of grammar enables us to propose that case assignments for internal arguments in the V-(s)ase causative form (as well as most complex predicates) can be formalized along the following lines.

(14)   Linking Rule for Complex Predicates [LRCP]
       When the Categorial Correspondence Condition is not satisfied in terms of the lower proposition, (i) invoke RS and (ii)
   a. if the base verb is transitive, mark the argument corresponding to the (more) proto-patient with an accusative case and the remaining argument with a dative/oblique case.
   b. if the base verb is intransitive, mark the sole argument as either an accusative or dative/oblique case by calculating its semantic (RS) role in the lower event.

---

[9] Ergative languages have a different order. I am of the opinion that the validity of the LCM hypothesis is better attested to by how sufficiently case assignments of ergative languages are handled. For a brief sketch, the interested reader is referred to Yuhara (2008).

A consequence of the LRCP is that there is no need to discuss case alterna-tions between -*ni and -o* as tied to syntactic configurations.[10] Equally im-portantly, *Hanako*, as in *Taro-ga [e] Hanako-o korosaseta* ('*Taro made [someone] kill Hanako*') in (11), is unambiguously interpreted as the victim of a murder case. The resulting crossing association lines are diagrammed in Figure 3.

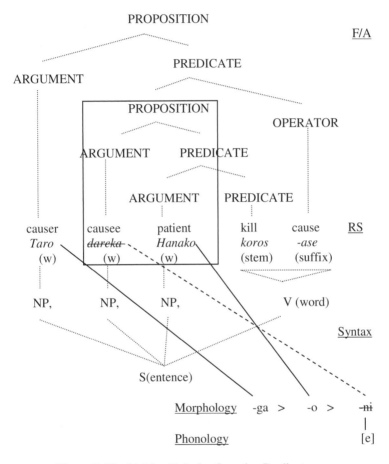

Figure 3. The Linking Rule for Complex Predicates

---

[10] Kuroda (1986) also suggests the possibility of eliminating the syntactic distinction between *ni*-causatives and *o*-causatives altogether (*ibid.* Footnote 8).

For explanatory purposes, I have provided a domain to which the LRCP applies and shown ellipsis *[e]* rendered in the phonological component in grammar above.[11]

A few expository remarks on the LRCP are in order. First, when the base verb is intransitive, there is no other competing participant role in the lower proposition, so that for argument realization, a certain semantic cut-off point is required in isolation, along the line of Dowtyan criteria for proto-agent and proto-patient properties. For instance, an inanimate entity, *ame* ('rain'), tends to receive *-o* when it is causativized, because it is difficult to imagine a world in which *rain* is eager to do something. Thus, *-ni* marking on *ame* is usually judged as unacceptable in the causative.

(15)   ame-o/*ni   fur-ase-ta
        rain-ACC/DAT fall-CAUSE-PAST
        [The shaman] made rain fall.

On the other hand, for the adversative passive, another kind of complex predicate in Japanese, the sole argument in the lower proposition, be it inanimate or animate, must receive *-ni* because the corresponding participant role is always the causer of the resulting, adversative event.

(16)   ame-ni/*o   fur-are-ta
        rain-DAT/ACC fall-ADVERSATIVE-PAST
        [I was] affected by rain having fallen (=I got rained on.)

What is needed here is to permit the grammar some device that reflects relatively a more proto-patientive/agentive argument (or a more typical direct/indirect object). Second, it is important to note that this position is not suggesting that cognitive-semantic factors determine all case markings. Rather, this analysis proposes a condition under which to invoke them in grammar. To put it differently, for predicates like *omou* ('think') and *iu* ('say'), which take a sentential complement, the LRCP is not applied. Rather, the default Categorial and Linear Correspondence Conditions suffice, as illustrated in Figure 4 (next page). Unlike complex predicates, there are two (matrix and embedded) Ss, each of which corresponds to the upper and lower propositions, respectively. The LCM rule hence applies to each S and twice in total. (Kuroda would say, the LCM applies cyclically to unmarked NPs in the domain of S.) In other words, nominative case assignments are always formal and blind to the RS representation.

---

[11] Thus, the presence of at least five different modules (F/A, Syntax, Morphology, RS, and Phonology) is assumed in ALS. For details, see Sadock (1991) and Yuhara (2008).

Third, as a head-final language, the division between monoclausal and biclausal sentences in Japanese is not always this sharp, as is contrasted in Figures 3 and 4.

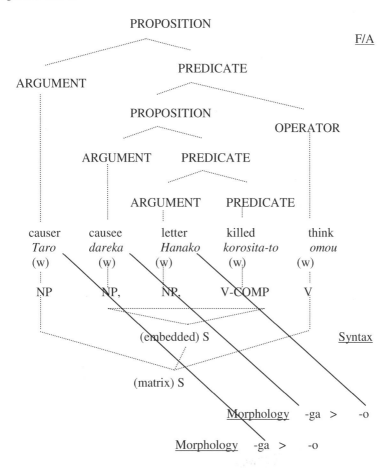

Figure 4. The LCM Rule for Biclausal Sentences in ALS

Since a predicate always comes at the end of a sentence, there are cases where the boundary between monoclausal and biclausal sentences becomes fuzzy. What I have in mind here is serial predicate constructions such as *V-te morau* ('receive a favor of someone's V-ing') and *A-ku omou* ('think something ADJ'), the latter of which may standardly be analyzed as a version of ECM and/or small clause constructions. In my view, they are all variants of complex predicates although they are morpho-phonologically not a unitary word. Hence, to the extent that these two adjacent predicates are judged as formally projecting a simplex sentence, the LRCP becomes invoked. The cardinal idea behind the LRCP is this: The more two predicates are integrated into one word, the flatter (or more monoclausal) a biclausal sentence becomes, thus increasing of the likelihood of resorting to the cognitive contents of arguments to assign case. I conjecture that this is a near-universal principle in natural languages.

Finally, while the LRCP enables grammar to weigh which argument is the relatively more-typical patient, it does not entirely exclude the possibility of representing two arguments with the same case particle. If they are calculated as having approximately the same number of, say, proto-patient properties, a grammar may allow a case particle to spread. I conjecture that this might be what happens in constructions like possessor ascension such as *Taro-ga Hanako-no/??-o yokogao-o utukusiku omotta* ('Taro thought Hanako's profile beautiful') but this issue is beyond the scope of this paper.

5. Concluding Remarks

In this article, I have argued for adopting Kuroda's (1978) LCM hypothesis reconfigured within the framework of ALS. Although this reconfiguration technically differs from Kuroda's original proposal, I have argued that (i) complex predicates must be analyzed as simultaneously bipropositional and monoclausal; (ii) case assignments should be independent from syntactic configurations so as to allow for the ranking of an argument as a relatively more direct or indirect object when there is a mismatch between the number of propositions and clauses; and (iii) the Double-*o* Constraint is insufficient to remove double-*o* if a grammar allows that form to surface. Read with a contemporary eye, Kuroda (1978) correctly addresses these points, and much of it is thoroughly new in conception. I therefore conclude that despite 30 odd years of neglect in generative studies of Japanese, Kuroda's analysis is deeply right, and no serious linguist should ever dismiss his works just because they do not fit current theory.

Acknowledgments

Thanks to the 19th Japanese/Korean Linguistics audience members for useful comments, especially Yoshihisa Kitagawa, Takashi Nakajima, William O'Grady, and Natsuko Tsujimura. My cordial thanks also go to Kazuhiko Fukushima, Jerry Sadock, and Heidi Waterfall, all of whom provided me much needed support in various forms.

References

Ackerman, F. and Moore, J. 1999. Syntagmatic and Paradigmatic Dimensions of Causee Encodings. *Linguistics and Philosophy* 22: 1-44.

Dowty, D. 1991. Thematic Proto-roles and Argument Selection. *Language* 67: 547-619.

Goldsmith, J. A. 1976. Autosegmental Phonology. Ph.D. dissertation. MIT.

Harada, S.-I. 1973. Counter-equi-NP-deletion. *Annual Bulletin* 7. The Research Institute of Logopedics and Phoniatrics. [Reprinted in *Papers in Japanese Linguistics* 9: 157-201.]

Jackendoff, R. 2002. *The Foundation of Language.* Oxford: Oxford University Press.

Kitagawa, Y. 1986. Subjects in Japanese and English. Ph.D. dissertation. University of Massachusetts, Amherst. [Published by Garland as Kitagawa 1994.]

Kuno, S. 1973. *The Structure of the Japanese Language.* Cambridge, MA: MIT Press.

Kuroda, S.-Y. 1965. Generative Grammatical Studies in the Japanese Language. Ph.D. dissertation. MIT. [Published from Garland as Kuroda 1979.]

Kuroda, S.-Y. 1978. Case Marking, Canonical Sentence Pattern, and Counter Equi in Japanese. In J. Hinds and I. Howard (Eds.), *Problems in Japanese Syntax and Semantics* (pp. 30-51). Tokyo: Kaitakusha.

Kuroda, S.-Y. 1981. Some Recent Issues in Linguistic Theory and Japanese Syntax. *Coyote Papers* 2: 103-122.

Kuroda, S.-Y. 1986. Movement of Noun Phrases in Japanese. In T. Imai and M. Saito (Eds.), *Issues in Japanese Linguistics* (pp. 229-271). Dordrecht: Foris.

Kuroda, S.-Y. 1992. *Japanese Syntax and Semantics.* Dordrecht, Kluwer.

Kuroda, S.-Y. 2003. Complex Predicates and Predicate Raising. *Lingua* 113: 447-480.

Miyagawa, S. 1999. Causatives. In N. Tsujimura (Ed.), *The Handbook of Japanese Linguistics* (pp. 236-268). Oxford: Blackwell.

Muraki, M. 1978. The *sika-nai* Construction and Predicate Restructuring. In J. Hinds and I. Howard (Eds.), *Problems in Japanese Syntax and Semantics* (pp. 155-77). Tokyo: Kaitakusya.

Polinsky, M. and Potsdam, E. 2002. Backward Control. *Linguistic Inquiry* 33: 245-282.

Sadock, J. M. 1991. *Autolexical Syntax: A Theory of Parallel Grammatical Representations.* Chicago: University of Chicago Press.

Shibatani, M. 1973. Semantics of Japanese Causativization. *Foundations of Language* 9: 327-373.

Shibatani, M. 1976. Causativization. In M. Shibatani (Ed.), *Japanese Generative Grammar* (syntax and semantics 5) (pp. 239-94). New York: Academic Press.

Shibatani, M. 1977. Grammatical Relations and Surface Cases. *Language* 53: 789-809.

Tonoike, S. 1978. On the Causative Constructions in Japanese. In J. Hinds and I. Howards (Eds.), *Problems in Japanese Syntax and Semantics* (pp. 3-29). Tokyo: Kaitakusya.

Ueno, Y. 1994. Grammatical Function and Clause Structure in Japanese. Ph.D. dissertation. University of Chicago.

Yip, M., Maling, J., and Jackendoff, R. 1987. Case in Tiers. *Language* 63: 217-50.

Yuhara, I. 2008. A Multimodular Approach to Case Assignment in Japanese: A Study of Complex and Stative Predicates. Ph.D. dissertation. University of Chicago.

Part III

Semantics

Partitive Particle *com* in Korean

JAEHEE BAK

University of Toronto / York University

So far, in Korean linguistics circles, the fact that Korean has the partitive particle has never been reported. I will give an account of the word *com*, which has only been believed to be a degree adverb and I will argue that *com* has another function: as a partitive particle in Korean.

In several dictionary definitions[1], the function of *com* as a partitive particle is never cited. Instead, *com* is principally defined as a degree adverb as in (1) or as a polite expression as in (2). The criteria for the distinction between these two definitions seem to be reliant on whether or not *com* can be replaced by the degree adverb *cokum* 'a little'.

---

* I deeply appreciate the valuable ideas and feedback on this paper which I received from B. Elan Dresher, Yoonjung Kang and Elaine Gold. I wish to extend my appreciation to Diane Massam and Peter Avery who fully supported this research.

[1] The definitions are from the standard Korean dictionary published by the National Institute of the Korean Language: http://www.korean.go.kr/06_new/dic, the Yensei Korean dictionary created by Korea Britannica Corporation: http://kordic.britannica.co.kr/ and Yahoo dictionary: http://kr.dic.yahoo.com/search/kor/

Japanese/Korean Linguistics 19.
Edited by Ho-min Sohn, Haruko Cook, William O'Grady, Leon A. Serafim, and Sang Yee Cheon.
Copyright © 2011, CSLI Publications

(1)   *Com* is the contraction form of the degree adverb *cokum* 'a little' and so
        its semantic meaning is 'a little': (henceforth *com1*)[2]

        mas-i   com1/cokum   pyenha-yess-eyo[3].
        taste-NOM   a little/a little change-PAST-DEC
        'The taste (of the food) has changed a little.'

(2)   *Com* makes an utterance polite when requesting something from someone
        and so its semantic meaning is 'please' (henceforth *com2*)

        changmwun-ul   yele-cwu-si-keyss-eyo,   com2/*com1(*cokum)?
        window-ACC   open-give-HON-FUT-REQ   please/*a little
        'Could you open the window, please?'

However, in addition to these two uses, native speakers frequently encounter another usage of *com* in daily life. This other usage of *com* is not
consistent with those of *com* in the dictionary definitions as this cannot be
interpreted as 'a little' or 'please' by any means. I propose to set apart this
com from *com1* and *com2* and label it *com3*. *Com3* is exemplified as in (3):

(3)   sensayngnim-kkeyse   kwail   com3/*com2/*com1(*cokum)
        teacher-NOM.HON   fruit   com/*please/*a little
        tu-si-ess-e?
        eat-HON-PAST-Q
        'Did the teacher eat the fruit?'

In (3), *com3* does not hold the meaning 'a little' or 'please' and it cannot
be replaced by the degree adverb *cokum* 'a little'. Thus, it leads to the questions: What is the key function of *com3*? and, What is the meaning of *com3*?
    In this paper I will clearly show that (i) *com3* should be classified as a
particle and (ii) in particular, that *com3* has the characteristics of a partitive
particle in Korean. The paper is organized as follows: in Section 1 I will
evaluate how *com3* has been treated in previous studies. In Section 2 I will
verify using empirical data that *com3* is a particle in Korean in terms of
morpho-phonological behaviors at the phrasal level. In Section 3 I will illus-

---

[2] In order to avoid ambiguity, I divide the word *com* into 3 types depending on its meaning
and function: *com1* 'a little' (degree adverb), *com2* 'please' and *com3* (partitive particle).

[3] Abbreviation: NOM (nominative), ACC (accusative), LOC (locative), TOP (topic), VOC
(vocative), PART (partitive), INST (instrumental), DIR (direction), HON (honorific), DEC
(declarative), IMP (imperative), REQ (request), QUES or Q (question), PAST (past tense),
PRES (present tense), FUT (future tense), REL (relative clause), H (high tone), L (low tone),
1sg (1st person singular)

trate the function of *com3* as a particle, which works as a partitive particle based on account of the Finnish partitive particle.

1. Previous Studies

In addition to *com1* 'a little' and *com2* 'please', the other usage of *com* (i.e. *com3* in this paper) has drawn a lot of attention in previous studies (Sohn (1989), Kwu (1998), and Cwu (2000, 2004)). However, these studies do not treat *com3* as a particle. Instead, *com3*, like *com2,* is still categorized as *com1* 'a little'. *Com3* and/or *com2* are regarded just as instances when *com1* gains certain additional semantic or pragmatic meaning in the discourse. Along this vein, Kwu (1998) and Cwu (2000) regard both *com3* and *com2* as grammatical words. Thus, the previous approaches assume that *com1* 'a little' is derived from the degree adverb *cokum* 'a little' and then, its semantic meaning develops into 'please' (i.e. *com2*) or other meanings (i.e. *com3*). In particular, Kwu (1998) insists that the various meanings of *com* occur through chronological language change (i.e. grammaticalization). Kwu's grammaticalization of *com* can be summarized as follows:

(4)   Grammaticalization of *com* in Korean (Kwu 1998):
         cokum 'a little' > *com1* 'a little' > *com2* 'please' or *com3*
                       (degree adverb)   (grammatical word)

Based on the grammaticalization proposed in Kwu (1998), *com1* 'a little' is formed as the result of the contraction of the degree adverb *cokum* 'a little'. In addition, the degree adverb *com1* 'a little' becomes a specific grammatical word via grammaticalization. This assumption makes sense if one is focusing only on dictionary definitions but in fact, it is challenged empirically and theoretically.

The first challenge is to determine what the term 'grammatical word' means and what kind of grammatical words *com2* and *com3* are as the previous studies do not explain in detail the notion 'grammatical words' as they pertain to Korean. Secondly, the notion of grammaticalization always accompanies chronological language change. If the assumption in (4) is true, historically, the degree adverb *cokum* 'a little' must have formed before *com1* 'a little' started being used. In a parallel line of thought, *com1* 'a little' has to appear much earlier than *com2* and *com3* in history. However, according to historical data, *com* is not derived from the degree adverb *cokum* 'a little' and *com2* does not come from *com1* 'a little'. As a concrete word form, *com* started to be used during the mid 19th century and interestingly, was used for expressing the meaning 'please' (i.e. *com2*) rather than 'a little' (i.e. *com1*). In fact, *com* started being used as 'a little' only during the late 19th or early 20th century.

(5)   a. *com2* 'please'[4]

...*mwulkoki-lul*   *com*   *kacyeola...*

...fish-ACC   please   bring

'Please, bring the fish...'

(*The New Testament* 1900: John 21,11)

b. *com1* 'a little'

... *com*   *tahayng*   *ha-n*   *il-i*   *toyya-se.*

a little   (good) luck   do-REL   work-NOM   become-DEC

'... (something) becomes a little bit of a good thing.'

(*Chwuwelsayk* 1914: 47)

In the 19th century, the main form of the degree adverb 'a little' was *cokom* (i.e. phonetically [tsokom]) instead of *cokum* 'a little'. From the mid 19th century, the form *cokum* [tsokɨm] 'a little' began to be used.

(6)   a. *cokom* 'a little'

pwul-ul   *cokom neh-un*   *hwu...*

fire-ACC   a little   put-REL   after

'After (I) put a little bit of fire in...'

(*Kwuhapchongse* 19c: 3b)

b. *cokum* 'a little'

cokum   *isstaka*

a little   later

'a little later'

(*Kwukhanhoye* 1895: 263)

Based on the data from the 19th or early 20th century, the word forms *com* and *cokum* 'a little' began to be used around the same period. Because of this, it is difficult to say that the word form *com* was derived from the degree adverb *cokum* 'a little' and assumption (4) should be revised.

One could suppose that the word form *com* may be derived from the degree adverb *cokom* 'a little' in the 19th century, then takes on various other functions. However, this assumption can be avoided without trouble by looking at Korean phonological change. If *com* [tsom] comes from *cokom* [tsokom] 'a little', two sound changes are necessary to explain this change between them as in (7):

---

[4] All data are found in Seycong Corpus. *The New Testament* (1900) was published by The Organization of Bible Translation. *Chwuwelsayk* (1914) as a new style novel was written by Chan-Sik Choi in 1912 but the version in the corpus was published in 1914. *Kwuhapchongse* (1809) was edited by pinghekak Lee but the author is anonymous. *Kwukhanhoye* (1895) as the dictionary was published by Cwunyeng Lee and 4 other authors.

(7)   Phonological change: *cokom* [tsokom] → *com* [tsom]
        a. [o] deletion (i.e. [o]→ Ø)
        b. [k] deletion (i.e. [k]→Ø)

The first rule in (7) seems to violate a natural Korean phonological rule. In Korean, [o] deletion is uncommon, unlike [ɨ] deletion. Thus, I assume that *com* does not come from the degree adverb *cokom* 'a little'. At this time, I am uncertain of the origin of the word form *com* in Korean, so I leave this as a future study topic.

Unlike the above studies, Mok (2001) clearly recognizes the existence of *com3* and the need to distinguish it from the degree adverb *com1* 'a little'. In his study, he attempts to define *com3* as a particle in Korean and assumes its main function as assigning 'focus' or 'new information' to the nominal expression. I believe that Mok is on the right track regarding the nature of *com3* but that his proposal needs more concrete evidence on why *com3* should be considered a particle in Korean. Thus, in the next section, I will verify the fact that *com3* is a particle in Korean.

2. *Com* as a Particle in Korean

Before discussing why *com3* can be categorized as a particle in Korean, I will look at the inherent features of particles in Korean. The characteristics of particles in Korean are well explained in Sohn (2001) as in (8):

(8)   Inherent features of Korean particles by Sohn (2001):
        a.   Particles in Korean are bound morphemes.
        b.   Particles in Korean are postpositional (i.e. they are found at the end of the phrase [noun/adverb+particle]).
        c.   Particles in Korean indicate the grammatical relations of the nominal expression (i.e. *kyek-cosa*: case particle) or delimiting the meanings of the nominal expressions or adverbial expressions (i.e. *po-cosa*: delimiter).
        d.   Particles in Korean build a phonological phrase with a nominal expression or an adverbial expression.

(9)   *Mary-ka*   *pap-man*   *mek-ess-ta.*
        M-NOM   rice-only   eat-PAST-DEC
        'Mary ate only rice.'

In (9), there are two particles (i.e. -*ka* and –*man*). The nominative particle –*ka* and the delimiter –*man* 'only' are bound morphemes which indicate grammatical relations such as subject (i.e. *Mary-ka*) or delimit the meaning of the noun such as 'nly rice' (i.e. *pap-man*) in a clause. Following Sohn (2001), a phrase which is made up of a particle and a noun (e.g. *Mary-ka* or *pap-man*) creates a phonological phrase but it is uncertain how it does so. Thus, we need supportive evidence to explain this.

2.1 The Phonological Phrase in Korean

In the studies of Mok (2001) and Sohn (2001), native speakers are intuitively aware of the fact that a phrase which is constructed by the combination of a noun stem and a particle builds a phonological phrase. However, it is uncertain what the phonological phrase looks like and how native speakers indicate the phonological phrase. Therefore, in order to confirm this intuition, it is necessary for us to find specific evidence.

According to Jun (1998) and Schafer and Jun (2002), it is obvious that a particle as a bound morpheme combines with its noun stem and this combination creates a phonological phrase in Korean. In the above studies, all utterances could be reformulated as intonational structures, which consist of three hierarchical structural levels as in (10).

(10)   Intonational structure:

High level:	Intonational Phrases (IP)
Intermediate level:	Accentual Phrases (i.e. phonological phrase (//), AP)
Low level:	Phonological Words (σ PW)

In this structure, the boundary of the intermediate level of representation (e.g. AP) coincides with the boundary of the low level of representation (e.g. PW) but the intermediate level boundary never occurs in the middle of a low level boundary.

In Seoul Korean, an AP is indicated by a tonal pattern where the initial tone is LH and the final tone is LH as in (11):

(11)   AP boundary tones: initial LH... final LH
        [$\sigma \sigma$...$\sigma \sigma$]$_{AP}$
        L H L H

However, when phrasal-initial segment is either aspirated or tensed, the initial tone is realized as HH rather than LH. If an AP is shorter than four syllables, the initial tone is realized as a L tone and the final tone is realized as a H tone.

Now let us turn to an example in Korean in (12), focusing on the phonological phrase constructed by the combination of particles and noun stems.

(12) a. *hyengnim-ney-nun*   *Younga-lul*   *silhe-han-ta.*
      brother-family-TOP   Younga-ACC   hate-PRES-DEC
      '(My) brother's family hates Younga.'

    b. Tonal pattern:
    ((hyengnim-ney-nun)$_{AP}$// *(Younga-lul)*$_{AP}$//   *(silhe-han-ta)*$_{AP}$)$_{IP}$
      (H-H-L-H)   (L-L-H)   (L-H-L-H):
                          (Schafer and Jun 2002:6)

In (12), the phrases built by the combination of noun stems and particles make APs (i.e. *Hyenim-ney-nun* 'brother-family-TOP' and *Younga-lul* 'Younga-ACC'). As mentioned before, at the end of these APs all tone patterns are realized as the LH as in (12b) and the particles simply contain a H tone.

By adopting the proposal put forth in Jun (1998), we can test whether or not *com3* is a particle in Korean. If *com3* is a particle, it must be a PW (σ) but not an AP. Thus, the AP boundary cannot come before *com3*. If *com3* is not a particle, it only functions as the degree adverb (i.e. independent morpheme), the same as *com1* 'a little' which makes an AP as well as a PW. In such a case, the AP boundary can come before *com3*.

(13)   *ku*   *acwumma-hanthey myelchi-lul* // *com*1 (///) *sa-ss-e.*
      that   lady-DAT   anchovy-ACC   a little   buy-PAST-DEC
      'I bought a few anchovies from that lady.'
                          (Kwu 1998: 5)

Com in (13) should be an example of *com1* 'a little' because it contains the meaning 'a little' and can be replaced by the degree adverb *cokum* 'a little'. In ordinary speech, native speakers recognize that the tonal patterns of *myelchi-lul* 'anchovy-ACC' and *com* in (13) are realized as a L-L-H pattern and a L-H pattern, respectively. In other words, an AP boundary falls between *myelchi-lul* 'anchovy-ACC' and *com* 'a little' and these two phrases build their own AP phrases. Based on this fact, we know that *com* in (13) is not a bound morpheme and it cannot make any phrase with the preceding phrase *myelchi-lul*. Based on this evidence, we can assert that *com1* is not a particle.

(14)   *changmwun-ul*   *yele-cwu-si-keyss-eyo,* // *com2/*com*1(*cokum)?
      window-ACC   open-give-HON-FUT-REQ please/*a little
      'Could you open the window, please?'

Com in (14) can be an example of com2 because it means 'please' in the clause and it cannot be replaced by the degree adverb cokum 'a little'. For most native speakers, the tone of com in (14) is realized as a L-H pattern rather than just a High tone. Clearly, the preceding phrase is an AP, thus, the AP boundary occurs before com2. As a result, com2 'please' like com1 is an AP as well as a PW.

(15)　　sensayngnim-kkeyse　　　　kwail　com3/*com2/*com1(*cokum)
　　　　teacher-NOM.HON　　　　　fruit　com/please/a little
　　　　tu-si-ess-e?
　　　　eat-HON-PAST-Q
　　　　'Did the teacher eat the fruit?'

Com in (15) may be categorized as com3 because the meaning of this com is not related to com1 'a little' or com2 'please'. Unlike the previous two examples in (13) and (14), com3 cannot construct its own AP. In normal speech, com in (15) seems to only hold a High tone, the same tone pattern of normal particles in the AP. The AP boundary does not occur before com in (15) because this com is a part of the AP kwail-com 'fruit com3' (i.e. tone pattern H-L-H). As a result, com3 acts the same as a normal particle and in fact, the preceding nominal expression and com3 combine to make an AP. Based on this observation, we find that the distinction between com3 and the other coms fully relies on the placement of the AP boundary.

2.2 The Sound Change: From [o] To [u]

According to Kang (1998, 1999), a phonological sound change takes place word or phrase final in Korean (i.e. [o] → [u] / _____#). This sound change is optional but not necessary. Native speakers can optionally pronounce [o] or [u] and the semantic meaning of word or phrase is not changed at all.

(16)　　The sound change from [o] to [u] word-internally:
　　　　a. [samchon]　　→　　[samchun]　　　'uncle'
　　　　b. [puco]　　　　→　　[pucu]　　　　'contribution'
　　　　　　　　　　　　　　　　(Kang 1997: 15-16)

In (16), the sound change from [o] to [u] happens word-internally; the [o] in a final syllable can optionally be pronounced [u]. This sound change is also found phrase final. For instance, when the particle contains the [o], this [o] often changes to [u] as in (17):

(17) a. *malkun*   *mwul-lo*   *ssis-ela.*
          clean   water-INST   wash-IMP
          'Wash (something) with clean water.'
          → mwul-lo 'water-INST': [lo] or [lu]
      b. *motwu*   *Seoul-lo*   *wase*   *salko.*
          all   Seoul-DIR   come   live
          'All come to Seoul to live.'
          → Seoul-lo 'Seoul-DIR': [lo] or [lu]
                                    (Kang 1997: 17-18)

In (17), the particle *–lo* [-lo] 'instrumental or direction' can be optional-ly pronounced as [-lu]. As can be seen in the previous subsection, the parti-cles occur in the phrase final position (i.e. postposition) and I think that Kang's proposal is on the right track.

In adopting Kang's (1997) proposal, if *com3* is a particle, it should oc-cur in the phrase final position and it could be acceptable to pronounce [tsum] as well as [tsom] (i.e. the [o] changes to the [u]). However, in the cases of *com1* and *com2*, this sound change never occurs.

(18) *kwuk-i*   *com1/*com3*   *cca-ta.*
      soup-NOM   a little/com3   salty-DEC
      'The soup is a little salty.'

Com in (18) may be included in *com1* because it has the chief meaning 'a little' and can be replaced by the degree adverb *cokum* 'a little'. Here, *com* [tsom] cannot be pronounced as [tsum], so the sound change from [o] to [u] does not happen. Based on this fact, the word *com* is not placed phrase final.

(19) *ipen*   *yehayng-un*   *pata-lo*   *ka-yo,*   *com2.*
      this time trip-TOP   sea-at   go-IMP,   please
      'During this trip, let's go to the beach   please.'

Com in (19) is *com2* because its basic meaning is 'please' in this exam-ple. As with *com1*, *com* 2 [tsom] 'please' cannot be changed to [tsum]. This confirms the fact that *com2* in (19) cannot occur in the phrase final position.

(20) *sinpal-com3*   *sa-ss-e?*
      shoes-com3   buy-PAST-DEC
      'Did you buy (the) shoes?'

Com in (20) seems to be *com*3 because it does not mean 'a little' or 'please' and the AP boundary cannot be placed between the noun and this *com*. For native speakers, the sound change from [tsom] to [tsum] in (20) does not have an influence on any meaning change in this phrase. In Kang (1997), the sound change from [o] to [u] happens in word final or phrase final position without any meaning change and so, *com*3 in (20) may be placed in the phrase final position. Thus, it is apparent that *com3* occurs in the phrase final position, as do other particles in Korean.

Based on the evidence from these two morpho-phonological examples, I categorize *com* 3 as a particle in Korean.

3. *Com* as Partitive Particle in Korean

In the previous section, I have verified why *com*3 should be classified as a particle in Korean based on the morpho-phonological evidence. In this section, I will examine the primary function of *com*3 as a particle. I assume that *com3* mainly functions as a partitive particle in Korean.

3.1 Characteristics of Partitive Particles

Partitive particles are found across languages and share certain common characteristics. According to Kiparsky (1998) and Lyons (1999), the features of partitive particles can be summarized as follows:

(21)   a. Partitive particles mostly occur with the direct object rather than the subject.

        b. Partitive particles are related to the quantificational meaning of the nominal expression (i.e. a part of).

        c. Partitive particles are someway related to aspectual property.

We know that *com*3 has the first two features in (21). Firstly, *com*3 primarily combines with a direct object rather than a subject in a clause. In other words, *com*3 replaces an accusative particle more commonly than a nominative particle.

(22)   *Mary-ka/*com3*   *sakwa-lul/com3*   *mek-ess-ta*
        M-NOM/com3   apple-ACC/com3   eat-PAST-DEC
        'Mary ate the apple.'

In (22), when the nominative particle –*ka* replaces *com*3, the sentence is bizarre. However, if the accusative particle replaces *com*3, the sentence is well formed. Thus, we see that *com*3 has the first feature of partitive particles presented in (21).

Secondly, the semantic meaning of *com3* often contains the meaning 'a part of' and hence, the object noun is interpreted as a part of this object noun in the clause. As a result, we can propose that the basic semantic meaning of *com3* is the 'partitive meaning'.

(23)   a. *Mary-ya,*   *kolay-lul*   *mancye*   *pwa.*
        M-VOC   whale-ACC   touch   try.to
        'Mary, try to touch the whale.'
        b. *Mary-ya,*   *kolay-com3*   *mancye*   *pwa.*
        M-VOC   whale-com3   touch   try.to
        'Mary, try to touch a part of the whale.'

In (23), *com3* and the accusative particle can optionally be marked on the object noun. When the object noun is marked with the accusative particle, the partitive meaning (i.e. a part of) does not hold as in (23a). However, when *com3* occurs with the object noun stem, the object noun phrase gains the partitive meaning. In (23b), the sentence can be read as "touch a part of the whale" after the object is marked with *com3*. Thus, *com3* possesses the second feature of partitive particles in (21).

According to the examples in (22) and (23b), it seems obvious that *com3* is a partitive particle in Korean. Nonetheless, certain examples in Korean make us hesitate to describe *com3* as a partitive particle because often the noun marked with *com3* does not have the partitive meaning. Thus, it is questionable whether or not *com3* should be included as a partitive particle as in (24).

(24)   *Mary-ya,*   *pang*   *chengso-com3*   *ha-yela.*
        M-VOC   room   cleaning-com3   do-IMP
        'Mary, clean your room.'

In (24), the noun *chengso* 'cleaning' is marked with *com3*. This noun as an event noun in Korean cannot intrinsically hold the partitve meaning 'a part of'. However, interestingly, *com3* can be attached to this event noun as in (24). In order to account for this phenomenon, I adopt from Kiparsky (1998) his account of the alternation between the accusative particle and the partitive particle in Finnish.

3.2 Boundedness and *com* in Korean

In Finnish, when the object contains the partitive meaning, a partitive particle should occur instead of the accusative particle as in (25). For instance, when the object noun is expressed with quantification (i.e. plural marking in (25)), it must be marked with the partitive particle.

(25)   NP with partitive meaning (Quantificational):
    a.   *saa-n*   *karhu-n/ karhu-t.*
            get-1sg   bear-ACC/bear-PL.ACC
            'I'll get the (a) bear/I'll get the bears.'
    b.   *saa-n*   **karhu-a/ karhu-j-a.*
            get-1sg   bear-PART/bear-PL-PART
            'I'll get the some bear/ I'll get bears.'
                                    (Kiparsky 1998: 268)

However, except for this case (i.e. the partitive particle marking because of the NP-related reason), the direct object can alternatively be marked with the accusative particle and the partitive particle in Finnish as in (26). In (26), the object noun does not have any quantificational meaning in the clause.

(26)   *Ammu-i-n*   *karhu-n/a.*
        shoot-PAST-1sg   bear-ACC/PART
        'I shot the (a) bear.'

                                  (Kiparsky 1998: 267)

According to Kiparsky (1998), 'boundedness' is related to aspect which is constructed by the combination of a verb and its object (i.e. VP). The alternation between the accusative particle and the partitive particle is fully dependent on the degree of boundedness in Finnish. When an entire VP (i.e. the object noun and verb) is expressed as a bounded event, object nouns must be marked with accusative particles. On the other hand, when a VP implies an unbounded event, the direct object should be marked with a partitive particle. Simply, a bounded event implies terminative, perfective aspect, a telic event, or a change of state in the direct object while an unbounded event implies duration, imperfective aspect, an atelic event or no change of state in the direct object. Thus, boundedness in Kiparsky (1998) is connected to both the verb and the direct object. This concept of boundedness is found in other languages. For instance, in English, a degree adverbial expression (i.e. *more, a lot, very much*) can occur with the verb or the noun related to an unbounded event.

(27)   Verbs with the unbounded event:
    a.   **The sportsman killed the bear some more.*
                                (Verb: bounded)
    b.   *The sportsman shot the bear some more.*
                             (Verb: unbounded)

(28)   NP with the unbounded event:

a.   *a lot of bear, *a lot of the bear
                               (Noun: bounded)

b.   a lot of bears, a lot of coffee
                               (Noun: unbounded)

In Finnish, when the sentence denotes an unbounded event because one of the verbs or the object is related to an unbounded event, the direct object should be marked with the partitive particle. On the other hand, when a sentence is expressed as a bounded event, both the verb and the object should contain the feature [+bounded]. In this case, the direct object must be marked with the accusative particle.

(29)   a.   *Ammu-i-n*   *karhu-n.*
              shoot-PAST-1sg   bear-ACC
              'I shot the (a) bear.'
                      (Accomplishment: 'to shoot dead')

        b.   *Ammu-i-n*   *karhu-a.*
              shoot-PAST-1sg   bear-PART
              'I shot at the (a) bear.'
                      (non-committal as to what happened to the bear)
                                       (Kiparsky 1998: 267)

In (29a), the sentence in Finnish means that the bear was killed after shooting. Thus, this sentence implies a bounded event (i.e. telic event or perfective aspect). In this case, the sentence also implies a change of state in the direct object (i.e. from living to dead). Thus, in (29a), the direct object should be marked with the accusative particle. Unlike (29a), in (29b) there is no tangible change of state in the bear and this implies an unbounded event according to Kirparsky (1998). Thus, the direct object should be marked with the partitive particle instead of the accusative particle.

I will look at the distribution of *com3* in Korean because *com3* alternates with the accusative particple in Korean. In fact, *com3* as a partitive particle seems to be deeply related to the concept boundedness in Kiparsky (1998) and Kiparsky's proposal helps to account for the inherent feature of *com3* in Korean. Simply speaking, if the entire VP is expressed as a bounded event, the accusative particle is obligatory but if the VP denotes an unbounded event, the direct object is optionally marked by the partitive particle *com3* or the accusative particle. Thus unlike Finnish, the partitive particle *com3* is not obligatory even in the unbounded event.

(30)   *Mary-ka [3-pen   mwuncey]-lul/*com3   haykyelha-yess-ta.*

      M-NOM   3-number problem-ACC/*com3   solve-PAST-DEC
      'Mary solved problem number 3.'

In (30), the entire VP is related to a bounded event and as such this sentence mainly means 'Mary completely solved problem number 3.' In particular, the object NP *3-pen mwuncey* 'problem number 3' as a definite expression may be included as a bounded NP following Kiparsky (1998). In addition, the verb is marked with the simple past (i.e. *-ess* 'past tense'), which is related to the concept of the telic event. Overall, the entire VP is obviously related to a bounded event. In this situation, the direct object can only be marked with the accusative particle and not *com3*. The unacceptability of *com3* in this construction is significant given the conditions surrounding the alternation between the accusative particle and the partitive particle in Finnish.

(31)   *Mary-ya,*   *[3-pen   mwuncey]-lul/com3*   *haykyelha-yela.*
       M-VOC   3-number problem-ACC/com3   solve-IMP
       'Mary, solve problem number 3!'

In (31), the direct object can optionally be marked with either the accusative particle or the partitive particle *com3*. Compared to example (30), the sentence in (31) changes from declarative to imperative. However, the sentence, including the direct object, has not changed at all. In (31), why can the direct object be marked with the partitive particle in Korean? Based on Kiparsky (1998), the sentence in (30) may be related to a bounded event whereas the sentence in (31) implies an unbounded event. When looking again at example (31), the verb ending is imperative. In general, imperative constructions naturally imply the imperfective aspect rather than the perfective aspect. As a result, the sentence in (31) expresses an unbounded event, by nature. Thus, as in Finnish, the partitive particle *com3* can be replaced by the accusative particle because the VP is an unbounded event.

    To sum up, in Korean, *com3* as a partitive particle is intrinsically related to the aspectual feature as is the partitive particle in Finnish.

4. Conclusion

In this paper I examined the inherent properties of another function of *com* in Korean. This particular *com* (i.e. *com3* in this paper) should be included as a particle in Korean rather than as a degree adverb. In addition, this particle should be categorized as a partitive particle because it shares the universal characteristics of partitive particles across languages.

References

Cwu, K-H. 2000. Com and Cokum. *Kwukehak* 36: 379-399.

Cwu, K-H. 2004. A Semantic and Pragmatic Study of the Grammaticalization of *Com*. *Kwukekyowuk* 115: 433-452.

Hopper, P. and Traugott, E. C. 2003. *Grammaticalization: Second Edition*. Cambridge: Cambridge University Press.

Im, Y-C. 1995. About Com and Cokum. *Hanyangemwun* 3: 1081-1101.

Jun, S-A. 1998. The Accentual Phrase in the Korean Prosodic Hierarchy. *Phonology* 15(2): 189-226.

Kang, H-S. 1998. [o]>[u] Change and Linguistic Fossilization: Focusing on the Cennam Dialect. *Kwuemwunhakhoy* 33: 5-27.

Kiparsky, P. 1998. Partitive Case and Aspect. *The Projection of Argument: Lexical and Compositional Factor*, ed. M. Butt., and W. Geuder, 265-307. CSLI.

Kwu, C-N. 1998. About the Discourse Marker Com. *Hankwukenemwunhak* 41: 411-434.

Mok, J-S. 2001. The Function of Com and its Grammaticalization. *Enehak* 28: 77-100.

Lyon, C. 1999. *Definiteness*. Cambridge: Cambridge University Press.

Schafer, A. J. and Jun, S-A. 2002. Effect of Accentual Phrase on Adjective Interpretation in Korean. *East Asian Language Processing*, ed. M. Nakayama, 223-255. CSLI.

Sohn, H-M. 2001. *The Korean Language*. Cambridge: Cambridge University Press.

Sohn, S-M-T. 1989. Semantic Meaning of Com. *Hankwukhaknoncip* 14: 477-508.

The Nature of Associative Plurality in Korean: Accounting for *Ney* and *Tul*

KYUMIN KIM
University of Toronto

SEAN MADIGAN
University at Buffalo

In this paper, we explore the nature of associative plurality in Korean. Using the so-called Japanese associative plural marker *tati* for comparative purposes, we show that the Korean plural markers *ney* and *tul* differ from *tati* in that the former is a pure associative, while the latter can have both an additive meaning and what we term a *weak associative meaning*. One important conclusion that stems from this analysis is that there is no strict one-to-one relationship between the type of plurality and available markers. Stemming from this, we argue for a redefining of associative plurality based on contextually determined referents. Finally, we examine the syntactic status of both *tul* and *ney*, drawing the conclusion that they belong to the category of classifiers and in addition head two separate phrases, namely *ney* heads an *Associative Phrase* and *tul* heads a separate *Number Phrase*.

Japanese/Korean Linguistics 19.
Edited by Ho-min Sohn, Haruko Cook, William O'Grady, Leon A. Serafim, & Sang Yee Cheon.
Copyright © 2011, CSLI Publications

1. Additive and Associative Plurality in Japanese and Korean

In this section, we outline a comparative analysis of the Korean plural markers *tul* and *ney*, with the Japanese marker *tati*. We show the differences between these markers with respect to whether or not they show properties of additive plurality or associative plurality.

Additive plurality differs from associative plurality in that it is referentially homogeneous, meaning that every referent of the plural form is also a referent of the stem. In addition to this, there seems to be no requirement as to group membership. In other words, in an additive plural, the referents of the plural form do not necessarily have to have a close-knit relationship with each other. Associative plurals exhibit the opposite behavior with regards to these properties. Before discussing these, however, we first provide an example of an additive plural in both Korean and Japanese in (1a-b).

(1) a. Ku   haksayng-**tul**-i   ku   kenmwul-ul   twullessassta.
    that   student-TUL-NOM   that   building-ACC   surrounded
    'Those students surrounded that building.'

    b. Gakusei-**tati**-ga   sono   biru-o   torikakonda.
    student-TATI-NOM   that   building-ACC   surrounded
    '(The) students surrounded that building.'

The plural DP *ku haksayng-tul* 'those students' in Korean is an additive plural in that it refers to a homogeneous group wherein all referents of the plural form must be students. In addition, there seems to be no particular restrictions concerning the relationship that the students must have with each other.

Regarding the Japanese example, the DP in question is also additive because it shows the same properties as the Korean example, namely that it is referentially homogeneous and there is no requirement placed on the relationship between the group members. In fact, Nakanishi and Ritter (2009) argue that this reading of *tati* is a "pseudo-additive" reading, achieved when it combines with a common noun that has a descriptive property (e.g. being a student). The associates denoted by *gakusei-tati* share this property. This will be discussed in more detail below. What is important at this point is that *tati* does indeed exhibit properties related to additive plurality.

An associative plural is a plural nominal construction consisting of a definite human noun and an associative plural marker, whose meaning consists of a closely related group of people whose central member (aka *focal referent*) is denoted by the proper noun (Moravcsik 2003). Korean has a dedicated associative plural marker, *ney*. Examples of associative plurals in

Korean are given in (2a-c). These examples show that *ney* can combine with a proper name, a common noun, and a pronoun.

(2) a. Jwuhi-ney-ka   ku   kenmwul-ul   twullessassta.
    Jwuhi-NEY-NOM   that   building-ACC   surrounded
    'Jwuhi and her family/associates surrounded that building.'

   b. Ku   haksayng-ney-ka   nolkoissta.
    DEM   student-NEY-NOM   playing
    'That student and his group over there are playing.'

   c. Kyay-ney-ka   pulse   ttenassta.
    3rd- NEY-NOM   already   left
    'They already left.'

The properties of associative plurality as they relate to distinguishing this reading from an additive one are that they are referentially heterogeneous, meaning that every referent of the plural form need not be a referent of the stem and they necessarily must form a close-knit group. More generally, the meaning of an associative plural is as in (3).

(3) Associative plural reading: *x* and those closely associated to *x*, where *x* and *x*'s associates are human.

Given this sort of meaning, the example in (2a) means Jwuhi and a group of people closely associated to her surrounded that building.

Recall that *tati* was shown above to provide an additive reading. Nakanishi and Tomioka (2004), however, argue that *tati* is always associative rather than additive. The examples in (4a-b) show an associative reading with a proper noun as well as a pronoun.

(4) a. Mika-tati-ga   sono   biru-o   torikakonda.
    Mika-TATI-NOM   that   building-ACC   surrounded
    'Mika and her friends/family/classmates surrounded that building.'

   b. Watasi-tati-ga   sono biru-o   torikakonda.
    I-TATI-NOM   that building-ACC   surrounded
    'We surrounded that building.'   (Nakanishi and Ritter 2009)

In (4a), *Mika-tati* refers to a focal individual named 'Mika' and her associates, where the associates are more or less closely associated to her. The explanation for why *tati* contributes to both an associative and additive reading has been attributed to the observation that an associative meaning exists when *tati* combines with an element lacking a descriptive property, e.g. a proper noun (Nakanishi and Ritter 2009). This will be discussed in more detail below.

While we showed above that Korean *tul* contributes to an additive reading, *tul* can in fact yield a kind of associative reading when combined with a third person pronoun.

(5) Ku-tul
3rdsing-TUL
'(lit.) That person and others.'

This type of fact was previously noted by Madigan et al. (2008) who illustrated that *tul* can be associative when combined with the long-distance reflexive *caki* in so-called *Inclusive Reference* contexts.[1]

(6) John-i   caki-tul-i   iky-ess-ta-ko mal-ha-yess-ta.
J-NOM   self-PL-NOM win-PST-DC   tell-do-PST-DC
'John$_1$ said that they$_{1+2}$ won.'   (Cho 1996)

Unlike *tati*, *tul* cannot be combined with a proper or common noun to create an associative reading.

(7) a.   Jwuhi-tul-i   ttenassta.
     Jwuhi-TUL-NOM   left
     'The people named Jwuhi (*Jwuhi and her family/associates) left.'

   b.   #Namca-tul-i   kathi   swukcey   hayssta.
     Man-TUL-NOM   together   homework did
     '(lit.) The man and those closely associated to him did the homework together.'

In summary, what we have illustrated in this section is that *tati* can be an additive or associative plural depending on whether it combines with an element containing a descriptive property or not. Regarding *ney*, it seems to yield only an associative reading. Finally, *tul* contributes to creating an additive reading when combined with common or proper nouns and an associative reading when combined with a third person pronoun or reflexive. In the following section, we compare these empirical facts in order to begin to

---

[1] *Inclusive Reference* refers to a construction where a singular antecedent binds a plural element (see Madigan and Yamada 2007).

tease apart what associative plurality in Korean actually is and where it stems from.

2. Comparing *tul*, *tati*, and *ney*

As mentioned above, Nakanishi and Ritter (2009) made the observation that when *tati* combines with a noun that lacks a descriptive property it has an associative reading and otherwise an additive reading. An intuitive question then, is whether or not the presence or lack of a descriptive property predicts the behavior of *tul* or *ney*? The relevant data is summarized below in Table1.

Table 1

	Tati		*Tul*		*Ney*	
	Additive	Associative	Additive	Associative	Additive	Associative
Element with Descriptive Property	Yes kagusei-tati	No	Yes haksayng-tul	No	No	Yes haksayng-ney
Element lacking Descriptive Property	No	Yes Mika-tati	Yes Juhwi-tul	No	No	Yes Juhwi-ney

It appears from the table above that if we base our analysis on descriptive properties, then we cannot extend the analysis of *tati* to *tul* or *ney*. In what follows we show that while this is true for *ney*, we may in fact be able to salvage the account of *tati* and apply it to *tul* depending on how we view the data. In order to tease these issues apart, first consider a summary of the data presented thus far, given in Table 2 which is organized with regards to noun types.

Table 2

	Tati		*Tul*		*Ney*	
	Additive	Associative	Additive	Associative	Additive	Associative
Proper Noun	No	Yes	Yes	No	No	Yes
Common Noun	Yes	No	Yes	No	No	Yes
Pronouns	Yes	No	No	Yes	No	Yes

The table above illustrates that *ney* appears to be a pure associative marker regardless of what it combines with, thus making a direct comparison to *tati* inappropriate as *tati* has both additive and associative readings. *Tul* and *ney* differ in all respects except pronouns. Finally, *Tati* differs from *tul* with respect to proper nouns and pronouns. At first glance, it would appear that one cannot extend Nakanishi and Ritter's (2009) analysis to *tul* or *ney*. In the following section, however, we show that it may in fact be possible to explain *tul* in a manner similar to that of Nakanishi and Ritter's (2009) explanation of *tati*.

3. Towards a More Complete Analysis of Associative Plurality

In this section, we provide an account of the above data. First, we consider Nakanishi and Ritter's (2009) semantics that explains why *tati* has an additive reading with common nouns, and thus why it is associative when it combines with a proper noun.

(8) $[[\ tati]]^c = \lambda x$: x is human. group(x)(c)   Type <e,e>

    $[[\ gakusei]]^c = \lambda x$. x is one or more students   Type <e,t>

        $[[\ gakusei]]^c = \{$Ann, Beth, AnnU_lBeth$\}$ (U_l is an individual sum operator)[2]

        $[[\ gakusei]]^c = AnnU_l$Beth

    $[[\ gakusei\text{-}tati]]^c = $group(Ann$U_l$Beth)(c)

    "a group that consists of AnnU_lBeth and their associates (who are also students)"   (Nakanishi and Ritter 2009)

The assumption in the above derivation is that the lexical meaning of the noun *gakusei* 'student' determines what property is common to both Ann and Beth and their associates. In this example, the property of being a student is what is common to all members of the group denoted by the plural noun. When *tati* combines with a proper name, however, there is no descriptive property, and an associative reading becomes available.

For Korean, we could say that, when *tul* combines with a noun that has a descriptive feature, an additive reading is obligatory, just as with *tati*. The question then is why is it that *tul* cannot have an associative reading with proper names? The basic information necessary to answer this question has been available for some time in the literature and has to do with the fact that *tul* must have a denotation like that in (9).

(9) $[[tul]] = \lambda$ P: Atomistic (P). λ x. $[P(x) \wedge \neg Atom(x)]$

The denotation above stipulates that *tul* only selects *non-atomic* individuals from a noun's extension, which contains both atomic and plural individuals (Song, 1975, Kim 2005). We will not provide the full argumentation

---

[2] Type-shifting is assumed to apply here.

here to support this but simply refer the reader to the cited references. In short, in Korean, bare nouns are ambiguous in number. Therefore, it is necessary to make the assumption that the extension of a bare noun in Korean contains both atomic and plural individuals (see Kim 2005). It thus becomes further necessary to postulate that *tul* has some sort of denotation that filters out atomic individuals when it combines with a common noun, thus providing a plural reading.[3] Moving on to why it is that *tul* has no associative reading with proper nouns, considering an example like (7a), this is a very special usage of a proper name. In this case, the proper name *Jwuhi* is really used as a common noun, in that the plural form *Jwuhi-tul* represents a set of individuals named Jwuhi. In a sense, there is a descriptive property shared among the members of the group, namely the property of being named Jwuhi. If *Jwuhi* is being treated as a bare noun with an extension that contains both atomic and plural individuals, as do all other bare nouns in Korean, then Nakanishi and Ritter's analysis can be extended to account for *tul* with respect to so-called proper noun+*tul* combinations.

Moving on, we now explain why it is that *tul* and *tati* behave differently with respect to pronouns. According to Nakanishi and Ritter (2009), Japanese 3rd person pronouns are definite descriptions that are composed of a descriptive gender feature and a definite determiner (Kratzer to appear). Consider the derivation in (10a-b):

(10)   a. $[[\ kanozyo]]^c$ = the unique female

     b. $[[\ kanozyo\text{-}tati]]^c$ = group(the unique female)(c)
"a group that consists of the unique female and her associates (who are also female) wrt c"

Just as with the common noun above, the lexical meaning of the noun determines what is shared between the unique female and her associates. The "lexical meaning" that is important here is the property of being a female. Since it is generally assumed that 3rd+PL forms are additive (Corbett 2000), this type of approach makes sense. However, Korean 3rd+*tul* is associative. The reason for this is rather simple and pertains to the fact that there is no common descriptive feature between the members of the groups. In other words, while the Japanese third person pronoun contains a descriptive feature, there is none in the Korean third person pronoun and it is instead a

---

[3] Not all studies assume that *tul* has a denotation like that in (9). In fact, Madigan et. al (2008) assumes that *tul* has no true denotation and is instead a morpho-syntactic spell-out of plural agreement. For the purpose of ease of discussion and lack of space, we will not discuss that option here.

simple variable. This is evidenced by the fact that *ku-tul* 'they' can refer to a group that consists of a mixed group of males and females (11).

(11)   Ku-tul
        3rd-PL
        'That man/girl and his associates (who are male or female or a mixture of both).

We make a similar assumption to Madigan et al. (2008) that when *tul* combines with a simple variable, it can function as a default plural marker to indicate plural agreement. The reading of plurality in this case would be created via a plural presupposition. In addition, we propose that *tul* can also have the denotational meaning provided above, but only when combined with a noun that has a descriptive feature.

Finally, in accounting for *ney* we assume the same explanation as Madigan et al. (2008) that n*ey* is simply a pure associative marker with the following denotation.

(12)   a. [[*ney*]]^c = λx. the plural entity that includes *x* and those associated with *x* in a context *c*

        b. [[*Jwuhi-ney*]] ^{c} = the plural entity that includes *Jwuhi* and those associated with *Jwuhi* in a context *c*

A denotation like (12a) above assures that every referent is not necessarily a referent of the stem, as illustrated in (13).

(13)   Ku   haksayng-ney-ka   ttenassta.
        that   student-NEY-NOM   left
        'Those students and their associates (where 'students' can be a mixture of students and nonstudents) left.'

In the following section, we discuss the nature of associative meanings and attempt to further clarify not only where the associative meaning comes from, but also various types of associative meanings.

4. Clarifying the Analysis: What do we mean by *Associative*?

Two questions that the above analysis raises are: What is the proper definition of associative plurality, and where does the so-called "associative reading" come from? In this section, we show that the defining feature of associative plurality is the fact that its referents are determined contextually and not necessarily any criteria about the nature of the relationship between the referents.

As mentioned above, we view *ney* as a "pure" associative marker. This marker is a "pure" associative in that it most closely matches the definitions of associative plurality provided in the literature. What becomes important then is what characterizes this type of associative plurality as different from that of *tul* and *tati*.

In our interpretation of the empirical analysis, the only difference between *ney* and *tati* is that *ney* requires the group it represents to be close-knit. Consider (14) below:

(14)   Inho-ney
    1. Inho and his family.
    2. Inho and his classmates.
    3. #Inho and a group of people he does not know.

In fact, *ney* seems to require that the group not only be close-knit, but that the focal referent must retain a status of equal or higher social position.

(15)   Inho-ney
    1. Inho and his classmates.
    2. Inho and his underclassman.
    3. #Inho and his superiors.

Therefore, a more accurate denotation of *ney* might be:

(16) $[[ney]]^c =$ $\lambda x.$ the plural entity that includes x and those **closely** associated with x, **where x is of equal or higher social status**, in a context c.

Tati, on the other hand, has much weaker requirements on the relationship the referents have with each other, requiring that the focal referent only be a representative of the group.

(17)   Mika-tati
    1. Mika and her family.
    2. Mika and her underclassmen.
    3. #Mika and a group of people whom she does not represent.

This notion of *tati* is correctly captured by Nakanishi and Tomioka's denotation of *tati*.

(18) $[[\textbf{tati}]] = \lambda x_e. \lambda Y_e. x \leq_i Y \ \& \ |Y| \geq 2 \ \& \ x \text{ represents } Y$

The associative reading of *tul* also does not require that the referents have any special sort of relationship.

(19)   Ku-tul
   1.   That person and his/her classmates.
   2.   That person and his/her underclassmen.
   3.   That person and his/her superiors.

Thus we can see that there appears to be at least two types of associative plurality in Korean, namely a *strong associative* reading as with *ney* and a *weak associative* reading in the case of *tul*. Depending on one's characterization of the data, Japanese *tati* could fall under the strong associative type or perhaps a type of its own.

From the above discussion, we draw the conclusion that while they may vary in their meanings, all markers have one thing in common, namely that the referents of the plural form are picked out from the context. In other words, associative plurality is not always a function of the meanings of specific plural markers, as with *ney*. Rather, associative plurality is really about picking up referents from the available context and *not* about the inherent closeness or not of the group. This is evidenced by the fact that *tul* can have a type of associative reading, which we term a *weak associative reading*. A weak associative reading then, refers to a plural where the referents are picked out of the context (as opposed to the extension of a noun), but there is no requirement that the group have any sort of special relationship to each other.

5. The Syntax of *ney* and *tul*

Borer (2005) and Nakanishi and Ritter (2008) assume that additive plural markers and classifiers belong to the same functional syntactic category. Therefore, they should never co-occur. According to Nakanishi and Ritter, *tati* can co-occur with classifiers because it is inherently an associative plural that heads its own phrase (20).

(20)   San-nin-no   gakusei-tati
       three-CL-GEN   student-TATI
       'three students'

The proposed account in this paper is that *ney* is associative and should therefore be able to combine with classifiers. However this is not the case as shown in (21).

(21) *Se-myeng-uy   ku   yeca-ney-ka   cinakassta.
      Three-CL-GEN   this   woman-NEY-NOM   passed by
      'The women and her two associates passed by.'

Likewise, the weak associative use of *tul* also shows the same pattern of being incompatible with classifiers:

(22) *Se-myeng-uy   ku-tul-i   cinakassta.
      Three-CL-GEN   this-TUL-NOM   passed by
      'The man and his two associates passed by.'

The additive usage of *tul* does not seem to be compatible with classifiers as predicted by the assumption that additive plurals and classifiers belong to the same category.

(23) *Se-myeng-uy   ku   yeca-tul-i   cinakassta.
      three-CL-GEN   this   woman-TUL-NOM   passed by
      'Three women passed by.'

If this assumption is correct, the data in (21)-(23) indicate that the associative marker *ney* and both uses of *tul* belong to the same syntactic category as that of classifiers. However, this does not seem to mean that *ney* and *tul* belong to a single category, as they can co-occur as illustrated in (24):

(24) Ai-ney-tul
      Child-NEY-TUL
      'The children'

We propose that *ney* heads an *Associative Phrase* and *tul* heads a separate *Number Phrase*, and both of them are subcategories of a classifier phrase (25).

(25)   ClassP

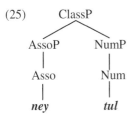

The differences between Korean and Japanese shown in this section thus may be due to a syntactic difference between the markers. In Korean, associative *ney* as well as *tul* function syntactically as classifiers, while in Japanese *tati* functions syntactically as an associative marker. Nevertheless, *ney* and *tul* have their own semantic functions, with the former being associative and the later being both weak associative and additive.

6. Remaining Issues: *Ney* and Pronouns

Finally, we also extend the proposed account to the distribution of *ney* with pronominal elements. The paradigm of pronoun+associative marker in Korean is given below in (26).

(26)

	1st	2nd	3rd
Sg+ney	*na-ney	ne-ney	ku-ney
Pl+ney	wuli-ney	nehuy-ney	ku-tul-ney

It is simple to see how the semantics for *ney* provided here allow for *ney* to combine with a pronoun. For instance, the second person when combined with *ney* gives the semantics in (27).

(27) $[[\text{ne-ney}]]^c$ = λx. the plural entity that includes *the addressee* and those associated with *the addressee* in a context c

However, one remaining issue is why $ney+1^{st}$ is out, as the semantics predicts this should be possible.

(28) $[[na\text{-}ney]]^c$ = λx. the plural entity that includes *the speaker* and those associated with *the speaker* in a context c

We provide a potential solution of the ungrammaticality of $ney+1st$ in terms of sociolinguistics. First, consider that the associative marker *ney* also has a possessive meaning as shown in (29).

(29)   Inho-ney   cha
       I-NEY   car
       'Inho and his family's car'

If *ney*'s possessive meaning is always carried with it, then $1^{st}+ney$ could be infelicitous on sociolinguistic terms. This may be so because, it is sociolinguistically inappropriate to have a possessive group headed by a singular 1st person. The Korean sense of ownership is most often expressed in terms of group ownership as shown in example (30).

(30)   Wuli   cip
       1stPL   house
       'Our house'

Given this line of reasoning, we propose that 1st-+*ney* may be out due to the fact that there is a conflict with the inherent possessive meaning of *ney* and the singular 1st person pronoun usage. Another, although less interesting, possibility is that *na-ney* is simply an accidental gap in the lexicon, as languages like Chinese and Japanese allow their associative markers to combine with a first person pronoun.

(31)   a.   Watasi-tati
            1st-PL
            'We'

       b.   Wo-men
            1st-PL
            'We'

Given these sorts of facts and the semantics of *ney* provided here, it may be the case then that *na-ney* is simply an accidental gap in the grammar. Further research is needed to clarify this issue.

7. Conclusion

What we have attempted to do here is to explore the nature of associative plurality in Korean as compared to Japanese. In doing so, we drew the conclusion that an associative plural may best be defined as a plural nominal that picks its referents out of the context of the utterance. However, within this class of associative plurals is at least two divisions, namely these markers that produce strong and weak associative meanings. Further research is needed to determine if this is indeed the proper conclusion. If it is proven to be so, then it would be very interesting to explore the range of associative plural readings in a typological manner.

References

Borer, H. 2005. *Structuring Sense. Volume 1: In Name Only*. Oxford: Oxford University Press.

Cho, D. 1996. Anaphor or Pronominal? *Language Research* 32: 621-636.

Corbett, G. 2000. *Number*. Cambridge: Cambridge University Press.

Kim, C. 2005. The Korean Plural Marker *tul* and Its Implications. Doctoral dissertation, University of Delaware.

Madigan, S. and Yamada, M. 2007. Inclusive Reference and Anaphoric Dependencies: A Crosslinguistic Analysis. *In the Proceedings of 30th Penn Linguistics Colloquium, Penn Working Papers in Linguistics.*

Madigan, S., Peng, A., and Masahiro, Y. 2008. Inclusive Reference in Korean and its Implications for Theory of Plurality. *Proceedings of the 12th Harvard International Symposium on Korean Linguistics.*

Moravcsik, E. 2003. A Semantic Analysis of Associative Plurals. *Studies in Language* 27: 469-503.

Nakanashi, K. and Tomioka, S. 2004. Japanese Plurals are Exceptional. *Journal of East Asian Linguistics* 13: 113-140.

Nakanishi, K. and Ritter, E. 2009. Plurality in Languages without Mass-count Distinction. Paper presented at Mass/Count workshop. University of Toronto.

Processing, Pragmatics, and Scope in Korean and English*

MISEON LEE
Hanyang University

HYE-YOUNG KWAK
Korea University

SUNYOUNG LEE
Korea University

WILLIAM O'GRADY
University of Hawai'i at Mānoa

1. Introduction

It is commonly observed that English sentences such as (1) are potentially ambiguous.

(1)   Mary didn't read all the books.

On the preferred reading, *not* has scope over *all*, giving an interpretation that can be paraphrased as 'Mary read (only) some of the books.' As illustrated by the diagram in figure 1, this reading divides the set of books into two subsets—those that have been read by Mary and those that she did not read. We will henceforth refer to this as the 'partitioned set interpretation.'

---

* We acknowledge with gratitude the helpful comments provided by Kevin Gregg and by various members of the audience at the Japanese-Korean Linguistics Conference.

Japanese/Korean Linguistics 19.
Edited by Ho-min Sohn, Haruko Cook, William O'Grady, Leon A. Serafim, and Sang Yee Cheon.
Copyright © 2011, CSLI Publications

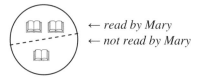

Figure 1. The partitioned set interpretation: 'Mary read some of the books.'

In contrast, on the 'full set reading' of (1), *all* has wide scope, giving the interpretation that can be paraphrased as 'All of the books were unread.' On this reading, depicted in figure 2, all members of the set of books are assigned the property of being unread by Mary.

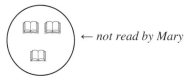

Figure 2. The full set interpretation: 'All of the books were unread.'

Interestingly, the opposite preference has been reported for Korean sentences such as (2) (Han, Lidz, and Musolino 2007, O'Grady, Lee, and Kwak 2009).

(2)   Mary-ka   motun chayk-ul   an ilk-ess-ta.
         Mary-Nom all   book-Acc not read-Pst-Decl
         'Mary didn't read all the books.'

In this paper, we focus on three questions raised by these facts.

i.   Why is the partitioned set interpretation of sentences such as (1) strongly preferred in English?
ii.   Why does Korean manifest a preference in the opposite direction?
iii.   Does bilingualism affect these scope preferences?

We will address each of these questions in turn in the sections that follow.

2. Why English Prefers the Partitioned Set Interpretation

One well known explanation for why English speakers prefer the partitioned set interpretation of *not–all* sentences comes from Musolino and Lidz (2006:834). The key idea is that when speakers of English hear a sentence such as (1), they reason as follows: if the speaker had intended to express the full set interpretation, s/he would have done so more directly, via an unambiguous pattern such as (3).

(3)   Mary didn't read any of the books.
        (full set interpretation only—all of the books were unread.)

Because the speaker uttered (1) rather than (3), so the reasoning goes, s/he must have intended to express the partitioned set interpretation. Hence the preference on the part of listeners for that interpretation.

We will henceforth refer to this chain of reasoning as the 'pragmatic calculus.' Although this proposal is not uncontroversial (see, e.g. Noveck et al. 2007 for an alternative proposal involving relevance theory), we will assume its essential correctness for the purposes of our discussion. This brings us to our second question, which has to do with why Korean differs from English in its interpretive preferences in scopal patterns that appear to fall within the purview of the pragmatic calculus.

3. Why Korean Prefers the Full Set Interpretation

As illustrated in (2), repeated here as (4), Korean permits sentences in which a negated verb takes a universally quantified direct object.

(4)   Mary-ka   motun chayk-ul   an ilk-ess-ta.
        Mary-Nom   all   book-Acc not read-Pst-Decl
        'Mary didn't read all the books.'

Yet, as noted at the outset, Korean speakers strongly prefer the full set interpretation of this sentence (all of the books were unread)—the precise opposite of what we find in English. This is somewhat puzzling since, like English, Korean has a competing pattern that permits only the full set interpretation.

(5)   Mary-ka   amwu chayk-to   an ilk-ess-ta.
        Mary-Nom   any book   -even not read-Pst-Decl
        'Mary didn't read any books.' (i.e. All the books were unread.)

This raises an obvious question: why doesn't the availability of (5), with its exclusive full set interpretation, lead to a preference for the partitioned set interpretation in the case of (4), in accordance with the pragmatic calculus? Put another way, why isn't Korean just like English? We believe that the answer lies in processing considerations.

3.1 A Processing Explanation

Our approach to processing is guided by the following two uncontroversial assumptions (e.g. Grodner and Gibson 2005: 262-63).

- As the processor works its way through a sentence, it immediately assigns each word and phrase an interpretation.
- The revision of a previously assigned interpretation is costly since it disrupts the normal linear operation of the processor, forcing it to go back and redo its work.

Consider in this regard how the processor goes about deriving the partitioned set interpretation in an English sentence such as *Mary didn't read all the books*. Two steps are of crucial importance:

(6)   Mary didn't read all the books.
    a.   As the processor moves through the sentence, it encounters the negative on the auxiliary verb *did*.

Mary did**n't**

    b.   Subsequently, upon encountering the quantified NP, the processor can immediately assign the partitioned set interpretation—in compliance with the pragmatic calculus and without backtracking.

Mary didn't read **all** the books.

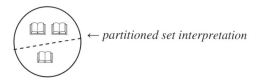 ← *partitioned set interpretation*

In sum, because the negative precedes the direct object in English, the partitioned set interpretation can be derived without the need for the processor to retrace its steps and modify an earlier interpretation.

Now consider how the processor will have to proceed if it is to derive the partitioned set interpretation for the equivalent sentence type in Korean. Once again, two steps are crucially important.

(7)   Mary-ka motun chayk-ul an ilkessta. ('Mary didn't read all the books.')

    a.   As the processor moves through the sentence, it quickly encounters the quantified NP and assigns it the default full set interpretation:

Mary-ka   **motun** chayk-ul ...
Mary-Nom all   book-Acc

    b.   Subsequently, the negative is encountered. If it is allowed to trigger the partitioned set reading, the previous interpretation of the quantified NP must be recomputed.

Mary-ka   motun chayk-ul **an** ilk-ess-ta
Mary-Nom all   book-Acc not read-Pst-Decl

The need for backtracking makes the partitioned set interpretation hard to process, in comparison to the full set alternative. On our view, this then nullifies the effects of the pragmatic calculus, which would otherwise favor the partitioned set interpretation, as it does in English.

A crucial feature of this proposal is the proposition that the partitioned set interpretation does in fact incur extra processing cost in Korean. As we will see next, experimental work by Lee (2009) provides independent evidence for this claim.

3.2 A Processing Experiment

Subjects

Thirty-eight native Korean-speaking adults (mean age 22;9) participated in Lee's experiment. They were all life-long residents of Korea.

Materials

Test sentences contained a universally quantified direct object and short-form (preverbal) negation, as illustrated by the sample item in (8).

(8)   Ecey pamey, Seyhee-ka   motun chospwul-ul an   khyessta ko
       last   night   Seyhee-Nom all   candle-Acc not light   that

       iyaki-nun malhaycwunta.
       story-Top says
       'The story says that Seyhee didn't light all the candles last night.'

All test sentences were preceded by one of two contexts—one supporting a full set interpretation and the other supporting a partitioned set interpretation, as illustrated below.

> Sample context favoring the full set interpretation:
> Last night Sehee worked late and came back home around midnight. Right after she took a shower, the electric lights suddenly went out. She found three candles on the table near the bed. However, since she was so tired, she didn't light the candles but went to sleep right away in the dark. [Test sentence is true on the full set interpretation, because all the candles were unlit.]

> Sample context favoring the partitioned set interpretation:
> Last night Sehee worked late and came back home around midnight. Right after she took a shower, the electric lights suddenly went out. She found three candles on the table near the bed. She took out one candle and lit it. Then she started reading a novel until she fell asleep. [Test sentence is true on the partitioned set interpretation, because one of the candles was lit, and two weren't.]

There were six test items per condition, arranged in a Latin square design so that none of the subjects heard the same test item in more than one context. (An additional two conditions, not relevant to the current discussion, tested the interpretation of sentences containing post-verbal negation.)

Procedure

After reading a context, the subjects pressed a button to call up the test sentence on the computer screen one region at a time (a moving-window self-paced reading task), as illustrated below.

(9)   1   2   3   4   5

Ecey pamey / Seyhee-ka / motun / chospwul-ul / an khyessta ko

last night   Seyhee- Nom all   candle-Acc   not light that

      6   7

iyaki-nun / malhaycwunta.

story-Top   says

'The story says that Seyhee didn't light all the candles last night.'

The subjects then identified the sentence as true or false by pressing the appropriate response key on a response pad.

It is well known that the truth of the full set (*all > not*) reading entails the truth of the partitioned set (*not > all*) reading: if it is the case that all of the candles are unlit, it must also be true that some of the candles are unlit. Of course, the converse does not hold: the fact that some of the candles are unlit does not entail that all of the candles are unlit. For this reason, judgments of the test items in the partitioned set context are especially important—a judgment of true unequivocally establishes the availability of the partitioned set interpretation.

Results

Three measures are relevant to our hypothesis that the partitioned set interpretation in Korean incurs more processing cost and is therefore less accessible than its full set alternative.

The first measure involves interpretive preference—whether Korean speakers prefer one reading over the other, even when each occurs in a natural context. Table 1 summarizes our results in this regard.

Table 1. Truth value judgments—was the test sentence true or false?

Full set context (all the candles are unlit)		Partitioned set context (one of the three candles is lit)	
True	False	True	False
94.4%	5.6%	54.6%	45.4%

As can be seen here, the full set interpretation is selected almost 95% of the time in contexts that favor it. In comparison, the partitioned set interpretation is adopted just 54.6% of the time in contexts that support it; in the remaining cases, the sentence is judged false—presumably because participants assign it the full set reading. Taken together, these results suggest that although the partitioned set interpretation is possible in Korean, it is the weaker reading.[1]

---

[1] Because test items are accepted as true far more often in the context supporting the full set interpretation, it is unlikely that this reading is selected simply because a situation in which none of the candles were lit is compatible with a situation in which not all the candles were lit.

A comparable asymmetry is reported by Han, Lidz, and Musolino (2007).

The second relevant measure involves the amount of time required to judge a test sentence to be true in each of the two types of contexts. (Response time is measured from the appearance of the final word on the screen to the point at which the subject presses the 'true' button.) Table 2 reports Lee's findings for this measure.

Table 2. Response time for judgments of truth

Full set context (all the candles are unlit)	Partitioned set context (one of the three candles is lit)
1571 ms	2412 ms

On average, it took 1571 ms to judge a sentence to be true in the context favoring the full set interpretation, compared to 2412 ms in the context that supports the partitioned set reading. The effect of context is significant $(F(1,35) = 93.89, p < 0.005)$, suggesting that the processing time for the full set interpretation is in fact faster.

The third and final measure of relevance to our hypothesis involves on-line reading times for each segment of the test sentence (see (9) above). Figure 3 (p. 305) depicts the region-by-region residual reading times.[2]

Of special interest here is region 5, which contains the negated verb and therefore constitutes the point at which an opportunity arises to derive the partitioned set interpretation by revising the full set reading that was previously assigned to the quantified NP, as outlined in the discussion of (7) above. As illustrated in figure 3, processing slows down at the negated verb in contexts that favor the partitioned set interpretation compared to those that favor the full set interpretation. (The effect of context is significant: $F(1,35) = 14.74, p < 0.005$.) This supports our hypothesis that the processor has to retrace its steps after encountering the negative and revise the earlier default full set interpretation of the quantified NP.

The full set interpretation appears to exist as an independent (and dominant) reading.

[2] Residual reading times are used to adjust for differences in subjects' reading rates or for differences in word length within conditions. To calculate residual reading times, a linear regression is estimated for each subject with raw reading times as the dependent variable and length in number of characters as the explanatory variable. The reading times predicted by the individual linear regression are then subtracted from the raw reading times. Thus, for a given region, 0 ms would provide average reading speed for the region of differing lengths across participants. A positive number shows that the reading time is slower than predicted on the basis of the length of the word, whereas a negative number shows that reading time is faster than expected.

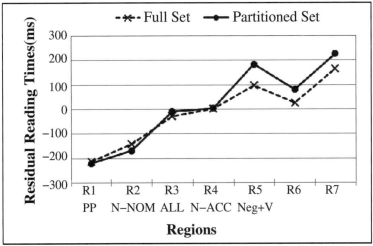

Figure 3. Region-by-region residual reading times

In sum, as predicted by the processing theory that we have put forward, the full set interpretation does indeed appear to be more accessible and less difficult than the partitioned set reading in Korean: it is selected more often, its truth is judged faster, and it manifests a shorter reading time at the region containing the negated verb. All of this is consistent with our proposal that processing considerations nullify the pragmatic calculus, which would otherwise lead to a preference for the partitioned set interpretation in Korean, just as it does in English.

4. The Effect of Bilingualism on Scope Preferences

We turn now to our third question, which focuses on whether bilinguals who learned Korean before English are able to employ the pragmatic calculus in computing scope interpretations in English, despite the irrelevance of this consideration to the comprehension of *not–all* patterns in Korean. We report here on two experiments that we conducted on this subject.

4.1 Experiment Involving Child Bilinguals

Subjects

Nine children (aged 6;0 to 11;9—mean age, 8;5) of Korean parents living in the United States participated in this experiment. The children had been exposed to English for at least four years; five had been born in the U.S. All were attending English-language schools and in accord with the classic profile of 'heritage language learners' (Montrul 2008) were English-dominant.

Procedure and Materials

The children's interpretive preferences were assessed with the help of short stories such as the ones illustrated below. Each story, which was presented orally and illustrated with pictures on a laptop computer, consisted of a context-setting situation and a test sentence, produced by a puppet. The child's task was to judge whether the sentence offered an accurate summary of the story.

Sample story supporting a full set interpretation:

Robert is working hard at home. His father wants him to clean three windows and to cut down three trees. Robert says, "Okay, I'll do that." Robert cleans the three windows right away. Then, Robert looks at the first tree. It is very big. So he doesn't cut it down. The second tree looks even bigger. So Robert doesn't cut it down either. Then, Robert looks at the third tree. It is smaller than the other trees. So he thinks that he can cut it down. However, when he is about to start, he realizes that it is his sister's favorite tree. So he doesn't cut it down either.

Test sentence: *Robert didn't cut down all the trees.*

Sample story supporting the partitioned set interpretation:

Robert is working hard at home. His father wants him to clean three windows and to cut down three trees. Robert says, "Okay, I'll do that."

Robert cleans the three windows right away. Then, Robert looks at the first tree. It is very big. So he doesn't cut it down. The second tree looks even bigger. So Robert doesn't cut it down either. Then, Robert looks at the third tree. It seems very big too. But he decides to try, and he manages to cut it down.

Test sentence: *Robert didn't cut down all the trees.*

There were three test items per condition, arranged in a Latin square design so that none of the subjects heard the same test item in more than one context. The experimental protocol also included two practice items and four filler items.

Results

Table 3 summarizes our results.

Table 3. Bilingual children's truth value judgments for sentences such as *Robert didn't cut down all the trees*

Full set context		Partitioned set context	
(all the trees are uncut)		(one of three trees was cut down)	
True	False	True	False
100%	0%	59%	41%

As can be seen here, our subjects manifested a strong preference for the full set interpretation in English, comparable to what is found in Korean.[3] Two explanations come to mind. On the one hand, it is possible that our subjects simply extend the interpretive preferences for Korean to English, overriding the pragmatic calculus that would normally favor the partitioned set interpretation in the latter language. On the other hand, it is also possible that our subjects are simply unaware of the pragmatic calculus at this point in their development, independent of their bilingualism. Evidence that children's pragmatic development can lag behind their syntactic skills comes from a study by Musolino and Lidz (2006), who investigated the ability of monolingual English-speaking children to interpret *not–every* sentences in basic descriptive contexts such as the following.

---

[3] In an independent experiment, not reported here for reasons of space, the same children were tested on Korean, in which they manifested a strong preference for the full set interpretation.

Sample test item from Musolino and Lidz (p. 836):
A strong guy tries to lift three dogs and three elephants one by one
and put them on a large table behind him. He begins with the dogs
and easily manages to place each of them on the table. He then
turns to the elephants and tries to lift the bigger one. Unfortunately,
the big elephant is far too heavy for the strong guy who cannot
even lift it off the floor. The strong guy then turns to the medium
elephant, hoping that it is lighter. Still no luck though— elephants
are heavy! Finally, the strong guy tries to pick up the smaller elephant but he still fails to lift it off the ground. In the end therefore,
the strong guy was able to put all the dogs on the table but none of
the elephants. At this point, the puppet describes what happened by
saying that ''The strong guy didn't put every elephant on the table''.

The 20 children in Musolino and Lidz's study (mean age 5;4) accepted the
full set interpretation (judging the test sentence to be true) about 75% of the
time,[4] suggesting a disregard for the pragmatic calculus. In contrast, adult
subjects accepted the full set reading just 20% of the time.

One way to further test the effect of age on the use of the pragmatic calculus is to consider the scope preferences of *adult* bilinguals, for whom the
possibility of a pragmatic lag is presumably irrelevant.

4.2 Experiment Involving Adult Bilinguals

Subjects

Seven adults (aged 23;8-30;8) who grew up in Korean immigrant families
living in the United States participated in this experiment. All had been born
in the U.S. or moved there before puberty. Like the child heritage learners
in the experiment described in section 4.1, they spoke Korean to varying
degrees at home, but attended English-language schools. All earned undergraduate degrees from English-language universities in the U.S., and considered English to be their stronger language.

Procedure and Materials

The interpretive preferences of adults were assessed using a written questionnaire, in which each test item was preceded by a context and accompanied by a picture that summarized the situation described in the context, as
in our experiment with child bilinguals. There were four test items per condition, arranged in a Latin square design so that none of the subjects heard

---

[4] However, Musolino and Lidz's test items involved the quantifier *every* rather than *all*.

the same test item in more than one context. The questionnaire also included two practice items and ten filler items.

Results

The results for our experiment are summarized in table 4.

Table 4. Bilingual adults' truth value judgments for sentences such as *Robert didn't cut down all the trees*

Full set context (all the trees are uncut)		Partitioned set context (one of three trees was cut down)	
True	False	True	False
86%	14%	54%	46%

As shown in table 4, the adult bilinguals resemble their child counterparts in manifesting a strong preference for the full set interpretation, which is accepted 86% of the time, compared to just 54% for the partitioned set interpretation. This preference is similar to one observed for Korean in a separate study with the same subjects, but differs sharply from the interpretive propensities manifested by monolingual speakers of English. Indeed, Lee (2009:126) reports mirror-image results for adult native English speakers—an acceptance rate of 45% in the full set context and of 90% in the partitioned set context.[5] We obtained similar results in a study that we did with nine English-speaking adults: the acceptance rate for our test sentences was 47% in the full set context and 97% in the partitioned set context.

In sum, the data from our adult subjects suggest that bilinguals differ from monolingual native speakers of English in two respects—they over-accept the full set interpretation and they under-accept the partitioned set interpretation. Both propensities point to a disregard for the pragmatic calculus, which favors the partitioned set interpretation in English at the expense of the full set reading. This in turn suggests that prior knowledge of Korean interferes with attention to pragmatic aspects of scope interpretation in English, even after many years of exposure to that language.

5. Concluding Remarks

We began by considering the question of why English speakers prefer the partitioned set interpretation of sentences such as *Mary didn't read all the books*. Following Musolino and Lidz (2006), we adopted the view that a pragmatic calculus shapes the comprehension of such sentences: listeners assume that the full set interpretation, if intended, will be expressed by an unambiguous pattern such as *Mary didn't read any of the books*, thereby

---

[5] Lee's sentences contained the quantifier *every* rather than *all*.

inferring that *Mary didn't read all the books* must have the partitioned set interpretation.

This led us to the question of why Korean doesn't exhibit the same preference in sentences containing a negated verb and a universally quantified direct object. We put forward the hypothesis that the pragmatic calculus is suppressed in Korean by processing considerations, which strongly favor the full set interpretation. We went on to report experimental evidence that offers independent support for the relative difficulty of the partitioned set interpretation in Korean, as predicted by our hypothesis.

Finally, we investigated the possible effect of bilingualism on scope interpretation in English, focusing on children and adults who had learned Korean before English became their dominant language. The key finding was that early exposure to Korean seems to interfere with learners' attention to the pragmatic calculus in English. This in turn suppresses the preference for the partitioned set interpretation that is otherwise characteristic of English, leaving a preference for the full set interpretation parallel to what is observed for Korean. Crucially, however, whereas the preference for the full set interpretation in Korean appears to be motivated by processing considerations, as demonstrated by the experimental work reviewed in section 3.2, there is no comparable motivation for this interpretation in English— the preference seems to come entirely from early exposure to Korean.

This finding raises potentially far-reaching questions about the relationship between processing and pragmatics in the course of language acquisition. Of special interest is the fragility of the pragmatic calculus, whose impact depends on the sensitivity of learners to alternative and more direct ways of expressing particular interpretations. As we have seen, this chain of observation and inference can be suppressed by processing considerations (as happens in Korean) and subsequently ignored in English by Korean-speaking child learners, who are not accustomed to computing its effects. Even more remarkably, the effects of this early inattention seem to last into adulthood, creating interpretive preferences in English-dominant adult speakers that are quite unlike those associated with their monolingual counterparts. It is hoped that research currently underway will shed further light on the nature and generality of this phenomenon.

References

Grodner, D. and Gibson, E. 2005. Consequences of the Serial Nature of Linguistic Input for Sentential Complexity. *Cognitive Science* 29:261-90.

Han, C.-H., Lidz, J., and Musolino J. 2007. V-Raising and Grammar Competition in Korean: Evidence from Negation and Quantifier Scope. *Linguistic Inquiry* 38:1-48.

Lee, S. 2009. Interpreting Ambiguity in First and Second Language Processing: Universal Quantifiers and Negation. Doctoral dissertation, University of Hawaii at Manoa.

Montrul, S. 2008. *Incomplete Acquisition in Bilingualism: Re-examining the Age Factor.* Amsterdam: John Benjamins.

Musolino, J. and Lidz, J. 2006. Why Children Aren't Universally Successful with Quantification. *Linguistics* 44:817-852.

Noveck, I., Guelminger, R., Georgieff, N., and Labruyere, N. 2007. What Autism Can Reveal about *Every ... Not* Sentences. *Journal of Semantics* 24: 73-90.

O'Grady, W., Lee, M., and Kwak, H.-Y. 2009. Emergentism and Second Language Acquisition. *Handbook of Second Language Acquisition*, ed. W. Ritchie and T. Bhatia. 69-81. Bingley, UK: Emerald Press.

Part IV

Pragmatics, Discourse, and Sociolinguistics

Linguistic Forms, Context of Use and the Emergence of Functions: The Case of the Japanese Quotative Expression *Tte*

SHIGEKO OKAMOTO
University of California, Santa Cruz

1. Introduction

The Japanese quotative particle *tte* have been studied with regard to its syntactic, semantic, and pragmatic properties (Martin 1975, Makino and Tsutsui 1986, Okamoto 1995, Suzuki 1999, 2008, Okamoto and Ono 2008). The present study further examines this particle with a focus on the question of how to account for its multi-functionality. The particle *tte* has been recognized as having more than one meaning or function. Are they part of the inherent meanings of the form *tte*? Or is there one basic function from which other functions are inferred as implications engendered in specific context? Asking these questions concerns larger theoretical issues concerning the relationship between form, meaning and the nature of grammatical categories (e.g. Hopper and Thompson 1980, Hopper 1987, Langacker 1987, Fischer 2006, Englebretson 2008).

Japanese/Korean Linguistics 19.
Edited by Ho-min Sohn, Haruko Cook, William O'Grady, Leon A. Serafim, & Sang Yee Cheon.

The data for this study are mostly drawn from several recorded and transcribed conversations. The paper is organized as follows: Section 2 presents five different uses of *tte* examined in this study; Sections 3 and 4 offer arguments for and against recognizing only one function and, hence, one grammatical category for the particle *tte*; and Section 5 draws a conclusion based on the findings in Sections 3 and 4.

2. Uses of the Particle *tte*

The particle *tte* is used in widely differing contexts, which seem to give rise to different functions of this morpheme (Okamoto 1995, Okamoto and Ono 2008, Suzuki 2008). However, there seems to be one function that is invariant in all uses of *tte*. It is the quotative function to indicate that what precedes *tte* is a reported or reproduced speech or thought. Are there other functions of *tte*? In Okamoto and Ono (2008), we identified five different but related patterns of use of *tte*:

    (i)   *tte* as an object complement marker [Example (1) below],
    (ii) *tte* as a conjunctive particle [Example (2)],
    (iii) *tte* as a topic marker [Example (3)],
    (iv) *tte* as a semi-sentence-final particle [Example (4)], and
    (v) *tte* as a sentence-final particle [Example (5)].

(1)   MS, talking with her friend about her work.

        MS: *moo   rainen   yameru **tte** itchatta kara.*
               already next year quit   said-PST[1] so
               'I'll quit (my job) next year **tte** I've already said, so'

(2)   NK, talking with MS about her work schedule.

1   NK: *de   yo-ji-han   ni   enchoo   matte,*
               and 4:30-p.m. at   director wait-and
               'And at 4:30, I wait for the director (of the
               kindergarten) and'
2   MS: *[u::n]*
               yeah
               'Yeah'

---

[1] The abbreviations used in this study are as follows: AH (addressee honorific); AUX (auxiliary verb); COP (copula); GM (genitive marker); HSFX (honorific suffix); NEG (negative); NOM (nominalizer); OM (object marker); PASS (passive); PL (plain form); PRG (progressive); PRT (particle); PST (past tense); Q (question marker); SM (subject marker); SFX (suffix); TM (topic marker).

3   NK: *[otsukare]sama deshita:: tatatata rokkaa itte, kigaete*
                  tiring-HSFX   COP-AH-PST   locker go-and change
                  *otsukaresama de::su **tte** kaetchau no.*
                  tiring-HSFX   COP-AH   go-home PRT
                      'I (say) *otsukaresamadeshita::* (It was tiring), and dashing to the locker like *tatatata*, and change, and (saying) *otsukaresama de::su **tte**,* go home.'

(3)   MS, looking at an advertisement in a catalog.

1   MS: *kono kaban hoshii kedo na:: nijuuni-man*
                  this   bag   want   but   PRT   220,000-yen
                  *ga juugo-man **tte** doo yuu   koto?*
                  SM   150,000-yen   what kind of   meaning
                      'I want this bag, but (what is usually) 220,000 yen is (now) 150,000 yen ***tte***, what does (that) mean?'

(4)   HS, asking MS if she will call her fiancé.

1   HS: *M ga denwa-sun no?*
                  SM   call   do PRT
                  'Are you (MS) going to call (him)?'
2   MS: *un.*
                  yeah
                  'Yeah.'
                  (0.3)
3   HS: *kaette kita yo **tte**.*
                  come back-PST PRT
                  'I'm back ***tte*** (saying, "I'm back")?'
4   MS: *soo.*
                  right
                  'Right.'

(5)   RO, talking about her classmate.

      RO: *okusan Nihonjin na n desu **tte**.*
                  wife   Japanese COP AUX-AH
                  'His wife is Japanese ***tte*** (I heard).'

Example (1) illustrates the use of *tte* that may be regarded as a marker of object complement for a verb of linguistic or cognitive activity, such as *yuu* 'say' and *omou* 'think.' Example (2) illustrates the use of *tte* that may be considered as a conjunctive particle that links the clause or phrase that precedes *tte* as serving as a manner or temporal adverbial [in (2), a manner of leaving the office] for what follows *tte*. Example (3) illustrates the use of *tte* that may be treated as a topic marker. Examples (4) and (5) respectively illustrate the use of *tte* that may be considered a semi-sentence-final particle and a (genuine) sentence-final particle.

In what follows, I examine if these five grammatical roles are inherent properties of the particle *tte* or if they are inferable from the core function of *tte* and the context of its use.

3. Arguments for the Particle *tte* as Having a Single Function/Meaning

In all five examples above, the particle *tte* serves to indicate the epistemic status of what precedes *tte* as reported or reproduced speech. Further, depending on the context, *tte* appears to play a different grammatical role. However, one may argue that these different grammatical roles are not part of the inherent properties of *tte* since they cannot be identified without recourse to its structural context. For example, *tte* in Example (1) may be regarded as an object complement marker because it occurs before the verb of saying (*itchatta*), which prompts one to interpret what precedes *tte* as the content, or 'object,'[2] of saying. In Example (2), on the other hand, *tte* is followed by the verb *kaechau* 'go home,' in which case, what precedes *tte* cannot be interpreted as the 'object' complement of the following verb, but it may be interpreted as a manner in which the action *kaechau* was performed (i.e. 'went home, saying *otsukaresamaa*'). Accordingly, *tte* in (2) may be treated as a conjunctive particle that follows an adverbial clause. In Example (3), what precedes *tte* is a topic of what follows *tte*, which then may be considered a topic marker (Okamoto and Ono 2008; Suzuki 2008). In Example (5), *tte* is used utterance-finally and does not have any clause/phrase linking function. Thus, it may be considered a sentence-final particle used as a modality marker for the utterance that precedes *tte*. In Example (4), too, *tte* occurs utterance-finally, but it is implicitly linked to the preceding utterance *M ga denwa-sun no?* (line 1) if we invert the order of clauses in lines 1 and 3 to *Kaette kita yo tte M ga denwa-sunn no?* What precedes *tte* may then be interpreted as a manner in which MS makes a phone call. Accordingly, *tte* in (4) could be considered a semi-sentence-final particle, or semi-conjunctive particle, that is, having a status between the third and fourth categories.

The foregoing discussion suggests that the grammatical roles associated with the particle *tte* depend on the relationship between what precedes *tte*

---

[2] As will be discussed in Section 5, what preceded *tte* is not a prototypical object.

and what follows it and where in the sentence *tte* occurs. In this respect, we may argue that *tte* has only one meaning—the quotative function—and its structural context determines the grammatical role of *tte*, and not vice versa. To further illustrate this point, let us look at Example (6), which includes six instances of *tte*.

(6) MS, talking with HS, her mother, about what her fiancé says about her.

1 MS: *tako, takona koto bakka yuu **tte**.*
     stupid things only say
     'I say only *takona*/stupid things ***tte*** (he says).'

2 HS: *tato, na, takona koto bakka itte **tte** doo yuu koto?*
          things only say what kind of meaning
     'What do you mean by saying only *takona* things?'

3 MS: *okaasan, wakannai no, tako **tte**.*
     mother understand-NEG PRT stupid
     'Mother, you don't understand (that)? *Tako **tte**?*'

4 HS: *tako **tte** aho **tte** yuu koto?*
          stupid say meaning
     '*Tako* means stupid?

5 MS: *soo. ampontan dakke na.*
     right stupid I think
     'Right. It means *ampontan*/stupid, I think.'

6 HS: *ara maa.*
     oh my
     'Oh, my!'

7 MS: *tako **tte** joodan de yutte n da yo.*
          joke as say-PRG AUX PRT
     'He says *tako **tte*** as a joke.'

One may categorize *tte* in line 1 as a sentence-final particle; *tte* in line 2 as a topic marker; *tte* in line 3 as a semi-sentence-final particle (or semi-topic marker); the first instance of *tte* in line 4 as a topic marker and the second one and *tte* in line 7 as object complement markers. But such categorizations are possible only after examining the structural context of *tte*. That is, these functions emerge only in specific contexts.

4. Arguments Against the Particle *tte* as Having a Single Function/Meaning

Given the foregoing observations, the argument that there is only one meaning of *tte* seems quite plausible. However, there are several pieces of evidence that do not support this argument and instead warrant the treatment of *tte* as comprising five different grammatical categories, each with a specific function. Drawing on Okamoto (1995) and Okamoto and Ono (2008), in this section, I discuss five criteria for distinguishing these five categories of *tte*: (1) the substitutability with the particle *to*; (2) the applicability of the sentence-final particle *yo*; (3) the target of addressee honorifics; (4) the paraphrasability with other phrases; and (5) specialized pragmatic functions.

The first criterion, the substitutability of *tte* with the particle *to*, a stylistically more formal variant of *tte*, allows us to distinguish *tte* as an object complement marker from the other uses of *tte*. That is, *tte* as an object complement marker, but not other uses of *tte*, can be substituted by *to*, as shown in Example (1a), a modified version of Example (1):

(1a) MS: *moo rainen yameru to itchatta kara.*
'I will quit (my job) next year *to* I've already said, so'

Examples (7) and (8) are additional examples attested in the data. They show that *tte* and *to* are interchangeable in that both occur in the same environment, that is, between *kana* and *omotteru n desu kedo*.

(7) HT, talking about her plans after her graduation.

HT: *shuushoku-guchi ga attara Amerika de hatarakitai*
employment　　SM exist if America in work want
kana　tte omotteru n desu kedo.
I wonder　think-PRG AUX-AH but
'If there is a job, I want to work in America *tte* I'm thinking, but …'

(8) HT, talking about the course she is thinking of taking.

HT: *de, sore totte miyoo kana to omotteru n desu kedo.*
'And I (should) take that (course) and see (how it is) *to* I'm thinking, but …'

The particle *to* cannot be used in the other four uses of *tte*, as shown by the asterisks indicating inappropriateness in Examples (2a)-(5a), modified versions of (2)-(5):

(2a) NK: *[otsukare]sama deshita:: tatatata rokkaa itte, kigaete*
*otsukaresama de::su tte/*to kaetchau no.*
'I (say) *otsukaresama deshita::* (It was tiring), and dashing to the locker like *tatatata*, and change, and (saying) *otsukaresama de::su tte/*to* go home.'

(3a) MS: *kono kaban hoshii kedo na:: nijuuni-man*
    *ga juugo-man **tte/*to** doo yuu koto?*
      'I want this bag, but (what is usually) 220,000 yen is
      (now) 150,000 yen ***tte/*to***, what does (that) mean?'

(4a) HS: *M ga denwa-sun no?*
    'Are you (MS) going to call (him)?'
   MS: *un.*
    'Yeah.'
    (0.3)
   HS: *kaette kita yo **tte/*to**.*
    'I'm back ***tte/*to***?'

(5a) RO: *okusan Nihonjin na n desu **tte/*to**.*
    'His wife is Japanese, ***tte/*to*** (I heard).'

These observations thus suggest that *tte* as an object complement marker should be distinguished from the other four uses of *tte* in that the particle *tte* has specialized functions for the latter.

The second criterion, the applicability of the sentence-final particle *yo*, concerns the use of *tte* as a sentence-final particle. The particle *yo* 'I'm telling you' can follow *tte* in certain cases in which *tte* is used utterance-finally in the fifth use, as illustrated in (5b), a modified version of (5), and also in (9), attested in the data:

(5b) RO: *okusan Nihonjin na n desu **tte yo**.*
    'His wife is Japanese, ***tte*** (I heard) ***yo***.'

(9) HS, commenting on the cakes that her daughter had bought.

   HS: *wa:: oneechan ikko gohyaku-en*
    wow older-sister-SFX one-piece five-hundred-yen
    *no keeki da **tte yo**.*
    GM cake COP PRT
    'Wow! Sister, these cakes are five hundred yen a piece ***tte***
    (I heard) ***yo***'

The particle *yo* cannot follow *tte* in the other four uses, as illustrated in (1b), in which *tte* may be considered an object complement marker.

(1b) MS: *moo rainen yameru tte *yo itchatta kara.*
    'I will quit (my job) next year ***tte *yo*** I've already said,
    so'

In Example (10) below, *tte* may be considered a semi-sentence-final particle. But it cannot be followed by *yo*, as shown in (10a). This suggests that even though *tte* appears utterance-finally in (10), it should be distinguished from the use of *tte* as a (genuine) sentence-final particle.

(10)   TT, talking with her son about his future work.

    TT: *u::n, naite kaette kuru yo,   mo::   ya::da::*   ***tte.***
       uh   crying come back   PRT any more cannot do (it)
       'Uh, you would come back (saying), "I can't do it any
       more" ***tte.***'

(10a)   TT: *u::n, naite kaette kuru yo, mo:: ya::da::*   ***tte *yo.***

The third criterion involves the use of addressee honorifics. As in the case of the second criterion, this also serves to distinguish the use of *tte* as a sentence-final particle from the other uses of *tte*. Compare, for example, line 3 of (2) and (5), reproduced below as (2b) and (5c):

(2b)   NK: *[otsukare]sama deshita:: tatatata rokkaa itte, kigaete*
           *otsukaresama de::su **tte**   kaetchau no.*
               COP-AH
           'I (say) *otsukaresama deshita::* '(lit.) It was tiring', and
           dashing to the locker like *tatatata*, and change, and *otsu-
           karesama de::su **tte***, and go home.'

(5c)   RO: *okusan Nihonjin na n desu*   ***tte.***
                      AUX-AH
           'His wife is Japanese, ***tte*** (I heard).'

(5d)   RO: *okusan Nihonjin na   n da*   ***tte.***
                     AUX-PL

(5e)   RO: *okusan Nihonjin na   n *deshita*   ***tte.***
                     AUX-AH-PST

In (2b), the addressee honorific *de::su* that precedes *tte* (as a conjunctive particle) is used for the addressee of the quoted speech, namely, the director of the kindergarten, and not MS, the addressee of the current speech. *Desu* also precedes *tte* in (5c), but its target is the addressee of the current speech, and not that of the reported speech. If RO were talking with a close friend, she would use the plain form *da* instead of *desu*, as in (5d). Further, the past tense form *deshita* cannot be used, as shown in (5e), since it is used to express politeness for the addressee of the current speech.

As in Example (2b), if an addressee honorific precedes *tte* in the other three uses (i.e. *tte* as an object complement marker, topic marker, or semi-sentence-final particle), its target is construed as the addressee of the reported speech, as shown in (1c), (3b), and (4b):

(1c)   MS: *moo   rainen   yame<u>masu</u> **tte** itchatta kara.*
                            quit-AH
              'I will quit (my job) next year *tte* I've already said, so'

(3b)   MS: *kono kaban hoshii kedo na:: nijuuni-man*
                *ga juugo-man   <u>desu</u>   **tte** doo yuu koto?*
                            COP-AH
              'I want this bag, but (what is usually) 220,000 yen is (now) 150,000 yen *tte*, what does (that) mean?'

(4b)   HS: *M ga denwa-sun no?*
                'Are you (MS) going to call (him)?'
        MS: *un.*
                'Yeah.'
                (0.3)
        HS: *kaette   ki<u>mashita</u>   yo   **tte**.*
                  come   back-AH-PST PRT
                'I'm back *tte*?'

The utterances that precede *tte* in Examples (2b), (1c), (3b), and (4b) thus represent direct speech with the addressee honorific used for the addressee of the original reported speech. Example (11) further supports this argument:

(11) YO, talking with her former student.

      YO: *kekkyoku dare no tame ni benkyoo-shite iru/*
            after all whom GM for   study-PRG-PRES
            <u>imasu</u> ka **tte yuu to jibun no tame desu   kara,*
              *AH Q   say if self GM for COP-AH so
            'After all, if one asks for whom one is studying *tte*, it's for oneself, so,'

Here, *tte* may be considered an object complement marker for the verb *yuu* 'say.' YO is making a general statement and the question he is asking in the reported speech is aimed at a non-specific person, for whom one need not be polite. Accordingly, it is awkward to use an addressee honorific, which, therefore, supports that the utterance before *tte* in this example is targeted at the addressee of the reported speech.

The fourth criterion is whether *tte* can be paraphrased by another expression. Let us first examine the use of *tte* as a conjunctive particle. For example, *tte* in (2) can be paraphrased as X *tte/to itte* 'saying that,' as shown in (2c) and (12):

(2c)   NK: *[otsukare]sama deshita:: tatatata rokkaa itte, kigaete*
                 *otsukaresama de::su **tte/tte itte**   kaetchau no.*
                                                saying
                 'I (say) *otsukaresama deshita::* '(lit.) It was tiring', and
                 dashing to the locker like *tatatata*, and change, and (say-
                 ing) *otsukaresama de::su **tte**, go home.

(12) MS, talking with her mother about her fiancé.

     MS: *futsuu atashi ga sa, sa, baibai **tte/tte itte** miokun*
             usually   I   SM PRT   bye-bye   saying see of
             noni,   A ni miokurarete,   Okayama de.
             although by see off-PASS and   in
                     'Although usually, (saying) bye-bye ***tte***, I see him off,
             (this time) I was seen off by A in Okayama.'

In (2c), the clause that precedes *tte* can be construed as a manner adverbial for the action described by the utterance that follows it. Further, *itte* is in the continuative form that links the clause that precedes *tte* to the clause that follows it, which supports the treatment of *tte* as a conjunctive particle. Example (12) illustrates the same point.

Example (13) illustrates a similar point, but in this case, *tte* is paraphrased as *tte omotte* 'thinking that.'

(13) TI, talking with her friend about the movie she saw recently.

     TI: *warau toko nan kana:: **tte/tte omotte**, watashi mo*
             laugh place COP I wonder   thinking I   also
             tsurarete   waratta kedo.
             following laughed but
                     '(Thinking) this may be a place one is supposed to
             laugh ***tte***, I also laughed following (those who were
             laughing), but ...'

Such paraphrasing is also possible for the use of *tte* as a semi-sentence-final particle, when the utterance that immediately precedes *tte* is interpreted as an adverbial for the preceding clause, as illustrated in (4c):

(4c)   HS: *M ga denwa-sun no?*
'Are you (MS) going to call (him)?'

        MS: *un.*
'Yeah.'
(0.3)

        HS: *kaette kita yo **tte itte**.*
                              saying
'I'm back ***tte itte***? (Saying, "I'm back")?'

However, the same kind of paraphrasing is not possible for the other uses of *tte*, as shown in (1d), (3c), and (5f):

(1d)   MS: *moo rainen yameru **tte *itte** itchatta kara.*
                                     saying
'I have already said I will quit (my job) next year ***tte * itte*** so'

(3c)   MS: *kono kaban hoshii kedo na:: nijuuni-man*
*ga juugo-man **tte * itte** doo yuu koto?*
                                 saying
'I want this bag, but (what is usually) 220,000 yen is (now) 150,000 yen ***tte *itte*** what does (that) mean?'

(5f)   RO: *okusan Nihonjin na n desu **tte *itte**.*
                                   saying
'His wife is Japanese ***tte *itte**.'

The fact the *tte itte* is not allowed in these three uses of *tte* suggests that the role of *tte* as a conjunctive particle is a specialized function associated with a particular structure. Further, if *tte* as a conjunctive particle were in fact derived from *tte itte* or a similar longer expression, its function as a conjunctive particle could not be regarded simply as a matter of contextual inference, although this point needs further study.

In the case of *tte* as a topic marker, it can be paraphrased as *tte/to yuu no wa*, which consists of the particle *tte* or *to*, the verb *yuu* 'say,' the nominalizer *no*, and the topic marker *wa* (Example (3d)).

(3d)   MS: *kono kaban hoshii kedo na:: nijuuni-man*
*ga juugo-man **tte/to yuu no wa** doo yuu koto?*
                                   say NOM TM
'I want this bag, but (what is usually) 220,000 yen is (now) 150,000 ***yen tte yuu no wa*** what does it mean? (What does it mean to say …)'

Although I will not show examples, such paraphrasing is not possible in the other four uses of *tte*, suggesting that *tte* as a topic marker must appear in a specific structural environment. Further, if it were the case that *tte* as a topic marker were in fact derived from, or motivated in, a longer expression, such as *tte yuu no wa*, this criterion would have validity for treating this type of *tte* as belonging to a different grammatical category, but this needs further study. These observations regarding the paraphrasability of *tte* suggest that the particle *tte* has acquired a special function as a conjunctive particle or a topic marker.

The fifth criterion concerns the particle *tte* that may be regarded as a sentence-final particle. In addition to the basic quotative function, *tte* in the fifth use has a special function of serving as a modality marker that indicates that what precedes *tte* is hearsay or what the speaker insists on. The former is illustrated by Examples (5g) and (14) and the latter by Examples (15) and (16):

(5g) RO: *okusan Nihonjin na   n desu **tte**.*
            'His wife is Japanese ***tte*** (I heard).'

(14)   MS, talking with her mother.

       MS: *nee,   Shaneru no tokei   juugo-man da   **tte**.*
             hey/look Chanel   GM watch   150,000   COP
             'Look, a Chanel's watch is 150,000-yen ***tte*** (they say).'

(15)   From a TV drama.

1   A: *ie   yo.*
             say PRT
             'Tell me about it.'
2   B: *nan demo nai   **tte**. Nan demo nai   yo.*
             anything NEG   anything   NEG PRT
             'It's nothing ***tte*** (I insist). It's nothing.

(16)   HS and MS, HS's daughter, arguing whether or not stores are already open (in the beginning of January).

1   HS: *datte, ka,   istuka made aitenai   **tte**.*
             but Tues(day) 5th   until open-NEG
             'But (stores) are not open until Tues(day), the 5th ***tte***.'
2   MS: *uso   da   yo. motto hayaku aiteru **tte**.*
             false COP PRT more   early   open
             'That's not true. They are open much earlier ***tte***.'

The particle *tte* in (5) and (14) indicates that what precedes *tte* is something the speaker heard from someone else. The speakers in (15) and (16), on the other hand, are not simply reporting what they heard, but rather emphasizing a particular point as true. In (15), for example, the speaker says *nan demo nai tte* 'it's nothing-*tte*' and repeats *nan demo nai*, indicating his insistence on the point he is making.

5. Non-discrete Subcategories of the Particle *tte*

The analyses presented in the preceding section seem to support the treatment of *tte* as consisting of five distinct grammatical categories. However, a closer look at the data suggests that the boundaries between these categories are not clear-cut. In addition to the fact that they all share the quotative function, there are cases in which *tte* does not exhibit prototypical properties of a particular grammatical role (e.g. object complement marker). Furthermore, there is within-category variation in that not all instances of *tte* playing the 'same' grammatical role exhibit the same syntactic, semantic, and/or pragmatic properties..

For example, *tte* in (1), reproduced below, and (7) may be considered an object complement marker:

(1)　　MS:　　*moo　　rainen　　yameru **tte** itchatta kara.*
　　　　　　　　'I will quit (my job) next year **tte** I've already said, so'

However, in the case of a prototypical object marker, the particle *o* is used. Also, what precedes the particle *o* must be a nominal element. Accordingly, if it is a clause, it must be nominalized by a nominalizer, such as *no* or *koto*, as illustrated in (1e) and (1f). These properties are, however, not applicable to the use of *tte* as an object complement marker (Okamoto and Ono 2008).

(1e)　　*Takada-san ga rainen　　yameru **koto　o**　　shiranakatta.*
　　　　　　　HSFX SM next year quit　　NOM OM know-NEG-PST
　　　　　　　'I didn't know that Ms. Takada will quit (her job) next year.'

(1f)　　*Takada-san ga rainen　yameru *o shiranakatta.*

Furthermore, there is variation within the use of *tte* as an object complement marker. The particle *tte* in (1) and (7) can be considered a complement (as opposed to an adjunct) in the sense that it is a constituent, or an obligatory element, for the verb *yuu* 'say' or *omotteru* 'thinking.' However, there are cases in which it is not clear whether or not the utterance that precedes *tte* is a complement.

(17)   YO, talking with his former student about one of his former professors.

    YO: *de, sono sensei ni soodan shi ni ittaraba, sono*
             and that professor to consult   to went when that
             *sensei   ga hahaha **tte/to** waratte,*
             professor SM   laugh and
             'And when I went to (see) that professor for consultation, ha-ha-ha *tte* he laughed and'

In (17), for example, *ha-ha-ha* can be construed as a manner adverbial (and hence adjunct) in that it specifies the manner of laughing. At the same time, however, *tte* in (17) meets the criteria for distinguishing *tte* as an object complement marker from *tte* in the other uses in that it is interchangeable with *to*, as shown in (17); and that it cannot be paraphrased as *tte itte*. Example (18) also presents a similar "problem":

(18)   TI, talking with her former professor YO about her experience as a graduate student in the United States.

1   TI: *demo u::n saisho no semesutaa da   kara   **tte/to***
             but   uh first GM semester   COP because
             'But uh because it's the first semester ***tte***'
2   YO: *un*
             yeah
             'Yeah'
3   TI: *jibun   o   nagusamete,*
             myself OM comfort-and
             'I comforted myself and'
4   YO: *un*
             yeah
             'yeah'

Is the instance of *tte* in (18) an object complement marker or a conjunctive particle? *Tte* here can be substituted by *to*, as shown in (18), suggesting it is a complement marker. But, *nagusamete* already has its object complement *jibun o*; further, it can be paraphrased by *tte itte*, in which case *tte* may be considered a conjunctive particle that links the manner adverbial clause to the verb *nagusameru*. These examples suggest that the particle *tte* is not a prototypical example of an object complement marker and also that there is variation within this use: in some cases, such as (17) and (18), it is unclear whether *tte* should be regarded as an object complement marker or a conjunctive particle, while in other cases, such as (1) and (7), such ambiguity does not exist.

With regard to the use of *tte* as a topic marker, I mentioned earlier the possibility of paraphrasing it with *tte/to yuu no wa*, as was illustrated in (3d). However, other paraphrases are also possible, as shown in (3f):

(3f)   MS: *kono   kaban   hoshii   kedo   na::   nijuuni-man*
             *ga juugo-man **tte yuu kedo, sore wa**   doo yuu   koto?*
                       say   but   that TM
             'I want this bag, but (what is usually) 220,000 yen is (now) 150,000 **yen tte yuu kedo,** what does it mean? (They say ... but what does it mean?)'

If *tte* were paraphrased with *tte yuu kedo, sore wa*, then it could be treated as a conjunctive particle. Further, there are cases in which *tte* may be regarded as a topic marker but cannot be paraphrased as *tte/to yuu no wa*.

(19)   TI, talking with her former professor while looking at old photos of the professor.

    TI: *kore **tte** sensei ga   tiineijaa no   toki   desu   ka?*
        this   professor SM teenager GM when COP-AUX Q
        'Is this when you were a teenager?'
(19a)   TI: *kore * **tte/to yuu nowa** sensei ga   tiineijaa   no*
        toki   desu   ka?

(20)   RS, talking with her friend about asking her acquaintances to do her a favor.

    RS: *dakara, nanka   ammari   shiriai   ni tanomu no   **tte***
        so   somehow not so acquaintance to ask   NOM
        iya   janai.
        undesirable AUX-NEG
        'So, asking my acquaintances **tte** is somehow not so desirable, right?'
(20a)   RS: *dakara, nanka   ammari   shiriai   ni tanomu no*
        ?tte/to   yuu no   wa *iya   janai.*

In (19) and (20), *tte* can be replaced with the topic marker *wa*, but not with *tte/to yuu no wa*, as shown in (19a) and (20a). These observations show that the use of *tte* as a topic marker is not monolithic.

The use of *tte* as a semi-sentence-final particle poses similar 'problems.' As the term *semi-* itself indicates that it is not a discrete category. For ex-

ample, *tte* in this category cannot be followed by another sentence-final particle *yo*, as discussed earlier. Nor can it be used as the same kind of modality marker as *tte* as a 'genuine' sentence-final particle. Further, the use of *tte*
as a semi-sentence-final particle is related to other uses of *tte* because the
utterance in question could be considered as resulting from the inversion of
the clauses/phrases in which *tte* is used as an object-complement marker, as
shown in (21) and (21a); a conjunctive particle, as shown in (10), reproduced below, and (10b); or a topic marker, as shown in (6), reproduced below and (6a).

(21) RM, a well-known writer, interviewing KM, a female high school
      student. [From Murakami 1998: 32]

1   RM: *nanka   iwarenai   no?*
            something   say-PASS-NEG PRT
            'Aren't you told something (by the teachers)?'
2   KM: *nyuugaku-shita toki   iwareta.   kami ga chairoku*
            entered school when say-PASS-PST   hair SM brown
            *natteru   n janai   ka **tte**.*
            has become AUX-NEG Q
            'When I entered the school, I was told, your hair has be-
            come brown, hasn't it **tte**.'
(21a) KM: *kami ga chairoku   natte   n janai ka **tte***
            nyuugaku-shita toki   iwareta.
            'Your hair has become brown, hasn't it **tte** I was told when
            I entered school.'

(10) TT: *u::n, naite kaette kuru yo, mo:: ya::da:: **tte**.*
            'Uh, you will come back, (saying), "I can't do it any
            more" **tte**.'
(10b) TT: *u::n, mo:: ya::da:: **tte** naite kaette kuru yo.*
            'Uh, (saying), "I can't do it any more" **tte** you will
            come back."

(6)   MS: *okaasan, wakannai   no, tako **tte**.*
            'Mother, you don't understand (that)? *tako **tte**?"*
(6a) MS: *tako **tte** okaasan   wakannai   no?*
            stupid   mother   understand-NEG PRT
            'Mother, *tako **tte*** you don't understand?'

At the same time, however, *tte* as a semi-sentence-final particle occurs
utterance-finally and does not have an explicit clause/phrase linking func-

tion, as in the case of *tte* used as an object-complement marker, conjunctive particle, or a topic marker. In addition, there is evidence that suggests that an utterance with *tte* as a semi-sentence-final particle is not a result of clause/phrase inversion.

(22) From a T.V. drama (Maynard 2001: 58)

> <u>koo</u>   *yuu* *n da,* *anta* *nanka*   <u>suki</u>
> this-way say AUX   you something-like love
> <u>ja-nai</u>   ***tte,***   <u>sukina wake nai **tte**.</u>
>   NEG   love   reason NEG
> '(She) says like this. I don't love you ***tte***, there's no reason why I love you ***tte***.'

(23) YO, talking with his former student about 7-Eleven, a convenience store chain.

> YO: <u>*sore wa*</u> *Nihon de wa* *dokka* *Itooyookadoo-kei* *ka*
>   that TM Japan in TM   somewhere   group or
>   *nanaka*   *da to omoimasu.* <u>*Sebun-irebun* ***tte***.</u>
>   Something COP   think-AH   7-Eleven
>   'I think in Japan that is (part of) the *Itooyookadoo* group or something. 7-Eleven ***tte***.'

For example, in (22), the complement of *yuu* is explicitly mentioned as *koo* 'this way' in the first clause, but it is rephrased in the following two clauses, each marked with *tte*. Likewise, in (23), the complement clause for *omoimasu* 'think' has an explicit topic *sore* 'that' marked by the topic marker *wa*, but then the speaker rephrases *sore* with *Sebum-irebun* in the subsequent utterance. Neither (22) nor (23) thus can be treated as the result of inversion, because if we reverse the order of clauses/phrases, the result will be unacceptable or marginal.

These observations suggest that the *tte* clauses/phrases in Examples (21), (10), (6), (22) and (23) are increments rather than the outcomes of inversion, which further supports the treatment of *tte* in these cases as a semi-sentence-final particle. Furthermore, these examples show that even within the use of *tte* as a semi-sentence-final particle, there is variation in that *tte* in Examples (22) and (23), in which inversion is not possible, may be considered closer to a 'genuine' sentence-final particle than that in Examples (21), (10), and (6), in which inversion is possible.

The use of *tte* as a sentence-final particle is not monolithic, either. Earlier, I discussed two pragmatic functions of the final *tte*: one for indicating that the information in question is hearsay and the other for the speech act of insistence. The former may be paraphrased as *tte kiita* 'I heard," while the latter may be paraphrased with an expression such as X *tte itteru desho* 'I'm telling you that X' or X *tte ieba* X 'if I say X, it's X.' In fact, the form *tte ba*, a contracted form of *tte ieba*, may be used to indicate the speaker's insistence, as shown in (24):

(24)   HS, asking MS, her daughter, to take some clothes and foods with her to her apartment.

1   HS: *anta ashita   sukoshi motte tte ne, iroiro yoofuku,*
             you tomorrow a little bit take   PRT various clothes
             gohan toka.
             food   etc.
             'Tomorrow, will you take various (things) like clothes
             and foods a little bit with you, OK?'
2   MS: *iranai   **tte ba::***
             need-NEG   if
             'I don't want them ***tte ba::***. (If I tell you I don't want
             them, I don't want them.)'
(24a) MS: *iranai   **tte**.*
             'I don't want them ***tte***. (I'm telling you I don't want
             them.)'

In (24), *tte ba::* in MS's utterance in line 2 may be replaced by *tte* without changing the meaning except that *tte ba::* may convey a stronger insistence than *tte* alone. It is unclear whether *tte* used for the speaker's insistence is in fact derived from *tte ba*, but if it is, it seems to further support the treatment of this use as distinct from the final *tte* used for hear-say, because *tte ba* cannot replace the latter use of *tte*.

6. Conclusion

In this paper, I have examined the structural and functional properties of the particle *tte* using conversational data. I now return to the question posed at the outset of this paper: Is there only one category of *tte* with one function? If that is the case, the additional functions are all considered inferable from the context of use. Or are there five distinct grammatical categories of the particle *tte*, each with different functions? The analyses presented in this paper suggest that the answer lies in between. As mentioned, the basic function of *tte* can be regarded as quotative. It is also undeniable that other functions of *tte* depend on the context of use, that is, the syntactic position of *tte* in an utterance and the functional relationship between what precedes *tte* and what follows *tte* (if there is any expression that follows *tte*).

At the same time, the foregoing observations suggest that the five categories of *tte* are not discrete or completely independent from each other. They suggest that the particle *tte* has been used creatively in a variety of contexts and that specialized functions have begun to be associated with the use of *tte* in each type of context with particular syntactic, semantic and pragmatic properties. However, these properties are partially overlapping, and moreover, there are cases that do not fit clear-cut categorization. Accordingly, it seems best to understand these categories of *tte* in terms of a continuum, recognizing prototypical and marginal examples of *tte* in each category. These categories thus may be regarded as mutually related and partially overlapping subcategories of the particle *tte*. This is not unique to the particle *tte* in Japanese. Previous studies have shown that grammatical categories in both Japanese and other languages are not discrete and rather they are more adequately understood in terms of a continuum (Minami 1974, Hopper and Thompson 1980, Haiman and Thompson 1984, Thomson and Mulac 1991, McGloin 2004, Englebretson 2008;). I hope this study serves as a further illustration of the non-discrete nature of grammatical categories and the fluidity, flexibility and multiplicity of the relationship between a linguistic form, its context of use and its functions.

Acknowledgments

I would like to thank the audience at the 19th Conference on Japanese/Korean Linguistics for their valuable comments.

References

Englebretson, R. 2008. From Subordinate Clause to Noun Phrase: *Yang-*Constructions in Colloquial Indonesian. *Crosslinguistic Studies of Clause Combining: The Multifunctionality of Conjunctions*, ed. R. Laury, 1-34. Amsterdam: John Benjamins.

Fischer, K. 2006. Frames, Constructions, and Invariant meanings: The Functional Polysemy of Discourse Particles. *Approaches to Discourse Particles*, ed. K. Fischer, 427-447. Amsterdam: John Benjamins.

Haiman, J. and Thompson, S. A. 1984. 'Subordination' in Universal Grammar. *Proceedings of the Tenth Annual Meeting of the Berkeley Linguistics Society*, ed. C. Brugmann & M. Macauley, 510-523. Berkeley CA: Berkeley Linguistics Society.

Hopper, P. and Thompson, S. A. 1980. Transitivity in Grammar and Discourse. *Language* 56: 251-299.

Hopper, P. 1987. Emergent Grammar. *Proceedings of the Tenth Annual Meeting of the Berkeley Linguistics Society*, ed. J. Aske, N. Beery, L. Michaelis, and H. Filip, 139-155. Berkeley CA: Berkeley Linguistics Society.

Langacker, R.W. 1987. *Foundations of Cognitive Grammar Vol. I: Theoretical*

Prerequisites. Stanford, CA: Stanford University Press.

Makino, S. and T Michio. 1986. *A Dictionary of Basic Japanese Grammar.* Tokyo: Japan Times.

Martin, S. E. 1975. *A Reference Grammar of Japanese.* San Francisco, CA: Yale University Press.

Maynard, S. 2001. *Koisuru Futari no "Kanjoo" Kotoba: Dorama-Hyoogen no Bunseki to Nihongoron* ("Emotional" Expressions of Lovers: Analysis of linguistic expressions in dramas and a theory of Japanese). Tokyo: Kuroshio Shuppan.

Minami, F. 1974. *Gendai-Nihongo no Koozoo [Structure of Modern Japanese].* Tokyo: Taishukan.

Murakami, R. 1998. *Yumemiru Koro o Sugireba: Murakami Ryu vs. Joshi-koosei 51-nin [After the Dreaming Period: Murakami Ryu vs. 51 Female High School Students].* Tokyo: Rikuruuto Davinchi.

Okamoto, S. 1995. Pragmaticization of Meaning in Some Sentence-Final Particles in Japanese. *Essays in Semantics and Pragmatics: In Honor of Charles J. Fillmore,* ed. M. Shibatani & S.A. Thompson, 219-246. Amsterdam: John Benjamins.

Okamoto, S. and Ono, T. 2008. Quotative *tte* in Japanese: Its Multifaceted Functions and Degree of "subordination." *Crosslinguistic Studies of Clause Combining: The Multifunctionality of Conjunctions,* ed. R. Laury, 205-230. Amsterdam: John Benjamins.

Suzuki, R. 1999. Grammticalization in Japanese: A Study of Pragmatic Particleization. Ph.D. dissertation, University of California, Santa Barbara.

Suzuki, R. 2008. Quoting and Topic-marking: Some Observation on the Qotative *tte* Construction in Japanese. *Crosslinguistic Studies of Clause Combining. The Multifunctionality of Conjunctions,* ed. R. Laury, 231-246. Amsterdam: John Benjamins.

Thompson, S. A. and Mulac, A. 1991. A Quantitative Perspective on the Grammaticization of Epistemic Parentheticals in English. *Approaches to Grammaticization Vol. II,* E.C., ed. Traugott and B. Heine, 313-329. Amsterdam: John Benjamins.

The Pragmatics of Pronoun Borrowing: The Case of Japanese Immigrants in Hawai'i

MIE HIRAMOTO
National University of Singapore

EMI MORITA
National University of Singapore

1. Introduction

Studying Japanese spoken outside of Japan can be very illuminating for the field of contact linguistics, yet currently there are only a handful of works documenting dialect/language contact or linguistic change in regards to Japanese immigrants' language.

This study investigates such issues of language change, focusing on the historical use of the English personal pronouns *me* and *you*[1] by Japanese immigrants in Hawai'i as exemplified below.

---

[1] These words appear their Rômanji forms of *mî* and *yû,* respectively, in the transcriptions appearing in this text.

Japanese/Korean Linguistics 19.
Edited by Ho-min Sohn, Haruko Cook, William O'Grady, Leon A. Serafim, & Sang Yee Cheon.

335

Example (1)[2]

1→ B: *Hô, mî wa Iwakuni ni modottoruka to...*
   'Oh, *I* (*me*) thought she was back in Iwakuni now...'

Example (2)

1   H: *Ewa no nangai aida otta nga,*
2 →   *ano yû-ra manda umarenai toki ni hayai koro strike nga atta no.*
   'I stayed at Ewa for a long time, but before *you* (*yû-ra*) were born, in the early days, there was a strike.'

As mentioned, existing studies on the actual use of Japanese by immigrants outside of Japan are quite scarce; however, there are some studies on the forms of Japanese spoken in Hawai'i by plantation immigrants and their descendants, and some of these studies do mention the use of *loanwords* – including English personal pronouns – by such immigrants (Higa 1970, 1975, 1976; Inoue 1975; Kurokawa 1983). Linguistically, Japanese is known for its alteration of pronouns to suit the relationship between interlocutors. Suzuki and Miura's (2001:162) discussion of the use of Japanese pronouns in self-referent situations describes an example of a person alternating between the Japanese first person pronouns *watakushi* (formal neutral register) and *boku* (less formal masculine register) both of which are equivalent to the English 'I'.

The choice of a particular self-reference term can be seen as a Japanese speaker's display of his or her understanding of their social role and relationship within society and towards one another at that moment in that given context. Each instance of self- and other- reference can thus be seem as an explicit performance of positioning of oneself within the social order. Studying the phenomenon of English personal pronoun borrowing in Japanese immigrants' speech should therefore reveal how these people negotiated both their new local identities, as well as their ongoing cultural ties to Japan.

The 'borrowability' of personal pronouns has been discussed in the field of contact linguistics as reviewed below. In this paper, we hope to contribute to this discussion by providing an examination of the rich data contained within the records of immigrants' actual language practice. Detailed analysis of their person referencing practices reveals that the use of English personal pronouns became a characteristic property of the *nikkeijin* 'people of Japanese ancestry.' However, such borrowing is not a 'fixed' property of immigrants' speech and our research shows that people in the *nikkeijin* communi-

---

[2] Data are transcribed according to Romanization system, using a modified version of the system described in Gail Jefferson (1974). All personal names have been replaced with pseudonyms. The list of symbols used is listed on page 14.

ty flexibly deploy different person pronouns in response to various sociopragmatic situations.

2. The Borrowability of Personal Pronouns

Scholars in the field of contact linguistics have long been examining the nature of cross-linguistic borrowability in language contact situations. A commonly held belief is that pronoun systems are relatively stable and thus hold low borrowability (e.g. Nichols and Peterson 1996). On the other hand, some scholars claim that given appropriate social circumstances, pronouns can be and are so 'borrowed'. For example, there are certain groups of languages that show great flexibility in the borrowing of personal pronouns (e.g. Campbell 1997; Foley 1986; Thomason and Everett 2005; Wallace 1985).

One rough grouping that they discuss in this regard is Court's (1998, cited in Thomason 2001: 83-83; Thomason and Everett 2005: 307) distinction between 'open' and 'closed' pronoun systems[3]. 'Closed' systems are those such as Indo-European languages that have a one-to-one correlation for each person/number combination. 'Open' systems are those that can have multiple expressions corresponding to each English personal pronoun. Japanese clearly falls under the 'open' system.

The personal reference terms of an open pronoun system are conceptually different from those of a closed pronoun system. Japanese terms of person reference, as one example of open pronoun system, developed over history by reflecting social differences and relationships. Social change affected even the closed pronoun system of English and resulted in the vanishing of the dual second-person pronoun system in the eighteenth century. Open pronoun systems are, not surprisingly, even more susceptible to social changes. In particular, in contact language situations involving at least one open pronoun system, the borrowing of person reference term from a genetically unrelated language may be just another way of adding new terms into the current system of personal referencing.

By looking at both previously available and recently collected data, we find that the use of English personal pronouns such as *me* and *you* are characteristically incorporated as alternative person reference terms in the Japanese language spoken by Japanese immigrants. Although such English personal pronoun borrowing is a phenomena largely limited to the English-speaking *nikkeijin* community, our data provides further evidence for the borrowability of personal pronouns to addition to the existing cases of pronoun borrowing in the languages of Southeast Asia, the Pacific, and the Americas (Thomason 2001). Unlike the majority of first-person pronouns in

---

[3] The original link cited in Thomason 2001, and Thomason and Everett 2005 is no longer available.

Japanese, English first-person pronouns are neither gendered, nor age re-stricted, nor do they indicate regional differences or formality of the situa-tion. Despite this conceptual difference in first person pronouns in the two languages, the relative 'neutrality' of the English system may have been a contributing factor to the documented adoption of these pronouns in the talk of immigrant Japanese. As members of a newly heterogeneous community in America – one where the regional differences that their dialectal form of Japanese person pronouns would 'mark' could be 'masked' by the use of the 'neutral' English first person pronoun – the use of English personal pro-nouns could also indicate such speakers' special access to English, hence indexing their bilingual status. The use of these terms to nonEnglish-speakers would, however, result in the violation of the existing linguistic norms of Japanese. Yet, eventually, in the Hawaiian context, it became the immigrant community's norm (Morita 2009). Thus, this study supports Thomason and Everett's claim that if speakers want to borrow one pronoun or a whole set of pronouns, they can do so and it is not the linguistic factors (such as structural similarity) restrict the borrowability. Before going into the discussion of English pronoun borrowing in the Japanese language spo-ken in Hawai'i, a brief background of Japanese immigration to Hawai'i will be mentioned.

3. Historical Background of the Japanese Immigration to Hawai'i

The demand for Hawaiian cane sugar was the result of two major events impacting the U.S. mainland: the dramatic population growth in California during the 1840's Gold Rush, and 1861's severe sugar shortage in the South, due to the American Civil War (Chinen and Hiura 1997: 9). By the time that the commercial cultivation of sugar cane began at Koloa Plantation on the island of Kaua'i in 1835 (Alexander 1937), the native Hawaiian population was already in decline after the arrival of Westerners. Yet the sugar econo-my was booming and the demand for manpower increased greatly during this time. According to Nordyke (1989: Table 3-1), while the precontact population of the Hawaiian Islands differs depending the views of the re-searcher, the total number of native Hawaiians was estimated to be 37,656, excluding 29,799 part-Hawaiians (cited in Kawamoto 1993: 193). Unable to secure the necessary numbers of laborers domestically, the sugar cane plantations began to become increasingly dependant upon foreign immigrant workers who began coming to Hawai'i from different parts of the world, especially after the mid 1800s. 'The Master and Servants Act of 1850,' notes Kawamoto, 'paved the way for massive labor immigration' at this time (1993: 198). Chinese nationals were the first to arrive in 1862, followed by the Portuguese in 1878, and the Japanese in 1885 (Sakoda and Siegel 2003:

4). The 1920 Census data reports that the major ethnic group in the state at that time to be the Japanese (42.7% of the total population), followed by Portuguese (10.6%), Hawaiians (9.2%), Chinese (9%), Filipinos (8.2%), Other Caucasians (7.7%), and Caucasian-Hawaiians (5%) (cited in Reinecke (1969/1988: 42).

Prior to 1900, men outnumbered women by four-to-one among Japanese immigrants (Clarke 1994: 18; *Hawaii Hochisha* 2001: 53). Yet unlike other plantation immigrants in Hawai'i, who intermarried with other immigrant groups or native Hawaiians, the Japanese group avoided interracial marriage for cultural reasons. As a result, many Japanese men started bringing over 'picture brides' from their hometowns, especially between 1908 and 1923 (*Hawaii Hochisha* 2001: 61; Odo 1998: 109). This practice, and the families that resulted, contributed to the maintenance of the Japanese language in Hawai'i. Many *issei* 'first generation Japanese immigrants' who left their hometowns as *dekasegi* 'temporary' laborers were uneducated farmers and fishermen from rural areas. For example, in 1910, 49,750 (79.0%) of Japanese who were ten years of age or older were monolingual (Reinecke 1969/1988: 124). The majority of *nisei* (or second generation Japanese) were bilinguals, and attended English-language using school systems. Yet the Japanese language was valued among Hawai'i-born *nisei* children at home and as the community language. A journalist of the time, William Carter, writes, that 'The Japanese men marry only Japanese women, and their children are habitually registered as Japanese with officials of their own government' (1921: 275). Accordingly, most Japanese immigrants had firm cultural ties to their homeland, and hoped that they or their children would someday return there. Carter also notes that 'A large proportion of them are sent back to Japan for part of their education. The younger children attend both the public schools of Hawai'i and private Japanese schools.'

The overwhelmingly large number of Japanese immigrants became a serious concern in Hawai'i, especially after a series of labor strikes in the early 1900's, and the Japanese immigration to Hawai'i officially ended in 1924 (e.g. Kawamoto 1993; Kotani 1985; Tamura 1993). Following the Pearl Harbor attack in 1941, the use of the Japanese language in Hawai'i ceased during World War II. During to the postwar recovery of Japan's economy in the early 1970's, however, Hawai'i experienced accelerated economic growth, resulting in a resurgence of the Japanese language. Thus, Japanese became the most widely-used second language in the state (Yamamoto 1973: 67). Yet unlike the prewar variety of Japanese, postwar Japanese language speakers switched to modern Standard Japanese (SJ). Consequently, younger generations of Japanese speakers in Hawai'i became more familiar with SJ than with the local Japanese dialects brought over and modified by plantation immigrants. The largest number of these immigrants came from

Hiroshima and Yamaguchi in western Honshû, where the Chûgoku dialect is spoken. Other large numbers of people came from Kyûshû Island in western Japan, primarily from Kumamoto and Fukuoka, where the Kyûshû dialect is spoken, as well as from the south-westernmost islands of Okinawa, where various Okinawan languages and dialects are spoken. The majority of non-western Japanese immigrants came from the Tôhoku dialect region of Fukushima and northern Niigata in north-eastern Honshû Island (see Hiramoto, in press).

4. Data and Methods

The data used in this paper were collected under the direction of Professor E. Smith at the University of Hawai'i at Mānoa between 1973 and 1982; hence, this corpus will be referred to as the Smith Project Data (SPD). The SPD were recorded by students attending advanced Japanese language courses taught by Professor Smith. The recordings are based on free conversations of *issei* and *nisei* speakers, and upon interviews of *issei* speakers by advanced learners of Japanese, most of them ethnically Japanese. The interview data are based on recordings of the students' own grandparents. As such, all data were collected by individuals who have good rapport with the speakers. The medium of the data varied between reel-to-reel tapes and cassette tapes which were converted to digital format before transcribing. The transcription and codification were conducted as part of a larger study of Japanese dialect contact in Hawai'i, and the data used for this paper, consisting of audio recordings collected between 1972 and 1975 from four speakers, represent only a subset of the SPD's total speakers.

All speakers hailed from a common rural farming environment and had minimum education; none had moved back to Japan after their immigration for an extended period of time; all speakers had been married to other *issei* speakers from their hometowns for at least thirty years, and conversation topics were limited to the speakers' memories of immigration and plantation life, visits to Japan, and their family members.

The Japanese spoken in Hawai'i during and after the plantation period was heavily influenced by Hawaiian and English loanwords due to the close contacts between Japanese immigrants and locals, and by the Chûgoku dialect of Japanese, due to the large population of immigrants are from that region (Higa 1970, 1985).

5. Analysis

Higa (1975) reports that English kinship and personal reference terms are frequently used among the *nikkeijin* in Hawai'i. The following speech data confirm Higa's observation.

Example (3)
(A conversation between a brother (B) and a sister (S) who were born in
Hawai'i, but went back to Yamaguchi, finished high school, and soon after
returned to Hawai'i. B was seventy-three years old and S was seventy years
old at the time of the recording in 1975 at S's house in Honolulu. B is talking about his barber's trip to Japan; S replies to B with her own stories about
visiting Japan)

1   B: *dakara nishûkan kankô shite ato wa inaka e iku wake.*
2   *â, yôtta yo.*
3   *dakara oi mo sanpatsu nanka yôsen yo.*
       'so, after two weeks of the group sightseeing trip, everyone goes to
       visit their relatives. That's what he said. That's why I can't have my
       hair cut.'

4 → S: *soredakara no, **mî** mo no, darenimo iwanto iku no yo.*
5   *hoidake ano Club 100⁴ dare mo iya sen yo.*
6 →   *'you folks Japan ikan no' yûte kara no,*
7   *kotoshi wa ikan de, rai-nen wa brother kuru ke ikan yo.'*
8   *damattorya mendô shinai kê no.*
        'So, I (*mî*) don't tell anyone when I go to Japan. Likewise, at Club
        100, nobody says when they will visit Japan. When someone asks,
        "you folks won't go to Japan?," they say things like "I won't go this
        year. My brother's coming to visit here next year, so, I won't go to
        Japan." If you keep quiet, there is no hassle.'

9   B: *Mendô shinai ka.*
       'There is no hassle, huh?'

Example (4)
(A conversation between H, a seventy years-old immigrant from Fukushima
who lived in Maui for a long time, and his sister-in-law (V). The recoding
was done in 1972 at his then residence in Wahiawa, central O'ahu. H is talking about his late younger brother, Genta, to V. V is his wife.)

1 → H: *hondake **mî-ra** yûtotta yo,*
2   *ano Genta nga itsuban oya no neki ni nangagu otta tameni,*
3   *are wa hausu utte moratta kê,*
4 →   *rakkî suta tte **wasu** yû no yo.*

---

⁴ Club 100 is a social organization for local Japanese in Honolulu.

'So, we (*me-ra*) said [to family members in Japan] that as Genta stayed with the parents the longest, they sold the house for him and he got lucky. I (*wasu*) told everyone [in Japan] that.'

In Example 3, as S explains why she does not tell people in her community club when she goes to Japan, she refers to herself with English person pronoun *me*. The use of English *me* as a term for the first person singular is common practice in *nikkeijin* community, yet the nominative case 'I' is never borrowed for use in their Japanese speech.[5] Additionally, when they refer to the first person plural, they use *mî*-ra – English *me* plus the Japanese plural suffix –*ra* (as in Example 4, line 1). If a specific case marking is necessary, postpositional particles are attached. Such data indicates that the English personal pronoun reference system has been borrowed not so much as a whole paradigm, but that from it, only a few words were selectively chosen to suffice for specific needs.

Also as shown in Example (3), the term used for the second person in the direct quotation of the other Japanese immigrant that is addressed to the speaker, is 'you folks'. Apparently, Japanese immigrants also picked up a casual colloquial way for referring to the second person plural in English and borrowed it in their Japanese speech.

Examining the *nikkeijin*'s lexical borrowing, Higa (1975) proposed four hypotheses in regard to the sociolinguistic and psycholinguistic principles underlying this language use. One of his hypothesis states that 'the use of loanwords among the *nikkeijin* is a linguistic device to create a new Japanese dialect – Hawaiian Japanese' [6] (Higa 1975: 81), indicating that Japanese immigrants formed a distinct group within the whole body of society, deliberately devising speech forms of their own. Moreover, such use of English pronouns as possible personal reference terms are not a validated community norm in mainland Japan, as it distinctively indexes a *nikkeijin* identity. In fact, the mere use of such English personal reference terms works well to mark those speakers as what they call *roko* 'local'.

Higa also notes that categories like personal reference are particularly susceptible to foreign influence, as they are 'unnecessarily borrowed', – i.e. there exists Japanese vocabulary already for those referents, and innovating new terms was not linguistically necessary. Yet the above example shows that it is not just the particular lexemes, but rather, a certain style of referencing people that the Japanese immigrants incorporated. Although what Higa said holds still true – i.e. that in order to acculturate oneself in a new

---

[5] The third person, himu 'him' and hâ 'her' are also observed in the data, though much less frequently.

[6] The term 'Hawaiian Japanese' is not used in the recent literature, as the use of the adjective *Hawaiian* should refer to something of a Hawai'i origin.

culture, it is minimally sufficient to familiarize oneself with that culture's most basic vocabulary, such as kinship terms, terms to indicate social relations, time, and quantity, etc. (Higa 1975: 86) – this deployment of English personal pronouns is not a uniform property of Japanese spoken in Hawai'i. Instead, our research shows that the speaker may still use Japanese personal pronouns as well. Example (5) below reflects this point.

Example (5)
(The speakers, B and S, are the same speakers as in Example 3. Here, the two are talking about S's latest trip to Japan.)

1   B: *hoijaga nanjaro, fuyu ittara ikan no ja ro, ano hô e wa?*
      'But, isn't that the case that when you visit during winter, you won't bother to go there?'

2 →S: =*no, **mî** wa ikan ga, a,*
3   *Yuki ra ga nani suru[ken*
      'No, I (***me***) won't go but Yuki and her folks are making arrangements...'

4   B: [*oh, iku no yo,*
5   =[*akko e?*
      'Oh, so, [Yuri and the folks are] going there?'

6   S: [*tomaru nê, hito ban.*
      '[They'll] stay for one night.'

7   B: *ho::.*
      'oh.'

8   S: *nani made itte no,*
9   *Kyûshû mawatte Iwakuni hitoban tomatte, (.8)*
10   *hitoban tomatte hâ akuruhi no jûji goro hâ nani*
      'I'll go over there, go around Kyûshû, then stay overnight at Iwakuni, stay overnight, then, already on the following day just about 10 o'clock, already, whatchumacallit...'

11   B: *modotte kuru no?*
      'Will be returning?'

12   S: *umm, modo[ranna ya.*
      'umm, need to return.'

13 B: [*Hmmm.*
            'hmm.'

14 S: *hôte Tôkyô e jûichiji ka nanbo jake,*
15 → **washi-ra** *no, kaukau*[7] *morôte kicharôka? tte yû ke,*
16 → **washi** *ga Mamoru ni kaite no,*
17   *kaukau morôte motte kite kurena yo yûte*
      (continues)
      'Then, when I was going to leave for Tokyo, [Mamoru] asked if he
      should bring our (**washi-ra** *no*) food, so I (**washi**) wrote Mamoru [a
      note] and told him do not bring us any food…'

As shown in above example, the same speaker S switches between the
English first person pronoun *me* (line 2) and the Japanese first person pronoun *washi* (line 15 and 16) as she speaks to her brother. Both S and B are
Japanese-English bilinguals, and often switch between English and Japanese.
We can speculate that S uses *me* to juxtapose her *nikkeijin* identity with that
of her relatives in Japan. When she switches to the Japanese pronoun *washi*
later (line 15 and 16), it seems that she feels that such juxtaposition is not
necessary. In this story, S describes the scene where she is in Japan interacting with her relatives. As a member of the family, she uses the Japanese first
person pronoun to 'unmark' the difference. This dialectal use of the Japanese first person pronoun could be used as a flexible sociopragmatic resource to index their specific regional identity. In the Hawaiian context, it
may also carry special meaning, by distinguishing its speakers from many
other dialect speakers. Thus, the first person pronouns used by Japanese
immigrants may change depending on the identity which is foregrounded by
its deployment at any given time or place.
    The next example also shows the speaker flexibly changing the term
used to refer to himself within a continuous turn of storytelling.

Example (6)
(The speaker, H is the same speakers as in Example 4. He is talking to the
same listener, V, about how his son, Jimmy, met his wife in mainland.)

1 H: *hosute arenga anô, enzunia ni natte kara ne,*
2   *mo tabi tabi kakuno yo.*
3   *Jacky, mainland ni koi koi tte.*
4   *otô-san ikitai ga sutori musuko,*
5 → **yû** *mainlan itte mainlan girl tsukamaitara otô-san kikando yûte.*

---

[7] *Kaukau* means 'food' or 'to eat' in Hawai'i Creole.

6 → *"degiru dage **yû**, Hawai gyôru kyacchi sê" tte **mî** yûta yo.*
7   *sosutara nani made itte,*
8   *togoro no musume kyacchi sutan jakê no, are.*
9 → *mama ga **wasu**-ra no tokoro no mon de.*
   'After becoming an engineer, he still wrote and asked Jacky to move
   to the mainland. So, he says "Dad, I want to go", but he is my only
   son. So, I (***me***) said, "if you (***you***) go to mainland and catch a mainland girl, I (***otô-san***) will not accept. You (***you***) find a Hawaii girl if
   possible". Then he went all the way to the mainland to catch a girl
   from my hometown. Her mama is from our (***wasu-ra no***) hometown.'

In this example, when H quotes his own speech to his son in line 5, he
refers to himself with *otô-san* as he takes his son's perspective - what Suzuki
calls an 'allocentric use of person reference term' (Suzuki 1978), which is a
typical Japanese way of shifting the speaker's perspective to the younger
person's view point. Next, in line 6, he refers to himself with *mî* in order to
describe his own action in this storytelling. Note that he changes his terms
for referring to himself for the third time in line 9. Interestingly, here he
switches to *wasu* – a dominant Japanese first person pronoun commonly
used among Japanese immigrants – when describing a woman from his
hometown in Japan. This form was acquired by H after his move to Hawai'i
through contact with other immigrants from a different dialect-speaking area.
We speculate that what is foregrounded with this use of the first person pronoun from H's newly adopted dialect is that his personal connection to this
woman is not so much as a Japanese in general, but rather as someone from
the same hometown in Japan who shares the same immigrant experience,
which was an important issue for the immigrants of that time. By contrast,
the use of the English second person pronoun *you* to refer to his own Ameri-
can-born son reveals a different relationship among his family.

As shown above, with the differentiating use of each term for himself,
the speaker flexibly positions himself vis-à-vis his 'relation to the person in
the story', his 'relation to his current interlocutor', and his 'relation to his
own community.'

Some examples show, moreover, that different terms may be used even
in sentences which have similar structure and whose contexts and topics are
the same.

Example (7)
[H talking to V about his good *issei* friend whom he knew when he was on
Maui.]

1 → H: *aregara **wasu** guffren nattan yo.*
   'Since then I (***wasu***) am good friend (of him).'

2 V: *oh.*
   'oh.'

3→H: *Hitosu Onoda nga **wasu** yorika daibun tosu …*
4   *eiji nga daibun tsugau yo,*
5→   *sore **mî**, mô, guffren yo.*
6   *hoide ano:, register no member, orchid register suru nomo*
7   *â, Maui no mono wa,*
8   *no more time toka iyâ, ah, I got to check,*
9   *dare ga yattoru ka yattoran ka check sennya igen [gara yûte.*
       'Hitoshi Onoda was much older than me (***wasu***)… (our) age was
       very different, but (he and) I (***me***) were good friends. When register-
       ing orchids for competitions, members of registrations, about the
       ones on Maui, [the organizers] say "I got to check" because [they
       were not sure of the] time and year [of the orchid competitions].'

10 V: [*hmm.*
                                               'hmm.'

11 H: *yatte kurenken damejaittara,*
12 →   *ossan "**mî** no togo ni hanâ ogure, **mî** yatte yaru kê*
       (continue)…
       'So, they don't help very much, I told him. Then, the old man said
       "send me (***me***) the flowers, I (***me***) will take care of them"…'

Here, first H refers to himself with the Japanese word *wasu* in lines 1
and 3. Then he switches to English *me* in line 5. Lines 1 and 5 have quite
similar propositional meanings; however, these two sentences play slightly
different roles in conversation. The sentence in line 1 is a 'first report' of
H's own personal experience. But then H provides more information, i.e.,
the age difference between H and Mr. Onoda, which justifies the 'tellability'
of this event. The reformatted utterance with emphatic marker *mô* in line 5
should be now reanalyzed by the participants. At the point of this conversation move, H switches to the English first person pronoun *me*. We may
speculate from the notional difference of these two terms that when the English first person pronoun *me* is used, the implied relationship of the speaker
and someone within the immigrant community in American context is more
explicitly highlighted.

6. Conclusion

We have observed that Japanese immigrants in Hawai'i flexibly deploy different personal pronouns both from English and Japanese. Although such
'borrowing' of English personal pronouns is a characteristics of their spoken

Japanese, it is not replacing the Japanese personal reference system or simplifying it, but rather adding to it another dimension whereby the speaker can locate themselves in the speech context. The speakers thus alter between Japanese and English person reference terms, depending on the different issues that surface in their talk. Such factors include the topic and location of the story, the interlocutors' relationship to the other people in the story, and the juxtaposition of different personal and social identities. As the Japanese pronoun system is categorized as 'open class', the English first person pronoun *me* is just another addition to many other possible reference terms for oneself that Japanese immigrants can choose from. Likewise, the second person *you* is a possible resource to acknowledge the interlocutor as a fellow member of the same community and to thereby construct a local community and context. In sum, this study provides yet more supporting evidence to what Thomason and Everett (2005) claim: the practice or nonpractice of pronoun borrowing is subject to the deliberate and conscious choices made by speakers to index sociopragmatic order.

Transcription Symbols:
. falling intonation
? rising intonation
[onset of overlapped talk
= latched talk
(.) short, untimed pauses

Acknowledgements

This study was funded by National University of Singapore Academic Research Fund (FY2008-FRC2-004). Our sincere thanks go to Ed Smith and William O'Grady for making the Smith Project Data available for us.

References

Alexander, A. 1937. *Koloa Plantation 1835-1935: A History of the Oldest Hawaiian Sugar Plantation*. Honolulu: Honolulu Star-Bulletin.

Campbell, L. 1997. Amerindian Personal Pronouns: A Second Opinion. *Language* 73: 339-351.

Carter, W. 1921. The Japanese in Hawaii. *Atlantic Monthly* 128: 255-257.

Chinen, K. and Hiura, A. 1997. *From Bento to Mixed Plate: Americans of Japanese Ancestry in Multicultural Hawaii*. Los Angeles: Japanese American National Museum.

Clarke, J. 1994. *Family Traditions in Hawai'i*. Honolulu: Namkoong Publishing.

Court, C. 1998. Untitled Posting on the SEALTEACH list. (cited in Thomason and Everett 2005 and Thomason 2001 below.)

Foley, W. 1986. *The Papuan Languages of New Guinea*. Cambridge: Cambridge University Press.

Hawaii Hochisha. 2001. *Aroha Nenkan: Hawai no Subete.* 11th ed. Honolulu: Hawaii Hochisha.

Higa, M. 1970. The Sociolinguistic Significance of Borrowed Words in the Japanese Spoken in Hawaii. *University of Hawaii Working Papers in Linguistics* 2: 125-40.

———. 1975. The use of loanwords in Hawaiian Japanese. *Language in Japanese Society: Current Issues in Sociolinguistics*, ed. F.C. Peng, 71-89. Tokyo: University of Tokyo Press.

———. 1976. Nihongo to Nihonshakai. *Iwanami Kôza Nihongo 1: Nihongo to Kokugogaku*, eds. T. Shibata, K. Shigeo, and S. Tsurumi, 99-138. Tokyo: Iwanami.

———. 1985. Hawaian Japanîzu. *Gekkan Gengo* 14: 72-74.

Hiramoto, M. 2011. Dialect Contact and Dialect Change among Plantation Immigrants from Northern Japan in Hawai'i. *Journal of Pidgin and Creole Linguistics* 25(2).

Inoue, F. 1975. Hawai Nikkeijin no Nihongo to Eigo. *Gengo Seikatsu* 236: 53-61.

Kawamoto, K. 1993. Hegemony and Language Politics in Hawaii. *World Englishes* 12: 193-207.

Kotani, R. 1985. *The Japanese in Hawaii: A Century of Struggle.* Honolulu: Hawaii Hochisha.

Kurokawa, S. 1983. Hawai no Nihongo. *Gendai Hôgengaku no Kadai: Shakaiteki Kenkyûhen*, ed. T. Hirayama, 199-220. Tokyo: Meiji Shoin.

Morita, E. 2009. Arbitrating Code-mixing: The Use of *Me* in Japanese Discourse. *Beyond Yellow English*, eds. A. Reyes and A. Lo, 175-194. Oxford: Oxford University Press.

Nichols, J. and Peterson, D. 1996. Amerind Personal Pronouns: A Reply to Campbell. *Language* 74: 605-14.

Nordyke, E. 1989. *The Peopling of Hawaii.* 2nd ed. Honolulu: University of Hawai'i Press.

Odo, F. 1998. *Hawai no Nisei. Hawaii Nikkei Shakai no Bunka to Sono Henyô*, ed. Y. Okita, 108-126. Tokyo: Nakanishya.

Reinecke, J. 1969/1988. *Language and Dialect in Hawaii: A Sociolinguistic History to 1935.* Honolulu: Social Science Research Institute and University Hawaii Press.

Sakoda, K. and Siegel, J. 2003. *Pidgin Grammar: An Introduction to the Creole Language of Hawai'i.* Honolulu: Bess Press.

Suzuki, T. 1978. Words for Self and Others. *Japanese and the Japanese*, 98-127. Miura, A. translator. Tokyo: Kodansha International.

Suzuki, T. and Miura, A. 2001. *Words in Context: A Japanese Perspective on Language and Culture.* Tokyo: Kodansha International.

Tamura, E. 1993. The English-only Effort, the Anti-Japanese Campaign, and Language Acquisition in the Education of Japanese Americans in Hawaii, 1915-40. *History of Education Quarterly* 33: 37-58.

Thomason, S. 2001. *Language Contact: An Introduction.* Edinburgh: Edinburgh University Press.

Thomason, S. and Everett, D. 2005. Pronoun Borrowing. *Berkeley Linguistic Society* 27: 301-315.

Wallace, S. 1983. Pronoun in Contact. *Essays in Honor of Charles F. Hockett*, eds. F. Agard, G. Kelly, A. Makkai and V. Makkai, 573-89. Leiden: E.J.Brill.

Yamamoto, E. 1973. *From* 'Japanee' to Local: Community Change and the Redefinition of Sansei Identity in Hawaii. Unpublished B.A. thesis, University of Hawaii.

Ikema Ryukyuan: Investigating Past Experience and the Current State through Life Narratives*

Shoichi Iwasaki
University of California, Los Angels

Tsuyoshi Ono
University of Alberta

1. Introduction

There are two goals in this paper. The first is to describe the current endangered status of one of the endangered languages spoken in Okinawa, Japan by identifying a set of factors that has affected this language. The second is to promote the life narrative approach that we have adopted to arrive at a reliable basic description which is necessary for documentation. We propose that the life narrative approach is an important framework for documenting all endangered languages.

* We would like to thank the people on Ikema Island and in Nishihara on Miyako Island for their help with this project. We would also like to thank Maggie Camp and Yuka Matsugu for their help in the preparation of this manuscript.

Japanese/Korean Linguistics 19.
Edited by Ho-min Sohn, Haruko Cook, William O'Grady, Leon A. Serafim, & Sang Yee Cheon.

The online edition of UNESCO's *Atlas of the World's Languages in Danger* (2009)[1] identifies four Ryukyuan languages as 'definitely endangered' (Miyako, Okinawa, Kunigami, and Amami) and two as 'severely endangered' (Yonaguni and Yaeyama) according to the following definitions. [2]

> **Definitely endangered**: Children no longer learn the language as mother tongue in the home.

> **Severely endangered**: Language is spoken by grandparents and older generations; while the parent generation may understand it, they do not speak it to children or among themselves.

In this paper, we examine the current state of endangerment surrounding one of the dialects of the definitely endangered language of Miyako Ryukyuan, Ikema. Ikema is named after the island where people speaking this dialect originally came from.[3] It is often reported that at this point only people in their 60s or older (the grandparents' generation) speak Ikema fluently. This suggests that the current parental generation does not speak the language anymore. If this is true, Ikema is moving from the 'definitely endangered' state to the 'severely endangered' status rapidly.

There are, however, somewhat conflicting reports being made. In 2005 and 2006, Heinrich, for example, surveyed speakers' use of their own local variety when addressing different types of speakers (i.e. spouse, children, parents, grandparents, neighbors, and colleagues), and found out that the vitality of Miyako, as well as Amami and Yonaguni, is stronger than that of Okinawa and Yaeyama (reported in Fija et al. 2009).[4] Some researchers also suggest that Ikema is relatively healthy (Shigehisa Karimata, personal communication).

Based on the above-mentioned survey by Heinrich, Fija et al. (2009) suggest that the vitality of Yonaguni is due to the strong sense of community resulting from its small size and isolation. In the case of Amami, they suggest that because its US occupation ended much earlier (in 1953) than other Ryukyu islands (in 1972), the impact of language shift there was less drastic,

---

[1] http://www.unesco.org/culture/ich/index.php?pg=00206
[2] http://www.unesco.org/culture/ich/index.php?pg=00139
[3] Besides Ikema, there are three to four major dialects of Miyako. Previous research on the Miyako language is mostly based on its central dialect spoken in Hirara on the island of Miyako (Shibata 1980, Izuyama 2002, Nevsky 2005), and descriptions of Ikema are limited to preliminary analyses of vocabulary, phonetics, phonology, morphology, and syntax (Hirayama 1983, Nakama 1992).
[4] The positions of Yonaguni and Okinawa are reversed when compared to the UNESCO report.

speakers on other islands felt shifting to Standard Japanese was essential for social mobility once they fully became Japanese citizens after the reversion in 1972. When it comes to the situation of Miyako, however, Fija et al. do not have a clear explanation.

> Miyako also did not experience radical language shifts, but for quite different reasons. … While a detailed account for this is not yet possible and would require *detailed field work*, the reasons seem to include the absence of in-migration and continuance of subsistence farming. (emphasis added)

While we leave to future research the 'absence of in-migration' and 'continuance of subsistence farming' as possible causes for slower language shift in Miyako, we take this statement as an appeal for a detailed sociolinguistic field work for the situation in Miyako.

Using a broad labeling such as a 'definitely endangered language' as a useful starting point, we propose to begin a more detailed examination of the situation. More specifically, we attempt to identify factors that influence the community's and individuals' language use.

The UNESCO report suggests the following six major factors:[5] (1) Intergenerational Language Transmission, (2) Absolute Number of Speakers, (3) Proportion of Speakers within the Total Population, (4) Trends in Existing Language Domains, (5) Response to New Domains and Media, and (6) Materials for Language Education and Literacy. The UNESCO Ad Hoc Expert Group on Endangered Languages, however, stresses that '(n)o single factor can be used to access a language's vitality' (2003: 7). To understand the intricacy of the interaction of factors, we have taken an approach in which we engaged speakers in extended life narratives during an interview session. We will discuss this approach in detail in section 3, but we will first introduce the community of Ikema speakers.

2. Ikema Speaking Communities

Currently, Ikema is spoken in three main communities. The original location of Ikema speakers is Ikema Island, which has a land area of 2.62 square miles and a current population of about 736. It is located north of Miyako Island, which is itself located 170 miles southwest of the main Okinawa Island and just 180 miles northeast of Taiwan. Until a 4675-foot bridge between Ikema and Miyako was opened in 1992, the island was only accessible by sea. It flourished as a port for deep sea bonito fishing until the mid

---

[5] The report also mentions the local and majority communities' attitudes towards an endangered language and the amount of available documentation materials as something that should be considered when the degree of endangerment is assessed.

1970's. However, fishery is no longer a vital industry on the island. In 1874, some residents were forced to relocate from Ikema Island to a new location in the northern part of Miyako. This second community was named Nishihara. The current population of Nishihara Village is 1034. The major industry is sugar cane farming. The third location where Ikema is spoken is Sarahama Village on Irabu Island, a community created approximately 300 years ago. The current population is 3264. Here fishing is still strong, unlike on Ikema Island. Irabu Island is currently only accessible by sea, but a bridge is under construction with the opening date set for 2013. Even after a long period of separation, speakers of the three disparate communities still identify themselves as *Ikema Minzoku* 'Ikema Race', and probably due in part to their strong identity, the profile of the Ikema language is distinct from other varieties spoken on Miyako. Our research team[6] has been conducting field work mostly in Ikema and Nishihara, but recently we have also started to explore the situation in Sarahama.

Before we conducted the current research, we made the following casual observations regarding the types of speakers. There is no monolingual Ikema speaker, though some speakers over 80 years old are more comfortable speaking in Ikema. People between 60 and 80 years old are bilingual speakers of Ikema and the local variety of Standard Japanese, and most people in this group can switch between the two languages smoothly depending on the social situations. People between 40 and 60 are diverse in terms of their linguistic ability, but most, if not all, have a high level of comprehension ability in Ikema. People younger than 40 are stronger in Standard Japanese, and the younger members may be completely monolingual in Japanese.

The current populations in the three communities, published in 2010, are 736 (Ikema), 1034 (Nishihara), and 3264 (Sarahama).[7] Among the community members, however, the number of children is small; only 8% of the population attend elementary or middle schools.

Table 1.

	Elementary school children	Middle school children	School children total	Total population	% of school children
Ikema	24	18	42	736	5.7
Nishihara	67	45	112	1034	10.8
Sarahama	163	93	256	3264	7.8
Total	254	156	410	5034	8.1

[6] The team consists of researchers from universities in Canada, Japan, and the U.S.

[7] http://www.city.miyakojima.lg.jp/site/view/contview.jsp?cateid=29&id=437&page=1

In contrast, the number of elders is extremely high. According to the 2005 census, on average the percentage of the population over 65 years old is greater than 33% (49.5% in Ikema, 37.2% in Nishihara, and 29.5% in Sarahama). These statistics show that the basis for continuing cultural and linguistic tradition is very weak. Our task in this paper, however, is not to predict the future of Ikema, but to explore whether our casual observations given above are confirmed. More importantly, we attempt to find out how the current language situation came about.

3. Life Narrative Approach

As found in a quote by Himmelmann, the ultimate goal of our current research is to fully document one dialect of an endangered language:

> A language documentation ... aims at the record of *the linguistic practices and traditions of a speech community* (Himmelmann 2002: 9)

To achieve this goal, it is not sufficient to work with a single 'good' speaker as is often done in a language description study. Instead we set our target as documenting Ikema used by the whole community. As part of the Ikema documentation project, we have been conducting in-depth interviews with community members regarding their language use in various situations throughout their lives, including language choice, code mixing, school policies, fluency, and bilingualism, among others. This has provided us with a rich array of information unobtainable in quantitative sociolinguistic surveys based on questionnaires.

Two related issues which we explore in the present study are:

a) Current state and degree of endangerment (e.g. the number of fluent speakers of Ikema and the status of Ikema/Japanese bilingualism)

b) Factors for language shift and the way in which they contributed to the current linguistic situation

In order to gather information regarding these issues, we initially prepared a set of questions concerning topics like age; birthplace and places of residency; family structure; primary caretaker; schooling; occupation; lifestyle; available language media including newspaper, radio and TV; and language use at various stages/places. Our original plan was to go over these interview questions quickly with a large number of community members (similar to the way data collection in quantitative sociolinguistics is typically conducted), but when we began interviewing people, it became immediately clear that we could effectively gather information only by engaging the interviewees in a conversation in which they talk about their experiences in the form of life narratives.

Obviously, reflecting actual language use, especially from several decades ago, is a daunting task. This is particularly difficult in determining which language variety was used in specific situations since people seem to switch between Ikema and Japanese rather unconsciously. In fact, we found out at the very beginning that our interviewees, in trying to answer our questions, recounted their experience in the form of conversational narratives. For this reason, we abandoned our original plan and switched to the standard methodology of oral history where we let the interviewees tell a narrative while we played an active role as conversational partners (Labov 1984: 32-42).

In the new approach, we normally started each interview by asking some of the questions mentioned above, but when the interviewees started telling a narrative, we let them take the floor. We tried to elicit answers to our questions at places which seemed appropriate. Naturally, as we spent more time talking to community members, relevant factors became increasingly clear. We then dealt with these factors by implementing a new set of more specific questions. This made it necessary for us to constantly revise our questions, and to have (sometimes multiple) follow-up sessions with our interviewees and new sessions with other community members (see the next section for more about this).

The actual format of the interview varied from session to session. When we talked with an interviewee alone, we used Japanese as all the interviewees can speak it. When there were one or more other Ikema speakers at the session, interviewees sometimes switched to Ikema when they needed to solicit information from others. Thus, this approach has made the process of data collection much slower than we had originally planned but allowed us to access more detailed and accurate information concerning language use in various situations, which is indispensable in identifying relevant factors and determining how those factors might have interacted among themselves to create a unique situation for each person in particular and to result in the current endangered state of Ikema in general.

In 2009, we interviewed 23 community members (11 from Ikema and 12 from Nishihara; 12 male and 11 female) who were between 39 and 69 years old. Unless otherwise noted, ages mentioned in this paper are from the summer of 2009. These interviews lasted a minimum of 45 minutes, with follow-up sessions as discussed above. These longer interviews were supplemented by additional shorter interviews with approximately 25 interviewees, including several from Sarahama. The shorter interviews were conducted to reconfirm factual information and to fill in information gaps.

4. Factors

In this section, we will discuss several factors which we have identified as relevant to the current endangered state of Ikema. As will become evident, it is often not easy to separate these factors because they co-occur and interact among themselves creating a unique situation for each individual, resulting in the current condition of endangered state of Ikema. The relevance of some of these factors became apparent only through the course of the conversational narratives which we had our interviewees engage in.

It is important at this point to define fluency as we refer to it throughout the paper. We determine fluency based on two criteria: a) assessment by community (typically elder and multiple) members and b) our observation of the person's ability to speak only in Ikema without code mixing.

4.1 Schooling

Education is always a strong means to implement governmental language policy. Even before Standard Japanese was officially defined by the Meiji government, local institutions were established in Okinawa in the 1880's to train teachers in the Tokyo dialect. The central government policy was endorsed so strongly by people in Okinawa that even a regulation to prohibit the use of 'dialects' on campus was established (Hokama 1971: 80).

Our interviewees received primary education during and after World War II, when language regulation was also strongly implemented. Their regular exposure to Standard Japanese started when they attended kindergarten in the village.[8] Since our oldest interviewee (born in 1939) attended kindergarten, we can conclude that it was already operational during the war, if not earlier. Thus children who were around five years old heard local teachers (from the same village) speaking Japanese, while at home most, if not all, of our interviewees spoke Ikema.

Our interviewees all attended local elementary and junior high schools during the post-war period in the village. With the defeat in the war, Japan began to transform itself into a modern democratic nation. The government saw as its responsibility educating its people for full participation in society, which was also strongly desired by people in Okinawa which was scheduled to return to Japan in 1972 after the post-war US control. A manifestation of the strong sentiment for this desire was the use of infamous *hogenfuda* 'dialect tag' at school (Hokama 1971: 59, Itani 2006, Kondo 2008).[9]

---

[8] We checked this with most of our main interviewees and found that they all attended kindergarten.

[9] The first use of *hogenfuda* was recorded in the late Meiji period (early 20th century), and reappeared before the Pacific War. *Hogenfuda* in the post-war period can be considered to be part of a more comprehensive measure adopted by schools and communities. Other measures

Hogenfuda was made out of a piece of wood or cardboard usually in a rectangular shape (2" x 6" to 7"). Some were painted red. On them, the phrase *hogenfuda* 'dialect tag' or *hogen shiyoosha* 'dialect user' was written. A student who was caught using even a single word of the 'dialect' was given the tag and had to wear it around his/her neck until a different student spoke a word of 'dialect.' This practice does not seem to have been regulated closely and different teachers appear to have used it in somewhat different ways, i.e. some were more strict and others more lenient. Although some interviewees reported that there was an element of playfulness,[10] most students took it seriously.

Although it may have actually been detrimental to young students' developing identities, this practice most likely resulted from the concern that parents, teachers, and community leaders had for their children's future well-being. In other words, it was not a top-down mandate in the education system, but rather a local practice that emerged only in Okinawa. However, the fear of being a non-fluent Japanese speaker is not without foundation as many elders experienced linguistic discrimination during the war and at locations of immigration.[11] This concern became more real when young speakers received strong incentive to seek employment in major cities during the 1960's when Japan was transforming itself from a war-torn nation into an economically powerful modern nation. Thus the language shift in the Okinawan context was motivated by a mixture of fear, an inferiority complex, a desire to be part of the mainstream society, and an effort towards upward social mobility.

The *hogenfuda* was already in use in 1920's on Ikema Island.[12] However, this infamous practice seems to have disappeared sometime in the first half of 1960's based on our interviewees' accounts. On Ikema Island, Ms. Y who started going to elementary school in 1961/2 experienced it, but Mr. F who started going to school in 1966 didn't. In Nishihara, Mr. I who started

---

include honoring households that use Japanese daily and appointing a student to watch over other students' language use. Except for unconfirmed report in the Tohoku (northeast) region in Japan (Itani 2006), the use of *hogenfuda* was reported only in Okinawa. This unique form of punishment is believed to have its origin in the 'punishment tag' used traditionally throughout Ryukyu in the Ryukyu Kingdom period (Itani 2006).

[10] Several speakers reported that when they had the tag, they would step on another student's foot to make her/him exclaim in Ikema, *agai* 'ouch', thereby forcing her/him to wear the tag.

[11] 'Dialect' speakers were viewed as spies during the war (Yakabi 2007: 161), and 'dialect' speakers were ridiculed by other Japanese immigrants in places like Hawaii and South America (Hokama 1971: 83).

[12] This information was obtained from an elderly woman on Ikema introduced to us by one of our consultants, Mr. Morio Iraha (2009). According to Itani (2006: 42), Kondo (1999: 49) also found a record of the earliest use of *hogenfuda* in Nishibe elementary school (in Nishihara) in the 1930's and 40's.

school in 1957 experienced it while Mr. SS who started school in 1962 did not.[13]

Based on this information, the following picture begins to emerge. At least until the early to mid 1960's, children entered elementary school still primarily speaking Ikema and the extreme measure of using *hogenfuda* was necessary to change this situation.[14] Because of this severe language control, students gradually became comfortable with Japanese after the mid 1960's, and perhaps this to some extent satisfied the parents' and teachers' desire to provide a better future for their children. This also explains the fact that people who are younger than 50 years old as of 2009 in general do not have the speaking facility of Ikema. The 1960's seems to be a critical decade for the language shift.

4.2 Media

Though *hogenfuda* disappeared in the early to mid 1960s, media in the form of TV seems to have taken over the role of promoting the use of Standard Japanese. The decline of Ikema is particularly apparent starting with people who are around 50 years old, which may be explained in part by the introduction of TV to the area in the late 1960s (most likely 1967 in Ikema and a few years earlier in Nishihara). Although TV sets were originally acquired by only some households, TV programs in Standard Japanese became immediately available to the community as a whole because TV sets were often placed facing the street to show the programs (and perhaps to show off the sets!) to neighbors. People who are 50 years old in 2010, for instance, had regular exposure to Standard Japanese through TV starting when they were first graders or younger. Researchers on endangered languages have discussed TV as being a 'cultural nerve gas' (Krauss 1992: 6) which eliminates minority languages, and the spread of this technology in Japan seems to have been very effective to this end, even on the remote islands of Okinawa.

---

[13] This estimate of time corresponds with a statement in Itani (2006: 161). Itani considers the emergence of Okinawan identity as the cause of the disappearance of *hogenfuda*, but if this is the case, the revitalization of Okinwan languages should have been voiced more strongly. On the contrary, Japanese became the language of choice.

[14] This does not mean, however, that all the children were using Japanese regularly even after the mid 1960's. We often heard mention of the slogan ("Let's use the Standard Language") written on the blackboard and specially selected students to told to watch over the use of language among students. One interviewer reported that she promised to promote the regular use of Japanese once she was elected class leader in the mid 1970's. Also, though *hogenfuda* may have disappeared, students were sometimes forced to stand in the back of the room, sit on the floor, or were pinched on the chest when they slipped into 'dialect'.

4.3 Primary Caretaker

Our interviewees and others often commented that those who were raised by grandparents (especially grandmothers) speak Ikema fluently. We do have several speakers who fit into this category: Mr. N (62 years old), Ms. O (61 years old), Ms. M (56 years old), and Ms. K (54 years old). However there are several exceptions as well. Mr. S (69 years old), for instance, is considered to be fluent even though he was raised by his parents. One might suggest that Mr. S is old enough to be fluent even without having been raised by his grandparents. Ms. Y (53 years old) and Ms. S (44 years old), on the other hand, are not fluent even though they were raised by grandparents. Perhaps they fall below this critical age for fluency. Interestingly, we found out that Standard Japanese was regularly used at Ms. S's home because her father came from Yaeyama where a different Ryukuan language is spoken and did not speak Ikema.

This suggests that what is more directly relevant to fluency in Ikema might be the way the speaker lived their life (i.e. lifestyle), which includes one's regular interaction with fluent speakers, perhaps especially when they were children. This will be further discussed in the following section.

4.4 Lifestyle

Four of our younger fluent speakers, two of them our youngest, were not raised by grandparents. Closer examination of their lifestyles reveals more direct causes for shaping speakers' fluency.

Mr. G (55 years old) in fact recalls the difficulty he had speaking Japanese when he first moved to Tokyo to work after high school, at the age of 18.[15] It turns out that his high school, located in the regional political and commercial center of Miyako Island, was a fishery school attended mostly by men, many of whom were Ikema speakers. As a result, Ikema was widely spoken at this high school. Mr. SS (53 years old), another fluent speaker, attended the same high school and had a similar linguistic experience there.

Mr. F (49 years old) went to college in Okinawa where he lived for several years with Ikema speakers in a place other Ikema speakers regularly gathered, a situation which might be best described as a mini-Ikema ghetto.

The life of Mr. TS, the last speaker in this category, is the most intriguing. He is the youngest (47 years old) among the four and just like the other three was not raised by his grandparents. However, he did grow up in an Ikema immersion environment where he was looked after by Ikema speaking apprentices who worked for his father, a master carpenter. He later worked on mainland Japan when he was 17-23 where he was again im-

---

[15] Mr. N (62 years old) recounts a similar experience when he moved to Okinawa to go to college.

mersed in an Ikema speaking environment while living with Ikema speaking relatives.

These accounts suggest that the way one lived her/his life is more directly relevant than the single factor of the grandparent's influence in shaping one's fluency of Ikema.

4.5 Gender

The four fluent speakers not raised by grandparents, discussed in the last section, are 47-55 years old, well below the commonly believed fluency cutoff age of 60. Interestingly, they are all men, which is in clear contrast with the two women (44 and 53 years old) discussed in 2.3. Those women were both raised by their grandmother but are not fluent in Ikema, suggesting that gender is another factor playing a role in shaping fluency, perhaps one which is more influential than merely living with grandparents.

Interestingly, we found that male students broke the rules and spoke Ikema at school more often than their female counterparts. As noted in section 4.4 above, some male students continued to use Ikema even at high school where Standard Japanese was the standard medium of communication. Perhaps for this reason, some men in fact had trouble speaking Japanese when they moved to the main island of Okinawa and mainland Japan after high school where they had to use Japanese. In general such an experience was not reported by female interviewees.

Several interviewees also noted that this type of gender difference still continues today. For instance, Mr. TS (47 years old), introduced in the last section, noted that he talks with his male *agu* 'neighborhood peer group'[16] in Ikema, but added that his female *agu* can't speak Ikema. Several other interviewees reported similar experiences. In fact, the use of Ikema seems to have a clear social implication or stereotype, which is most vividly expressed in a comment by Mr. F (also introduced in the last section): *hogen da to josei rashiku nai* 'if you use the dialect, you are not feminine.' It is particularly interesting to note that Mr. F, though relatively young (49 years old), himself is a fluent speaker.

Finally, we recently met three junior high school students in Sarahama who are surprisingly fluent in Ikema.[17] Although the exact fluency of these students needs to be determined, they are all first year students in junior high school (12 or 13 years old). Interestingly, they are all male students and spend much of their time interacting with local fishermen, which again supports the roles of both gender and lifestyle in shaping the fluency of Ikema.

---

[16] People in the Ikema community, starting from childhood, practice a number of social activities with their *agu* 'neighborhood peer group'.

[17] There are likely to be more students with some fluency of Ikema yet to be discovered.

The faster switch among women than men from Ikema to the dominant language of Japanese fits with the observation that, in some societies, women are "more sensitive to the social significance of social-class-related linguistic variables" (Trudgill 1974: 93). The situation of Ikema is reminiscent of Monchak (a minor Mongorian language) where "young Monchak men continue to speak the language in far greater numbers and with greater fluency that do females" (Harrison 2007: 97).

4.6 Social/Religious Events

The three Ikema speaking communities of Ikema, Nishihara, and Sarahama are known for having numerous religious and social events. These include both community-based official events and more smaller scale and/or private gatherings, including those organized by the associations for elderly people and the above-mentioned *agu* groups. In these events and gatherings, the use of Ikema is encouraged, or even required. Based both on the interviews which we conducted for the current study and on our own experience in participating in many of these events/gatherings, we feel that these occasions positively influence the maintenance of Ikema: participating in them and using Ikema mutually reinforce peoples' identity as belonging to each community in particular and *Ikema Minzoku* 'Ikema Race' in general.

Obviously, not everyone in the community participates in these activities, and people's lifestyles undoubtedly play a role in their level of participation, but it is our impression that a large portion of the community members do actively participate in them perhaps partly due to social obligation. It is worth pointing out that these activities seem to be much more actively practiced in the two new settlements of Nishihara and Sarahama than the original community of Ikema, and interestingly it is the impression of both community members and ourselves that Ikema is better maintained in these new settlements than on Ikema,[18] suggesting that cultural and language maintenance might be influencing each other. It should be remembered here that the three junior high school students who we discussed in the last section are all from Sarahama, whose fluency in Ikema points to the possible connection between lifestyle, gender, and social/religious events.

---

[18] A higher maintenance level of Ikema in Sarahama may be related to the following three factors: 1) Sarahama is more geographically isolated than Ikema and Nishihara from the regional political and commercial center of Miyako Island because it is on Irabu Island which can only be accessed by sea. 2) Sarahama hosts a much larger population than Ikema and Nishihara. 3) Finally, Ikema speaking people in Sarahama are a linguistic majority on Irabu Island compared to a smaller number of speakers of Irabu, another dialect of Miyako.

5. Conclusions

Our ultimate goal of the larger Ikema project is "to record the linguistic practices and traditions" of this speech community (Himmelmann 2002: 9). To this end, gathering information from community members at large was a necessary step. We believe our life narrative approach is a successful method to achieve this goal.

It has provided us with insight into the influencing factors for the current situation surrounding Ikema, which include schooling, including kindergarten, exposure to television, primary caretakers, gender, and lifestyle. We have found that there are still some fluent speakers of Ikema who are in their late 40s and 50s, which goes against the common belief that fluent speakers are limited to 60 years old or above. These younger speakers are often inconspicuous and hard to find. Only through our narrative-based approach have we been able to obtain these findings.

In the process of engaging community members in conversation through life narratives, we have also been provided with a web of new and useful information for our continuing project, including (a) who we might want to work with in collecting and analyzing data in terms of who is fluent, available, and appropriate and (b) what kind of data we might want to collect which is relevant not just to linguists but to the community. In particular, considering that our ultimate goal is to come up with a good representation of "the linguistic practices and traditions of a speech community" (Himmelmann 2002: 9), deciding on the type of data to collect and who to represent in it in discussion with the community is essential.

a) We can also summarize important additional (and somewhat unexpected) outcomes of our life narrative approach as follows:Better Rapport: In the process, we were able to establish a good rapport with community members, which we believe is a critical step toward fully documenting a language. This was achieved because the life narrative approach created opportunities where interviewees and researchers actively interacted as conversational partners. Obviously, there is nothing surprising about this because we create a relationship with others by actually interacting with them.

b) Better Understanding: It seems that people whom we interviewed for the present project now have a better understanding of what we are interested in and what we are trying to accomplish, which is again crucial for our documentation project to become successful. Again, this was because our questions about interviewees' past and current experiences were what non-linguists could easily relate to. We thus suggest that if one's goal is to document a language, they should start a project by asking questions similar to ours rather than jumping into questions purely of linguistic nature (such as sound inventory, clause structure, etc.).

c) More Interest: Through talking with us, our interviewees seem to have developed a curiosity in their past and current experiences, particularly of their language use. Some of them have started discussing their experience with their family members and friends and volunteering further information to us.

References

Fija, B., Brenzinger, M., and Heinrich, P. 2009. The Ryukyus and the New, but Edangered, Languages of Japan. *The Asia-Pacific Journal: Japan Focus* 3138.

Harrison, D. 2007. *When Languages Die.* Oxford: Oxford University Press.

Himmelmann, N. 2002. Documentary and Descriptive Linguistics. Unpublished manuscript.

Hirayama, T. (ed.) 1983. Ryukyu *Miyako Shotoo Hoogen Kiso Goi no Soogooteki Kenkyuu.* Tokyo: Oofuusha.

Hokama, S. 1971. *Okinawa no Gengoshi.* Tokyo: Hoseidaigaku Shuppankyoku.

Itani, Y. 2006. *Okinawa no Hogenfuda.* Naha: Borderink.

Izuyama, A. 2002. A Study on the Grammar of Miyako Hirara Dialect of Luchuan. *Grammatical Aspects of Endangered Dialects in Japan* (1), ed. S. Sanada, 35-97. Tokyo: ELPR.

Kondo, K. 1999. Kindai Okinawa ni okeru hogenfuda (3). Aichi kenritsu daiga kubungakubu ronshu 48.

Kondo, K. (ed.) 2008. *Hogenfuda.* Tokyo: Shakaihyooronsha.

Krauss, M. 1992. The World's Languages in Crisis. *Language* 68: 4-10.

Labov, W. 1984. Field Methods of the Project on Linguistic Change and Variation. *Language in Use*, eds. J. Baugh and J. Sherzer, 28-53. New Jersey: Prentice Hall.

Nakama, M. 1992. *Ryukyu Hogen no Kosoo.* Tokyo: Daiichishoboo.

Nevsky, N. 2005. *Miyako Hogen Nooto.* Miyako, Japan: Okinawaken Hirarashi kyooikuiinkai.

Shitaba, T. 1980. Okinawa Miyokogo no Goitaikei. *Gekkan Gengo* 9:1-9:12.

Trudgill, P. 1974. *Sociolinguistics.* London: Penguin.

UNESCO Ad Hoc Expert Group on Endangered Languages. 2003. Document submitted to the *International Expert Meeting on UNESCO Programme Safeguarding of Endangered Languages.* Paris, 10–12 March 2003.

UNESCO 2009. Atlas of the World's Languages in Danger.

Yakabi, O. 2007. "Nihongo" "Nihonminzoku" no Hensei de Ikani Honroo saretaka: Okinawa no Kyoodoshika Shimabukuro Zenpatsu no Kiseki. *Taiwan, Kankoku, Okinawa de nihongo wa nani o shita no ka*, eds. C. Furukawa et al., 155-173. Tokyo: Sangensha.

Declination in Japanese Conversation: Turn Construction, Coherence and Projection

Ross Krekoski
Nanyang Technological University

1. Introduction

Turn construction and completion practices in general are broadly understood to possess syntactic, pragmatic and intonational dimensions. There have been a large number of recent studies exploring the ways that speakers utilize these resources in interaction (for example, see Auer 1996, Couper-Kuhlen and Ono 2007, Ford and Thompson 1996, Tanaka 2000). Comparatively little work however has been done on developing a precise description of the intonational resources that are employed in turn construction and completion. This is largely due of course to the fact that intonation in real discourse is inherently complex to begin with, and a host of environmental, discourse and practical factors (overlap, background noise, variable pitch ranges, recording quality, to name just a few) often interfere with what pitch data is available, and the result is that our understanding of intonational resources in turn taking is relatively underdeveloped.

Japanese/Korean Linguistics 19.
Edited by Ho-min Sohn, Haruko Cook, William O'Grady, Leon A. Serafim, & Sang Yee Cheon.
Copyright © 2011, CSLI Publications

Investigating ordinary Japanese face-to-face conversation, this study attempts to add to current understanding of intonational resources of relevance to turn construction and completion, with F0 declination being examined in specific.[1] Turn constructional units, the basic interactional units of speech (henceforth TCUs,) and the primary units of analysis in this paper, usually consist of multiple intonation units (see Du Bois et al. 1992) in sequence.[2] Declination, or the general tendency for the average F0 (henceforth pitch) of a particular utterance to drop over time, is generally found to occur across sequential intonation units (Schuetze-Coburn et al. 1991, Nagahara and Iwasaki 1995), yielding the potential implication that declination therefore may be a process that is relevant to turn taking.[3] This possibility is certainly suggested by evidence from studies which show that declination is perceptually salient ('t Hart et al. 1990) and subject to conscious control (Ohala 1978, 't Hart et al. 1990). Schuetze-Coburn et al. (1991) also pursues this possibility and investigates the intersection of turns with what their study terms 'declination units'.[4] As the examination of precise declination practices in talk-in-interaction necessitates a detailed acoustic analysis of all of the data in question, the data set for this study is relatively small, consisting of only approximately 215 turn units taken from three separate recordings. This analysis therefore should be taken as very preliminary and exploratory. The approach taken here was first to segment the conversations into turn units at what Ford and Thompson (1996) term 'complex transition

---

1 The collection of recordings used for this study was compiled by Tsuyoshi Ono and his associates at UC Santa Barbara and the University of Arizona. I would like to express my sincere appreciation to him for making them available for this study.

2 This study makes the methodological assumption that TCUs are delimited by speaker changes and CTRPs. Although this may possibly be an oversimplification of the underlying process, a more nuanced approach is far beyond the scope of this paper.

3 Declination is not to be confused with catathesis. Catathesis is a similar but distinct phenomenon and occurs at the domain of the intonation unit. Catathesis is the compression of the absolute pitch range towards the right boundary of the unit. Although often this does result in an absolute lowering of average pitch towards the right boundary it is a completely different process. Figure 1 actually illustrates this distinction— the entire utterance in the figure is comprised of three intonation units with boundaries roughly at i, ii, and iii respectively. Although a compression of pitch range towards the right boundary can be seen in each consecutive intonation unit, illustrating catathesis, the overall drop in average pitch across the whole utterance, at pitch troughs i, ii, iii illustrates declination.

4An important distinction however between the methodology of the present study and that in Schuetze-Coburn et al. (1991) is that a turn in their study was treated as a stretch of speech by a given speaker: turn boundaries are marked with the beginning of a new turn by a different speaker. In the present study a given speaker's 'turn' (in the sense of Schuetze-Coburn et al. 1991) could, and frequently did consist of multiple TCUs. TCU boundaries here are CTRPs and not necessarily speaker changes, though of course speaker changes frequently occur at CTRPs.

relevance places (CTRPs). CTRPs are understood to be points of convergence of syntactic, pragmatic and intonational completion. Syntactic completion is operationalized as a stretch of speech being interpretable in its context as a complete clause, with an overt or recoverable predicate. Intonational completion points occur at the end of intonation units where a clear 'final' intonation is heard, and correspond to a period or question mark in the transcription convention used here (Du Bois et al. 1992) Points of pragmatic completion are identified by the occurrence of intonational completion if the stretch of speech in question is construable as a complete conversational action.[5] After segmenting the data, intonation contours, both within and across sequential turns by a given speaker were examined. In other words, although the data here was segmented into TCUs through the distribution of CTRPs which depend upon an auditory dimension, the examination of declination itself was an acoustic, rather than an auditory analysis.[6] Something as complex as intonation should, I feel, be examined from a variety of analytic perspectives. Since the overarching goal is to identify specific features of intonation of relevance to turn taking, so long as speakers are both orienting towards the use of, and also utilizing the acoustic features in question as an interactional resource, the inclusion of both types of data here is not seen as problematic.

2. Declination

Although declination is arguably simple to identify impressionistically by looking at pitch contours, or by listening to recordings, the intrinsic complexity of pitch movement coupled with the relative messiness of pitch in real discourse make the automation of calculating declination a somewhat complex matter. Schuetze-Coburn et al. (1991), investigating English discourse, measure declination using a best-fit, downwards sloping parallelogram which forms an envelope around both pitch peaks and pitch troughs. Nagahara and Iwasaki (1995) however make the point that measuring declination by observing pitch values only at troughs is also a very viable approach. Motivations for such an approach are that pitch troughs are less affected by variable pitch ranges than peaks, they are relatively unaffected by catathesis and defocusing, and are also relatively unaffected by NP-focusing. Nagahara and Iwasaki's approach served to suit the present data more judiciously and so was adopted here. When attempting to measure declination certain segments of the data needed to be excluded from the analysis outright. These included very short utterances such as backchannels or turns

---

5 See Ford and Thompson 1996 for a more detailed discussion of CTRPs.
6 Schuetze-Coburn et al. 1991, in their investigation of declination in conversation also utilize both dimensions of analysis.

that were otherwise too short to measure a declination effect, quotative expressions which generally have marked prosody and any other examples of marked prosody such as highly emotional speech, and examples such as laughter tokens and other non-speech vocalizations. In addition to excluded segments, there also exist a fairly significant number of cases of segments where the pitch was unextractable. In the majority of cases, a stretch of speech could be observed to be undergoing declination at pitch troughs, but the final few seconds of speech exhibit overlap, or are uttered quietly and consequently the pitch value at the end of the segment could not be extracted.[7] Other cases also exist where pitch in general could not be extracted due to the quality of a given speakers speech, background noise, overlap throughout the utterance or a variety of other factors. These were excluded from all analyses. The following, example (1), exemplifies a typical declination contour in this database. A pitch trace (Figure 1) follows. The speaker here is simply explaining how she doesn't like having to look through other people's belongings. The bracketed roman numerals in the example correspond to their respective pitch levels in Figure 1. Declination is clearly present with each consecutive pitch trough being uttered at a progressively lower pitch than the previous.

(1)   yabai   yo (i) ne nanka,
             dangerous FP   FP something
             'It's freaky you know, like,'

             hito   no   mono o koo nanka (ii)
             people GEN thing o this something
             'looking through other people's stuff,'

             miteru   mitai de ya janai   nanka (iii)
             look-prog like   hate COP-:neg something
             'don't you hate it?'

---

7 These cases were included for the analysis discussed in section three if the final pitch was clearly audible. The analysis regarding turn projection in section four which is quantitative and requires precise pitch measurements at the end of utterance did not include these cases.

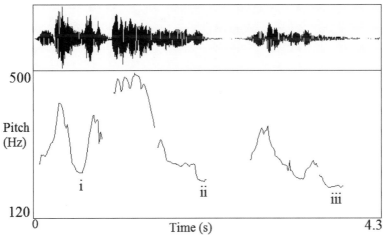

Figure 1: Pitch contour of example (1). The pitch at points i, ii, and iii is 223Hz, 201Hz, and 186Hz respectively.

3. Declination as a Coherence Resource

One of the first findings that materialized from the present database was that there was only one case where the end of a declination contour did not coincide with the occurrence of a CTRP. [8] This immediately suggests that speakers are aligning their use of declination with the moment to moment construction of turns, and that material produced within a given declination contour somehow 'belongs together'. This is further verified by a closer examination of the data, which indeed indicates that declination commonly seems to serve a coherence function. This is illustrated in the following segment where the speaker is talking about things that women have to do around the house. The bracketed roman numerals in the transcription again correspond to their respective pitch levels in Figure 2:

(2)   datte (i) tsukuru dake ja   sumanai mon. (ii)
        but   prepare only   live-NEG FP
        'but (women) don't only prepare (meals)'

        ..katazukeru mon. (iii) ...kaimono mo suru mon. (iv)
        tidy   fp shopping also do   FP
        '(they/we/I) tidies up (the house) (and we) also do the shopping.'

---

8 This was a case of a fairly long stretch of speech by a single speaker who was strongly indicating that further talk was forthcoming.

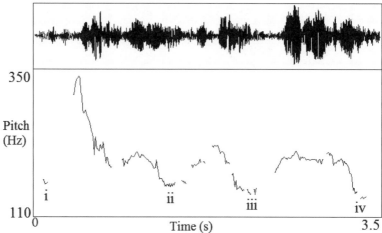

Figure 2: Pitch contour of example (2). The pitch at points i, ii, iii, and iv is 162Hz, 157Hz, 145Hz and 138Hz respectively.

In this example we have three consecutive clauses, each with a construably final intonation contour, that occur together within a single declination contour and comprise together a single conversational action: the speaker is responding to her husband's assertion that cooking is creative work. The semantic information expressed by the second and third clauses (*katazukeru mon,* '(they/we/I) tidy the house', and *kaimono mo suru mon,* '(they/we/I) also do the shopping', respectively) is a further specification of the information expressed by the first clause, and all three clauses share a common subject argument (*onna no hito,* 'women', expressed previously in the discourse).[9] It is important to note that although each respective clause is interpretable as being syntactically complete, the second and third clauses here are of course strongly retrospectively oriented, and depend upon the preceding information uttered within this particular contour to be interpretable. What is also interesting is that although there is no intervening talk in the entire segment, the end of this segment represents a no-gap transition; the current speaker's husband begins speaking immediately afterwards. The following example is in many respects similar to the previous. The speaker here, M, is talking about her brother's recent purchase of a sports car. She

---

9 The translation gloss provided references the subject argument as 'they/we/I' rather than 'women'. This is because although 'women' is acting as a syntactic argument, the speaker here is actually talking about women in general, including herself.

does not approve of it, believing it to be a wasteful and extravagant purchase. She is saying here that she does not know what type of car it is:

(3)   nan da   ka   wa(i)kannai,   shiranai   atashi. (ii)
        what COP NOM understand-neg   know-neg   I
        '(I) don't know what (kind of car it is), I don't know."

        mada oboekirenai. (iii)
        still   recall:-neg
        'I still can't recall.'

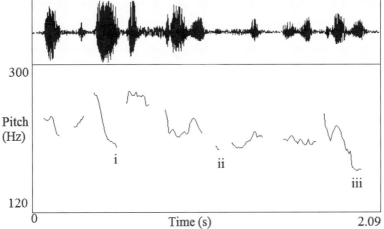

Figure 3: Pitch contour of example (3). The pitch at points i, ii, and iii is 195Hz, 190Hz, and 164Hz respectively.

Again, as with the previous example, this is a case of three consecutive clauses under a single declination contour, hearable as a single conversational action. Like the previous example, each consecutive clause is a further specification of the speaker's mental state of not knowing (and feeling somewhat dismissive and disdainful about the whole ordeal). In addition, as with the previous example they all share the same arguments and the second two clauses are both retrospectively oriented.

In addition to declination serving as a coherence resource, two specific prosodic patterns were commonly observed, each with a correlating function. Declination resets, when they occurred within the context of a single speaker talking, tended to correlate with the creation of new conversational actions, and new TCUs. Turn continuations on the other hand, or the addition by speakers of new material to an already completed turn, seem to be marked with the production of additional content with pitch troughs exhibiting values comparable with the minimum pitch value observed at the end of the preceding unit.[10] Consider the following example:

(4)   soo soo nan da   kedo, kotowanno. (i)
          right right that COP but   refuse FP
          'that's right but I still refuse (to use them).'

          ... a dakedo nanka   ima erina wa (ii) inai   jan, (iii)
            oh but   something now erina TOP   exist-neg FP
          'oh, but now erina isn't here.'

          ima ruumumeeto inai   jan. (iv)
          now roommate   exist-neg FP
          '(My) roommate isn't around right now.'

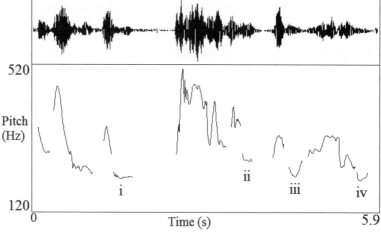

Figure 4: Pitch contour of example (4). The pitch at points i, ii, iii, and iv is 203Hz, 242Hz, 203Hz and 195Hz respectively.

In this example the speaker, Y, who is a student living with her roommate, starts out by responding to a query by S who expresses that he is surprised that she refuses to use daily household items that belong to her roommate, even though her roommate gave Y permission to use them. This

---

10 Luke and Zhang (2007) mention that turn continuations or extensions are often marked with what they term subordinate prosody, defined as material being uttered with a combination of 'lowered pitch, reduced loudness, and quickened tempo', but this is not with direct reference to declination.

is represented by the material up to point (i). Perhaps not wanting to continue with the discussion of why she continues to refuse to utilize household items, Y changes the focus of the discussion, initiating a new conversational action, and a new TCU. Point (i) is marked by strong syntactic, pragmatic and intonational completion. It is interesting that the material after point (i) is marked not only by a declination reset and a corresponding new declination contour, but also by the introduction of a topic: Erina, (Y's roommate), rather than Y herself, and a new discourse function: relating news rather than responding. In this case then, the declination reset marks the creation of a new TCU and the initiation of a new conversational action.

This contrasts with the following example, taken from the same conversation. The speaker here, again Y, is now talking about how she will not answer the phone if her roommate is around. At this point in the conversation she sounds a little bit defensive, as S is questioning her as to why she wouldnt just pick up the phone if it rings. After explaining how her roommate will answer the phone anyway Y reaches a point of syntactic, pragmatic and intonational closure at point (iii). She then adds to the turn, extending the current conversational action with the inclusion of the assertion that she definitely will not answer the phone (implying that her roommate understands this anyway). What is interesting about this example is that the addition of material here to an existing turn is not accompanied by a declination reset. Shown in figure 5, the additional material has a pitch trough (at point iv, 186Hz) at a level that is almost equivalent to that reached at the closure of the preceding turn unit (at point iii, 183Hz). Turn continuations, or the extension of conversational actions seem to be marked not by a declination reset, but by the production of material at a comparable pitch level.

(5)   demo (i) denwa nattara erina okiru   shi, (ii)
            but   phone ring   erina wake up and
            'but if the phone rings, erina will wake up (anyway).'

            soshitara   koo toru   no. (iii)
            in that case this pick up FP
            'in that case, she'll pick it up (like this).'

            ...asshi zettai   toranai   shi. (iv)
               I   definitely pick up:neg and
            'and I definitely won't pick it up.'

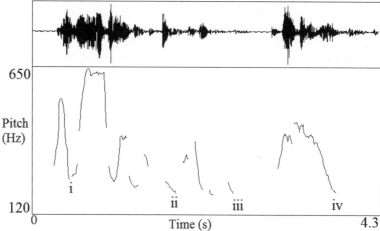

Figure 5: Pitch contour of example (5). The pitch at points i, ii, iii, and iv is 229Hz, 188Hz, 183Hz and 186Hz respectively.

4. Unit Projection through Declination Contours

One of the more suggestive possibilities here was that, in addition to serving a coherence function in discourse, declination may also be acting to project turn unit completion. This possibility is implicitly suggested in the findings of previous research. A number of studies have previously suggested that the rate of declination is a function of the length of the utterance in question (Bruce 1982; Cooper and Sorenson 1981;'t Hart et al. 1990, Schuetze-Coburn et al. 1990; Weitzman 1970). In other words, short utterances seem to undergo declination at a proportionately faster rate than longer ones. If we consider this conversely, there is the resultant implication that the rate of declination thus gives some cue as to the length of the initial TCU. Superficially, this may seem to be a problematic implication as one of the more elegantly beautiful elements of the turn taking system is the provision for speakers to add material to previously completed turns causing, of course, the total length of a given action to be contingent on a host of factors often negotiated on a moment-to-moment basis by speech participants. This however does not preclude the possibility of speakers being cognicent of at least the general form that the **initial** TCU will take. Figure 5 in fact shows an example of just this: the material up to point (iii) comprises a single TCU and a single declination contour. The addition of new material to the same TCU afterwards is done with a final trough level comparable to the previous minimum. It was thus reasoned that if declination indeed serves to project the end of a turn unit, that a logical cue for doing so would be the overall percent drop in pitch. Such would certainly explain the findings of research mentioned above which associate the rate of declination with the length of utterance: if the overall drop in frequency over the course of a declination contour is static and an element of the turn taking system, this will cause longer utterances to undergo declination at a slower relative rate than shorter ones. Under such a scenario therefore, prosodic projection of a turn's completion would be logically then realized both through the overall rate of declination, as well as through the potential existence of a target pitch level which would be expected by the listener well before the completion of the initial TCU. This prosodic projection then would serve to signal completion along with syntactic and pragmatic resources.

Perception of pitch is an exponential function, and an analogy of this is in the perception of music. The pitch in Hz of a note of a particular octave is always precisely double the pitch of the same note of an immediately lower octave. In addition, the ratio of pitch of two immediately neighboring notes is a static value[11] and thus a given percent drop in pitch will always be perceived by listeners as the same. The percent drop in pitch of the first pitch trough and the final pitch trough of all turn units which had pitch contours that were completely measureable for the entire utterance (n=35) was calculated.[12] The smallest % drop in pitch observed was approximately 13%, and the largest % drop in pitch was approximately 25%. It should be mentioned that both of these values should be considered outliers. The overall average was an 18% drop.[13] The standard deviation was a mere 3%, with approximately 78% of values occurring within one standard deviation of the mean, making this a fairly tightly distributed data set. This is also significant when we consider that in this data set, pitch variations of at least an octave within a turn are the norm, and there are several cases of pitch variations of two octaves (see Figure 5) within a single turn. Although the data set here is rather small, it is nevertheless an interesting possibility that a pitch ratio serves to signal the closure of a turn. More research on this is clearly necessary.

5. Conclusions

The implications suggested by the data here seem to indicate that declination may be acting as an important resource for the construction of turns. Declination contours were found to correlate closely with the distribution of

---

11 That is, one musical half step or semitone is equivalent to the 12th root of 2, or approximately 1.0595.

12 According to the formula 1-F0f/F0i where F0f is the final pitch trough and F0i is the initial pitch trough.

13 Interestingly, an 18% drop is almost precisely 3 musical semitones.

CTRPs. In addition, declination seems to serve as a coherence device, with material produced within a single declination contour often also occurring as single conversational actions. New TCUs seem to be marked with corresponding declination resets, and turn continuations are associated with the production of new material with pitch troughs at levels comparable to previous minimums. Finally the possibility that declination may be also serving a turn projection function is suggested by the data. It needs to be emphasized however that the present study is very preliminary, and the findings here should be further explored with a larger database.

It should also mentioned that although Hz values at pitch troughs was used here as a means of automating declination measurements, it is at least conceivable that pitch values at troughs may not be the only declination cue that listeners perceive as relevant. This also clearly needs more research.

References

Auer, P. 1996. On the Prosody and Syntax of Turn-continuations. *Prosody in conversation: Interactional studies,* eds. E. Couper-Kuhlen and M. Selting. 57-100. Cambridge: Cambridge University Press.

Auer, P. 2005. Projection in Interaction and Projection in Grammar. *Text* 25(1): 7-36.

Bruce, G. 1982. Textual Aspects of Prosody in Swedish. *Phonetics* 39: 274-287.

Cooper, W. and Sorenson, J. M. 1981. *Fundamental Frequency in Sentence Production.* New York: Springer-Verlag.

Couper-Kuhlen, E. and Ono, T. 2007. Incrementing in Conversation. A Comparison of Methods in English, German and Japanese. *Pragmatics* 17: 513-552.

Du Bois, J. W., Cumming, S., Schuetze-Coburn, S., and Paolino, D. 1992. *Discourse Transcription (Santa Barbara Papers in Linguistics, vol. 4)* ed. S. Thompson. Santa Barbara: University of California, Department of Linguistics.

Ford, C. E, and Thompson, S. A. 1996. Interactional Units in Conversation: Syntactic, Intonational, and Pragmatic Resources for the Management of Turns. *Interaction and Grammar.* eds. E. Ochs, E.A. Schegloff and S.A. Thompson, 134-184. Cambridge: Cambridge University Press.

Fox, B.A. 2001. An Exploration of Prosody and Turn Projection in English Conversation. *Studies in Interactional Linguistics.* eds. M. Selting and E. Couper-Kuhlen, 287-315. Amsterdam: Benjamins Publishing Company.

't Hart, J., Collier, R., and Cohen, A. 1990. *A Perceptual Study of Intonation.* Cambridge, UK: Cambridge University Press.

Luke, K. K. and Zhang, W. 2007. Retrospective Turn Continuations in Mandarin Chinese Conversation. *Pragmatics* 17: 605-635

Nagahara H. and Iwasaki, S. 1995. Tail Pitch Movement and the Intermediate Phrase in Japanese. Ms.

Ohala, J. 1978. Production of Tone. *Tone: A Linguistic Survey,* ed. V. Fromkin. New York: Academic Press.

Schegloff, E. A. 1987. Analyzing Single Episodes of Interaction: An Exercise in Conversation Analysis. *Social Psychology Quarterly* 50 (2): 101-114.

Schuetze-Coburn, S., Shapley, M., and Weber, E. G. 1991. Units of Intonation in Discourse: a Comparison of Acoustic and Auditory Analyses. *Language and Speech* 34: 207–234.

Tanaka, H. 2000. Turn-projection in Japanese Talk-in-interaction. *Research on Language and Social Interaction* 33(1): 1-38.

Wells, B. and Macfarlane, S. 1998. Prosody as an Interactional Resource: Turn-Projection and Overlap. *Language and Speech* 41: 265-298.

Weitzman, R. S. 1970. "Word Accent in Japanese." *Studies in the Phonology of Asian Languages 9.* Los Angeles: University of Southern California Acoustic Phonetics Research Lab.

How to Tell a Story: Comparison of L1 Japanese/Korean and L2 Japanese Narratives

YUKO NAKAHAMA
Keio University

Within the framework of functional linguistics, successful management of referents in a story plays a major role in achieving coherence in narrative discourse. In narrating a story, forms are selected in order to show certain functions by the speakers. The present study was conducted to examine how native speakers (NS) of Japanese and Korean attain form-function relationships in storytelling and to find out how the possible similarities/differences between the two languages affect learner discourse of Japanese as a second language (L2). In particular, the study addresses how differing task types trigger diverse implementations of referent tracking scheme among NS and nonnative speaker (NNS) discourse, as it has been maintained in related literature that task complexity influences the style of narrative formation.

1. Background

According to Givón (1983), most continuous topics in a story should be marked with a zero anaphora, while most discontinuous topics should be

Japanese/Korean Linguistics 19.
Edited by Ho-min Sohn, Haruko Cook, William O'Grady, Leon A. Serafim, & Sang Yee Cheon.
Copyright © 2011, CSLI Publications

marked with full noun phrases (hereafter NPs). Givón (1983) further argues 'the iconicity principle' that claims 'The more disruptive, surprising, discontinuous or hard to process a topic is, the more coding material must be assigned to it.' (Givón 1983: 18). The simplified topic continuity scale for Japanese and Korean is as follows; NP+*ga* → (NP+*wa* →) Zero Anaphora for Japanese, NP+*ka/i* → (NP+*(n)un* →) Zero Anaphora for Korean (See Hinds,1983 for Japanese, and Sohn, 1999, for Korean). NP+*wa*, NP+*(n)un* are in parenthesis because when a referent is introduced for the first time, it is marked by *ga*, then subsequently zero anaphora unless there are other competing referents. If there were such cases, the topic would be marked by *wa/(n)un* in Japanese and Korean, respectively.

Choice of perspective has influence on the selection of grammatical devices in marking a referent in a story (Berman and Slobin 1994). Kim (2001) revealed that Japanese and Korean speakers tell a story from different perspectives and this is reflected in their narrative structures. To be specific, Japanese speakers place their focus on the main characters of a story and tell the story from their perspectives. Koreans, on the other hand, focus on action that is taking place in each scene, and thus, they switch subjects quite frequently among the story characters. Japanese speakers tend to keep the protagonist in the subject position, and the antagonist in the agent position, by using the passive voice. Due to these differing perspectives in relating events between the two languages, Korean learners of Japanese produce fewer occurrences of passives as compared with their Japanese NS counterparts (e.g. Kim 2001; Nakahama 2009; Tashiro 1995; Watanabe 1996).

In Nakahama (2009), Korean learners of Japanese benefited from the shared topic management style between Japanese and Korean in producing appropriate particles to introduce and maintain referential topics during their oral story telling activity using a picture book. Conversely, the different perspectives in story telling between the two languages resulted in Korean learners' production of fewer passive expressions and frequent switch of subjects in their L2 Japanese discourse, compared to NS of Japanese.

Many of the investigations of perspective setting in L2 Japanese story telling activities utilized narration of the series of picture to elicit the data (e.g. Kim 2002, Nakahama 2009, Taguchi 1995). It is possible that different types of tasks would trigger different ways in which the speakers related events in the story. In fact, Nakahama (2003) and Nakahama (2009) investigated the introduction and the maintenance of referential topics in L2 Japanese, using silent film retelling and narration of consecutive pictures, respectively. The appropriate marking of a referent in the most continuous context (i.e. the use of zero anaphora) appeared to be more difficult for the low level English speaking L2 learners of Japanese in a film retelling task, as compared to a picture narration task. The two studies used different methods to measure the learners' proficiency levels, and thus the results might only be partially comparable, however, the finding is worth investigating further.

Several researchers (e.g. Gilabert 2007, Ishikawa 2007, Robinson 1995, 2003) have investigated the relationship between task complexity and the style of narrative formation of L2 English, and the general consensus of these studies was that a more complex task (referring to something in the displaced context: 'there and then' context, T/T hereafter) triggers higher complexity and accuracy in their English L2 narratives, as compared to referring to something that is in front of them ('Here and Now' context, H/N hereafter). Retelling a story in T/T setting is considered more complex than in H/N, as speakers would need to code, store and retrieve the content of the story in viewing the film and re-telling the story afterward, thus cognitively more challenging than the H/N setting.

Robinson (1995) reported that his participants showed higher accuracy in production of articles in T/T context than H/N contexts. The researcher argues that the speakers paid more attention to forming a coherent story by connecting propositions, and as a result, produced higher accuracy in terms of article selections. The findings of these studies are worth exploring in other L2s, especially with focus placed not only on grammatical accuracy but also on discourse perspective, such as how the speakers refer to new and known information in narratives and make connected stories.

The current study aims to document how NS of closely related languages, Japanese and Korean to be specific, attain form-function relationships in storytelling and to find out how the possible linguistic and conceptual similarities/differences between the two languages affect L2 Japanese discourse. In particular, the study addresses whether task complexity triggers diverse implementation of referent tracking scheme among Japanese/Korean NS as well as NNS discourse. The following research questions were asked:

Research Question (1) How do the linguistic similarities and conceptual differences between Japanese and Korean affect the L2 acquisition of topic management styles in Japanese oral narratives?

Research Question (2) Does task complexity affect topic management styles of Japanese and Korean NSs as well as Korean learners of Japanese?

2. Study

2.1 Participants

NS of Japanese (JNS, N=10) and Korean (KNS, N=10) and Korean learners of Japanese (intermediate level (JSL-INT, N=10)) and advanced level (JSL-ADV, N=10)) participated in the study. The Simulated Oral Proficiency

Interview (SOPI)[1] was partially administered to participants, and those who were grouped into intermediate-mid and intermediate-high levels served as intermediate level learners, and those who were rated as advanced-low, advanced-mid, advanced-high served as advanced level learners in the current study. The average length of Japanese studies and stay in Japan for the learners were JSL-INT: 18.9 months, 9.5 months, and JSL-ADV: 57.3 months, 18.3 months, respectively.

2.2 Tasks and Procedure

The participants constructed two types of narratives; one narrating a wordless picture book (*Frog, Where are You?* written by Mayer 1969) while looking at a series of pictures, and the other reconstructing a story after viewing a silent film (*Winter Carousel*). The book, *Frog, Where Are You?* is comprised of twenty-four consecutive pictures, and the plot involves main characters (a little boy, his dog and his pet frog) as well as various peripheral characters that interfere with the protagonists' actions. The characters move from place to place through time, resulting in production of very rich connected discourse. The silent film also has three major characters (which are animals but act like humans) and they encounter miscellaneous characters during the story. The movie is twelve minutes long, but in order not to challenge the memory capacity of the speakers, the first six minutes was shown to the participants for later story telling. Picture narration task is intended to elicit storytelling in H/N context, that is, to discuss something within the realm of consciousness of the speaker/listener. In the second task, in contrast, the speakers are referring to something in the displaced context: T/T. I managed to interview all ten NS and three JNS-INT learners and two JNS-ADV learners. I could not obtain information from KNS. These participants listened to their own narration on the tape and were asked questions about the use of *wa*, *ga*, zero anaphora, passive forms, and so on.

2.3 Analysis

Data was coded in the following ways. How all the animate referents were introduced into the story was coded as Referent Introduction. Reintroduction of a known referent in a subject position was coded as Topic Switch. Referent was coded as Topic Continuation, if they remain to be a topic after being reintroduced into discourse. Finally all occurrences of passive expressions were coded.

---

[1] Unlike Oral Proficiency Interview (OPI), SOPI does not have an interlocutor. The testees listen to questions on the tape and record their responses, as if they are talking to someone. The SOPI raters listen to the tapes afterwards and rate the learners' proficiency levels, according to the ACTFL guidelines.

In sentence (1), Referent Introduction is marked in bold with underline.

(1) *Otoko no ko* **_ga_**   *kaeru* **_o_** *tsukamaete kite sore o bin ni iremashita*
     Boy   NOM frog ACC catch come   it ACC jar in put-PAST
     'A boy caught and brought home a frog and put it in a jar.'

In Sentence (2), Topic Switch is marked in bold with underline, whereas Topic Continuation is marked within a parenthesis.

(2) *Inu **ga**   mado   kara tobiorite shimaimashita.   Otoko no ko* **_wa_**
     Dog NOM window from jump unfortunately-PAST Boy   TOP
     okotteimasu. (φ) mori no   naka e   itte (φ) ana o sagashimashita.
     angry   Forest GEN inside into go and hole ACC look-PAST
     'A dog jumped out of the window, and the boy is angry. (The boy) went
     into a forest and looked into a hole.'

In (1), *ga* and *o* are coded as referent introductions of the boy and the frog, respectively. Utterance (2) appeared a couple of utterances after the first mention of the boy and the dog, and these characters have been established in the narrative. Here, the dog was reintroduced as a topic and therefore *ga* is marked as Topic Switch but the topic of discourse was switched to the boy afterwards with *wa*, therefore, this *wa* is also marked as Topic Switch. The boy remained to be the topic with the use of zero anaphora thereafter. These two anaphoras are coded as Topic Continuation.

In order to ensure reliability of coding, I randomly selected 30% of data to be coded by two coders, and the Pearson's correlation was .995 indicating high correlation between coders. The proportional use of each marker (in comparison with all the forms used in the context) was calculated and compared between groups with the use of ANOVA. The total frequency of the occurrences of passive expressions were coded and compared between groups.

3. Results and Discussion

The forms that were used to mark referents in each context (Referent Introduction, Topic Switch and Topic Continuation) will be shown in tables and notable tendencies of marking the referents will be discussed. The occurrences of passive expressions will be discussed in the end of the results section.

3.1 Referent Introduction

Table 1 illustrates the forms used in the context of referent introduction.

Table 1.Referent introduction(Numbers indicate percentage use of the form)

	NP+	*ga,* *ka/i* (NOM)	*wa,* *n(un)* (TOP)	*o,* *r(ul)* (ACC)	*ni,* *hanthey* (by)	*mo,* *doo* (also)	particle drop	Others
KNS	H/N	56.6	0.9	21.1	2.3	1.8	0	17.2
	T/T	60.4	3.4	9.4	5.1	1.1	3.0	17.5
JNS	H/N	52.9	0	19.7	11.1	4.5	0	13.3
	T/T	63.0	0	0	7.4	5.2	0	24.5
JSL-INT	H/N	63.1	0	14.6	2.0	2.9	0	17.5
	T/T	71.8	3.1	5.0	4.2	6.4	0	9.5
JSL-ADV	H/N	50.5	4.5	12	7.8	2	0	21.2
	T/T	65.2	1.7	0	6.7	4.5	5.0	17.0
Average	H/N	55.8	1.4	16.8	5.3	2.8	0.0	16.5
	T/T	65.1	2.0	3.6	5.8	4.3	2.0	14.7

As can be seen in Table 1, for referent introduction, JNS and KNS tended to use the canonical forms for coding a new entity (i.e. *ga* and *ka/i*, respectively) for both H/N and T/T venues. However, the average percentage use of the indefinite markers was greater for T/T than H/N (65.1% and 55.8%, respectively) across the groups, and the difference was significant ($F(1,36)= 4.3$, p =.045). The lower percentage use of NP+*ga* might be an artifact of higher use of NP+*o* (*ul*) in H/N context, in which speakers tended to use *o* (*ul*) to mark the frog, the main character's pet. Another assumption could be that the speakers introduce a new character into story by 'cautiously' accessing their stored memory in T/T setting, and in so doing, they are bound to use the most typical form for coding new information in the subject position, that is NP+*ga* (*ka/i*). The latter premise would support what Robinson (1995) found in his data, in that the speakers tend to pay more attention to sentence constructions in T/T context and thereby more frequent use of indefinite markers were found.

Previous studies (e.g. Doi and Yoshioka 1990, Nakahama 2003, 2009, Sakamoto 1993) revealed that the acquisition of *ga* is found to be difficult for English speaking learners of Japanese. However, the current study showed that the Korean speaking learners of Japanese had no difficulty in producing NP+*ga* in an appropriate context. Given that KNS used the Korean equivalent NP+*ga* (i.e. NP+*ka/i*) as a canonical marker to code new information in their first language (L1) narratives, it seemed that Korean speaking learners made use of their L1 coding scheme when they were speaking in their L2.

In order to clarify this assumption, a question was asked regarding how the learners differentiate NP+*ga* and NP+*wa*. It was revealed that five Korean learners of Japanese are aware of the parallel use of NP+*ga*, *wa* and NP+*ka (i)*, *(n)un*, respectively and apply the knowledge when they speak in Japanese. This result is a typical example of the benefit that learners receive when their L1 and L2 are typologically close to each other. JNS, on the other hand, used NP+*ga* and NP+*wa* without knowing their functions; they stated that both NP+*ga* and NP+*wa* are subject markers and could not explain the different uses of them but were producing them appropriately.

3.2 Topic Switch

The uses of NP+*ga*, NP+*wa*, NP+*mo*, Particle drop, and Zero anaphora were found in the context of Topic Switch. Table 2 shows the percentage use of each form.

Table 2. Topic switch (Numbers indicate percentage use of the form)

	NP+	*ga,* *ka/i*	*wa,* *n(un)*	*mo,* *doo*	particle drop	zero anaphora
KNS	H/N	29.1	39.6	5.3	0.6	25.4
	T/T	53.5	25.8	4.5	5.2	11.0
JNS	H/N	25.1	33.1	2.3	0	39.6
	T/T	40.0	30.5	2.9	2.1	24.1
JSL- INT	H/N	33.5	43.4	1.6	0	21.5
	T/T	45.3	31.9	0.9	4.2	17.8
JSL-ADV	H/N	29.7	44.8	1.8	0	23.7
	T/T	46.7	23.4	1.9	6.0	22.0
Average	H/N	29.4	40.2	2.7	0.1	27.5
	T/T	46.5	27.9	2.5	4.3	18.7

In the context of topic switch, two noteworthy tendencies were found. First, particle drop was observed only for T/T setting but not for H/N except for once by a speaker in KNS narratives. Although the percentage of particle drop was rather low (ranging from 2.1% to 6.0% across groups), nine out of ten KNS dropped particles at least once in T/T setting.

In conversations, particle drop is commonly practiced, but in monologues, it can be considered rather uncharacteristic. In reintroducing a known referent back into discourse via topic switch, the speakers delve into their memory in terms of what the character did and how the story line continues from then on. Unlike the introduction of a new character, the relationship between the current topic and the reintroduction of the known topic is intricate and requires careful deliberation. It seemed that after the struggle of attempting to retrieve the information from their memory, the speakers ended up dropping the particles. In H/N setting, on the other hand, the speakers- with the pictorial support- know who they are switching the topic to and what action the referent will take and this certainty led to no confusion of particle selection.

Another noteworthy trend found in the topic switch context was that the percentage use of zero anaphora was significantly higher in H/N than T/T type narrative ($F (1, 36) = 6.3, p = .016$). Switching topics possibly involves altering the direction of a story, and therefore requires a great deal of attention from both the speakers and the listeners. Under the H/N condition, both speakers and listeners share information because they have the pictorial support in front of them, so the listeners could infer who the speakers were referring to without having to mention the subject. Under T/T condition, on the other hand, the speaker would have to make sure that the listener follows the narrative, thus triggering the speaker to be more explicit especially when they switch the topic of discourse. Interestingly, it was found that the majority of topic switch (over 90 % in all four groups) was done in order to bring back the main character into the topic of story, and all the occurrences of topic switch with zero anaphora (except for three cases by JSL-INT speakers) were found in switching the topic to the main characters, irrespective of task types. This result parallels what Clancy (1992) calls 'ellipsis for hero' strategy, which denotes that speakers use ellipsis (zero anaphora) when they switch discourse topics to main characters of story.

3.3 Topic Continuation

As was in the context of Topic Switch, the uses of NP+*ga*, NP+*wa*, NP+*mo*, Particle drop, and Zero anaphora were found in Topic Continuation. Table 3 shows the percentage use of each form.

Table 3. Topic continuation (Numbers indicate percentage use of the form)

	NP+	*ga,ka/i*	*wa,n(un)*	*mo,doo*	particle omit	zero anaphora
KNS	H/N	9.1	7.6	0	0	81.9
	T/T	11.9	3.8	7.4	0.6	76.2
JNS	H/N	0.7	4.1	0	0	95.1
	T/T	7.2	8.9	1.1	1.8	80.9
JSL-INT	H/N	3.0	11.4	0	0	85.6
	T/T	10.1	8.2	0.6	1.0	80.0
JSL-ADV	H/N	1.6	3.6	0	0	94.8
	T/T	9.3	8.5	0	1.4	80.7
Average	H/N	3.6	6.7	0	0	89.4
	T/T	9.7	7.4	2.3	1.2	79.5

The form most frequently used for marking the highest topic continuity (i.e. in the context of topic continuation) was zero anaphora for both H/N and T/T, as expected from previous studies and Givón's (1983) 'the iconicity principle'. However, as in the topic switch context, the higher use of zero anaphora was observed in H/N than T/T in this context, and the difference was significant (F $(1,36)$ = 9.5, p = .004). The follow-up interview revealed that although no speakers intentionally maneuvered use and non use of zero anaphora depending on the task types, they all said they paid attention to making their narration easy to follow for the listeners in T/T context.

In contrast, making a story with pictorial support (both for the speaker and the listener) reduced the burden and they can just tell the story naturally and without particular effort. With this interview result, it is argued that for topic switch and topic continuation, the speakers attempted to avoid ambiguity and used full NPs when referents were not in sight in order to be more explicit, though that might not be a conscious choice by the speakers (see comparable argument in Clancy's (1997) analysis of Korean children's L1 data).

By analyzing how referent was introduced, gain topicality and maintained to be a topic, it was found that speakers' narrative formation was affected by two different task types, H/N and T/T. There were no big differences between Japanese and Korean NS narratives in coding referents in each context, and that might explain the similar results found in NNS data, irrespective of their proficiency levels. What follows next is the discussion of passive expressions found in the data.

3.4 Passive Expressions

Table 4 shows the number of occurrences of passive expressions found throughout the narratives of all four groups.

Table 4. Passive exressions (in total frequences)

	H/N Task	T/T Task	Total
KNS	17	2	19
JNS	25	24	49
JSL-INT	6	4	10
JSL-ADV	18	7	25

As Table 4 shows, the number of occurrences of passive expressions was much fewer in narratives by KNS and JSL than JNS. Interestingly, task types triggered no difference in passive productions in JNS narratives (H/N: 25, T/T: 24) but H/N context generated more passive forms in KNS narratives (H/N: 17, T/T: 2). JSL-ADV displayed similar pattern (H/N: 18, T/T: 7), though JSL-INT did not show a big difference between task types with very low instances of passives for both types (H/N: 6, T/T: 4). Micro analysis of JSL-INT data revealed that these speakers of lower proficiency faced linguistic snags in constructing passive forms and hence lead to low production of passive forms, irrespective of narrative types. Excerpt (1) illustrates this pattern.

(1) Narrative by JSL-INT

Bii tachi ni... bii tachi ni... bii tachi ga... inu o tsuite..tsuite
Bee plural by bee plural by bee plural NOM puppy ACC follow
'Bees by...bees by... bees follow the puppy'

The topic of the utterance before this was the dog, and the speaker had an attempt to keep the dog as the topic by introducing the bees in the agent position, preceding *ni* 'by'. However, the speaker could not produce a proper conjugation of the verb, and thereby switched the topic from the dog to the bees with the subject marker, *ga*. Successful formation of passives were found in JSL-ADV narratives. Excerpt (2) shows one example.

(2) Narrative by JSL-ADV
    Soko ni shika ga   ite... Φ   sono shika no atama... no ue ni
    There at deer NOM exist (boy)   that deer   GEN head GEN above at
    noserarechaimasu
    carry-PASS-unfortunately
    'A deer was there and (the boy) got carried on the deer's head.'

This advanced level speaker introduced the deer in the topical position with *ga*; however, he switched the topic to the boy (marked with zero anaphora), accompanied by passivization of the verb, *noseru*.

Excerpt (3) shows how passive expression was used by KNS.

(3) Narrative by KNS

    Φ beol dul hanthey jjyok m ul   bat-gguyo
    bee plural by   go after ACC receive polite
    'Lit: (the dog) received 'following' by the bees'

This KNS speaker did not use passivized verb but instead expression that depicts passivization. Many of the KNS passive expressions were found to be lexical passives like this one. While several successful passive expressions were found in JSL-ADV narratives, the tendency was that both KNS and JSL-ADV speakers switch subjects when new actions take place in the story, as they view the story focusing on actions, not the central characters. Japanese speakers, on the other hand, are inclined to place their viewpoint on protagonists and as a result, the speakers keep the main character in the subject position as a patient in the passive structure when contextually appropriate.

I compared the plots of H/N and T/T stories carefully and realized that the storyline in H/N would prompt more passives, as the main characters went into difficulties created by the antagonists of the story, whereas T/T story did not have obvious trouble causing activities in its plot. Thus, it appeared that the different numbers of occurrences of passive expressions in the KNS and JSL-ADV narratives between the two tasks were the outcome of the different story plots. However, JNS still produced almost equal amount of passive structures in both types of narratives, irrespective of the differences in the plots. This would be indicative of a strong tendency of the Japanese speakers to focus on relating the events from the viewpoint of the main characters in the story. As a result, these different ways of 'thinking for speaking' (see Slobin 1991) reflected in the Korean learners' L2 Japanese narratives.

Five Korean participants (who narrated JSL narrative) were interviewed after storytelling activities, and it was revealed that although they had the syntactic and semantic knowledge of passive forms in Japanese, they did not know its functions on the discourse level. In other words, they were not aware of the relationship between the use of passive forms and the perspective of relating events.

4. Conclusion

In summary, two research questions posited for the study can be answered as follows.

(1) How do the linguistic similarities and conceptual differences between Japanese and Korean affect the L2 acquisition of topic management styles in Japanese oral narratives?

Similarities in coding referents in the contexts of 'referent introduction', 'topic switch' and 'topic continuation' were observed in Japanese and Korean NS data. These similarities had a positive influence on Koreans' constructing their L2 Japanese narratives, and the positive effects were confirmed even at the lower proficiency level learners. The conceptual difference was observed in JNS and KNS narratives, in terms of how they view stories, as expected from relevant literature. To be specific, Japanese speakers placed their viewpoint on the main characters and told the story from their perspectives, while Korean tend to take a somewhat neutral perspective in telling the story by switching subjects when introducing the new happenings into the story. This difference resulted in fewer occurrences of passive expressions in both KNS and JSL data. The occurrences of passives by lower proficiency level learners were very few, regardless of the task types, and this seemed to be caused by the linguistic difficulties that they encountered.

(2) Does task complexity affect topic management styles of Japanese and Korean NSs as well as Korean learners of Japanese?

The most discernible difference between tasks was the use of zero anaphora. In the context of Topic Switch and Topic Continuation, higher percentage use of zero anaphora was found in H/N than T/T narratives across all four groups. It is argued that the speakers were trying to ensure that the listeners could follow the story in T/T setting by explicitly stating the topic of discourse, as there is no pictorial support in front of them. In terms of production of passive forms, different tasks did not trigger different numbers of incidence in JNS data; however Korean speakers produced fewer occurrences of passive expressions in T/T tasks in their L1 narratives as well as their L2 Japanese narratives. It seemed that the way learners view events in their L1 affects the way they tell a story in their L2.

5. Pedagogical Implications

Given that the learners who responded to the follow-up interview were not aware of the function of the passive forms on the discourse level, the findings of the present study might be used as a pointer for pedagogical intervention to teach how to tell a story in an easy-to-understand and convincing manner in L2 Japanese, as well as raising the consciousness of form-function mapping skills in L2 discourse in general. Before I close this article, I will give one example of pedagogical intervention to teach narrative construction. A teacher can arrange a lesson in which learners narrate a story (with or without pictorial support) freely. Then they will listen to a pre-recorded baseline narration by NS of Japanese. The teacher can have the learners write down (or discuss) possible differences between their narratives and the NS baseline narratives. In so doing, the teacher can ask the learners who they think the topic of the discourse is, in any given context. With this consciousness raising activity, the learners are encouraged to 'notice' the difference of narrative structure between theirs and the baseline. Reviewing passive conjugation or any other forms that have relevance to viewpoint setting (, giving/receiving verbs) is encouraged, depending on the learners' proficiency levels. Finally they will be asked to re-tell a story with the new knowledge of story-telling strategy.

References

Berman, R. and Slobin, D. 1994. *Relating Events in Narrative: A Crosslinguistic Developmental Study.* Hillsdale, NJ: Lawrence Elbaum Associates.

Clancy, P. 1992. Referential Strategies in Narratives of Japanese Children. *Discourse Processes* 15: 441-467.

Clancy, P. 1997. Discourse Motivations for Referential Choice in Korean Acquisition. *Japanese/Korean Linguistics.* Volume 6, eds. H. Sohn and J. Haig, 639-660. Stanford: CSLI Publications.

Doi, T. and Yoshioka, K. 1990. Joshi no shuutoku ni okeru gengo unyoojoo no seiyaku: Pienemann–Johnson moderuno nihongo shuutoku kenkyuu e no ooyoo [Speech processing constraints on the acquisition of Japanese particles: Applying the Pienemann–Johnson model to Japanese as a second language]. *Proceedings of the 1st Conference on Second Language Acquisition and Teaching,* 23-33. Niigata: International University of Japan.

Gilabert, R. 2007. Effects of manipulating task complexity on self-repairs during L2 oral production. *IRAL* 45(3): 215–240.

Givón, T. 1983. Topic Continuity in Discourse: Quantitative Cross-language Studies. Amsterdam: John Benjamins.

Hinds, J. 1983. Topic continuity in Japanese. Topic Continuity in Discourse: Quantitative Cross-language Studies, ed. T. Givón, 47-93. Amsterdam: John Benjamins.

Ishikawa, T. 2005. Investigating the Relationship between Structural Complexity Indices of EFL Writing and Language Proficiency: A Task-based Approach. *JACET Bulletin* 41: 51-60.

Kim, K. 2001. Danwa koosei ni okeru bogowasha to gakushuusha no shiten- Nikkan ryoogengo ni okeru shugo to dooshi no mochiikata o chuushin ni. [The expression of viewpoint in discourse by learners and native speakers: Contrasting the choice of subjects and verbs between Japanese and Korean]. *Nihongo Kyooik,* 109: 60-69.

Mayer, M. 1969. *Frog, Where Are You?* New York: Dial Press.

Nakahama, Y. 2003. Development of Reference Management in L2 Japanese: Silent Film Retelling Task. *Studies in Language and Culture* 25(1): 127–146.

Nakahama, Y. 2009. Cross-Linguistic Influence on Reference Introduction and Tracking in Japanese as a Second Language. *Modern Language Journal* 93(2): 241-260

Robinson, P. 1995. Task Complexity and Second Language Narrative Discourse. *Language Learning* 45(1): 99-140.

Robinson, P. 2003. Attention and Memory during SLA. *The Handbook of Second Language Acquisition,* eds. C. J. Doughty and M.H. Long, 631-678. Blackwell Publishing.

Sakamoto, T. 1993. On Acquisition Order: Japanese Particles WA and GA. *Proceedings of the 3rd Conference on Second Language Acquisition and Teaching*, 105-122. Niigata: International University of Japan.

Slobin, D. 1991. Learning to Think for Speaking: Native Language, Cognition, and Rhetorical Style. *Pragmatics* 1: 7-25.

Sohn, H. 1999. *Korean Language.* New York: Cambridge University Press.

Tashiro, H. 1995. Chuu jookyu nihongo gakushuusha no bunshoo hyoogen no mondaiten: Fushizensa wakarinikusa no gen-in o saguru [Problems in literal expressions in written discourse: Investigation of unnaturalness and incomprehensibility]. *Nihongo Kyooiku* 85: 25–37.

Watanabe, A. 1996. *Chuu Jookyuu nihongo gakushuusha no danwa tenkai.* [Discourse development of intermediate- and advanced-level Japanese learners].Tokyo: Kuroshio Publisher.

Speech Style Shifts and Teacher Identities in Korean Language Classroom Discourse

MIYUNG PARK
University of Hawai'i at Mānoa

1. Introduction

By applying the interactional approach together with the indexicality principle (Lyons 1977; Silverstein 1976), this paper examines a teacher's speech style shifts in Korean as a foreign language (KFL) classroom discourse. In particular, this paper focuses on the use of two Korean speech styles, *-e/a (-e/a?)* and *-(u)p-si-ta*, using the *-yo* form as a baseline.[1] A sequential analysis of discourse in a KFL classroom reveals that the teacher often shifts her speech styles to the *-e/a (-e/a?)* and *-(u)p-si-ta* forms during the lesson, while using the *-yo* form to deliver the content of instruction. From the tradi-

---

[1] The reason that the *-yo* form is used as a baseline is because, during classroom instruction, the teacher generally uses it when delivering the content of the lesson (Lee and Ramsey 2000). The *-yo* form is traditionally considered a polite speech style. It seems to be employed because the student audience is viewed collectively and thus is treated with greater respect.

Japanese/Korean Linguistics 19.
Edited by Ho-min Sohn, Haruko Cook, William O'Grady, Leon A. Serafim, & Sang Yee Cheon.

tional approach that assumes a strict hierarchy of speech styles, this occurrence can be seen as jumping from one extreme style to the other by moving
upwards and downwards repeatedly within the speech style system. The
question then arises as to how to explain the occurrence of speech style
shifts when a speaker is interacting with the same interlocutor(s) within a
given context. This study investigates how and why alternations among specific speech styles in Korean are utilized as a linguistic resource in the context of language learning and teaching. The teacher shifts speech styles, calling on the -e/a (-e/a?) form and the -(u)p-si-ta form as she shifts between
social identities at different points in the classroom interaction. The -e/a
(-e/a?) form indexes the teacher's personal identity, and the -(u)p-si-ta form
indexes her professional identity.

Korean speech styles are determined by sentence-final suffixes[2] attached
to verbs and adjectives. They have been traditionally characterized in terms
of social relationships and formality. Previous studies discussed the prototypical usage of each speech style (e.g. Choo 2008; Lee and Ramsey 2000;
Sohn 1999; Song 2005). It is often asserted that the -e/a (-e/a?) form is used
between intimates who feel comfortable with one another (e.g. siblings,
close friends, spouses) or when talking to someone younger (e.g. by an adult
to a child). The -(u)p-si-ta form is known as a propositive form used among
adults of similar age and status who are familiar with each other, or when
addressing someone in an inferior position (e.g. by age or social rank) with a
certain amount of courtesy. -(u)p-si-ta sounds highly formal when the proposal is directed to a general audience. Thus, the -e/a (-e/a?) form implies a
context of social closeness and informality, and the -(u)p-si-ta form signals
the use of the more formal style.

However, there is a growing understanding that Korean speech styles
serve a greater range of social functions than being formal/informal markers
or being grammatical encodings of the relative social status between interlocutors (e.g. Eun and Strauss 2004; Kim and Suh 2007; Strauss and Eun
2005). For instance, Eun and Strauss (2004) and Strauss and Eun (2005)
examined alternation between the -yo form and -(su)p-ni-ta form, based on
the status of information being delivered and the semantic features of ±
boundary. Their analysis of a large corpus of casual and public discourse
illustrates that the -yo form indexes shared information and a common
ground between speaker and addressee whereas the -(su)p-ni-ta form index-

---

[2] Sentence-final suffixes are often labeled based on their corresponding metapragmatic meaning (e.g. 'intimate', 'polite', 'deferential'). The degree of deference and formality is the main
criterion for this labeling. These labels represent the stereotypical belief that a single meaning
exists for each suffix ending while overlooking other potential meanings that are contextually
derived. In this paper, to avoid predetermining any particular metapragmatic meaning of the
-e/a form and -(u)p-si-ta form, specific labels are not applied to these forms.

es new information and distance between the two. The current study expands the knowledge of diverse speech style shifts among *-e/a (-e/a?)*, *-yo*, and *-(u)p-si-ta* forms by extending analysis of such shifts into another context, that of KFL classroom discourse. It demonstrates how mixed uses of Korean speech styles can function as an interactive strategy that enables the teacher to construct different social identities and accomplish communicative goals.

2. Data

The data of this study consist of eight hours of naturally occurring teacher-student interactions in a fourth year KFL classroom. Participants include a female Korean teacher and her twelve students. The teacher is in her mid-thirties with more than three years of Korean teaching experience at an American university. Ten of her students are Korean-American students who had some prior exposure to the language at home. The remaining two students are non-Korean students who lived in Korea for more than a year. The data is transcribed according to the conventions of Conversation Analysis (Atkinson and Heritage 1984) and romanized using the Yale system. A microanalytic qualitative research approach is used for data analysis because it clearly shows the process of speech style shifts. The teacher's speech style shifts are dependent on the topics being discussed. On-task talk is talk directly related to the academic content of the lesson assigned by the teacher whereas off-task talk is talk that is not related to the lesson (Potowski 2007). When engaging in off-task talk, the context becomes more informal and conversational, and when engaging in on-task talk, the context becomes more formal and task-oriented. In the following section, specific examples of the shifts to the *-e/a* form and the *-(u)p-si-ta* form are provided.

3. Speech Style Shifts as a Device for Displaying Social Identities

This data set shows that the teacher occasionally shifts to the *-e/a* and *-(u)p-si-ta* forms during instruction to construct her preferred social identities. The use of the *-e/a* form indexes a personal identity whereas the use of the *-(u)p-si-ta* form indexes a professional identity. When the teacher is engaged in multiple social roles during instruction, crossing the boundary between personal and professional identities is inevitable.

In the following sections, I describe the sequential environments in which shifts to the *-e/a* form occur and demonstrate that the *-e/a* form is used as a linguistic resource to express personal identity and build interpersonal solidarity with students. Showing what takes place before, within, and after the use of the *-e/a* form on a turn-by-turn basis makes it possible to thoroughly examine how shifts to the *-e/a* form are triggered and organized within interactions. The *-e/a* form tends to occur during discussions of solidarity-building topics such as when the teacher and students are sharing personal feelings with each other. In this paper, solidarity refers to degrees of intimacy and familiarity.

3.1 -e/a Form as Solidarity Marker

Excerpt (1) below presents the teacher's use of the -e/a form during off-task talk regarding homework submission. The conversation is off-task because the teacher places an on-going activity on hold and displays her affective state in reaction to students' good behavior, by stepping out of her objective teacher role. This on-going activity is to formulate sentences based on newly introduced expressions.

In order to better understand Excerpt (1), the preceding discussion should be considered. Previously, the teacher had asked her students to formulate their own sentences using the target expressions. While students were composing their sentences, the teacher reminded students to turn in their homework. This reminder seemed to puzzle the students. The teacher sensed this confusion, and, because the homework had been announced by email the day before class, she asked her students whether or not they had checked their email. Many students gave a negative response, and the teacher offered a deadline extension. Half of the students actually had finished their homework, and they requested extra credit for early homework submission. Subsequently, the teacher agreed.

Excerpt (1) below begins with the teacher telling her students that they deserve an A+ for their effort. The teacher[3] extended this praise after observing her students' enthusiastic request for extra credit in order to earn a better grade.

(1) Homework submission

1 → T: *cengmal i-pan ey-nun*   *eyiphullesu*   *nao-nun*
        really this-class in-TC   A+   get-RL
2   *salamtul-i manh-keyss-e. ta*   *eyiphullesu*
        people-NM many-will-*e*   everyone   A+
        'Many students will get an A+ in this class. A+ for everyone.'
3 SO: *eyiphullesu*
        'A+'
4 T: *eyiphullesu?*
        'A+?'
5 SO: *ani-ey.yo. ce-nun mangha-l soci-ka*   *iss-e.yo.*
        no-POL I-TC   ruin-PRL possibility-NM exist-*e.yo*
        'No, there is a possibility of ruining my chances to get a good grade.'

---

[3] In the excerpts, the capital letter T represents the teacher. The two-uppercase letters are the abbreviations for the student names. For example, Ha Young is abbreviated as HY. The abbreviation Ss means "students."

6   ((students take out their homework to submit.))
7 → T: ↑*e* *ta*   *hay-ss-canh-**a**.::: =
        oh everyone   do-PST-you see-***a***
        'Oh, everyone did his/her homework.'
8 → T: =*na soki-n-kes*   *kathun*   *kipwun-i-y**a**.::: =
        me cheat-RL-NM   like   feeling-be-***ya***
        'I feel like you cheated me.'
9   Ss: ((quietly laughing))
10→T: *ilelswu-n*   *epsnun-ke-y**a**. :::   *sok-ass-**e**.* (1.0)
        This way-TC   can't-fact be-***a***   be cheated-PST-***e***
        'It can't be this way.   I was cheated.'
11   JH: *sensayngnim, ce-nun chayk-eyta hay-ss-e.yo.*=
        teacher   I-TC   book-in   do-PST-*e.yo*
        'Teacher, I did the homework in the textbook.'
12   T: =*chayk-eyta hay-ss-e.yo?*   *okheyi.*
        Book-in   do-PST-*e.yo*   Okay
        'Did you do it in the textbook? Okay.'
13   T: *ca*   *kulemyen*   *yelepwuntul*   *mwuncang-ul*
        alright then   everyone   sentence-AC
14   *yelsimhi*   *mantul-ko*   *iss-cyo:::?*
        hard   make-and   be-*cyo*
        'Alright, then, are you trying your best to make a sentence?'

The teacher uses the *-e/a* form to praise her students' behavior (line 1). The use of the *-e/a* form along with the humorous tone frames the statement as an affect-loaded compliment rather than an objective assessment. The teacher's lexical choice of "A+" encodes her positive evaluation of students, thereby inviting social intimacy into their relationship. In line 6, the students willingly respond to their teacher's prior request to submit homework by taking out their assignment. The teacher then notices that many of the students had completed their work despite the late email notification. In lines 7–10, we see the use of the *-e/a* form again, whereby the teacher shares her affective state at a personal level in reaction to students' unexpected behavior. Her surprise is evidenced by the use of the discourse marker "*e*," the Korean equivalent of English "oh." "*E*" in Korean is used as an indicator of a change in state (Heritage 1984).

The teacher expresses her personal identity by engaging her students through conversation in a friendly, approachable, and even comical way. In lines 8 and 10, the teacher jokingly accuses students of fooling her into believing that they did not do their homework, as described in *ilelswu-n epsnun-ke-ya.::: sok-ass-e.* ("It can't be this way. I was cheated"). Attitudinal vocabulary, *sok-ass-e* ("was cheated"), is used in a cordial way to share her personal feelings with the students and not meant to be an evaluative comment. When the teacher makes playful and humorous remarks, the students' immediate response is laughter (line 9). Thus, there is a feeling of solidarity between the teacher and her students. To laugh at the humor is to be involved in the interaction (Eggins and Slade 2005). Laughter generates a frame shift (Goffman 1974, Tannen 1993). By laughing, the teacher and students co-produce a non-serious, informal frame that is on a different trajectory from explicit orientation to the task or academic content. This dialogue sequence opens up a space where the teacher effectively establishes her friendly persona, which consequently contributes to creating a relaxed atmosphere in class and rapport building with the students.

It is also important to note that the shift to the *-e/a* form occurs along with other affect-loaded linguistic elements, such as the elongation of the sentence enders (*"a"*), the use of the plain form of the first person pronoun (*"na"*), and the informal content of the talk. First, the elongation of the sentence ender *"a"* is visible in the teacher's statements (lines 7, 8, and 10). This signals a casual, ongoing conversation supported by the teacher's cheerful and friendly attitude. In this off-task interaction, the teacher uses the plain form of the first person pronoun (*"na"*) in line 8 to refer to herself. In Korean, different personal pronouns reflect relative social hierarchy between the speaker and the addressee (Sohn 1999). When talking to the students during on-task talk, the teacher uses the first person humble form *ce* (*"I"*) to show greater respect toward students or *sensayngnim* (*"teacher"*) to indicate her role as a teacher. Therefore, her use of the first person plain form *na* (*"I"*), a pronoun used when addressing a child or a close friend, is highly noticeable. By selecting the use of this particular pronoun, the teacher brings herself closer to her students and creates a relationship of familiarity.

The teacher closes the off-task dialogue on homework submission and shifts back to the *-yo* form to resume the main activity by asking whether or not they are working on their sentences (line 13–14). Here, the teacher creates a more distanced and objective stance while projecting herself as someone responsible for checking students' performance on the ongoing task.

Another example of the shift to the *-e/a* form is observed in Excerpt (2). Excerpt (2) is taken from an off-task conversation on a student's personal matter. Here, the teacher requests a student, JW, to show his new haircut to the class.

(2) Haircut
　　1　T:　*ca*　　*kuntey*　　　*yelepwuntul,*　*swuep sicak-haki*　*ceney*
　　　　　　Alright　by the way　everyone　　　class start-NOM　before
　　2　　　　*JW-i*　　　*meli-cal-l-ass-nun-ke*
　　　　　　JW-NM　　hair-cut-PST-RN-NM
　　3 →　　　*hanpen*　　*po-y-e-cwu-l-kka?*

```
        one time    see-PAS-give-PRS-a
        'Alright, everyone. JW, before getting started, would you show your
        new haircut?'
4   JW:  a:::::
         'ah'
5   CH:  po-ko       siph-e.yo.
         see-NOM    want-e.yo
         'I want to see.'
6 → T:   ku-cyo?          wuli i-kes-to      kukello-ha-l-kka?
         that-cyo         we this-one-also that-do-PRS-kka
         'Right? Should we also do this (extra credit)?'
7   SO:  Extra credit. Give him one point. hheh heh heh
8   Ss:  ((quietly laughing))
9 → T:   kulehkey-ha-l-kka?
         That way-do-PRS-kka
         'Shall we do that?'
10  JW:  It's not worth a point.
11  T:   ((looking at JW wearing a hat)) °hanpen pesepo-ki° silh-e.yo?
                             one time take off-NOM   dislike-e.yo
         'Don't you at least want to try taking off your hat?'
12       (1.0)
13 →T:   kep       an-cwu-l-kkey.         twayss-e.yo. twayss-e. hheh heh
         pressure not-give-PRS-kkey     fine-e.yo     fine-e    hheh heh
         'I won't pressure you. That's fine. That's fine. huh huh'
14  JW:  hahahaha
```

The teacher orients the class attention toward a student's new haircut by addressing the entire class, as in *yelepwun-tul* ("everyone") in line 1. Also, in order to draw students' attention effectively, she uses other discourse markers in sentence-initial position, such as the transition marker, *ca* ("alright"), and the contrastive marker, *kuntey* ("by the way"). Then, the teacher gently asks JW to take off his hat and present his new hairstyle to the class. Here, the teacher uses the *-e/a* form to show her friendliness and involve JW more personally in the conversation. Because a request is a speech act that may be considered to be imposing on others, the use of the *-e/a* form with the interrogative sentence helps mitigate its imposition. By engaging a student in a dialogue on seemingly unimportant daily subjects in a casual way, the teacher presents her role as a member of the classroom community. She shows interest in learning more about students' daily lives and chatting with students about common life events.

Upon hearing this request, the student JW produces a minimal expression, *a:::::* ("ah:::::"), with sound stretching so as to indicate his hesitance to participate in that action. In line 5, CH joins the discussion pertaining to the haircut by telling the teacher that she also wants to see JW's new haircut.

Then, in line 6, the teacher echoes with a tag question and invites agreement from the class. However, up to this point, JW remains silent and does not provide any personal opinions. The teacher attempts to encourage JW to show his new haircut by revealing her willingness to give him extra credit while shifting back to the -*e/a* form (line 6). The teacher uses the first person plural pronoun, *wuli* ("we"), with the -*e/a* form to convey relatively inclusive and friendly feelings to the students. By including her students in the decision making process, the teacher diminishes the power difference and emphasizes shared membership and values. In response to the teacher's attempt to negotiate by granting extra credit to JW, SO playfully answers by asking her to give one point to JW (line 7). SO starts laughing and other students immediately respond by laughing. JW states that showing his haircut is not worth a point in line 10, and his reluctance to show it is apparent.

In line 11, the teacher confirms JW's reluctance to show his haircut by asking a question in the -*yo* form, °*hanpen pesepo-ki*° *silhe-yo?* ("Don't you at least want to try taking off your hat?"). Here, the teacher reformulates her initial question uttered in lines 1–3 by turning the positive question into a negative. This reformulation of the question still does not elicit any response from JW. JW does not use any words to make his rejection explicit, but, rather, stays silent. This silence is a display of discomfort and noncompliance. Due to lack of collaboration from JW, the teacher constructs a disengagement sequence by saying *kep an-cwu-l-kkey. twayss-e.yo. twayss-e. huhhh* ("I won't pressure you. That's fine. That's fine."). JW engages in the next turn with laughter. This provides insight into JW's awareness that the teacher wants to stop pressuring him.

To summarize this section, the use of the -*e/a* form is employed during off-task talk for solidarity-building purposes. Shifts to the -*e/a* form demonstrate broader social relationships that go beyond the contextually constrained student and teacher roles. The -*e/a* form tends to occur while the teacher is closely involved in interactions such as sharing feelings or commenting on students' personal matters. These rapport-building conversations lessen the seriousness of the classroom conversation and enable the teacher to reveal her personal identity. During rapport-building talk, the teacher keeps the lines of conversation open and takes on an interactive role as a facilitator and a member of the classroom community rather than as a sole knowledge transmitter. Solidarity-building speech is indicated not only by the use of the -*e/a* form but also by careful choice of other appropriate linguistic devices that convey various aspects of her personal identity (Geyer 2008). Using intimate language along with being personable effectively creates a friendly and social environment for learning.

3.2 -*(u)p-si-ta* Form as Organizational Marker

This section examines the use of the *-(u)p-si-ta* form. The *-(u)p-si-ta* form is a propositive form equivalent to the English expression "let's." It consists of three morphemes: the addressee honorific (*-(u)p*), the requestive (*-si*), and the propositive marker (*-ta*) (Sohn 1999). The form is used to invite someone to participate in a joint action, usually those who have lower status (e.g. by age or social rank). When the *-(u)p-si-ta* form is used in the context of a KFL classroom, it designates the boundaries of on-task topics or sequences within the same topic and conveys the teacher's professional identity.

Consider the next example, in which the *-(u)p-si-ta* form functions to open a new discussion topic. Excerpt (3) continues from where Excerpt (2) ends. Here, the teacher closes the off-task talk about a student's haircut and launches a new on-task topic about the *hanlyu* phenomenon ("Korean wave"). *Hanlyu* literally means Korean wave; it refers to the surge of popularity of South Korean culture throughout the world.

(3) *Hanlyu* (Korean wave)

16	T:	*ca*	*kulemyen*	*hanlyu-ey*	*tayhayse*	
		Alright	then	Korean wave-in	about	
17 →		*hanpen*	*hay-po-**p-si-ta**.*			
		one time	do-try-**p-si-ta**			
		'Alright, then, let's try talking about *hanlyu* now.'				
18		*hanlyu-ka*		*mwen-ci*	*al-ko iss-e.yo?*	
		Korean wave-NM		what-NOM	know-and exist-e.yo	
		'Do you know what *hanlyu* is?'				
19	SO:	yes				
20	JW:	Korean [wave				
21	JD:	[Korean wave				
22	T:	*hanlyu*	*yelphwung*			
		'Korean wave popularity'				
23	T:	*yekise han-un*	*hankwuk-i-la-nun*	*mal-i-cyo?*		
		Here han-TC	Korea-be-DC-RN	meaning-be-cyo		
		'Here *han* means Korea. Right?'				
		((lines omitted))				
29	T:	*kuleh-key*	*ha-myen toy-ko.*			
		That way-AD	do-if okay-and			
		'Having said that'				
30	T:	*um::: objective-lul*	*haksupmokphyo-lul*			
		well objectives-ACC	objectives-ACC			
31 →		*hanpen*	*ilke-po-**p-si-ta**.* =			
		one time	read-see-**p-si-ta**			
		'Well, let's read the objectives.'				
32		=*payksipil-ccok il.il.il ey HY-i-ka hanpen ilk-e-po-l-kka-yo?*				
		111-page	111	eh HY-NM one time	read-INF-try-Q-yo	
		'In page 111, would you read, HY?'				

The teacher introduces a new lesson topic on *hanlyu* by shifting to the

-(u)p-si-ta form. The shift to the *-(u)p-si-ta* form indicates the opening of on-task talk, signaling the teacher's intent to move ahead to the next phase of instruction. The *-(u)p-si-ta* form indexes the teacher's objective attitude and professional persona because it indicates the teacher's attempt to organize her instruction by controlling the flow of information. There is a social distance between the teacher and her students. The shift to the *-(u)p-si-ta* form occurs along with other contextualization cues (Gumperz 1992) in the utterance-initial position: *ca* ("alright") and *kulemyen* ("then"). These discourse markers work together with the *-(u)p-si-ta* form to help the students recognize a discourse boundary where a new on-task topic starts.

The teacher continues with instruction in line 18 by asking a question that assesses students' background knowledge. This question is delivered with the *-yo* form. SO provides a minimal positive confirmation in English, "yes." In lines 20–21, JW and JD answer what *hanlyu* means by saying "Korean wave" in overlap. While the teacher is transitioning from off-task talk to on-task talk, there is a change in the students' participation pattern. The cheerful and playful behavior gradually becomes calm and serious. Upon shifting to on-task talk, the class directs their quiet attention to the teacher's directions and answers her questions. No noise or side conversations between students are heard. From line 24 to line 28, which are omitted for the sake of space, the teacher delivers information on the definition of *hanlyu* in relation to the semantic components of its Chinese characters, with the persistent use of the *-yo* form. Here, she indicates her role as an expert on the topic. After the explanation, the teacher closes the sequence of the activity in line 29 by saying *kuleh-key ha-myen toy-ko* ("having said that").

The teacher progresses to the next stage of the activity, reading lesson objectives, by shifting back to the *-(u)p-si-ta* form in line 31. The teacher uses the *-(u)p-si-ta* form to have the students engage in reading the objectives together. The teacher possibly uses the *-(u)p-si-ta* form here instead of a declarative sentence to effectively suggest that both the speaker (herself) and the hearers (her students) are engaged in a joint action of moving onto the next stage of the activity. The *-(u)p-si-ta* form can successfully denote specific instructional focus because the delivery of instruction is usually characterized by the *-yo* form and therefore the use of *-(u)p-si-ta* is highly noticeable. In line 32, the teacher shifts back to the *-yo* form while nominating an individual student, HY, to read the objectives out loud for the class. As shown in Excerpt (3), by using the *-(u)p-si-ta* form as a formulaic expression, the teacher fulfills her social function of being a professional language teacher. The *-(u)p-si-ta* form serves as a useful interactional technique to deliver step-by-step directions that students are asked to follow. Because the *-(u)p-si-ta* form clearly highlights the new content to be learned, the students' attention to the new instruction is heightened.

The following excerpt contains another example of the -*(u)p-si-ta* form used in negotiating a topic shift. Explicitly stating a topic shift from one discussion topic to another, the teacher enables the students to pay attention to the structures of the activities and reduces the possibility of misunderstanding of what exactly is being discussed. In the conversation below, the teacher tells the students the examination date and moves onto the new discussion topic, the World Cup.

(4) World Cup

1	T:	*kuliko*	*tto*	*ha-l-kes-un*		*swuyoilnal yelepwuntul sihem*	
		And	also	do-PRS-thing-NM		Wednesday everyone	exam

2 *chi-nikka kongpwu hay-se o-ko, al-keyss-e.yo?*
  take-because study do-and come-and know-think-e.yo
  'And another thing to do is since you are taking an exam on Wednesday, come prepared. Okay?'

3 Ss: *ney*
    'yes.'

4 → T: *okwa hanpen phye po-**p-si-ta**. sakwa*
    Lesson 5 once open look-**p-si-ta** lesson 4
    'Let's turn to lesson 5. Lesson 4.

5 *ca weltukhep-i encey ilena-ss-e.yo?*
   alright World Cup-NM when happen-PST-e.yo
   'Alright, when did World Cup happen?'

6 (1.0)

7 *encey kaychoy toy-ess-e.yo?*
   when take place-PST-e.yo
   'When did it take place?'

8 JD: *icheninyen*
    '2002'

The teacher reminds her students of the upcoming examination date in order to ensure her students' adequate preparation (lines 1–2). After the students' acknowledgement in line 3, the teacher shifts to the -*(u)p-si-ta* form to open a new discussion on the World Cup by saying *okwa hanpen phye po-p-si-ta. sakwa* ("Let's turn to lesson 5. Lesson 4."). Using this form, the teacher unites herself with her students to collectively propose a course of action. The use of the -*(u)p-si-ta* form in an on-task context frames the utterance as an official statement (see Geyer 2008) and reinforces the institutional student-teacher roles. By shifting to the -*(u)p-si-ta* form, the teacher delivers instruction in a more formal and straightforward way. The teacher's statements marked by the -*(u)p-si-ta* form contain no hedging devices or obvious pauses. The teacher expresses her professional identity by remaining objective, disengaged, and rational in dealing with subject matter. During the on-task talk, the teacher controls most of the speech turns by asking the class questions and by selecting specific students to respond. The ways in which the turns are determined indicate a formal institutional context where the power differential is co-constructed by the teacher and students.

Once the teacher launches a new topic in the *-(u)p-si-ta* form, she shifts back to the *-yo* form to continue with her instruction in lines 5–7. Because the propositive *-(u)p-si-ta* form has a function of engaging someone in an action, it is often used in formulaic expressions such as *hap-si-ta* ("Let's do…") and *pop-si-ta* ("Let's take a look at…"). These expressions are formulaic because they typically occur in a specific sequence in classroom interaction and are linked to particular functions of organizing instruction.

In summary, the teacher's shifts to the *-(u)p-si-ta* form tend to emerge when there is a transition between topics or within activity sequences. This linguistic resource provides the students with knowledge of the boundaries of the topics being discussed. These boundaries are essential; they help students to properly follow instructions and to understand what is going on in class. In my data, the *-(u)p-si-ta* form is only found during on-task talk. This means that the *-(u)p-si-ta* form is not used to share topics beyond the on-task subject matter. As shown in Excerpts (3) and (4), the teacher's objective and professional identity is realized not only by using the *-(u)p-si-ta* form but also by deciding the topic of conversation and the structure of the activity carried out during the lesson. This leaves little possibility for negotiation on what is being discussed. Because the teacher has control over topic management (Edwards 1981), the students seem to understand both what they are supposed to be doing and the importance of keeping the teacher's talk free of interruptions.

4. Conclusion

A sequential analysis of Korean language classroom discourse reveals the complex indexical relationships between speech styles shifts and construction of social identities. The teacher creatively utilizes different speech styles to construct her social identities and achieve her interactional goals (Cook, 2008). For example, the teacher tends to use the *-e/a* form in more emotionally laden utterances to display her personal identity whereas she tends to use the *-(u)p-si-ta* form in a more formal context to display a professional identity. These two dimensions of the teacher's identity are equally significant in the classroom environment. Being personable to students helps to mediate tensions that build up during academic engagement and provides a relaxed social atmosphere. Having a professional identity helps the teacher to organize topics/activities and establish herself as a leader in the classroom. Regardless of the teacher's shifts to a variety of speech styles, the students typically maintained the use of the *-yo* form to present their institutional student roles. The *-yo* form, a form used in contexts where politeness is called for, is motivated by the dominant institutional ideology that affirms power dynamics in teacher/student relationships.

It is also important to point out that language is merely one of the semiotic resources that create social identities. Bodily conduct, such as gesture or gaze, provides another essential dimension of contextual information, and therefore should be taken into account in future discussions in order to grasp a deeper and more holistic understanding of speech style shifts. Further study should look at the alternation of speech styles in a wider range of classroom situations.

References

Choo, M. 2008. *Using Korean: A Guide to Contemporary Usage.* Cambridge, UK: Cambridge University Press.

Cook, H. 2008. Style Shifts in Japanese Academic Consultations. *Style Shifting in Japanese*, eds. K. Jones and T. Ono, 9–38. Amsterdam: John Benjamins.

Eggins, S. and Slade, D. 2005. *Analysing Casual Conversation.* London: Equinox Publishing.

Eun, J. and Strauss, S. 2004. The Primacy of Information Status in the Alternation between Korean Deferential and Polite Forms in Public Discourse. *Language Sciences* 26: 251– 272.

Geyer, N. 2008. Interpersonal Functions of Style Shift: The Use of Plain and Masu Forms in Faculty Meetings. *Style Shifting in Japanese*, eds. K. Jones and T. Ono, 39–70. Amsterdam: John Benjamins.

Goffman, E. 1974. *Frame Analysis.* New York: Harper & Row.

Gumperz, J. 1992. Contextualization and Understanding. *Rethinking Context: Language as an Interactive Phenomenon*, eds. A. Duranti and C. Goodwin, 229–252. Cambridge, UK: Cambridge University Press.

Heritage, J. 1984. A Change-of-state Token and Aspects of Its Sequential Placement. *Structures of Social Action. Studies in Conversation Analysis,* eds. J. M. Atkinson and J. Heritage, 299–345. Cambridge, UK: Cambridge University Press.

Atkinson, J. M. and Heritage, J. 1984. *Structures of Social Action: Studies in Conversational Analysis.* Cambridge, UK: Cambridge University Press.

Kim, K-H. and Suh, K. H. 2007. Style Shift in Korean Pedagogical Discourse. *The Sociolinguistic Journal of Korea* 15(2): 1–29.

Lee, I. and Ramsey, S. 2000. *The Korean Language.* New York: State University of New York.

Lyons, J. 1977. *Semantics.* Cambridge, UK: Cambridge University Press.

Potowski, K. 2007. *Language and Identity in a Dual Immersion School.* Clevedon, UK: Multilingual Matters.

Silverstein, M. 1976. Shifters, Linguistic Categories, and Cultural Description. *Meaning in Anthropology*, eds. K. Basso and H. Selby, 11–56. Albuquerque: University of New Mexico Press.

Sohn, H.-M. 1999. *The Korean Language*. Cambridge, UK: Cambridge University Press.

Song, J. J. 2005. *The Korean Language: Structure, Use, and Context*. London and New York: Routledge.

Strauss, S. and Eun, J. 2005. Indexicality and Honorific Speech Style Choice in Korean. *Linguistics* 43: 251–651.

Tannen, D. 1993. *Framing in Discourse*. New York: Oxford University Press.

The Manifestation of Intrasentential Code-Switching in Japanese Hip Hop

NATSUKO TSUJIMURA
Indiana University

STUART DAVIS
Indiana University

1. Introduction

The use of English has been a typical phenomenon in Japanese pop music for the past several decades, and it is particularly prevalent in Japanese hip hop. For the most part, however, the use of English has been restricted to the borrowing of words or phrases. This includes words and phrases that have not yet been nativized for general use. For example, ロマンス (romance), ラブソング(love song), and フリスキー(frisky), all appear in hip hop lyrics, ranging from solidly nativized to not yet nativized. As Manabe (2006) observes, Japanese rappers often use English interjections such as "yes, yes, y'all", "check it out", "Oh yeah", "oh no", and "all right", to name a few. There are additionally some instances in which English is used innovatively for the specific purpose of rhyming (Tsujimura and Davis 2009).

Japanese/Korean Linguistics 19.
Edited by Ho-min Sohn, Haruko Cook, William O'Grady, Leon A. Serafim, & Sang Yee Cheon.
Copyright © 2011, CSLI Publications

The innovative way of using English for rhyming purpose can be illustrated by the rapper Dragon Ash. The underlined parts in (1) are intended to rhyme, and the last rhyming unit, "Don't stop," is altered in its pronunciation so that it rhymes with the remaining three underlined parts.

(1) saa kakenukeyoo ze <u>dooshita</u>
     yuri no moto tsudotta <u>dooshitachi</u>
     yo ima dakara koso <u>tooshidashi</u>
     Don't stop tomo ni mezasu eikoo e ikoo

In our previous work (Tsujimura and Davis 2009), we discussed how the notion of rhyming, which is absent in Japanese traditional poetry, has been adopted and adapted into Japanese hip hop lyrics. We specifically refer to such rhyming as "moraic assonance". This is because moraic heads (vowels, coda nasals, and geminates) in rhyming words need to be identical although accompanying onset consonants can differ or need not be present.

A very interesting manifestation of the use of English in hip hop lyrics world-wide is code-switching phenomena as implemented by bilingual rappers. It has been argued that code-switching plays an important role as an identity marker, although the identity issue will not be discussed in this paper. An example comes from a Quebec French rap group (Sarkar 2009). The underlined words in (2) are in Quebec French.

(2) J'check <u>Rob</u>: 'What up dog?'
     -- 'What up yo! Shit, <u>les rues sont</u> fucked up!
     Enough talk. Check <u>le reste du</u> squad.
     <u>On</u> set <u>un</u> get <u>ce soir</u>. Peace. Hang up the phone. (Sakar 2009: 145)

This is a particularly interesting example in that it illustrates intrasentential code-switching, in which within a single clause, both English and French words appear with respective native pronunciations. This contrasts with intersentential code-switching, in which all the elements in a single clause are from one language, but there can be language switching between clauses. In our discussion of Japanese hip hop, we will focus more on intrasentential code switching.

In the remainder of this paper, we will examine the nature of intrasentential code-switching as exhibited by Japanese-English bilingual hip hop musicians. We shall begin by giving a brief introduction to the research devoted to code-switching phenomena in general. After outlining biographical information of a few bilingual musicians, we will present examples of the types of code-switching that are manifested by these artists. We will finally discuss how our data relate to previous work on Japanese-English code-switching.

2. Background

In general, in considering linguistic aspects of code-switching, the primary goal of the theoretical models "is to predict which utterances containing code switches are well formed or not, and to explain why certain kinds of mixture are either permitted or blocked." (Winford 2003: 126) Probably the most influential model of code-switching is the Matrix Language-Frame (MLF) model of Myers-Scotton (1993, 2001). The MLF model is based on the assumption that one of the languages involved in code-switching sets the grammatical frame for the sentence or, more accurately, the clause. The language that sets the grammatical frame is referred to as Matrix Language (ML). The other language involved in code-switching is called Embedded Language (EL). As will be seen, it is sometimes very difficult to discern what constitutes the ML in Japanese-English code-switching.

When a matrix language sets the grammatical frame of a clause with code-switching, certain function or system morphemes must be in the ML. Specifically, the type of function morphemes that must be in the ML are agreement markers and case markers. These are morphemes that depend on grammatical information outside their maximal projection for their realization. For instance, "John-ga eats" (John-Nom eats) or "Taroo-ga taberu-s" (Taro-Nom eat-3Psg) are expected not to occur since the Nominative Case particle *–ga* and the 3rd person agreement marker *–s* are relevant function morphemes within the same clause, but are in different languages. "The kodoo" (the-heartbeat), on the other hand, is acceptable because the determiner "the" does not depend on grammatical information outside the NP for its realization. Content morphemes, which can include certain particles like postpositions and perhaps the topic marker, could either be in the matrix language or the embedded language.

The next theoretical issue is distinguishing between code-switching and borrowing. This is especially important when there is only one word within a clause that is realized in the other language, i.e. EL. According to Myers-Scotton, a single word from the EL constitutes code-switching, and not borrowing, if it is morphosyntactically integrated into the ML or if it is a bare form. MacSwan and Colina (to appear), in contrast, claim that the difference between borrowing and code-switching should be based on the phonology. In code-switching, words display the phonology of the source language whereas in borrowing the pronunciation of the source-language word is modified to fit the phonology of the other language. To illustrate the distinction proposed by MacSwan and Colina, the Spanish-English example in (3) serves the purpose (MacSwan and Colina, to appear).

(3) Hablamos de   mi **b**ook yesterday
    we talked about my

Based on natural and experimental data from Spanish-English bilingual code-switchers, they show that the first consonant of the word "book" in (3) is always pronounced as a stop [b] as in English and crucially not as the fricative [β], which would be the case if it were borrowed into Spanish in this context.

In our observation, we generally agree with the importance of the phonological criteria for determining Japanese-English code-switching. A specific example is taken from the dual use of the word "love", as is demonstrated by the Japanese bilingual singer Hikaru Utada in her song, First Love. In this song, she pronounces the phrase "love song" as a borrowing—ラブ ソング—whereas elsewhere in the song, she pronounces the word "love" as English, which would then be considered code-switching.

3. Observations

Our observations of code-switching in Japanese hip hop lyrics come from examinations of three bilingual groups, Heartsdales, RIZE, and m-flo. Heartsdales are a two-sister group, Yumi and Emi Sugiyama. They were born in Japan, but moved to the US in their early childhood. They spent 14 years in New York before returning to Japan. The main artist of RIZE, Jesse, has a Japanese father and a western mother. He grew up in Japan, but attended international schools. M-flo is a duo of a Korean-Japanese and a Japanese, both of whom attended an international school in Tokyo and then received post-secondary education in the US before returning to Japan. Jesse in RIZE and m-flo each collaborate with other bilingual artists.

We now present some of the types of code-switching that we found in these bilingual hip hop groups. We will restrict ourselves to only a few examples of various types. Note also that although we tried to classify our observations into various types, the classification may not always be straightforward. In all our examples below, Japanese words are italicized.

First, the English determiners with Japanese nouns and vice versa are well attested, as is illustrated in (4).

(4) a. feel the *kodoo*   [Heartsdales]
          heartbeat

  b. make a *zaisan*   [Heartsdales]
          fortune

  c. *namae* with the *kashiramoji*   [m-flo]
          name   initial (letter)

  d. I push it to the *genkai*   [RIZE]
          limitation

These examples show that the determiner *the* and the article *a* appear with Japanese nouns, and code-switching is detected within a noun phrase. A reverse situation of this is also observed, as in (5).

(5) a.   *sono* love story *misete hoshii*   [m-flo]
          that   show want
     b.   *sonna*   hot boy-*wa* *dare*?   [Heartsdales]
          that kind of   -Top who

In these examples, Japanese demonstrative words like *sono* and *sonna* are immediately followed by English nouns. Crucially *love story* and *hot boy* are both pronounced as English phrases. Although it needs to be confirmed by additional data, it seems that when the determiner is in English, the ML of the clause tends to be English, while when the determiner is in Japanese, the ML tends to be Japanese. This is consistent with Myers-Scotton's original theory of code-switching (1993) in which all functional morphemes are predicted to be in the ML.

Winford (2003: 163) has observed that bilinguals often resort to the strategy of fronting or dislocation to facilitate code-switching. This is attested by our data. We observe a number of right-dislocated phrases as the target of code-switching. This is consistent with Manabe's (2006) observation that Japanese hip hop lyrics amply make use of right-dislocated "fragments," leading her to the term "broken syntax." (p. 9) To illustrate, consider the phrases in (6).

(6) a.   *asobitai*   with you   [Heartsdales]
          want to play
     b.   flow-*wa tokuchuu*   for you   [m-flo]
          -Top special order
     c.   *hikaru* like the *taiyoo*   [RIZE]
          shine   the sun

(6a) contains the Japanese verb, which suggests that the ML is Japanese. We should then expect that the PP *with you* should appear to the left of the verb, as would be the general word order pattern in Japanese. The position of *with you* in this example, thus, amounts to an instance of right dislocation. The other two examples are similar.

Myers-Scotton discusses the cases to which she refers as "double-morphology", in which "a switched item is marked simultaneously by an EL and ML system morpheme expressing the same meaning" (Winford 2003: 148). Her examples, however, only seem to show bound morphemes as in the Lingala-French example below, where plurality is marked both by the Lingala prefix *ba-* and French suffix *–s*.

(7) <u>ba</u>-jeunne-<u>s</u>   "young people"

While we do not find double-marking that is achieved strictly in the form of bound morphemes as in (7), we see quite a few instances of this phenomenon in our data, even more widely than at the morpheme level. To start with, the examples in (8) show double-marking between two independent words or between a preposition and a postposition.

(8) a. every time *me-ga   au   tabi*   [Heartsdales]
             eye-Nom meet every time
     b. *sukina koto*   do it   [m-flo]
             what you like
     c. *karada-ga*   it's breaking apart   [m-flo]
             body-Nom
     d. so fly with Ryoohei-*to*   [m-flo]
                -with

(8a) exhibits repeated independent words with identical meaning from each language, *every time* and *tabi*, consistent with the word order of each language. In (8b) and (8c), the pronoun *it* refers back to the Japanese words, *koto* and *karada*, respectively. (8d) involves the commitative marking by both the English preposition *with* and the Japanese postposition *to*. This type of example is also noted by Nishimura (1986) in her work on Japanese-English code-switching. Muysken (2000: 104-105) further notes similar examples in Finnish-English code-switching suggesting that this type of code-switching occurs only from a VO language to an OV language.

The examples in (9) show double-marking between an English free morpheme and a Japanese bound morpheme.

(9) a. Please *norina*   [RIZE]
             get on
     b. let's *sawag-oo*   [m-flo]
             make a racket-let's

In (9a) *na* in *norina* is an imperative ending and *please* has an imperative force, resulting in double-marking. In (9b) English *let's* is repeated by a Japanese verbal suffix *–oo*.

Finally, the example in (10) is a particularly interesting case since it can arguably be interpreted as double-marking at a deeper level.

(10)   I drift *yuraari yurayura*   [m-flo]

In lexical-semantic terms, the English verb *drift* lexicalizes motion and manner in the sense of Talmy (1985). It is the manner component that is doubly marked by the Japanese mimetic words *yuraari* and *yurayura*, both describe drifting manner. (See also Muysken (2000: 289-91) for semantic doubling in code-mixing.)

It is interesting to note that double-marking of the types shown above has also been reported to occur in the code-switching speech of bilingual children. The sample speech of English-Japanese bilingual children in (11) is taken from Patschke et al. (2001).

(11) a.   [When I was trying to *chakuriku-suru-toki*] I always have to get weight and then I could go down.

    b.   um…well I thought [*gojikan-me ga ne, taiku to omottandayo ne* but it was *ongaku* and I always take my…

    c.

In (11a) the English word *when* is repeated by its Japanese counterpart *toki*; and in (11b) the English verb *thought* corresponds to the Japanese *omotta(ndayo)*.

The rappers make innovative use of idiomatic expressions through code-switching. We mean here that an idiomatic phrase from one language may incorporate an element from the other language. Some examples that illustrate this point are given in (12).

(12) a.   make a *zaisan*   [Heartsdales]
            fortune

    b.   signed, sealed, *deribarii*   [m-flo]
              delivery

    c.   *dakara itsumo* cats love this like I'm *hurisukii*   [m-flo]
        so   always   frisky

(12b) comes from the English phrase *signed, sealed, and delivered*, but we analyze the change from delivered to *deribarii* to be intended to achieve rhyming with *jealousy*, which appears in the neighboring lyric line. As this example shows, sometimes in hip hop code-switching, word choice and pronunciation are influenced by rhyme. (12c) presents another intriguing case. The English word *frisky* in the matrix frame is nonetheless pronounced in the Japanese manner *hurisukii*. This pronunciation achieves a rhyme with *yamitsuki* "addicted" in the neighboring lyric line in a way that the English pronunciation *frisky* would not.

We have further observed some instances in which bound morphemes in one language are affixed to words or phrases of another language. This is illustrated in (13).

(13) a. the *ryuusei*'s flowing this year
      shooting star
   b. I believe that *subete*'s *guuzen ja nai*
             all   accident isn't
   d. It's all I got-*na yume*
               dream
   d. *moo*-speed   [m-flo]
      extra

In (13a) and (13b) the English *is* is contracted to the preceding Japanese word. Note that *is* and *ja nai* in (13b) can be considered another example of double-marking although the latter is a copula that is negatively conjugated. In (13c) while *–na* is commonly used for a loanword modifier for a Japanese noun, as in *rich-na hito* "a rich person", *-na* in this phrase is cliticized onto *all I got*. (13d) has the Sino-Japanese morpheme *moo* prefixed to the English *speed*, which the artist indeed pronounces as an English word.

Finally, code-switching in the comparative and superlative structures is not very common across musicians, but the examples from Heartsdales in (14) are quite intriguing.

(14) a. I take *otona yori* dirty *yanchana* boy
           adult than   playful
   b. *shikamo*   we the most *ikareta kyoodai*
      moreover   crazy sisters
   c. make you want more *jirasu*
                 ansy

(14a) takes English as ML, parallel to *I take a boy dirtier and more playful than adults*, but the comparative phrase, which would have been placed to the right of *boy* instead appears to the left of it by following the Japanese comparative construction pattern. The other two examples combine the English superlative and comparative markers, *most* and *more*, with Japanese descriptive expressions. While this type of switch can be accounted for by most theories of code-switching, what would be unexpected is the attachment of the bound comparative and superlative suffixes *–er* and *–est* to Japanese words. Such combination is not attested in our data.

As a note in passing, the English of (14b) and (14c) display characteristics of African American Vernacular English (AAVE). *We the most* shows copula absence and *make you want more* shows lack of 3rd person agreement *–s*. All our bilingual hip hop artists exhibit both pronunciation features and morphosyntactic features of AAVE.

4. Discussion

As Winford (2003) has stated, the goal of linguistic models of code-switching is to predict which utterances with code-switching are permitted and which are blocked. Myers-Scotton (2001) seems to make a specific prediction for Japanese-English code-switching that on the surface a clause with an English verb should not have a subject that is marked with *–ga* nor an object marked with *–o*. This prediction seems to be verified in the bilingual hip hop lyrics that we have examined. However, what we observe are various ways of avoiding this pattern. Consider the examples in (15).

(15) a.   *karada-ga* it's breaking apart   [m-flo]
            body-Nom
      b.   *sono yukue-wa*   nobody know   [m-flo]
            that whereabout-Top
      c.   I spray *kashi*   [Heartsdales]
            lyrics
      d.   sunset-*o*   check *shite*   [m-flo]
            -Acc   do

In (15a) we find a subject NP marked with Nominative *–ga* with an English verb, but the subject is repeated in the form of English pronoun *it*. In (15b) the object NP *sono yukue* is topicalized. In (15c) the object NP is not marked with the Accusative marker *–o*. The last example, (15d), looks as though the English verb, *check*, takes an o-marked object, but the Japanese light verb *suru* puts the sentence frame in Japanese. All these indicate strategies for avoiding the pattern in which Japanese *ga*-marked subject and *o*-marked object directly appear with independent English verbs.

An interesting proposal is made by Azuma (2001) on Japanese code-switching. Although we do not detail his theory here, he predicts first that English code switched adjectives require *–na* suffixation so as to make them nominal; and second, that English code switched verbs take *suru* so that they are like verbal nouns. We examined these predictions with our data. Considering *na*-suffixation, most of our data on English code switched adjectives support Azuma's hypothesis, as the first group of examples in (16) show. However, there are some instances, where the English adjectives do not take *–na*, as the second group of examples illustrate although this pattern is far fewer than the first.

(16) a. X-na Y

  kininaru kimi-wa hot hot-*na* B-Boy   [Heartsdales]
  kimi-no tooboe sexy-*na baion noboru sora*   [RIZE]
  it's all I got-*na yume*   [m-flo]
  b. X-∅ Y
  cool *midashinami*
  red *kaapetto*   [m-flo]

Concerning code-switching of English verbs, as the examples in (17) indicate, they always take *suru*, as Azuma would predict.

(17) a. *kono* vibe-*no mama* ride <u>*shitai desu*</u> to the breakadown
  b. *sabishigariya-na* love, escape <u>*shimasu*</u>
  c. *sukina mono* buy <u>*shite*</u>   [m-flo]

The underlined words in (17) are morphological variants of the verb *suru*. We have no examples of English verb form with Japanese verbal inflection.

5. Summary

To sum up, we have presented a preliminary examination of code-switching phenomenon in Japanese hip hop lyrics. Most of the aspects of code-switching that we discussed in this paper are consistent with what various theories predict, and with what has been said about Japanese code-switching. Nonetheless, we find phenomena in our data that have not been given extended discussions, such as the use of double marking. In future research, focus should be placed on issues such as how various theories of code switching pertain to our data, how rhyme interacts with code-switching, and how bilingual artists use AAVE.

References

Azuma, S. 2001. Functional Categories and Codeswitching in Japanese/English. *Codeswitching Worldwide II*, ed. R. Jacobson, 91-103. Berlin: Mouton deGruyter.

MacSwan, J. and Colina, S. to appear. Some Consequences of Language Design:Codeswitching and the PF Interface. *Grammatical Theory and Bilingual Code switching*, ed. J. MacSwan. Cambridge, MA: MIT Press.

Manabe, N. 2006. Globalization and Japanese Creativity: Adaptations of JapaneseLanguage to Rap. *Ethnomusicology* 50: 1-36.

Muysken, P. 2000. *Bilingual Speech: A Typology of Code Mixing*. Cambridge: Cambridge University Press.

Myers-Scotton, C. 1993. *Duelling Languages: Grammatical Structure in Code-Switching*. Oxford: Oxford University Press.

Myers-Scotton, C. 2001. The Matrix Language Frame Model: Developments and Responses. *Codeswitching Worldwide II*, ed. R. Jacobson, 23-58. Berlin: Mouton de Gruyter.

Nishimura, M. 1986. Intra-sentential Code-switching: The Case of Language Assignment. *Language Processing in Bilinguals: Psycholinguistic and Neuropsychological Perspectives*, ed. J. Vaid, 123-143. Hillsdale, NJ: Lawrence Erlbaum.

Patschke, C., Shirai, J., and Shirai, H. 2001. The Development of the Hybrid Complement Clause Structure by Bilingual Children. *Code-Switching by Japanese/English Bilinguals.* Report of Research Results. Chukyo University.

Sarkar, M. 2009. "Still reppin por mi gente": The Transformative Power of Language Mixing in Quebec Hip Hop. *Global Linguistic Flows*, ed. H. S. Alim et al.139-157. New York: Routledge.

Talmy, L. 1985. Lexicalization Patterns: Semantic Structure in Lexical Forms. *Language Typology and Syntactic Description 3: Grammatical Categories and the Lexicon*, ed. T. Shopen, 57-149. Cambridge: Cambridge University Press.

Tsujimura, N. and Davis, S. 2009. Dragon Ash and the Reinterpretation of Hip Hop: On the Notion of Rhyme in Japanese Hip Hop. *Global Linguistic Flows*, ed. H. S. Alim et al. 179-193. New York: Routledge.

Winford, D. 2003. *An Introduction to Contact Linguistics*. Malden, MA: Blackwell.

The Polite Voice in Korean: Searching for Acoustic Correlates of *contaymal* and *panmal*

BODO WINTER
University of Hawai'i at Mānoa

SVEN GRAWNDER
Max Planck Institute for Evolutionary Anthropology

1. Introduction

Politeness is an integral part of everyday communication (Brown and Levinson 1987). In speaking to different people, we constantly adjust our behavior, our body language, the words and sentence structures we use, and our tone of voice. In line with current trends in expressive speech research (see Tatham and Morton 2004, Erickson 2005), we suggest that the speech signal alone – independent of the choice of lexical items or grammatical constructions – conveys some of the social meaning of an utterance. While many studies in the field of expressive speech have sought to characterize the "prosodic profile of emotions" (e.g. Banse and Scherer 1996, Scherer 2003), or how emotions are expressed through a speaker's tone of voice, we set out to characterize the "prosodic profile of politeness".

Japanese/Korean Linguistics 19.
Edited by Ho-min Sohn, Haruko Cook, William O'Grady, Leon A. Serafim, and Sang Yee Cheon.

We conducted a speech production task with 16 native speakers of Korean who spoke short utterances in either *contaymal* (polite or formal speech) or *panmal* (informal speech). In our analysis, we focus on three dimensions of phonetic differences between these politeness registers: First, we analyze aspects of speech rate, pauses and fillers. Second, we analyze aspects of pitch and pitch variability. Third, we analyze voice quality. Prior studies on phonetic aspects of politeness have each focused on only a limited amount of different phonetic measurements (e.g. Ofuka 2000, Ohara 2001, Ito 2004, Shin 2005). This study seeks to provide a more holistic perspective on the phonetic and acoustic correlates of politeness by taking several phonetic dimensions into account.

Investigating vocal aspects of politeness is important for many reasons. First, it has practical applications, such as in speech synthesis or second language teaching. If specific vocal characteristics correlate reliably with different politeness registers, one can implement these phonetic dimensions in computer speech and one can teach these phonetic dimensions in classroom contexts. The possible significance of vocal aspects of politeness in second language acquisition is highlighted by a study of Ogino and Hong (1992). These researchers found that sentences uttered by learners of Japanese with the intention of being polite were actually judged as polite by only about 50% of Japanese native speakers. Finding out what exactly the phonetic parameters of politeness are might help in improving this score and promoting intercultural understanding.

Finally, a phonetic study of politeness has the advantage of relating to concrete physiological and acoustic parameters which can be connected to biological hypotheses of voice production (e.g. Ohala 1983, 1984, 1996). Such a connection cannot be made when focusing solely on morphosyntactical and lexical differences between politeness registers. In the long run, these connections might feed back into theoretical notions of politeness.

2. Background

2.1 Phonetic Aspects of Politeness

The vocal parameter "fundamental frequency" (f_0, the acoustic correlate of pitch) has received most attention in phonetic studies of politeness. In a study on Japanese, Ohara (2001) found that female speakers tended to express politeness by raising average f_0, whereas male speakers avoided the use of an elevated f_0. The study suggests that this might be because a high-pitched voice is associated with femininity. Shin (2005) shows that – differently from Japanese speakers – female Korean speakers tended to lower their average f_0; male speakers showed only little to no variation in pitch.

These findings can be related to the "frequency code" as formulated by Ohala (1983, 1984, 1996), a hypothesis which states that high pitch is associated with subdominance and low pitch with dominance in all kinds of mammals, including humans. If this hypothesis can be transferred to politeness, one would expect an increase in pitch when speaking to superiors. In this regard, Japanese women behave in line with the frequency code hypothesis, Korean women do not (Shin 2005). However, the Korean data was based on only very few speakers. We therefore intend to extend this work by recording a larger number of speakers and by doing so, we hope to give patterns of pitch differences in male speech a greater chance to emerge.

Ofuka and colleagues (2000) took a different approach to vocal politeness. Instead of looking at overall f_0 differences, they looked at f_0 movement on the final vowel of Japanese utterances and found that the direction of f_0 movement was used consistently to indicate politeness registers. In yet another study, Ito (2004) notes that aspiration noise (which could be a reflection of breathiness) is perceptually associated with relatively more polite speech in Japanese. However, as noted by Ito (2004: 216) herself, "We cannot see what kind of voice quality has the most effect on changing the impression of politeness." By looking at several voice quality parameters in this study, we hope to further understanding of which voice quality parameters matter for politeness distinctions.

2.2 Politeness in Korean

The Korean language is widely known for its extremely elaborate system of honorification:

> "No doubt in all societies, people have some awareness that different ways of speaking can convey different social messages. In the Korean case, however, this kind of awareness is obviously more explicit and more specific than in most other societies." (Yoon 2004: 204)

The grammatical system forces speakers of Korean to make choices for every single sentence depending on the relationship with their interlocutors (Yoon 2004: 194). The large variety of differentiated linguistic forms means that in Korean, one can hardly say anything without choosing between options regarding different levels of politeness. This was one of the main reasons why we chose Korean as the language for our phonetic analyses: we thought politeness distinctions would be easier to elicit and expressed more readily in a language and culture where politeness is so entrenched.

Also, Korean provided us with an easy way to operationalize politeness for the purposes of this study: We decided to define politeness as the distinction between formal speech to superiors (*contaymal*) and informal speech to inferiors and peers (*panmal*) (for a discussion of the lexical and morphosyntactic differences between these speech styles see also Sohn 2001: 407-417). By sticking to this culturally recognized distinction rather than theoretical notions such as "positive" or "negative" politeness (Brown and Levinson 1987), we avoid the long-lasting controversy surrounding politeness theory (see e.g. Xie et al. 2005) and we investigate categories which are known and meaningful to our Korean participants.

3. Methodology

3.1 Participants

Nine female and seven male speakers (age: 21-31, median: 23.5) were recruited via internet forums and a local Korean church community located in Cologne, Germany. The speakers volunteered to be recorded and received ten euros for a thirty minute session. Of the sixteen speakers, all but three were from Seoul metropolitan area and reported to speak standard Korean. At the time of the recording, all participants had resided in Germany for a mean time of four years and all but one reported to use Korean on a daily basis.

3.2 Procedure and Materials

Participants were seated in a sound-proof booth at the Institute of Phonetics, University of Cologne and were informed about the procedure by a native speaker of Korean. Instructions were also presented in written form (Hankul) on a computer screen. After reading out a newspaper extract to make them acquainted with speaking into the microphone, each participant performed two different tasks. First, a Mailbox Task was performed in which the participants were given a note in paper format. They had to use the main points of this note (e.g. "meeting at 10.30 am, in front of Starbucks") to formulate a coherent message which they had to leave on an imaginary cellphone mailbox (cf. the task in Shin 2005). Second, a verbal version of the Discourse Completion Task (cf. Byon 2006 for a written version) was performed in which speakers were given contexts which served as a basis for initiating role-played dialogues.

All contexts and written materials except the note in the Mailbox Task were presented on a computer screen using Microsoft PowerPoint. Through a window in the booth, the researchers maintained eye-contact with the participants who were free to ask clarification questions at any time. As soon as the participants read and understood a context passage, they gave a visual signal through the window and a picture of the imagined interlocutor appeared on the screen inside the booth. 2200ms after display of the picture, participants heard a beep which served as a signal for participants to deliver their response.

Each context appeared in slightly different versions in a *panmal* and a *contaymal* condition. In the Mailbox Task, there were two contexts. One involved leaving a message on a mailbox about an appointment, the other involved leaving a recipe on a mailbox. In the Discourse Completion Task, there were five different contexts: requesting a letter of recommendation (*contaymal* condition) from a professor or a language textbook from a friend (*panmal* condition); giving an excuse for coming too late; giving directions; correcting a mistake; congratulating someone on a music performance.

The Discourse Completion Task has often been criticized with respect to its ecological validity (Bodman and Eisenstein 1988, Bardovi-Harlig and Hartfold 1993, Yuan 2001). It has been argued that the results do not reflect real language patterns and heavily depend on the participants' role-playing abilities. The pictures presented after each context passage served to counteract these methodological confounds. These pictures depicted either elderly and authoritative-looking or else young and casual-looking male interlocutors, i.e. people with whom a Korean speaker would unambiguously use either *contaymal* or *panmal*. This made it easier for our participants to switch between politeness registers.

3.3 Recordings

All recordings were done via a head-set microphone AKG C420 (linear characteristic) with 48kHz/16bit sampling. The distance and orientation of the actors to the microphone, as well as the input level of the sound recording, was held constant. For each participant, a whole session was recorded continuously but we excluded material before restarts from subsequent analysis.

4. Results and analysis

In general, participants accustomed to the task easily and used all morpho-syntactic markers of *contaymal* and *panmal* appropriately. In total, we collected 2.6 hours of spoken material. All phonetic analyses were conducted with Praat (Boersma 2001); statistical analyses with SPSS 16.0.0. Analyses are based on both tasks (Discourse Completion and Mailbox) for the acoustic analysis but only on the Discourse Completion Task for the analyses of pauses, fillers and speech rate[1]. Data were analyzed using analysis of variance (ANOVA) across participants (F_1) and items (F_2) with gender as between-participants factor.

---

[1] These phonetic dimensions are highly susceptible to differences in "reading fluency" and are therefore likely to be influenced by the note in the Mailbox Task.

4.1 Pauses, Fillers and Speech Rate

We used a pause detection script by Mietta Lennes (www.helsinki.fi/ ~lennes/ praat-scripts/) which automatically labelled all silent pauses which are longer than 200ms. It is common practice to take 100ms as the minimum threshold for pauses (e.g. Butcher 1981; Trouvain 1999; Trouvain and Grice 1999) but we decided to go with comparatively large 200ms in order to avoid interpreting the closure durations of Korean tensed stops as pauses. All results of the script were checked manually.

In addition to silent pauses, we analyzed filled pauses. These were further classified into fillers (such as *ahh* and *ohh*), "hissing sounds" and the discourse particle *yey*[2]. All our analyses are based on pause and filler *rates*: for the participants analysis, we divided the sums of pauses and fillers through each speaker's average speaking duration. For the items analysis, we divided the sums through the average speaking duration of each item. We measured speech rate by sentences per second, words per second and syllables per second. We measured articulation rate by syllables per second, excluding pauses.

There was no relevant difference in respect of silent pauses between *contaymal* and *panmal*, either by participants ($F_1(1,14)=1.529$, p=0.237) or by items ($F_2(1,8)=2.376$, p=0.162). However, there was a significant difference in respect of filled pauses between the politeness registers ($F_1(1,14)=6.825$, p=0.02; $F_2(1,8)=7.907$, p=0.023): the rate of fillers is almost twice as high in the *contaymal* (0.09 ± 0.026 fillers/second[3]) as in the *panmal* condition (0.05 ± 0.028 fillers/second).

There also was a significant difference in regard to hissing sounds; these were more than twice as likely to occur in *contaymal* speech (0.034 ± 0.012 hissing sounds/second) as in *panmal* speech (0.013 ± 0.018 hissing sounds/second); both by participants ($F_1(1,14)=7.556$, p=0.016) and by items ($F_2(1,8)=15.096$, p=0.005)[4]. These sibilant-like hissing sounds have a large amount of energy in the higher frequency range and are produced with an ingressive airstream. This airstream is often sucked in laterally (to the side of the tongue).

---

[2] We are aware of the fact that *yey* and the pauses and fillers can occur in different contexts and serve different pragmatic functions. However, our quantitative approach does not look into these differences and treats *yey*, fillers and pauses alike.

[3] All results will be reported with ± 2 standard errors.

[4] Interestingly, there was a near-significant interaction between gender and attitude by items ($F_2(1,8)=5.076$, p=0.054) but not by participants ($F_1(1,14)=2.886$, p=0.111). Across items, the hissing sounds were more used by men in the *contaymal* context than by women. Separate paired t-tests reveal that the hissing sounds are more reliably used by men than by women to indicate politeness (for men: $t_1(6)=2.291$, p=0.062; for women: $t_1(8)=1.130$, p=0.291).

The discourse particle *yey* was used only in the *contaymal* condition ($F_1(1,14)$=4.897, p=0.044, $F_2(1,8)$=53.055, p<0.001). Also, it was only used by men, as shown by an interaction between the factors gender and attitude ($F_1(1,14)$=4.897, p=0.044, $F_2(1,8)$=53.055, p<0.001). It seems to be the case that the use of *yey* to indicate politeness registers is a gender-specific strategy.

Speech rate as measured by words per second is significantly slower in the *contaymal* than in the *panmal* condition ($F_1(1,14)$=18.048, p=0.001; $F_2(1,8)$=56.709, p<0.001). However, when one looks at speech rate as measured by syllables per second as well as articulation rate (syllables per second without pause time), this difference disappears (speech rate: $F_1(1,14)$=0.333, p=0.573; $F_2(1,8)$=1.540, p=0.25; articulation rate: $F_1(1,14)$=0.013, p=0.91; $F_2(1,8)$=0.699, p=0.427). Therefore, participants utter more words in a given amount of time when speaking *contaymal* as compared to *panmal*, but they do not utter relatively more syllables.

4.2 Pitch

We analyzed the fundamental frequency means and standard deviations of each trial with Praat's automatic pitch-tracking algorithm (with standard autocorrelation settings of Praat version 5.1.23). The mean f_0 and median f_0 were lower in the *contaymal* condition by about two to three semitones. This difference was significant by participants ($F_1(1,14)$=33.515, p<0.001) and items ($F_2(1,12)$=9.863, p=0.009). The f_0 standard deviations were also lower in the *contaymal* condition than in the *panmal* condition , however only for participants ($F_1(1,14)$=14.344, p=0.002; $F_2(1,12)$=0.001, p=0.98).

4.3 Intensity

Intensity is the acoustic correlate of perceived loudness. Mean intensities were lower in *contaymal* speech than in *panmal* speech, both by participants ($F_1(1,14)$=17.220, p=0.001) and items ($F_2(1,12)$=5.032, p=0.045). This difference was statistically significant but extremely small in magnitude: in our data set, *panmal* speech was only 1dB ± 0.235dB louder than *contaymal* speech. This difference is therefore unlikely to play a great role for the impression of politeness on the part of the listener.

4.4 Voice Quality

Voice quality refers to "the quality of a sound by which a listener can tell that two sounds of the same loudness and pitch are dissimilar" (ANSI 1973). We measured perturbation by amplitude (shimmer), perturbation by fundamental frequency period (jitter), and the differential energy of the first harmonic to the second harmonic (H1-H2).

We found a significant decrease in shimmer ($F_1(1,14)$=23.928, p<0.001; $F_2(1,12)$=11.313, p=0.006) and jitter ($F_1(1,14)$=16.375, p=0.001;

$F_2(1,12)=6.332$, p=0.027) in the *contaymal* condition. In this condition, there also was a significant increase in H1-H2 ($F_1(1,14)=15.444$, p=0.002; $F_2(1,12)=16.143$, p=0.002). This difference in H1-H2 is the only acoustic parameter where a significant interaction effect between gender and politeness register occurred ($F_1(1,14)=16.38$, p=0.001; $F_2(1,12)=17.176$, p=0.001). Whereas women clearly increased H1-H2 when speaking *contaymal*, the H1-H2 values of men did not change to the same extent, as can be seen in figure 1.

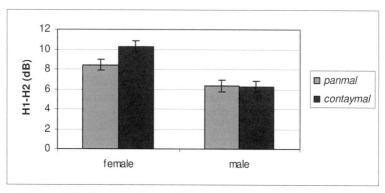

Figure 1. H1-H2 values for female and male participants in relation to politeness condition

5. Discussion

5.1 Pauses, Fillers and Speech Rate

The fact that fillers but not silent pauses differed consistently between the politeness registers suggests that for Korean, audible fillers are more likely to acquire social meaning than non-audible speech pauses. The hypothesis that in Korean, audible fillers are more relevant for politeness than silent pauses generates predictions which can be tested in subsequent perceptual experiments. In general, we interpret the increase in fillers as a stylized way of marking insecurity.

Our speech rate analyses suggest that words per second, which is sometimes used as a measure of speech rate, might not be an apt reflection of relevant rate differences. In Korean, words have consistently more syllables in *contaymal* than in *panmal* speech[5] (for participants: $F_1(1,14)=30.164$, p<0.0001; for items: $F_2(1,8)=35.083$, p<0.0001). This results in speech rate

---

[5] To our knowledge nobody has yet investigated whether differences in word length have an effect on the perception of speech rate.

differences when words per second are measured which disappear when syllables per second are measured.

5.2 Pitch

The lowering of fundamental frequency in Korean polite speech has also been recognized by Shin (2005). This study confirms that f_0 in *contaymal* speech is lower than in *panmal* speech. This is a different pattern from Japanese (e.g. Ohara 2001). If Ohala's frequency code (1983, 1984, 1996) applies to human politeness distinctions (as is suggested by e.g. Shin 2005), it would predict speech to superiors (as is the case with *contaymal* speech) to be higher in average pitch than speech to peers. Korean does not follow this prediction. This might show that the frequency code cannot be directly applied to politeness phenomena.

Even though it was not our intention to analyze the data in regard to Politeness Theory, it is also interesting to relate our pitch results to a comment made by Brown and Levinson (1987: 267-268):

> "We predict (...) that a sustained high pitch (maintained over a number of utterances) will be a feature of negative-politeness usage, and creaky voice a feature of positive-politeness usage, and that a reversal of these associations will not occur in any culture."

To the extent that politeness usage in Korean can be analyzed as reflecting mainly negative politeness (or "politeness-as-deference", cf. Pinker 2007) rather than positive politeness ("politeness-as-sympathy"), our data seem to contradict Brown and Levinson's prediction[6].

5.3 Voice Quality

Voice quality measures are notoriously difficult to directly relate to differences in perception and physiological settings. Our clearest results are exhibited by the harmonics-to-noise ratio which has been taken as an indicator of breathiness (Klatt and Klatt 1990): women use a relatively more breathy-sounding voice when speaking *contaymal* than when speaking *panmal*. Men do not seem to employ breathiness in a similar way; they do not exhibit consistent differences between the two politeness registers.

This is interesting because in other languages, a breathy voice quality has been found to be associated with "femaleness" or "effeminacy". In American English (Klatt and Klatt 1990) and Spanish (Mendoza et al. 1996),

---

[6] However, one should note that at the time this prediction was made, the necessary exploratory work of looking at a number of different languages and their respective vocal patterns of politeness had not been conducted. One has to look at more languages before universalist hypotheses like these can be made.

it has been found that female voices are relatively more breathy than male voices. Sulter and Peters (1996) found that this difference in "breathiness" can be a reliable cue for gender discrimination. For Dutch, van Borsel and colleagues (2009) found that breathy vowels are perceived as being more feminine than modal vowels uttered by the same speaker.

We currently think that because breathiness has been repeatedly found to be associated with femaleness, it is a politeness strategy that is not available to male speakers who probably do not want to sound "effeminate". This is similar to the Japanese men in Ohara's (2001) study who did not employ a high-pitched voice in polite speech. It might be the case that breathiness, by virtue of being associated with femininity, gains a kind of taboo status for men[7].

Finally, it should be noted that in Johnstone and Scherer (1999), a decrease in jitter was perceptually associated with an increase in perceived tension of the speaker. It might be that the decreased jitter values in *contaymal* (and possibly the decreased shimmer values as well) are perceived as indicating 'tensedness' or insecurity of the speaker.

6. Conclusions

When one takes a broader perspective on the different phonetic parameters we measured, one realizes a certain pattern: a number of measures which are taken to indicate perturbation of the speech signal are decreased. Perturbation by period (jitter), perturbation by amplitude (shimmer) and pitch variability are all decreased. Together with the slight decrease in loudness, we think that this creates the impression of "dampness", a speech style which is more subdued and monotonous than modal voice.

This characterization is related to the finding that the variability of an acoustic signal leads to differences in the perception of loudness. Moore et al. (1998) and Neuhoff et al. (1999) point out that pitch changes and changes in loudness can influence each other and musicians report that one of the functions of vibrato, which is a relatively slow (3 to 8 Hz) modulation of the fundamental frequency of a voice or an instrument, is to make a sound appear more expressive or loud (see also Fletcher and Munson, 1933). A decrease in pitch variability leads to a decrease in perceived loudness and perceived expressiveness (see e.g. Traunmüller and Eriksson 1995). The same could apply to differences in voice quality; however, we currently do not know of any studies which investigate possible relationships between perceived loudness and differences in perturbation measures.

---

[7] However, one would need to test the way breathiness is produced and perceived in Korean to substantiate this claim.

To summarize, our data show that politeness affects many phonetic parameters, ranging from intensity and pitch to speech rate and voice quality. Taken together, these parameters and the differences in speech pauses and fillers produce audible phonetic differences between the politeness registers. Subsequent studies can test the perceptual relevance of these phonetic differences and they can investigate how much each parameter contributes to the auditory impression of politeness.

Traditionally, the field of politeness studies has focused on lexical and morphosyntactic aspects of politeness. These studies are very important to demonstrate how politeness is realized in everyday interactions; however, by not studying "vocal politeness" we miss a certain part of what politeness is. Instead of relying solely on hedging constructions, honorific markers and lexical items, politeness is simultaneously and redundantly expressed in the voice. Phonetics is thus an aspect of politeness which deserves more attention to arrive at a richer understanding of politeness and how it is realized in different cultures.

Acknowledgements

We thank Bernard Comrie, Katie Drager and Clive Winter for helpful comments and suggestions. We thank Roger Mundry, Benjamin Bergen and Katie Drager for helping with statistical issues. Special thanks belongs to all our participants, as well as to Joelle Kirtley, James Grama and Franziska Goetzke. This project would not have been possible without the generous help of Oh Ju-Young and Kim Won-Hee. Only the authors are responsible for any remaining errors.

References

ANSI, American National Standards Institute. 1973. "Psychoacoustical terminology," Technical Report, S.3.30, American National Standard Report.

Banse, R. and Scherer, K.R. 1996. Acoustic Profiles in Vocal Emotion Expression. *Journal of Personality and Social Psychology* 70: 614-636.

Bardovi-Harlig, K. and Hartfold, B. 1993. Refining the DCT: Comparing Open Questionnaires and Dialogue Completion Tests. *Pragmatics and Language Learning*, ed. Bouton, L.F. and Kachru, Y. (Monograph 4), 143-165. Urbana, IL: University of Illinois at Urbana-Champaign, Division of English as an International Language.

Bodman, J. and Eisenstein, M. 1988. May God Increase Your Bounty: The Expression of Gratitude in English by Native and Non-native Speakers. *Cross Currents* 15, 1-21.

Boersma, P. 2001. Praat, A System for Doing Phonetics by Computer. *Glot International* 5: 341-345.

van Borsel, J., Janssens, J. and de Bodt, M. 2009. Breathiness as a Feminine Voice Characteristic: A Perceptual Approach. *Journal of Voice* 23: 291-294.

Brown, P. and Levinson, S. 1987. *Politeness: Some Universals in Language Usage.* Cambridge: Cambridge University Press.

Butcher, A. 1981. Aspects of the speech pause: phonetic correlates and communicative functions. *Arbeitsberichte Phonetik Kiel* 15, Kiel.

Byon, A.S. 2006. The role of linguistic indirectness and honorifics in achieving linguistic politeness in Korean requests. *Journal of Politeness Research* 2: 247-276.

Campbell, N. and Mokhtari, P. 2003. Voice Quality: the 4th Prosodic Dimension. *Proceedings of the 15th International Congress of Phonetic Science*, Barcelona.

Erickson, D. 2005. Expressive Speech: Production, Perception and Application to Speech Synthesis. *Acoustical Science and Technology* 26: 317-325.

Fletcher, H. and Munson, W. A. 1933. Loudness, Its Definition, Measurement and Calculation. *Journal of the Acoustical Society of America* 5: 82-108.

Ito, M. 2004. Politeness and Voice Quality - The Alternative Method to Measure Aspiration Noise. *Proceedings of Speech Prosody 2004*, 213-216.

Johnstone, T. and Scherer, K. R. (1999). The Effects of Emotions on Voice Quality. *Proceedings of the 14th International Congress of Phonetic Sciences*, San Francisco.

Klatt, D. and Klatt, L. 1990. Analysis, Synthesis and Perception of Voice Quality Variations among Female and Male Talkers. *Journal of the Acoustical Society of America* 87: 820-857.

Mendoza, E., Valencia, N., Muñoz J., and Trujillo, H. 1996. Differences in Voice Quality between Men and Women: Use of the Long-term Average Spectrum (LTAS). *Journal of Voice* 10: 59-66.

Moore, B.C.J., Launer, S., Vickers, D. and Baer, T. 1998. Loudness of Modulated Sounds as a Function of Modulation Rate, Modulation Depth, Modulation Waveform and Overall Level. *Psychophysical and Physiological Advances in Hearing*, ed. Palmer, A.R., Rees, A., Summerfield, A.Q. and Meddis, R., 331-342. London: Whurr.

Neuhoff, J. G., McBeath, M. K., and Wanzie, W.C.1999. Dynamic Frequency Change Influences Loudness Perception: A Central, Analytic Process. *Journal of Experimental Psychology: Human Perception and Performance* 25: 1050-1059.

Ofuka, E., McKeown, J. D., Waterman, M. G., and Roach, P. J. 2000. Prosodic Cues for Rated Politeness in Japanese Speech. *Speech Communication* 32: 199-217.

Ogino, T. and Hong, M. 1992. Nihongo onsei no teineisa ni kansuru kenkyuu (A study on politeness in Japanese speech). *Nihongo intonation no jittai to bunseki* (The State-of-the-art and Analysis of Japanese Intonation), ed. T. Kunihiro, 215-258. Tokyo: Monbushou.

Ohala, J. J. 1983. Cross-language Use of Pitch: An Ethological View. *Phonetica* 40: 1-18.

Ohala, J. J. 1984. An Ethological Perspective on Common Cross-language Utilization of f0 of Voice. *Phonetica* 41: 1-16.

Ohala, J.J. 1996. The Frequency Code Underlies the Sound Symbolic Use of Voice Pitch. *Sound Symbolism*, ed. Hinton, L. and J. Nichols, 325-347. Cambridge: Cambridge University Press.

Ohara, Y. 2001. Finding One's Voice in Japanese: A Study of the Pitch Levels of L2 Users. *Multilingualism, Second Language Learning, and Gender*, eds. Pavlenko, A., Brackledge, A., Piller, I. and M. Teutsch-Dwyer, 231-254. New York: Mouton de Gruyter.

Pinker, S. 2007. The Evolutionary Social Psychology of Off-record Indirect Speech Acts. *Intercultural Pragmatics* 4: 437-461.

Scherer, K. 2003. Vocal Communication of Emotion: A Review of Research Paradigms. *Speech Communication* 40: 227-256.

Shin, S. 2005. Grammaticalization of Politeness: A Contrastive Study of German, English and Korean. Doctoral dissertation, University of California, Berkeley.

Sohn, H.-M. 2001. *The Korean Language*. Cambridge: Cambridge University Press.

Sulter, A. M. and Peters, H. F. 1996. Perceptive Characteristics of Speech of Untrained and Trained Subjects, and Influences of Gender. *Variation of Voice Quality Features and Effects of Voice Training in Males and Females*, ed. A.M. Sulter, 73-94. Groningen: Groningen University.

Tatham, M. and Morton, K. 2004. *Expression in Speech: Analysis and Synthesis*. Oxford: Oxford University Press.

Traunmüller, H. and Eriksson, A. 1995. The Perceptual Evaluation of F0 Excursions in Speech as Evidenced in Liveliness Estimations. *Journal of the Acoustical Society of America* 97: 1905-1915.

Trouvain, J. 1999. Phonological Aspects of Reading Rate Strategies. *Phonus* 4, Research Report Phonetics Saarbrücken, 15-35.

Trouvain, J. and Grice, M. 1999. The Effect of Tempo on Prosodic Structure. *Proceedings of the 14th International Congress of Phonetic Science*, San Francisco.

Xie, C., He, Z. and Lin, D. 2005. Politeness: Myth and Truth. *Studies in Language* 29: 431-461.

Yoon, K-J. 2004. Not Just Words: Korean Social Models and the Use of Honorifics. *Intercultural Pragmatics* 1: 189-210.

Yuan, Y. 2001. An Inquiry into Empirical Pragmatics Data-gathering Methods: Written DCTs, Oral DCTs, Field notes, and Natural Conversations. *Journal of Pragmatics* 33: 271-292.

Part V

Historical Linguistics and Grammaticalization

The Historical Development of the Korean Suffix –*key*

Minju Kim
Claremont McKenna College

1. Introduction

In this study, I will examine the historical development of the Korean suffix -*key*. In Present Day Korean, the suffix -*key* is found in five different grammatical markers; see (1) through (5).

(1)   Adverbial suffix -*key*
        Mina-nun cemsim-ul   masiss-key mek-ess-ta[1]
        Mina-TOP lunch-ACC <u>delicious-*key*</u> eat-PAST-DEC

---

[1] The transliteration system adopted in this study is an extended Yale system based on Samuel Martin (1993) and Seongha Rhee (1996) to suit the transliteration of Middle Korean (e.g. · for A). Chinese characters in historical texts are transliterated as capital letters and pronounced as in Present Day Korean. The abbreviations used in this study are ACC (Accusative), AD (Additive), CAUS (Causality), COND (Conditional), CONN (Connective), COP (Copular), DEC (Declarative), DEF (Deferential), DESIRE (Desiderative), FUT (Future), GEN (Genitive), HON (Honorific), IMP (Imperative), IND (Indicative), INS (Instrumental), INT (Intransitive), LOC (Locative), NF (Non-finite), NOM (Nominative), PASS (Passive), PAST (Past, Old anterior), PERM (Permission), PRES (Present tesne), PROG (Progressive), RES (Resultative), RETRO (Retrospective), RL (Relativizer), and TOP (Topic).

Japanese/Korean Linguistics 19.
Edited by Ho-min Sohn, Haruko Cook, William O'Grady, Leon A. Serafim, & Sang Yee Cheon.
Copyright © 2011, CSLI Publications

'Mina enjoyed her lunch.'
(literal translation: Mina ate her lunch deliciously)

(2)   Purposive connective *-key*
        chayk <u>sa-key</u> man-won-man   cwu-seyyo
        book <u>buy-key</u> 10,000-won-only give-REQ
        'Please give me 10,000 won to buy a book.'

(3)   Imperative ender *-key*
        nayil   ilccik <u>o-key</u>
        tomorrow early <u>come-key</u>
        'Please come early tomorrow.'

(4)   Causative *-key ha-*
        Mina-ka   ku-eykey chayk-ul   <u>ilk-key</u>   ha-yess-ta
        Mina-NOM him-DAT book-ACC <u>read-key</u> do-PAST-IND
        'Mina made him read the book.'

(5)   Epistemic modal *-keyss-*
        nayil   pi-ka   <u>o-keyss-ta</u>
        Tomorrow rain-NM <u>come-keyss</u>-DEC
        'It will probably rain tomorrow.'

First, as in (1), it is used as an adverbial suffix which converts adjectives to adverbs. It is also used as a purposive marker as in (2) and as an imperative sentence ender as in (3). In the remaining two cases, *-key* constitutes part of a grammatical construction: *-key* is used in the causative construction *-key ha-* as in (5) and in the epistemic modal marker *-keyss-* as in (6).

In this study, based on evidence from a diachronic corpus of Korean and on Haspelmath's (1989) study on cross-linguistic universals of infinitive markers, I will propose that 1) the different uses of *-key* are semantically and developmentally related; 2) among various functions, the purposive meaning served as the original source meaning; 3) derived from that use, the core semantics of the suffix *-key* is projected futurity and this meaning made other functions of *-key* possible; and 4) although Korean does not have an infinitive construction (e.g. English *to*, German *zu*) per se, the core semantics and development of *-key* show important similarities with those of infinitive constructions.

Figure 1 shows the developmental path of the Korean *-key* proposed in this study. I suggest that *-key* first started out with the purposive meaning. Then with the meanings of purpose and projected futurity, *-key* could contribute to the emergence of four additional grammatical markers.

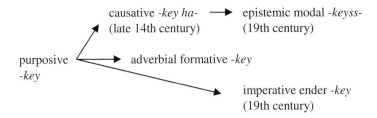

Figure 1. Proposed developmental path of *-key*

2. Replacement of *-i* with *-key*

With respect to the emergence of the suffix *-key*, what should be first noted is that the adverbial suffix *-key* emerged replacing the existing adverbial suffix *-i*. Based on *Kwukyel* data, J.Y. Chung (1998) showed that during the 14th century, the most productive adverbial suffix was *-i* and the next most productive one was *o* (e.g. *oAlo* 'fully', *kolo* 'equally'). However, over time, these suffixes gradually became recessive while the use of *-key* increased. As the result of the increased popularity of *-key* and its subsequent replacement of *-i*, some adverbs with *-i* are no longer in use in Present Day Korean as in (6a) while others sound archaic as in (6b).

(6a)
　　tyoh-i> coh-key 'well' *kh-i> khu-key* 'largely' *cyak-i> cak-key* 'small'
　　cop-i> cop-key 'narrowly' *nep-i> nel-key* 'widely' *nuc-i > nuc-key* 'late'
　　olh-i> olh-key 'in a right way' *pAlk-i> palk-key* 'brightly'
　　　　　　　　　　　　　　　　　　　　　　　　　　(from S.W. Lee 1984)

(6b)
　　i-li> ileh-key 'like this' *ce-li > celeh-key* 'like that'

The remainder of the study will show that the two suffixes *-key* and *-i* have much in common and that the historical development of *-key* could be influenced by analogy with that of the pre-existing suffix *-i*.

3. Purposive Meaning of *-key* as Source

Previous studies on *-key* often concluded that it denotes the meaning of "causing a situation" (S.N. Yi 1980: 328) or "reaching to a state" (W. Huh 1975: 601). I agree that its core semantics is projected futurity. Then where did this meaning come from? I propose that the suffix *-key* originated from the purposive use.

First, as shown in figure 1, the imperative *-key* and the modal *-keyss-* appeared between the 17th and 19th century. Also, the purely adverbializing function of -*key* with a weak meaning of projected futurity as shown in (1) is a later development. Then, between the two remaining functions of the periphrastic causative -*key ha*- and the purposive -*key*, it seems more reasonable to allocate the purposive meaning as the source rather than the syntactically more complex -*key ha*-.

Examples (10) through (12) show that from the earliest Korean language documents, -*key* could denote the purposive meaning of 'in order to', combined with both adjectives and verbs.

(7) *kutuy ka-a*   *alatut-key*   *nilu-la*
     you go-CONN understand-*key* say-IMP
     '(The king said to Tayayto) 'you go and tell (Yaswu) for her to understand''   (*Sekpo sangcel* 1447, 6:6b)

(8) *poli* *nik-key* *posk-uni*
     barley cook-*key* stir:fry-CONN
     'Stir-fry barley to get cooked...'   (*Kwukup kani* 1489, 3:35b)

(9) *sAlko-psi*   *sop tas-hop* *kem-key* *posk-a*
     apricot-pit inside five-hop black-*key* stir:fry-CONN
     'Stir-fry five *hop* (unit of volume) of apricot pit insides to become black...'   (*Kwukup kani* 1489, 6:41b)

(10) *kAcang khu-key mAyngk-Ala*   (*Welin sekpo* 1459, 25:106a)
     most   big-*key* make-CONN
     'Make it biggest...'   (i.e. make it to become biggest)

-*Key* is suffixed to verbs in (7) and (8) and to adjectives in (9) and (10). It has been a common practice that -*key* used with verbs is considered as a purposive connective while that used with adjectives is considered as an adverbial suffix. However, the semantics of purpose that -*key* conveys and the syntactic structure involving -*key* in these four examples are very similar; for instance, see (8) and (9). For this reason, I will refer to the use of -*key* that is suffixed to adjectives and delivers a clear sense of purpose or projected futurity, as in (7) and (8), as a 'purposive-adverbial suffix'.

The second piece of evidence supporting my proposition that the purposive use served as the source of -*key* comes from Haspelmath (1989); see Figure (2).

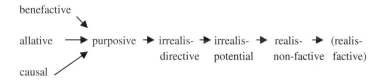

Figure 2. Grammaticalization of the infinitive (Haspelmath 1989: 298)

Drawing on data from a variety of languages including Indo-European, Turkic, Finno-Ugric, and Bantu languages, Haspelmath proposed in his article "From Purposive To Infinitive" (1989) that infinitives develop from purposive markers. The purposive markers can in turn be traced back to an allative, benefactive, or causal element. The purposive marker subsequently undergoes four phases of development as a complement clause; these phases are different from each other in their modalities. The differences result because over time the later development comes to lose much of the purposive and irrealis meanings (i.e. through desemanticization; Heine, Claudi, and Hünnemeyer 1991). Examples in (11) illustrate Haspelmath's proposals.

(11)
    a) Allative: Mary went to Sabina's apartment
    b) Purposive: He went to marry Jane. He bought a camera to take photos.
    c) Irrealis-directive: 'to' infinitive used with 'order', 'cause'
    d) Irrealis-potential: 'to' infinitive used with 'be possible', 'be able'
    e) Irrealis-non-factive: 'to' infinitive used with 'think', 'say'
    f) Realis-factive: 'to' infinitive used with 'know', 'realize'

Figure 2 shows some similarities to figure 1. Although it is not yet possible to pinpoint the stage before the purposive -*key* in Korean, we can at least identify the purposive stage, in which -*key* denotes the meaning of 'in order to'.[2] Next, the stage of the "irrealis directive" which is "the modality of complements to manipulative verbs like 'order', 'ask', 'cause'" (Haspelmath 1989: 298) can be applied to the use of -*key* in the causative construction. Also, in a later development when -*key* functioned as the adverbializing suffix, it demonstrates the loss of the irrealis meaning; for examples, see (1),

---

[2] Based on figure 2, the Korean dative –*eykey*, which originated from the combination of the genitive –*Ay* plus *key* "there", could have been assigned as the source for the purposive –*key*. However, it is difficult to argue that possibility because no examples of –*key* suffixed to a noun can be found in historical documents.

(19), and (20). Finally, as infinitives (with its meaning of projected futurity) often contribute to the coinage of epistemic modal markers (Bybee et al. 1994: 185), the suffix *-key-* also participated in the making of the epistemic modal *-keyss-*. In sum, the historical development of *-key* exhibits similarities with that of the infinitives and these similarities also support the proposal that the purposive meaning served as the source for the different functions of *-key*.

In terms of textual evidence, it is unfortunate that I could not find examples of the purposive *-key* in *Kwukyel* documents of 14th and 15th centuries, although examples of causative *-key ha-* were witnessed at that time. One of the reasons behind this discrepancy seems to be that most *Kwukyel* texts are Buddhist texts, which tend to frequently use causative constructions (e.g. 15th century Buddhist texts).

4. Causative Construction *-key ha-*

Next, the purposive meaning of *-key* could lead to the emergence of the causative construction *-key ha-*. As shown in (14), the compositional meanings of *-key* and *ha-* 'do' (or its older form *hA-*) can easily induce the causative meaning 'make (causee) do X'. Korean at first used causative suffixes (i.e. morphological causative) but with the spread of *-key*, the periphrastic construction *-key hA-* (i.e. syntactic causative) started to appear in the late 14th or early 15th century (D.J. Choi 2000).

(12) *kulh-ketun cuzuy   as-ko   kAcang te-i hA-ya*
      boil-COND dregs remove-CONN most hot-*i* make-CONN
      'When it boils, remove the dregs (of the medicine) and make it
      very hot...'   (*Kwukuppang* 1466, 2:33b)

(13) *cyeki tep-key hA-ya   SIKCEN-ey   meki-la*
      little hot-*key* make-CONN before.meal-LOC feed-IMP
      'Make it a little hot and feed (the patient) before meals'
                                            (*Kwukuppang* 1466, 1:13a)

(14) *tye POSAL-i   w-a   na-lAl po-key hA-syosye*
      That saints-NOM come-CONN I-ACC see-*key* make-DESIRE
      'Please make the Buddhist saint come and see me.'
                                            (*Pephwakyeng* 1463 7:16a)

Examples (12), (13), and (14) seem to suggest a kind of developmental continuum. As mentioned earlier, *-key* emerged, replacing *-i*; this is shown in (12) and (13). Also (13) expresses the meaning of the purposive while taking the form of the causative, suggesting the close relationship between the two functions.

Examples (15), (16) and (17) also render supporting evidence for the close relationship between purposive and causative functions. It is generally believed that unlike the suffix -*key*, the suffix -*i* is combined only with adjectives. However, in historical documents we can find rare examples in which the suffix -*i* is combined with verbs and denotes the purposive meaning, as in (15) and (16), and even the causative, as in (17). Since these examples are very rare, we cannot make any general conclusion. Nevertheless, these examples seem to be in support of my proposal that the purposive meaning could contribute to the development of the causative. In addition, these examples hint that the similarity between the suffix -*i* and -*key* are not limited to the adverbial formative use and that the historical development of -*key* is influenced by analogy with that of the older adverbial suffix -*i*.

(15)   *ku namo-s pwulhwi-lAl spayhhy-e   kuwul-i pwul-e*
       that tree-GEN root-ACC pull-CONN <u>bend-i</u> blow-CONN
       '(The wind) blows to pull and bend the tree's root.'
                                          (*Sekpo sangcel* 1447, 6: 30b)

(16)   *CENGKECHEN-ey   nilul-i pichwi-si-ni*
       CENGKECHEN-LOC <u>reach-i</u> shed-HON-CONN
       '(He) shed light to reach the sky of Cengkechen.'
                                          (*Sekpo sangcel* 1447, 3: 25b)

(17)   *KU-lul   HANGPOK LYENG <u>i-ha</u>-lti*
       he-ACC surrender CAUS <u>-i ha</u>-CONN
       '(Palamil) made him (a pagan) to surrender,,,'
                 (from *Kwukyel* text *Kumkwang* mid-13th century, 5: 21-22)

5. Adverbial Formative -*key*

When -*key* is suffixed to adjectives, we tend to treat them uniformly as the same adverbial formatives. However, in this study, I am proposing that it is possible to classify them into two groups: the first kind of -*key* (which I called the purposive-adverbial suffix) contains the meaning of purpose or projected futurity and the second kind of -*key* is devoid of such meaning. For instance, in (18) *kkaykkusha-key* means 'to become clean' or 'in order to be clean', and hence -*key* contains the purposive meaning. However, -*key* in (19) and (20) do not contain the purposive meaning because 'be heard in order to be loud' or 'stare at someone in order to be strange' does not make sense. Between the two different kinds of -*key*, I propose that the first one with the purposive meaning is an earlier development, while the second is derived from the first through desemanticization.

(18)   *kkaykkusha-key takk-ala*
        <u>Clean-*key*</u>   wipe-IMP
        'Wipe it (to become) clean.'

(19)   *soli-ka*   <u>*khu-key*</u> *tul-li-n-ta*
        sound-NOM <u>big-*key*</u> hear-PASS-IND-DEC
        'Sounds are heard big (i.e. sounds are loud).'

(20)   *ku-nun Minho-lul*   <u>*isangha-key*</u> *chyetapo-ass-ta*
        He-TOP Minho-ACC <u>strange-*key*</u>   stare-PAST-DEC
        'He stared at Minho strangely.'

Historically, in the 15th century, *-key* could denote the purposive meaning of 'in order to' as shown earlier in example (13). At that time, however, examples like (19) and (20), which are mostly devoid of the purposive meaning, were rare. This is in support of the proposal under discussion. Grammaticalization theory explains that over time and use, a word loses its concrete semantic details and peculiarities while retaining its more abstract meaning (Heine et al. 1991). In the same vein, Haspelmath (1989) proposed that with time, the meanings of futurity and irrealis gradually disappear from infinitive constructions. In the case of *-key* as well, it seems that *-key* was originally used to deliver the purposive meaning (e.g. *khu-key* in (13)). Over time, however, the original semantics of purpose faded out of *-key* and what came to remain is its syntactic concomitant that changed adjectives to adverbs (e.g. *khu-key* in (19)). This function spread and emerged as a new function of *-key*.

Another piece of supporting evidence is shown in Table 1. It is well-attested in historical documents that as an adverbial formative, *-i* was still more dominant than *-key* in the 15th C. For instance, table 1 shows the ratio of *-i* and *-key* when used with the adjective *coh-* (old form *tyoh-*) 'be good'. Table 1 demonstrates that it was much later than the 15th century when *-key* became the primary adverbial formative.

Table 1. The ratio of adverbial suffixes -*i* and -*key* used with the adjective *coh*- 'good'

coh-*	-*i*		-*key*	
	raw	percentile	raw	percentile
15th century	157	(72%)	61	(28%)
17th century	163	(79%)	43	(21%)
19th century	22	(47%)	25	(53%)

* The older form of *coh*- is *tyoh*-. Both forms were examined.

The adverbial formative -*key* emerged in the presence of the existing adverbial formative -*i*. As a result, presently there are some adjectives that can take both adverbial formatives. S.W. Park (1993) showed that in those cases, the older marker -*i* denotes more abstract and secondary meanings while the newer marker -*key* denotes more literal meanings. For instance, the adjective *tantanha*- 'be hard' can be converted into adverbs by both -*i* and -*key*. The difference is that with -*key*, the adverb *tantanha-key* denotes the more literal meaning 'hard' while with -*i*, the adverb *tantanh-i* can convey both the literal meaning of 'hard' and its derived meaning, 'very'; see (21). In the same way, the adjective *sensenha*- 'be cool' can be converted into two kinds of adverbs: *sensenha-key* denotes the more literal weather-related meaning 'coolly' while *sensenh-i* can express both the weather-related 'coolly' and the attitude-related 'willingly'; see (22).

(21)   *Mina-nun <u>tantanh-i</u> hwa-ka   na-ss-ta*
         Mina-TOP <u>very</u>   anger-NOM appear-PAST-IND
         'Mina got very angry.'

(22)   *totwuk-un kyengchal-uy yokwu-ey   <u>sensen-hi</u> unghay-ss-ta*
         thief-TOP police-GEN demand-LOC <u>willingly</u> comply-PAST-IND
         'The thief complied with the policeman's demand willingly.'
                                        (from S.W. Park 1993: 91)

This difference in semantics between the older form -*i* and the newer form -*key* can be explained by desemanticization and subjectification. Subjectification (Traugott 1989) refers to the tendency in semantic change to move from more concrete meanings to meanings that are more anchored in the speaker's stance and attitude. This tendency arose because speakers tend to encode their stance and attitude in their use of the language (e.g. *sensenha*- 'be cool' => *sensenh-<u>i</u>* attitude-related 'willingly', *tantanha*- 'be hard' => *tantanh-i* degree word 'very'). In the same vein, Brinton and Traugott

(2005: 132-136) explain that the derivation of adverbs with the addition of -*ly* in English often results in changes from more literal to more abstract meanings, such as those of degree adverbs (e.g. *high* => *highly*, *real* => *really*). In the case of Korean, the older form -*i* seems to have been more advanced in this development than the newer form -*key*.

6. Imperative Ender -*key*

The purposive connective -*key* also engendered the imperative ender -*key*. With the purposive meaning of -*key*, -*key* plus *hA*- 'do' could mean 'do to do X' or 'make efforts to do X'. For instance, -*key hA*- in (23) and (24) is not used as a causative construction but is used to mean 'make efforts to do X' combined with the imperative enders -*so* and -*ela*.

(23)   [context: husband's letter to his wife]
        Swui   o-so
        Quickly come-IMP
        'Come quickly'

        (approximately one line omitted)

        yumwu-ey   cAsyey kuypyelhA-so
        letter-LOC in:detail inform-IMP
        'Inform me in detail (of your arrival date) in the letter.'

        putAy swui   o-key hA-so
        Please quickly come-*key ha*-IMP
        'Please come quickly.'   (*Cincwu Ha letters* 17th C)

(24)   [context: grandmother's letter to her grandson]
        kwake-to po-ko   cwuk-e ka-ten hanmi-to   po-ko
        exam-AD take-CONN die-PROG-RL grandma-AD meet-CONN
        'To take the exam, to meet your aging grandma and'

        atAl-to po-ko   kyemhikyemhi o-a   tAnnyeka-key hA-yela
        son-AD meet-CONN multiply come-CONN visit-*key ha*-IMP
        'to meet your son, for these multiple reasons, please visit (me).'
                                (*Kim Ilkun Letters*, ca. 1744, po 13)

(23) is an illuminating example. In the letter, in which a husband is asking his wife to come to him, in the first line, the husband uses the imperative ender –*so*, but in the last line, he asks more sincerely, using -*key hA-so* and *putAy* 'please'. Between the 17th and 19th century, the '*key hA*- plus imper-

ative' construction was frequently used in making requests with the meaning 'please try to do X'. S.H. Lee (2004) proposed that this frequent use led to the reduction of *hA-* and the imperative enders (e.g. *-key* [*hA-so*]) and that the remaining *-key* eventually functioned as a new imperative marker starting from the mid 19th century. The new imperative ender *-key* became productively used, replacing the old imperative ender *-so*.

(25) 17th C   mid 19th C
      o-key hA-so   =>   *o-key* [*hA-so*]   => *o-key*
      come-*key* hA-IMP
      'Please come.'

7. Epistemic Modal *-keyss-*

The last grammatical marker to be examined is the epistemic modal suffix *-keyss-* 'probably'. As Bybee et al. (1994) showed, infinitive constructions with the semantics of projected futurity and irrealis often form part of obligation or predestination constructions, which subsequently engender epistemic modal markers. In Korean as well, with the meaning of projective futurity, *-key* participates in the coinage of the modal *-keyss-*.

The source form of *-keyss-* is well-documented as *-key hAyes-*, which is the causative construction *-key hA-* plus the anterior/past tense marker *-yes-* (K.K. Lee 1987, K.H. Park 1990). M. Kim (2008) examined the development of *-keyss-* and proposed that the causative *-key hA-* could express the quasi-passive meaning in the 15th and 16th centuries before *-key toy-* was coined and took over this meaning.[3] (26) shows the quasi-passive use of *-key hA-*. This example describes what will be the fate of those women who abort their conceived children. The subject of *-key hA-* in the first line is the same as that of *mannA-n-ta* 'meet' or 'suffer' in the second line and that is a woman who aborted her child and hence will suffer the ill-fate described in this passive sentence.

(26)   *isAyng-aysye-to   khun pyeng-ul   et-e*
         this:life-LOC-AD big disease-ACC get-CONN
         'In this life, receiving a great illness,'

---

[3] In the 15th century, the difference in the number of tokens of *-key hA-* and *-key toy-* was drastic: while 1943 tokens of *-key hA-* were observed, only 23 tokens of *-key toy-* were found. On this basis, M. Kim (2008) proposed that the *-key toy-* construction just started to emerge in the 15th century, modeled after *-key hA-*. In the 15th and 16th century, when the use of *-key toy-* was not yet productive, *-key hA-* could express the meaning of the quasi-passive which is now carried by *-key toy-*.

mokswum-i <u>*tyelA-key hA*</u>*-mye*
life-NM   <u>short-key hA</u>-CONN
'her life is to be shortened and,'

cwuk-e apitiok-ay   pteleti-ye khun koloon i-lAl   mannA-n-ta
die-CONN hell-LOC fall-CONN big painful thing-AC meet-IND-
DEC
'after death, she falls into hell and suffers great pain.'
                                     (*Cangswu* 16th century, 7b-8a)

In Korean, the subject of a sentence was commonly omitted. In the use of the causative *-key hA-*, when the subject (causer) was omitted, the remaining human participant (causee) could be in focus; the switch of focus to the causee could give rise to a passive-oriented reading. Besides Korean, the development of passives from causatives has been commonly observed across different languages (Haspelmath 1990).

The anterior marker *-yes-* was added to emphasize the definiteness of a current imposition resulting from a past action, and starting in the 16th century, *-key hAyes-* was used to report a destined future. In (27) and (28) both *-key hAyes-* and *-key toyyes-* denote the meaning of predestined future of 'come to'.

(27)   *Nay ahAy cyangchAs* <u>*cwuk-key hAyesi*</u>*-ni*
        My child soon   <u>die-key hAyes</u>-CONN
        'My child is soon about to die…'
                            (*Tongkwuk sinsok* 1617, *yel* 6: 62b)

(28)   *Yesyun-uy pyengtul-e keuy* <u>*cwuk-key toyyet*</u>*-kenAl*
        60-at sick-CONN   almost <u>die-key toyyes</u>-CONN
        'At the age of 60, (the grandfather) got sick and was almost about
        to die…'   (*Tongkwuk samkang* 1617, *hyo* 2: 34b)

The meaning of a destined future of *-key hAyes-*, which carries senses of both external binding and futurity, could engender the epistemic modal meaning starting in the 17th century. Both *-key hAyes-* and *-keyss* in (29a) and (29b) express the probability meaning. These examples are drawn from two different translations of the same Japanese text and show the transformation from *-key hAyes-* to *-keyss-*

.

(29a)   *Tolichay-lul mAyntAl-aya thacak-ul <u>hA-key hAyes</u>-sApnAy*
          Flail-AC make-CON   threshing-AC <u>do-key hAyes</u>-DEC
          'Only after we make a flail, could we do the threshing.'
                                             (*Kyolin chephay* 1881)

(29b)   *Tolikay-lul mAyntul-eya thacak-ul   <u>hA-keys</u>-sApnAy*
          Flail-AC   make-CON threshing-AC <u>do-keys</u>-DEC
          'Only after we make a flail, could we do the threshing.'
                                             (*Cungkyo chephay* 1904)
                                             (from K.H. Park 1990)

8. Conclusion

In this study, I have examined the historical development of the Korean suffix -*key* on the basis of a diachronic corpus of Korean and of Haspelmath's (1989) study on cross-linguistic universal of infinitive markers. I have attempted to show that the purposive use of -*key* served as the source and that with the semantic properties of purpose and projected futurity, -*key* could contribute to development of four additional functions, the adverbial formative -*key*, the imperative ender -*key*, the causative -*key ha*-, and the epistemic modal -*keyss*-. In particular, based on its historical development, I have suggested that although when suffixed to adjectives, -*key* has been uniformly considered as an adverbial suffix, those cases that have a clear purposive meaning (purposive-adverbial suffix) emerged first and those that do not have such a meaning resulted later through desemanticization of the purposive meaning.

I have also attempted to demonstrate that although Korean does not have an infinitive construction *per se* such as English *to* and German *zu*, the semantics as well as the historical development of -*key* show important similarities with those of infinitive constructions. Therefore, as infinitives often participate in the coinage of other grammatical markers such as causative and modal constructions with the sense of projected futurity, the semantic properties of -*key* also contributed to the emergence of additional grammatical markers.

Acknowledgements

I would like to thank Professors Sung-Ock Sohn, Jae-young Chung, John Whitman, Phunghyon Nam and Ross King for their insightful comments at the 19th Japanese Korean Linguistics Conference. Any remaining errors are my own.

References

Brinton, L. and Traugott, E. C. 2005. *Lexicalization and Language Change*. Cambridge, UK: Cambridge University Press.

Bybee, J. L., Perkins, R., and William, P. 1994. *The Evolution of Grammar: Tense, Aspect, and Modality in the Languages of the World*. Chicago: University of Chicago Press.

Choi, D. J. 2000. Kwuke satong kwumwun uy thongsicek pyenhwa (Historical Development of Korean Causative Constructions). *Enehak* 27: 303-326.

Chung, J. Y. 1998. Kolye sitay uy i pwusa wa pwusahyeng (*i* adverbs and adverbs types in Korye Dynasty). *Kwuke ehwi uy kipan kwa yeksa (On the formation of the Korean words)*, ed. J. K. Sim, 737-784. Seoul: Tayhaksa.

Haspelmath, M. 1989. From Purposive to Infinitive — A Universal Path of Grammaticization. *Folia Linguistica Historica* 10: 287-310.

Haspelmath, M. 1990. The Grammaticization of Passive Morphology. *Studies in Language* 14: 25-71.

Heine, B., Claudi, U., and Hünnemeyer, F. 1991. *Grammaticalization : A Conceptual Framework*. Chicago: University of Chicago Press.

Huh, W. 1975. *Wuli yeymalpon* (Middle Korean). Seoul: Saym.

Kim, M. 2008. The Emergence of the Korean Modal *-keyss-*: From Causative to Epistemic and Volitive Modal. *Tamhwa wa inci* (Discourse and Cognition) 15:1-27.

Lee, J. T. 1993. 15 seyki kwuke ipumpep kwa haimpep (The Causative and Passive Constructions in the 15th Century). Unpublished master's thesis, Yonsei University.

Lee, K. K. 1987. Miceng uy ssikkuth uli wa keyss uy yeksacek kyochey (The Historical Replacement of the Probability Marking *uli* by *keyss*). *Mal* 12: 161-197.

Lee, S. H. 2004. Myenglyenghyeng congkyel emi key uy hyengseng ey tayhan kwanken (The Development of Imperative Sentence-finite Ending -key). *Kwukehak* 44: 109-131.

Lee, S. W. 1984. Cwungseye i pwusahwa wa ilpwu uy phye e hyensang (On the *i* Adverbs and Its Partial Loss). *Tongyanghak* 14: 1-24.

Martin, S. E. 1992. *A Reference Grammar of Korean*. Rutland, Vermont: Charles E. Tuttle Company.

Park, K. H. 1990. Senemal emi keyss ey kwanhan yenkwu (Study on the Suffix -*keyss*). Unpublished master's thesis, Kyungkwuk National University.

Park, S. W. 1993. -i pwusa wa -key pwusahyeng-ey tayhaye (On the -*i* and -*key* Adverbial Suffixes). *Hansengemwunhak* 12: 83-98.

Rhee, S. H. 1996. *Semantics of Verbs and Grammaticalization: The Development in Korean from a Cross Linguistic Perspective*. Seoul: Hankuk.

Traugott, E. C. 1989. On the Rise of Epistemic Meanings in English: An Example of Subjectification in Semantic Change. *Language* 65: 31-55.

Yi, S. N. 1980. *Cwungse Kwuke Mwunpep* (Middle Korean Grammar). Seoul: Ulyu.

On the Origins of the Old Japanese *kakari* Particles, *ka, zö,* and *kösö,* and their Okinawan Counterparts: An Iconicity-based Hypothesis

LEON A. SERAFIM
University of Hawai'i at Mānoa

RUMIKO SHINZATO
Georgia Institute of Technology

1. Introduction

The purposes of this paper are three-fold. First, we point out that there exist two distinct groupings of KM from a comparative analysis of *kakari musubi* (henceforth, KM) constructions in Old Japanese (OJ) and Okinawan (Ok):[1] One group has cognates in both lineages, and the other has representations only in OJ. We recognize the first group as having existed in Proto-Japonic (PJ) as KP, and reconstruct their deictic-based progenitors. Secondly, after laying out the correspondences between the KPs' deictic distance, functions, and *musubi* conjugation, we tackle an important but nonetheless very rarely

---

[1] We offer our thanks to Alexander Vovin, John Bentley, John Whitman, Shigehisa Karimata, and Yukiko Shimabukuro for their discussion and comments during the writing of this paper.

Japanese/Korean Linguistics 19.
Edited by Ho-min Sohn, Haruko Cook, William O'Grady, Leon A. Serafim, & Sang Yee Cheon.

raised question: Are such correspondences arbitrary? This question merits discussion no matter which KM origin hypothesis one subscribes to (inversion, insertion, or biclausal); and yet it has escaped serious investigation, with Quinn (1997) on OJ *ka* and *sö* an important exception. We claim that the correspondences between KP and their respective functions are iconically motivated. Thirdly, to support our iconicity-based hypothesis, we present known instances of grammaticalization.

2. A Typology of KM

2.1 Origins of KPs

In the Japanese literature, it has been pointed out that the KPs in Group A (below) originate in demonstratives, while those in Group B, in interjectional/interpersonal particles (Ōno 1993, Sakakura 1993, Nomura 2002, *inter alia*).[2]

(1) KPs originating in demonstratives (Group A): |ka| , |zo|, |koso|
     KPs originating in i./i. ptcles (Group B): |ya| , |namu|

In the Okinawan literature (cf. Hokama 1981, Mamiya 2005, Takahashi 1991, Uchima 1994), cognations between OOk (= Old Okinawan) KPs and their Japanese counterparts have been explicitly suggested for Group A. Our study of Pan-Ryukyuan data (Serafim and Shinzato [henceforth S&S] 2009), confirmed this typology, since no single dialect evinces either |ya|[3] type or |namu| type KM. Illustrative examples follow in OJ-OOk order.

(2) |ka| / |ga|
     Type I (|ka| / |ga| correlating with inferentials)
     a. NABARI.nö.YAMA-wo   KYEPU **-ka** KWOY- **-ur-am-u**[4]
        Mount.Nabari-through today **-KP** cross- **-SE-IA-RT**
        '(Where is my love traveling?) I wonder if it is today that he will cross over Mt. Nabari.' (MYS 1: 43)

     b. taa **-ga**   tur-y[i-   **-y]ur-a**   taa **-ga** 'uc-y[i-   **-y]ur-a**[5]
        who **-KP**   hold-RY-   **-SE-IA**   who **-KP** beat-RY-   **-SE-IA**

        'I wonder who could be holding [the drum]. I wonder who could be beating it.' (OS 12: 1157)

---

[2] |α| = name for *kakari* particle (e.g. |do| Ok KP *-du*, *-dö*; |koso| Jp KP *-kösö*, *-koso*).

[3] An Ok sentence-final particle forming a yes/no question is cognate to this morpheme. This fact leads us to posit this particle as a Sentence-final Particle in PJ (Cf. S&S 2009).

[4] Small caps in the OJ text signal non-phonographic material; however, small caps in glossing lines indicate function morphs.

[5] This agreement pattern is known to be almost exceptionless even to this day (Uchima 1994).

Type II (Ikal / Igal correlating with regular RTs)

c. NWOPEY-NÖ   YAMABUKYI TARE-**ka** tawor-i-   **-si**
   the wild-GEN   globeflowers who **-KP** pick-RY- **-PST**$_{RT}$

   '…Who is it that picked the wild globeflowers?' (MYS 19: 4197)

d. nuu myi-cyee- **-ga**   'u[u]-yi-k-y[i-   **-y]ur-u** (OS12: 731)
   what see-RSLT- **-KP**   chase-RY-come-RY- **-SE-RT**

   '(The long-billed bird:) What has it seen that it is chasing (it) down?'

(3)   Izol / Idol

   a. KYEPU **-sö** WA[-GA]   KÖ[**-SI**]
      today **-KP** I-SUB   come **-PST**$_{RT}$

      'It is today that I came (to see you).' (MYS 10: 2216)

   b. syiyuryi furu 'ami-ya sidi-myizi   **-du** fur-y[i- **-y]u-ru**
      Shuri   fall rain-TOP purified-water **-KP** fall-RY-**-SE-RT**

      'The rain falling on Shuri: it is *pure* water that falls.' (OS 7: 386)

(4)   Ikosol / Isul

   a.MUKASI **-kösö** YÖSÖ-ni-mo   myi **-sika**
     long ago **-KP**   strange-ly,-even think**-PST**$_{IZ}$ (MYS 3: 474)

     'Though it's long ago (not now) that I saw it as strange, …'

   b. faci-nyisya   **-si** mac-yu-tar-   **-i**
     first-north-wind **-KP** await-SE-PST- **-IZ**

     'It was the first north wind itself that we awaited.' (OS 13: 899)

By working out phonological and morphological incongruities these pairs present, we reconstructed their PJ progenitors (S&S 2000, 2005, & 2009):

(5) KPs: Ikosol/Isul (<*kö#swo*) Izol/Idol (<*työ*) Ikal/Igal (<*ka*)
     Deictics: *kö* = proximal   *työ* = mesial   *ka* = distal

Both Ikal/Igal and Izol/Idol originate in distal and mesial deictics, and Ikosol(/Isul, OOk *si*) fused from *kö-* '(proximal)' and *swo* '(nominalizer)', but pre-OOk lost *kö*, leaving only the nominalizer (cf. S&S 2005, and sec. 2.4).

    The KP labels proximal, mesial, and distal lack universal acceptance. Below we will address this issue first.

2.2 The OJ Demonstrative System

The most influential work on OJ demonstratives is Hashimoto's (1982: 224-8), which has two categories (6). The proximal deictic *kö* belongs to the former, and the deictic *sö*, to the latter. From a handful of available examples, he characterizes *ka* as referring to an object that is visually obscure.

(6)   Hashimoto's (1982) Typology
       kankakuteki shiji 'direct experience'   :   *kö* (proximal) vs. *ka* (distal)
       kannenteki shiji 'indirect experience' :   *sö*

The deictics *kö* (= proximal) and *ka* (= distal) seem to be in opposition, but the few *ka* examples led Hashimoto to conclude that *ka* had not yet become a distal deictic. (7) is one of his three phonographically written examples. The other two (MYS 3565 & 4384) are dialect poems. Two additional examples have logographic spelling (彼), MYS 2240 & 2545. He further asserts that OJ *ka* derives from OJ *kö*, because OJ had many *a* :: *ö* alternations.

(7)   a-ga-mop-u   kyimyi-ga   myi-pune-kamo   **kare**(加礼)
       I-SUB love-RT   my.lord-GEN   EX-boat-KP   **that one**
       'Could that be the boat of my esteemed lord?'   (MYS 18: 4045)

Hashimoto's account raises the following questions:

(8)   a. Does the paucity of |ka| necessarily suggest its inception?
       b. Is |ka| derived from |ko|?
       c. How does the alleged under-development of |ka| reconcile with its
          claimed existence in PJ as a KP *ka*?

Ri (2002: 156; 317) disputes point (8a), taking the under-development of *ka* to refer to Pre-OJ, not OJ. Yasuda (1928: 69-70) takes the paucity of *ka* examples to mean that the distal *ka(re)* is nearly obsolete. He further suggests that the mesial *sö* may once have had a distal deictic meaning, due to the character for the first syllable of *So-no-ki* (彼杵), a Nagasaki place name, being written with the same character 彼 as the distal deictic, *ka*. Similarly, Quinn (1997: 66) attributes the relative paucity of *ka* in the Nara period to the wealth of the Heian data both in variety and sheer volume.

   Point (8b) is countered, too. Quinn (1997: 66, n11) rejects the claimed evolutionary scenario of *ka* from *kö*. Diessel (1999: 50), based on extensive cross-linguistic data, states that "All languages have at least two demonstratives that are deictically contrastive." Additionally, he (p.c., 2002.9) says he is unaware of "any language in which a distal demonstrative directly derived from a proximal demonstrative."

   Issue (8c) is difficult to resolve if we assume the existence of |ka| KM in PJ, and that KP *ka* is related to distal *ka*. Since the distal origin of KP *ka* is well-accepted by researchers (Ōno1993; Sakakura 1993, *inter alia*), the question is whether KM was just emerging in OJ, and did not exist in PJ. In our previous work (S&S 2000, 2005 and 2009), we argued extensively for the presence of KM in PJ. In brief, assuming OJ, OOk, and Pan-Ryukyuan KM to be independent developments has to assume too many coincidences.

Further, an actual distal deictic **kare* exists in Southern Ryukyuan (cf. 2.3).

In contrast to Hashimoto, Vovin (2005: 266-269) treats the OJ demonstrative system as a three-term system, namely proximal *kö*, mesial *sö*, and distal *ka*. However, unlike Middle and Modern Japanese, all distances are reckoned from the point of view of the speaker, thus not (yet) associating the mesial *sö* with the hearer. Vovin adds (2005: ibid.) that *sö* is commonly used as a discourse anaphor. Thus *sö* has an anaphoric as well as a spatial function.

(9)   Vovin's (2005) Typology   *köre*: proximal
                                        söre: mesial / anaphoric
                                        kare: distal

2.3 The OOk Demonstrative System

Just like OJ, the OOk demonstrative system also presents a challenge with its mesial and distal deictics. As seen in (10), *kuri* 'this one (proximal)' is straightforward, and its cognation to OJ *köre* '(id.)' is readily explainable phonologically in terms of loss in earlier Ryukyuan of the A/B distinction, followed by simple raising, the reconstruction then easily yielding a proximal **kö-* in PJ.

(10) | Deictics | OJ | OOk | KPs (| OJ | / | OOk) |
|---|---|---|---|---|---|---|
| proximal | *köre* | *kuri* | | \|koso\| | / | \|su\| |
| mesial | *söre* | *'uri* (*[x]suri*) | | \|so\| | / | \|do\| |
| distal | *kare* | *'ari* | | \|ka\| | / | \|ga\| |

The contrast of distal *'a-* of N. Ryukyuan with S. Ryukyuan *ka-* is best explained (Vovin 2006 and p.c., 2009) as an intrusion through the Shuri/Naha culture center by MJ-and-later *a-*, replacing PR **ka-*. Thus PR had **ka-*: PR **ka-* → pre-OOk **ka-/*a-* → OOk *'a-*. The relationships between KPs \|ka\|/\|ga\| and \|koso\|/\|su\| and their corresponding deictics are also readily explained (see S&S 2000, 2005). However, the relationship between OOk mesial *'uri* and KP \|do\| is not to be explained phonologically. The lack of correlation between OJ *sö-* and OOk *'u-* (not *[x]su*) now requires discussion.

Table 1. Shifts in mesial deictic patterns in Ok-language prehistory

Stage	KP	deictic	Reflexive Deictic	Question Deictic
1	*-tö-$_{KP'}$	*tö-$_{'that'}$	*ö-$_{'self'}$	*idwo-$_{'which?'}$
2	*-tö-$_{KP'}$	*tö-$_{'that'}$	*ö-$_{'self'}$	*dwo-$_{'which?'}$
3	*-dö-$_{KP'}$	*dö-$_{'that'}$	*ö-$_{'self'}$	*dwo-$_{'which?'}$
4	*-do-$_{KP'}$	***do-$_{'that'}$**	*o-$_{'self'}$	***do-$_{'which?'}$**
5	*-do-$_{KP'}$	*o-$_{'that'}$[6]	*dou-$_{'self'}$ (<$_{'torso'}$)	*do-$_{'which?'}$

We claim that proto-Ryukyuan *tö-based mesial deictics were replaced by the original *reflexive* deictic system, to avoid a merger between the mesial and question deictic systems (see items in bold at Stage 4 in the table).

Here is the scenario: In prehistory the voiceless initial of the mesial KP and the mesial deictic became voiced (Stage 3). This voicing spread to the mesial deictics in general. Now we would have e.g. *dö 'that' ⇔ *dwo 'which?' by only the A/B feature, a minimal pair. The vowels merged, as in Japanese (cf. 2.4), yielding *do (Stage 4), leading to confusion. Therefore, the mesial deictic system came to be represented by *o-, not *do- (Stage 5). The replacement salvaged the three-way system by replacing one deictic with a member of the reflexive system (cf. discussion by Vovin 2006: 269; also, cf. meanings of NJ *onore* 'self; I; you; you s.o.b.!').[7]

2.4 Frellesvig and Whitman (F&W)'s PJ Demonstrative System

Oddly enough, our deictic-replacement argument looks remarkably similar to an argument put forth in F&W (2004: 288) on the OJ deictic system.

(11)		PROXIMAL	MESIAL	DISTAL	INTERROG
MK		*i*	*ku*	*tye*	*e*
		PROXIMAL	MESIAL	DISTAL	INTERROG
pJ		*i̵	*ki̵	*si̵	*e
		PROXIMAL	MESIAL	DISTAL	INTERROG
pre-OJ. a		*i̵	*ki̵	*si̵	*i̵

---

[6] The word *öre* in OJ means 'you', and in MJ, 'I'; conversely, *önöre* in OJ means 'oneself', in early MJ, 'I', and in later MJ, 'you'. Note that (1) the original reflexive is seen at different times in J as reflexive (typically first person?), first person (equivalent to proximal), second person (equivalent to mesial); (2) in Japanese, too, a SJ word *jibun* (*jishin*) has replaced the original reflexive. While the Ryukyuan reflexive slipped into mesial deictic position, the Japanese reflexive slipped into the personal pronoun system, as either first- or second-person pronoun.

[7] A totally unlooked-for benefit of this hypothesis is that it also explains the use of the new reflexive morpheme, (*dou >) duu, which is found in Japanese only as a Sino-Japanese morph meaning 'body' or 'torso'. It has long seemed odd to observers that the Sino-Japanese morpheme should be used in ordinary colloquial Ryukyuan in this meaning. It must be added, however, that Nakamoto's (1990) etymology for *'uNzyu* 'you (polite); (your)self (polite); your body/health (polite)', namely *ore-no-syu[u] 'self's group', should be put aside in favor of the more straightforwardly explainable etymology *o-myi-dou 'EX-EX-self/body' (cf. Handa 1999: 104, 587-8). For the latter, see also Serafim (2004).

	PARTICIPANT	NONPARTICIPANT		INTERROG
pre-OJ. b	*kɨ	*sɨ		*i
	SPEAKER	NONSPEAKER		INTERROG
OJ	ko (~ i)	so		i- ~ idu-
	PROXIMAL	MESIAL	DISTAL	INTERROG
EMJ	ko	so	ka	i- ~ idu-

Agreeing with the claim of earlier demonstrative *i, as in *ima* 'now' ← *i* 'this' + *ma* 'interval', they (ibid: 288) assume that "OJ *i* descends from an earlier proximal pronoun, ... displaced by the ancestor of OJ *ko*." They support this scenario through matching the MK demonstrative system with that of Japonic: the PJ (our Proto-Japonic) system was upset by the new homonymy between the Pre-OJ proximal *i (< PJ *i) and interrogative *i (< pJ *e), but (ibid: 289) "resolved by proximal *i being ... retained only in fossilized compounds ... and mesial *kɨ and distal *sɨ ... reinterpreted as speech-event participant and nonparticipant ... (pre-OJ. b)."

F&W's proposed PJ deictic system is at odds with our hypothesized origin of KPs in (5). We agree that the *i ⇔ *e merger created an unstable system, and that the instability was resolved with a new proximal deictic. We are struck, however, with the fact that even their system does not take account of *ka. We believe that a reconceptualization of Hashimoto's (1982) axes of direct vs. indirect and of proximal vs. distal improves both the Hashimoto hypothesis and the F&W hypothesis.

(12) Our reconceptualization, for Pre-PJ, of Hashimoto's (1982) typology:

		proximal	non-proximal
direct experience	:	*kö	*ka
indirect experience	:	*i	*työ[8]

Loss of *i due to *i-/*e- merger destabilizes this system, resulting in a reconfiguration of the system to one of proximal, mesial, and distal, in which *kö remains proximal, *työ (> *sö) is a new mesial (also with ana-phoric functions), and *ka is the sole distal, finally yielding the PJ system.

(13)

	Proximal	mesial	distal	interrog
pJ	*kö ~ (*i)[9]	*sö	*ka	*i

OOk evidence supports proximal *i* alternating with KP |sul (*swo, dealt with in S&S 2005), in prehistory involving proximal *kö*. At its inception, both *i* and *kö* participated in KM, but *kö* won out in OJ. Thus OJ does not evince *i* as a KP, but OOk does, as shown in the parallel lines in example

---

[8] The placement of *työ in the non-proximal slot finds support from the *So-no-ki* example.
[9] By now *i is falling into disuse, and is present mostly in lexicalizations such as *ima* 'now'.

(14), from OS 5, and OS 123 respectively.

(14) a. katana 'uc-yi- **-yi** dya-kunyi tuyum-y[-i-y]uwar **-i** (5)
    b. katana 'uc-yi- **-si** dya-kunyi tuyum-y[-i-y]uwar **-i** (123)
      sword strike-RY- **-KP** great-land resound-RY-EX **-IZ**
    'It is with sword at his side that he is renowned in the great land.'

We assume that: KM at first had KP *i#swo 'this one' with the earlier indirect-experience proximal deictic *i, then with the direct-experience proximal deictic *kö: PJ *i/*kö + swo. (14a) is a trace of *i in Ryukyuan. Since Ryukyuan had also lost the original *i- as a *deictic* element (but *not* as an element in the KP complex), coming to be replaced with deictic *kö-, there developed a rift between deictic and KM usages. The *kö- deictic eventually developed into ku-, but the KP *i#swo dyad developed two free alternants, one *-i, and the other *-swo. Two facts undermined the continued use of *i: first, there already was a particle (*)-yi (< *-ye), a question particle; second, like *-ye, the proximal-derived KP *-yi remained in hiatus from its preceding vowel. Thus it fell out of use. The remaining free alternant, *-swo, continued in use until the KP + IZ construction itself was abandoned.

3. KPs and Their Functions: An Iconicity-based Account

3.1 Correspondences of KP Origin, Form, Function, and Meaning

Based on the foregoing, and adding the *musubi* conjugational forms, and their respective functions, we obtain Table 2. The characterization of 'strong assertion' for |kosol/|sul, as opposed to 'mere assertion' of |zol/|dol, comes from Ōno's (1993) work on OJ, and Mamiya's (2005) work on OOk.

Table 2. KPs and their form-function correspondences

KPs		Deictic	Functions	Conjugational
PJ	*OJ/Ok*	meanings		forms
kö#swo	|kosol/|sul	Proximal	Strong assertion	IZ
työ	|zol/|dol	Mesial	Assertion/ *Wh*-question	RT
ka	|kal/|gal	Distal	(*Wh*)-question /Doubt	OJ: RT -am-u Ok: MZ (= RT -am -u w/o ...mu)

In contrast to previous studies, which paid little attention to *musubi*-shape differences (besides IZ for |kosol/|sul), we emphasize the epistemic differences between the three *musubi* forms, namely IZ, regular RT, and inferential RT -am-u, as in (15). Realis/Irrealis here is not an aspectual distinction, despite the Japanese terms Izen and Mizen; rather, it is the speaker's evaluation, i.e. her/his certainty about the propositional content.

(15) IZ (both with & w/o preceding IA)::   Realis (Strong certainty)
      RT (non-inferential)   :: Realis (illocutionless, non-subjective)
      RT (with preceding IA)   ::   Irrealis (Uncertainty)

Certainty embodied in non-inferential IZ forms is perhaps not controversial (see Ogawa 1993), but the same treatment for the inferential -*am-ey* may be debated. The epistemic certainty -*am-ey* expresses is illustrated in the syntactic minimal pair in (16), where both predicates have the auxiliary -*(a)m-*, co-occurring with a *wh*-word, but without a KP. The RT form -*(a)m-u* in (16a) shows the speaker *wondering*, and *uncertain* as to the location where her love might shelter her in case of an unfavorable turn of events, while the IZ -*(a)m-ey* in (16b) expresses the speaker's *strong conviction* that her husband will not leave her behind (cf. MYS 14: 3577 also).

(16) a. WA[-GA]   se.kwo-pa   **IDUKU**   YUK-**ur-am-u** ...
          I-GEN   male.lover-TOP **where**   go-SE-**IA-RT**

          'I wonder where my love is traveling. (I wonder if it is today that he is crossing over the mountains [that are hidden like seaweed in the offing].)' (MYS 1: 43)

      b. WA[-GA]   SEKWO-wo   **IDUTI**   YUK-A**m-ey**   -tö
          I-GEN   love-SUB   **where**   go-**IA-IZ**   -QT

          '[Thinking,] "where would my husband go? [— nowhere]," (I refused him in our bed, and now, too late, I grieve.)' (MYS 1412)

A similar epistemic distinction is also applicable to OOk MZ -*a* < *-*(a)m-u* and IZ -*(a)m-i* (OS 1451, OS 1411 for MZ vs. IZ). In OS, IZ -*(a)m-i* and its regular IZ counterpart paraphrase each other in a single poem, as in (17). This can be interpreted as IZ -*(a)m-i* showing the speaker's certainty just as much as its non-inferential counterpart.

(17) 'ura-nu kazɨ   kyimyi-gyimyi **-syu**   mabur   **-i**
      village-'s number priestess-es **-KP**   protect **-IZ**
      syiyuryi-muryi   kyimyi-gyimyi **-syu**   mabur   **-am-i**
      Shuri-grove   priestess-es **-KP**   protect **-IA-IZ**

      'It is the priestesses of the inlet villages who are to protect (the ship in its voyage); it is the priestesses of the Shuri sacred grove, ...who will surely protect it. (OS 853)

Let us explain the characterization of non-inferential RTs as illocutionless and non-subjective in (15). They form a proposition, assumed, referential, and known as true to the speaker. Thus, in that sense, they are *realis* (cf. Ogawa 1993). *Rentai shūshi bun*, RT-ending sentences, are interpretable as exclamation, explanation, or question. Such diverse meanings obtain precisely because RT is illocutionless (i.e. the sentence is not predetermined to express particular meanings such as assertion, question, exclamation, etc.). RT sentences are nominals in essence, and thus, the meanings they convey are context-dependent (Onoe 1982, Iwasaki 1993). As shown in (18) from Shinzato (in press), the noun SNOW is variously interpretable, and so are RT sentences.

(18)   a. <<Look!>> Snow!
       b. <<You are wearing a heavy coat.>> Snow?
       c. <<I thought it was cold. I see why.>> Snow.
       d. <<So what is it? Something white...>> Snow.
       e. <<The Genie commands it to....>> Snow!

Recall also Nomura's (2002: 27) claim that a KP, having its own illocution (assertion, interrogation) to form a KM, could govern a RT clause because RT is illocutionless. Similarly, a KP did not couple with SS, since SS expresses its own illocution, i.e. the speaker's judgment.

This illocutionless-ness and lack of speaker judgment are the elements with which some scholars (Yoshida 1973, *inter alia*) associate the non-subjectivity of the RT form. That RT can have exclamatory tone may appear to suggest its subjectivity, but exclamation is not the intrinsic RT meaning (cf. Quinn 2001), but rather is yielded by the context. Just as the noun 'snow' itself in (18) has no subjective coloring, neither does RT. RT is illocutionless, or colorless, and precisely because of that, subjective coloring can be added when put into a context. We argue that non-inferential RTs differ from inferential RT (= *am-u* < *-am-wo*), which embodies uncertainty as its intrinsic meaning.

Based on the semantics of conjugational forms, Table 2 is now revised.

Table 3. KP origins, form, function, and meaning correspondences

KP Deictic meanings	Functions	Conjugational forms	Semantic characterization
Proximal |koso|/|su|	Strong assertion	IZ	Realis: strong certainty
Mesial |zo|/|do|	Assertion/ *Wh*-question	RT	Realis (illocutionless, non-subjective)
Distal |ka|/|ga|	(*Wh*)-question	OJ: RT without IA	Realis (illocutionless, non-subjective)
	/Doubt	OJ: RT-IA OOk: MZ (= RT-IA, without ...*mu*)	Irrealis: uncertainty Irrealis: uncertainty

Standing out from the above are the correspondences of deixis, functions, and semantic characterization, as below:

(19) Proximal :: Assertion (=A) :: Realis (certainty)
Mesial :: A & Q :: Realis (illocutionless / non-subjective)
Distal :: Question (=Q) :: Irrealis (uncertainty)

The distal row in (19) *could* have the feature *Realis* (certainty) as in Table 3, because of the non-inferential RT form. But it was simplified here, since the majority of the \|ka\|-type KM in OJ end with inferential auxiliaries (S&S 2000), the norm in MOk and NOk. Just as in Ok, in the Hachijō dialect (Kaneda 1998: 70), a direct descendant of the OJ Eastern dialect, the KP *ka*[10] obligatorily calls for the auxiliary *noo*, a corollary of -*(a)m*-.[11]

(20) Dai-**ka**   yokiita   n   **noo**. (Hachijō dialect,
who-**KP**   sent   NOM[12]   **IA**   while opening a box)

'I wonder who sent it to me.'

KP \|zo\|/\|do\| come between \|koso\|/\|su\| and \|ka\|/\|ga\|, in their mesial deictic meaning. Functionally, they are also in the middle, because on the one hand, they *assert*, like \|koso\|/\|su\|, and on the other, they *question*, like \|ka\|/\|ga\|. This duality also recalls the character of its *musubi*: the non-inferential RT expresses *realis* information, referential, and assumed to be true, but its information is not what the speaker takes sides on, either for or against; thus, in that sense, it is non-subjective and non-committal.

---

[10] This particle is not the same as the other KP *ka*, which has IZ as its *musubi*, Kaneda's suggested correspondent to OJ *kösö*.

[11] The sequence *yokiitannoo* in (20) consists of — in effect — **yokositaruramu*.

[12] Historically, it makes more sense to see this as a remnant of **ru*: **yokos-yi-tar-ur-am-u*. Our glossing follows Kaneda's Japanese glosses.

At this point, a question might arise as to the form-function-meaning correspondences of KPs: Are they accidental, or have they emerged based on some principle? This is a legitimate question whether one subscribes to insertion, inversion, or biclausal origin hypotheses, but nonetheless, it has not garnered much attention. The next section will take up this question in the context of the grammaticalization of demonstratives into focus particles and temporal copulas.

4. An Iconicity-based Account

The correspondence in (19) is not accidental; rather, it reflects the conceptual transfer of the deictic center from the spatial to the epistemic domain, since such a correspondence is cognitively sound, and finds corroboration in world-language grammaticalization: demonstrative $\rightarrow$ focus markers, and demonstrative $\rightarrow$ tensed copulas. These are shown below with examples.

A. demonstratives $\rightarrow$ **focus markers**
    proximal   ::   **assertion**
    distal   ::   **question**

(21)   AMBULAS, (Wilson 1980: 334-5, 172-3)[13]

   a. **ken**   wunat   kaperedi   waasa   ...   naadaka   (< ken 'this')
      FOCUS   to.me   very.bad   dog   ...   they.say.and
      'It is to me that they say, "very bad dog, ...," and...'

   b. **wan**   samu   bene   y-o   (< wan 'that')
      FOCUS   what   you$_D$ do-PR
      'What is it that you two are doing?'   (ibid: 172-3)

This distribution of *ken* and *wan* is certainly reminiscent of OJ/OOk |kosol/|su| vs. OJ/OOk |ka|/|ga|, which form strong assertion and inquiry respectively.

In all of the following examples, the proximal demonstratives associate with present or immediate future tense copulas, while distals associate either with past (Kilba & Napare), or future (Cemuhî).

B. demonstratives $\rightarrow$ **copulas**
    distal   ::   **past-tense copula**
    proximal   ::   **present-tense copula**
    distal   ::   **future-tense copula**

Schu (1983) reports on the association of proximal *nà* with the present tense

---

[13] Although Wilson (1980) gives no detailed account as to the difference between the two, from the data, it seems *wan can* appear in a question, while *ken* is reserved for a strong assertion.

and the distal *ndà* with the past tense.

(22) KILBA (Chadic language, Gongola State, Nigeria), (Schu 1983: 318)
a. àlí **nà** (proximal)
'It's Ali (e.g.referring to someone talking on the phone).'
b. àlí **ndà** (distal)
'It's Ali (e.g. said after speaking to someone and hanging up).'

Yet another example comes from Gildea (1993), who reports two Napare demonstratives grammaticalized as tense markers. The proximal deictic, *këj*, representing something within the sphere of perception, was grammaticalized as a present or immediate future marker. In contrast, the distal deictic, *nëj* became a past or distant future marker.

(23) NAPARE, Gildea (1993: 60-61)
a. maestro **këj** mëj
teacher **ANIM$_{\mathbf{PROX}}$** ANIM$_{\mathrm{VISIB}}$
'This guy **is** a teacher here' [He (PROX) is (PROX) a teacher.]
b. maestro **nëj** mëj
teacher **ANIM$_{\mathbf{DIST}}$** ANIM$_{\mathrm{VISIB}}$
'This guy **was** a teacher here' [He (PROX) is (DIST) a teacher.]

In a similar vein, de Haan (2005: 27) illustrates cases where spatial deictic meanings extend to temporal deictics. For instance, Cèmuhî (New Caledonia, citing Ozanne-Rivierre 1997:97 and Rivierre 1980:156-7) evinces the following correlation between spatial and temporal deixis:

(24) CÈMUHÎ (New Caledonia): de Haan (2005: 27)

	SPATIAL	TEMPORAL
cè	'near speaker'	**present tense**
ne	'distant, visible'	
naa	'distant, invisible'	**future tense**

Patterns A and B above recall Fleischman's (1989) account of an inverse relationship between temporal and modal (i.e. our epistemic) distance (C): the further the temporal distance in either direction, the harder for the speaker to vouch for the truth of the proposition. (25a-c) illustrates a cross-linguistic inverse relationship (e.g. Spanish & French): present :: 'probable' (25a), past :: 'improbable' (25b), and pluperfect :: 'impossible' (25c).

C. Temporal distance :: Modal (i.e. our epistemic) distances
Past: Less easy to vouch for
Present: Easy to vouch for (Undoubtedly true)
Future: Impossible to vouch for

(25) a. If I have time, I'll write to you
      b. If I had time, I would write to you.
      c. If I had had time, I would have written to you.

Emerging from Patterns A-C is the close relationship among spatial, temporal, and epistemic distance. It is realized on the one hand as the alignment of 'here', 'now', and 'certainty/strong commitment', and on the other, 'there', 'past/future', and 'uncertainty/weak commitment'. Not surprisingly, they all measure from the same deictic center, 'here', 'now', and 'I' (Büler 1982 [1934]).

Similarly, in the relationships in (19), the liaison between proximal *kö, the assertion-making function of |kosol/|sul, and their epistemic meaning of Realis (i.e. certainty) is what one would expect. In contrast, the distal *ka aligns with the question function of |kal/|gal, and their Irrealis meaning, uncertainty, as in the case of Ok, and of OJ and Hachijō dialects. Noteworthy is Givón's (1982: 44) iconicity-based proximity hierarchy: things near the scene are subjectively more certain than things away from the scene. In this sense, for the KP |zol/|dol of mesial deictic origin to take the dual functions (i.e. assertion and question), and to share them both with |kosol/|sul and |kal/|gal is also iconically reasonable.

5. Conclusion

A clear typological division of KPs has emerged from a comparative analysis of KM constructions in OJ, Ok, and Pan-Ryukyuan. The KPs shared in both branches are deictically based, and also, in a crosslinguistic context of deictic grammaticalization patterns, the correlations between KPs' origins, *musubi*, functions, and epistemic meanings turned out to be iconically motivated.

Abbreviations and Conventions

EMJ	Early Middle Japanese	NOM	nominalizer
EX	exalting	PST	past
GEN	genitive	RSLT	resultative
GER	gerund	RT	*rentai(kei)*
IA	inferential auxiliary	RY	*ren'yō(kei)*
IZ	*izen(kei)*	SE	stative extension marke
KP	*kakari* particle	SS	*shūshi(kei)*
MK	Middle Korean	SUB	subject
MZ	*mizen(kei)*	TOP	topic

References

Büler, K. 1982 [1934]. The Deictic Field of Language and Deictic Words. Abridged translation of K. Büler, 1934, *Sprachtheorie*, pt. 2, chs. 7, 8. *Speech,*

Place, and Action: Studies in Deixis and Related Topics, eds. R. Jarvella and W. Klein, 9-30. New York: John Wiley.

De Haan, F. 2005. Encoding Speaker Perspective: Evidentials. *Linguistic Diversity and Language Theories*, eds. Z. Frajzyngier, A. Hodges and D. Rood, 379-397. Amsterdam: John Benjamins.

Diessel, H. 1999. *Form, Function, and Grammaticalization* (Typological Studies in Language 42). Amsterdam: John Benjamins.

Frellesvig, B., and Whitman, J. 2004. The Vowels of Proto-Japanese. *Japanese Language and Literature* 38: 281-299.

Fleischman, S. 1989. Temporal Distance: A Basic Linguistic Metaphor. *Studies in Language* 13(1): 1-50.

Gildea, S. 1993. The Development of Tense Markers from Demonstrative Pronouns in Panare (Cariban). *Studies in Language* 17(1): 53-73.

Givón, T. 1982. Evidentiality and Epistemic Space. *Studies in Language* 6(1): 23-49.

Handa, I. 1999. *Ryūkyūgo Jiten* (Dictionary of Ryukyuan). Tokyo: Daigaku Shorin.

Hashimoto, S. 1982. Shijigo no Shiteki Tenkai (The historical development of deictics). *Kōza Nihongogaku*, vol. 2, eds. K. Morioka and H. Miyaji, 217-240. Tokyo: Meiji Shoin.

Hokama, S. 1981 [1972]. Omoro-go *i* no Bunpō-teki Seikaku (The grammar of the *omoro* word *i*). *Okinawa no Kotoba*, S. Hokama, 219-237. Tokyo: Chūō Kōronsha.

Iwasaki, S. 1993. Functional Transfer in the History of Japanese Language. *Japanese/Korean Linguistics* 3, ed. S. Choi, 20-32. Stanford: CSLI.

Kaneda, A. 1998. Gendai Nihongo no Naka no Kakari Musubi: Hachijōjima Hōgen no Rei o Chūshin ni (*Kakari musubi* in modern Japanese, focusing on examples from Hachijōjima dialect). *Gengo* 27(7): 67-73.

Mamiya, A. 2005. *Omoro Sōshi no Gengo* (The language of the *Omoro Sōshi*). Tokyo: Kasama Shoin.

MYS = *Man'yōshū*.

Nakamoto, M. 1990. *Nihon Rettō Gengoshi no Kenkyū* (Studies in the history of the languages of the Japanese archipelago). Tokyo: Taishūkan Shoten.

Nomura, T. 2002. Rentaikei ni Yoru Kakari Musubi no Tenkai (Development of *kakari musubi* from adnominal forms). *Nihongogaku to Gengo Kyōiku*, ed. H. Ueda, 11-37. Tokyo: Tōkyō Daigaku Shuppankai.

Ogawa, E. 1993. Jōhō Kōzō to Shite no Kakari Musubi (*Kakari musubi* as information structure). *Kokugo Kokubungaku* 32: 1-16.

Ōno, S. 1993. *Kakari Musubi no Kenkyū* (A study of KM). Tokyo: Iwanami Shoten.

Onoe, K. (1982), Bun no Kihon Kōsei: Shiteki Tenkai (Basic structure of sentences: Their historical development). *Kōza Nihongogaku*, vol. 2, eds. K. Morioka and H. Miyaji, 1-19. Tokyo: Meiji Shoin.

OS = *Omoro Sōshi*.

Quinn, C. J. 1997. On the Origins of Japanese Sentence Particles *ka* and *zo*. *Japanese/Korean Linguistics* 6, eds. J. Haig and H. Sohn, 61-89. Stanford: CSLI.

Quinn, C. J. 2001. Why Early Japanese Rentaikei Sentences Didn't Mean "...*koto*". *Cognitive-Functional Linguistics in an East Asian Context*, eds. K. Horie and S. Sato, 303-331. Tokyo: Kuroshio Publishers.

Ri, C. 2002. *Nihongo Shiji Taikei no Rekishi* (The history of deixis in the Japanese language). Kyoto: Kyōto Daigaku Gakujutsu Shuppankai.

464 / LEON A. SERAFIM & RUMIKO SHINZATO

Sakakura, A. 1993. *Nihongo Hyōgen no Nagare* (The trend of expression in Japanese over time). Tokyo: Iwanami Shoten.

Schu, R. G. 1983. Kilba Equational Sentences. *Studies in African Linguistics* 14: 311-326.

Serafim, L. A. 2004. The Shuri Ryukyuan Exalting Prefix **myi-* and the Japanese Connection, *Japanese Language and Literature* 38(2): 301-322.

Serafim, L. A. and Shinzato, R. 2000. Reconstructing the Proto-Japonic *Kakari Musubi, *ka ...(a)m-wo. Gengo Kenkyū* 118: 81-118.

Serafim, L. A. and Shinzato, R. 2005. On the Old Japanese Kakari (Focus) Particle *Koso:* Its Origin and Structure. *Gengo Kenkyū* 127:1-49.

Serafim, L. A. and Shinzato, R. 2009. An Overview of *Kakari Musubi* in Pan-Ryukyuan. Presented at the 1st Ryūkyūan Workshop, UCLA, Oct. 23-26, 2009.

Shinzato, R. To appear. Nominalization in Okinawan: From a Diachronic and Comparative Perspective. *Nominalization in Asian Languages: Diachronic and Typological Perspectives. Volume II: Asia Pacific Languages. Typological Studies in Language*, eds. F. H. Yap and J. Wrona. Philadelphia: Benjamins.

Takahashi, T. 1991. *Omoro Sōshi no Kokugogakuteki Kenkyū* (A linguistic/philological study of the *Omoro Sōshi*). Tokyo: Musashino Shoin.

Uchima, C. 1994. *Ryūkyū Hōgen Joshi to Hyōgen no Kenkyū* (A study of particles and expression in the Ryukyuan dialects). Tokyo: Musashino Shoin.

Vovin, A. 2005. *A Descriptive and Comparative Grammar of Western Old Japanese Part I: Sources, Script and Phonology, Lexicon, Nominals.* Folkestone, Kent: Global Oriental.

Wilson, P. R. 1980. *Ambulas Grammar.* Ukarumpa, Papua New Guinea: Summer Institute of Linguistics.

Yasuda, K. 1928. *Kokugohō Gaisetsu* (An overview of Japanese grammar). Tokyo: Chūkōkan.

Yoshida, K. 1973. *Jōdaigo Jodōshi no Shiteki Kenkyū.* (A historical study of Old Japanese auxiliary verbs). Tokyo: Meiji Shoin.

Rendaku in Sino-Japanese: Reduplication and Coordination

TIMOTHY J. VANCE
National Institute for Japanese Language and Linguistics

1. *Rendaku*

Many Japanese morphemes have one allomorph that begins with a voiceless obstruent and another allomorph that begins with a voiced obstruent. When a morpheme shows this kind of alternation, the allomorph that begins with a voiced obstruent can appear only when it is not the first morph in a word. For example:

(1) a. /tane/ 種 'seed'
    b. /tane+imo/ 種芋 'seed potato' (cf. /imo/ 'potato')
    c. /hi+dane/ 火種 'spark' (cf. /hi/ 'fire')

Notice that the morpheme meaning 'seed' is realized as /tane/ in (1a) and in (1b) but as /dane/ in (1c). The appearance of the voiced obstruent /d/ in /hi+dane/ is an instance of what is known in Japanese linguistics as *rendaku* 連濁—a technical term for which Martin (1952:48) suggested 'sequential voicing' as an English translation. In recent years the phenomenon has become widely known among linguists around the world, and it is typically

Japanese/Korean Linguistics 19.
Edited by Ho-min Sohn, Haruko Cook, William O'Grady, Leon A. Serafim, & Sang Yee Cheon.
Copyright © 2011, CSLI Publications

referred to in English-language publications as *rendaku* voicing, Japanese *rendaku*, or just *rendaku*.

The examples in (2) illustrate all the relevant phoneme alternations, including an additional instance of the /t/~/d/ alternation exhibited by the morpheme meaning 'seed'.[1]

(2) a. /f/~/b/   /fune/ 船 'boat'   /kawa+bune/ 川船 'river boat'
    b. /h/~/b/   /hako/ 箱 'case'   /haši+bako/ 箸箱 'chopstick case'
    c. /t/~/d/   /tama/ 玉 'ball'   /me+dama/ 目玉 'eyeball'
    d. /k/~/g/   /kami/ 紙 'paper'   /iro+gami/ 色紙 'colored paper'
    e. /c/~/z/   /cuka/ 塚 'mound'   /ari+zuka/ 蟻塚 'anthill'
    f. /s/~/z/   /sora/ 空 'sky'   /hoši+zora/ 星空 'starry sky'
    g. /č/~/ǰ/   /či/ 血 'blood'   /hana+ǰi/ 鼻血 'nosebleed'
    h. /š/~/ǰ/   /šika/ 鹿 'deer'   /ko+ǰika/ 子鹿 'young deer'

As these examples show, a voiceless obstruent and its *rendaku* partner differ in more than just the absence versus presence of voicing in many cases. These complications are due to well-known changes in Japanese pronunciation over the centuries (Vance 1987:133–148).

When it comes to spelling in *hiragana*, however, *rendaku* is a uniform phenomenon.[2] The relationships between *hiragana* symbols with and without the *dakuten* 濁点 diacritic (゛)mirror the alternations in (2). For example, the diacritic is added to the symbols for /fu/ ふ, /ha/ は, /ta/ た, and /ka/ か to write the syllables /bu/ ぶ, /ba/ ば, /da/ だ, and /ga/ が. Because of historical mergers, each of the syllables /zu/, /ji/, /ǰa/, /ǰo/, and /ǰu/ has two possible spellings.[3] Since the spelling reforms of 1946, the diacritic is usually added to /su/ す, /ši/ し, /ša/ しゃ, /šo/ しょ, and /šu/ しゅ to write /zu/ as ず, /ji/ as じ, /ǰa/ as じゃ, /ǰo/ as じょ, and /ǰu/ as じゅ. But when a morpheme affected by *rendaku* has a voiceless allomorph that begins with one of /cu/ つ, /či/ ち, /ča/ ちゃ, /čo/ ちょ, and /ču/ ちゅ, the practice is to write its voiced allomorph by just adding the diacritic and writing /zu/ as づ, /ji/ as ぢ, /ǰa/ as ぢゃ, /ǰo/ as ぢょ, and /ǰu/ as ぢゅ.[4] As a result, in terms of *hira-*

---

[1] The surfacy phonemic transcription used in this paper is the one worked out in Vance (2008b).
[2] The examples in this paper can also be spelled in *katakana*, and the corresponding *katakana* spellings are parallel in the relevant respects.
[3] The present-day *rendaku* pairings of /z/ with both /c/ and /s/ and of /ǰ/ with both /č/ and /š/ reflect the historical mergers of voiced affricates and voiced fricatives. The symbols じ, ぢ, ず, and づ, and the sounds they have represented over the course of history, are traditionally referred to as the *yotsugana* 四つ仮名 'four kana', and the mergers took place about 400 years ago in the Tokyo region (Toyama 1972: 198–202).
[4] Seeley (1991: 104–125, 153–154) describes the differences between the old spellings in use before the reforms (*kyū-kanazukai* 旧仮名遣い) and the new spellings adopted in 1946 (*gendai-kanazukai* 現代仮名遣い).

gana spelling, *rendaku* is just the addition of the diacritic, as in ありづか for (2e) /ari+zuka/ 'anthill' (cf. つか for /cuka/ 'mound') and はなぢ for (2g) /hana+ji/ 'nosebleed' (cf. ち for /či/ 'blood').

In some cases, a word contains a voiced obstruent that is etymologically a case of *rendaku* but is not recognized as such by ordinary speakers. An example is /cumazuku/ 躓く 'to trip', which originated as a compound of /cuma/ (~/cume/) 爪 'finger-/toe-nail' and /cuku/ 突く 'to thrust'. When the old *hiragana* spelling of such an example had づ or ぢ, it was replaced by ず or じ:

(3) /cumazuku/: つまづく > つまずく in 1946.

Rendaku is fundamentally irregular (Okumura 1955; Vance 1987:135–136, 2005a:8–9), but there are several well-known tendencies. One is that reduplicated native words (e.g. /toki+doki/ 時々 'sometimes') strongly favor *rendaku* (Martin 1952:49), unless the constraint called Lyman's Law (which prohibits *rendaku* in an element that contains a medial voiced obstruent) would be violated (e.g., 度々 /tabi+tabi/ 'often').[5] Another tendency is that native coordinate compounds strongly disfavor *rendaku* (Okumura 1955; Sakurai 1966:41). For example, /oya+ko/ 親子 'parent & child' lacks *rendaku*, even though the morpheme meaning 'child' often shows *rendaku* in noncoordinate compounds (e.g., /toši+go/ 年子 'children born a year apart'). Mimetic morphemes consistently resist *rendaku* (Martin 1952:49; Okumura 1955), even when reduplicated (e.g., /teku+teku/ てくてく 'tramp-tramp'), and non-Chinese borrowings resist almost as consistently (Nakagawa 1966:307–308; Irwin 2005:132–133). But when it comes to Sino-Japanese elements, the situation is more complicated.

2. Sino-Japanese

Sino-Japanese vocabulary items present some difficult challenges for a synchronic description of *rendaku* (Vance 1996). First consider binoms (*niji-jukugo* 二字熟語), which are certainly the prototypical Sino-Japanese words in modern Japanese. A binom is written with two *kanji*, each of which at least arguably represents a morpheme. Many binoms, although only a minority, exhibit *rendaku* when they appear as non-initial elements in compounds (Vance 1996:23–25). For example (using a dot rather than a plus sign to mark the boundary between elements within a binom):

(4) a. /mizu+deQ·poH/ 水鉄砲 'squirt gun'
    cf. /teQ·poH/ 'gun'
  b. /uN·doH+bu·soku/ 運動不足 'lack of exercise'
    cf. /fu·soku/ 'insufficiency'

---

[5] For details on Lyman's Law, see Vance (2005b, 2008a).

Within binoms, however, it is doubtful that historical instances of *rendaku* should be treated as *rendaku* in a synchronic analysis of modern Japanese. In some cases, binom-medial obstruent voicing simply continues voicing in the original borrowing from Chinese. This kind of voicing is known as *hondaku* 本濁 'original voicing'. Two examples of such original voicing are /mei·ǰiN/ 名人 'master' and /kei·ba/ 競馬 'horse racing'. In other cases, binom-medial obstruent voicing developed within Japanese after borrowing. This kind of voicing is known as *shindaku* 新濁 'new voicing'. Two examples of such new voicing are /yoH·ǰiN/ 用心 'caution' and /kaN·baN/ 看板 'signboard'. The /ǰiN/ written 心 cannot appear word-initially, and the Sino-Japanese pronunciation most commonly associated with this *kanji* is /šiN/, as in /šiN·pai/ 心配 'worry' and /aN·šiN/ 安心 'ease'. In contrast, the /ǰiN/ written 人 can appear word-initially, as in /ǰiN·koH/ 人口 'population', and this *kanji* never represents /šiN/. Given this difference in distribution (i.e., the possibility or impossibility of word-initial appearance), it might seem a simple matter to distinguish original voicing from new voicing and treat the latter as synchronic *rendaku*, but Sino-Japanese doublets muddy the waters considerably.

Consider the *kanji* 神, which can represent either /šiN/ or /ǰiN/. In this case, either pronunciation can occur word-initially:

(5) a. /šiN·wa/ 神話 'myth'   c. /sei·šiN/ 精神 'spirit'
    b. /ǰiN·ǰa/ 神社 'shrine'   d. /sui·ǰiN/ 水神 'water god'

The /ǰiN/ in (5b) /ǰiN·ǰa/ is an older borrowing (*goon* 呉音). The /šiN/ in (5a) /šiN·wa/ 神話 is a more recent borrowing (*kan'on* 漢音).[6] But how can we tell whether the /ǰiN/ in (5d) /sui·ǰiN/ is original voicing or new voicing? And is it realistic to expect an ordinary native speaker of modern Japanese to keep things straight?

3. *Hiragana* Spelling of Sino-Japanese Binoms

The 1946 spelling reform provides a hint that modern speakers do not think of binom-internal new voicing as *rendaku* (Vance 1996:27–28). Consider the examples in (6).

(6) a. /boH·zu/ 坊主 'Buddhist monk'   b. /yuH·zui/ 雄蕊 'stamen'
    ばうず > ぼうず in 1946   ゆうずゐ > ゆうずい in 1946

The /z/ in (6a) is new voicing (cf. /hoQ·su/ 法主 'high priest'), whereas the /z/ in (6b) is original voicing (since the *kanji* 蕊 never represents /sui/). In both (6a) and (6b), the second morph was spelled with ず (す /su/ plus the

---

[6] On *goon* vs. *kan'on*, see Miller (1967: 91, 102–104) and Tōdō (1977: 129–130).

diacritic) before 1946 and is spelled with the same letter today. Now compare (7).

(7) a. /soH·zu/ 僧都 'high-ranking cleric'   b. /cu·do/ 都度 'every time'
    そうづ > そうず in 1946   つど (no change in 1946)

The /z/ in (7a) is new voicing. As noted in Section 1, the 1946 reformers retained the spelling づ (つ /cu/ plus the diacritic) in clear cases of *rendaku*, as in ありづか for the native+native compound (2e) /ari+zuka/ 蟻塚 'anthill' (cf. つか for /cuka/ 'mound'). In contrast, the present-day spelling of the /zu/ in (7a) /soH·zu/ as ず rather than づ indicates that the reformers did not see it as an instance of *rendaku*.

Irwin (2005:121) uses the term 'mononom' to refer to a Sino-Japanese morpheme (written with a single *kanji*) that occurs alone as an element in a compound, and mononoms provide an interesting contrast with binoms. The examples in (8) illustrate with /zaN/~/saN/ 算 'calculation'.

(8) a. /taši+zaN/ 足し算 'addition'
       cf. native /taši/ 'adding'
    b. /neN·rei+zaN/ 年齢算 'age calculation problems'
       cf. Sino-Japanese /neN·rei/ 'age'
    c. /aN·zaN/ 暗算 'mental calculation'
       cf. Sino-Japanese /aN/ 'dark; unseen'
    d. /saN·suH/ 算数 'arithmetic'
       cf. Sino-Japanese /suH/ 'number'

The /z/ in (8a–c) is new voicing; the kanji 算 always represents /saN/, never /zaN/, in word-initial position, as in (8d). In both (8a) and (8b), the final element /zaN/ is a mononom, whereas the /zaN/ in (8c) is the second half of a binom. The obvious question to ask here in connection with mononoms is how words with diagnostic *hiragana* spellings were treated in the 1946 reforms, but there are very few relevant examples. These examples contain Sino-Japanese /ǰa/ 茶 'tea' (cf. /ča/ 茶 'tea') or /ǰuH/ 中 'during; throughout' (cf. /čuH/ 中 'during, within'), in which the /ǰ/ is new voicing.

For /ǰa/ 茶 'tea', consider the examples in (9).

(9) a. /kuči+ǰa/ 口茶 'adding tea leaves'
       cf. native /kuči/ 'mouth'
    b. /me+oto+ǰa·waN/ 夫婦茶碗 'paired teacups'
       cf. native /me+oto/ 'married couple'
       Sino-Japanese /ča·waN/ 'teacup'

The final element in (9a) is a mononom, and it was spelled ぢや (cf. ちや for

/ča/) before 1946.[7] This spelling was retained by the reformers, which suggests that they saw the /ǰ/ in /kuči+ǰa/ as an instance of *rendaku*.[8] As mentioned above in Section 2, some Sino-Japanese binoms exhibit *rendaku*, and /ča·waN/ 'teacup' is one of these. As expected, the pre-1946 spelling of /ǰa/ as ぢや was retained in examples like (9b) /me+oto+ǰa·waN/. Given the spelling change in examples like (7a) /soH·zu/ 僧都 'high-ranking cleric', the expectation is that the modern *hiragana* spelling of /ǰa/ 'tea' as the second element of a Sino-Japanese binom would be じや (cf. しや for /ša/) rather than ぢや. Unfortunately, this element meaning 'tea' does not seem to have developed new voicing as the second element of any binom. Thus, there are no examples containing /ǰa/ 'tea' that are parallel to (8c) /aN·zaN/ 暗算 'mental calculation'.

For /ǰuH/ 中 'during; throughout', consider the examples in (10).

(10) a. /mači+ǰuH/ 町中 'all over town'
  cf. native /mači/ 'town'
  b. /se·kai+ǰuH/ 世界中 'throughout the world'
  cf. Sino-Japanese /se·kai/ 'the world'
  c. /neN·ǰuH/ 年中 'throughout the year'
  cf. Sino-Japanese /neN/ 'year'

The final element in (10a) and (10b) is a mononom. The composition of (10a) /mači+ǰuH/ is like that of (8a) /taši+zaN/ 足し算 'addition' and (9a) /kuči+ǰa/ 口茶 'adding tea leaves': each contains a native element followed by a Sino-Japanese monomom. The composition of (10b) /se·kai+ǰuH/ is like that of (8b) /neN·rei+zaN/ 年齢算 'age calculation problems': both contain a Sino-Japanese binom followed by a Sino-Japanese mononom. The composition of (10c) is like that of (8c) /aN·zaN/ 暗算 'mental calculation': both are Sino-Japanese binoms. The /ǰuH/ in (10a–c) was spelled ぢゆう (cf. ちゆう for /čuH/) before 1946, but this spelling was changed to じゆう (cf. しゆう for /šuH/) by the reformers in all three cases. Notice in particular the changed spelling of the mononom in (10a) and (10b), in contrast to the unchanged spelling of the mononom in (9a) /kuči+ǰa/. The changed spelling in (10a–c) suggests that the reformers did not see the /ǰ/ in any of these words as an instance of *rendaku*.

---

[7] Note the full-size second letter in the old spellings. Only the first letter is relevant here, so old ぢや and new ぢや, and all parallel cases, are considered the same spelling.

[8] The word /kuči+ǰa/ is rather obscure, but no better example is available. Matsumura (1995) lists only one other word containing the mononom /ǰa/ meaning 'tea': /ha+ǰa/ 葉茶 'leaf tea' (cf. native /ha/ 'leaf'). This second word is just as obscure and, furthermore, has the alternative pronunciation /ha+ča/, without new voicing (see, e.g., the entry for /ha+ǰa/ in Matsumura 1995 and the entry for /ha+ča/ in Nihon Kokugo Daijiten Dainihan Henshū Iinkai 2000–02).

To summarize the apparent contradiction, the unchanged spelling ぢゃ of the /ǰa/ in (9a) /kuči+ǰa/ 口茶 indicates that new voicing in a Sino-Japanese mononom should be treated synchronically as an instance of *rendaku*, whereas the changed spelling じゅう of the /ǰuH/ in (10a) /mači+ ǰuH/ and in (10b) /se·kai+ǰuH/ indicates that new voicing in a Sino-Japanese mononom should not be treated synchronically as an instance of *rendaku*. However, it is probably a mistake to treat the /ǰuH/ written 中 in (10) as analogous to the /ǰa/ written 茶 in (9) and the /zaN/ written 算 in (8), because the /čuH/ and /ǰuH/ written 中 have diverged semantically. Compare the examples in (11) below with those in (10).

(11) a. /hanaši+čuH/ 話し中 'in the midst of talking'
      cf. native /hanaši/ 'talking'
   b. /go·zeN+čuH/ 午前中 'during the A.M.'
      cf. Sino-Japanese /go·zeN/ 'A.M.'
   c. /kuH·čuH/ 空中 'midair'
      cf. Sino-Japanese /kuH/ 'air'

As the crude glosses given earlier suggest, /ǰuH/ 中 tends to have the meaning 'throughout, all over', whereas /čuH/ tends to have the meaning 'during, within'. The well-known tendency for alternative pronunciations of a vocabulary item to develop distinct meanings has been labeled 'semantic bifurcation' (Bolinger 1968:110; Vance 2002). Dictionaries ordinarily do not even list morphs that exhibit new voicing, but it is typical to find separate entries for the suffix-like uses of /ǰuH/ and /čuH/ exemplified in (10) and (11) (see, e.g., the entries for *-chū* and *-jū* in Masuda 1974 and the corresponding entries in Matsumura 1995).[9]

Given the semantic bifurcation in /čuH/ versus /ǰuH/, it seems reasonable to take the *hiragana* spelling of the mononom /ǰa/ in (9a) /kuči+ǰa/ 口茶 'adding tea leaves' as the relevant hint in deciding whether or not to analyze typical examples of new voicing in Sino-Japanese mononoms as synchronic instances of *rendaku*. As already noted, since the 1946 reformers did not change the spelling of /ǰa/ as ぢゃ (cf. ちゃ for /ča/) in /kuči+ǰa/, they presumably saw the /ǰ/ in /kuči+ǰa/ as a case of *rendaku*. Thus, if we follow this hint in analyzing (8a) /taši+zaN/ 足し算 'addition' and (8b) /neN·rei+zaN/ 年齢算 'age calculation problems', the conclusion is that the /z/ in each is a synchronic instance of *rendaku*.

---

[9]As Jorden and Noda (1988:4) point out, the bifurcation is not complete, since /ǰuH/ and /čuH/ are synonymous in some examples, such as /kyoH+ǰuH/ 今日中 'during today' (cf. native /kyoH/ 'today') versus /hoN·ǰicu+čuH/ 本日中 'during today' (cf. Sino-Japanese /hoN·ǰicu/ 'today').

On the other hand, if we accept the suggestion offered at the beginning of this section that cases of binom-internal new voicing are not synchronic instances of *rendaku*, then we have to attribute the /z/ in (8c) /aN·zaN/ 暗算 'mental calculation' to something other than *rendaku*. As noted at the end of Section 2, it does not seem realistic to imagine that ordinary native speakers can distinguish new voicing from original voicing in Sino-Japanese binoms. The natural way to treat Sino-Japanese doublets is just to say that the two morphs realize different morphemes, although those morphemes are typically synonyms (Vance 1987: 172–174). This treatment applies to cases such as /ǰiN/ (original voicing) 神 'god' versus /šiN/ 神 'god' in (5), where the pronunciation difference matches a *rendaku* alternation (2h), as well as to cases such as /ǰiN/ (original voicing) 人 'person' versus /niN/ 人 'person', where the pronunciation difference does not match a *rendaku* alternation. The 1946 spelling reforms are consistent with this analysis. Consider the binom examples in (12).

(12) a. /či·ri/ 地理 'geography'   c. /hei·či/ 平地 'flat land'
     b. /ǰi·šiN/ 地震 'earthquake'   d. /ro·ǰi/ 露地 'open field'

The /ǰ/ in (12b) is original voicing, since it is word-initial, and the /ǰ/ in (12d) is probably original voicing too, although it is hard to be sure, since /č/~/ǰ/ is one of the *rendaku* alternations (2g). In any case, the /ǰi/ in both words was spelled ぢ (cf. ち for /či/) before 1946, but the reformers changed it to じ (cf. し for /ši/). This spelling change is in line with expectations on the assumption that /či/ 地 'land' and /ǰi/ 地 'land' in (12) are different (though synonymous) morphemes. If we treat unambiguous cases of new voicing in Sino-Japanese binoms in parallel fashion, then, for example, /zaN/ (new voicing) in (8c) /aN·zaN/ 暗算 'mental calculation' and /saN/ in (8d) /saN·suH/ 算数 'arithmetic' realize different (though synonymous) morphemes.

The proposed morphological relationships between the instances of /zaN/ and /saN/ in (8) are shown in (13) (see Vance 2007:60–62).

(13)

```
          ┌─ /saN/ in /saN·suH/ 算数 (8d)
     ┌─ = ├─ /zaN/ (rendaku) in /taši+zaN/ 足し算 (8a)
     │     └─ /zaN/ (rendaku) in /neN·rei+zaN/ 年齢算 (8b)
  ≠  │
     └─ /zaN/ (not rendaku) in /aN·zaN/ 暗算 (8c)
```

(13) shows clearly how the reasoning followed above leads to a highly counterintuitive conclusion. However, if we assume instead that examples like (8c) /aN·zaN/ 暗算 'mental calculation' do involve synchronic instances of *rendaku*, we are led to a different undesirable conclusion. Consider the examples in (14).

(14) a. /soN·zai/ 存在 'existence'   c. /zoN·buN/ 存分 'one's fill'
   b. /sei·zoN/ 生存 'survival'

The /z/ in (14c) /zoN·buN/ 存分 'one's fill' must be original voicing, since it is word-initial. It is hard to be sure about the /z/ in (14b) /sei·zoN/ 生存 'survival', since /s/~/z/ is one of the *rendaku* alternations (2f), but regardless of its historical status, assume that it is a synchronic instance of *rendaku*. On this assumption, the /zoN/ in (14b) /sei·zoN/ realizes the same morpheme as the /soN/ in (14a) /soN·zai/ 存在 'existence', but the /zoN/ in (14c) /zoN·buN/ 存分 'one's fill' has to be the realization of a different morpheme, since a word-initial voiced obstruent cannot be an instance of *rendaku*, as noted in Section 1. The proposed morphological relationships between the instances of /zoN/ and /soN/ in (14) are shown in (15) (see Vance 2007:62).

(15)

    = ⌈ /soN/ in /soN·zai/ 存在 'existence' (14a)
      ⌊ /zoN/ (*rendaku*) in /sei·zoN/ 生存 (14b)

  ≠ ⌊ /zoN/ (not *rendaku*) in /zoN·buN/ 存分 (14c)

The conclusion shown in (15), namely, that the /zoN/ in (14b) and the /zoN/ in (14c) are realizations of different morphemes, seems just as counterintuitive as the conclusion in (13). To avoid the counterintuitive aspects of both (13) and (15), we would have to assume that speakers manage to distinguish original voicing from new voicing and, in the case of the examples in (8) and (14), treat the /saN/ and /zaN/ written 算 in (8) as realizations of the same morpheme while treating the /soN/ and /zoN/ written 存 in (14) as realizations of different morphemes. As the rhetorical question at the end of Section 2 suggests, it seems unlikely that ordinary speakers can do this. I'll return to this issue in the conclusion below in Section 6.

4. Reduplicated Sino-Japanese Binoms

It is fairly easy to search the modern Japanese vocabulary systematically for reduplicated Sino-Japanese binoms. The number of phonemic forms that can realize a Sino-Japanese morph is quite small, and many of these forms are not relevant for present purposes because they do not begin with a voiceless obstruent. A search using an electronic version of *Kōjien* 「広辞苑」 (a widely used, comprehensive Japanese dictionary) yielded 206 examples of what appear to be reduplicated Sino-Japanese binoms with an initial voiceless obstruent (Vance 2007:8).[10] There is no danger of violating Lyman's Law (Section 1) in a Sino-Japanese binom because no Sino-Japanese morph contains a medial voiced obstruent. Of the 206 examples, only eight are listed

---

[10] The electronic version used for the search is based on the 4th edition of *Kōjien* (Shinmura 1998).

with medial voicing in the dictionary. One of these eight is /saN·zaN/ 散々 'severely'. Among the 198 examples without medial voicing is /taN·taN/ 淡々 'calmly'.

Of these 198 examples without medial voicing, 29 are common vocabulary items in the modern language, where 'common' is defined as 'listed in the *Genius Japanese-English Dictionary*「ジーニアス和英辞典」 (a medium-sized Japanese-English dictionary included in many electronic dictionaries)'.[11] Of the eight examples with medial voicing, four are common vocabulary items by this same definition:

(16) a. /saN·zaN/ 散々 'severely'   c. /sei·zei/ 精々 'at best'
    b. /šu·ǰu/ 種々 'variety'   d. /hoH·boH/ 方々 'all over'

The four examples with medial voicing in (16) are all quite salient, taking 'salient' to mean 'familiar even to the non-native-speaking author of this article'. In any case, it is probably better to count only common vocabulary items and use 4/33 (12%) rather than 8/206 (4%) as a measure of the rate of medial voicing in reduplicated Sino-Japanese binoms. Either way, if these instances of medial voicing are treated as *rendaku*, it is obvious that reduplicated Sino-Japanese binoms do not in general behave like reduplicated native words. As noted above in Section 1, reduplicated native words strongly favor *rendaku*, as long as Lyman's Law is not violated.

There are also two adjectives of the form SJbinom+/ši-i/ that have what looks like new voicing:

(17) a. /soH·zoH+ši-i/ 騒々しい 'noisy'[12]
    b. /fuku·buku+ši-i/ 福々しい 'plump and happy looking'[13]

Both (17a) and (17b) are common vocabulary items by the definition given in the preceding paragraph. In most adjectives consisting of a reduplicated base followed by /ši-i/, the reduplicated morpheme is native:

(18) a. /hana·bana+ši-i/ 華々しい 'glorious'
    b. /karu·garu+ši-i/ 軽々しい 'frivolous'
    c. /toge·toge+ši-i/ 刺々しい 'acrimonious'

---

[11] The electronic version used for the search is based on the 2nd edition of the *Genius* dictionary (Konishi and Minamide 2003).

[12] I am grateful to Satoshi Kinsui for pointing out to me that the base in (17a) /soH·zoH+ši-i/ is etymologically not Sino-Japanese. For suggestions that the interpretation of /soH/~/zoH/ as Sino-Japanese 騒 'noise' is a folk etymology, see the entries for *sōzōshii* in Matsumura 1995 and in Nihon Kokugo Daijiten Dainihan Henshū Iinkai 2000–02. Synchronically, this word can presumably be considered a relevant example.

[13] Leon Serafim has suggested to me that the base in (17b) may not be etymologically Sino-Japanese either. The /fuku/ in /fukuyoka/ 膨よか 'plump' is a plausible native source (cf. also the attested synonyms /fukuyaka/ 膨やか and /fukuraka/ 膨らか).

These examples with native bases all exhibit *rendaku*, as in (18a) and (18b), unless it would violate Lyman's Law, as in (18c).

The question that confronts us is: How should we analyze the four words in (16) and the two words in (17) synchronically? Should we treat them as instances of *rendaku*? None of them had a spelling involving a relevant letter (づ or ぢ) before the 1946 reform, so there is no direct evidence for the intuitions of the reformers.

5. Coordinate Sino-Japanese Binoms

It is not so easy to search systematically for coordinate Sino-Japanese binoms, since determining whether a word is coordinate requires consideration of its meaning. Of course, for present purposes, the only items of interest are those that have a second element beginning with an obstruent. If the second element in such a binom begins with a voiceless obstruent, it is an example that could have developed new voicing but did not, as in /soN·toku/ 損得 'loss & gain'.

Thanks to the publication of reverse-lookup (*gyakubiki* 逆引き) counterparts to comprehensive Japanese dictionaries, it is possible (though quite time-consuming) to find all the coordinate Sino-Japanese binoms listed in such a dictionary that did develop new voicing. As mentioned in Section 4, the number of phonemic forms that can realize a Sino-Japanese morph is fairly small, and the number that begin with a voiceless obstruent is, of course, even smaller. The search reported here used the reverse counterpart of *Daijirin*「大辞林」(another widely used, comprehensive Japanese dictionary), which groups words ending the same way by the *kanji* used to write their final elements.[14]

The search method was very simple-minded. To illustrate with a concrete example, consider the Sino-Japanese elements /šiN/ and /ǰiN/, both meaning 'heart; mind' and both written with the *kanji* 心. The /ǰ/ in this /ǰiN/ is an instance of new voicing. All the *Daijirin* headwords that end with /šiN/ or /ǰiN/ written 心 are grouped into a single list in the reverse-lookup *Daijirin*. All that is necessary is to scan the *hiragana* spellings of the words on that list and pick out the binoms that end じん, which spells /ǰiN/. In this particular case, there are 329 words on the list, 202 of which are Sino-Japanese binoms (excluding proper names). Of those 202 binoms, seven end with /ǰiN/, including /šiN+ǰiN/ 信心 'belief'. And of those seven that end with /ǰiN/, one is coordinate: /kaN+ǰiN/ 肝心 'essential' (literally 'liver & heart'). The great majority of the binoms on this list (195/202) do not have new voicing, that is, they end with /šiN/ rather than with /ǰiN/. In fact, this is

---

[14] This reverse-lookup dictionary (Sanseidō Henshūsho 1997) is based on the 2nd edition of *Daijirin* (Matsumura 1995).

the general pattern: of all the Sino-Japanese binoms of interest, only a small minority have new voicing. Consequently, finding all the coordinate binoms listed in *Dajirin* that did develop new voicing is a manageable task, because the number of items that have to be checked for coordinate meaning is relatively small. The results of this search are reported below. In contrast, to find all the coordinate binoms that did not develop new voicing would require going through a much larger number words and checking each one for coordinate meaning. Since this more daunting task has not been carried out, it is not possible to provide even a rough estimate of the proportion of coordinate Sino-Japanese binoms that actually have new voicing.

Of the coordinate Sino-Japanese binoms that did develop new voicing, eight are common vocabulary items by the definition given in Section 4 (i.e., listed in the *Genius Japanese-English Dictionary*). These eight examples are given in (19).

(19) a. /iN·ga/ 因果 'cause & effect'
    b. /toH·zai/ 東西 'east & west'
    c. /koN·ǰaku/ 今昔 'past & present'
    d. /šuN·ǰuH/ 春秋 'spring & autumn'
    e. /ši·ǰuH/ 始終 'always' (literally 'beginning & ending')
    f. /kaN·ǰiN/ 肝心 'essential' (literally 'liver & heart')
    g. /moN·doH/ 問答 'question & answer'
    h. /naN·boku/ 南北 'south & north'

Incidentally, examples like /keN·go/ 堅固 'firm, solid' (literally 'solid+firm') are not considered coordinate here. Unlike the examples in (19), and also unlike coordinate compounds consisting of native elements, the two elements in /keN·go/ are synonyms.

In any event, it is clear that coordinate Sino-Japanese binoms have not resisted new voicing as strongly as native coordinate compounds have resisted *rendaku*. The only convincing example of *rendaku* in a native coordinate compound is in /aši+de+matoi/ 足手纏い 'hindrance'.[15] There is no independent word /aši+de/ 'feet & hands', but this element is clearly coordinate in {{/aši/+/de/}+/matoi/}.

As for whether the examples of new voicing in (19) should be analyzed as synchronic instances of *rendaku*, none of them had a spelling involving a relevant letter (づ or ぢ) before the 1946 reform. Thus, just as in the case of

---

[15] I am grateful to Nobue Suzuki for bringing this example to my attention many years ago. Nihon Kokugo Daijiten Dainihan Henshū Iinkai 2000–02 lists only *ashi-te-matoi*, without *rendaku*, as a headword, but the entry gives the form with *rendaku* is an alternative pronunciation. The form without *rendaku* seems to be obsolescent or obsolete in Tokyo today.

the reduplicated binoms in (16) and (17) in Section 4, there is no direct evidence for the intuitions of the reformers.

6. Conclusion

One possible synchronic analysis is to say that a medial voiced obstruent in a Sino-Japanese binom is never an instance of *rendaku*. As we saw in Section 3, in those cases where the *hiragana* spelling changes adopted in 1946 are diagnostic, they are consistent with this analysis. We saw in Section 4 that new voicing occurs in reduplicated Sino-Japanese binoms, but only rarely. In contrast, reduplicated non-mimetic native compounds strongly favor *rendaku*, whereas reduplicated mimetic compounds consistently resist it. If medial voicing in a reduplicated Sino-Japanese binom is not an instance of *rendaku*, the disparity is not a problem for a synchronic analysis of *rendaku*.

As we saw in Section 5, new voicing occurs in some coordinate Sino-Japanese binoms and does not seem to be unusual, although it is hard to estimate how prevalent it is. In contrast, coordinate native compounds strongly disfavor *rendaku*. Here again, if medial voicing in a coordinate Sino-Japanese binom is not an instance of *rendaku*, the disparity is not a problem for a synchronic analysis of *rendaku*.

A synchronic analysis that does treat instances of new voicing in Sino-Japanese binoms as instances of *rendaku* will, of course, have to relativize the account of *rendaku* so that the constraints, rules, or whatever apply differently to different categories of vocabulary items. Furthermore, the daunting problem of how (and whether) to distinguish new voicing from original voicing has to be dealt with in an analysis that identifies new voicing with *rendaku* (Vance 1996, 2007).

Finally, leaving synchronic analysis aside, we need a plausible diachronic story for the development of new voicing. It does not seem satisfactory to view new voicing as just the haphazard analogical spread of *rendaku* into borrowed (i.e., Sino-Japanese) vocabulary items, since it has been known for a long time that an immediately preceding nasal was a strong promoting factor (Hamada 1952:18–19; Okumura 1952:11–13; Endō 1966: 70–71). In fact, it was perfectly obvious during the search described in Section 5 that the great majority of instances of new voicing in Sino-Japanese binoms developed following an initial element that ended in a nasal. When this nasal was Chinese /m/ or /n/, modern Japanese has /N/, and when it was Chinese /ŋ/, modern Japanese has vowel length or the second half of a VV sequence (Miller 1967:204–205; Okumura 1972:73–78, 82–87). Of the eight examples of new voicing in (19), seven involved an immediately preceding nasal, including (19b) /toH·zai/ 東西 'east & west' (cf. modern Mandarin *dōng* 東). On the other hand, no such nasal was involved in (19e) /ši·juH/ 始終 'always' (cf. modern Mandarin *shǐ* 始). And, as noted above in Section 5, of all the Sino-Japanese binoms that could have developed new voicing, most did not, including many with an initial element that ended in a nasal. In short, the relationship between nasals and new voicing is no more than a tendency.

References

Bolinger, D. 1968. *Aspects of Language.* New York: Harcourt, Brace & World.

Endō, Y. 1966. Rendakugo no yure (Variability in *rendaku* words). *Kokugo Kokubun* 35(5): 68–77.

Hamada, A. 1952. Hatsuon to dakuon to no sōkansei no mondai (On the correlation between mora nasals and voicing). *Kokugo Kokubun* 21(4): 18–32.

Irwin, M. 2005. Rendaku-Based Lexical Hierarchies in Japanese: The Behaviour of Sino-Japanese Mononoms in Hybrid Noun Compounds. *Journal of East Asian Linguistics* 14: 121–153.

Jorden, E. H. and Noda, M. 1988. *Japanese: The Spoken Language, Part 2.* New Haven: Yale University Press.

Konishi, T. and Minamide, K. eds. 2003. *Genius Japanese-English Dictionary* [*Jīniasu waei jiten*], 2nd ed. Tokyo: Taishūkan Shoten.

Masuda, Koh, ed. 1974. *Kenkyusha's New Japanese-English Dictionary* [*Shin waei daijiten*], 4th ed. Tokyo: Kenkyūsha.

Martin, S. E. 1952. *Morphophonemics of Standard Colloquial Japanese.* Supplement to *Language* (*Language Dissertation No. 47*).

Matsumura, A., ed. 1995. *Daijirin*, 2nd ed. Tokyo: Sanseidō.

Miller, R. A. 1967. *The Japanese Language.* Chicago: University of Chicago Press.

Nakagawa, Y. 1966. Rendaku, rensei (kashō) no keifu (The genealogy of sequential voicing and [as a provisional term] sequential voicelessness). *Kokugo Kokubun* 35: 302–314.

Nihon Kokugo Daijiten Dainihan Henshū Iinkai, ed. 2000–02. *Nihon Kokugo Daijiten* (Great dictionary of the Japanese national language), 2nd ed. Tokyo: Shōgakukan.

Okumura, M. 1952. Jion no rendaku ni tsuite (On *rendaku* in Sino-Japanese elements). *Kokugo Kokubun* 21(6): 8–22.

Okumura, M. 1955. Rendaku. *Kokugogaku jiten*, ed. Kokugo Gakkai, 961–962. Tokyo: Tōkyōdō.

Okumura, M. 1972. Kodai no on'in (Old Japanese phonology). *Kōza Nihongoshi 2: On'inshi, mojishi*, ed. N. Nakata, 63–171. Tokyo: Taishūkan Shoten.

Sakurai, S. 1966. Kyōtsūgo no hatsuon de chūi subeki kotogara (Matters requiring attention in the pronunciation of the common language). *Nihongo hatsuon akusento jiten*, ed. Nihon Hōsō Kyōkai, 31–43. Tokyo: Nihon Hōsō Shuppan Kyōkai.

Sanseidō Henshūsho, ed. 1997. *Kanjibiki, gyakubiki Daijirin* (*Kanji*-lookup and reverse-lookup *Daijirin*). Tokyo: Sanseidō.

Seeley, C. 1991. *A History of Writing in Japan.* Leiden: E. J. Brill.

Shinmura, I., ed. 1998. *Kōjien*, 4th ed. Tokyo: Iwanami Shoten.

Tōdō, A. 1977. Kanji gaisetsu (An outline of *kanji*). *Iwanami kōza Nihongo 7: Moji*, ed. S. Ōno and T. Shibata, 61–157. Tokyo: Iwanami Shoten.

Toyama, E. 1972. Kindai no on'in (Early modern phonology). *Kōza Nihongoshi 2: On'inshi, mojishi*, ed. N. Nakata, 173–268. Tokyo: Taishūkan Shoten.

Vance, T. J. 1987. *Introduction to Japanese Phonology*. Albany: SUNY Press.

Vance, T. J. 1996. Sequential Voicing in Sino-Japanese. *Journal of the Association of Teachers of Japanese* 30: 22–43.

Vance, T. J. 2002. Semantic Bifurcation in Japanese Compound Verbs. *Japanese/ Korean Linguistics 10*, ed. N. Akatsuka and S. Strauss, 365–377. Stanford: CSLI.

Vance, T. J. 2005a. Nihongo kyōiku ni okeru rendaku (*Rendaku* in Japanese language education). *Gengogaku to Nihongo kyōiku IV*, ed. M. Minami, 1–11. Tokyo: Kuroshio Shuppan.

Vance, T. J. 2005b. Sequential Voicing and Lyman's Law in Old Japanese. *Polymorphous Linguistics: Jim McCawley's Legacy*, ed. S. S. Mufwene, E. J. Francis, and R. S. Wheeler, 27–43. Cambridge: MIT Press.

Vance, T. J. 2007. Reduplication and the Spread of *Rendaku* into Sino-Japanese. *KLS 27: Proceedings of the Thirty-First Annual Meeting*, 56–64. Osaka: Kansai Linguistic Society.

Vance, T. J. 2008a. Have We Learned Anything About *Rendaku* that Lyman Didn't Already Know? *Current Issues in the History and Structure of Japanese*, ed. B. Frellesvig, M. Shibatani, and J. C. Smith, 153–170. Tokyo: Kurosio Publishers.

Vance, T. J. 2008b. *The Sounds of Japanese*. Cambridge: Cambridge University Press.

Part VI

Psycholinguistics and L1/L2 Acquisition

Contrastive Focus Affects Word Order in Korean Sentence Production

HEEYEON Y. DENNISON
University of Hawai'i at Mānoa

AMY J. SCHAFER
University of Hawai'i at Mānoa

1. Introduction

This paper presents results of a sentence production experiment in Korean that investigated speakers' preferences in word order. Despite the existence of so-called "canonical" order for certain types of sentences, Korean exhibits flexible linear word orders that maintain constant grammatical relations (Sohn 1999). For example, a dative sentence describing an object transfer can have various word orders above and beyond those described in (1), while (1a) is considered as the canonical order.

(1)   a. Subject—Indirect Object (IO)—Direct Object (DO)—Verb.
       b. Subject—DO—IO—Verb.
       c. IO—Subject—DO—Verb.
       d. IO—DO—Subject—Verb.
       Etc.

Japanese/Korean Linguistics 19.
Edited by Ho-min Sohn, Haruko Cook, William O'Grady, Leon A. Serafim, & Sang Yee Cheon.
Copyright © 2011, CSLI Publications

Given the flexibility permitted in the language along with the existence of the canonical order, we can ask which factors lead native speakers of Korean to produce one word order versus another in the course of online sentence production. Previous studies using psycholinguistic experiments have identified several factors affecting speakers' word order choices in online production. For example, *information status* of the noun phrases matters: people tend to mention given information before new information (e.g. Ferreira and Yoshita 2003). *Imageability* of the referent also affects word order. Bock and Warren (1985), for example, found that noun phrases with more imageable or concrete referents are mentioned earlier than less imageable referents. *Phrasal length* is also a factor, but its influence is in the opposite direction in English and Korean/Japanese, arguably due to differences in verb placement across these languages (Hawkins 2004). English speakers tend to mention short phrases before long phrases (e.g. Arnold, Wasow, Losongco, and Ginstrom 2000, Stallings, MacDonald, and O'Seaghdha 1998), while Korean and Japanese speakers mention long phrases before short phrases (e.g. Dennison 2008, Yamashita and Chang 2001).

Another factor that has received much attention is the *animacy* of the referent. Various studies have demonstrated that people prefer to mention animate entities before inanimate entities (e.g. Chang, Kondo, and Yamashita 2000, Dennison 2008, Pra-Sala and Branigan 2000, Branigan, Pickering, and Tanaka 2008). Dennison (2008), for example, investigated how animacy of the dative argument affects speakers' preference for the canonical order [S–IO–DO–V] in Korean. Materials included sentences like (2), where the direct object (DO) was always inanimate and the indirect object (IO) was either animate (2a) or inanimate (2b).

(2)   a. Yengswu-ka   **samchon**-hanthey phica-lul paytalhaysseyo.
          Yengswu-NOM **uncle**-DAT   pizza-ACC delivered.
          'Yengswu delivered pizza to uncle.'

    b. Yengswu-ka   **yuchiwen**-ey   phica-lul paytalhaysseyo.
          Yengswu-NOM **kindergarten**-DAT pizza-ACC delivered.
          'Yengswu delivered pizza to kindergarten.'

The results from a sentence production experiment found that speakers produced the canonical order [S–IO–DO–V] 67% of the time when the indirect object was animate. When the indirect object was *in*animate, however, this canonical order preference was significantly reduced to 48%. Instead, people produced an order that switched the order of the internal arguments [S–DO–IO–V] for 44% of the productions, a substantial increase from 27% with the animate IO. These results suggest that the canonical order could be an artifact of a more general preference to mention animate entities before inanimate entities.

Researchers have strived to provide processing-oriented reasons for word order preferences and have argued that this set of factors and their influences on word order can be captured by the construct of conceptual accessibility: the ease with which the mental representation of some potential referent can be activated in or retrieved from memory (Bock and Warren 1985: 50). Consider how this fits with current models of human sentence production.

Levelt (1989) and others have observed that humans produce speech at the impressive rate of three to five words per second. Speakers do so by uttering words and phrases as they become available, instead of waiting for a full sentence to be prepared (e.g. Ferreira 1996, Ferreira and Dell 2000). This is because the sentence production system allows incremental processing of the material within a sentence, as well as simultaneous processing across multiple levels of linguistic analysis (see Branigan et al. 2008, for a detailed description).

The accessibility of a concept affects the incremental output of the sentence production system. A concept that is more quickly accessed or activated will have a chance to complete the necessary processing earlier, hence taking higher grammatical relations as well as earlier linear positions (e.g. Branigan et al. 2008, Bock and Warren 1985, Chang et al. 2000, McDonald, Bock, and Kelly 1993, Prat-Sala and Branigan 2000). Therefore, variation in conceptual accessibility can affect sentence word order due to the incremental nature of the sentence production mechanism. More specifically, phrases that present highly accessible material, such as information that is given, imageable, or animate, will tend to occur early in the sentence, because its processing can be completed before that for other phrases.

Given that conceptual attributes are influential in speakers' word order, we investigated the role of another conceptual factor: contrastive focus. Contrastive focus can be seen in Korean sentences employing -*man*, a particle conveying the meaning of 'only' as in (3) below (e.g. Jackson 2008).

(3) Yumyengin-i yuchiwen-ey-**man** khetalan sikyey-lul senmwulhaysse.
     celebrity-NOM kindergarten-DAT-**only** big clock-ACC presented.
     'A celebrity presented a big clock only to a kindergarten.'

The sentence's surface meaning highlights that a celebrity presented (i.e. gave as a present) a big clock to the focused entity *kindergarten*. However, the sentence also implies that a celebrity did not give a big clock to any other organizations like an elementary school or high school. The unmentioned set of items that is implicitly in contrast with the focused target is called the alternative set.

Recently, many researchers have investigated how contrastive focus is understood in the mind of speakers (e.g. Ito and Speer 2008, Sedivy 1997). This work has found that contrastive focus is conceptually rich and that the mental calculation of the alternative set is quite fast (e.g. Rooth 1992, Sedivy, Tanenhaus, Eberhard, Spivey-Knowlton, and Carlson 1995). It seems that contrastive focus may increase conceptual saliency. For example, Both Watson, Tanenhaus, and Gunlogson (2008) and Ito and Speer (2008) found faster eye movements in English to the referents of phrases marked with the L+H* pitch accent, which is used to convey contrastive focus. Contrastive focus can be seen as a linguistic device that marks the mentioned information as highly salient while also contrasting it with the alternative set.

If contrastive focus increases conceptual accessibility, we would expect it to influence linear phrasal ordering in Korean sentence production. However, conceptual accessibility is not the only plausible determinate of an effect of contrastive focus on Korean word order. The following sections describe two distinct predictions for the ordering of contrastively focused material. We then present a sentence production experiment that tests these predictions.

2. The Current Study

The current study tested the effect of contrastive focus on Korean word order production using a phrase-assembly task similar to Dennison (2008) and Yamashita and Chang (2001). We identified two competing hypotheses, drawing from theories of sentence production and syntactic typology.

First, with the *Conceptual Accessibility Hypothesis*, we predicted that a contrastively focused item should tend to be placed on the left periphery of the sentence. This pattern fits with what the current theory of sentence production anticipates: the more salient or accessible a concept is, the earlier it will appear in the sentence, because information is processed in an incremental fashion (e.g. Branigan et al. 2008). The Conceptual Accessibility Hypothesis is consistent with previous findings for the comprehension of Korean sentences, which has shown that phrases which are contrastively focused (and marked by –*man*) are more likely to be interpreted as having been scrambled – that is, moved to an earlier position in the sentence (e.g. Hwang, Schafer, and O'Grady 2010).

However, other research suggests that a contrastively focused element may tend to appear immediately before the verb. Kim (1988), among others, has argued that the preverbal position is a focus position in Korean as well as in many head-final languages. Kim observed that wh-words such as 'who' and 'what', which are considered to be in focus, usually take the preverbal position. If this pattern extends to contrastively focused phrases (versus "regular focus" or "rhematic focus"), then instead of moving to the left-periphery (or perhaps, to a more leftward position), a contrastively focused phrase should tend to be the rightmost of the preverbal phrases. We call this the *Head Proximity Hypothesis*, where proximity is operationalized as linear proximity of the contrastively focused phrase to the sentence-final verb. This hypothesis follows from a separation of topic and focus (or theme and rheme) in which topic is normally placed early in the sentence, and focused information occurs late in the sentence, even though other factors can easily alter this general pattern (e.g. Kim 1988, Lambrecht 1996).

These two hypotheses make opposing predictions about contrastively focused phrases. The Conceptual Accessibility Hypothesis predicts that the focused phrase will be produced early in the sentence, while the Head Proximity Hypothesis predicts it will occur late, and specifically just prior to the verb.

To test these hypotheses, we developed three types of dative sentences as in (4). Dative sentences provide good testing cases since their three preverbal arguments allow multiple possibilities for word order. Moreover, the existence of and possible reasons for the canonical order for the dative structure has been explored using the same or similar experimental tasks (e.g. Dennison 2008), so the current results have bases for further comparison. Here, the sentences are shown in the canonical order, but this is not how participants received the materials (see the materials section).

(4)   a. No contrastive focus marker (Broad Focus)
        Yumyengin-i yuchiwen-ey   khetalan sikyey-lul senmwulhaysse.
        celebrity-NOM kindergarten-DAT   big clock-ACC presented.
        'A celebrity presented a big clock to a kindergarten.'

        b. Contrastive focus marker on the dative argument (IO Focus)
        Yumyengin-i yuchiwen-ey-**man** khetalan sikyey-lul senmwulhaysse.
        celebrity-NOM kindergarten-DAT-only big clock-ACC presented.
        'A celebrity presented a big clock only to a kindergarten.'

        c. Contrastive focus marker on the accusative argument (DO Focus)
        Yumyengin-i yuchiwen-ey   khetalan sikyey-**man** senmwulhaysse.
        celebrity-NOM kindergarten-DAT big clock-only   presented.
        'A celebrity presented only a big clock to a kindergarten.

All sentences in each test condition contained a subject, an indirect object (IO), a direct object (DO), and a ditransitive verb. Moreover, only inanimate referents were chosen for both IOs and DOs to avoid any unintended variability due to an animacy difference for these two phrases. Instead, the critical manipulation was the presence of the contrastive focus marker *-man* on the IO, the DO, or neither phrase. If participants are sensitive to the conceptual aspect of the contrastive focus, or to the need for head proximity, then we should be able to observe word order variation depending on the presence or absence of the contrastive focus marker *–man*.

More specifically, the *Broad Focus* condition in (4a) served as a baseline condition to collect the default word-order preference for the experimental materials. Based on Dennison's (2008) results, we anticipated a weak preference for the canonical order since the dative and accusative arguments were both inanimate.

The *IO focus* and *DO focus* conditions allowed a direct testing of the two hypotheses described above. For the Conceptual Accessibility Hypothesis, we predicted two patterns of evidence: strong and weak. Strong evidence for a conceptual accessibility effect would be obtained if the focused element reliably takes the earliest possible position in the sentence. Therefore, in the *IO focus* condition we should find a higher percentage of the [*IO*–S–DO–V] order than other grammatical options, whereas in the *DO focus* condition we should find a higher portion of the [*DO*–S–IO–V] order.

Weaker evidence for the conceptual accessibility hypothesis would come from results where the focused element takes the second earliest possible position in the sentence: hence, the preferred order should be [S–*IO*–DO–V] in the *IO focus* condition and [S–*DO*–IO–V] in the *DO focus* condition. (Since the subject phrase was always animate, this pattern might suggest that animate phrases have higher accessibility than contrastively focused inanimate phrases.)

However, the Head Proximity Hypothesis predicts that the preverbal position is the focus position. If this is true, we should find the focused item immediately before the verb, and the preferred orders should be [S–DO–*IO*–V] in the *IO focus* condition and [S–IO–*DO*–V] in the *DO focus* condition. (5) – (7) summarize the dominant production pattern predicted for each condition. Note that because past results have shown a mix of word orders with broad-focus presentation, options (6b) and (7c) could potentially occur for a significantly greater number of productions than in the broad-focus condition that serves as a baseline.

(5)   Strongest evidence for the Conceptual Accessibility Hypothesis
      a. Broad Focus: S–IO–DO–V.
      b. IO focus: *IO*–S–DO–V.
      c. DO focus: *DO*–S–IO–V.

(6)   Weaker evidence for the Conceptual Accessibility Hypothesis
      a. Broad Focus: S–IO–DO–V.
      b. IO focus: S– *IO*–DO–V.
      c. DO focus: S– *DO*–IO–V.

(7)   Strongest evidence for the Head Proximity Hypothesis
      a. Broad Focus: S–IO–DO–V.
      b. IO focus: S–DO– *IO*–V.
      c. DO focus: S–IO– *DO*–V.

2.1 Participants

Eighteen native Korean speakers at the University of Hawai'i at Mānoa participated in a sentence production experiment and received $10 each in compensation. They were all born and raised in Korea and came to the United States for higher education.

2.2 Materials and Task

The experiment employed a phrase-assembly task that was disguised as a phrase-recognition task (Dennison 2008; Stallings et al. 1998; Yamashita and Chang 2001). Each critical sentence (similar to (4) above) was separated into four phrases and presented in four boxes on the computer screen (see panel A in Figure 1).

For all critical trials, the subject and verb locations were fixed at the bottom-right and top-left corners respectively. However, the IO and DO locations on the computer screen were balanced between the bottom-left and top-right boxes in order to monitor any possible influence of the phrase location on word order preferences. Counterbalancing two levels of screen locations and three types of sentences (i.e. Broad Focus, IO focus, DO focus) yielded six experimental conditions. These conditions were rotated through the experimental items across six presentation lists following a Latin-square design.

Each experimental list included thirty critical sentences along with ninety filler sentences that varied in type and length (e.g. transitives, intransitives, instrumentals, wh-questions).

2.3 Procedure

After signing a consent form, each participant sat in front of a computer and read instructions for the goal and procedure of the experiment. The experiment goal was described as a memory test measuring how quickly participants would recognize sentence parts that they saw in previous trials. For this reason, forty percent of the fillers were presented twice during an experimental session.

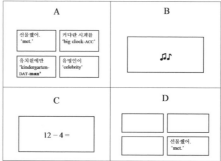

Figure 1. A sequence of a trial in one of the IO focus conditions
(The English translation was not given in the actual task.)

After the instructions, all participants received ten practice trials. For each trial, a fixation mark '+' was replaced with a screen showing four boxes that contained sentence fragments (as in panel A in Figure 1). If the sentence parts were exactly the same as the ones in any of the previous trials, then participants pressed a button as quickly as possible to indicate that they recognize these parts. This button press allowed a jump to the next trial.

However, if the sentence parts were new to the participants, then they connected the fragments to create a sentence in whatever order made sense to them and pressed a key to indicate the sentence completion. This key press led to a 1500 ms "pause" screen (panel B in Figure 1), which was replaced with a simple math problem (panel C). This secondary task was to prevent any immediate recall from the visual buffer and encouraged sentence production based upon meaning (Dennison 2008, Yamashita and Chang 2001). After participants typed an answer to the math problem, the last screen of a trial displayed only the verb portion of the sentence fragments (panel D in Figure 1). Using this verb as a cue, participants spoke out loud the sentence they had prepared. Each production was recorded into a digital voice recorder for later coding and analysis.

Each participant experienced 120 trials including thirty critical ones and ninety fillers including the repeated materials. The order of presentation was pseudo-randomized, with the constraint that no two experimental items were shown consecutively. Each session took about one half hour on average with a range from 25 to 40 minutes. Nobody expressed any difficulty in understanding the task.

2.4 Accuracy Coding

Sentences produced by participants were first classified into two accuracy-coding categories: incorrect and correct productions. Incorrect trials included (1) items that were skipped due to false recognition, (2) productions with the focus marker attached to an incorrect argument, and (3) productions with any missing arguments. Correct trials included productions where all grammatical markers including the focus marker were realized without any discrepancy from the original items. The only mistake that was accepted was lexical suppletion where proper names like John were substituted with similar names like Jake. Overall, ninety-six percent of the test items were produced correctly according to these criteria and there was no difference in accuracy across conditions. All correctly produced items were then coded for their word orders.

2.5 Results

The primary dependent measure was the percentage of sentences produced with the canonical order [S–IO–DO–V] in each experimental condition. We first performed two-way repeated measures of ANOVA tests to evaluate any effects of the two independent variables—sentence type and phrase location on the screen. The percentage of canonical orders varied significantly depending on the sentence type (a main effect of sentence type: $F_1(2, 34)=8.518$, $F_2(2, 58)=8.225$, both at p=.001). In addition, for each sentence type there were more productions of the canonical order when the indirect object was presented at the bottom-left corner of the computer screen (a main effect of phrase location: $F_1(1, 17)=7.119$, p=.016; $F_2(1, 29)=10.064$, p=.004). More importantly, however, the effect of sentence type did not interact with the effect of phrase location (no interaction effect: $F_1(2, 34)=.352$, p=.706; $F_2(2, 58)=1.485$, p=.235).

The uniform effect of phrase location enabled us to reduce the six testing conditions into just three, which allowed further explication of the sentence-type effect. Figure 2 below shows the percentages of word orders produced by participants (i.e. y-axis) in each sentence-type condition (i.e. x-axis). Each portion of the stacked bars represents word orders in three categories: the grey portion for the canonical order [S–IO–DO–V], the striped portion for the clause-internal scrambled order [S–DO–IO–V], and the black portion for all the other orders produced by participants.

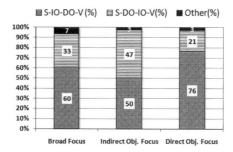

Figure 2. Proportions of word orders produced in each condition

One-way ANOVA tests on both participants and items found that percentages of canonical word order differed significantly depending on the sentence type ($F_1(2, 34)=8.774$, p=.001; $F_2 (2, 58)=6.147$, p=.004). When there was no focus marker in anywhere in the sentence (i.e. *Broad Focus* condition), participants produced the canonical order for 60% of the correct trials while producing the shifted order for 33% of the time.[1]

When the contrastive focus marker *–man* was attached to the indirect object (i.e. the *IO focus* condition), however, speakers' preference for the canonical order was reduced to only 50%. Instead, the number of productions in the order that placed the focused indirect object immediately preceding the verb (i.e. [S–DO–*IO*–V]) was significantly increased to 47% (pairwise comparison of *Broad Focus* and *IO focus*: $t_1=2.11$, p=0.07; $t_2=2.05$, p=0.01). This supports the Head Proximity Hypothesis. Participants rarely produced word orders that placed the focused element at the sentence beginning: only 1.9% of trials carried the [IO–S–DO–V] order and only 0.6% showed the [IO–DO–S–V] order. These results disconfirm the strong version of the Conceptual Accessibility Hypothesis.

As for the *DO focus* condition, we again found no support for the strong Conceptual Accessibility Hypothesis. There were no productions in this condition that placed the focused DO at the sentence beginning. Moreover, productions that placed the focused DO at the second position of the sentence (i.e. [S–*DO*–IO–V]) decreased significantly from both the baseline condition (pairwise comparison of *Broad Focus* and *DO focus*: $t_1=2.11$, p=0.02; $t_2=2.05$, p=0.15) and the *IO focus* condition (pairwise comparison of *IO focus* and *DO focus*: $t_1=2.11$, p<0.001; $t_2=2.05$, p<0.001). This goes

---

[1] This general preference for the canonical order was stronger in the current study than in the comparable condition in Dennison (2008, 48%). It could be that participants interpreted inanimate datives metonymically more often in the current study than in Dennison (2008). Participants in the current study experienced only inanimate datives, whereas people in the previous study received both animate and inanimate datives.

against the weaker version of the Conceptual Accessibility Hypothesis. Instead, we found a significant increase in the number of productions with the focused direct object in the preverbal position ([S–IO–*DO*–V], pairwise comparison of *Broad Focus* and *DO focus*: $t_1=2.11$, p=.009; $t_2=2.05$, p<.000). This supports the Head Proximity Hypothesis.

3. General Discussion

The current study found that contrastive focus exerts a strong influence on speakers' word order choices. Moreover, the direction of the influence aligned closely with the predictions of the Head Proximity Hypothesis but failed to support the Conceptual Accessibility Hypothesis. Speakers' preference for the canonical order in the Broad-Focus condition was diminished in the IO-focus condition and boosted in the DO-focus condition to place focused materials in the preverbal position.

Therefore, the current study provided behavioral evidence that the preverbal position is indeed a focus position in Korean, confirming the previous observation made from studies of syntactic typology (e.g. Kim 1988). Interestingly, while Kim laid out the discussion in terms of rhematic focus, our results suggest that the preference to place focused phrases pre-verbally extends to contrastive focus.

However, it might seem surprising that contrastive focus, as a conceptual factor, does not seem to affect conceptual accessibility during sentence production. One possible explanation for the lack of a conceptual accessibility effect could be the nature of the phrase assembly task. The task allows good control of the sentential material, but at a cost of naturalness. It is possible that the artificiality of an assembly task might minimize conceptual accessibility effects. While we cannot completely rule out this possibility, we note that an identical task was successful in detecting effects of animacy on word order in Dennison (2008).[2]

---

[2] Prat-Sala and Branigan (2000) have proposed that the ultimate influence of an entity's conceptual accessibility is in fact the added influence from two types of conceptual accessibility. One type is inherent accessibility, which is determined by an entity's inherent semantic properties such as animacy, prototypicality, and concreteness. Due to its intrinsic nature, inherent accessibility remains constant across contexts.

The other type is derived accessibility. That is, an entity's inherent accessibility can be influenced by extrinsic factors such as linguistic or non-linguistic contextual factors. Both given information and contrastive focus fall into this later category of accessibility.

Using two sentence production experiments, Prat-Sala and Branigan (2000) showed that derived accessibility can supplement the influence of inherent accessibility. Speakers in their experiments preferred word orders that allowed an early mention of entities that had been discussed in the previous discourse. Moreover, this pattern was stronger when the previously mentioned items were animate entities rather than inanimate entities. Their results suggest that

We suggest that the conceptual complexity inherent to contrastive focus mitigates its conceptual accessibility. Take the example in (8).

(8) Visiting the home of the Simpsons, Santa gave a gift only to Lisa.

The meaning that this sentence conveys is not just that Lisa received Santa's gift. There is also a strong implication that some other children did not get the gifts. Anybody who is familiar with the TV show *The Simpsons* will understand that the children are specifically Bart and Maggie (while someone unfamiliar with the show might infer one or more unidentified children).

As such, understanding contrastive focus involves computation of both the focused target and the alternative set. Computing the alternative set depends heavily on the potential candidates in a projected discourse context. The complexity involved in these additional processes may impose a processing burden to the production system, hence working against early mention. The demands of constructing an alternative set would presumably have been particularly high in our task, which did not provide contexts to aid the establishment of alternative sets.

We noted above that given information is also treated as conceptually salient. Given information likewise requires consideration of the discourse context, but it is arguably much easier to track what has already been mentioned or implied than to construct an alternative set. An important next step in this line of research is to examine the effects of contrastively focused versus given information in more natural contexts.

One final consideration is that in this study, the subject was always animate, and both the indirect object and the direct object were always inanimate. Under these circumstances, speakers preferred to place the contrastively focused items immediately before the verb. It may be the case that the conceptual accessibility of the animate subject made it particularly well-suited for early mention, competing successfully with the contrastively focused phrase for that position. Another avenue for future research is to explore these effects with varying animacy across the argument phrases.

The current study's findings together with the previous results suggest that sentence production is simultaneously influenced by multiple factors (both universal and language-specific factors). Despite the overall results

derived accessibility is a transitory property that is tied to particular linguistic or non-linguistic discourse factors.

The animacy effect found in Dennison (2008) is an effect of inherent accessibility. Korean speakers produced more canonical order [S-IO-DO-V] when the indirect object was animate than when it was inanimate. It is possible that the phrase-assembly task can detect effects of inherent accessibility, but not those of derived accessibility.

supporting the Head Proximity Hypothesis, we found a mix of word orders in each condition. In particular, the 50% of productions in canonical order [S–*IO*–DO–V] in the IO-focus condition suggests some competition among multiple factors during sentence production.

First of all, we saw a preference for the canonical order, which may have been shaped from speakers' general tendency to mention animate-like recipients in describing an object transfer event (i.e. an overgeneralization from typical patterns of animacy). Second, the structural patterns in the grammar of Korean and people's experiences with those patterns may justify the preverbal position as a focus position in Korean. Lastly, although the saliency of contrastive focus may indeed have increased the accessibility of the phrase in some respects, the need to compute an alternative set may have increased the processing time needed for the phrase and worked against its early mention.

For efficient processing, the production system needs to simultaneously satisfy as many constraints as possible. One order that was highly favored by the participants in this study (occurring with 76% of productions) was [S–IO–*DO*–V] for contrastively focused direct objects. This order satisfied (1) the canonical order constraint, (2) the head-proximity constraint for a focused element, and (3) late mention of conceptually complex information. This is a clear piece of evidence that linear word order in sentence production results from the competition among multiple factors.

Acknowledgements

This work was supported by a Graduate Scholarship from the Center for Korean Studies (CKS) at the University of Hawai'i at Mānoa. We express our gratitude to the organizing committee as well as the audience at the 19th conference on Japanese/Korean linguistics.

References

Arnold, J. E., Wasow, T., Losongco, A., and Ginstrom, R. 2000. Heaviness vs. Newness: The Effects of Structural Complexity and Discourse Status on Constituent Ordering. *Language* 76(1): 28–55.

Bock, J. K. and Warren, R.K. 1985. Conceptual Accessibility and Syntactic Structure in Sentence Formulation. *Cognition* 21: 47–67.

Branigan, H. P., Pickering, M. J., and Tanaka, M. 2008. Contributions of Animacy to Grammatical Function Assignment and Work Order during Production. *Lingua* 118: 172–189.

Chang, F., Kondo, T., and Yamashita, H. 2000. Conceptual Accessibility Influences Scrambling in Japanese. Poster presented at the CUNY conference on Human Sentence Processing, San Diego.

Dennison, H. Y. 2008. Universal versus Language-specific Conceptual Effects on Shifted Word-order Production in Korean: Evidence from Bilinguals. *Working Papers in Linguistics* 39(2), University of Hawai'i.

Ferreira, V. S. 1996. Is it better to give than to donate? Syntactic Flexibility in Language Production. *Journal of Memory and Language* 35(5):724–755.

Ferreira, V. S. and Dell, G. S. 2000. Effect of Ambiguity and Lexical Availability on Syntactic and Lexical Production. *Cognitive Psychology* 40(4):296–340

Ferreira, V. S., and Yoshita, H. 2003. Given-new Ordering Effects on the Production of Scrambled Sentences in Japanese. *Journal of Psycholinguistic Research* 32(6):669–692.

Hawkins, J. A. 2004. *Efficiency and Complexity in Grammars*. New York, NY: Oxford University Press.

Hwang, K., Schafer, A. J., and O'Grady, W. 2010. Contrastive Focus Facilitates Scrambling in Korean Sentence Processing. *Japanese and Korean Linguistics, Volume 17*, ed. S. Iwasaki, H. Hoji, P. M. Clancy, and S.-O. Sohn, 167-181. Stanford, CA: CSLI Publications.

Ito, K. and Speer, S. R. 2008. Anticipatory Effects of Intonation: Eye Movements during Instructed Visual Search. *Journal of Memory and Language* 58: 541–573.

Jackson, K. H. 2008. The Effect of Information Structure on Korean Scrambling. Doctoral dissertation, University of Hawai'i at Manoa.

Kim, A. H.-O. 1988. Preverbal Focusing and Type XXIII Languages. *Studies in Syntactic Typology*, ed. M. Hammond, E. Moravcsik, and J. Wirth, 147-169. Amsterdam: John Benjamins Publishing Company.

Lambrecht, K. 1996. *Information Structure and Sentence Form: Topic, Focus, and the Mental Representations of Discourse Referents*. Cambridge, UK: Cambridge University Press.

Levelt, W. J. M. 1989. *Speaking: From Intention to Articulation*. Cambridge, MA: MIT Press.

McDonald, J. L., Bock, K., and Kelly, M. H. 1993. Word and World Order: Semantic, Phonological, and Metrical Determinants of Serial Position. *Cognitive Psychology* 25: 188–230.

Prat-Sala, M., and Branigan, H. P. 2000. Discourse Constraints on Syntactic Processing in Language Production: A Cross-linguistic Study in English and Spanish. *Journal of Memory and Language* 42(2): 168–182.

Rooth, M. 1992. A Theory of Focus Interpretation. *Natural language semantics* 1: 75–116.

Sedivy, J. C., Tanenhaus, M. K., Eberhard, K. M., Spivey-Knowlton, M., and Carlson, G. N. 1995. Using Intonationally-marked Presuppositional Information in On-line Language Processing: Evidence from Eye Movements to a Visual Model. *Proceedings of the annual conference of the Cognitive Science Society* 17: 375–380.

Sedivy, J. C. 1997. A Model-based Psycholinguistic Study of Semantic Contrast. Doctoral dissertation, University of Rochester.

Sohn, H-M. 1999. *The Korean Language*. New York: Cambridge University Press.

Stallings, L. M., MacDonald, M. C., and O'Seaghdha, P. G. 1998. Phrasal Ordering Constraints in Sentence Production: Phrase Length and Verb Disposition in Heavy-NP Shift. *Journal of Memory and Language* 39: 392–417.

Watson, D. G., Tanenhaus, M. K., and Gunlogson, C. A. 2008. Interpreting Pitch Accents in Online Comprehension: H* vs. L+H*. *Cognitive Science* 32: 1232-1244.

Yamashita, H. and Chang, F. 2001. "Long before Short" Preference in the Production of a Head-final Language. *Cognition* 81: B45–55.

Does Noun Phrase Accessibility Matter? A Study of L2 Korean Relative Clause Production

SORIN HUH
University of Hawai'i at Mānoa

1. Introduction

Since Keenan and Comrie's (1977) noun phrase accessibility hierarchy (NPAH) was proposed, a considerable amount of research has been conducted to test the hypothesis in first language (L1) and second language (L2) acquisition. Although the acquisition order predicted in the NPAH has been supported in most of the SLA research conducted in English and European languages, recent studies in East Asian languages (EALs) have reported mixed findings. Specifically, a few studies conducted in Korean (Jeon and Kim 2007; O'Grady, Lee, and Choo 2003; O'Grady et al. 2000) have reported favorable findings for the NPAH, whereas studies on Japanese, on which studies have been most productively conducted, have shown different results. In response to the perplexing findings regarding relative clauses (RCs) of the EALs, Comrie (1998, 2002) has revoked the initial NPAH and postulated that the RCs found in the EALs are attributive clauses rather than RCs as in European languages. However, with the small number of studies

Japanese/Korean Linguistics 19.
Edited by Ho-min Sohn, Haruko Cook, William O'Grady, Leon A. Serafim, and Sang Yee Cheon.
Copyright © 2011, CSLI Publications

conducted in Korean, it seems still too early to conclude that the acquisition order of Korean RCs is consistent with the NPAH, let alone whether Korean RCs should be regarded as RCs or attributive clauses.

The purpose of this study is to examine whether L2 learners of Korean acquire Korean RCs in accordance with the order predicted in the NPAH. While previous studies conducted on Korean RCs limited their investigation to the acquisition of subject and direct object RCs, the scope of investigation in this study was expanded to the acquisition of oblique RCs.

2. Noun Phrase Accessibility Hierarchy

The noun phrase accessibility hierarchy (Comrie 1989; Hawkins 2004; Keenan and Comrie 1977), predicts the relativizability of a noun phrase (NP) in the order of subject (SU) > direct object (DO) > indirect object (IO) > oblique (OBL) > genitive (GEN) > object of comparison (OComp). In other words, if a language permits relativization of a lower position in the hierarchy, then it also allows relativization of all the higher positions in the hierarchy (i.e. positions to the left in the hierarchy). For instance, if IO can be relativized in a language, then SU and DO should be able to be relativized as well in that language.

The NPAH, which was originally proposed as a typological generalization, was extended to second language acquisition with the purpose of predicting the difficulty order of RC acquisition. A considerable amount of research has been conducted in the acquisition of RCs of European languages such as English (Doughty 1999; Eckman, Bell, and Nelson 1988; Gass 1979; Izumi 2003), Italian (Croteau 1995), French (Hawkins 1989), and Swedish (Hyltenstam 1984), and researchers have reported supporting evidence for the NPAH. Accordingly, the NPAH has been regarded as a universal hierarchy that predicts the developmental order of RCs. However, most of the studies that tested the NPAH were conducted in a few European languages, all of which have postnominal RCs, and thus it has remained unknown whether the NPAH is also observed in the acquisition of EAL RCs, which are prenominal.

Recently, studies have been conducted on the acquisition of EAL RCs, and these have shown a somewhat different picture than the acquisition of European RCs, challenging the universality of the NPAH. Among the EALs, studies have been most extensively conducted on Japanese RCs. Researchers have examined the acquisition of Japanese RCs in various gap positions (i.e. SU, DO, IO, and OBL), and by using various types of tasks, such as a grammaticality judgment task (Tarallo and Myhill 1983), a listening comprehension task (Kanno 2000, 2007), a sentence combining task (Ozeki and Shirai 2007), and an oral production task (Hasegawa, 2002). The findings have been contradictory; while some studies (Kanno 2000, 2001, 2007; Sakamoto and Kubota, 2000 cited in Kanno, 2007) supported the NPAH, others (Hasegawa 2002; Ozeki and Shirai 2007; Roberts 2000) did not. It seems that, despite the considerable number of studies carried out on Japanese RCs, it is still uncertain whether the development of Japanese RCs is constrained by the NPAH or not.

Only a small number of studies have been conducted on the acquisition of Korean RCs (Jeon and Kim 2007; O'Grady Lee, and Choo 2003; O'Grady et al. 2000). The studies explored the acquisition of SU and DO in listening comprehension (O'Grady, Lee, and Choo 2003) and oral production (Jeon and Kim 2007; O'Grady et al. 2000), and the findings were consistent with the NPAH. It is very interesting that despite the structural similarity between Korean and Japanese RCs, dissimilar patterns of acquisition were evidenced; whereas studies on Korean RCs generally supported the NPAH, Japanese studies did not. However, it should be noted that the number of studies conducted on Korean RC acquisition was quite small and their investigation was mostly confined to the acquisition of SU and DO, leaving the acquisition of more marked RCs such as IO, OBL, and GEN uncovered. Therefore, more research is required in order to examine whether the acquisition order predicted by the NPAH still holds in the acquisition of Korean RCs, particularly in the acquisition of more marked ones such as IO, OBL, and GEN.

3. Characteristics of Korean Relative Clauses

Korean RCs exhibit unique characteristics that are not shared with the RCs of European languages (Jeon and Kim 2007; Sohn 1999). First, the Korean RC is prenominal. In other words, the modifying clause precedes the head noun (HN) it modifies. Second, no relative pronoun is involved. Instead, relativization is signaled by a set of adnominal verbal suffixes such as *-(u)n, -nun,* and *-(u)l,* which also express the tense of the RC. Third, unlike European RCs, movement and pronominalization are not involved. Only the noun coreferential with the HN is omitted together with the case particle.

In Korean, subjects (1), direct objects (2), indirect objects (3), and obliques (4) can be relativized:

(1)   Subject (SU):
        [$_{NP}$ [t_i *aki-lul   po-nun*]   *yeca$_i$*]
        baby-ACC see-REL.PRES woman
        'The woman who looks at the baby'

(2)   Direct object (DO):
        [$_{NP}$ [$yeca$-ka t_j po-nun] aki_j]
            woman-NOM   see-REL.PRES   baby
        'The baby who the woman looks at'

(3)   Indirect object (IO):
        [$_{NP}$ [$namca$-ka t_k $phyenci$-lul ssu-nun] $yeca_k$]
            man-NOM   letter-ACC   write-REL.PRES   woman
        'The woman to whom the man writes a letter'

(4) Oblique (OBL):
        [$_{NP}$ [$namca$-ka t_l $phyenci$-lul ssu-nun] $pheyn_l$]
            man-NOM   letter-ACC   write-REL.PRES   pen
        'The pen with which the man writes a letter'

In this study, acquisition of SU, DO, and OBL RCs will be examined. It should be noted that, following Eckman, Bell, and Nelson (1988), dative constructions will be regarded as OBL. Unlike in English, dative constructions in Korean are not structurally different from OBL except that the HN is animate, as shown in (3) and (4).

4. Research Questions

This study aims to investigate whether L2 acquisition of Korean RCs is constrained by the NPAH. Especially, this study examines whether oral and written productions of Korean RCs elicited from L2 learners are in accordance with the acquisition order predicted in the NPAH. Unlike previous studies that were limited to the acquisition of SU and DO, the scope of investigation will be extended to the acquisition of OBL in this study. The following research question was developed:

> Do L2 learners of Korean produce Korean RCs following the order predicted in the NPAH? In particular, are OBL RCs indeed more difficult than DO for learners to produce?

5. Methods

5.1 Participants

In total, thirty-six L2 learners of Korean were solicited in this study from two major Korean language institutions located in Seoul. Because the target structure was introduced in Level 2 (equivalent to high beginning) at the institutions, learners from the end of Level 2 to Level 4 (equivalent to high intermediate) participated in this study. There were twenty-three female and thirteen male learners, ranging in age from nineteen to thirty-eight (M = 23.7). Their average length of previous study of Korean was 1.2 years (4 months to 4.2 years), and their average length of residency in Korea was six months (two months to three years). The learners were from various L1 backgrounds: Chinese (19), Japanese (10), English (5), Mongolian (1), and Russian (1).

5.2 Materials

Two elicitation tasks were employed in this study: a sentence combination task (SCT) and an oral production task (OPT). The SCT is a written task which requires learners to combine two sentences into one using an RC, and the OPT asks learners to describe objects or people depicted in a set of similar pictures. These are the most frequently used tasks in previous RC acquisition studies (see Eckman, Bell, and Nelson 1988; Gass 1979; Ozeki and Shirai 2007, for the SCT; and Doughty 1988; Hyltenstam 1984; Pavesi 1986, for the OPT), although they were rarely employed in previous studies on Korean RC acquisition (only the OPT has been used in O'Grady et al., 2000). In total, eighteen items were developed for each task, with six sentences for each of the three (SU, DO, and OBL) RC conditions.

The SCT was developed by adapting the sentences used in Ozeki and Shirai (2007). An example of an SCT item is shown in (5):

(5)   Sentence Combination Task

    a.   Sentence A
        Yeca-ka   kongwen-eyse chinkwu-lul mannayo.
        Woman-NOM   park-LOC   friend-ACC   meet-PRES-POL
        'A woman meets a friend at a park.'

    b.   Sentence B
        Ku yeca-nun   acwu yeyppeyo.
        The woman-TOP   very   pretty-PRES-POL
        'The woman is very pretty.'

    c.   Combined Sentence
        Kongwen-eyse chinkwu-lul manna-nun   yeca-nun
        Park-LOC   friend-ACC   meet-REL. PRES woman-TOP
        acwu yeyppeyo
        very   pretty-PRES-POL
        'The woman who meets a friend at a park is very pretty.'

Each SCT item was composed of two sentences: (a) sentence A, which contained a subject, a verb, a direct object, and an adverbial noun phrase (NP); and (b) sentence B, which was an equational copular sentence. Since OBL required one more NP than the other types of RCs, an adverbial NP indicating place, time, instrument, or indirect object was added to SU and DO to make the number of NPs the same. In sentences B, an adverb or an adjective (e.g. *acwu* 'very') was occasionally added to make a sentence sound more natural. The participants were instructed to always start with sentence A to ensure that they produced a sentence containing an RC (e.g. 'the woman who meets a friend at a park is very pretty') rather than simply converting sentence B into an adjective (e.g. 'a very <u>pretty</u> woman meets a friend at a park').

The OPT materials were adapted from Hyltenstam (1984) and consisted of nine sets of four pictures depicting people involved in similar activities, as shown in Figure 1:

Figure 1. Oral production task

In each picture, there was an object or person to which a particular number was assigned, and the participant's task was to describe the object or person that was asked about by number. In order to ensure that RCs were elicited, the participants were encouraged to answer in a certain sentence format (e.g. 1 *pen-un yeca-ka po-nun aki-yeyyo.* 'number 1 is the baby whom the woman looks at'), and a set of specific elicitation techniques was employed as well, adapting Doughty (1988). The learners were allowed to ask for words when they could not think of appropriate ones. When the learners needed help with a verb or an adjective, only the bare forms of the predicates were provided.

5.3 Coding

All OPT data were transcribed and coded by the researcher. When learners repeated the same expression after a pause or vowel lengthening, it was regarded as repetition or self repair, and only the second utterance was included in the analysis, following Jeon and Kim (2007). All SCT and OPT answers for each item were coded as either right (1) or wrong (0), and no partial score was given.

6. Results

In total, 630 and 610 responses were elicited from the learners in the SCT and the OPT respectively. The mean accuracy scores for each RC type are presented in Table 1. The highest scores were obtained from SU, regardless of the task type, followed by DO and then OBL. Overall, the SCT scores were higher than the OPT scores, and the accuracy scores decreased more rapidly in the OPT as the RC type changed from SU to OBL, as shown in Figure 2. In addition, greater variation was shown among the learner responses as the markedness of the RC increased: the standard deviation (SD) increased as RC type changed from SU to OBL in both tasks, except OBL in the OPT, whose mean score was already very low.

Table 1. Mean accuracy scores for RC conditions

RC	SCT		OPT		Total	
Type	M	SD	M	SD	M	SD
SU	5.34	1.08	5.06	1.56	9.97	2.50
DO	5.03	1.62	3.74	1.94	8.42	2.96
OBL	4.23	1.75	1.79	1.30	5.81	2.41
Total	14.19	4.43	10.0	4.32	24.19	6.74

Note. Maximum score = 6.00, N = 35 (OPT), 34 (SCT)

A two-way repeated measures ANOVA was performed to determine the effects of RC type and task, with the alpha level set at .05. Significant main effects of RC Type, $F (2, 32) = 49.201$, $p = .00$, and task, $F (1, 33) = 16.586$, $p = .00$, were found. Significant interaction effects were found among the factors as well ($F (2, 32) = 12.583$, $p = .00$). Post hoc comparisons of the mean accuracy scores of the three RC types were conducted with the Bonferroni correction in order to examine where the difference occurred among the RC types. The mean accuracy score differences among the three RC types were all found to be significant ($p = .00$), resulting in the accuracy order of SU > DO > OBL.

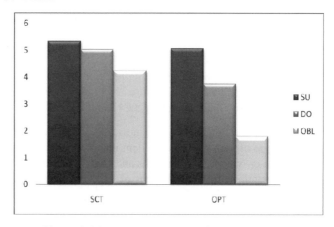

Figure 2. Mean accuracy scores for RC conditions

Table 2 displays the frequency of the non target RCs produced in each RC type for each task. The frequency of the non target RCs shows how often the learners deviated from the target RC type and produced a non target type of RC. In total, there were 145 instances of non target RCs (i.e. RC type changes). Among them, 129 changes were made in the OPT, and only sixteen changes were identified in the SCT. Considering the nature of the tasks, it is natural that the learners made more RC type changes in the OPT than the SCT. In the OPT, the learners had to determine the relationship between the HN and the argument inside an RC to decide which type of RC they needed to produce, whereas, in the SCT, the relationship was already delineated by the verb given in the sentence.

Table 2. Frequency of non target RCs in each RC target context

	Target RC	RC Produced				
		SU	DO	OBL	Total	(%)
SCT	SU	0	3	0	3	(19)
	DO	0	0	1	1	(6)
	OBL	10	2	0	12	(75)
	Total	10	5	1	16	(100)
OPT	SU	0	0	1	1	(1)
	DO	31	0	0	31	(24)
	OBL	49	48	0	97	(75)
	Total	80	48	1	129	(100)

The most frequently occurring pattern of changes was to produce either SU or DO instead of OBL. This pattern comprises approximately 75% of the total RC type changes found in both tasks (twelve instances for the SCT and ninety-seven instances for the OPT). Interestingly, the learners predominantly produced SU (ten instances, 83.3%) instead of OBL in the SCT. By comparison, a similar proportion of SU (forty-nine instances, 50.5%) and DO (forty-eight instances, 49.5%) were observed in the same context in the OPT. However, further examination of the individual items revealed that the context and the type of verb given in the item mattered more than whether the tasks were oral or written. Certain verbs and contexts were more conducive to the interpretation of particular types of RCs. For instance, the verb *give* can be easily converted to *receive* promoting SU interpretation. In addition to the changes from OBL to SU or DO, conversion of DO into SU was also observed thirty-one times (24%) in the OPT. In general, the learners made changes from marked RCs (OBL and DO) to less marked ones, implying that marked ones are more difficult to produce than less marked ones. Indeed, there were only five instances of RC type changes made in the opposite direction, from less marked RCs to more marked ones.

The frequency of miscombination errors found in the SCT also suggests that OBL RCs were more difficult for the learners to produce than other types of RCs. The learners made a larger number of miscombination errors in OBL (ten instances) than when SU and DO were combined (five instances). Further examination of the individual learner's responses showed that the learners who made such errors were able to combine the two sentences in the right order in the other contexts. However, when OBL was targeted, they combined the sentences in the wrong order and produced a simple sentence rather than a complex sentence that contained an RC. It seems that OBL constructions were too difficult for these learners and thus they chose an easier way to combine the two sentences by changing the order of combination even though this did not result in an RC as they had been instructed. To summarize, all the evidence discussed here, including the accuracy scores of each RC type, the direction of RC type change, and the frequency of miscombination errors, demonstrates that SU RCs are easier for the learners to produce than DO/OBL, and in the same way DO RCs are easier than OBL, in alignment with the acquisition order predicted by the NPAH.

7. Discussion and Conclusions

The results of this study confirmed the RC acquisition order predicted in the NPAH. This is in accordance with the findings of the previous studies (Jeon and Kim 2007; O'Grady, Lee, and Choo 2003; O'Grady et al. 2000) and extends the evidence to OBL RCs. The L2 learners of Korean who participated in this study produced SU more frequently and accurately than any other type of RC in both oral and written tasks (Tables 1); DO was also produced more often and accurately than OBL. The direction of RC type changes shown in Table 2 also provides additional supporting evidence for the NPAH. The learners often made RC type changes when marked ones were targeted, producing less marked RCs instead (i.e. SU or DO instead of OBL and SU instead of DO). In addition, the learners made a larger number of miscombination errors in OBL than in SU and DO. All of this evidence indicates that the marked RCs were more difficult for the learners to produce than less marked ones.

It is very intriguing that despite the structural similarity between Korean and Japanese RCs, distinctive patterns of findings have been reported in previous studies on the acquisition of RCs. With regard to the incongruent findings of Japanese RC acquisition studies, Kanno (2007) suggested that the differences might be caused by the tasks employed in the studies. She carefully examined the previous Japanese RC acquisition literature and noticed that while favorable findings were found in production tasks in general (Hasegawa, 2002; Roberts, 2000), the findings were split in the comprehension studies (Hasegawa 2002; Kanno 2000, 2001, 2007; Roberts 2000).

In Korean, with the findings of the current study, we can more confidently say that the NPAH is observed in the production of Korean RCs. The comprehension studies conducted so far (O'Grady, Lee, and Choo 2003; O'Grady et al. 2000) also have reported findings that are in accordance with the NPAH, although the studies did not include comprehension of OBL RCs. Nevertheless, with the paucity of studies conducted so far in both production and comprehension of Korean RCs, we do not have enough evidence to conclude whether the differences between the two structurally similar languages are due to the types of tasks employed in the previous studies, as Kanno speculated, or due to other structural or processing factors that have not been examined yet. This question is left to future research to answer.

In conclusion, the present study offers support for the claim that acquisition order of L2 Korean RCs are in accordance with the NPAH. In particular, the evidence for this claim was extended to the acquisition of OBL RCs in this study. For the L2 learners of Korean who participated in the study, SU was easier to produce than DO/OBL and DO was also easier than OBL. This was true of both a more controlled, written and a less controlled, oral production task.

Acknowledgements

I would like to thank Lourdes Ortega and William O'Grady for their helpful comments on this paper.

References

Cho, S. 1999. The Acquisition of Relative Clauses: Experimental Studies on Korean. Doctoral dissertation, University of Hawai'i at Mānoa.

Comrie, B. 1989. *Language Universals and Linguistic Typology.* Chicago: University of Chicago.

Comrie, B. 1998. Attributive Clauses in Asian Languages: Towards a Real Typology. *Sprache in Raum und Zeit: In Memoriam Johannes Bechert, Band 2,* ed. W. Boeder, C. Schroeder, K. Wagner, and W. Wildgen, 51–60. Tübingen: Gunter Narr.

Comrie, B. 2002. Typology and Language Acquisition: The Case of Relative Clauses. *Typology and Second Language Acquisition,* eds. A. G. Ramat, 19–37. Berlin: Mouton de Gruyter.

Croteau, K. C. 1995. Second Language Acquisition of Relative Clause Structures by Learners of Italian. *Second Language Acquisition Theory and Pedagogy,* eds. F. Eckman, D. Highland, P. Lee, J. Mileham, and R. Weber, 115–128. Mahwah, NJ: Erlbaum.

Doughty, C. 1988. The Effect of Instruction on the Acquisition of Relativization in English as a Second Language. Doctoral dissertation, University of Pennsylvania.

Doughty, C. 1991. Second Language Instruction Does Make a Difference: Evidence from an Empirical Study of SL Relativization. *Studies in Second Language Acquisition* 13: 431–469.

Eckman, R., Bell, L., and Nelson, D. 1988. On the Generalization of Relative Clause Instruction in the Acquisition of English as a Second Language. *Applied Linguistics* 9: 1–20.

Gass, S. M. 1979. Language Transfer and Universal Grammatical Relations. *Language Learning* 29: 327–344.

Hasegawa, T. 2002. The Acquisition of Relative Clauses by Children Learning Japanese as a Second Language. Unpublished manuscript, University of Hawai'i at Mānoa.

Hawkins, J. 2004. *Efficiency and Complexity in Grammars.* Oxford: Oxford University Press.

Hawkins, R. 1989. Do Second Language Learners Acquire Restrictive Relative Clauses on the Basis of Relational or Configurational Information? The Acquisition of French Subject, Direct Object and Genitive Restrictive Relative Clauses by Second Language Learners. *Second Language Research* 5: 158–188.

Hyltenstam, K. 1984. The Use of Typological Markedness Conditions as Predictors in Second Language Acquisition: The Case of Pronominal Copies in Relative Clauses. *Second Languages: A Cross-linguistic Perspective,* ed. R. Andersen, 39–60. Rowley, MA: Newbury House.

Izumi, S. 2003. Processing Difficulty in Comprehension and Production of Relative Clauses by Learners of English as a Second Language. *Language Learning* 53: 285–323.

Jeon, K. and Kim, H. 2007. Development of Relativization in Korean as a Foreign Language. *Studies in Second Language Acquisition* 29:253–276.

Kanno, K. 2000. Sentence Processing by JSL Learners. Paper presented at the Second Language Research Forum, Madison, WI.

Kanno, K. 2001. On-line Processing of Japanese by English L2 Learners. *Acquisition of Japanese as a Second Language* 4: 23–28.

Kanno, K. 2007. Factors Affecting the Processing of Japanese Relative Clauses by L2 Learners. *Studies in Second Language Acquisition* 29: 197–218.

Keenan, E. and Comrie, B. 1977. Noun Phrase Accessibility and Universal Grammar. *Linguistic Inquiry* 8: 63–99.

Kim, Y. 1987. The Acquisition of Relative Clauses in English and Korean: Development in Spontaneous Production. Doctoral dissertation, Harvard University.

Lee, K. 1991. On the First Language Acquisition of Relative Clauses in Korean: The Universal Structure of COMP. Doctoral dissertation, Cornell University.

Lee, S. 2005. Relative Clauses and Subject-drop in KSL Learner's Writing: Sentence Processing Approach. *Language Research* 41: 405-435.

O'Grady, W., Lee, M., and Choo, M. 2003. A Subject-object Asymmetry in the Acquisition of Relative Clauses in Korean as a Second Language. *Studies in Second Language Acquisition* 25: 433–448.

O'Grady, W., Yamashita, Y., Lee, M., Choo, M., and Cho, S. 2000. Computational Factors in the Acquisition of Relative Clauses. *Paper presented at the International Conference on the Development of the Mind*, Tokyo: Keio University.

Ozeki, H., and Shirai, Y. 2007. Does the Noun Phrase Accessibility Hierarchy Predict the Difficulty Order in the Acquisition of Japanese Relative Clauses? *Studies in Second Language Acquisition* 29: 169–196.

Pavesi, M. 1986. Markedness, Discourse Models, and Relative Clause Formation in a Formal and Informal Context. *Studies in Second Language Acquisition* 25: 99–126.

Roberts, M. A. 2000. Implicational Markedness and the Acquisition of Relativization by Adult Learners of Japanese as a Foreign Language. Doctoral dissertation, University of Hawai'i at Mānoa.

Sohn, H. M. 1999. *The Korean Language*. Cambridge: Cambridge University Press.

Tarallo, F., and Myhill, J. 1983. Interference and Natural Language Processing in Second Language Acquisition. *Language Learning* 33: 57–76.

Negotiating Desirability: The Acquisition of the Uses of *ii* 'good' in Child-Mother Interactions in Japanese

CHIGUSA KURUMADA
Stanford University

SHOICHI IWASAKI
University of California, Log Angeles

1. Introduction

Conditional construction has been examined extensively in connection with the question of the relationship between the development of grammars and a child's ability of logical reasoning. In English conditionals are learned relatively late, at around the ages of two and a half to three years (Bates 1976, Bowerman 1986, Reilly 1982, 1986). Based on Slobin's (1973) work on the cognitive-based order of acquisition, some studies concluded that the late development of conditional is associated with the complexity it imposes on children's cognition. On the other hand, drawing on data from a variety of languages, Bates (1976), Reilly (1986) and Bowerman (1986) suggest that

Japanese/Korean Linguistics 19.
Edited by Ho-min Sohn, Haruko Cook, William O'Grady, Leon A. Serafim, and Sang Yee Cheon.
Copyright © 2011, CSLI Publications

children appear to have cognitive, linguistic, and pragmatic abilities needed for expressing the conditional relationship between two events well before the morpho-syntax of conditionals first appears in their speech.

Akatsuka and Clancy (1993) and Clancy et al. (1997) illuminated the possibility that a high frequency of input can alleviate the difficulty of learning of conditional expressions. They showed that Japanese and Korean speaking children begin using conditional constructions before they turn two. The timing of acquisition is thus significantly earlier compared to children speaking English and other Indo-European languages. Akatsuka and Clancy (1993) and Clancy et al. (1997) attribute this difference to the frequent use of conditional expressions in child-directed speech by Japanese and Korean speaking adults. For example, Japanese speaking mothers often use what they call 'deontic conditionals', as in (1) and (2).

(1) *koo   shitara   ii.*
    this-way   do-IF   good
    'If (you) do it this way, (it is) good (You should do it this way)'
(2) *sore nage-cha   dame.*
    that throw-if bad
    'If (you) throw it, it is bad. (Do not throw it.)'

By means of this type of conditional expressions, adult speakers express positive or negative judgments towards an event expressed in the antecedent clause and thereby express deontic modality such as permission, suggestion, prohibition and obligation. These studies further suggested that what adults convey with this type of structure is not the logical reasoning between the antecedent and consequent. Instead, they encode contingencies between two events in terms of 'desirability' -- What is desirable (e.g. you do it this way) leads to a desirable state, whereas what is undesirable (e.g. if you throw it) leads to an undesirable state. Such utterances are conceptually simpler than ones expressing a hypothetical reasoning (e.g. If it is sunny tomorrow, we will go to the park). Moreover, since the deontic conditionals have the immediate consequence of controlling children's behavior, they are considered to be pragmatically relevant and hence easy to grasp for children as young as two years old.

Based on these assumptions, Akatsuka and Clancy (1993) presented the hypothetical sequence of development for conditional expressions in child speech (189-190). First, children learn the simple evaluative terms (e.g. *ii* 'good' and *dame* 'bad') that appear in the consequent clause of the conditionals. From this foundation, children begin to understand the adults' uses of deontic conditionals. In the next stage, children are expected to link the deontic conditionals to conditional constructions of a more general kind.

The consequent clauses begin to involve a wider variety of expressions (e.g. *kooshitara kiree da yo*. 'If you do it this way, it will be pretty. = 'You should do it this way to make it pretty'). It is after this stage that children avail themselves of conditional expressions that express abstract conditional reasoning between the antecedent and consequent clauses.

Their analysis highlights the important relationship between the high frequency of input and the pragmatic function of the target utterances. The adults' intention to control and discipline their children results in the affluent input of the morpho-syntax of deontic conditional expressions. Presumably, such a highly frequent exposure accelerates the acquisition of Japanese (and Korean) conditionals. This was a pioneering discussion since recent studies based on usage-based approaches to language acquisition have discovered the significant effects of input frequency (Bybee and Hopper 2001, Cameron-Faulkner, Lieven and Tomasello 2003, Gulzow and Gagarina 2007, Tomasello 2003, Diessel 2007 among others).

However, to empirically assess the validity of Akatsuka and Clancy's (1993) hypothesis about the course of development, we pose the following two questions.

[Question 1]   Regarding the claim presupposes compositionality of the structure and the meaning, they assume that children learn the adjective *ii* as an evaluative term and later combine it with the antecedent. Is this valid?

They do not provide any evidence that the evaluative meaning of the adjectives *ii* 'good' or *dame* 'bad' is already available for two year-olds. Investigating the adult usage of the adjective *ii*, Ono and Thompson (2009) pointed out that adult speakers of Japanese use *ii* in various fixed and semi-fixed expressions recurrently used in conversational discourse. The pragmatic meaning of *ii* differs significantly depending on its embedding contexts. For example, the literal meaning of *X ga ii* (X is good) could be an evaluation of the property of X as good, but it is most commonly understood as an expression of the speaker's desire for the intended referent (I want X) and is often treated as an instrumental utterance (Give me X). Interestingly, *ii* also appears in a prefabricated expression which signals a lack of need or desire, i.e. *moo ii* ((I am) already good = I don't need it.). Observing the wide variety of pragmatic meanings that *ii* can convey leads us wonder whether two year-olds have a unitary notion of *ii* as 'the evaluative' expression, as the previous papers suggest.

[Question 2]   Is behavior management the only functional motivation
                 for mothers to use the adjective *ii* 'good', and deontic
                 conditionals including *ii*?

It is the core argument of the previous studies' analysis that a mother
(=authority) expresses her desirability to a child (=subordinate) because
"(Y)oung children are expected to carry out adult wishes, (…) and they are
obliged to do what adults tell them to do (Akatsuka and Clancy 1993: 180)."
However, a closer examination of the actual utterances they provide calls
this statement into question.

(3)   *akereba   ii   no*?   (by Mother)
        open-COND   good   FP
        'Is opening good? = Should I open this?'

In example (3), the mother is asking the addressee's (i.e. child's) opinion rather than expressing her own assessment of desirability. Rather, the
mother is inquiring about the child's intention in order to align her own behavior. If Japanese speaking caretakers use many of these question forms to
inquire about the addressee's assessment of desirability, it becomes difficult
to maintain the previous studies' argument about the functional motivation.

To wrap up, the previous studies fall short by not providing compelling
empirical evidence for the effects of adult input on the acquisition of deontic
conditionals. These problems stem in part from their research methodology.
They restrict their attention to conditional constructions, without looking
into how the children and mothers express 'desirability' through a wider
variety of related constructions. In this paper, we broaden our perspective to
include a variety of constructions which are formed with the adjective *ii* to
provide a better idea of how desirability is expressed in mother-child interaction. Also, the previous research focused on adult input and paid less attention to the adjacent utterances, especially the children's responses. In this
paper, we investigate both the children's as well as the adults' utterances
with an emphasis on the functional motivation for them to use the various
constructions including the adjective *ii*.

Our analysis attempts to tackle the above mentioned possible problems
in the following two modes of inquiry.

   1) How is *ii* used by children as well as mothers BEFORE the deontic
      conditionals come about?
   2) How often do mothers use the adjective *ii* to express their own desir-
      ability – and how often do they not?

2. Method

2.1 Data

The data for this study were drawn from the CHILDES corpus (Oshima-Takane et al. 1998) and consist of three sets of mother-child conversations collected longitudinally when the children were aged eighteen- to thirty-six-months. Each mother-child dyad was individually video- and audio-recorded during free-play naturalistic interactions in the home. Mothers were instructed to let their children speak as much as possible but otherwise to play and talk with their children as they usually do. The play sessions were held once a week and recorded for approximately one hour in the cases of Aki and Ryo, and forty minutes in the case of Tai.

2.2 Coding

A total of 3054 utterances containing the adjective *ii* were found and classified into five types.

	Types	Examples	
1	*ii* + (final particle(FP)) [1]	*ii* *yo* . good FP	'Good/OK'
2	NP (case/topic particle) + *ii* +(FP)	*kotchi ga* *ii* . this NOM good	'This is good. 'I like/want this one.'
3	Verb-*te ii* +(FP)	*akete* *ii* *yo* . open:TE good FP	'Opening this is good. 'You can/may open it.'

4	Verb-Conditional[2] + *ii* + (FP)	*koko kara haire-ba* *ii* *n* *da* *yo*.
		 Here from enter-COND good NOML COP FP
		         'If you enter from here, it will be good'
		         'You should enter from here.'	

	Others	*Ryo-kun ii* *ko* ? 'Are you a good boy, Ryo?' Ryo good child	

2.3 Analysis

All speech produced by the children and their mothers during the recorded sessions was transcribed according to the JCHAT (Japanese) transcription system (Oshima-Takane, MacWhinney, Shirai, Miyata and Naka 1998). CLAN programs (MacWhinney 2000) were used for the quantitative analysis of the data.

---

[1] The elements in parentheses are optional.
[2] The conditional markers include: *-tara, -(r)eba, -nara, -temo, -to.*

3. Results and Discussion

3.1 Compositionality and Constructional Nature of *ii* Utterances

Our first question is regarding the compositionality of the deontic conditionals. We would like to know in what context the mothers and children use the adjective *ii*. In order to construct a general picture of the development of the utterances including *ii*, we plotted the onset of the uses of the four major formal types we introduced in Section 2.2. Table 1 summarizes the onset of the uses of these four types. The order is common to the three boys: *ii* + F(inal) P(article) and NP +*ii* → V(erb)-te *ii* → Verb-Conditional + *ii*.

Types	Aki	Ryo	Tai
ii	[2;01;10]	[2;00;08]	[1;6;19]
NP + *ii*	[2;03;00]	[2;00;08]	[1;6;19]
Verb-*te ii*	[2;07;05]	[2;02;29]	[1;8;13]
Verb-Conditional + *ii*	[2;07;19]	[2;09;06]	[1;10;20]

[years; months; days]

Table 1. The onset of the use of the four construction types

Seemingly, the order of acquisition supports the claim of compositionality – children initially use *ii* as a predicate only with a final particle, or with a noun preceding it. Later they begin using it with a linking form of a verb (i.e. V-*te*) to create a rather complex predicate, and then with a conditional marker to create what is normally analyzed as a complex clause.

However, the utterances tells us that the meaning of *ii* is, even at the earliest stage, nowhere close to uniform. Even before they reached the stage of using verbs with *ii*, the children make skillful uses of simple utterance forms to express a variety of pragmatic meanings. To illustrate this point, let us examine a following excerpt. In this example, Ryo uses only three types of structures: *ii* + (FP), N + *ii*, and the prefabricated expression *moo ii* (already good = no need). However, he manages to express various pragmatic meanings. Responding to his mother's question, he expresses acceptance (line 30), makes an offer (line 31), declares no need for an object (lines 34 and 36-37), and states his preference and thereby request for his intended object (line 39). The earliest uses of *ii* are thus simple in structure while variable in functions.

(4) Ryo and his mother are talking about toy motorbikes [Ryo 27 months]
29 Mother: *Oneechan ni kashiteagete ii* ?
30 Ryo: *ii yo* .
31 Ryo: *kore ii* .

M gives motorbike to Y (Ryo's sister); Ryo runs into the kitchen
and throws his motorbike on the floor

34	Ryo:	*kore Ryookun moo ii* .
35	Mother:	*moo ii no?*
36	Ryo:	*moo ii* .
37	Ryo:	*moo ii no* .

Ryo goes to Y, who was drawing at a table

39	Ryo:	*kore ga ii no* .

Mother:	'Can I give this to your sister?'
Ryo:	'Good/OK.'
Ryo:	'This is good.'

Ryo:	'I'm already good = I don't need this.'
Mother:	'Are you already good? (Don't you need it?)'
Ryo:	'I'm good. (I don't need it.)'
Ryo:	'I'm good (I don't need it.)'

Ryo:	'(because) this is good. = I want this one'

Given the wide variety of pragmatic meanings, it is not plausible to assume that two year-olds manage to abstract out the evaluative meaning of *ii* 'good' that generalize across contexts of use. In order for such generalization to be possible, the child would have to have a fine-grained knowledge of the other parts of the utterance. For example, to extract the evaluative meaning of 'good' from the utterances *kore ga ii* (This is good = I want this) and *moo ii* ((I am) already good (without this)), they would need to understand that the latter utterance has an elided subject (i.e. 'I') which should be topical in this context. However, an independent line of research has shown that solid understanding of the distinction between topical and non-topical phrases is beyond of the capacity of two year-olds (Hatano 1979; Tahara and Ito 1985). In addition, they should understand the pragmatic intention of the speaker based on a scalar implicature associated with the use of the adverb *moo* 'already' (i.e. 'I am *already* good' means anything additional to the current condition would not be needed). Together these factors indicate that it is a stretch to suppose that two year-olds have access to the meaning of the adjective *ii* by analyzing the whole structure based on the syntactic cues.

A more straightforward hypothesis would be that children attend to the multi-word sequences and understand them in terms of their pragmatic meanings. For example, ~ *ga ii* and *moo ii* are stored as distinct units matched up with holistic pragmatic meanings of 'expressing preference/desire for an object' and 'declaring lack of need' respectively. This way of reasoning is in accordance with the recent studies' attempts to reassess the compositionality of language and to shed a new light on an importance of sentence constructions and multi word sequences (Locke 1993 1995, Clark and Kelly 2006, Diessel 2006, Diessel and Tomasello 2005, Tomasello 2003).

Looking at the utterance as constructions enables us to sort the utterances based not only on their forms but also on their functions. In this way, we can clearly see that the formally distinct utterances have commonality in their functions. Most importantly, deontic modality, which is associated with early conditionals, has already been introduced in mother-child conversation through the uses of simpler structures. For example, the following examples compare one of the mother's uses of *ii* at two different time points: when the child was 26 and 33 months old. In both cases, she grants permission by means of N *mo ii* 'N is also good'. However, in the latter case, she rephrased the message by means of a deontic conditional (*tara ii*). Thus, the deontic modality typically associated with the early conditionals appears to have its roots in earlier uses of simpler constructions.

(5) Aki's mother tells Aki to bring a book to read [26 months]

	575	Mother:	*buumbuumbuum tsuiteru hon mottekite* !
	576	Aki:	*atta*!
	587	Aki:	*aomushichan*!
→	588	Mother:	*aomushichan mo ii yo.*
	589	Mother:	*mottoide* !

Mother: 'Go get the one[book] with boon-boon-boon'
Aki: 'Found it!'
Aki: 'Caterpillar [name of a book]!'
Mother: 'Caterpillar is also good/OK'
Mother: 'Bring it here'

(6)Aki and his mother are making a pile with toys [33 months]

	1232	Aki:	*kore wa*?
→	1233	Mother:	*sore mo ii.*
	1234	Aki:	*kasa wa*?
	1235	Aki:	*kore kasa wa*?
→	1236	Mother:	*sore dattara ii.*

Aki: 'How about this?'
Mother : 'It's also good/OK'
Aki: 'How about an umbrella?'

Aki: 'How about this umbrella?'
Mother: 'It that is it, (it will be) good = it will be good/OK'

To sum up, in this section, we argued that there are few compelling reasons to assume compositionality in comprehension of deontic conditionals. We illustrated that utterances with *ii* are used for various pragmatic functions from the earliest stages on. For two year-olds, conjoining two concepts are usually considered to be above their cognitive capacity.[3] Rather, we suggest that the children are attending to an utterance level constructions.[4] They are a more cognitively attainable level of abstraction for the young children because each of the constructions is matched up with a concrete pragmatic function such as the mothers' granting them permission to take a particular action. In this sense, the deontic conditionals do not have to be analyzed as bi-clausal structures. They are much simpler structures in which the main propositional content is modified by deontic modal markers indicating permission or obligation. This would be done by modal auxiliaries (e.g. can, may, should) in English, which are available to two year-olds.

3.2 Interactional Use of *ii*

Our second question pertains to the declarative and interrogative uses of *ii*. The previous study suggested that the motivation for the mothers to use deontic conditionals is to control children's behavior by stating what they assess as 'desirable'. This is mainly done by declarative sentence. However, as suggested in Section 2, this does not hold in the cases of interrogatives, which inquire about the addressee's assessment of desirability. In Figure 1, we plotted the percentages of interrogative utterances containing *ii* (against all the utterances that have *ii*) produced by the three mothers. It clearly shows that the proportion of the questions against all the utterances including *ii* reaches 50% as children turn two years of age. The percentages are highest when the children are 27-30 months old: mothers ask questions more often than they tell the children what they think is desirable. This finding is astounding in that it sharply contradicts the previous studies' assumptions.

---

[3] Recent studies on formulaic language have suggested that children at the earlier language acquisition phase up to two years of age rely heavily on the strategy of holistic processing. (e.g. Locks 1993, Wray and Perkins 2000: 19-22).

[4] In fact, Clancy (1985) already pointed this out, rejecting the account that early conditionals include a linking of two concepts. She suggests that Japanese children's exceptionally early acquisition of conditionals is made possible because 'the meanings encoded are accessible, the linguistic structure simple, and the total number of words required within the child's productive capacity.'

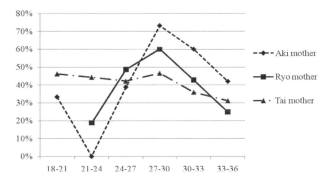

Figure 1. The percentages of interrogatives in the mothers' utterances

This observation naturally leads us to inquire about why the mothers are asking so many questions with utterances including *ii*. To answer this, we extracted all the questions and categorized them into five types according to the speech-acts the mothers tried to achieve: 1) asking preference or need for an object (e.g. *dore ga ii no* ? 'Which one is good / Which one do you want?'), 2) requesting permission (e.g. *Okaasan mo yatte ii* ? 'Is Mommy's doing it good? / Can Mommy do it?'), 3) providing and soliciting suggestions (e.g. *doo yattara ii ka naa*? 'What should we do to make it good? / How should we do this?'), 4) teaching (e.g. *Sonna koto shite ii no kana*? (e.g. 'Is doing such a thing good? /Do you think it is a good thing to do?'), 5) others.

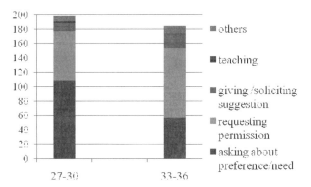

Figure 2. Frequency of the mothers' question types

Figure 2 shows the frequencies of the five types of questions produced by the three mothers when the children were at the ages of 27-30 months and 33-36 months. Clearly, the mothers' frequent use of question forms we saw in Figure 1 was due to their tendencies to ask about the children's needs and preferences. The questions ranged from simple Yes-No questions (e.g. *kore ga ii no*? 'Is this one good? / Do you want this one?) to wh-questions (e.g. *dore ga ii kanaa*? 'Which one is good for you? Which one do you want?'). In the later stage, however, the mothers were more inclined to use questions to ask for permission (e.g. *tsukatte ii no*? 'Is my using this good? / Can I use this?'). Together with the times when they use *ii* to give or solicit suggestions, the later instances of the mothers' uses of *ii* were mainly for inviting children's opinion about future events.

Contrary to what is suggested in the previous research, it is clear that the mothers are not controlling the children's behavior by simply asserting what is *good*. In fact, as illustrated in (7), it is often the case that the children's initial response to the mothers' questions (line 341) is non-compliant, and then she had to reinitiate or modify her question (line 345). This is another source of the mothers' frequent uses of questions and it is through such question-answer sequences that the process of negotiation between the mothers and children are established. Desirability, in this sense, is not expressed only by the mothers, but constructed by the mother and child through question-answer sequences.

(7) Aki's mother is asking whether Aki agrees to give one of his toys to his sister (Aki 29 months old)

341	Mother:	*kore ii ,, hitotsu kashiteyatte* ?
342	Aki:	*Akichan* .
343	Mother:	*sore Akichan no* ?
344	Aki:	*un* .
345	Mother:	*kore wa ii* ?
346	Aki:	*ii wa* .

Mother:	'Is giving this (to your sister) good/OK? / Can I give this (to your sister)?'
Aki:	'Aki.'
Mother:	'Is that Aki's (yours)?'
Aki:	'Yes.'
Mother:	'Is this Good/OK?'
Aki:	'Good/OK.'

Philosophical discussion of deontic modality has typically been based on the analysis of isolated sentences (e.g. 'Open the window.' 'You should do it this way'). In this framework, one is easily led to the conclusion that speakers choose to use this type of sentence to convey their modal intensions in a uni-directional way. Akatsuka and Clancy's (1993) and Clancy et al.'s (1997) analysis on child directed speech follows this tradition. However, in the actual context of discourse, each speaker has her own will, and her needs and wants often conflict with those of others. Therefore, it is not always effective to simply state what the speaker thinks the other person should do. Inevitably, speakers often resort to more skillful uses of language to induce the partner to cooperate in their acts and thereby make the intended event happen. In (7) above, the mother's intention was to let the siblings share their toys. By requesting the child's consent ('Is giving this to your sister OK?') and negotiating, rather than directly expressing obligation ('You should share it with your brother'), the mother achieves the goal.

As they mature, children also learn this interactional strategy and start to ask for the mothers' permissions through questions. This function was often achieved through the use of the structure 'V-*te ii*', as in (8).

(8) Ryo and his mother are talking about toy blocks (Ryo 30 months)
     Ryo: *Mama, tsumiki* .
➔   Ryo: *yatte ii* ?
     Mother: *ii yo* .

     Ryo   'Mom, blocks'
     Ryo: 'Is doing it good/OK? / Can I do it?'
     Mother: 'Good/Sure.'

As soon as the children start using this construction, the percentage of interrogative sentences in general increases dramatically[5]. Until this point, the vast majority of their utterances with *ii* are declaratives with functions mainly to express their own desire, need of an object (or lack thereof), or consent to the mothers' suggestions (see (3) in 3.1). However, the use of V-*te ii*? with the permission request function opens a channel to ask about the mothers' opinions toward their own behavior (e.g. *Is* (my) *doing this good/OK?*). The utterance including *ii* thus becomes a useful device both for the children and the mothers to coordinate each others' behavior through an exchange of asking and granting permissions.

The cognitive complexity associated with the comprehension of conditional construction, V-COND(itional)-*ii*, appears to be minimized by its formal and functional similarity to the V-*te ii* construction. With the earliest conditional constructions, the mothers and the children continue requesting

---

[5] We calculated the percentage of questions using *ii* against the total utterances including *ii*. During the three months prior to the first use of V-*te ii*, the percentages for the three children were 13% (Aki), 7% (Ryo) and 0% (Tai). These increased to 49% (Aki), 33% (Ryo) and 38% (Tai) in the following three months after they began using V-*te ii*.

and granting permission to each other (e.g. *kotchi yat-tara ii?* 'Can I do this one?' [Aki, 35 months-old]). In addition, they begin engaging in pragmatically more sophisticated ways of behavior control such as suggesting a solution (*koko kara haire-ba ii n da yo.* [Tai, 32 months-old]), and soliciting an opinion (e.g. *Hiro-kun tte yobeba ii no?* 'Should I call him Hiro-kun?' [Ryo, 33 months-old]).

From this functional perspective, we see that the mothers' and children's use patterns of grammatical structures change over time as they develop a wider range of communicative sequences. In the second year of life, children reach the developmental stage in which they begin to actively express their likes and dislikes. The mothers appear to be sensitive to this change, and start questions to gauge their children's desire and preferences. This may reinforce, if not actually creates, the children's understanding of instrumental property of their language use. That is, the children become aware that they can use language to satisfy their wants and needs, and that there is more than one way to do so.

In the following developmental stage, the children, too, begin to ask for adult permission. The 'V-te *ii*' form, as well as some of the conditional constructions, is best matched with this function. Consequently, the children became capable of carrying out their wishes in an interaction with their conversational partners. We argue that it is through this process of socialization that children learn to use new linguistic units, including conditional expressions, which allow them to better manage the negotiation (Ochs 1986; Burdelski 2006; Cook 2008).

4. Conclusion

This paper was inspired by Akatsuka and Clancy's (1993) and Clancy et al.'s (1997) pioneering work on the deontic modality in early mother-child interactions in Japanese. By extending the data to an earlier stage of development and taking interactional use of language into consideration, we were able to build a more comprehensive view on the acquisition of conditionals.

Our study has shown that the utterances including *ii* came about in children's repertoire in strong association with ontogenetically basic functions such as expressing their wants and needs. On the pragmatic ground of mother-child interactions, such expressions of desire were typically interpreted as an act of making requests. Similarly, declaring a lack of need or interest had the illocutionary force of rejection of an offer or deterrent of an action. The acquisition of the utterances with the adjective *ii* thus plays an important role in the children's learning of culturally attested ways to perform the speech-acts.

We argued against the idea that an apprehension of deontic conditionals presupposes the understanding of the evaluative meaning of *ii* 'good'. Given the wide variety of pragmatic functions it serves, we suggested that early uses of *ii* are better understood as parts of differently sized constructional structures. Children's understanding of *ii* at the early stage may be formed around concrete pragmatic meanings realized in actual uses of these constructions. Deontic modality, which is associated with the early conditionals, had already been introduced by the structurally simpler constructions. Therefore, the understanding of the deontic conditional is more likely to be formed by adding complexity to such existing constructions, rather than by compositionally combining the conditional antecedent (i.e. *if~*) and the evaluative meaning of *ii* (i.e. good).

Our analysis also showed that the mothers and children were actively using *ii* to ask the other person's opinion and preference. That is, the adjective *ii* was not used only to assert the speaker's desire; it was also used to ask about the other person's opinion to negotiate the needs and wants. This is likely to be closely related to the children's growing awareness that they can use language to get others to satisfy their wants. Similarly, they come to understand that other people also use language to restrict their behavior. Such behavioral control of, or instrumental, aspects of language can be one of the most fundamental properties of human linguistic communication. Much more research should be done to address issues regarding the relationship between a child's linguistic and pragmatic abilities.

References

Akatsuka, N. and Clancy, P. M. 1993. Conditionality and Deontic Modality in Japanese and Korean; Evidence from the Emergence of Conditionals. *Japanese/Korean Linguistics* 2: 177-192. Stanford: CSLI.

Bates, E. 1976. *Language and Context: The Acquisition of Pragmatics.* NY: Academic Press.

Bowerman, M. 1986. First Steps in Acquiring Conditionals. *On conditionals,* eds. E. Traugott, A. Meulen, J. Reily and C. Ferguson, 333-372. Cambridge: Cambridge University Press.

Burdelski, M. 2006. Language Socialization of Two-year old Children in Kansai, Japan: The Family and Beyond. Doctoral dissertation, University of California, Los Angeles.

Bybee, J. L. and Hopper, P. 2001. *Frequency and the Emergence of Linguistic Structure.* Amsterdam: John Benjamins.

Cameron-Faulkner, T., Lieven, E., and Tomasello, M. 2003. A Construction Based Analysis of Child Directed Speech. *Cognitive Science,* 27: 843-873.

Clancy, P. 1985. The Acquisition of Japanese. *The Crosslinguistic Study of Language Acquisition,* vol.1, ed. D.I. Slobin, 373–524. Mahwah NJ: Lawrence Erlbaum Associates.

Clancy, P., Akatsuka, N., and Strauss, S. 1997. Deontic Modality and Conditionality in Discourse: A Cross-linguistic Study of Adult Speech to Young Children. *Di-*

rections in Functional Linguistics, ed. A. Kamio, 19-57. Amsterdam: John Benjamins.

Clark, E. V. and Kelly, B. 2006. *Constructions in Acquisition*. Stanford: CSLI.

Cook, M. H. 2008. Language Socialization in Japanese. *Encyclopedia of Language and Education*, 2nd ed., vol. 8, eds. P. A. Duff and N. H. Hornberger: 313-326. Springer Science+Business Media LLC.

Diessel, H. 2004. The Acquisition of Complex Sentences. [Cambridge Studies in Linguistics 105]. Cambridge University Press.

Diessel, H. and Tomasello, M. 2005. A New Look at the Acquisition of Relative Clauses. *Language* 81: 882-906.

Gulzow, I. and Gagarina, N. 2007. *Frequency Effects in Language Acquisition: Defining the Limits of Fderequency as Explanatory Concept*. Mouton De Gruyter.

Hatano, E. 1979. Kodomo-ni okeru yoshi *wa/ga* no kakutoku no kenkyu (A Study on the Acquisition of the Particles *Wa* and *Ga* by Children). *Japanese Journal of Educational Psychology* 27: 160–168.

Locke, J. L. 1993. *The Child's Path to Spoken Language*. Cambridge, MA: Harvard University Press.

Locke, J. L. 1995. Development of the Capacity for Spoken Language. *The Hand-Book of Child Language*. eds. P. Fletcher and B. MacWhinney, 278-302. Boston MA: Blackwell.

Ochs, E. 1986. Introduction. *Language Socialization across Cultures*. eds. B. B. Schieffelin and E. Ochs, 1-13. New York: Cambridge University Press.

Ono, T. and Thompson, S. A. 2009. Fixedness in Japanese Adjectives in Conversation: Toward a New Understanding of a Lexical ('part-of-speech') Category. *Formulaic Language (Typological Studies in Language)*. eds. B. Corrigan, E. Moravcsik, H. Ouali and K. Wheatly, 117-143. Amsterdam: John Benjamins.

Oshima-Takane, Y., MacWhinney, B., Shirai, H., Miyata, S., and Naka, N. 1998. *CHILDES for Japanese,* 2nd ed. Nagoya: Chukyo University.

Reilly, J. S. 1986. The Acquisition of Temporal and Conditionals. *On conditionals,* eds. E. Traugott, A. Meulen, J. Reily and C. Ferguson, 309-331. Cambridge University Press.

Slobin, D. I. 1973. Cognitive Prerequisites for the Development of Grammar. *Studies of child language development*. eds C. Fergason and D. Slobin. NY: Holt, Rinehart, Winston.

Tahara, S. and Ito, T. 1985. Joshi *wa*-to *ga*-no danwakinoo-no hattatsu (The Development of the Discourse Functions of *Wa* and *Ga*). *Japanese Journal of Psychology* 56: 208–214.

Tomasello, M. 2003. *Constructing a Language: A Usage-based Theory of Language Acquisition*. Cambridge, MA: Harvard University Press.

Wray, A. and Perkins, M. 2000. The Function of Formulaic Language: An Integrated Model. *Language and Communication* 20: 1-28.

A Trihedral Approach to the Overgeneration of "no" in the Acquisition of Japanese Noun Phrases*

KEIKO MURASUGI
Nanzan University and University of Connecticut

TOMOMI NAKATANI
Nanzan University

CHISATO FUJI
Nanzan University

1. Introduction

It is very well known that Japanese-speaking children around ages one to four overgenerate *no* between the sentential modifier and the head NP, as shown in (1).

(1) a. howasi   ookii *no   howasi (=ohasi) (2;1)
       chopstick big   NO   chopstick
       'chopsticks, the big ones, chopsticks' (Nagano 1960)

* We would like to thank the organizers, participants and the anonymous reviewers of JK 19, and scholars involved in the activities of Center for Linguistics at Nanzan University, especially Michiya Kawai, Tomoko Hashimoto, Mamoru Saito, Koji Sugisaki, Daiko Takahashi, and Yurie Tsuruhara, for valuable discussions on the topic discussed in this paper. The research presented here was supported in part by Nanzan University Pache Research Grant I-A and by JSPS Grant-in-Aid at Nanzan University (#20520397).

Japanese/Korean Linguistics 19.
Edited by Ho-min Sohn, Haruko Cook, William O'Grady, Leon A. Serafim, & Sang Yee Cheon.

b. maarui *no   unti (2;0)
round   NO poop 'a round poop' (Yokoyama 1990)
c. Yuta-ga   asyon-deru *no   yatyu wa   kore, kore (Yuta 2;3)
Yuta-Nom playing-is   NO thing Top this this
'The thing that Yuta (I) is playing with is this (train).'

In (1a) and (1b), children insert *no* between the adjective (e.g. *ookii* (big) and *marui* (round)) and the head nominal (e.g. *howasi* (chopsticks) and *unti* (poop)) at around two years of age. Later, at two to four years of age, as in (1c), Japanese-speaking children insert *no* between the sentential modifier *Yuta ga asyon-deru* (Yuta is playing) and the head nominal *yatyu* (thing).

In adult Japanese, there are mainly three types of *no*.

(2) a. [Yamada] no   hon (Genitive Case marker)
              Gen book 'Yamada's book'
    b. akai   no (Pronoun)
       red (+present) one 'the red one'
    c. Emi-ga   hazimete   robusutaa-o tabe-ta no   wa
         -Nom for the first time lobster-Acc ate   Comp Top
       Bosuton de da (Complementizer)
       Boston in Copula
       'It is in Boston that Emi ate a lobster for the first time.'

(2a) is the genitive case marker, which roughly corresponds to *'s* or *of* in English. (2b) is a pronoun, which roughly corresponds to *one* in English. A complementizer in (2c) is the head of the presuppositional phrase in the cleft sentence, which corresponds to *that* in English.

In the history of Japanese acquisition, three contradictory analyses, the Pronoun Hypothesis, the Genitive Case Hypothesis, and the Complementizer Hypothesis have been proposed regarding the syntactic status of the over-generated *no*. Accordingly, the age children overgenerate *no* is contradictory: Some say it happens when children are one year old (e.g. Nagano 1960), but some say it lasts until four years old (e.g. Murasugi 1991).

In this paper, mainly based on our longitudinal study with a Japanese-speaking child, Yuta, and the corpus analysis of CHILDES (Sumihare and Jun), we argue that the mysteriously long overgeneration phenomenon of *no*, in fact, stems from three distinct sources, as proposed by Murasugi (2009). We show that three contradictory hypotheses (i.e. Pronoun, Genitive Case, and Complementizer) proposed in the past acquisition researches, are basically all correct. First, a pronoun *no* is used due to the limit in production at the two-word stage. Second, the genitive Case marker *no* is inserted because of the miscategorization of adjectives as nominals. Third, a complementizer *no* is overgenerated due to the parameterization in the structure of relative clauses. The overgeneration of *no*, which looks like a single phenomenon, is reanalyzed as a trihedral phenomenon, and each phase represents one of the crucial developmental stages in language acquisition.

2. The Complementizer Hypothesis: Relative Clause Parameter (Murasugi 1991)

Murasugi (1991), based on her longitudinal and experimental study with Japanese-speaking children at two to four years of age, proposes that the overgenerated *no* is a complementizer. According to her analysis, a structure of a sentential modifier is parameterized; either CP or TP depending on the languages. Murasugi argues that sentential modifiers in adult Japanese (and Korean) are TPs, unlike CP relatives in English. However, Japanese-speaking children initially hypothesize that Japanese relative clauses are CPs, and overgenerate a complementizer between the sentential modifier and the head nominal.

Children's first complex NPs are found after two years of age, and they are usually a fixed expression without overgeneration (Murasugi and Hashimoto 2004). Our subject Yuta's first complex NPs were also fixed expressions. The relevant examples are shown in (3).

(3) a. Tottan-ga   katte kure-ta purezento da   yo (2;0)
     father-Nom buy   gave   present   Copula Int
     '(This is) the present that my father bought (for me).'

    b. Kore, Yuki-tyan-ga   kure-ta purezento na   no (2;0)
      this,   -Nom gave   present   Copula Int
      'This is the present that Yuki-tyan gave (to me).'

In (3), the verbs were limited to *katte kureru* (buy and give) and *kureru* (give) only. The head NP was also limited to the NP, *purezento* (present).

Later, some children overgenerate *no* on sentential modifiers. Yuta started to overgenerate *no* productively not only in complex NPs as in (4a) and (4b), but also after adjectives as in (4c), after 2;2.

(4) a. Kare-teru *no   hana da   yo (2;2)
     wither-is   NO flower Copula Int '(I have) a withered flower.'

    b. Yuta-ga   asyon-deru *no yatyu wa kore, kore (2;3)
        -Nom playing-is NO thing Top this   this
      'The thing that Yuta (I) is playing with is this (train).'

    c. Kore nagai *no yatyu da   ne (2;3)
      this   long   NO one Copula Int 'This is a long one.'

In (4a), Yuta inserted *no* between the modifier *kare-teru* (is withered) and the head nominal *hana* (flower). Similarly, in (4b), Yuta (playing with a train in front of the box with the picture of the train, and comparing the toy and the picture of it), overgenerated *no* between the sentential modifier *Yu-ta-ga asyon-deru* and the head NP, *yatyu*. In (4c), he overgenerated *no* after the adjective *nagai* (long).

Murasugi (1991) reports that children at around two to four years of age overgenerate a complementizer *no* between the head NP and all types of sentential modifiers, as exemplified in (5).

(5) a. tigau *no outi (3;0)
    differ NO house 'the different house'
  b. Emi-tyan-ga kai-ta *no sinderera (2;11-4;2)
         -Nom drew NO Cinderella 'the Cinderella that Emi drew'
  c. ookii *no tako (2;11-4;2)
    big NO octopus 'a big octopus' (Murasugi 1991)

In (5a), *no* is inserted between the inflected verb, *tigau* (differ) and the head nominal, *outi* (house), and in (5b), it is inserted between the sentential modifier and the head nominal. In (5c), *no* is overgenerated after the adjective, *ookii* (big), as well.

Crucially, however, she reports that those children, who overgenerated *no*, sometimes undergenerated the genitive Case marker on PPs, as in (6), although they can correctly insert it between two NPs, as in (7).

(6) Tokyo made [φ] basu (3;2)
       to *(Gen) bus 'the bus to Tokyo' (Murasugi 1991)
(7) a. Emi-no hon (Emi:2;9) b. megane-no ozityan (Miki: 2;4)
      -Genbook   glasses-Gen man
    'Emi's book'   'the man with eye glasses'(Murasugi 1991)

Thus, the overgeneration takes place when the genitive Case marking is not fully acquired.

One piece of direct empirical evidence for the Complementizer Hypothesis was found in Toyama dialect in Japanese as in (8a) and Korean as in (8b).

(8) a. *Anpanman tui-toru *ga koppu (Ken 2;11)
    (a character) attaching-is GA cup
    'the cup which is pictured with "Anpanman"' (Murasugi 1991)

b. Acessi otopai   tha-nun *kes soli ya (2-3 years old) (Kim 1987)
   uncle motorcycle riding-is KES sound is
   'Lit. (This) is the sound that a man is riding a motorcycle.'

The overgenerated item is a complementizer, for instance, *ga* in Toyama dialect, and *kes* in Korean, but not the genitive case marker (*no* in Toyama dialect nor *uy* in Korean).

Thus, not only Japanese-speaking children but also Korean-speaking children initially hypothesize that their relative clauses are CPs, and overgenerate a complementizer between the sentential modifier and the head nominal.

Murasugi and Hashimoto (2004), however, argue that the Complementizer Hypothesis alone cannot fully explain the overgeneration phenomenon of *no*. In fact, the overgeneration of *no* is observed with very young children, even at around the age of one, when they start producing two-word utterances. Crucially, then, not only T or C related items, but also, even the genitive Case marker is not produced. Murasugi and Hashimoto point out that it is very unlikely that the same type of overgeneration lasts for four years, and conclude that there are two types of overgeneration of *no*: A pronoun and a complementizer.

3. The Pronoun Hypothesis In Addition To the Complementizer Analysis (Nagano 1960, Murasugi and Hashimoto 2004, 2006)

The Pronoun Hypothesis was in fact originally proposed by Nagano (1960) fifty years ago. His argument is very simple and clear: The overgenerated *no* cannot be the genitive Case marker, because the overgeneration takes place when there is no genitive Case marker found in the child production, but only pronoun *no* is produced. Examples in (9) are cited from Nagano (1960).

(9) a. howasi   ookii *no   howasi (=ohasi) (2;1)
       chopstick big   one chopstick 'chopsticks, the big ones, chopsticks'
    b. Amuna (=Harumi) tittyai *no Amuna (2;1)
                       small   one
    'Harumi, the small one, Harumi' (Nagano 1960)

In (9a) and (9b), *no* looks like to be erroneously inserted between the adjective (e.g. *ookii* (big) and *tiisai* (small)) and the NP (e.g. *howasi*, which is *ohasi* (chopsticks) and *Amuna*, which is *Harumi*) at 2;1. The overgeneration in question appears just after the pronoun *no* starts to be correctly produced at 2;1, as in (10), but before the genitive Case marking is fully acquired, as in (11).

(10) a. Ookii no (2;1)   b. Tittyai no (2;1) (Nagano 1960)
    big one 'The big one(=bus).' small one 'The small one(=leaf)'
(11) ke...mama   [φ] ke, mama   [φ] ke, mama (2;0)
    hair Mommy *(Gen) hair Mommy *(Gen) hair Mommy
    'hair...Mommy's hair, Mommy's hair, Mommy' (Nagano 1960)

In (11), the child omitted the genitive Case marker *no*, although it should be inserted between *mama* (Mommy) and *ke* (hair) in the adult grammar. It is only one month later, at 2;2, that the genitive Case marker appears in the natural production, as shown in (12).

(12) Papa-no   buton (=zubon) (2;2)
    Daddy-Gen pants 'Daddy's pants' (Nagano 1960)

    The parallel developmental stage was observed by Murasugi and Hashimoto's (2004) longitudinal study with Akkun, and our longitudinal study with Yuta. Both subjects started overgenerating *no* before the genitive Case marker was inserted between NPs.

(13) a. akai no at-ta (2;3)   b. Akkun no. Akkun [φ] ohuton (2;3-2;5)
    red onethere-was   one.   bed
    '(I) found the red one' '(This is) Akkun's. Akkun('s) bed.'
                                 (Murasugi and Hashimoto 2004)

    Furthermore, both Akkun and Yuta put a brief pause between the NP headed by the pronoun *no* and the referential NP. (14) shows Akkun's data taken from Murasugi and Hashimoto (2004).

(14) a. Akkun tiityai no konkonkon (2;4)
          small-is one hammer 'Akkun's (/My) small hammer'
    b. [Akkun//pause//[tiityai no]//pause//konkonkon]

They argue that the utterance consists of two parts (i.e. *tiityai no* (small one) and *konkonkon* (hammer)), and this is very different from the overgeneration of a complementizer.

    Similarly, the subject we examined in the present study, Yuta, started overgenerating *no* at around 1;10, when he just started combining two words in the utterances. An example is given in (15).

(15) a. Hon, atarasii no, hon da (1;10)
        book new   one book Copula
        'a book, a new one, (this is) a book'
    b. [hon //pause// [atarasii no] //pause// hon da]

The analysis of Praat[1] clearly shows that there is a pause between *no* and the reference NP, thereby confirming Murasugi and Hashimoto's (2004) observation.

Figure 1. A pause found between *no* and the referential NP

pronoun_mov_mono

In Figure 1, the pitch contour shows that there is a pause of 0.48 seconds between *no* and the referential NP, *hon* (a book). Thus, this result indicates that the utterance consists of two parts.

In contrast, as for the overgeneration of a complementizer given in (4b) found after two years of age, there is no pause between *no* and the head NP.

Figure 2. No pause found between *no* and the head NP with the overgeneration of a complementizer

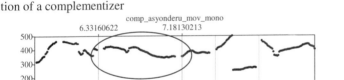
comp_asyonderu_mov_mono

The Praat analysis in Figure 2 indicates that there is no separation of any kind, and *asyonderu (ashon-deru) no yatyu* is produced as a unit.

Hence, Murasugi and Hashimoto (2004, 2006) argue that Nagano's (1960) Pronoun Hypothesis is supported, and the overgenerated *no* at the age of one and early age of two is a pronoun. They analyze that this *no* is, in fact, not an error, but reflects the production strategy of very young children to combine two elements. When children cannot create the modification

---

[1] Praat is a program for doing phonetic analyses and sound manipulations (Boersma and Weenink 2009).

structure, they produce an NP headed by the pronoun *no* (one) first, to provide a frame for an NP, and the modifier, or the head nominal is realized as the second independent NP. Children use this strategy since the genitive Case marker is not yet acquired at the beginning of the two-word stage. Murasugi (2009) further proposes that this stage reflects the earliest morphological realization of the operation of merger, and that the onset of the merger starts with the phrases headed by the smaller category (*no* (one) as N') with less semantic content. This hypothesis holds as there is a pause between the pronoun *no* and the second NP.

The argument given so far shows that there are at least two sources for the apparently same "overgeneration" phenomenon. The one observed in ages one and two is a pronoun, and the other observed in ages two through four is a complementizer.

However, another empirical problem arises. *No* is overgenerated when children have already acquired the genitive case marker, have no problem in combining two elements, and produce no relative clauses. The mysterious *no* associated with those characteristics is exemplified in (16).

(16) a. atarasii *no kami (Yuta 1;11)   b. siroi *no gohan (Yuta 2;0)
       new   NO paper 'a new paper'   white NO rice 'white rice'
     c. Tiisai *no buubuu tootta yo (Sumihare 1;11)
        small NO car   passed Intensifier 'A small car passed.'

Crucially, the overgeneration is found after the two-word stage, at around the age of two, with limited adjectives such as color, size, shape, and state.

At this mysterious stage, the genitive Case marker between two NPs is productively and correctly used. For example, as in (17), Yuta started to produce the genitive Case marker between NPs at 1;11, and Sumihare started at 2;0.

(17) a. Ko otoosan-no hanasi da   yo (Yuta 1;11)
        this father-Gen story Copula Int 'This is a story of father.'
     b. Ringo-no ozityan-ga... (Sumihare 2;0)
        apple-Gen man-Nom 'The man (who sells) apples is...'

Praat analysis reveals that unlike the case of a pronoun, there is no pause found between *no* and the NP following it. In Figure 3, no separation has been made between *siroi no* (white one) and *gohan* (rice), and they are produced as a unit.

The facts shown above cannot be explained by the Complementizer Hypothesis either. This mysterious *no* is produced by children who have not acquired complex NPs yet, and the cleft sentences are hardly observed. Moreover, as noted above, the overgeneration is found only with the present-tensed adjectives of color, size, and state.

Figure 3. No pause found between *no* and the head NP
with the mysterious overgeneration of *no*

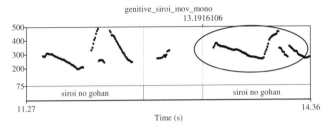

In the next section, we argue that children, at around the age of two, have difficulties in acquiring "the category of adjectives," and some adjectives are treated as nominals, and some, as verbs. Those "nominal-like adjectives" never inflect with tense, and children, who already know the genitive Case marker insertion between the nominal projections, correctly insert the genitive Case marker between the "nominal-like adjectives" and the head nominal. This would be the mysterious stage of overgeneration of *no* found before a relative clause is acquired. (See Murasugi (2009) for details.)

4. The Genitive Case Marker Hypothesis

The Genitive Case Marker Hypothesis has been proposed by many researchers in the past fifty years (Iwabuchi and Muraishi 1968, Harada 1980, 1984, Clancy 1985, Yokoyama 1990, Ito 1998, among others). Among those, Yokoyama's (1990) generalization is quite important. He argues that the erroneous *no* is a genitive Case marker, and it is overgenerated only with the adjectives referring to color, size, and shape (e.g. *akai* (red), *ookii* (big), *maarui* (round)), but never with other adjectives (e.g. *abunai* (dangerous), *yasasii* (kind)), as shown in (18).

(18) a. ookii *no   sakana (1;8)   b. maarui *no   unti (2;0)
    big   NO fish 'a big fish'   round   NO poop 'a round poop'

Yokoyama's apparently curious generalization is further confirmed by Murasugi and Hashimoto (2004). They find that the adjectives of color, size, and shape do not inflect with tense, but appear only in present-tense forms.

This generalization is further supported by our longitudinal study with Yuta and also by our corpus analysis of Sumihare. The overgeneration occurs only with the adjectives which refer to color, size, shape, and state, but it never occurs with such adjectives as *itai* (is painful), *omoi* (is heavy), or *kowai* (is scary), which only appear in the predicative form with tense (i.e. present and past) but never in the prenominal form. As these adjectives never appear in the prenominal form, there is naturally no chance that the overgeneration should take place. Rather, these adjectives are not associated with the overgenerated *no*, and behave like verbs, as in (19).

(19) a. Oisii,   kore. Oisii,   kore (Yuta 1;10)
      delicious this   delicious this 'This is delicious.'
    b. Koko babatii yo ne (Sumihare 2;0)
      here   dirty   Int Int '(It is) dirty here.'
    c. Okaatyan pompo   itai no (Sumihare 2;0)
      Mommy   onomatopoeia ache Q
      'Mommy, is (your) stomach aching?'

In (19), the adjectives, *oisii* (delicious), *babatii* (dirty), *itai* (painful), are used as predicates, conjugating with tense as shown in Tables 1 and 2.

Table 1 shows that the past-tense forms of nominal-like adjectives are produced relatively late, but those of verb-like adjectives are produced relatively early in the case of Yuta.

Table 1. The age of the first appearance of the present- /past-tense forms of adjectives by Yuta

Nominal-like Adjectives (of Touch and Sight)			Verb-like Adjectives		
Adjectives	Present-tense	Past-tense	Adjectives	Present-tense	Past-tense
ookii 'big'	*ooki-i* (1;8)	*ookik-atta* (2;0)	*itai* 'painful'	*ita-i* (1;11)	*itak-atta* (1;11)
tiisai 'small'	*tiisa-i* (1;11)	*tiisaik-atta* (2;1)	*oisii* 'delicious'	*oisi-i* (1;10)	*Oisik-atta* (1;10)
kuroi 'black'	*kuro-i* (2;0)	*kurok-atta* (2;4)	*kowai* 'scary'	*kowa-i* (1;10)	*kowak-atta* (2;2)

The contrast between nominal-like adjectives and verb-like adjectives is clearer in the case of Sumihare, as shown in Table 2.

Table 2. The age of the first appearance of the present- /past-tense forms of
adjectives by Sumihare (CHILDES)

Nominal-like Adjectives (of Touch and Sight)			Verb-like Adjectives		
Adjectives	Present-tense	Past-tense	Adjectives	Present-tense	Past-tense
ookii 'big'	*ooki-i* (1;11)	*ookik-atta* (2;9)	*itai* 'painful'	*ita-i* (1;8)	*itak-atta* (2;0)
akai 'red'	*aka-i* (1;11)	*akak-atta* (4;0)	*omoi* 'heavy'	*omo-i* (1;8)	*omok-atta* (2;2)
siroi 'white'	*siro-i* (2;2)	*sirok-atta* (3;6)	*kusai* 'smelly'	*kusa-i* (2;2)	*kusak-atta* (2;3)

Sumihare produced only the present forms for nominal-like adjectives, but
never the inflected forms, when he inserted *no* between the adjectives of
touch and sight (e.g. color, size, shape, and state) and the head nominals. On
the other hand, the verb-like adjectives (e.g. *itai* (painful), *omoi* (heavy),
kusai (smelly)), which are not erroneously genitive Case marked, inflected
with tense much earlier.

There are several pieces of evidence to show that the adjectives referring to the sense of touch and sight are used as nominals. For example, as
shown in (20), these adjectives are used as referential noun phrases.

(20) a.*Kiiroi   to   *akai to (Sumihare 2;9)
        yellow   and   red   and
        '(They're) a yellow (crayon) and a red (crayon).'
     (Adult form: kiiroi/akai-no (yellow/red one), / kiiro/aka (yellow/red))
     b.*Tiisai koo-te   ya (Sumihare 2;7)
        small buy-Request Int 'Please buy a small (dog).'
     (Adult form: tiisai-no (small one))

In (20a), Sumihare erroneously used the adjectives *kiiroi* (yellow) and *akai*
(red) to refer to the concrete objects, a yellow crayon and a red crayon. Similarly in (20b), he used the adjective *tiisai* (small) to refer to a small dog.

These nominal-like adjectives appear in the argument position being
Case marked as well.

(21) *Tittyai-ga atte *maarui-ga   atte...konna *ookii-ga atte...(Yuta 2;2)
      small-Nom be   round-Nom be   such   big-Nom be
      'There is (a) small (circle), (a) round (one), and such (a) big (one)...'
      (Adult form: Tittyai/maarui/ookii no (small/round/big one))

Yuta uttered as in (21), while he was repeatedly drawing circles. The adjectives, *tiisai* (small), *marui* (round) and *ookii* (big), appear in the subject position associated with the nominative Case marker *ga*.

The most valid generalization to be drawn from the description so far is
that the adjectives referring to the sense of touch and sight are miscatego-

rized as nominals (Murasugi 2009). Hence, those children who already know the system of genitive Case marking between two NPs, "correctly" assign the genitive *no* to the "nominals" which are, in fact, adjectives in adult grammar.

Then, why do children miscategorize certain adjectives? We conjecture that adjectives referring to color, size and shape share the properties of concrete nominals in that they are consistent, absolute, and evidential, compared with other types of adjectives such as emotion and evaluation (cf. Berman 1988, Mintz and Gleitman 2002). And as argued by de Villiers and de Villiers (1978), a certain set of adjectives of size and shape go together as colors in child language.

Furthermore, acquiring adjectives is difficult because it is "a fluid category" (Gassar and Smith 1998, Berman 1988, Polinsky 2005, among others). As shown in (22), the position where the adjective *big* appears in adult English can be occupied with the verb *dropped* or the noun *a dog*. Thus, the syntactic cue is ambiguous for children.

(22)   a. It's [big]   b. It [dropped]   c. It's [a dog]

The syntactic cue is ambiguous in Japanese, too. Both adjectives and nominals can be followed by the polite sentence-ending marker *desu*, as in (23), while both adjectives and verbs inflect with tense, as in (24).

(23) a. akai   desu (Adjective)
        is-red (Adj) Polite '(It) is red.'
     b. aka   desu (Nominal)
        a red color (Nominal) Polite '(It) is a red color.'

(24) a. ooki-i   ookik-atta   b. aka-i   akak-atta   (Adjectives)
        big-Pres big-Past   red-Pres   red-Past
     c. tabe-ru   tabe-ta   d. nom-(r)u   non-da   (Verbs)
        eat-Pres eat-Past   drink-Pres drink-Past

In this sense, the Japanese adjective is also "a fluid category," and this could make adjectives difficult to be acquired.

Note here that even if we assume that children's miscategorization of certain adjectives causes the genitive Case marker insertion, the Complementizer Hypothesis should be still maintained. For example, remember the overgeneration phenomena in Toyama dialect in Japanese and Korean. As in (8a) and (8b), repeated below, the overgenerated item is a complementizer, but not the genitive Case marker.

(8) a. *Anpanman   tui-toru   *ga   koppu (Ken 2;11)
       (a character) attaching-is GA   cup
       'the cup which is pictured with "Anpanman"' (Murasugi 1991)
    b. Acessi otopai   tha-nun *kes soli ya (2-3 years old)(Kim 1987)
       uncle motorcycle riding-is KES sound is
       'Lit. (This) is the sound that a man is riding a motorcycle.'

Thus, the Complementizer Hypothesis we discussed in Section 2, should be maintained, and there are three distinct stages of the "overgeneration" of *no*.

The hypothesis that there are three stages in the "overgeneration" of *no* is further supported by our corpus analysis of Jun. First, Jun, at 2;2, produced a pronoun but not the genitive Case marker. He produced (25a) and (25b), where there was a brief pause between *no* and the head nominals, *basu* (bus) and *okaasan* (mother). This is exactly the Pronoun stage as is discussed in Section 3.

(25) a. Ookii   no   [pause] basyu(=basu) wa? (2;4)
       big   N'(one)   bus   Top '(Where) is the big bus?'
    b. ookii no   [pause] okaasan (2;5)
       big   N' (one)   mother 'the big one, mother'

Then, at around 2;5, when the genitive Case markers were productively used as in (26), he inserted *no* between adjectives referring to color, size and shape and the head nominals, without making any pauses, as in (27).

(26) Kokko-no   outi   ya (2;5)
       chicken-Gen house Int '(This is) a chicken's house.'
(27) a. Hore, ookii *no   torakku atta zo hore (2;6)
       hey   big   NO truck   was   Int hey 'Hey, there is a big truck.'
    b. tiisai*no akatyan (2;6)   c. kuroi *no   zidoosya (2;6)
       small NO baby 'a small baby'   black   NO car 'a black car'

Just like Yuta and Sumihare, the overgeneration occurs only with the adjectives of touch and sight, and those adjectives are sometimes used as nominals as well.

(28) a.*Ookii-ga   otiru (2;7) (Adult: ookii-kuruma-ga / ookii-no-ga)
         big-Nom   fall 'The big (toy car) is falling.'
    b. FAT: Kore-wa nan desu ka
             this-Top what Cop Q'What is this?'(Showing CHI a new toy)
       CHI:Atarasii *no*akai (2;8) (Adult: atarasii akai-no)
           new   NO red '(It's) new red.'

In (28a), the adjective *ookii* (big) appears in the subject position associated with the nominative Case marker *ga*. In (28b), he used the adjective *akai* (red) to refer to the concrete object, a red toy. Hence, those adjectives are treated as nominals, and the overgenerated *no* in (27) is the genitive Case marker, being "correctly" inserted between two NPs.

Finally, as in (29), he started overgenerating *no* with relative clauses at around 2;8.

(29) a. koware-ten *no yatu   zidoosya (2;8)
        is-broken   NO thing car '(This is) a broken car.'
     b. Omosiroi *no   yakiimo   ya kore
        funny   NO   baked sweet potato Int this
        'This is a funny baked sweet potato.' (2;10)

In (29a), *no* is overgenerated between the modifier *koware-ten* (=*teru*) (is broken) and the head nominal *yatu* (thing). (29b) shows that the overgeneration occurs with any kind of adjectives at this stage. Thus, this is the Complementizer stage, where Jun hypothesizes that Japanese relative clauses are CPs (Murasugi 1991).

Thus, the longitudinal studies with Akkun and Yuta, and the corpus analysis of Sumihare and Jun (CHILDES) indicate that Japanese-speaking children through three stages of "overgeneration" of *no*.

5. Conclusion

In this paper, we argued that there are three stages of Japanese-speaking children's overgeneration of *no*, in line with Murasugi (2009). The overgeneration of *no*, which apparently looks like a single phenomenon includes three parts: *No* as (i) a pronoun (N') at the late age of one, (ii) the genitive Case marker at around the age of two, and (iii) a complementizer (C) at around the age of two through four. The only case that we can truly name as overgeneration is the third stage, or the overgeneration of C. In the other two, *no* is actually used "correctly".

The fifty-year-debate in the field of Japanese acquisition has never ended because of the belief that the overgeneration takes place for a single reason. However, the overgeneration of *no* is due to three independent reasons, is a trihedral phenomenon, and informs us of the important phases in the stages of grammar acquisition, i.e. the immature merge operation, the miscategorization of adjectives, and the setting of the relative clause parameter.

References

Berman, R. 1988. Word Class Distinctions in Developing Grammar. *Categories and Processes in Language Acquisition* eds. Y. Levy, I. Schlesinger and M.D.S. Braine, 45-72. Hillsdale: Lawrence Erlbaum Associates.

Boersma, P. and Weenink, D. 2009. *Praat: Doing Phonetics by Computer* (Version 5.1.23) [Computer Program]. Retrieved October 31, 2009, from http://www.praat.org/

de Villiers, J. G. and de Villiers, P. A. 1978. *Language Acquisition.* Cambridge, MA: Harvard University Press.

Gasser, M. and Smith, L. 1998. Learning Noun and Adjective Meanings: A Connectionist Account. *Language and Cognitive Processes Special Issue: Language Acquisition and Connectionism* 13: 269-306.

Iwabuchi, E. and Muraishi, S. 1968. Kotoba no Syuutoku [Acquisition of Language]. *Kotoba no Tanzyoo: Ubugoe kara Go sai made* [The Birth of Speech: From Newborn Babies to 5-year-olds], eds. E. Iwabuchi, K Hatano, J. Naito, I. Kirikae, T. Tokizane, M. Sawashima, S. Muraishi, and T. Takizawa, 109-177. Tokyo: Nihon Hoosoo Shuppan Kyookai.

Kim, Y. 1987. *The Acquisition of Relative Clauses in English and Korean: Development in Spontaneous Production.* Doctoral dissertation, Harvard University.

Mintz, T. and Gleitman. L. 2002. Adjectives Really Do Modify Nouns: The Incremental and Restricted Nature of Early Adjective Acquisition. *Cognition* 84: 267–293.

Murasugi, K. 1991. Noun Phrases in Japanese and English: A Study in Syntax, Learnability and Acquisition. Doctoral dissertation, University of Connecticut.

Murasugi, K. 2009. The Onset of Complex NPs in Child Production. Presented at WAFL 6. Nagoya University. September 5th.

Murasugi, K. and Hashimoto, T. 2004. Two Different Types of Overgeneration of 'no' in Japanese Noun Phrases. *Proceedings of the 4th Asian GLOW in Seoul*, ed. Hang-Jin Yoon, 327-349. Seoul: Hankook.

Murasugi, K. and Hashimoto, T. 2006. Gengo Kakutoku ni okeru Meisikunai deno Kazyooseisei [The Overgeneration of 'no' in the Acquisition of Japanese Noun Phrases]. *KSL* 26: 12-21. Kansai Linguistic Society.

Nagano, S. 1960. Yooji no Gengo Hattatsu - Tokuni Joshi 'no' no Shuutokukatei nituite [Language Development: A Case Study of Japanese 'no'. *Kansai Daigaku Kokubun Gakkai: Shimada Kyooju Koki Kinen Kokubungaku Ronsyu*, 405-418.

Noji, J. 1973-1977. *Yooziki no Gengoseikatu no Zittai* [The Language Use by Children]. I-IV. Tokyo: Bunka Hyoron Syuppan.

Polinsky, M. 2005. Word Class Distinctions in an Incomplete Grammar. *Perspectives on Language and Language Development*, eds. D. Ravid and H. Bat-Zeev Shildrkrodt, 419–36. Dordrecht: Kluwer.

Yokoyama, M. 1990. Yoozi no Rentai Syuusyoku Hatuwa ni okeru Zyosi 'no' no Goyoo [Errors of Particle 'no' in Young Japanese Children's Adjective-Noun Constructions]. *Hattatu Sinrigaku Kenkyuu* 1, 2-9.

Index